A History of *Music* in Western Culture

THIRD EDITION

VOLUME TWO

The Classical Era through the Present

Mark Evan Bonds

Department of Music
University of North Carolina at Chapel Hill

Prentice Hall
Upper Saddle River   London   Singapore
Toronto   Tokyo   Sydney   Hong Kong   Mexico City

Editor-in-Chief: Sarah Touborg
Executive Editor: Richard Carlin
Project Manager: Sarah Holle
Editorial Assistant: Emma Gibbons
Director of Marketing: Tim Stookesberry
Senior Marketing Manager: Kate Mitchell
Marketing Assistant: Jennifer Lang
Senior Managing Editor: Mary Rottino
Production Editor: Macmillan Publishing Solutions/
   Teresa Christie
Project Management Liaison: Joe Scordato
Senior Operations Supervisor: Brian Mackey
Senior Art Director: Pat Smythe

Interior and Cover Designer: Laura Gardner
Cover Photo: Philip Alexius de Laszlo Miss; Lisa Minghetti, 1933
   (oil on canvas)/Bridgeman Art Library
Director, Image Resource Center: Melinda Patelli
Manager, Rights and Permissions: Zina Arabia
Manager, Visual Research: Beth Brenzel
Manager, Cover Visual Research and Permissions:
   Karen Sanatar
Image Permission Coordinator: Debbie Latronica
Composition: Macmillan Publishing Solutions
Full-Service Management: Macmillan Publishing Solutions
Printer/Binder: The Courier Companies
Cover Printer: Phoenix Color Corp.

This book was set in 10/13 Janson Text by Macmillan Publishing Solutions and was printed and bound by
The Courier Companies. The cover was printed by Phoenix Color Corp.

Credits and acknowledgments borrowed from other sources and reproduced, with permission, in this textbook appear on appropriate
page within text.

Library of Congress Cataloging-in-Publication Data

Bonds, Mark Evan.
   A history of music in Western culture : combined volume / Mark Evan Bonds.—3rd ed.
      p. cm.
   Includes bibliographical references and index.
   ISBN 0-205-66172-6 (v. 1 : paper)—ISBN 0-205-66173-4 (v. 2 : paper)—
   ISBN 0-205-64531-3 (combined : case)
   1. Music—History and criticism. I. Title.
   ML160.B75 2009
   780.9—dc22

                                        2008041660

10 9 8 7 6 5 4 3 2 1

Prentice Hall
is an imprint of

www.pearsonhighered.com

ISBN 10: 0-205-66173-4
ISBN 13: 978-0-205-66173-2

To Dorothea, Peter, Andrew

Brief Contents

Contents

Preface

This book rests on the premise that the best way to convey the history of music is to focus squarely on the music itself. The text is organized around a carefully selected repertory of works, integrating the requisite names, dates, and concepts around specific compositions. Once familiar with a representative body of music, students can better grasp the evolution of musical style and music's changing uses within the Western tradition. Even more importantly, they will have a sound basis from which to explore other musical works and repertories.

A History of Music in Western Culture builds its narrative around the core repertory represented in the accompanying *Anthology of Scores* and the corresponding set of compact discs. The text is not an encyclopedia. My goal, rather, has been to help students gain a broad understanding of the nature of music, its role in society, and the ways in which these have changed over time.

Finally, *A History of Music in Western Culture* seeks to challenge students to think critically about its subject. The history of music is too often presented (and learned) as one long series of indisputable facts. I have tried to integrate into this text enough primary source documents—excerpts from composers' letters, contemporary reviews, theoretical treatises, and the like—to demonstrate the ways in which the raw materials of history can be open to conflicting interpretations. Indeed, the most interesting historical issues tend to be precisely those about which experts disagree.

NEW ORGANIZATION

In response to requests from students and professors, *A History of Music in Western Culture* is now available in two formats:

1. The original single-volume complete text;

2. Two individual volumes that correspond in coverage to the two volumes of the Score Anthology:

   A *History of Music in Western Culture*: Antiquity through the Baroque Era

   A *History of Music in Western Culture:* The Classical Era to the Present

   For schools that teach the history sequence over two or more semesters, this gives added flexibility to the students and professors who may wish to purchase only the relevant volume.

FEATURES OF THE TEXT

The narrative of *A History of Music in Western Culture* is closely integrated with the accompanying *Anthology of Scores* and compact discs. Every work in the *Anthology* gets a discussion in the text, called out with an icon in the margin cross-referenced to both the scores and recordings.

Following a Prologue on the music of classical Antiquity, the text is divided into six parts, each corresponding to a major era in music history: Medieval, Renaissance, Baroque, Classical, 19th century, and 20th century. The text concludes with a brief Epilogue on music today. Each part begins with a **prelude**—with one or more **maps**—that summarizes the historical and social background of each era, and the first chapter in each part provides an overview of the major stylistic characteristics and theoretical concerns of the music of the era.

The text also offers a variety of features and pedagogical tools:

- An **outline** at the beginning of each chapter gives students an overview of the content of the chapter.

- The opening pages of each prelude include a **comparative timeline** that lists major musical events side-by-side with other significant historical events.

- A graphic **summary of style differences** in each part highlights the principal differences in musical style between each era and the one immediately preceding (Renaissance vs. Medieval; Baroque vs. Renaissance, etc.).

- **Key terms** are highlighted in each chapter and defined in a **glossary** at the end of the book.

- Significant composers are featured in extended **Composer Profiles** that include key biographical information and a survey of principal works.

- **Primary Evidence** boxes contain excerpts from relevant contemporary documents, exposing students to some of the raw materials of music history. A brief introduction places each selection in its context and challenge students to think about the interpretation of historical evidence.

- **Focus** boxes highlight important information that expands on aspects of the core narrative.

- **Performance Practice boxes** examine in detail an alternative performance of the same work. Students will thereby have the opportunity to compare and discuss strikingly different ways of bringing to life the same notes on a page. In the Baroque era, for example, students can hear excerpts from Bach's "Goldberg" Variations as performed by Trevor Pinnock, playing on a harpsichord such as the composer would have played, and as performed by Glenn Gould, playing on his 20th-century concert grand piano.

- Numerous **examples, tables,** and **diagrams** help students grasp key points and visualize musical structures.

- The last chapter in each part concludes with a set of **discussion questions** designed to stimulate reflection on broad issues in music history.

NEW FEATURES OF THE THIRD EDITION

This text has been expanded, corrected, and updated, with more Focus boxes, added primary sources, and improved graphics. Other key changes include:

- **Full-color images throughout the text.** *A History of Music in Western Culture* is richly illustrated with carefully chosen images drawn from the period under discussion. Detailed captions reveal the wealth of information—about music, composers, and their role in society—embedded in these artworks. More than 25 new illustrations have been added to the Third Edition; in addition, many images previously published in black and white are now in color.

■ **Expanded repertory.** New works in the Third Edition include Isaac's "Innsbruck, ich muss dich lassen," Farmer's "Fair Phyllis," and Byrd's *Pavana, the Earle of Salisbury* (integrated into an expanded discussion of 16th-century music), two new works by Baroque women composers (Elisabeth Jacquet de la Guerre and Isabella Leonarda), new excerpts from Pergolesi's *La serva padrona* and Mozart's *Requiem*; 19th-century works by Edvard Grieg, Fanny Mendelssohn Hensel, and Clara Wieck Schumann; 20th-century works by Prokofiev, Ruth Crawford Seeger, Copland, Britten, John Cage, Hugh Le Caine, and Arvo Pärt; and works by George Gershwin and Miles Davis as well as new performances by Louis Armstrong (as part of an expanded discussion of American jazz, its sources, and its influences).

FEATURES OF THE SCORE ANTHOLOGY

The works in the *Anthology of Scores to A History of Music in Western Culture* have been carefully selected to represent the developments in music history discussed in the text. Every selection in the *Anthology of Scores* is discussed in the text. Volume I covers Antiquity through the Baroque Era; Volume II covers music of the Classical Era to the present.

Key features of the Score Anthology include

■ **Integrated commentary.** Excerpts from the text are integrated into the score anthology at the end of each selection, providing students with basic information and a brief discussion of every work.

■ **Cross-referencing to text and recordings.** Each selection in the anthology opens with a clear cross-reference to the recorded version of the work (disc and track number) and to the discussion of the work within the text (page number). In addition, the score and recordings in the anthology correspond exactly within their chronological span (Volume One of each through the Baroque Era; Volume Two of each since the Classical Era).

New to the Score Anthology

■ **New works.** New selections illustrating 16th-century styles, 19th-century nationalism, and 20th-century pluralism have been added to the anthology of scores. There are six new works by women composers, ranging from the Baroque Era to the present day.

■ **Improved editions.** The emphasis on using new editions of selected works have continued, including a conductor's score for Sousa's King Cotton March that illuminates the composer's scoring to a greater degree than previously possible.

■ **New Software for Cuing the Recordings.** To follow complex, longer scores, the Anthology offers several "cue points" in these works so students may locate where they are while listening to the accompanying CDs. To locate these cues, a

free software package is offered as part of the accompanying website, MyMusicHistoryKit.

FEATURES OF THE RECORDED ANTHOLOGY

Fifteen compact discs complement the text and *Anthology of Scores*. These recordings draw on the resources of many different recording labels and feature some of the most distinguished artists and ensembles of our time, such as Sequentia, Anonymous 4, Hilliard Ensemble, Orlando Consort, Les Arts Florissants, Huelgas Ensemble, Gothic Voices, La Chapelle Royale, Consort of Musicke, Tashi, La Petite Band, Tallis Scholars, Concentus Musicus Wien, Theatre of Voices, English Baroque Soloists, Orchestre Révolutionnaire et Romantique, and Concerto Köln. Representative soloists include Paul O'Dette, Emma Kirkby, Davitt Moroney, Thomas Quasthoff, Trevor Pinnock, Malcolm Bilson, Ruggiero Raimondi, Kiri Te Kanawa, Roberto Alagna, and Jessye Norman.

The discs are arranged chronologically and mirror the content and structure of the *Anthology of Scores*:

■ Volume I: Antiquity through the Baroque Era (6 discs).

■ Volume II: The Classical Era to the Present (9 discs).

New to the Recorded Anthology

■ **New works.** New selections illustrating 16th-century styles, 19th-century nationalism, and 20th-century pluralism have been added to the recordings, in addition to six new works by women composers, ranging from the Baroque Era to the present day.

■ **Alternative performances.** In several cases, a work is provided with an alternative performance. In Volume I of *Recorded Anthology*, for example, the frottola *El grillo*, ascribed to Josquin des Prez, is first performed in its notated version by four voices, followed by a very different realization of this work by a solo singer accompanying herself on the lute. There are also new works in the *Recorded Anthology* in which a traditional piece is followed by a larger work derived from it (Grieg's "Halling" from *Peer Gynt* and the "Hoe-down" from Copland's *Rodeo*. Students are thereby encouraged to think about the many options available to them as performers for music of all eras.

AN EXPANDED LIBRARY OF RESOURCES FOR STUDENTS AND INSTRUCTORS

A History of Music in Western Culture comes with a variety of supplementary print and multimedia materials for both instructors and students.

Instructor's Resource Manual

The *Instructor's Resource Manual with Tests* provides the following:

■ Sample syllabi

■ Exam schedule and grade points that can be earned for each exam

- Chapter outline
- Chapter summary
- Key terms
- Class projects
- Discussion questions, essay questions
- A list of about three to five websites that could be used for research
- A list of publications which can be used for research
- Other media sources that can be helpful such as movies and DVDs of live concerts/performances

Prentice Hall MyTest

Suitable for both Windows and Macintosh environments, this commercial-quality, electronic test-management program allows instructors to select questions from the bank of test questions and design their own exams.
ISBN 0205657044 or 9780205657049

PowerPoint Lecture Slides

Mirroring the organization and content of the text a set of PowerPoint slides provides a useful tool for lectures and class-room presentations. The value of the slides is further enhanced by the inclusion of some of the book's photos, maps, tables and charts.
ISBN 0205657036 or 9780205657032

MyMusicHistoryKit   PEARSON mymusichistorykit

MyMusicHistoryKit provides students an opportunity to delve more deeply into the ideas and personalities discussed in the text. Students can evaluate their progress with study and essay questions and report the results to the instructor. The site also includes an array of historical documents to complement those in the text. Many of the documents that appear in abbreviated form in the text appear complete on the site. Essay questions accompany each of these documents.

In addition, students may download a free software package that will enable them to follow the cues in the Score Anthology when listening to the longer works.

Acknowledgments

I am grateful to the many scholars who reviewed the manuscript for this book and its revisions at various points in its development. Their thoughtful and often detailed comments were invaluable at every stage in the process:

Bruce Alan Brown
University of Southern California

Walter Bailey
Rice University

Jonathan Bellman
University of Northern Colorado

Elizabeth Bergman
Princeton University

Lester Brothers
University of North Texas

Kellie D. Brown
Milligan College

Michael J. Budds
University of Missouri

Anna Celenza
Georgetown University

Vincent Corrigan
Bowling Green State University

Cynthia Cyrus
Vanderbilt University

Patricia Debly
Brock University

Andrew Dell'Antonio
University of Texas, Austin

Matthew Dirst
University of Houston

Lawrence Earp
University of Wisconsin

Sean Gallagher
Harvard University

Howard Goldstein
Auburn University

Floyd Grave
Rutgers University

David Haas
University of Georgia

Brian Harker
Brigham Young University

Robert Haskins
University of New Hampshire

Sara Heimbecker
University of Northern Colorado

Jan Herlinger
Louisiana State University

Elizabeth Keathley
University of North Carolina at Greensboro

Tammy Kernodle
Miami University

Kenneth Kreitner
University of Memphis

Charles Larkowski
Wright State University

James Leger
New Mexico Highlands University

Susan Lewis
University of Victoria

Stan Link
Vanderbilt University

Virginia Lile Boaz
East Texas Baptist University

Harry Lincoln
Binghamton University

John E. Lindberg
Minnesota State University

Eleanor McCrickard
University of North Carolina at Greensboro

Stephen Meyer
Syracuse University

Sterling Murray
West Chester University

Massimo Ossi
Indiana University

Tom Owens
George Mason University

Eftychia Papanikolaou
Bowling Green State University

James Parsons
Missouri State University

Georgia Peeples
University of Akron

Heather Platt
Ball State University

E. Harrison Powley
Brigham Young University

James Randall
University of Montana

Mary Scanlan
Grand Rapids Community College

Roberta F. Schwartz
University of Kansas

Deborah Schwartz-Kates
University of Miami

Christopher Smith
Texas Tech University

Murray Steib
Ball State University

Patricia Taylor Lee
San Francisco State University

Judith Tick
Northeastern University

Joshua Veltman
Union University

Susan Weiss
John Hopkins University

Douglas Wheeler
Clayton State University

Jeremy Yudkin
Boston University

Charles Youmans
Pennsylvania State University

I am also grateful to many colleagues and students at the University of North Carolina at Chapel Hill for their help at many points along the way. Fellow faculty members Tim Carter, John Covach, Annegret Fauser, Jon Finson, Sean Gallagher, Anne MacNeil, Jocelyn Neal, Severine Neff, and Tom Warburton all offered helpful advice (and an ear) at various stages of the project. I was also fortunate to be able to draw on the able help of several students in preparing the manuscript: Christina Tuskey, Jennifer Germann, Michelle Oswell, Seth Coluzzi, Ethan Lechner, Joseph Singleton, Douglas Shadle, and above all Peter Lamothe. The staff of the Music Library—particularly Dan Zager, Phil Vandermeer, Diane Steinhaus, and Eva Boyce—were unfailingly helpful and efficient.

Thanks, too, to Ruell Tyson and his staff at the Humanities Institute at the University of North Carolina at Chapel Hill. My fellowship there in the spring of 1999 provided the time and mental space needed to launch this project, and my weekly conversations with the other fellows that semester helped me think through some of the more basic issues associated with writing a textbook of this kind.

I am grateful as well to Massimo Ossi (Indiana University) for his comments on an early version of the Baroque section of the text; to Suzanne Cusick (New York University) for her help in matters pertaining to Francesca Caccini; and to Diane Parr Walker and Jane Edmister Penner (University of Virginia) for their help in securing a reproduction of Thomas Jefferson's request for music by Carlo Antonio Campioni. J. Samuel Hammond (Duke University Libraries) and Jeremy Yudkin (Boston University) also provided help and advice at many points along the way. Margaret Murata (UC-Irvine) and Barbara Haggh-Huglo (University of Maryland) were very generous in suggesting improvements for the Second Edition.

My editors at Prentice Hall have been a delight to work with from the very beginning. I first discussed the project with Bud Therien. Bud's successor as Music Editor, Chris Johnson, was the prime mover in this enterprise. Richard Carlin, the current Music Editor, has helped make the third edition even better. David Chodoff, my development editor, was indispensable in turning a text into a textbook, as was Joe Scordato, Production Editor for Humanities and Social Sciences at Prentice Hall. Teresa Nemeth provided many useful ideas for improving early drafts of the manuscript. Elsa Peterson helped with the development of the 20th-century chapters and coordinated the compilation of the anthology manuscript. Francelle Carapetyan and Diana Gongora were unflagging in their effort to track down the needed illustrations. For the Third Edition specifically, I owe my greatest debt of thanks to Richard Kassel, whose keen eye and imaginative approach have improved the text at many levels. Tom Laskey (Sony BMG Music Entertainment) expertly coordinated the revised package of recordings. I am also grateful to Jeanne Fischer and Beth Tomlin for their performance of Johann Friedrich Reichardt's *Italien* and to Paul Cole for engineering its recording.

Finally, my deepest thanks go to my family. My parents were not directly involved in producing this book, but they made it possible in ways that go well beyond the obvious. My brother Bob gave invaluable advice at an early stage of the process; I regret that the 23 pages of text originally devoted to Bruckner had to be deleted for reasons of space. And it is to Dorothea, Peter, and Andrew that I dedicate this book, with love.

About the Author

Mark Evan Bonds is the Cory C. Boshamer Distinguished Professor of Music at the University of North Carolina at Chapel Hill, where he has taught since 1992. He holds degrees from Duke University (B.A.), Christian-Albrechts-Universität Kiel (M.A.), and Harvard University (Ph.D.). His publications include *Wordless Rhetoric: Musical Form and the Metaphor of the Oration* (1991), *After Beethoven: Imperatives of Symphonic Originality* (1996), and *Music as Thought: Listening to the Symphony in the Age of Beethoven* (2006). He has also published essays on the music of Haydn and Mozart and has served as editor-in-chief of *Beethoven Forum*.

Why Study Music History?

Why study music history? This is a fair question, one you have likely asked yourself, particularly if you happen to be using this book as part of a required course. Here are a few reasons:

■ **A greater understanding of music's emotional power and its role in society.** Music is one of the most powerful yet least understood of all the arts. It has played a significant role in every known culture in human history. In the Western world, people have used it in widely varying contexts. It has provided entertainment, played a central role in many forms of religious worship, and has long been considered important to a well-rounded education. It has been admired since ancient times for its therapeutic benefits and it is used in shopping malls today for its ability to put people in the mood to buy. Political candidates identify themselves with theme songs, and patriotic music helps promote feelings of national unity. Music has even been used for torture. Entire generations have defined themselves according to the music they have enjoyed. And today, music drives a multibillion-dollar industry.

■ **A richer understanding of music's basic elements.** Composers and musicians have combined a few basic elements—rhythm, melody, harmony, texture, timbre, and form—in a remarkable variety of ways since ancient times. The polyphony of the 13th century sounds quite different from early-20th-century ragtime, but both are composed from the same building blocks. Studying music history helps us understand how these elements have been manipulated over time to create such a diversity of effects. And in the process, it can make us better listeners.

■ **A sense of changing musical styles across time.** Why, within the space of less than a hundred years, did Bach write in one style, Mozart in another, and Chopin in yet another? Why is so much of the music written after 1900 difficult to grasp on first listening? Why do musical styles change at all? Although we do not have to be able to answer these kinds of questions to enjoy the music of any composer or period, our attempts to do so can increase our understanding of it and deepen the pleasure it brings us.

■ **A basis for exploring new works and repertories.** Familiarity with a wide range of representative works from different historical periods enhances our ability to learn and understand new works and repertories of different kinds, including those of non-Western cultures. All of us are looking to expand our playlists in one way or another.

■ **A greater ability to talk and write about music.** Music, the most abstract of all the arts, is notoriously difficult to describe in words. If we could identify exactly what a work of music is "about" or translate its meaning into words, why would we bother with the music at all? Still, the fact that we can never capture in prose the essence of music does not mean that we should remain silent on the subject. The very process of trying to write about music can help us appreciate what distinguishes it from fiction, poetry, drama, painting, dance, architecture, or any other form of human expression.

Part IV

The Classical Era

Prelude

The Classical era in music—roughly 1750 to 1800—corresponds to a period of intense ferment and change in European history. Powerful intellectual currents bearing notions of liberty and progress challenged the established order. Conflict on a global scale among the great powers of Europe undermined the finances of Great Britain and France, loosening Britain's hold on its American colonies and triggering a cataclysmic revolution and the collapse of the monarchy in France. Advances in technology led to the beginning of the Industrial Revolution.

THE AGE OF ENLIGHTENMENT

The 18th century saw the emergence of an intellectual outlook that stressed the power of humanity, through the application of reason, to understand and improve its condition, and the power of the individual, granted sufficient liberty, to use reason in pursuit of self-fulfillment. The advocates of this outlook considered it to be enlightened, and the period in which they flourished is known as the Age of Enlightenment.

The German philosopher Immanuel Kant (1724–1804) defined Enlightenment as "man's emergence from his self-imposed immaturity. Immaturity is the inability to use one's understanding without guidance from another. This immaturity is self-imposed when its cause lies not in a lack of understanding, but in a lack of resolve and courage to use it without guidance from another."

This call for courage, which Kant summed up in the expression *sapere aude!* ("dare to know!") is an important element of Enlightenment thought. Leading figures of the Enlightenment were ready to follow reason wherever it might take them, even if that meant risking their lives and welfare in attacking such established institutions as the monarchy and the church.

The origins of this remarkable new outlook can be traced to late-17th-century England. The Glorious Revolution of 1688 had led to the establishment of a constitutional monarchy in which royal power was constrained by an elected parliament. In 1690, the English philosopher John Locke published two treatises in which he articulated the principle that government exists as a result of a contract with the governed to protect their natural rights to liberty and property. If the government violates that contract with oppressive policies, the governed have a right to rebel and replace it. The French writer François-Marie Arouet, better known as Voltaire (1694–1778), spent over two years (1726–29) in exile in England, where he was deeply impressed by the ideas of Locke, the scientific accomplishments of Isaac Newton, and the relative freedom of English society, with its emphasis on the dignity of the individual. He returned to France with a firsthand knowledge of English philosophy and social thought. Voltaire became a leader among a group of French thinkers who called themselves *philosophes* (but whom today we might call social critics). Foremost among these were Charles Montesquieu (1689–1755), Denis Diderot (1713–84), and the Swiss-born Jean-Jacques Rousseau (1712–78).

The *philosophes* of the Enlightenment were almost unfailingly optimistic. Human beings, they believed, were innately good, and society could be perfected if reason was permitted to replace superstition and tradition in the shaping of the social order. Their newfound confidence in reason as a means to self-fulfillment ultimately led to a new outlook on the relationship between the individual and the state, and between the individual and God. The *philosophes* challenged the claim of monarchs to rule by divine right and objected to organized religion for promoting intolerance and diverting attention from the rational pursuit of human and personal betterment in this life.

The political views of the *philosophes*, although generally rooted in the concept of natural rights and the social contract, were varied. They ranged from the reformist ideas of Montesquieu—an admirer of Britain's constitutional monarchy and the first to argue for the separation of powers in government—to the more radical democracy advocated by Rousseau. According to Rousseau, the "noble savage"—humanity in a state of primitive nature before government—was morally superior to the civilized individual hobbled by the arbitrary laws and conventions of society, its division into social classes, and its religions. "Man was born free," Rousseau observed in his *Social Contract* of 1762, "and everywhere he is in chains."

Enlightenment ideals found expression in the revolutionary movements of the end of the 18th century. The leaders of the American Revolution were all steeped in Enlightenment thinking, as reflected in the Declaration of Independence of 1776, a thoroughly Enlightenment manifesto. Consider the "truths" that the Declaration asserts to be self-evident: "that all men are created equal; that they are endowed by their Creator with certain unalienable Rights; that among these are life, liberty, and the pursuit of happiness. That to secure these rights, governments are instituted among men, deriving their just powers from the consent of the governed." Each is a characteristically Enlightenment proposition; none would have been thought self-evident 100 years earlier.

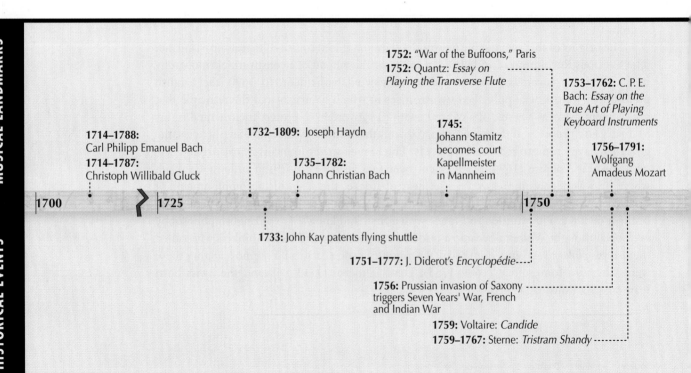

Despite the revolutionary implications of their ideas, however, many Enlightenment thinkers supported Europe's existing monarchies, and even the idea of absolutism (discussed in the Prelude to the Baroque Era). But they advocated an "enlightened" absolutism, led by an "enlightened despot," a powerful ruler who exercised restraint and who worked consistently for the good of the larger whole, as opposed to his or her self-aggrandizement. Several late-18th-century monarchs sought to apply certain Enlightenment principles along these lines. Both Frederick the Great in Prussia and Catherine the Great in Russia carried on a decades-long correspondence with Voltaire that often touched on ideas about governance; Voltaire even served for a time at Frederick's court in Berlin. In Austria, Joseph II instituted reforms driven by Enlightenment attitudes toward religion, forbidding long services and elaborate music and imposing in their place a form of worship that was simpler, more direct, and less burdened with ritual.

Consistent with their belief in the power of reason to promote progress, the *philosophes* of the Enlightenment were deeply committed to the pursuit of scientific knowledge. Quite aside from its potential for practical applications, the understanding of nature was seen as the key to self-enlightenment, a kind of religion in its own right. Scientific knowledge was considered a principal means of overcoming superstition. Thomas Jefferson (1742–1826), the leading advocate of the Enlightenment in the new United States, established the University of Virginia in the early 19th century on the basis of what he called "the illimitable freedom of the human mind. For here we are not afraid to follow the truth wherever it may lead, nor to tolerate any error so long as reason is free to combat it."

In order for the fruits of Enlightenment thought to reach the widest possible audience, it had to be synthesized and published. The desire of the *philosophes* to distribute their knowledge made the Enlightenment the great age of encyclopedias. The

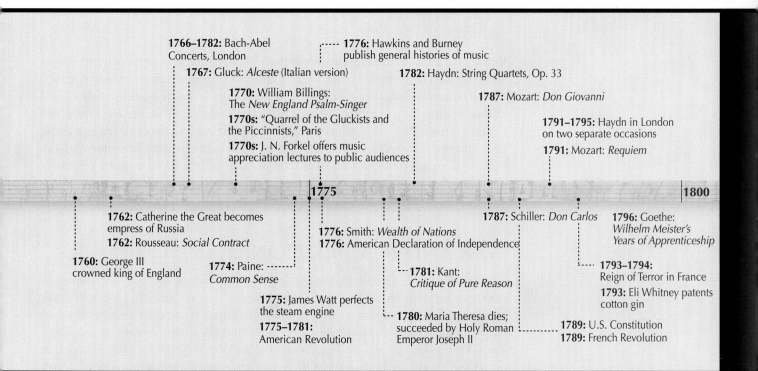

FOCUS — Key Figures in Enlightenment Thought

In France, the self-styled *philosophes* conducted an ongoing debate, much of it in public, about the nature of humanity and the structure of the ideal society. In his essays and satires, **Charles Louis de Montesquieu** (1689–1755) argued for increased individual liberties through institutional reform. **Voltaire** (1694–1778) was the leading figure of the age, writing histories, dramas, satires, political tracts, and scientific treatises with equal zeal. **Jean-Jacques Rousseau** (1712–78) was born in Geneva, in the French-speaking part of Switzerland. He wrote the entries on music for Diderot's *Encyclopédie* and composed music as well. His most important writings are the *Discourse on the Origin and Foundations of Inequality amongst Men* (1754) and the *Social Contract* (1762), both of which argue that society has corrupted the individual. Rousseau's novel *Emile* (1762) was influential in shaping ideas about the nature and goals of education. **Denis Diderot** (1713–84), the chief architect of the *Encyclopédie*, was a particularly adamant critic of religion as an opponent of reason.

In Great Britain, the philosopher and political theorist **John Locke** (1632–1704) argued that toleration of differing viewpoints makes a state stronger, not weaker. Locke also argued for the right of a people to overthrow a government that violates their natural rights. Locke's ideas had a significant impact on subsequent Enlightenment ideas about government. He greatly influenced **Thomas Paine** (1737–1809), whose pamphlet *Common Sense* (1774) argued in favor of American independence and self-government. **Adam Smith** (1723–90), the leading economic theorist of the 18th century, opposed Great Britain's mercantile, or protectionist, trade policies, arguing they stifled the unrestrained economic competition that was the true source of a nation's wealth; his *Wealth of Nations* (1776) put the discipline of economics on a rational footing. **Mary Wollstonecraft** (1759–97) was one of the first to argue for educational equality for women in her *A Vindication of the Rights of Woman* (1792). She died giving birth to her daughter, who, under her married name Mary Shelley, would later gain fame as the author of the novel *Frankenstein* (1818).

Benjamin Franklin (1706–90) and **Thomas Jefferson** (1742–1826), two leading American exponents of the Enlightenment, were instrumental in framing the Declaration of Independence of 1776, a document that succinctly captures more than a century of social thought about the rights of the individual. Both were also actively involved with music, Franklin as the inventor of an improved version of the glass harmonica, Jefferson as an avid violinist (see Chapter 12).

In Germany, **Gotthold Ephraim Lessing** (1729–81) preached religious tolerance in his play *Nathan the Wise* (1779). **Immanuel Kant** (1724–1804) reconciled reason with empirical experience and as such laid the foundations for modern philosophy. **Johann Wolfgang Goethe** (1749–1832) and **Friedrich Schiller** (1759–1805) are widely regarded as the two greatest poets and playwrights of the German language; both contributed to the fields of philosophy and aesthetics as well.

foremost example of this movement was the 33-volume *Encyclopédie*, edited by Diderot and published between 1751 and 1777. This massive compendium, bearing the subtitle *A Systematic Dictionary of Sciences, Arts, and Crafts*, contains approximately 72,000 entries written by more than 140 contributors, including Voltaire, Rousseau, and Diderot himself. Rousseau, who was also a composer, wrote almost all the entries on music for the *Encyclopédie* and would later use them as the basis for his influential dictionary of musical terms, published in 1768. In England, the more modest *Encyclopedia Britannica* first appeared in 1768–1771. The German-language *Brockhaus* encyclopedia began publication in 1796.

WAR AND REVOLUTION

Throughout the 18th century, the major powers of Europe jockeyed for advantage over one another both at home and in their now far-flung colonies. In 1756, a Prussian invasion of Saxony triggered a global conflict between France and Great Britain over their colonial claims in North America, India, and elsewhere. Known as the Seven Years' War in Europe and the French and Indian War in North America, it ended in defeat for France in 1763, leaving Britain in undisputed control of most of North America east of the Mississippi. The enormous expense of the war, however, strained

Europe in 1763

the finances of both countries. Britain, as a result, sought to impose new taxes in its American colonies, ultimately provoking the American Revolution of 1775–81 that led to the creation of the United States.

In France, left on the verge of bankruptcy by the war, the consequences were cataclysmic. After more than a decade of ineffectual attempts to address the financial crisis, Louis XVI was forced in 1789 to summon the Estates General, a representative body that had not met for more than 150 years. Thereafter events spun out of the king's control. The French Revolution, inspired by Enlightenment doctrines, resulted in the overthrow of the monarchy. Relatively bloodless at first, the revolution turned on itself during the Reign of Terror (1793–94), during which an estimated 250,000 suspected opponents of the revolution were arrested and about 1,400 executed in public by the guillotine. Louis XVI and his queen, Marie Antoinette, were among the victims.

The violent overthrow of what had long been regarded as Europe's most powerful monarchy shocked the rest of Europe. After 1789, no social or political institution could be taken for granted. Ideas about democracy and public self-determination had of course been in the air long before: ancient Greece and Rome offered a remote image of democratic rule, and Britain's monarchs had been ceding power gradually for many years. The American Revolution had provided yet another model for change. Still, the United States was perceived at the time to occupy the edge of a great wilderness, far removed from the centers of civilization. Paris, by contrast, was in many respects the capital of Europe, one of the leading centers of progress in science and the arts.

FOCUS   Music in the French Revolution

The French Revolution marks a new chapter in the use of music by the state. The ideals of the Revolution—liberty, equality, fraternity—called for an approach to music that was essentially public and nonelitist. The revolutionary government encouraged the singing of songs by enthusiastic crowds as a way to spread revolutionary ideology in much the same way that Martin Luther had used the congregational singing of hymns to spread the word of the Reformation in the 16th century.

The French Revolution had not one but two anthems. *Ça ira* ("This Shall Be"), with its denunciation of the aristocracy ("We'll string up the aristocrats! Despotism will die, Liberty will triumph. This shall be, this shall be!"), was sung endlessly by the crowds in the streets. *La Marseillaise*, composed in 1792 by Claude-Joseph Rouget de Lisle, an army captain, became the French national anthem on July 14, 1795, the sixth anniversary of the Revolution. Its capacity to inspire revolutionary ardor led several subsequent regimes—including those of Napoleon, Louis XVIII (after 1815), and Napoleon III (in the 1850s and 1860s)—to ban its performance. It would be reinstated as the French national anthem in 1879.

But the government's role went well beyond encouraging the use of one or two songs. The annual festivals commemorating the anniversary of the revolution made music a participatory event, not merely a spectacle for the entertainment of audiences. These enormous, open-air gatherings featured numerous secular hymns and political songs. Various constitutions of the new state were actually set to music—mostly to well-known tunes—for the express purpose of disseminating their content in a way the common person could understand.

The new government also established a national Conservatory of Music to train composers, performers, and teachers, who were, in turn, to create, perform, and propagate music for the national festivals and for the army. The agenda of the new institution was unabashedly nationalistic. The composer François-Joseph Gossec (1734–1829) argued for the establishment of such a school as a bulwark against those "foreign musicians, who, having no attachment to our country, corrupt our language and pervert our taste, . . . It is therefore advantageous—or to put it better, necessary—that we have a truly national music, and to achieve this end we need an Academy of Music." Gossec later became the conservatory's first director.

In the end, the goals of the French government were far loftier than its accomplishments. Within a few years, Paris was once again attracting foreign musicians of talent, and the emphasis on political music soon declined. But the use of music, even for a brief period, as a tool of the state would provide a powerful model for subsequent revolutions and regimes throughout the world.

The French Revolution, with its Enlightenment call for liberty, equality, and fraternity, marked the beginning of a gradual decline in the strict hierarchy of class structure across Europe. The change occurred more rapidly in some places (London, Berlin) than in others (Vienna) but was palpable everywhere. The loosening of social hierarchies meant increased opportunities for individuals of talent, who could choose their occupations with greater freedom than ever before.

But the violence of the revolution led many to question the Enlightenment ideals that motivated it. After the Terror, it was harder to believe in the inherent goodness of the individual and the perfectability of society.

THE INDUSTRIAL REVOLUTION

Another revolution, more subtle but no less significant, was taking place at this time in the world of industry. The Industrial Revolution, as it would later be known, was driven by new technology. New machines were making manufacturing more efficient and economical. In the textile industry, John Kay's flying shuttle, patented in 1733, allowed one weaver to do the work of two. The traditional spinning wheel, used in western Europe since the 14th century, could produce only a single thread at a time, but James Hargreaves's spinning jenny, developed during the 1760s, turned out 8 and later 16 threads at once. Eli Whitney's cotton gin (1793) made the cost of producing cotton so economical, the output of cotton from the American South increased tenfold in the years between 1793 and 1800. (Because southern planters relied on slave labor to cultivate cotton, an unfortunate consequence of Whitney's invention was to strengthen the institution of slavery in the South.) All these and other discoveries combined to accelerate the growth of textile mills in England, the United States (beginning in the 1790s), and throughout the Western world.

The most important invention of the Industrial Revolution was the steam engine. The first practical steam engine was invented by Thomas Newcomen and put to use in 1712 to pump water out of underground mines. Improvements by James Watt in the mid-1760s permitted the application of steam power to virtually any industry. Factories that once would have been located near streams and powered by running water could now be located anywhere with access to coal. Within a few short decades, the coal-producing Midlands region of England (including the cities of Manchester, Birmingham, and Sheffield) became the center of a highly industrialized economy that exported textiles, steel, machinery, and finished goods to every corner of the world. Over time, other Western nations would follow England's lead in making the transformation from an agrarian to an industrialized economy.

The social consequences of the Industrial Revolution were profound. Workers operating heavy machinery in large factories increasingly did work that had once been done in the home. Cities grew up around these new factories, often in the most haphazard fashion. Squalid living conditions and poor sanitation were commonplace, as were outbreaks of communicable diseases like tuberculosis, typhoid fever, and cholera. But as national economies increased in size and scope, more and more workers followed job opportunities from the agrarian countryside to the industrialized city.

Music engraving. Music engraving, although not new in the 18th century, made tremendous advances during this time and became the preferred method for publishing music. It offered the advantages of mass production while at the same time allowing for a considerable degree of freehand notation. This plate from Diderot's *Encyclopédie* illustrates the process of music engraving. The tool labeled Fig. 1 was used to engrave staves. Fig. 2 shows two staves engraved on a metal plate. The straight edge (labeled b) kept the stave engraving tool straight as it was drawn against the plate. Various punches (Fig. 5, Fig. 6, and Fig. 7) produced standard notational elements. The punch labeled Fig. 5, for example, created the treble clef sign. The notes could be either punched or drawn freehand.

Source: Courtesy of the Library of Congress

MUSIC IN ENLIGHTENMENT SOCIETY

Both directly and indirectly, music benefited from Enlightenment ideals and the many advances in commerce, technology, and transportation during the 18th century. Reflecting the Enlightenment impulse to produce encyclopedic compendiums of knowledge, the first comprehensive histories of music date to the Classical era (see Focus: The First Histories of Music). Technological advances in engraving improved the efficiency of music publishing, and the music trade became truly international in the second half of the 18th century. Improved manufacturing techniques made musical instruments like the piano increasingly affordable to middle- and upper-middle-class households. The growth of cities and entrepreneurial enterprise, particularly in England, was accompanied by an increasing demand for public concerts and an increase in the number of venues in which to hold them.

Audiences also wanted to know more about the music being performed at these concerts. Enterprising publishers filled this need with a steadily increasing number of music periodicals. In the 1770s, the German composer and theorist Johann Nikolaus Forkel (1749–1818) delivered a series of public lectures that represent one of the earliest attempts to educate the general public in music appreciation. Audiences also wanted to learn about composers themselves. John Mainwaring's *Memoirs of the Late G. F. Handel* (1760) was the first separately published biography of a composer. Several biographies of Wolfgang Amadeus Mozart appeared shortly after his death in 1791. This trend reflects the emergence of composers as cultural icons, their growing independence from aristocratic patronage, and their growing dependence on a paying public. When Joseph Haydn arrived in London the same year as Mozart's death, his reputation preceded him. Earlier in his career he had been a liveried servant for his aristocratic employer; now he was welcomed into the highest levels of society. By the time he returned permanently to Vienna in 1795, he had become a cultural hero and national treasure (see "The composer as a cultural hero: Haydn's farewell performance," on page 328).

Despite these trends, most music was still performed for the courts and residences of the royalty and aristocracy during the second half of the 18th century. The variety and quality of music at any given court thus depended entirely on the tastes and financial resources of the titled patron who presided over it. Composers likewise remained

---

FOCUS   The First Histories of Music

The first large-scale attempts at a comprehensive history of music appeared during the Classical era. The most important of these are by Giovanni Battista Martini, John Hawkins, Charles Burney, and Johann Nikolaus Forkel.

Martini never completed his monumental *Storia della musica* ("History of Music"). The three volumes he did complete, published 1757–81, cover only the ancient world. They are full of speculation about the music of the Egyptians, Hebrews, Greeks, Romans, and other ancient cultures.

Hawkins's *A General History of the Science and Practice of Music*, published in five volumes in 1776, was the first major history of music written in English. Hawkins was a lawyer by profession. His work is somewhat drier than Burney's, but on the whole fairly reliable and still useful for its portrait of 18th-century concert life in London.

Burney, himself an organist and composer, traveled widely to gather material for his four-volume *A General History of Music*, published 1776–89. Burney's travel diaries and autobiography also make for fascinating reading. His daughter, Fanny Burney (1752–1840), won fame as a novelist and diarist.

Forkel is best known for his early (1801) biography of Johann Sebastian Bach. He completed only two volumes of his *Allgemeine Geschichte der Musik* ("General History of Music"). Published in 1788–1801, these cover only through the middle of the 16th century. They nevertheless exposed German readers to musical repertoires previously unknown to most of them.

Audience participation. Like every good caricature, this scene from the performance of an Italian opera in London in the late 18th century is based on reality. Several members of the audience are singing along: the gentleman in the front box, in fact, seems to be attracting more attention than the *primo uomo* on stage. The orchestra director looks at the competing singer with despair. The musicians, judging from the expressions on their faces, have seen and heard it all before.

Source: Thomas Rowlandson, "John Bull at the Italian Opera." 1811. 44 × 28 cm. V & A Picture Library

mostly dependent on the patronage of the nobility and church for their livelihoods. Haydn was fortunate to have a princely employer committed to music making of high quality who had the resources to pay for it. He was able to live independently later in his career only because he had become an international celebrity. Other composers, like Mozart, were not so lucky. Independent by default because he was unable to secure a lucrative appointment, Mozart cobbled together an income from a variety of sources. He taught piano and composition, gave concerts from time to time, wrote works on commission, and sold the rights to works of all kinds to various music publishers. He was finally granted a minor position at the Imperial court in Vienna late in life, but the income it provided was insufficient to support him and his family.

Vienna thrived as a musical center during the Classical era because it was home to many noble and aristocratic families with the resources and the desire to maintain their own musical ensembles. As the capital of the Austrian Empire, it was also home to many foreign embassies, each seeking to impress the others with sophisticated music. Haydn, who had lived in Vienna during the winter months for most of his career, moved there after the death of his long time patron in the 1790s. Mozart moved there in the early 1780s to take advantage of its opportunities and in search of an appointment at the Imperial court. By the time the young Ludwig van Beethoven (1770–1827) arrived in 1792, Vienna had established a well-earned reputation for welcoming musicians and composers of talent. Aristocratic patrons vied for Beethoven's services, in part because they liked his music, in part to demonstrate their own cultural sophistication.

CHAPTER

11

The Art of the Natural

Like all the other period labels we have encountered so far, the label *Classical* was applied retrospectively. In this case, the designation dates to the middle of the 19th century. It was then that music historians began to look back on the late 18th century as a musical golden age that produced works of enduring value, hence "classical." Certainly it is easy today to think of the music of composers like Haydn and Mozart this way. They, however, thought of themselves as modern composers writing in the modern style. And their contemporary audiences had little concern for enduring value. On the contrary, listeners of this time routinely demanded—and got—a steady stream of new music. As in earlier periods, it would have been unusual during the Classical era to hear music written more than a generation before. Haydn and Mozart's contemporaries—and perhaps even the composers themselves—would be astonished to know that people are still listening to their works more than two hundred years later.

The term *classical*, however, also refers to Greek and Roman antiquity and the aesthetic values associated with it—balance, proportion, clarity, and naturalness. In this sense the term is aptly descriptive, because late-18th-century composers and audiences did indeed value these qualities in music. This was an era that on the whole preferred understatement to overstatement, clarity to obscurity. Although composers had long since given up the idea of recreating the music of antiquity, they found broad parallels between their musical ideals and the sculpture and architecture of ancient Greece and Rome, which for the most part avoided excessive ornamentation and decoration.

MUSIC AND THE IDEA OF NATURE

The aesthetic of the Classical era is deeply rooted in ideas about nature and, more specifically, ideas about the difference between nature and art, the natural and the artificial. Beginning around 1730, a preference for the natural over the excessively artful, or artificial, became increasingly widespread. The appeal of nature and the natural created a climate in which the ornate gave way to the simple, the opulent to the straightforward. In 1737, for example, the music critic Johann Adolph Scheibe (1708–76) disparaged the music of Johann Sebastian Bach as "turgid" and "confused." The composer would win wider acclaim, Scheibe maintained, if he did not "darken the beauty" of his works with "an excess of art." Scheibe compared Bach to a now-forgotten poet of the time, a Herr von Lohenstein, and concluded that "turgidity has led them both from the natural to the artificial, and from the lofty to the somber; and in both one admires the onerous labor and uncommon effort—which, however, are vainly employed, since they conflict with Nature."[1]

The ideal work of art, according to the predominant aesthetic of the 18th century, must imitate nature in some way. In the words of the influential French critic Jean-Baptiste Dubos (1670–1742), "Music, like painting, has but a single goal: to present to the mind the truth of nature."[2] Dubos and other similarly minded writers believed that what art could project from nature was first and foremost the human passions. This goal, as we have seen, was also basic to Baroque musical aesthetics. The difference was that by the middle of the 18th century, the emphasis had shifted from the musical expression of the affect inherent in a poetic, dramatic, or religious text to a more straightforward, "natural" representation of the passions. Once again, a critic's comments on the music of Johann Sebastian Bach provide a yardstick by which to measure this changing aesthetic. No less a figure than Johann Mattheson (1681–1754; see Focus: The Emergence of Tonal Harmony, in Chapter 7) chastised Bach—although not by name—for his practice of repeating individual words over long stretches of music. Mattheson singled out the cantata *Ich hatte viel Bekümmernis*, BWV 21, for special ridicule with this mocking transcription of the text underlay in one movement:

> I, I, I, I had much grief, I had much grief, in my heart, in my heart. I had much grief, etc., in my heart, etc., etc., I had much grief, etc., in my heart, etc., I had much grief, etc., in my heart etc., etc., etc., etc., etc. I had much grief, etc., in my heart, etc., etc." Then again: "Sighs, tears, sorrow, anguish (rest), sighs, tears, anxious longing, fear and death (rest) gnaw at my oppressed heart, etc." Also: "Come, my Jesus, and refresh (rest) and rejoice with Thy glance (rest), come, my Jesus (rest), come, my Jesus, and refresh and rejoice . . . with Thy glance this soul, etc.[3]

Bach, like many composers of his generation, had repeated the same words many times over to give full expression to their associated musical affect. But during the 18th century, this kind of attention to individual words, basic to so much Baroque vocal music, came to be viewed with increasing distaste. By the time Bach died, even his sons considered his music old-fashioned. It was too ornate, too elaborate—in a word, too artful.

At the same time, 18th-century critics recognized that music, as an art, is distinct from nature, and although it may convey "the truth of nature," as Dubos put it, it requires technique and craft. Music that seems natural and effortless, in other words, requires art and effort. According to the aesthetic theory of the time, this dichotomy between art

---

1. Quotation from Johann Adolph Scheibe, *Der critische Musikus*, 14 May 1737, trans. in *The New Bach Reader: A Life of Johann Sebastian Bach in Letters and Documents*, edited by Hans T. David and Arthur Mendel; revised and enlarged by Christoph Wolff (New York: Norton, 1998), p. 338. Copyright 1998 by Christoph Wolff. Used by permission of W. W. Norton & Company, Inc.

2. Jean-Baptiste Dubos, *Réflexions critiques sur la poésie et sur la peinture*, 3 vols. (Paris, 1719), II, 113.

3. Quotation from Johann Mattheson parody of BWV 21 text, trans. in *The New Bach Reader: A Life of Johann Sebastian Bach in Letters and Documents*, edited by Hans T. David and Arthur Mendel; revised and enlarged by Christoph Wolff (New York: Norton, 1998), p. 325. Copyright 1998 Christoph Wolff. Used by permission of W. W. Norton & Company, Inc.

and nature plays itself out in the person of the artist, who must combine genius (nature) with technique (art) and bring both to bear on the raw material of nature to produce a work of enduring quality. Other aspects of this dichotomy can be summarized as follows:

Nature versus Art in 18th-Century Aesthetics	
NATURE	**ART**
Genius	Technique
Inspiration	Craft
Unconscious	Conscious
Effortlessness	Hard work
Divine	Human
Not teachable	Teachable

Many accounts of the compositional process from the Classical era reflect these ideas about the connections and tensions between nature and art. In his "Introduction to the Rules of Musick" published at the beginning of his collection *The New England Psalm-Singer* (1770), the Boston-born composer William Billings sums up the matter quite neatly:

> Perhaps it may be expected by some, that I should say something concerning Rules for Composition; to these I answer that *Nature is the best Dictator*, for all the hard dry studied Rules that ever was prescribed, will not enable any Person to form an Air any more than the bare Knowledge of the four and twenty Letters, and strict Grammatical Rules will qualify a Scholar for composing a Piece of Poetry, or properly adjusting a Tragedy, without a Genius. It must be Nature, Nature must lay the Foundation, Nature must inspire the Thought. But perhaps some may think I mean and intend to throw Art intirely [sic] out of the Question, I answer by no Means, for the more Art is display'd, the more Nature is decorated. And in some sorts of Composition, there is dry Study requir'd, and Art very requisite. For instance, in a *Fugue*, where the Parts come in after each other, with the same Notes; but even there, Art is subservient to Genius, for Fancy [i.e., fantasy, imagination] goes first, and strikes out the Work roughly, and Art comes after, and polishes it over. . . . Therefore . . . for me to dictate, or pretend to prescribe Rules of this Nature for others, would not only be very unnecessary, but also a great Piece of Vanity.[4]

Billings goes on to describe in some detail the necessary mechanical rules of music, such as scales, basic harmony, and so on, because a certain familiarity with such conventions is a prerequisite for sharing almost any form of expression. Other composers of the time voiced similar ideas. Haydn drew a sharp distinction between the (natural) invention of a melody and its (artificial) working out. When asked late in his life how he went about composing, Haydn responded,

> I sat down [at the keyboard] and began to fantasize, according to whether my mood was sad or happy, serious or playful. Once I had seized an idea,

4. William Billings, "Introduction to the Rules of Musick," from his *The New England Psalm-Singer* (1770), in *The Complete Works of William Billings*, vol. 1, p. 32, ed. Karl Kroeger (© 1981 American Musicological Society and the Colonial Society of Massachusetts).

Mozart's most revealing statement on the relationship between genius and technique in composition appears in a letter he wrote from Paris to his father about one of his pupils. The young lady grasps the rules of voice leading and harmony well enough, he reports, but he doubts she will ever have an original idea of her own.

———◆—◆———

I think I told you in my last letter that the Duc de Guines, whose daughter is my pupil in composition, plays the flute extremely well, and that she plays the harp *magnifique*. She has a great deal of talent and even genius, and in particular a marvelous memory, so that she can play all her pieces, actually about two hundred, by heart. She is, however, extremely doubtful as to whether she has any talent for composition, especially as regards invention or ideas. But her father (who, between ourselves, is somewhat too infatuated with her) declares that she certainly has ideas and that it is only that she is too bashful and has too little self-confidence. Well, we shall see. If she gets no inspirations or ideas (for at present she really has none whatever), then it is to no purpose, for—God knows—I can't give her any. Her father's intention is not to make a great composer of her. "She is not," he said, "to compose operas, arias, concertos, symphonies, but only grand sonatas for her instrument and mine." I gave her a fourth lesson today and, so far as the rules of composition and harmony are concerned, I am fairly well satisfied with her. She filled in quite a good bass for the first minuet, the melody of which I had given her,

and she has already begun to write in three parts. But she very soon gets bored, and I am unable to help her; for as yet I cannot proceed more quickly. It is too soon, even if there really were genius there, but unfortunately there is none. Everything has to be done by rule. She has no ideas whatever, nothing comes. I have tried with her in every possible way. Among other things I hit on the idea of writing down a very simple minuet, in order to see whether she could not compose a variation on it. It was useless. "Well," I thought, "she probably does not know how she ought to begin." So I started to write a variation on the first bar and told her to go on in the same way and to keep to the idea. In the end it went fairly well. When it was finished, I told her to begin something on her own, only the treble part, the melody. Well, she thought and thought for a whole quarter of an hour and nothing came. So I wrote down four bars of a minuet and said to her: "See what an ass I am! I have begun a minuet and cannot even finish the melody. Please be so kind as to finish it for me." She was positive she couldn't, but at last with great difficulty something came, and indeed I was only too glad to see something for once. I then told her to finish the minuet, I mean, the treble only. But for *homework* all I asked her to do was to alter my four bars and compose something of her own. She was to find a new beginning and use, if necessary, the same harmony, provided that the melody should be different. Well, I shall see tomorrow what she has done.

Source: Mozart to his father, 14 May 1778; transl. MEB

my entire effort went toward elaborating and sustaining it according to the rules of art. . . . And this is what is lacking among so many of our young composers; they string together one little bit after another, and they break off before they have barely begun, but nothing remains in the heart when one has heard it.[5]

The genius of inspiration—the idea—is an essential first step in the process, but it is not an end in itself. Indeed, Haydn implies it is all too easy to string together a series of appealing—"natural"—melodies, but that such efforts rarely leave a lasting impression on the listener.

MUSIC IN THE CLASSICAL ERA: A STYLISTIC OVERVIEW

Opinions vary widely as to just when the Classical era began. Some music historians trace its origins as far back as the 1720s, others as late as the 1780s. The date used in this book, 1750, splits the difference between these extremes.

---

5. Georg August Griesinger, *Biographische Notizen über Joseph Haydn*, ed. Karl-Heinz Köhler (Leipzig: Reclam, 1975; 1st edition 1810), p. 78. Transl. MEB.

Harmony as a structural principle. Johann Philipp Kirnberger's *Die Kunst des reinen Satzes in der Musik* ("The Art of Strict Musical Composition," 1771–79) devotes considerable attention to the relationship between voice leading and harmony, arguing that "all music which cannot be reduced to a natural progression of both kinds of fundamental chords"—that is, triads and seventh chords—"is composed unintelligibly, hence incorrectly and contrary to the strict style of composition." To illustrate the importance of harmony within even the most contrapuntal structures, Kirnberger reduces the B-minor fugue from Book I of J. S. Bach's *Well-Tempered Clavier* to a series of harmonic progressions. The uppermost system shows Bach's original (mm. 66–67); the middle system shows a skeletal reduction of all parts with a figured bass; the next-to-bottom line shows a slightly different figured bass, including all dissonances; and the bass line at the bottom shows the harmony reduced to its fundamental components as defined by Rameau (triads and chords of the seventh). Although such a reduction might seem unremarkable today, Kirnberger's method manifests a fundamental shift in theoretical thought from the Baroque to the Classical era.

Source: Courtesy of the Library of Congress

The wide range of opinion about the beginning of the Classical era reflects the mixture of styles prevalent throughout the middle decades of the 18th century. Elements of Baroque style coexisted with elements of Classical style for some time, often within a single work. Styles also varied widely from region to region within Europe, and even from one work to another by the same composer. One of the hallmarks of the Baroque style, basso continuo, continued to be cultivated throughout the Classical era in sacred music and in secco recitative of all kinds, both sacred and secular. Fugues and dense contrapuntal textures, often associated with the later stages of the Baroque era, abound at the end of the 18th century as well.

The end of the Classical era is equally difficult to pinpoint. Some historians extend the period to the death of Beethoven in 1827; others prefer to treat Beethoven's late style (from about 1815 onward) as part of the Romantic era. Still others have argued that the Classical and Romantic eras together constitute a single stylistic epoch. The end date used in this book, 1800, is based less on changes of style than on changes in attitudes toward the nature of music, the profession of the composer, and the perceived role of music in society. As we see in Chapter 14, these new attitudes fundamentally changed the way music was produced and consumed.

The Elements of Classical Style

With these qualifications in mind, we can examine the most important stylistic developments in the Classical era. One early marker is the emergence of genuine homophony—in which a subordinate voice or voices support a single prominent melodic line—as opposed to the continuo homophony of the Baroque era. More and more, the melodic focus moved to the top line and the bass line ceased to function as an independent voice. Over the course of the Classical era, the basso continuo largely disappeared. Not coincidentally, the two genres in which it did survive—sacred music and, in opera, secco recitative—were among the most stylistically conservative.

The increasing prevalence of homophony, however, did not mean the end of counterpoint. Many composers continued to cultivate canon and fugue. And even within essentially homophonic textures, more subtle forms of counterpoint became increasingly prevalent in the 1770s and 1780s with the emergence of the **obbligato accompaniment,** in which secondary voices contribute material essential to a work's musical fabric. Although subordinate to the melody, these accompanimental voices establish their own distinctive profile. For example, in the opening of Haydn's String Quartet in C Major, op. 33, no. 3 (Anthology; discussed again in Chapter 12), the principal melodic line lies firmly in the first violin part, but the second violin, viola, and cello contribute material that, although apparently subordinate at first (mm. 1–3), becomes motivically distinctive as it progresses (mm. 4–6).

Periodic phrase structure, basic to the dance music repertories of earlier eras, became increasingly common in all musical genres of the Classical era. The more or less symmetrical juxtaposition of antecedent and consequent musical statements is found in operas, songs, symphonies, concertos, and all forms of chamber music from the second half of the 18th century. Related to this development was a shift away from paratactic forms, in which discrete thematic ideas follow each other in sequence (A, B, C, D), to syntactic forms, in which a few thematic ideas are manipulated in various ways over an entire movement. The most important new syntactic structure to emerge in the Classical era was *sonata form*, described later in the chapter, which, like periodic phrase structure, has its roots in the structure of earlier dance and dance-related music. Another new syntactic structure, **rondo form,** described in Chapter 12, became popular in the 1780s, particularly for instrumental finales. Composers regularly exploited both forms, often with great ingenuity and wit, creating patterns that were at once distinctive and easily recognizable.

Another characteristic of Classical style, this one emerging around the middle of the 18th century, was a relative slowing of **harmonic rhythm**—that is, the rate of harmonic change within an individual phrase or series of phrases. In most music of the Baroque era, harmonies often change from beat to beat; this is much less common in music of the Classical era, when harmonic shifts tend to occur less frequently, only once or twice in a measure, for example. This change reflects the growing emphasis on homophony, which demanded a decrease in the distinctiveness of all voices other than the melody. As composers came to rely increasingly on areas of broad harmonic contrast and repetition in large-scale forms, the polarity between tonic and dominant became particularly strong during the Classical era. In the binary and ritornello structures of the Baroque era, in contrast, the return to the tonic often occurs just before the end of a movement (see, for example, the binary form aria of J. S. Bach's *Goldberg Variations*, Anthology, or the ritornello-based A section of Cleopatra's aria "Non disperar" from Handel's *Giulio Cesare*, Anthology). In the larger-scale structures of the Classical era like sonata form and rondo form, such a brief return of the tonic would sound incomplete and unsatisfying.

The Illusion of Order

In making such broad generalizations about Classical style, we should keep in mind that Newton's third law of motion applies to musical as well as physical objects: every

The original title page from Mozart's "Musical Joke." "A Musical Joke for Two Violins, Viola, Two Horns, and Bass, written in Vienna on the 14th of June, 1787, by W. A. Mozart. Op. 93," published by Johann André in 1802. The artwork fits the music perfectly, for in this sextet Mozart lampoons many of the conventions of Classical style. The part writing is intentionally faulty at times, rhythms and harmonies are displaced, and the closing fugue never quite gets off the ground. Buyers are nevertheless assured that this publication has been "edited according to the original manuscript of the author." By the end of the 18th century, consumers were beginning to demand editions of works that were accurate and genuine—that is, written by the composer named on the title page and not by someone else. André knew the exact date of composition because he had acquired many of Mozart's manuscripts, including his personal thematic catalog, from the composer's widow, Constanze. **Source:** Dover Publications, Inc.

action produces an equal and opposite reaction. The sense of balance and proportion that characterizes the Classical style is equally countered by an undercurrent of asymmetry and irregularity. Just as syncopation is possible only within a defined metrical pattern, so too did the naturalness favored by 18th-century aesthetics make room for a subversion of balance and proportion. The apparent order on the surface of much of this music often covers a more complex subsurface.

This illusion of order is captured in Jean-Honoré Fragonard's well-known painting of 1767 entitled *The Pleasant Dangers of the Swing*. At first glance, this painting appears to depict an orderly scene of simple and innocent playfulness, a young man pushing a young woman on a swing. Closer inspection, however, reveals an undercurrent of sexual tension. Similar contrasting levels operate in music as well: what we hear on the surface may seem orderly and straightforward, yet below the surface—often not so very far down—the music is turbulent and unpredictable. Haydn, Mozart, and their contemporaries wrote music that abounds with irregularity, humor, and irony. The opening of Haydn's String Quartet in C Major, op. 33, no. 3, for example, is anything but regular. The music starts and stops and starts again in unpredictable ways, with gestures that function within—yet at the same time against—the framework of periodic phrase structure. Mozart's Piano Concerto in E♭, K. 271 (Anthology; see Chapter 12), introduces the solo instrument in the second measure, long before any listener of the time would have expected to hear it. And no one at the premiere of Haydn's Symphony no. 103 in E♭ (Anthology) in London in 1795 could possibly have anticipated the very loud and unprepared drumroll with which it begins.

The Classical era is often misunderstood as an age in which composers were somehow shackled by rules. This view, like the label *Classical* itself, arose in the 19th century. But there were in fact no rules to follow or break, only conventions to observe

The illusion of order. In his *Les hasards heureux de l'escarpolette* ("The Pleasant Dangers of the Swing") of 1767, Jean-Honoré Fragonard (1732–1806), a contemporary of Haydn, captures perfectly the kind of artistic playfulness and ambiguity so typical of late 18th-century art. The image works on several levels: it is at once innocent, erotic, and comic. The virtuous-looking young man on the right pushes the young lady on the swing (he uses ropes, for it would be improper actually to touch her). His earnestness contrasts with the rapture of the young man—a rival for her affections?—spying voyeuristically on the scene from the bushes on the left. How are we to understand the young lady's strange expression? Is she aware of the man on the left? Has she lost her shoe by accident, or kicked it off deliberately, and if deliberately, is it to reward or punish her concealed admirer? Much of the music of this era moves back and forth between order and disruption in an analogous manner. The music of Haydn, in particular, is often simultaneously regular and irregular, serious and humorous.

Source: Jean-Honoré Fragonard (1732–1806), "The Swing," oil on canvas/Musée Lambinet, Versailles, France/Bridgeman Giraudon/Lauros/Bridgeman Art Library

or bend. The young Beethoven who arrived in Vienna in 1792 was considerably more conservative than the elderly Haydn, who in his time was renowned for his idiosyncratic wit and unpredictability. During his own lifetime Haydn was repeatedly compared to Laurence Sterne, the author of *Tristram Shandy*, one of the most anarchical works in all of English literature. Sterne uses—and at the same time breaks—every known convention of narrative, repeatedly making his readers aware they are reading a book. Much of the music written during the Classical era, as we will see, adopts this same approach. In a style that was supposedly natural—at least on the surface—we are repeatedly reminded of the artifice behind the effect.

FORM AND STYLE IN THE MID-18TH CENTURY

The hallmarks of Classical style began to emerge as early as the 1720s, becoming increasingly evident around the middle of the century. Music historians have used several terms to describe the stylistically diverse music of the decades between the 1720s and the 1750s. Some call it *Preclassical*, but this term carries an unfortunate (if unintended) value judgment, suggesting the music of this time is somehow not yet up to the standards of the full-fledged Classical style. Others, borrowing from art history, use the terms **Galant** and **Rococo**. Both imply a sense of grace and elegance, aptly capturing the more transparent textures evident in many works of this time.

Another term, **Empfindsamkeit**—German for "sensibility"—describes a characteristic aesthetic associated with the new style. In the 18th century, to be a person of sensibility or "sentiment," as it was also called, was to be attuned to nuance and detail, delighting in small things. The author Laurence Sterne mocked this aesthetic in his 1768 novel *A Sentimental Journey through France and Italy*, in which the central character is so sensitive to details that he remains blind to larger and more consequential events. The term is nevertheless fitting for much of the music written around the middle of the 18th century, which tends to focus on detail and avoid thick textures and grandiose gestures.

The Emergence of Sonata Form

The most important formal innovation of the Classical era was **sonata form.** Although the term for it dates to the middle of the 19th century, this structural device had become firmly entrenched by the late 18th century. It applies to the organization of individual movements in a variety of genres—including sonatas, symphonies, and quartets—not to any sonata, symphony, or quartet as a whole.

Sonata form is essentially an expanded binary form that always modulates within the first reprise and usually involves more than one theme. The first reprise is called the **exposition** because it exposes the thematic ideas that will be manipulated in the second reprise. The exposition begins with one or more themes in the tonic, or primary key area (P), followed by a transitional (T) modulation to one or more themes in the secondary key area (S), usually the dominant (if the movement is in a major key) or the relative major (if the movement is in a minor key). The thematic material first stated in the primary key area is conventionally labeled P (or 1P, 2P, and so on, if there are multiple themes in this key). The thematic material first stated in the secondary key area is conventionally labeled S (or 1S, 2S, and so on). The transitional material, which can have its own themes, is conventionally labeled T.

The first part of the second reprise is called the **development** because it develops the thematic ideas of the exposition. Harmonically, the development tends to be unstable and can move to almost any key other than the tonic. The harmonic instability and unpredictability of the development is counterbalanced by the **recapitulation**—the second part of the second reprise—which reestablishes the tonic. The onset of the recapitulation is usually marked by a simultaneous return to the tonic key and a restatement of the opening theme of the exposition (1P). A recapitulation typically follows the order of the exposition, sometimes closely, sometimes freely, but always with one important difference: the thematic material (S) that was first stated in the secondary key is now restated in the tonic. In other words, the recapitulation, unlike the exposition, does not modulate, but remains in the tonic, providing a sense of harmonic balance and stability. The effect is to resolve the movement's harmonic contrasts and bring it to a satisfying close. Some sonatas conclude with a **coda** (Italian for "tail") after the recapitulation. Codas, like tails, range from short to long, but they always end on the tonic.

A typical sonata-form movement, then, might be diagrammed as follows:

Sonata Form				
Section	Exposition	Development	Recapitulation	(Coda)
Themes	‖: 1P 2P . . . T 1S 2S . . .	:‖: any theme(s) from exposition	1P 2P . . . T 1S 2S . . . :‖	
Key	I or → V or	unstable	I or	I or
	i III		i	i

In practice, no two manifestations of sonata form are entirely alike. The only constant elements are the modulation from a primary to a secondary key area in the exposition, a departure from these harmonic areas in the development, and the simultaneous return of the opening idea and the primary key area in the recapitulation. These predictable conventions provided listeners with easily recognized signposts with which they could orient themselves within a sonata form movement.

The First Movement of Monn's Symphony in B Major

Section	Exposition				Development			Recapitulation			
Themes	‖:1P	2P	T	1S	:‖:1P	2P		1P	2P	T	1S :‖
Measure	1	9	19	26	32	39		59	67	79	86
Key	I			V	V	ii (unstable)		I			

CD7, Track 1
MONN
Symphony in B Major
Score Anthology II/99

The first movement of Georg Matthias Monn's Symphony in B Major is an early example of sonata form. Probably written around 1740, the symphony exhibits both Baroque and Classical features. The first movement begins with two four-measure phrases in which the figure stated in the first phrase by the first violins is repeated in the second phrase by the second violins. This kind of periodic phrase structure can be found in the music of both eras; but the bass line is decidedly un-Baroque, in that it provides harmonic underpinning but very little in the way of an independent voice. With its steady drumlike rhythm and repetition of single notes for up to two measures, the bass line also acts to slow the harmonic rhythm of the movement.

The exposition sets out two different themes in the tonic (1P and 2P), another within the transition from the tonic to the secondary key area (T), and another (1S) in the secondary key area, F♯ major, the dominant of B. The development begins with 1P but now in the dominant. (Note that themes retain the identity assigned them in the exposition throughout a movement as a whole, regardless of the key in which they might subsequently appear.) The development then circulates through a series of harmonies, none of which establishes an area of clear stability. From measure 39 until the end of the development, a variant of the musical idea 2P predominates. At measure 59, the recapitulation begins with the return of the opening theme (1P) in its original key. At measure 67, we hear what is recognizably 2P, but in a different form. Beginning in measure 79 we hear a variant of the transitional theme (T), which this time remains in the tonic, leading to a restatement of 1S (m. 86), likewise in the tonic. The movement has no coda and ends with the recapitulation.

Not all binary form movements from this period bear the hallmarks of sonata form. Most of Domenico Scarlatti's one-movement sonatas for keyboard lack a clear recapitulation. The Sonata in D Major, K. 492, written in the 1750s toward the end of the composer's life (1685–1757), features two areas of harmonic stability (tonic and dominant) in the first reprise but lacks a clear return of the opening idea in the tonic within the second reprise. The material originally presented in the dominant, however, is restated in the tonic in the second reprise, beginning in measure 91.

CD7, Track 2
DOMENICO SCARLATTI
Sonata in D Major, K. 492
Score Anthology II/100

Like the first movement of Monn's symphony, Scarlatti's sonata features mixed elements of Baroque and Classical styles. The periodic phrase structure, relatively slow harmonic rhythm, and transparent textures look forward, whereas the virtuosic runs (mm. 35–42, 91–97) and sequential passages (mm. 10–16, 36–42, etc.) are more characteristic of the earlier part of the 18th century.

CD7, Track 3
STAMITZ
Symphony in D Major, op. 3, no. 2
Score Anthology II/101

The first movement of Johann Stamitz's Symphony in D Major, op. 3, no. 2 (ca. 1752–55) shares the Classical elements of the Monn and Scarlatti; the sequences still appear, but are more abbreviated and take unexpected turns. As this movement demonstrates, however, binary form is not the only historical antecedent to sonata form: another is the ritornello structure of the typical Baroque aria or concerto, which features a modulation from a primary to a secondary key area, followed by a period of harmonic instability and a return to the tonic at the end. The first movement of Stamitz's symphony states its opening (ritornello) theme twice in the tonic (at mm. 5 and m. 103) and once in the dominant (m 53). In between are areas of tonic instability and opposition. The first modulation begins in measure 18, ending in the dominant, A Major, confirmed by a distinctive second theme area (m. 37); this element suggests sonata form (or at least something other than a concerto grosso). Yet the lack of repeat signs (found in the previous two pieces) makes interpretation as a Classical sonata form problematic.

The return of the opening theme in the dominant (m. 53) initiates a transition that soon reestablishes the tonic; here, Stamitz incorporates previous material (compare mm. 29 and 77; more subtly, the ritornello theme, m. 44, and m. 82); the tonic returns definitively with the second theme in measure 87, which reinforces the sense of a sonata form. The return of the opening theme (m. 103) does not coincide with the return of the tonic, however, and in this sense, the recapitulation is diffused; the section that leads to it is more transitional than developmental. Many movements from the mid-18th century feature such mixed elements of old (ritornello) and new (sonata) forms. Even in the later decades of the 18th century, composers frequently departed from the standard conventions of sonata form.

Relationship of Ritornello Structure and Sonata Form in the First Movement of Stamitz's Symphony in D Major, op. 3, no. 2													
Ritornello structure	Ritornello I						Ritornello II			Ritornello III			
"Sonata form"	"Exposition"						"Development"			"Recapitulation"			
Themes	1P	2P	1T	2T	1S	2S	1P	2P	2T	1S	2S	1P	2P
Measure	5	13	18	29	37	44	53	61	77	87	94	103	111
Key	I				V		V		(IV-V)	I			

CD7, Track 4
J. C. BACH
Sonata in D Major, op. 5, no. 2
Score Anthology II/102

By the 1760s, sonata form had established itself as the structural framework for the first movements of most instrumental works, and for some slow movements and many finales as well. Except for concertos, the influence of ritornello structure had largely disappeared. The opening movement of Johann Christian Bach's Keyboard Sonata in D Major, op. 5, no. 2, first published in 1766, is typical for its time, and not just from the standpoint of form. The simple, straightforward melodies, textures, and rhythms create a movement that is unpretentious in the best sense of the word. The first movement of this sonata offered what 18th-century critics perceived as a natural form of expression that was unforced, without overt displays of contrapuntal, rhythmic, or textural artifice.

FOCUS   Mannheim's "Orchestra of Generals"

Johann Stamitz (1717–57) wrote his Symphony op. 3, no. 2, for his orchestra at the court of Mannheim, in southwestern Germany. The ensemble was renowned for its virtuosos. The critic and historian Charles Burney, who experienced firsthand almost every major ensemble of his time, wrote that this orchestra had "more solo players and good composers . . . than perhaps . . . any other orchestra in Europe; it is an army of generals, equally fit to plan a battle as to fight it." Another contemporary observer, C. D. F. Schubart, observed that "its forte is like thunder, its crescendo like a waterfall, its diminuendo is like a distant plashing brook, its piano like a breath of spring." In the 1770s, Mozart sought to find a position at the Mannheim court. He failed, but he did meet Constanze Weber, his future wife, there.

In the early 20th century, the German music historian Hugo Riemann championed the composers of what he called the "Mannheim School"—Stamitz, Franz Xaver Richter (1709–89), Ignaz Holzbauer (1711–83), and others—for their forward-looking orchestral scoring: extended crescendos (evident in Stamitz's symphony in the opening measures), tremolos, and an advanced integration of winds and strings. More recent research has shown that many of these devices originated in Italy and were transmitted to Mannheim through prominent operatic composers of the day.

The castle at Mannheim. Now the central building of the city's university, this imposing structure was the home of Europe's most renowned orchestra in the middle of the 18th century.
Source: © Achim Bednorz, Köln

The sharp contrast between this movement by J. C. Bach and a work like his father Johann Sebastian Bach's "Goldberg" Variations, written only 25 years earlier, illustrates the generation gap that divided Classical from Baroque style. In the opening air of the "Goldberg" Variations, the theme is in the bass and remains there through all subsequent variations; the melody in the soprano is of only momentary significance. In the opening measures of the son's work, in contrast, the lowest voice consists of repeated figurations on a series of triadic harmonies. This **Alberti bass**—so called because it was a favorite device of an otherwise obscure Italian composer named Domenico Alberti (1710–ca. 1740)—provides harmonic support for the melody in the upper voice but is not itself very engaging. The frequent repetition of the same broken chord necessarily leads to a harmonic rhythm slower than that typically found in music from the Baroque era. J. C. Bach's sonata also avoids the kind of sequential repetition so basic to much of his father's music.

Typically for music of the 1760s, the dimensions of J. C. Bach's movement are relatively small. The exposition presents only one theme in the primary key area (1P, mm. 1–8), and the transitional theme (T) suggests a move away from the tonic as early as

COMPOSER PROFILE

Carl Philipp Emanuel Bach (1714–88) and Johann Christian Bach (1735–82)

Today, Johann Sebastian Bach's reputation overshadows that of his children, but in the late 18th century this was not the case. Indeed to the extent the senior Bach was known at all, it was primarily as the father of Carl Philipp Emanuel Bach (the "Berlin Bach") and Johann Christian Bach (the "London Bach"). The two were actually half brothers. Carl Philipp was the second surviving son of Maria Barbara Bach, who died in 1720; Johann Christian was the youngest surviving son of Anna Magdalena Bach, whom Johann Sebastian had married in 1721. Both boys, along with their many siblings, learned to perform and compose from their father, but they developed distinctive styles consistent with their times. Carl Philipp, after all, was a near contemporary of Gluck, whereas Johann Christian was actually three years younger than Haydn.

KEY DATES IN THE LIFE OF CARL PHILIPP EMANUEL BACH

1714	Born in Weimar on March 8, second surviving son of J. S. Bach
1723	Moves with his family to Leipzig and continues to study music under his father
1740	Appointed chamber musician and clavecinist to Frederick the Great at the court in Berlin
1753–1762	Publishes his *Essay on the True Art of Playing Keyboard Instruments*
1767	Succeeds Telemann as music director of the principal church in Hamburg
1788	Dies in Hamburg, December 14

C. P. E. Bach. Carl Philipp Emanuel Bach (center) drops in on Christoph Christian Sturm, one of the leading clerics in the city of Hamburg, who in turn is having his portrait done by the artist Andreas Stöttrup. Sturm had written a number of poems on religious themes that C. P. E. Bach would later set to music. The scene thus represents a meeting of art, music, and poetry.

Source: Andreas Stoettrup, pen and ink- wash sketch, 1774, showing Bach and Sturm. Hamburger Kunsthalle, C. P. E. Bach. Bildarchiv Preussisher Kulturbesitz.

In 1740, C. P. E. Bach was appointed chamber musician and clavecinist to the court of Frederick II ("The Great") at Potsdam, just outside Berlin. The post gave him the freedom and resources to compose and perform in an almost ideal setting. One of his colleagues was Johann Joachim Quantz, the greatest flutist of his time and a composer of wide renown. In 1752, Quantz published what was then the definitive treatise on flute technique. The following year, C. P. E. Bach published the first volume of a two-volume treatise on harpsichord technique. Both treatises have considerable information on composition and aesthetics. In 1750, C. P. E. Bach sought to succeed his recently deceased father as Kantor of St. Thomas's Church in Leipzig, but the town council there rejected his application. In 1767, he assumed the duties of music director for the city of Hamburg, succeeding another celebrated musician of the time, Georg Philipp Telemann (1681–1767). Bach's responsibilities in this new capacity included providing music for the city's five main churches, so not surprisingly, he wrote most of his sacred music during these last years of his life. C. P. E. Bach rivaled his father's prodigiousness, leaving behind more than 200 works for solo harpsichord, more than 50 concertos, 18 symphonies, dozens of chamber works, two oratorios, and 22 Passions.

After a visit to C. P. E. Bach in Hamburg in 1772, the music historian Charles Burney wrote the following account of the composer at the clavichord:

After dinner . . . I prevailed upon him to sit down again to a clavichord, and he played, with little intermission, till near eleven o'clock at night. During this time, he grew so animated and *possessed*, that he not only played, but looked like one inspired. His eyes were fixed, his under lip fell, and drops of effervescence distilled from his countenance. He said, if he were to be set to work frequently, in this manner, he should grow young again. He is now fifty-nine, rather short in stature, with black hair and eyes, and brown complexion, has a very animated countenance, and is of a cheerful and lively disposition. His performance today convinced me of what I had suggested before from his works; that he is not only one of the greatest composers that ever existed, for keyed instruments, but the best player, in point *of expression*, for others, perhaps, have had as rapid execution: however, he possesses every style; though he chiefly confines himself to the expressive.[6]

Johann Christian Bach. Unlike his father, who never traveled outside central and northern Germany, Johann Christian Bach was a true cosmopolite who felt equally at home in Germany, Italy, and England. During his years in London, from 1762 until the end of his life, he enjoyed the patronage of the royal family, particularly Queen Charlotte, wife of George III. This connection led to a commission for the portrait shown here from one of the leading artists of the time, Thomas Gainsborough (1727–88).

Source: © Archivo Iconografico, S.A./CORBIS

Johann Christian Bach lived for a time in Milan (in northern Italy) but in 1762 moved to London, where he served as music master to Queen Charlotte, the wife of King George III. His graceful compositions, most of which are within the technical grasp of amateur performers, enjoyed great popularity in their time. The "London Bach" wrote in almost every genre of his era: opera, oratorio, sacred music, symphony, chamber music, and above all keyboard music. When the young Mozart visited the English capital with his father Leopold in 1764–65, J. C. Bach played a key role in introducing them to fellow musicians and influential patrons.

PRINCIPAL WORKS OF CARL PHILIPP EMANUEL BACH

C. P. E. Bach composed in almost all the same genres as his father, but was perhaps most prolific in his works for keyboard. These include sonatas, concertos, trio sonatas, and many individual pieces such as rondos, fantasias, and dance movements. He also wrote symphonies, songs, and many large-scale works for chorus and orchestra, including passions, oratorios, and motets.

PRINCIPAL WORKS OF JOHANN CHRISTIAN BACH

J. C. Bach was renowned in his lifetime not only as a composer of keyboard music, particularly sonatas and concertos, but also as one of the leading composers of opera seria, of which he wrote more than a dozen. He wrote symphonies, concertos, and much sacred music as well.

KEY DATES IN THE LIFE OF JOHANN CHRISTIAN BACH

1735	Born in Leipzig on September 5, the eleventh and youngest surviving son of J. S. Bach
1750	After his father's death, continues his musical studies with his brother Carl Philipp Emanuel Bach, in Berlin
1754	Appointed music director to Count Antonio Litta in Milan, Italy
1762	Moves to England and is soon appointed music master to Queen Charlotte
1782	Dies in London, January 1

6. Charles Burney, *An Eighteenth-Century Musical Tour in Central Europe and the Netherlands*, ed. Percy A. Scholes (London: Oxford University Press, 1959), p. 219.

its second measure (with the A♯ in the bass at the end of m. 10) before cadencing clearly on V of V in measure 18. The first theme in the secondary key area (1S, beginning in m. 19) presents a strong contrast to the opening theme, and the exposition as a whole ends with a clearly articulated cadence (m. 42). During the development, the themes appear in fragments. The end of 1S, for example, appears at the beginning of the development in measure 43, and the beginning of T can be heard in measure 48. In measure 60, the harmony reaches what later theorists would call a "point of furthest remove" from the tonic, in this case B minor. The music then gathers itself for a retransition back to the tonic and the opening theme, which arrives with great emphasis at measure 73, the beginning of the recapitulation. In typical sonata form fashion, the themes are presented in the same order as in the exposition, but this time all in the tonic and with only small variations and embellishments.

Sonata form appealed to composers and listeners alike. Composers used it as a framework for large-scale movements incorporating multiple and often contrasting thematic ideas. Audiences, too, benefited from hearing ideas presented in a more or less predictable order and fashion. An 18th-century listener hearing a work like J. C. Bach's Sonata op. 5, no. 2, for the first time, for example, could readily apprehend the overall structure of the opening movement based on its adherence to the conventions of sonata form. In this sense, sonata form functions more as a broad outline than a strict plan, rather like the form of a murder mystery, with its predictable sequence of characters and events: a crime, followed by a series of clues unraveled by an investigator sorting through a string of suspects, and ending with a solution. Yet no two sonata form movements are exactly alike, just as no two murder mysteries follow exactly the same plot, even though they follow the same general and predictable outline.

The Fantasia

To appreciate the function of formal conventions in a structure like sonata form, it helps to consider the one genre without any: the fantasia. For a composer to designate a work or movement a fantasia was to alert listeners that it would provide them with no predictable framework. In the 18th century, theorists often claimed the fantasia had "no theme." This is not literally true, of course, in that every fantasia has at least one theme, and most of them have quite a few. What theorists meant by this claim is that the fantasia typically lacks a *central* theme around which the work as a whole is organized. Eighteenth-century theorists also liked to compare the fantasia to that part of the compositional process identified with inspiration, the invention of ideas. Haydn himself said that when he began to compose, he sat down at the keyboard and *fantasized* until he latched on to a theme.

In this sense, the fantasia is like a search for themes, often opening with rhapsodic, quasi-improvisatory flourishes on the triad. At the beginning of Carl Philipp Emanuel Bach's Fantasia in C minor (originally published as the finale to a three-movement keyboard sonata in 1753), we hear a series of broken arpeggios and seemingly aimless passagework. The music conveys a mood of contemplation. Indeed, it struck the poet Heinrich Wilhelm von Gerstenberg as grappling with issues of life and death, inspiring him to set an elaborate text to this music based on the celebrated soliloquy in Shakespeare's *Hamlet* ("To be, or not to be: that is the question . . ."). Gerstenberg later set a second text to it as well, this one based on the dramatic moment when Socrates drinks poison rather than compromise his ethical principles. One reason for the serious reaction this work provoked is its dramatic trajectory: it begins with a mood of resigned contemplation, becomes agitated, recedes to a lyrical tone (the Largo section), and concludes with agitated force (Allegro moderato).

Like many fantasias of the time, C. P. E. Bach's is full of abrupt changes and unexpected events. Such musical rhetoric reflects similar forces in the German literary movement known as *Empfindsamkeit*. This term, usually translated as "sensibility" or "expressivity," was first applied to German literary works of the third quarter of the 18th century, and later to the English novel (as "sentimentality" or "sensitivity"). *Empfindsamkeit* refers to keen awareness of and empathy for the experience of others, rather than the mawkishness associated with these terms today. It was seen as a reaction to, or at least as a compensation for, the rationalism of 18th-century Enlightenment and manifested itself in music through an unusual degree of attention to small-scale gestures, unexpected rests, rapidly shifting moods, and rhythmic freedom. C. P. E. Bach's Fantasia exemplifies this style of writing. It features long stretches without any bar lines, emphasizing the rhythmic freedom with which it is to be performed. The notated meter at the opening—allegro moderato—seems almost irrelevant. Only in the middle section do we hear a recognizable theme in a recognizable meter; but this proves transitory.

CD7, Track 5
C. P. E. BACH
Fantasia in C minor
Score Anthology II/103

CONCLUSION

What we now think of as the Classical style emerged gradually over the course of several decades during the middle of the 18th century: many works from this period resist easy stylistic classification. But by the 1760s, an aesthetic of naturalness had come to predominate, favoring lighter textures, slower harmonic rhythms, and periodic phrase structure.

Summary of Style Differences between Music of the Baroque and Classical Eras

	BAROQUE	CLASSICAL
Style	Two styles, the *prima prattica* and the newer *seconda prattica*.	Sacred music tends to be somewhat more conservative, preserving basso continuo and imitative writing, but most music is written in what was then called the modern style.
Text Setting	Relatively freer projection of texts with greater attention to the declamation of individual words.	Greater emphasis on sense of natural declamation; less focus on the projection of individual words.
Texture	Polyphonic (in the *prima prattica*) or homophonic (in the *seconda prattica*) with a strong sense of polarity between the two outer voices ("continuo homophony").	Predominantly homophonic, especially in the early years of the Classical era, although with increasing use of nonimitative counterpoint ("obbligato accompaniment") in later decades.
Rhythm	A cultivation of extremes between simplicity and complexity, typically determined in vocal works by the text. The tactus gives way to a stronger sense of meter with fixed units of "strong" and "weak" beats.	Periodic phrase structure predominates, but this supposedly natural symmetry is often inflected by subtle irregularities.
Melody	More openly virtuosic, with more opportunities for embellishment by soloists. A growing differentiation between vocal and instrumental idioms.	Predominantly lyrical, with emphasis on periodic phrase structure. Virtuosity remains an option, but an aesthetic of naturalness predominates.
Harmony	Primarily tonal, especially by the end of the 17th century, with harmony conceived of as a progression of vertical sonorities. Relatively freer treatment of dissonance and voice leading.	A relatively slower harmonic rhythm, with limited and carefully controlled use of dissonance. The growing polarity of tonic and dominant allows composers to create movement-length forms on the basis of large-scale areas of harmonic stability.
Form	Both paratactic and syntactic, that is, with subunits connected rhythmically, harmonically, and thematically. Increasing use of ostinato patterns, binary form, and the ritornello principle.	Syntactic forms predominate, particularly binary form and its outgrowth, sonata form; rondo form becomes increasingly popular in finales after 1780. The only significant paratactic form is the set of variations on a theme.
Instrumentation	Composers have the option of either a cappella or concertato scoring, the latter with independent instrumental parts that complement rather than double the vocal lines. Vocal and instrumental idioms become increasingly differentiated.	A clear distinction between vocal and instrumental parts becomes the norm. The nucleus of the modern orchestra (strings, winds, brass, percussion) emerges as the standard ensemble for large instrumental works.

Instrumental Music in the Classical Era

Public demand for instrumental music grew steadily over the course of the Classical era, driven in part by the increasing internationalization of the music publishing trade, in part by the growing affluence of middle- and upper-middle-class musical amateurs. These amateurs sought out the latest chamber music, and publishers were there to sell it to them. A string quartet by Mozart printed in Vienna would now be readily available in, say, London or Paris. And composers kept publishers and musicians alike supplied with a remarkable outpouring of new works.

THE LANGUAGE OF INSTRUMENTAL MUSIC

Since antiquity, theorists and musicians had considered vocal music superior to purely instrumental music. Most Enlightenment thinkers who had something to say about music concurred in this evaluation. Jean-Jacques Rousseau, for example, writing in the 1760s, criticized instrumental music on much the same grounds as Plato had more than two thousand years before. Without words, Rousseau argued, music could please the senses, but it could not embody concepts or reason:

> The words to be sung usually provide us with the means to determine the object being imitated, and it is through the touching sounds of the human voice that this image awakens in the depth of our souls the sentiment it is intended to arouse. Who does not feel how far the pure symphony [instrumental music]—which seeks merely to make instruments sound brilliant—is from this energy? Can all the trifles of [the celebrated virtuoso] Monsieur Mondonville's violin move me as much as two sounds from [the celebrated diva] Madame Le Maure's voice? The symphony animates the song and adds to its expression but cannot supplant it. To understand what all the tumult of sonatas might mean . . . we would have to follow the lead of the coarse painter who was obliged to write underneath that which he had drawn such statements as "This is a tree," or "This is a man," or "This is a horse." I shall never forget the exclamation of the celebrated Fontenelle, who, finding himself exhausted by these eternal symphonies, cried out in a fit of impatience: "Sonata, what do you want of me?"[1]

1. Jean Jacques Rousseau, *Dictionnaire de musique* (Paris: Veuve Duchesne, 1768), article "Sonate." Transl. MEB.

Thomas Jefferson, music collector. In addition to being author of the Declaration of Independence, president of the United States, and founder of the University of Virginia, Thomas Jefferson was also an accomplished violinist. "Music," he once declared, "is the favorite passion of my soul." This note, probably a copy of one sent to a London music dealer, asks for more sonatas by the Italian composer Carlo Antonio Campioni (1720–1788). Jefferson writes, "On this paper is noted the beginning of the several compositions of Campioni which are in possession of T. Jefferson. He would be glad to have everything else he has composed of Solos, Duets, or Trios. Printed copies would be preferred; but if not to be had, he would have them in manuscript."

In Jefferson's time (and for many decades afterward) there were virtually no thematic catalogs available for any composers (see Appendix 1). Jefferson's laborious set of incipits—the first few measures of each piece—cost him time, but he had no other way to identify Campioni's works precisely. European publishers placed arbitrary opus numbers on whatever group of works they had before them. Thus Campioni's Trio Sonatas, op. 4 as published by Walsh of London around 1762 are altogether different from his Trio Sonatas, op. 4 as published by Hummel of Amsterdam at around the same time. Musicians in the United States relied almost entirely on European publishers for printed music, especially for chamber and orchestral works.

Source: Monticello Music Collection on deposit from the Thomas Jefferson Foundatin (3177-a), Special Collections, University of Virginia Library

The German philosopher Immanuel Kant likewise deemed instrumental music to be "more pleasure than culture."

At the same time, instrumental music was winning newfound respect. Although it lacked vocal music's ability to convey meaning, commentators agreed that it nonetheless constituted a "language of the heart," governed by its own rules of syntax and rhetoric. The idea that instrumental music had a syntax and rhetoric of its own, analogous to the syntax and rhetoric of language, emerged, as we saw, in the early 1700s (see Focus: Musical Rhetoric, in Chapter 10). By the second half of the century, this idea had become widely accepted.

In 1787, the composer and theorist Heinrich Christoph Koch (1749–1816) published a textbook on composition in which he taught students how to construct melodic sentences from two- to four-measure-long phrases. According to Koch, just as a linguistic sentence consists of a subject and predicate, the basic components of a musical sentence, or melody, are a subject phrase followed by a predicate phrase. In a series of examples, Koch shows a variety of techniques for expanding a simple musical sentence like the one in Example 12–1a. In Example 12–1b, for example, he substitutes a more elaborate alternative predicate for the original. And in Example 12–1c, he substitutes expanded versions of both the subject and predicate phrases. He then goes on to show how to join musical sentences into larger units of musical syntax—paragraphs—that cohere by virtue of their common melodic material.

Example 12–1 Examples of simple and expanded phrases in a musical "sentence," from Koch's *Introductory Essay on Composition*, vol. 2 (Leipzig, 1787).

According to Koch and other theorists, an entire movement must carefully combine elements to produce what was called "unity in variety"—a sufficient degree of contrast within an integrated whole. To burden a short movement, for example, with four "completely different melodic units," Koch argued, would create so much variety that it "would destroy a still more basic element of the piece, namely its unity and symmetry."

What is at issue here is the way composers repeat, vary, and contrast melodic elements over whole movements within the constraints of syntactic structures like sonata form. The quality of "unity in variety" is fundamental to the way composers approached all such forms during the Classical era. Without sufficient unity, a work would sound incoherent; without sufficient variety, it would sound tedious. Only the fantasia, which lacks a central theme (see Chapter 11), was exempt from this requirement.

A key concept in the Classical analysis of instrumental music in rhetorical terms is that of the *Hauptsatz* (German for "head sentence," or more idiomatically, "topic sentence"). The inner coherence of an instrumental work, according to Koch and his contemporaries, depends on the way the composer manipulates and sustains the *Hauptsatz.* They compared its function to that of a gospel reading for a church sermon. Just as all the points in a well-structured sermon always relate directly or indirectly to the reading, so all the thematic material in an instrumental movement relate directly or indirectly to the *Hauptsatz* (see Primary Evidence: The Musical Theme as a Topic Sentence).

FORM AND GENRE IN THE INSTRUMENTAL MUSIC OF THE CLASSICAL ERA

The most important genres of the Classical era—sonata, string quartet, symphony, concerto—consisted of three or four movements that provided distinct contrasts of tempo. First and last movements were normally fast; the middle movement (or one of the middle movements) was slower. Slow movements could take many forms: sonata form, theme and variations, and ternary (ABA) are the most common.

In four-movement cycles, one of the interior movements (usually the third) was almost always a **minuet.** This kind of movement was often rollicking and sometimes

PRIMARY EVIDENCE   The Musical Theme as a Topic Sentence

Johann Philipp Kirnberger (1721–83), a pupil of J. S. Bach, wrote important treatises on composition, counterpoint, and harmony. Here he explains the importance of a musical movement's opening theme—its *Hauptsatz*, or topic sentence—and the theme's relationship to subsequent ideas within the movement.

A *Hauptsatz* is a period within a musical work that incorporates the expression and the whole essence of the melody. It appears not only at the beginning of a movement, but is repeated frequently, in different keys and with different variations. The *Hauptsatz* is generally called the "theme," and [Johann] Mattheson compares it not inappropriately to the [scriptural] text that provides the basis of a sermon, which must contain in a few words that which the discourse will develop more fully.

Music is actually the language of sentiment, whose expression is always concise, for sentiment in itself is something simple, something that can be presented in a few brief utterances. Thus, a very short melodic phrase of two, three, or four measures can express a sentiment so definitely and correctly that the listener understands exactly the emotional state of the person who is singing. If, then, a musical work had no other purpose than to present a sentiment clearly, such a brief phrase, if well thought out, would suffice. But this is not the goal of music; it should engage the listener for a period of time in the same emotional state. This cannot be achieved through the mere repetition of the same phrase, no matter how splendid it may be, for the repetition of the same thing becomes boring and destroys the attentiveness of the listener. Therefore, one had to invent a type of melody in which one and the same sentiment, with appropriate variety and different modifications, could be repeated often enough to make the appropriate impression upon the listener.

It is in this manner that the form of most of our usual current musical works has arisen: concertos, symphonies, arias, duets, trios, fugues, etc. They all have this in common: they are based on a *Hauptsatz* presented in a main period, brief and appropriate to the expression of a sentiment; this *Hauptsatz* is supported or interrupted by smaller, interpolated ideas [*Zwischengedanken*—literally "in-between thoughts"] appropriate to it; this *Hauptsatz* and these interpolated ideas are repeated often enough, in different harmonies and keys, and with small melodic variations, so that the spirit of the listener is sufficiently captivated.

Source: Johann Philipp Kirnberger, "Hauptsatz," in Johann Georg Sulzer, ed., *Allgemeine Theorie der schönen Künste* (Leipzig: Weidmann, 1771–74). Trans. MEB

downright boisterous, adding a touch of levity to what might otherwise be a mostly serious work. Derived from a Baroque dance form, the minuet is always in triple meter and almost always consists of two juxtaposed binary forms. The first of these binary forms is called the **minuet proper,** and the second is called the **trio.** At the end of the trio, the minuet proper is repeated, as in a da capo aria. The trio often presents a contrasting mood and typically has a distinct theme or themes of its own; it might also be in a different key or mode.

Finales, too, can take on a variety of forms, the most common of which are sonata form and (particularly from the 1780s onward) **rondo,** a type of movement associated largely with finales and found in many different instrumental genres, including symphonies, string quartets, concertos, and sonatas. Like the minuet, the rondo derives from a Baroque dance form, used for a lively round dance. Rondos appear in many guises, but they always involve the alternation of a recurring theme with contrasting material. In the simplest terms, this pattern can be diagrammed as ABACADA, with A representing the opening, recurring idea (often called the **refrain**), and B, C, and D representing contrasting ideas (known as **episodes,** or **couplets**).

The opening theme, or refrain, of a rondo movement is typically brief and catchy. It is almost always a closed, self-contained unit consisting of an antecedent and consequent phrase with a cadence in the tonic. The first contrasting episode, or couplet, tends to be brief, thereby giving listeners an early return to the refrain. Longer digressions from the refrain usually appear later in a movement.

As with sonata form, composers used the basic rondo structure as a point of departure for any number of related formal schemes. They might, for example, have bundled more than one contrasting episode between refrains to create a pattern like ABACDAEFBA. They also overlaid aspects of sonata form on the rondo to create what eventually came to be known as **sonata-rondo form.** In this synthesis, the first episode (B) is presented in a secondary key, like a theme in the secondary key area of a sonata-form exposition; when this theme reappears toward the end of the movement, it is transposed to the tonic, as in a sonata-form recapitulation. In general terms, then, a sonata-rondo form might look like this:

Sonata-Rondo Form							
Theme	A	B	A	C	A	B	A
Key	I	V	I	X (unstable)	I	I	I

In practice, movements rarely follow this form strictly. Rondo, like sonata form, provided composers with a general framework for the presentation of ideas, not an unchangeable design.

Sonata

The sonata remained the quintessential domestic genre of instrumental music in the Classical era. The keyboard sonata, in particular, flourished throughout the second half of the 18th century, thanks to the growing availability of the piano (see Performance Perspective: The Fortepiano).

The keyboard sonata by Johann Christian Bach (op. 5, no. 2; Anthology II/102), discussed in Chapter 11, is typical of the genre at midcentury. It is light-textured and small in scale, can be played equally well on harpsichord or piano, and places only limited technical demands on the performer.

The same cannot be said of Haydn's Sonata in C minor, Hob. XVI:20, published in 1771, only five years after Bach's. This three-movement work is indicative of the increasing scale of late-century sonatas. Compared to Bach's it is longer, more varied musically and emotionally, and more demanding of the performer. Given its many rapid shifts between *forte* and *piano*, the work is clearly intended for the fortepiano (or clavichord) rather than the harpsichord. A harpsichord, for example, would be incapable of the rapid dynamic changes in measures 13–14.

The first eight measures of the sonata also illustrate Haydn's ability to create irregular patterns even within the constraints of periodic phrase structure. The opening two measures present a standard tonic to dominant progression, leading the listener familiar with this kind of pattern to expect the next two measures to lead back from the dominant to the tonic, completing a closed unit. But Haydn delays the **half cadence** (a cadence on the dominant) by repeating the turning figure sequentially to create an antecedent phrase of four rather than two measures. The next two measures (5–6) reiterate the tonic, but this time in a lower register—register will be a very important compositional element in this movement—and after a surprise flourish in measure 6, the music returns to the tonic in measure 8. This initial point of harmonic and rhythmic closure, however, is not very strong. The composer does not yet want the music to come to a complete stop, so he creates the expectation of continuity by placing the tonic cadence on the third beat of the measure rather than the downbeat

CD7, Track 6
HAYDN
Piano Sonata in C minor,
Hob. XVI:20
Score Anthology II/104

and also by leaving it harmonically "empty"—that is, as unharmonized octave Cs. We may be at the end of a sentence, Haydn is telling us, or even of a paragraph, but certainly not the end of a chapter or an entire work. In one sense, then, this opening eight-measure unit fulfills all our expectations about melodic and rhythmic structure. The first four measures take us from the tonic to the dominant, and the second four bring us back to the tonic. Haydn, however, has manipulated the inner workings of this larger progression in ways that are full of small surprises. Again, the music is rather like Fragonard's painting of the girl on the swing—it seems simple on the surface but on close inspection reveals subtle complications.

Haydn's sonata also features a style of writing that some commentators today refer to as **Sturm und Drang** ("storm and stress"). The term comes from the title of a play written in the late 18th century and applies to a small but significant body of music written during the late 1760s and early 1770s by such composers as Haydn, Mozart, Gluck, and Johann Baptist Vanhal (1739–1813). The characteristics of *Sturm und Drang* music include a predilection for the minor mode and such extreme gestures as large melodic leaps, jagged syncopations, and sudden dynamic contrasts. The overall result is a sense of heightened emotional intensity and drama. Haydn wrote several works that fit this description during the late 1760s and early 1770s, including, in addition to the Piano Sonata in C minor, the Symphonies nos. 45 in F♯ minor and 49 in F minor and the String Quartet in F minor, op. 20, no. 5. Mozart's Symphony in G minor, K. 183, and his Quartet in D minor, K. 173, both of which were written in the early 1770s, also fit the *Sturm und Drang* profile.

String Quartet

Although composers had written chamber works for four instruments during the Baroque era—some trio sonatas, for example, fall into this category—the string quartet is new to the Classical era. Two features in particular distinguish it from most earlier genres. Its performance forces—two violins, a viola, and a violoncello—are all from the same family, giving it a homogeneous timbre, and it has no basso continuo line. Although manuscript copies of some early string quartets include a figured bass, the cello and viola lines together provide the necessary harmonic underpinning that in earlier times would have been supplied by the basso continuo.

The limited timbral variety of the string quartet posed a special challenge to composers but also contributed to the genre's prestige. Contemporaries compared a good quartet to an intimate conversation among a close group of friends, in which the participants exchange ideas. It was a domestic genre, designed for performance in the house or salon to a small and select audience. During the Classical era, string quartets were rarely performed at public concerts. Some of Haydn's string quartets may have been performed publicly in London in the 1790s, but this would have been an exception.

String quartets of the Classical era typically consist of three, four, or five movements, with the four-movement format emerging as the standard in Haydn's works around the late 1760s. Mozart, too, preferred four movements, although other popular composers of the day—notably Carl Dittersdorf (1739–99) and Ignace Pleyel (1757–1831)—favored three (usually in the sequence fast-slow-fast).

The quartets of Haydn and Mozart surpass those of their contemporaries in textural richness and technical difficulty, qualities that did not always impress critics. Mozart's quartets in particular came under fire for being overly elaborate and complex. One anonymous critic, for example, although professing admiration for the composer, complained that Mozart "aims too high in his artful and truly beautiful writing, in order to become a new creator, so that little is gained for feeling and for the heart. His

PERFORMANCE PERSPECTIVE

The Fortepiano
CD7   Track 6

Malcolm Bilson's performance on a fortepiano of the first movement of Haydn's Sonata in C minor, Hob. XVI:20, illustrates the striking difference in sound between the instrument during Haydn's lifetime and the modern-day piano. Bilson plays on an original fortepiano made by the Schantz brothers; we know that Haydn purchased an instrument from this Viennese workshop about 1788. Compared to the modern grand piano, the instrument is smaller in every respect, with a span of about only five octaves and a narrower dynamic range. Yet the fortepiano features a lighter mechanism and a more transparent sound: what it lacks in power it makes up for in finesse, and many players today prefer this kind of instrument for repertory of the late 18th and early 19th centuries.

There were many varieties of fortepiano during Haydn's lifetime. The two most important types were the English and the Viennese (or German). The English pianos manufactured by Broadwood used an intermediate lever to throw the hammer at each set of three strings with considerable force. The resulting sound was distinctively loud, a feature Haydn exploited to great effect in the sonatas he wrote in London in 1791–95.

The Viennese pianos manufactured by such firms as Stein and Walter provided three strings only for the highest notes, two for the rest. Their sound, as a result, was not as powerful as that of the English instruments, but they were more responsive to the player's touch. The most valued feature of the Stein piano was its superior escapement action, which allowed each hammer to return to its original position almost immediately after striking the string. This in turn allowed performers to play rapid and repeated notes more easily than on English instruments. Mozart sent a glowing report of a new Stein instrument's light action to his father in 1777:

> Before I had seen any pianofortes made by Stein, those made by Späth had been my favorites. But now I prefer Stein's, for they dampen the sound much better. . . . When I hit a key forcefully,

the sound vanishes at once, regardless of whether I hold my finger on the key or lift it. I can attack the keys in any way I wish; the tone is always consistent. It does not mangle, get louder or softer, and it certainly does not fail to sound altogether. In a word, everything is even. Granted, he will not sell such a pianoforte for less than 300 gulden, but the care and energy he puts into them are priceless. His instruments distinguish themselves from all others in that they are made with an escapement. Only one in a hundred persons cares about this. But without an escapement it is impossible for a pianoforte to avoid jangling or reverberating unduly. When one strikes the keys, Stein's hammers fall back the moment after they have struck the strings, whether one holds the key down or releases it. When he has made such an instrument (as he told me himself) he sits down at it and tries all kinds of passages, runs, and leaps, and he whittles away and works on the instrument until it can do everything. For he works for the benefit of music and not for his personal benefit alone, otherwise he would be finished with his work right away.[2]

Piano by Johann Andreas Stein, Augsburg, 1790. Mozart praised the responsive action of Stein's pianos, which had a keyboard of 61 notes, from the F two-and-a-half octaves below middle C to the F two-and-a-half octaves above. The dampers were controlled by a sideways-moving lever operated by the player's right knee.

Source: Courtesy of the Library of Congress

---

2. Mozart, letter to his father, October 17, 1777, in Wolfgang Amadeus Mozart, *Briefe und Aufzeichungen*, ed. W. A. Bauer and O. E. Deutsch, vol. 2 (Kassel: Bärenreiter, 1962), p. 68. Transl. MEB.

FOCUS To Repeat or Not to Repeat?

Early examples of sonata-form movements regularly include repeat signs at the end of both the first reprise (the exposition) and the second reprise (the development and recapitulation). Over the course of his long career, however, Haydn gradually stopped calling for a repeat of the second reprise, starting a trend that would continue into the 19th century. By the 1820s, for example, Beethoven was inclined to drop the repeat sign even for the exposition sections of his sonata-form movements.

Today, many performers of Classical-era instrumental music observe some repeat signs when they are present in the music but ignore others. In sonata-form movements, for example, the exposition is routinely repeated, but it has become common to ignore the repeat of the second reprise. But the gradual decline in the use of the repeat sign by composers themselves suggests the signs should be respected when present. When composers didn't want a reprise repeated, in other words, they said so. Some composers, for example, would occasionally indicate that

the two reprises of a minuet proper should not be repeated when the minuet proper is played da capo. Performers today tend to abbreviate this return automatically, but when 18th-century composers did not want such repetitions in performance, they explicitly indicated as much.

Impatience with what sometimes seems excessive repetition, however, is not unique to performers today, as is evident from the comments of André Grétry (1741–1813), one of the leading operatic composers of his day:

A sonata is a discourse, an oration. What are we to think of a man who, dividing his discourse in half, repeats each half? "I was at your house this morning; yes, I was at your house this morning to talk with you about something; to talk with you about something." . . . I speak above all of the long reprises that constitute the halves of a [musical] oration. Reprises may have been good at the birth of music, at a time when the listener did not comprehend everything until the second time around. I know that an oration is often divided into two sections; but one certainly does not present each one twice.[3]

3. André Ernest Modeste Grétry, *Mémoires, ou Essais sur la musique*, 3 vols. (Paris: Imprimerie de la République, 1797), III, 356–7. Transl. MEB.

CD7, Track 7

HAYDN
String Quartet in C Major, op. 33, no. 3
Score Anthology II/105

new quartets for two violins, viola, and cello, which he has dedicated to Haydn, are certainly too highly seasoned—and what palate can endure this for long?"[4]

The first movement of Haydn's String Quartet in C Major, Op. 33, No. 3 illustrates the characteristic textural richness of his quartets. The repeated notes in the second violin and viola parts in the opening measures seem at first to be preparing us for the entry of a more engaging melodic line, which does indeed begin to emerge in the first violin in measure 2. Yet the surprising changes of pitch in this seemingly innocuous pulsing figure give it a growing significance: the C and E in the opening measures shift to F and D in measure 7, and B♭ and D in measure 13. What appears to be a subordinate figure, at first static in its pitch and rhythm, gradually emerges as a motivic idea in its own right, blurring the boundary between melody and accompaniment. That boundary is similarly ambiguous in the interaction between the first violin and the cello from measures 18 to 26. Are the two parts exchanging the melody from measure to measure, or is the cello figure merely accompanying the longer note values of the violin's melody? What these examples illustrate is the truly obligatory nature of the obbligato accompaniment in this quartet. Blending counterpoint with homophony, Haydn has created a texture in which accompaniment and melody are inextricably linked.

The lively second movement of this quartet, which Haydn labeled "scherzo," follows the typical structure of a minuet, with measures 1 to 34 constituting the minuet proper, measures 35 to 51 the trio. (Why Haydn chose to call this movement and its counterparts in the other quartets in op. 33 scherzos rather than minuets is not clear; he returned to the designation "minuet" in his subsequent quartets.) The duet between the first and second violin in the trio provides another example of the blending of homophony and counterpoint. The first violin clearly carries the melody within

4. Cramer's *Magazin der Musik*, 23 April 1787, Transl. MEB.

this simple two-voiced texture, but the second violin line provides nonimitative counterpoint to the melody.

The slow third movement of Haydn's quartet is in **sonata form with varied reprise.** In this variant of sonata form, the exposition is not repeated note for note, but instead written out and changed in subtle ways. The varied reprise in this particular movement begins with the return to the tonic in measure 30 and a restatement of the opening theme with new melodic embellishments, especially in the first violin. The modulation to the dominant, confirmed in measure 14 in the first statement of the exposition, is repeated in the second statement in measure 43, again with an elaboration in the first violin part. The effect is similar to that of a da capo aria, in which the singer was expected to embellish a reprise the second time through. In this case, however, Haydn specified the embellishments, rather than leaving them up to the performer. After a short development section (measures 59–64), the music returns to the tonic (measure 65) at the onset of the recapitulation, which repeats the themes of the exposition, but this time all in the tonic.

The last movement, a rondo, illustrates one of Haydn's favorite devices in this form—to incorporate thematic material from the opening refrain (the A section) within a contrasting episode. The A section (measures 1–22) and the B section (measures 23–36) are clearly distinct. The material in measures 37 to 72, however, which leads back to a second statement of A, is as long as the A and B sections combined and based on material from A. By manipulating harmonies and fragmenting the thematic material into increasingly small units, Haydn makes the return to A at measure 72 a significant event, even though it offers no thematic contrast to what precedes it. What, then, is the formal status of the material in measures 37 to 72? Because it is based on thematic material from A, it could be considered a statement of A within a typical rondo structure. Functionally, however, it is more like an extended retransition—a return to the opening idea—or even (in sonata-form terms) a development section. The finale as a whole can also be analyzed as a type of sonata-rondo form, as in the following diagram:

Sonata-Rondo Form in the Fourth Movement of Haydn's String Quartet in C Major, op. 33, no. 3								
Theme	A	B	retransition	A	B	retransition	A	Coda
Measure	1	23	37	72	93	107	125	147
Key	I	vi	x (unstable)	I	i	x → V	I	

These overlapping interpretations of a single movement reflect the way Haydn, like many composers of the Classical era, manipulated established conventions, working within the parameters of these forms but never constrained by them.

Symphony

In the early decades of the 18th century, the terms "symphony" and "overture" were synonymous. Sometime around the 1720s, however, these one- or three-movement works (fast-slow-fast) began to appear outside the theater, independent of any opera or oratorio for which they had originally been written. The earliest independently composed symphonies are believed to have been written in the 1720s by the Italian composer Giovanni Battista Sammartini (1701–75). The concert symphony was cultivated intensely throughout the Classical era: composers across Europe wrote a staggering

FOCUS   Cyclical Coherence

Cyclical coherence—sometimes called *cyclical unity*—refers to the manner in which the various movements of a sonata, quartet, symphony, or any other instrumental genre relate to one another. At the most basic level, the movements of any Classical era work almost always cohere on the basis of their performance forces and tonal relationships. The performance forces stay the same from movement to movement and the key at the beginning and end are almost invariably the same, although the mode (major or minor) may be different.

Beyond these basics, however, there are no consistent patterns in the way movements relate to one another as part of a larger whole. Sometimes we find composers explicitly repeating themes from one movement to another. Haydn did this in the last two movements of his Symphony no. 46 in B Major (1772), and Beethoven would do much the same thing in his Fifth Symphony from 1808. But these are exceptions, not the rule. Cyclical coherence generally expresses itself more subtly in Classical era works.

Haydn's String Quartet, op. 33, no. 3, provides a case in point. On a fairly obvious level, three of the four movements feature birdlike themes (movement 1, opening measures; movement 2, in the trio; movement 4, throughout). These themes account for this quartet's nickname, "The Bird" (a nickname that, like almost every other connected to Haydn's works, did not come from the composer himself). More subtly, the opening themes of the two outer movements are characterized by an unusual amount of repetition on a single note or a single figure. More subtly still, the unusual voicing of the first movement's opening is replicated in the first measures of the scherzo. Both movements begin with a first inversion of a C-major chord. By itself, this parallel might be coincidental. But it seems less so when we observe that the second phrase of each movement (measure 7 in the first movement, measure 5 in the scherzo) begins with a D-minor triad, again in first inversion. And just as the first movement veers unexpectedly to a B♭/D dyad in measure 13, so too does the scherzo move without preparation to a B♭ triad in measure 15.

Was Haydn aware of these connections? Probably, although we cannot be certain. But does it matter? A work of art is usually the result of both conscious and unconscious thought processes. A more important question is whether such connections, to the extent we can identify them, are significant enough to enrich our understanding and appreciation of a work. Here there is ample room for reasonable disagreement. A determined analyst will likely find connections between movements in any given cycle that a more skeptical observer will deny. As is often the case in matters of aesthetic judgment, there are no right and wrong answers for questions like these.

number of such works for performance at courts, in churches, and increasingly in public concerts (see Focus: The Rise of the Public Orchestral Concert). One recent scholar has catalogued more than twelve thousand symphonies written between roughly 1720 and 1810.

The quality of orchestras varied widely within Europe, but their size grew steadily during the second half of the 18th century. Haydn's symphonies, which span some four decades from the 1750s through the 1790s, provide a convenient reflection of this trend. His early symphonies typically call for strings (first and second violins, violas, cellos, double basses) and two oboes, with an occasional flute (sometimes two) or a pair of bassoons, or both. Relatively few of these early symphonies call for horns, trumpets, or timpani. From the late 1760s on, two horns became standard. By the mid-1780s, trumpets and timpani were routinely added to the mix. Haydn was relatively slow to accept clarinets into the orchestra, but in his last four symphonies, written in the mid-1790s, he included them as well. Mozart, in contrast, had scored clarinets into his symphonies of the late 1780s, and the Belgian composer François-Joseph Gossec (1734–1829) had been using them since the 1770s.

Like other composers, Haydn also used special instruments or combinations of instruments from time to time to give a distinctive color to individual symphonies. In his Symphony no. 22 in E♭ Major (nicknamed "The Philosopher" by a later generation of listeners), for example, he substitutes two English horns for the oboes. His Symphony no. 39 in G minor, from the late 1760s, uses four horns. And in his Symphony no. 100 in G Major from 1794 ("Military"), he incorporates a number of so-called Turkish instruments for special effect at certain points. (These instruments,

---

FOCUS   The Rise of the Public Orchestral Concert

The first regularly scheduled public concerts of orchestral music date to the Classical era. The range and nature of offerings, however, varied from city to city.

London, with a variety of concert-producing organizations, enjoyed Europe's most active and publicly accessible musical life. The Bach-Abel Concerts, organized jointly by Johann Christian Bach and Carl Friedrich Abel, flourished from 1766 to 1782. The Concerts of Ancient Music, founded in 1776, were unusual for their time in that they played no music less than twenty years old and were particularly committed to music by Handel. The Professional Concerts (1783–93) were organized by the Italian Muzio Clementi and the Germans Wilhelm Cramer and Johann Peter Salomon. In 1786, Salomon formed his own organization and five years later brought Haydn to London. Occasional concerts organized for special events provided yet another venue for the public consumption of music. Less formal but no less important were the many performances held in the city's "pleasure gardens"—a sort of genteel amusement park—that appealed to a still wider audience.

The focus of musical life in **Paris** continued to be the court and the residences of the aristocracy. The public *Concerts spirituel* series and the *Concerts de la Loge Olympique* were nevertheless important institutions in prerevolutionary Paris. It was for the latter of these that Haydn was commissioned to write his "Paris" symphonies (nos. 82–87) in 1785–86.

Vienna, where private orchestras thrived in the 1780s and 1790s, followed much the same pattern as Paris. There were, however, a few regular public concert series, and occasional concerts open to a paying public also became increasingly common during this period. Mozart, for example, organized and performed in a number of such concerts in the 1780s, often playing his own piano concertos. His father, Leopold Mozart, reported approvingly to his daughter after one such event that "a great many members of the aristocracy were present. Each person pays a gold sovereign or three ducats for these concerts. Your brother is giving them in the Mehlgrube [a local theater] and pays only half a gold sovereign each time he uses the hall. The concert was magnificent and the orchestra played splendidly."[5]

In **Berlin,** concert life outside the court was relatively slow to develop. The opera was open to the public, but instrumental music enjoyed little support. A civic choral society, the *Singakademie*, played an important role in reviving the music of Johann Sebastian Bach in the early 19th century and provided a model for other German cities to follow in establishing their own amateur musical societies.

---

5. Leopold Mozart, letter of 16 February 1785 to Maria Anna Mozart. Transl. MEB.

which include the bass drum, cymbal, tambourine, and triangle, were associated with the style of Turkish music.)

Although we tend to think of the Classical symphony as a four-movement form (fast-slow-minuet-fast), these works, the early ones in particular, actually display considerable variety in the sequence and number of movements. Many of Haydn's early symphonies, for example, have only three movements, a pattern derived from one of the genre's antecedents in the theater—the so-called **Italian overture**—which consisted of three movements in the order fast-slow-fast. (Many Classical era operas featured overtures of this kind.) In addition, the finales of early symphonies are not always fast. Some are minuets or in the minuet style. A look at the movement structure of Haydn's first 27 symphonies (before 1768; see table on page 327) indicates the extent of their variety.

The now familiar four-movement structure became standard for the symphony after about 1768. This structure can be summarized as follows:

- *First movement.* Typically the weightiest of the four and sets the expressive tone for the symphony as a whole. It is usually in sonata form, sometimes with a slow introduction.

- *Slow movement.* Usually the second movement, but sometimes exchanges place with the minuet movement to come third. Slow movements take a variety of forms, including sonata form, sonata form without a development (sometimes called "slow movement sonata form"), theme and variations, or some variety of ABA. Slow movements are usually in a key other than the tonic—most commonly the subdominant—providing tonal contrast with the rest of the cycle.

Two ways of holding the violin. Leopold Mozart's *Treatise on the Fundamental Principles of Violin Playing* was the standard violin manual of its day. Published six months after the birth of his son, Wolfgang, this book would go through multiple editions and be translated into several different languages by the end of the 18th century.

The frontispiece shows Leopold himself demonstrating the "relaxed" position of holding the instrument. "Here the violin . . . is held chest-high, slanting. . . . This position is undoubtedly natural and pleasant to the eyes of the onlookers but somewhat difficult and inconvenient for the player as, during quick movements of the hand in the high position, the violin has no support . . ." This position is still used today in bluegrass and old-time fiddling in the United States.

Another plate from the treatise shows the alternative method of holding the instrument, one that more closely resembles modern technique, "whereby the violin remains unmoved in its place even during the strongest movements of the ascending and descending hand." The ever-increasing demands on violinists to shift positions rapidly on the fingerboard eventually led to the almost exclusive adoption of this position among concert violinists.

Source: Art Resource/The New York Public Library

▬ *Minuet.* Dance-inspired movement in minuet form, usually the third movement. Symphonic minuets are often more rhythmically irregular (and certainly faster) than minuets written expressly for dancing.

▬ *Finale.* Last movement, usually relatively light, is often in sonata form, rondo, or sonata-rondo form.

Interior of a brass instrument workshop in Paris, ca. 1760.
The scale of this workshop is small compared to the instrument factories of the mid-19th century. In the 18th century, instruments were made by licensed masters who took on journeymen and apprentices learning their trade. Workshops like this one had no external source of power. Pounding, shaping, and polishing were all done entirely by hand.

Source: Dover Publications, Inc.

NEW MUSICAL FUND,

Under the PATRONAGE of Their ROYAL HIGHNESSES

The PRINCE of WALES and DUKE of YORK.

At the KING's THEATRE, in the HAY-MARKET,

On MONDAY the 20th of APRIL, 1795,

WILL BE PERFORMED

A Grand Miſcellaneous Concert

OF

VOCAL AND INSTRUMENTAL MUSIC,

FOR THE BENEFIT OF

The New Muſical Fund,

ESTABLISHED FOR

The Relief of Decayed Muſicians, their Widows and Orphans,

RESIDING IN ENGLAND.

Leader of the Band, Mr. CRAMER.

Conductors, Dr. HAYES and Dr. MILLER,

Dr. HAYDN will preſide at the Forte Piano.

Mr. GREATOREX at the Organ, built for the Occaſion, by Mr. ELLIOTT, with the Long Movement.

N. B. The Band will conſiſt of Four Hundred Performers, for which an Orcheſtra will be erected on the Stage.

ACT I.	ACT II.
GRAND CHORUS in the Dettengen Te Deum HANDEL.	GRAND SYMPHONY, M. S. HAYDN.
SONG, Mrs. SECOND	and performed under his immediate Direction
CONCERTO GRAND FORTE PIANO,	SONG, Mr. HARRISON
Mr. SMART, Jun. CRAMER.	PLEYEL'S CELEBRATED CONCERTANTE
SONG, Mr. BARTLEMAN	(by deſire) Meſſrs. CRAMER, F. CRAMER,
CONCERTO VIOLONCELLO, Mr.	H. SMART, SMITH, &c.
LINDLEY	A Favorite GLEE
SONG, Madam BANTI, with Violin Obligato,	SONG, Mrs. HARRISON
Mr. CRAMER	CONCERTO VIOLIN, Madam GILLBERG, be-
CONCERTO GERMAN FLUTE, Mr. ASHE	ing her Second Public Performance in England
AIR and GRAND CHORUS, " Glory to	GRAND CHORUS, " How excellent Thy
God" HANDEL.	Name" (Saul) HANDEL.

PIT and BOXES, 10s. 6d.   GALLERY, 5s.

☞ The Doors to be opened at SEVEN o'Clock, and the Performance begin at EIGHT precisely.

Subſcriptions are received, and Tickets delivered, at Meſſrs. Ranſom, Moreland, Hammerſley, and Co.'s, Bankers, Pall Mall; Meſſrs. Longman and Co.'s Muſic Warehouſes, Cheapſide and Haymarket; Meſſrs. Thompſon's, St. Paul's Church-yard; Mr. Fentum's, No. 78, Strand; Mr. Forſter's, No. 348, ditto; Mr. Preſton's, ditto; Mr. Buckinger's, ditto; Meſſrs. Lewis, Houſton, and Hide's, Holborn; Mr. Birchall's, New Bond Street; Mr. Miller's, Stationer, Old Bond Street; Meſſrs. Bett's, Royal Exchange; at the Se-cretary's, Mr. H. King, No. 358, near the Pantheon, Oxford Street; and of the Society's Treaſurer, Mr. Smart, at his Muſic Warehouſe, Corner of Argyll Street, Oxford Street.

N. B. A Subſcriber, paying ONE GUINEA, will have TWO TICKETS, each of which will admit One Perſon to any Part of the Houſe.

Such LADIES and GENTLEMEN as may be deſirous of encouraging the Society, by ſubſcribing to the Annual Performance, are reſpectfully informed, that Tickets (emblematical of the Inſtitution, and which may be re-tained by Subſcribers) are ready for Delivery at the above-mentioned Places.

The Subſcribers to the OPERA, who may wiſh to retain their Boxes for the above Benefit, are reſpectfully intreated to ſignify their intentions to Mr. SHELMANDINE, at the Theatre, on or before Tueſday, April 14th, otherwiſe they will be diſpoſed of.

SAMPSON LOW, Printer, No. 7, Berwick Street, Soho, oppoſite the Chapel.

A copy of the handbill for the charity concert at the King's Theatre, Haymarket, 20 April 1795; on this occasion Haydn, as well as presiding 'at the Forte Piano', conducted one of his own Symphonies – as was customary in his London concert appearances – immediately after the interval.

The miscellaneous nature of 18th-century concerts. As this advertisement indicates, The "Grand Miscellaneous Concert" presented at the King's Theatre, Haymarket, on April 20, 1795, included choruses, solo songs, concertos, and a symphony. Such heterogeneity was standard in Haydn's time and well into the 19th century. The program is remarkably long by today's standards. But audiences were freer to come and go back then, and the strictures of concert decorum were not nearly so rigid. Note that Haydn is honored here as "Doctor," a title he earned when Oxford University bestowed an honorary degree on him in 1792. The note that Haydn would "Preside at the Forte Piano" indicates only that he would conduct from there, not necessarily that he would actually play continuo for his own symphonies. The program does not specify which Haydn symphony is being performed, only that it is still in manuscript ("M.S.").

Source: British Department of the Environment, Transport, and the Regions

The Variety of Movement Structures in Haydn's Early Symphonies (before ca. 1768)

THREE MOVEMENTS

F-S-F (8)	F-S-M (2)	S-F-M (1)	S/F-M-F (1)
1, 2, 10, 12, 16, 17, 19, 27	9, 26	18	25

FOUR MOVEMENTS

F-S-M-F (7)	S-F-M-F (5)	S/F-S-M-F (2)	S/F/S-M-S-F (1)
3, 8, 13, 14, 20, 23, 24	4, 5, 11, 21, 22	6, 7	15

F = fast movement; S = slow movement; S/F = fast movement with a slow introduction; M = minuet.

The composer as a cultural hero.
Haydn last appeared in public at a performance of his oratorio *The Creation* in Vienna on March 27, 1808, just a few days before the composer's 76th birthday. Haydn, seated at the center, receives a gift from Princess Marie Hermenegild, wife of Prince Nikolaus Esterházy, scion of the family that Haydn had served for so many years. Trumpeters play a fanfare during the presentation, and all eyes are on the composer. The Viennese public, including even the aristocracy and nobility, acknowledged Haydn as a cultural hero. Such a scene would have been unthinkable during the many decades in which Haydn was in daily service to the Esterházy family; by 1808, attitudes toward composers had changed considerably.

Source: Copyright by Direktion der Museen der Stadt Wien

CD7, Track 11
HAYDN
Symphony no. 103
Score Anthology II/106

By the early 1770s, the concert symphony had begun to distinguish itself from other genres of instrumental music by its lofty tone as well as the number of performers it required. The first movements of "the best chamber symphonies," according to the composer and critic Johann Abraham Peter Schulz (1747–1800),

> contain grand and bold ideas, free handling of compositional techniques, apparent irregularity in the melody and harmony, strongly-marked rhythms of various sorts, powerful bass melodies and unisons, concerting middle voices, free imitations, often a theme handled fugally, sudden transitions and shifts from one key to another, which are the more striking the weaker the connection is, bold shadings of *forte* and *piano*, and particularly the *crescendo*, which has the greatest effect when used with a rising melody and its climax. To this is added the art of weaving all the voices in and out of one another in such a way that all parts, when played together, create a single melody that is incapable of accompaniment, but rather one in which every voice is making its own particular contribution to the whole. Such an Allegro in a symphony is like a Pindaric ode: it elevates and moves the soul of the listener in the same way, and it requires the same spirit, the same sublime imagination, and the same knowledge of art to be fully appreciated.[6]

Schulz went on to point out that the symphony as a whole "is especially suited to the expression of the grand, the solemn, and the sublime." Like his contemporaries, Schulz avoided using the term "beautiful" in accounts of this genre. Critics of the time defined as beautiful anything that was pleasing, and "agreeable" (to use a favorite 18th-century term). The sublime, however, was associated with that which was imposing, powerful, and perhaps even a bit frightening. A favorite example of the sublime in nature for 18th-century critics was a storm at sea, because it combined beauty with power and unpredictability. The sublime, in this view, appeals to a level of the soul that is above and beyond reason. The merely beautiful might be worthy of contemplation, but the truly sublime inspires awe.

The powerful, sudden, and wholly unexpected drumroll that opens Haydn's Symphony no. 103 in E♭ Major illustrates what critics like Schulz had in mind when they wrote of the sublime in music. It would have struck contemporary listeners as

---

6. Johann Abraham Peter Schulz, "Sinfonie," in Johann Georg Sulzer's *Allgemeine Theorie der schönen Künste* (Leipzig, 1771–1774). Transl. MEB.

loud, bizarre, and portentous, surely a signal announcing some great event, but what kind of event? It gets our attention but not necessarily our sympathy. The musical idea that follows is dark, fragmented, and difficult to grasp, like a painting of a scene shrouded in mist. Only later will we realize that what we are hearing at this point is a premonition of themes to come.

The opening theme in the low strings reinforces the mysterious air of this slow introduction. The first two measures sound very much like the opening of the *Dies irae* ("Day of wrath") from the plainchant Mass for the Dead (see Example 12–2). (Thirty-five years later, Hector Berlioz would use the complete *Dies irae* melody in the finale of his *Symphonie fantastique*; see Chapter 15.)

Example 12–2 Plainchant Sequence *Dies irae* from the Mass for the Dead.

Di - es ir - ae, di - es il - la, Sol - vet sae - cu - lum in fa - vil - la

Day of wrath, day that will dissolve the world in ashes

The slow introduction ends with what contemporary audiences must surely have perceived as a bizarre pounding on the notes G and A♭ (measures 35–39). But what sounds dark and ominous at the end of the slow introduction is immediately transformed into a bright and airy theme at the beginning of the Allegro con spirito that follows. Progressions like this—from somber to bright, dark to light, obscurity to clarity—are another manifestation of what 18th-century critics considered sublime. The sudden deflection from the dominant of C minor to E♭ Major is likewise another portent of things to come, this time of the many other sudden and unexpected modulations that abound in this sonata-form first movement. The return of the slow movement's opening in the coda of the first movement (at measure 202) is even more unexpected.

Haydn corrects Beethoven's counterpoint exercises. Most of Beethoven's studies with Haydn in 1792–93 involved exercises in strict counterpoint, a reflection of the enduring importance of counterpoint in the Western musical tradition. Haydn taught it in virtually the same way it is taught today. He provided his student, in this case Beethoven, with a cantus firmus voice (marked "C.f." at the left-hand side of three of the four systems here), and the student filled in the remaining voices. The cantus firmus alternates between alto and tenor in the exercises. Haydn has marked infelicities of voice leading with an "x" above the staves at various points, and to the right of the uppermost example he has written out a preferred solution. When he did these exercises, Beethoven was 23 years old and had already published several compositions of his own. He would later study counterpoint with two other teachers as well.

Source: Dover Publications, Inc.

COMPOSER PROFILE   Joseph Haydn *(1732–1809)*

Haydn's father made wagon wheels for a living, but his family and their neighbors in the village in which he was born recognized the boy's musical talent and sent him to Vienna when he was 8 years old. There he sang in the choir at St. Stephen's Cathedral and absorbed the repertory of the late Baroque and early Classical eras. When Haydn's voice broke, he was no longer of any use to the chorus at St. Stephen's and was, by his own account, thrown out on the street. He survived by giving music lessons and eventually drew the attention of the aristocratic Morzin family, who hired him as their music director in 1758. Three years later, he was lured away by Prince Paul Anton Esterházy, who was in the process of assembling what by all accounts was one of the best orchestras in Europe at the time. Prince Paul Anton died in 1762, but his brother and successor, Prince Nikolaus, was willing to spend even *more* money on music.

Haydn was thus in an ideal position to create new music. Late in life, he told one of his biographers, "My Prince was satisfied with all of my works and I received applause. As the director of an orchestra, I could make experiments, observe what elicited or weakened an impression, and thus correct, add, delete, take risks. I was cut off from the world, no one in my vicinity could cause me to doubt myself or pester me, and so I had to become original." A lesser composer might easily have fallen into a comfortable routine, churning out symphonies, sonatas, and quartets according to his patron's requirements, but Haydn imposed astonishing demands on himself. Beyond certain outward similarities, every one of his works seems to define its own issues and standards.

Haydn's first contract with the Esterházy family required him to "compose such music as His Serene Highness may command, and neither to communicate such compositions to any other person, nor to allow them to be copied, but he shall retain them for the exclusive use of His Highness, and not compose for any other person without the knowledge and gracious permission of His Highness." He was obliged to "appear daily . . . in the antechamber before and after midday, and inquire whether His Highness is pleased to order a performance of the orchestra." Haydn was also required "to instruct the female vocalists, in order that they may not forget in the country what they have been taught with much trouble and expense in Vienna."[7]

In spite of all this, Haydn soon became more famous than even he himself realized. Unscrupulous publishers in Paris pirated his music or placed his name on music that others had written. Haydn nevertheless spent most of his professional life writing music on demand. When his prince became obsessed with the baryton, a curious instrument rather like a viola da gamba, Haydn set to work writing literally dozens of trios for baryton, viola, and cello. When the prince was bitten by the opera bug and built a new opera house a few years later, Haydn dutifully composed new operas year after year.

The death of Prince Nikolaus in 1790 opened a new chapter in the composer's life. Johann Peter Salomon, a German-born impresario living in London, persuaded Haydn to make two extended tours to England, where he composed symphonies, songs, and a number of works for piano. After he returned to Vienna for good in 1795, he produced two highly successful oratorios (*The Creation* and *The Seasons*), a handful of Masses, and several of his finest string quartets.

A note on the composer's name: Although baptized "Franz Joseph Haydn," he never used his first name, even in legal documents. (The same is true for Wilhelm Richard Wagner, Fortunino Giuseppe Verdi, and a host of other composers.) Haydn's last name was often misspelled in his own lifetime—as "Hayden," "Haidn," or, as it appeared on his first contract with the Esterházy family, "Heyden"—but always in a manner consistent with the correct pronunciation (roughly, *hidin'*, with the accent on the first syllable).

PRINCIPAL WORKS

SYMPHONIES Haydn's 106 authentic symphonies span almost his entire career. Some of the early ones are openly programmatic (nos. 6, 7, and 8 bear the subtitles "Morning," "Noon" and "Night," respectively). Others are based on plainchant themes: the Symphony no. 26, for example, uses themes from a widely performed plainchant setting of the Lamentations of Jeremiah. Still others are downright bizarre. The most famous of these is the so-called "Farewell" Symphony in F♯ minor—one of only two known 18th-century symphonies in this key—in which the musicians exit one by one in the finale. Haydn was apparently trying to remind Prince Nikolaus that his musicians had stayed too long at Esterháza in the summer of 1772 and were eager to return to their families in Eisenstadt.

Many of Haydn's "London" symphonies (nos. 93–104) feature a gimmick guaranteed to resonate with the widest possible audience. Examples include the drum stroke in the slow movement of the "Surprise" Symphony (no. 94), the

---

7. Karl Geiringer, *Haydn: A Creative Life in Music*, 3rd ed. (Berkeley and Los Angeles: University of California Press, 1982), pp. 65–7.

KEYBOARD SONATAS   Haydn's career coincides with the rise of the piano as the principal instrument of domestic music making. The earliest of his 36 surviving sonatas were written with the harpsichord in mind, but from the mid-1760s onward, he was clearly attracted to the piano's greater dynamic range.

SACRED MUSIC   When he returned from England to Vienna in 1795, Haydn was still officially in the employ of the Esterházy family, even though his orchestra had long since disbanded. For several years in a row, Prince Nikolaus's successor commissioned Haydn to write a setting of the Mass Ordinary in honor of his wife's birthday. These late Masses contain some stunning vocal writing and music every bit as dramatic as the late symphonies. *The Creation*, an oratorio, also dates from this last period of Haydn's career.

Haydn composes. This painting is consistent with what Haydn himself said of the way he composed: "I sat down [at the keyboard] and began to fantasize, according to whether my mood was sad or happy, serious or playful. Once I had seized an idea, my entire effort went toward elaborating and sustaining it according to the rules of art." The blank music paper underneath the inkwell, juxtaposed with the work now on the stand, suggests a work in progress. Haydn was an extremely prolific composer and proud of his ability to write quickly and efficiently.

Source: Dagli Orti (A)/Picture Desk, Inc./Kobal Collection

tick-tock of the slow movement of the "Clock" (no. 101), and the opening of the slow movement of Symphony no. 98, which begins like "God Save the King," only to continue in a different fashion. At the premiere, some members of the audience must surely have begun to rise when they heard it, only to sit down foolishly a moment later.

STRING QUARTETS   Haydn played an important role in the emergence of the string quartet as a genre during the 1750s and 1760s. Even his earliest quartets (from the mid-1750s) have no need of a supporting basso continuo: the four voices alone combine to create the necessary sonorities and harmonies. Altogether, he wrote 67 complete and indisputably authentic string quartets. The set known as "Opus 3" is probably not by Haydn.

KEY DATES IN THE LIFE OF HAYDN

1732	Born in Röhrau (Austria) on March 31.
1740	Sent to Vienna, where he sings in the choir at St. Stephen's Cathedral.
1748	Forced to leave St. Stephen's; ekes out a living giving music lessons; composes first works.
1758	Appointed music director to Count Morzin in what is now the Czech Republic.
1761	Appointed assistant music director to Prince Paul Anton Esterházy in Eisenstadt.
1766	Becomes music director to Prince Nikolaus, Paul Anton's successor.
1790	Prince Nikolaus dies and Haydn leaves for England.
1791–1792	First English tour. Feted as a genius; receives an honorary degree from Oxford University.
1793–1794	Back in Vienna, gives lessons in harmony, counterpoint, and composition to Beethoven.
1794–1795	Second English tour; finishes the last of his twelve "London" symphonies.
1796–1801	Writes his final works, including the last quartets, two oratorios, and several Masses.
1801	Suffers the first of several strokes.
1809	Dies in Vienna on May 31.

PRIMARY EVIDENCE   Haydn in London

Written a week after Haydn's arrival in England, this fascinating letter to Maria Anna von Genzinger, a talented pianist who lived in Vienna, reminds us of the physical and emotional distance the composer had traveled from his native Austria. When Haydn arrived in London, he was already a celebrity. He granted interviews to three newspapers and received invitations to dine at the highest levels of English society. Only a few months before, he had been going about his daily routine in remote Esterháza.

London, 8th January 1791

Nobly born, Gracious Lady!

I hope that you will have received my last letter from Calais. I should have written you immediately after my arrival in London, but I wanted to wait a few days so as to be able to write about several things at once. So I can tell you that on . . . New Year's Day, after attending early Mass, I boarded the ship at 7:30 A.M. and at 5 in the afternoon I arrived, thank God! safe and sound in Dower [i.e., Dover]. At the beginning, for the first 4 whole hours, we had almost no wind, and the ship went so slowly that in these 4 hours we went no further than one single English mile, and there are 24 between Calais and Dower. Our ship's captain, in an evil temper, said that if the wind did not change, we should have to spend the whole night at sea. Fortunately, however, towards 11:30 o'clock a wind arose and blew so favorably that by 4 o'clock we covered 22 miles. Since the tide, which had just begun to ebb, prevented our large vessel from reaching the pier, 2 smaller ships came out to meet us as we were still fairly far out at sea, and into these we and our luggage were transferred, and thus at last, though exposed to a middling gale, we landed safely. The large vessel stood out to sea five hours longer, till the tide turned and it could finally dock. Some of the passengers were afraid to board the little boats and stayed on board, but I followed the example of the greater number. I remained on deck during the whole passage, so as to gaze my fill at that mighty monster, the ocean. So long as it was calm, I wasn't afraid at all, but towards the end, when the wind grew stronger and stronger, and I saw the monstrous high waves rushing at us, I became a little frightened, and a little indisposed, too. But I overcame it all and arrived safely, without vomiting, on shore. Most of the passengers were ill, and looked like ghosts, but since I went on to London, I didn't feel the effects of the journey at once; but then I needed 2 days to recover. Now, however, I am fresh and well again, and busy looking at this endlessly huge city of London, whose various beauties and marvels quite astonished me. I immediately paid the necessary calls, such as to the Neapolitan Ambassador and to our own; both called on me in return 2 days later, and 4 days ago I luncheoned with the former—N.B. at 6 o'clock in the evening, as is the custom here.

My arrival caused a great sensation throughout the whole city, and I went the round of all the newspapers for 3 successive days. Everyone wants to know me. I had to dine out 6 times up to now, and if I wished, I could dine out every day; but first I must consider my health, and 2nd my work. Except for the nobility, I admit no callers till 2 o'clock in the afternoon, and at 4 o'clock I dine at home with Mon. Salomon. I have nice and comfortable, but expensive, lodgings. My landlord is Italian, and also a cook, and serves me 4 very respectable meals; we each pay 1 fl. 30 kr. a day excluding wine and beer, but everything is terribly expensive here. Yesterday I was invited to a grand amateur concert, but I arrived a bit late, and when I showed my ticket they wouldn't let me in but led me to an antechamber, where I had to wait till the piece which was then being played in the hall was over. Then they opened the door, and I was conducted, on the arm of the *entrepreneur*, up the center of the hall to the front of the orchestra, amid universal applause, and there I was stared at and greeted by a great number of English compliments. I was assured that such honors had not been conferred on anyone for 50 years. After the concert I was taken to a handsome adjoining room, where a table for 200 persons, with many places set, was prepared for all the amateurs; I was supposed to be seated at the head of the table, but since I had dined out on that day and had eaten more than usual, I declined this honor, with the excuse that I was not feeling very well, but despite this I had to drink the harmonious health, in Burgundy, of all the gentlemen present; they all returned the toast, and then allowed me to be taken home. All this, my gracious lady, was very flattering to me, and yet I wished I could fly for a time to Vienna, to have more quiet in which to work, for the noise that the common people make as they sell their wares in the street is intolerable. At present I am working on symphonies, because the libretto of the opera is not yet decided on, but in order to have more quiet I shall have to rent a room far from the center of town. I would gladly write you in more detail, but I am afraid of missing the mail-coach. Meanwhile I am, with kindest regards to your husband, *Fräulein* Pepi, and all the others, most respectfully,

Your Grace's
most sincere and obedient servant,

JOSEPH HAYDN

Source: *The Collected Correspondence and London Notebooks of Joseph Haydn,* ed. and trans. H.C. Robbins Landon (London: Barrie and Rockliff, 1959), pp. 111–13.

In addition to their musical qualities, slow introductions served a practical purpose: to dampen the noise of the audience. In Haydn's time, audiences did not sit in breathless attention awaiting the beginning of a work. But with a slow introduction like that of his Symphony no. 103, Haydn could write an opening theme in the Allegro con spirito that would otherwise be barely audible. (Beethoven would later use two loud chords at the beginning of his "Eroica" Symphony to set up the soft main theme that follows; see Chapter 15.)

As is typical of slow introductions in general, the slow introduction to Symphony no. 103 follows no established conventions of form; instead, it represents something along the lines of a fantasia. It nonetheless shares important elements with the body of the first movement that follows. The down-and-up half-step motion of the *Dies irae*-like theme in the introduction, for example, resurfaces in the opening theme of the Allegro con spirito. The opening drumroll itself prefigures a remarkable number of themes in the first movement (and the symphony as a whole) that incorporate repeated notes. Among these are the principal theme of the sonata-form section of the movement (measures 40–41) and the transitional theme beginning at measures 59–60. The opening idea of the finale also features repeated notes, as does the theme of the second reprise of the minuet.

Concerto

As in the Baroque era, the concerto was the principal genre for instrumental virtuosos to showcase their talents during the Classical era. Concertos for keyboard—harpsichord or piano—were an important new addition to the repertory of the late Baroque and early Classical eras. Johann Sebastian Bach was one of the first to write concertos for the harpsichord, and his sons followed in his footsteps. Like the sonata (but unlike the symphony after about 1770), most concertos of the Classical era are in three movements (fast-slow-fast), without a minuet.

The ideals of spontaneity and improvisation exerted a powerful influence on the concerto genre. Cadenzas in every movement, particularly the first, were expected to be (or at least appear to be) moments of intense improvisation, giving performers free rein to exercise their fancy. Although Mozart wrote out many of his own cadenzas, these were presumably for friends and students. Not until Beethoven's last piano concerto, written in 1809, did composers begin to write obligatory cadenzas, and even then only sporadically.

The first movements of many concertos of the Classic era, including Mozart's piano concertos, employ a variant of sonata form called **double-exposition concerto form.** As the name implies, this structural convention presents two expositions, the first for the full orchestra (the tutti exposition) and the second for the soloist (the solo exposition). The tutti exposition does not modulate and remains essentially in the tonic throughout. The solo exposition begins in the tonic and then moves to the secondary key area, as in a conventional sonata-form exposition (I to V or i to III). Development and recapitulation proceed along the lines of conventional sonata form, at least harmonically, with the addition of an opportunity for a solo cadenza toward the end of the recapitulation.

Double-Exposition Concerto Form				
Section	Tutti exposition	Solo exposition	Development	Recapitulation	Cadenza & coda
Key	tonic	tonic → secondary	unstable	tonic	tonic

A keyboard concerto, 1777.
Although women rarely enjoyed easy access to formal instruction in composition, they could—and did—excel as performers, especially in singing and in playing the harpsichord and piano. Vienna was particularly rich in women keyboard virtuosos during the last three decades of the 18th century. The setting here happens to be domestic: a small and exclusive audience in a private setting. Some in the audience are listening, others conversing.

Source: Zentralbibliothek Zürich

CD7, Track 12

MOZART
Piano Concerto in D Major, K. 107, no. 1
Score Anthology II/107

The first movement of Mozart's Piano Concerto no. 1, based on Johann Christian Bach's Keyboard Sonata in D Major, op. 5, no. 2 (discussed in Chapter 11), illustrates the relationship between sonata form and double-exposition concerto form. (It also reflects Mozart's admiration for Bach as well as the familiar concept of composing from a model.) For the first eight measures, Mozart closely follows Bach's sonata (Anthology II/102), adding additional accompaniment in the inner voices (second violins and violas) but making no structural changes. At the beginning of the transition, however (measure 9), when the sonata modulates to the dominant, the concerto stays in the tonic. Mozart then abbreviates much of what J. C. Bach had presented in the secondary key area, adding a cadential figure of his own (measures 24–28) to close out the tutti exposition. All this time the soloist has been playing as a member of the basso continuo, filling in harmonies according to Mozart's figured bass.

The soloist assumes an altogether different function in the solo exposition, which begins at measure 29. Now the melody moves to the piano, the accompaniment moves to the strings, and the basso continuo drops out altogether. In the solo exposition Mozart also follows J. C. Bach's sonata much more closely, modulating to the dominant on the transitional theme (measures 37–46) and staying there to introduce all the themes J. C. Bach had presented in the secondary key area. (In retrospect, we can now see why Mozart abbreviated the tutti exposition: the music would have stayed in the tonic for far too long in proportion to the movement as a whole.)

The first movement of this concerto can also be analyzed in terms of ritornello structure, a form that Mozart never wholly abandoned in his concertos. As in a Baroque concerto, the movement as a whole consists of alternating tutti and solo sections. The contrasting tutti and solo sections are easy to identify in the score with a quick look at the keyboard part: figured bass notation—indicating the solo instrument is acting as a basso continuo—signals a tutti section; the absence of figured bass notation signals a solo section. Mozart appears to have composed the cadential figure first heard at measures 24–28 precisely in order to demarcate tutti from solo sections. The tutti sections are brief in comparison to the solo sections, but they nevertheless articulate the individual sections of the whole. In the diagram here, the labels applied to the themes in the tutti exposition (which does not modulate) are based on the appearances of these themes within the solo exposition (which does modulate).

The Structure of Mozart's Piano Concerto in D Major, K. 107, First Movement										
Ritornello structure	Rit. I				Solo 1					Rit. 2
Double-exposition concerto form	Tutti exposition				Solo exposition					
Theme	P	[T	1S	5S]	P	T	1S	2S	3S	4S	5S
Measure	1	9	17	24	29	37	47	54	59	62	70
Key	I				I	→	V				

Ritornello structure	Solo 2				Rit. 3					Solo 3	Rit. 4
Double-exposition concerto form	Development				Recapitulation					Cadenza	Coda
Theme	1S	T	4S	1S	P	T	1S	2S	3S	4S	(improvisation on earlier themes)	5S
Measure	75	80	84	93	105	113	120	128	132	135	143	147	148
Key	unstable		V		I								

These same patterns of double-exposition concerto form and ritornello structure are equally evident in Mozart's later concertos, including the Piano Concerto in E♭ Major, K. 271 (1777). The very opening of this concerto reminds us (yet again) that composers were constantly playing with conventions, for here the soloist enters quite unexpectedly as a soloist almost at once (measures 2–7) before receding back into the framework of the basso continuo. (The subsequent marking of *tasto solo* indicates the soloist is to play only the notes indicated, not any harmony above it, until the resumption of the figured bass markings in measure 12.)

To modern ears, accustomed to concertos that showcase the soloist, it may seem strange to hear the soloist shift repeatedly from foreground to background. The modern conception of the soloist's role, however, did not begin to emerge until the early 19th century in the piano concertos of Beethoven and did not become dominant until later in the century with the concertos of such composers as Weber, Mendelssohn, Chopin, and Schumann. During the Classical era, although the soloist certainly was given opportunities to shine, the relationship between soloist and orchestra was more collaborative.

From a thematic point of view, Mozart's Piano Concerto, K. 271 is tightly organized: almost every idea relates in some fashion to the opening theme, or *Hauptsatz* (Example 12–3a). The three most distinctive elements of the opening idea (1P) are

CD8, Track 1

MOZART
Piano Concerto in E♭ Major, K. 271
Score Anthology II/108

Example 12–3 The thematic ideas in the first movement of Mozart's Piano Concerto in E♭ Major, K. 271.

the arpeggiated upward leap (marked with an X in Example 12–3a), the threefold repetition of the B♭ (y), and the stepwise progression from the first scale degree (E♭) up to the fifth scale degree (B♭) and back down again (z). As early as measure 7, Mozart begins to manipulate these elements. The second theme in the primary key area (2P; Example 12–3b) emphasizes the repeated B♭ in its first half, the stepwise motion from E♭ to B♭ and back down again in its second half. The theme labeled 3P (Example 12–3c) expands on the upward arpeggiated figure (X) found in 1P. With its opening half note, 1S (Example 12–3d) picks up on the original rhythm of 1P; the upper notes of 1S outline yet another stepwise progression from the tonic to the fifth scale degree (here, in the key of B♭, the span from B♭ to F). The next theme presented in the secondary key area, 2S (Example 12–3e), syncopates the rhythm of themes 1P and 1S.

Mozart's music in general, and his piano concertos in particular, are renowned for their abundance of thematic ideas, in contrast to the music of Haydn, who tended to develop a smaller number of ideas more thoroughly. Yet Mozart's abundant themes are almost invariably linked in some way. Like all composers of his era, he took care to assure both unity and variety in his music.

CONCLUSION

Composers of instrumental music working in the second half of the late 18th century developed or refined a variety of genres and forms that would remain in use throughout the 19th and even 20th centuries. The string quartet and symphony took their place alongside such established genres as the sonata and concerto. Sonata form, rondo, and double-exposition concerto form provided broad frameworks for the presentation of musical ideas. By 1800, instrumental music had established itself as a language without words. Theorists borrowed from the terminology of grammar and rhetoric (period, phrase, antecedent, consequent) to suggest that even without words, music could function as a language in its own right.

Vocal Music in the Classical Era

*I*n spite of the rising status of instrumental music in the Classical era, vocal music, bolstered by the Enlightenment's emphasis on reason and rational persuasion, retained its traditional position of aesthetic supremacy. Without a text, instrumental music could appeal only to the emotions (the so-called language of the heart), whereas vocal music—sacred or secular—could appeal to both heart and mind at once.

The opera house, in particular, was a center of intense musical activity—and controversy—at any court or in any city with claims to cultural prominence. Opera's high status in the cultural hierarchy made it a subject of great critical interest and a magnet for the most talented singers, composers, stage designers, and poets of the day. Like movie stars today, these people often found themselves the focus of gossip and adulation.

Unfortunately, very few operas of the Classical era are performed with any regularity today. Other than the operas of Mozart and a handful by Christoph Willibald Gluck (1714–1787), the bulk of this enormous repertory remains largely unknown to all but a few specialists. Yet in their day the works of the leading opera composers—Johann Adolph Hasse (1699–1783), Baldassare Galuppi (1706–1785), Niccolò Jommelli (1714–1774), Tomasso Traetta (1727–1779), Niccolò Piccinni (1728–1800), François-Joseph Gossec (1734–1829), André-Ernest-Modeste Grétry (1741–1813), Domenico Cimarosa (1749–1801), and Antonio Salieri (1750–1825)— were familiar to almost every music enthusiast.

THE RISE OF OPERA BUFFA

As early as the 1720s, a new style of opera was beginning to emerge in Italy. **Opera buffa**—comic opera—featured many elements not found in opera seria. Its subject matter was humorous rather than serious. The libretto of the typical opera buffa centered on everyday characters rather than heroes, rulers, and gods. Singers included basses (largely absent in opera seria) but not castrati. Opera buffa gave more emphasis to ensemble singing (duets, trios, quartets), again in contrast to opera seria, which featured mostly solo arias. Opera buffa also avoided da capo arias and other opportunities for elaborate vocal improvisations. Melodies were on the whole simple and straightforward, with increasing evidence of periodic phrase structure.

The origins of opera buffa lie in the tradition of the **intermezzo,** a work intended for performance between the acts of a larger (serious) opera. Giovanni Battista Pergolesi's intermezzo *La serva padrona* ("The Maidservant as Mistress") was written in 1733 and first performed in Naples between the acts of an opera seria also written by Pergolesi. Over time, this intermezzo and others like it became so well known that they were performed alone rather than between the acts of larger works, thus giving rise to opera buffa as a separate genre.

La serva padrona tells the story of a maidservant who, through guile and cunning, becomes mistress of the household in which she had been employed. In contrast to the elaborate cast of characters found in many opere serie of the time, Pergolesi's intermezzo makes do with only two singers, Uberto (a bass), the master of the house, and Serpina (a soprano), the maidservant. (The character of Vespone, a manservant, is entirely mute and limited to mime.) The orchestra consists of string and basso continuo; the texture is homophonic with a great deal of doubling of voice part by the orchestra, although there are a few moments of independence. In the first of two acts, Serpina is hoping to raise her station by marrying her master (although she is in fact his former ward), but the negotiation between them becomes a psychological game: can Uberto marry and still retain his self-respect, and can Serpina marry and still retain her power over him?

In the duet that closes the act, "Lo conosco a quegl' occhietti" (I see it in your eyes), the two "discuss" the question in comic style. Serpina opens with a melody (G Major) that modulates to ends on A Major; Uberto's reply remains in A Major, using music derived from Serpina's opening. The development of the melody through the repetition of short simple phrases is a formula that gives opera buffa much of its character; what better way to suggest stubbornness on the part of both characters? The octaves (Serpina: "furbi, ladri," measure 10; Uberto: "troppo," measure 20) provide a simple but effective comic emphasis. The next section is marked by chromatic motion, first descending in the bass (Serpina, measures 28ff.), then ascending in Uberto's response, doubled by the bass (measures 40ff.). The resulting tension devolves into quicker dialogue, culminating in the first duet (measures 51ff.) ending in D Major.

A brief orchestral interlude suggests that the dominant major will remain the key, but when Serpina enters, it is soon clear that G Major is once again the tonic. The music from the opening returns, but the comic dialogue supersedes the original longer phrases as motives are reused and repeated. This effect is especially effective in Uberto's plaintive G-A-B♭ motive beginning in measure 80 ("Quanto và che me la fa!"); this idea briefly becomes his characteristic motive to the extent that Serpina mocks him with it in measures 94–97. The concluding section featuring more argumentative (or playful) exchanges between the protagonists; when the two actually repeat one another (measures 104ff.) and the octaves return in the tonic, the discussion reaches its (unsettled) end.

Somewhat surprisingly, the orchestra concludes the duet not with its introduction, but with a transposition and expansion of the interlude in measures 55–57. This is forward-looking in that the ritornello idea common to Baroque music has been subverted; instead, a brief interlude in the dominant is repeated in the tonic key, resolving harmonic tension (much as a secondary theme in the dominant close of an exposition would be transposed into the tonic at the end of a recapitulation). Furthermore, the change reinforces the development of the characters as the duet progresses. The motivic repetitiveness does not occur at the larger structural level of the Baroque da capo aria; similarly, many of Mozart's and Rossini's arias are set with similar characterization and psychological progression in mind. The work as a whole points toward the lighter style of the mid-18th century, but also to a less monolithic approach to musical expression.

OPERA WARS

Admired in some quarters, reviled in others, opera buffa provoked controversy throughout Europe. Advocates considered it a breath of fresh air that would reinvigorate a genre grown otherwise stale; opponents considered it an affront to established traditions.

The debate raged with particular virulence in France. The dispute known as the War of the Buffoons (*Guerre des Bouffons*) was ignited by the debut of Pergolesi's *La serva padrona* in Paris in 1752 in a performance by a troupe calling itself the Bouffons ("the Comedians"). In an era when political dissent was severely limited, this dispute had implications far beyond the issues at hand. Like many other artistic and philosophical controversies, it provided an opportunity for competing social groups to jockey for influence and a pretext for some to question established authority without directly confronting it. The War of the Buffoons pitted partisans of King Louis XV against those of Queen Marie, defenders of French culture against advocates of Italian style, and the entrenched aristocracy against the intellectual bourgeoisie. The king and his conservative followers sought to uphold the traditions of the French *tragédie lyrique* as represented by the stately, serious works of Lully and Rameau (see Chapter 9). Their opponents sought to use the model of opera buffa to promote a new, lighter style of musical theater in France. The philosopher and amateur composer Jean-Jacques Rousseau weighed in with his own *Le devin du village* ("The Village Soothsayer") of 1752, an opera in French about a shepherd and a shepherdess that drew on the conventions of Italian opera buffa. With its simple, unpretentious music, the work was immensely popular.

The traditionalists ultimately lost the War of the Buffoons, and in its aftermath, French composers began to incorporate elements of comic opera into their works. The most notable among them was André Grétry (1741–1813), who came to be called "the French Pergolesi." By the 19th century, comic opera would emerge as a mainstay of French musical culture.

Opera nevertheless remained a forum for public controversy in prerevolutionary Paris. In the late 1770s, another heated debate erupted, this one dubbed the Quarrel of the Gluckists and Piccinnists. Once again the debate pitted Italian against French culture, although in this case the composers at the center of the dispute—Christoph Willibald Gluck and Niccolò Piccinni—were both foreigners. Piccinni was an Italian composer who came to Paris in 1776. Gluck, who was born in the Bohemian region of the Austrian Empire and spent most of his professional life in Italy and Vienna, moved to Paris in 1773. The Parisian music-loving public saw Gluck as a worthy successor to Lully and Rameau in the French tradition of *tragédie lyrique*; Piccinni, in turn, was perceived to represent the Italian tradition of opera seria. Benjamin Franklin, the American envoy to France at the time, found the intensity of the debate both amusing

A riot at Covent Garden Theater. Although today we tend to think of opera as an elite art, earlier audiences in many locales considered it popular entertainment. In London, the King's Theatre catered to a higher social class, but Drury Lane and Covent Garden attracted a more diverse audience. Here, at Covent Garden, members of the audience storm the stage because of management's refusal to admit spectators at half price after the intermission. The musicians are beating a hasty retreat for the door leading under the stage. The opera being performed, *Artaxerxes* by Thomas Arne (1710–88), was one of many 18th-century works based on so-called Turkish themes (the era's term for anything Middle Eastern). At the time, Britain and other European nations were consolidating their empires abroad, and the public was fascinated with representations of exotic locales and peoples.

Source: English School (18th Century), "Riot at Covent Garden" (engraving)/Bridgeman Art Library

and bewildering, comparing it to a debate among flies that consumes most of their short lives:

> We have been shown numberless skeletons of a kind of little fly, called an ephemera, whose successive generations, we are told, were bred and expired within the day. I happened to see a living company of them on a leaf, who appeared to be engaged in conversation. You know I understand all the inferior animal tongues. . . . I listened through curiosity to the discourse of these little creatures; but as they, in their national vivacity, spoke three or four together, I could make but little of their conversation. I found, however, by some broken expressions that I heard now and then, they were disputing warmly on the merit of two foreign musicians, one a *cousin*, the other a *moscheto* [French and Italian, respectively, for "mosquito"]; in which dispute they spent their time, seemingly as regardless of the shortness of life as if they had been sure of living a month. Happy people! thought I, you live certainly under a wise, just, and mild government, since you have no public grievances to complain of, nor any subject of contention but the perfections and imperfections of foreign music.[1]

1. Benjamin Franklin, *Writings*, vol. 7, ed. Albert Henry Smyth (New York: Macmillan, 1907), p. 207.

Clearly, to an outsider like Franklin, the issues that separated the two sides of this debate were trivial; his own nation was fighting for its independence when he wrote these lines. But within the upper classes of French society, the debate was quite serious indeed.

GLUCK AND THE REFORM OF OPERA

While the new genre of opera buffa challenged its dominance from without, opera seria was also facing challenges from within. A growing number of poets, composers, and critics maintained that the time-honored conventions of opera seria, designed to showcase the virtuosity of individual singers, were unnatural impediments to dramatic action. One critic, for example, writing in 1755, criticized the opening ritornello of most arias as "tediously prolix" and "often superfluous." "For can anything be more improbable," he asked, "than that, in an air expressive of wrath, an actor should calmly wait with his hand stuck in his sword belt until the ritornello be over, to give vent to a passion that is supposed to be boiling in his breast?"[2] Other writers pointed out that virtuoso settings of texts—in which a single syllable might endure for dozens of notes—compromised both the intelligibility and dramatic weight of the words.

In response to these concerns, several composers deliberately set out to reform opera seria to make it more natural and dramatically coherent. Notable composers working in this direction include Niccolò Jommelli, Tomasso Traetta, and, most prominently, Christoph Willibald Gluck (see "Composer Profile: Christoph Willibald Gluck").

In the preface to his opera *Alceste* (1769), Gluck spelled out the basic principles behind his efforts to eliminate the "abuses" that had "disfigured" Italian opera (see Primary Evidence: Gluck's Operatic Manifesto). In many respects, Gluck's aesthetic closely resembles the principles of the Florentine camerata (see Chapter 7), whose members insisted that the words should be the mistress of the music and not vice versa. The music of opera, in Gluck's view, should never serve a purely musical purpose but instead always help further the dramatic action. Many of the characteristic features that distinguish so-called reform opera from opera seria follow from this fundamental premise. These features include the following:

- no da capo arias

- little or no opportunity for vocal improvisation or virtuosic displays of vocal agility or power

- no long melismas

- a more predominantly syllabic setting of the text to make the words more intelligible

- far less repetition of text within an aria

- a blurring of the distinction between recitative and aria, declamatory and lyrical passages, with altogether less recitative

- accompanied rather than secco recitative

- simpler, more flowing melodic lines

---

2. Francesco Algarotti, *An Essay on the Opera* (Glasgow: R. Urie, 1768), p. 41.

PRIMARY EVIDENCE   Gluck's Operatic Manifesto

Gluck's preface to the published score of *Alceste* is a manifesto of his artistic beliefs, setting out the principles by which he sought to "restrict the music to its true purpose of serving to give expression to the poetry." *Alceste* was sufficiently different from all previous operas, in Gluck's own view, as to warrant careful explanation.

***

When I began to write the music for *Alceste*, I resolved to free it from all the abuses which have crept in either through ill-advised vanity on the part of the singers or through excessive complaisance on the part of composers, with the result that for some time Italian opera has been disfigured and from being the most splendid and most beautiful of all stage performances has been made the most ridiculous and the most wearisome. I sought to restrict the music to its true purpose of serving to give expression to the poetry and to strengthen the dramatic situations, without interrupting the action or hampering it with unnecessary and superfluous ornamentations. I believed that it should achieve the same effect as lively colors and a well-balanced contrast of light and shade on a very correct and well-disposed painting, so animating the figures without altering their contours. So I have tried to avoid interrupting an actor in the warmth of dialogue with a boring intermezzo or stopping him in the midst of his discourse, merely so that the flexibility of his voice might show to advantage in a long passage, or that the orchestra might give him time to collect his breath for a cadenza. I did not think I should hurry quickly through the second part of an air, which is perhaps the most passionate and most important, in order to have room to repeat the words of the first part regularly four times or to end the aria quite regardless of its meaning, in order to give the singer an opportunity of showing how he can render a passage with so-and-so many variations at will; in short, I have sought to eliminate all these abuses, against which sound common sense and reason have so long protested in vain.

I imagined that the overture should prepare the spectators for the action, which is to be presented, and give an indication of its subject; that the instrumental music should vary according to the interest and passion aroused, and that between the aria and the recitative there should not be too great a disparity, lest the flow of the period be spoiled and rendered meaningless, the movement be interrupted inopportunely, or the warmth of the action be dissipated. I believed further that I should devote my greatest effort to seeking to achieve a noble simplicity; and I have avoided parading difficulties at the expense of clarity. I have not placed any value on novelty, if it did not emerge naturally from the situation and the expression; and there is no rule I would not have felt in duty bound to break in order to achieve the desired effect.

These are my principles. Happily all my intentions fitted admirably with the libretto, in which the famous author [Ranieri d' Calzabigi, the librettist], having devised a new plan for the lyrical drama, had replaced florid descriptions, superfluous comparisons, sententious and frigid moralization with the language of the heart, with strong passions, interesting situations and an ever-varied spectacle. My maxims have been vindicated by success, and the universal approval expressed in such an enlightened city [Vienna] has convinced me that simplicity, truth and lack of affectation are the sole principles of beauty in all artistic creations.

Source: Hedwig and E. H. Mueller von Asow, eds., *The Collected Correspondence and Papers of C. W. Gluck* (London: Barrie and Rockliff, 1962), pp. 22–4.

- an overture that is linked by theme or mood to the ensuing action

- more prominence for the chorus, giving it, in imitation of classical Greek drama, an important role commenting on the events unfolding on the stage

Gluck's *Alceste* translates all of these principles into music. The overture, which sets the tone for the action to come, flows directly into the opening scene. Aria and recitative are for the most part readily distinguishable, but the boundaries between the two are far less pronounced than in opera seria. And although the vocal roles for the soloists are demanding, they are by no means ostentatious. The chorus plays a prominent role throughout the entire opera, reacting to the events as they unfold on stage.

Very much in the tradition of opera seria, the libretto is based on a Greek legend, that of Queen Alceste's extraordinary devotion to her husband, King Admetus of Thessaly. When the dying Admetus learns from an oracle that he will be saved if

CD8, Track 3
GLUCK
Alceste
Score Anthology II/110

another mortal agrees to die in his place, Alceste resolves to sacrifice herself for him. Admetus recovers and Alceste is summoned to the underworld, but Hercules, with the blessing of Apollo, brings her back and she is restored to life. Unlike other operas based on Greek drama, Gluck's *Alceste* does not require a "happy ending" tacked on (compare his *Orfeo ed Euridice*), although Euripides' *Alcestis* has both darker and lighter elements not found in the libretto.

In the excerpt that appears in the anthology (from Act II, scene iii) Admetus learns that Alceste is the one who will die for him and he pleads with her to change her mind. (The opera was originally performed in Italian in Vienna in 1767; the excerpt in the anthology is from the French version Gluck prepared for performance in Paris in 1776.) In this scene, Gluck skillfully weaves together accompanied recitative, chorus, aria, and duet into a musically continuous dramatic sequence.

- Accompanied recitative (measures 486–524). In the opening dialogue, Admète (French for Admetus) pleads with Alceste to reveal who has agreed to die for him. She resists but in the end admits that she herself is the victim.

- Chorus (measures 525–38). At the climactic moment when Alceste reveals that she is to be the sacrificial victim, the chorus interjects with an outcry of "*O Dieux!*" ("O ye gods!"). This is in keeping with principles of ancient Greek tragedy, in which the chorus reflects the perspective of the community as a whole, transcending that of any individual character. After Admète registers his own astonishment, the chorus sings a lament for Admète and praises Alceste for her courage and love toward her husband.

- Accompanied recitative (measures 538–90). The dialogue resumes. Admète admonishes Alceste, telling her she will be breaking her marriage vows by abandoning him if she dies and leaves him alone. He calls on the gods to intercede. Alceste answers these protestations calmly, ending the dialogue (in measures 589–90) with the pleading phrase "*Ah, cher époux*" ("Ah, dear husband").

- Aria (measures 591–638): Without fanfare or ritornello, the accompanied recitative flows into an aria, sung by Admète, who proclaims his love for Alceste and tells her that he cannot live without her. The aria does not adhere to conventional structure, except to repeat text. There is no suggestion of a da capo aria; the music instead follows the sense of the text. In measure 623, for example, when Admète declares that death is his only salvation, the music shifts abruptly from andante and 3/4 time to alla breve presto. Even the text repetitions are handled in a dramatic manner (compare the music on "Barbare," upbeat to measure 591, then upbeat to measure 615).

- Interruption (measures 638–39). Just before the end of Admète's aria, Alceste interrupts with a simple but dramatic repetition of her earlier plea, "*Ah, cher époux.*"

- Return of the aria's opening section (measures 639–44). The tempo shifts to moderato, the meter back to 3/4, and Admète closes by repeating the key phrase from the opening part of his aria just before leaving the stage: "Je ne puis vivre, tu le sais, tu n'en doutes pas" (I cannot live [without you], you know it, you have no doubt of that). By returning to earlier material at the end of the aria, Gluck is to some extent following the conventions of the da capo aria, including even the exit convention. But the differences here are more revealing than the similarities: the return is extremely brief, and virtuosity for its own sake plays no role at all. The repetition reinforces the text, reminding us that in spite of Admète's desire to die, his overwhelming emotion is one of grief at the thought of losing Alceste.

COMPOSER PROFILE   Christoph Willibald Gluck *(1714–1787)*

Like Handel before him, Gluck was a cosmopolitan composer who seemed to be at home almost anywhere in Europe. He was born in the Upper Palatinate region of Bavaria, moving as a child with his family to Bohemia, then part of the Austrian Empire of the Hapsburgs. He settled in Milan in 1737, where he studied and wrote music, and subsequently received commissions to write operas for Dresden, London, Copenhagen, Vienna, Prague, and Paris, where his former student Marie Antoinette became his patron. Gluck achieved extraordinary success in Paris, presenting many of his Italian operas in revised French versions.

Like other 18th-century composers, however, Gluck composed on commission, and even in the midst of writing the most famous of his reform operas (*Orfeo ed Euridice*, 1762; *Alceste*, 1767; *Iphigénie en Aulide*, 1774; *Iphigénie en Tauride*, 1779), he continued to write opere serie as the occasion demanded. Although he wrote some trio sonatas that were widely performed in his day, Gluck devoted himself mostly to opera and was known then and is remembered now as one of the greatest of all composers for the stage. In the 19th century, Richard Wagner (see Chapter 17) looked upon Gluck, not Mozart, as his principal forerunner, because Gluck, like Wagner, was striving for a synthesis of music and drama. Gluck's operas would serve as models for 19th-century French grand opera and have remained in the repertory continuously to the present day.

PRINCIPAL WORKS

Aside from a set of six trio sonatas and some ballets, Gluck's output is almost entirely vocal. He wrote dozens of operas, some in Italian, some in French; many exist in versions in both languages. His most acclaimed operas include *Demofoonte* (1742), *Orfeo ed Euridice* (1762), *Alceste* (1767), *Iphigénie en Aulide* (1774), *Armide* (1777), and *Iphigénie en Tauride* (1779).

Gluck composes. Gluck is seated at the clavichord, a small, intimate instrument traditionally associated with the studio rather than the salon or concert hall. His gaze—directed upward to the muses for inspiration—tells us he is composing and not performing. Note the similarity of this image to Haydn composing at the keyboard (Chapter 12).

Source: Joseph Siffrede Duplessis (1725–1802), "Christoph Willibald Gluck at the spinet," 1775, oil on canvas, 99.5 cm. × 80.5 cm./Kunsthistorisches Museum, Vienna, Austria/The Bridgeman Art Library

KEY DATES IN THE LIFE OF GLUCK

1714	Born in Erasbach (now in Germany) on July 2.
1736	Moves to Vienna, plays violin for Prince Lobkowitz (a member of the same family that would support Beethoven), and later travels extensively in Italy.
1741	Composes his first opera, *Artaserse*, in the tradition of opera seria. Travels extensively, including important stays in Paris and London.
1762	Premiere of *Orfeo ed Euridice*, in Vienna.
1767	Premiere of *Alceste*, in Vienna.
1773	Moves temporarily to Paris; becomes embroiled in the "Quarrel of the Gluckists and Piccinists."
1779	With his new opera *Echo et Narcisse* a failure and in poor health, returns to Vienna.
1787	Dies in Vienna on November 15.

Gluck's approach to opera was soon imitated by other composers seeking a more natural approach to the genre. Still, conventional opera seria did not disappear overnight. On the contrary, it continued to flourish well into the 19th century. Mozart's last completed opera, *La Clemenza di Tito* (1791), for example, was an opera seria, with the title role written for a castrato. Gioacchino Rossini (1792–1868) was still writing in the genre in the 1820s. Even Gluck himself wrote several opere serie in the last decades of his life. Note that the principles of Gluck's manifesto are open to varied interpretation. *Alceste*, for example, is full of ballets. Do these sometimes lengthy numbers unnaturally interrupt the flow of the drama, or do they intensify it? There is no hard and fast answer.

MOZART AND THE SYNTHESIS OF OPERATIC STYLES

Of all the genres in which Mozart worked—and he wrote in virtually every genre of his day—his operas are justly celebrated as his greatest achievements. And of all the opera composers of his day, he stands out for two accomplishments: his ability to create psychologically complex characters and his ability to synthesize and transcend the boundaries of buffa, seria, and other operatic styles. Mozart was a keen student of human behavior, with a sharp and a wicked sense of humor. The characters in his most celebrated operas—nobles and commoners alike—are believable, three-dimensional human beings, not the heroic but essentially two-dimensional nobles who populate an opera seria like Handel's *Giulio Cesare*, or even Gluck's *Alceste*, or the stock servants and peasants who predominate in the typical opera buffa. (See Composer Profile: Wolfgang Amadeus Mozart.)

In his early operas, those written before he moved to Vienna in 1781, Mozart tried his hand at a variety of styles and traditions, including opera seria (both conventional and in Gluck's reform style), opera buffa, and singspiele (German-language plays with songs, akin to modern-day musicals). He was thus ideally positioned to synthesize the previously separate serious and comic strands of musical drama, which he did in four late operas: *Le Nozze di Figaro*, *Don Giovanni*, *Così fan tutte*, and *Die Zauberflöte*. The first three, which he wrote in collaboration with the librettist Lorenzo da Ponte (1749–1838), are generally considered his greatest, in no small part because their texts and music probe so deeply into that great central human concern: love and war between the sexes. (For *Die Zauberflöte*, see under "Song" later in this chapter.)

The plot of *Don Giovanni* is based on the legend of Don Juan, a nobleman and notorious libertine. Da Ponte's libretto is both comic and serious; he called it a *dramma giocoso*, a "comic drama." The plot pits men against women, nobles against commoners, individuals against the community. The title character is at once malevolent and alluring, a man who openly flaunts conventional morality, pursuing instead his own pleasure under the guise of "liberty." At the beginning of the opera he slays the Commendatore (Commandant), the father of Donna Anna, a woman who has just fought off Don Giovanni's attempted assault. At the end of the opera, the statue of the Commendatore consigns the unrepentant Don Giovanni to the flames of hell.

The overture and first three scenes of *Don Giovanni*, which together constitute some 20 minutes of continuous music and seamless dramatic action, demonstrate the way Mozart integrates buffa and seria elements. True to the principles of Gluck's operatic creed, Mozart uses the overture (not in the Anthology) to set the tone of the opera as a whole, with its unpredictable juxtaposition of tragedy and farce. The opening,

CD8, Track 4
MOZART
Don Giovanni, K. 527
Score Anthology II/111

with its slow tempo and heavy dotted rhythms, conveys a sense of ominous foreboding, heightened by the sinuous chromaticism that follows; the impression is given that this is a deeply serious opera. But at the beginning of the longer, sonata-form second section (measure 31), the tempo becomes faster and the mood changes abruptly from gravity to gaiety. In a broad sense, these contrasting sections symbolize the Commendatore and Don Giovanni, who will soon defend their respective moral poles (literally): the world of the Commendatore in which law prevails, crime is punished, and damnation is the sure consequence for unrepented sin, versus the world of Don Giovanni, with his devotion to pleasure and liberty.

The overture segues directly into the first scene. Leporello, the servant of Don Giovanni, stands guard outside a nobleman's house while his master attempts to seduce yet another woman. Even before Leporello sings a single note, the music announces he is a commoner: the opening theme, which Leporello picks up when he begins his aria-monologue, bounces back and forth between tonic and dominant. There is nothing sophisticated about this theme harmonically, rhythmically, or melodically. Leporello is complaining to himself about the wicked ways of his master while at the same time longing to be a "gentleman" himself. With its relentlessly syllabic text underlay and vehement repetitions of "No, no, no," the aria sounds appropriately comical.

But as in the overture, the juxtaposition of comedy and tragedy occurs without warning. Leporello's monologue segues into a frantic duet between two members of an altogether different class: the noblewoman Donna Anna and the nobleman Don Giovanni. Donna Anna pursues the unknown man (Don Giovanni), who attempts to escape unrecognized. Almost at once, the duet becomes a trio as Leporello joins their agitated exchange with more of his melodically simple line, this time commenting on the action and predicting his master's philandering will bring his own ruin.

A new dramatic unit begins with the arrival of the Commendatore, Donna Anna's father. He demands a duel with the unknown intruder. Don Giovanni reluctantly accepts and deals the Commendatore a mortal wound. Again, Leporello comments on the scene as it transpires before him, this time with an even greater sense of gloom. There follows a brief dialogue in secco recitative between Don Giovanni and Leporello, after which they exit. We then move directly into another dramatic unit, still with no real break in the music. Donna Anna returns, having summoned the aid of her kindhearted but rather boring fiancé, Don Ottavio. During the accompanied recitative that follows, they discover her father's body and she faints. Don Ottavio revives her so efficiently, however, that she is soon able to launch into her part of a powerfully dramatic duet ("Fuggi, crudele, fuggi") at the end of which they swear together to avenge her father's death. The music, agitated and virtuosic, comes from the world of opera seria. Mozart fuses the reflective power of aria (Donna Anna's shock at the death of her father) with the interchange of duet (Don Ottavio's promise of consolation and revenge), all interrupted at unpredictable moments by powerful outbursts of accompanied recitative.

Clearly, Mozart wanted to create a sense of dramatic continuity for the entire opening sequence of events, for it is only now, at the end of this extended duet, that he gives the audience its first opportunity to applaud. The arias and ensembles are not, as is so often the case in opera seria, reflections on events that have already happened. On the contrary, they are part of the action, propelling it forward. The events of the drama, in other words, move through the music.

One of the devices Mozart uses to structure this extended series of units is tonality (see table). The sequence begins and ends in D minor, and the choice of key in between is closely coordinated with the drama unfolding on stage. Each dramatic unit has its own distinctive key, different from yet related to the one before and the one after.

The integration of music and drama is evident as well in the two subsequent numbers. The first of these, "Ah, chi mi dice mai" ("Ah, who shall ever tell me"), begins like an aria. Donna Elvira, who had been seduced and abandoned by Don Giovanni long before the curtain has gone up, is asking herself if she will ever again find that "barbarian," promising to "cut out his heart" if she does. Her demanding vocal line, full of large leaps and covering a wide range, is that of a character who would be at home in an opera seria. As she is singing, Don Giovanni and Leporello see her from a distance, and the aria becomes a trio. Don Giovanni does not at first recognize her (a curious reversal from the previous scene in which he escaped unrecognized) and so is unaware it is he she is raging about. With another seduction clearly in mind, he steps forward to console her. The moment they recognize each other, the ensemble ends. The music changes without a pause to secco recitative, and the drama presses on. Once again Mozart deprives the audience of an opportunity to applaud. Instead, we

The Structure of the Opening Sequence of Mozart's *Don Giovanni*

	VOCAL NUMBER	KEY	TYPE	DRAMATIC ACTION
Overture		D minor/major	Instrumental	Slow introduction and sonata form. Leads directly into Scene i.
Scene i	1: Introduction	F Major	Aria	Leporello alone.
		B♭ Major	Duet/Trio	Don Giovanni and Donna Anna enter. The two noble characters struggle, singing in counterpoint. Leporello stands safely apart, commenting, in the bass, in his own diatonic and decidedly nonimitative way.
		G minor	Duet	The Commendatore enters and Donna Anna exits. The Commendatore challenges Don Giovanni to a duel.
		D minor	Instrumental	Sword fight between the Commendatore and Don Giovanni
		F minor	Trio	Slow death of the Commendatore. The Commendatore, Don Giovanni, and Leporello each expresses his own thoughts in what amounts to three simultaneous monologues. Leads directly into Scene ii.
Scene ii		G Major B♭ Major	Secco recitative	Don Giovanni and Leporello alone. Exit from stage, but with an immediate musical segue into Scene iii.
Scene iii		D Major	Secco recitative	Donna Anna returns with Don Ottavio and servants.
	2: Recitative and duet	G minor	Accompanied recitative	Donna Anna reacts to her father's death; Don Ottavio directs removal of the corpse.
		D minor	Duet	(a) Alternation between Donna Anna, who swears revenge, and Don Ottavio, who offers consolation; (b) Both characters swear revenge in true duet fashion, singing simultaneously.

Two scenes from Mozart's *Don Giovanni*. These two scenes from Act I of *Don Giovanni* were engraved by Johann Heinrich Ramberg in 1825. The illustration on the left captures the moment when Donna Anna faints at the sight of the father, who has just been murdered in a duel with an unknown assailant—Don Giovanni, as it turns out. Don Ottavio comforts her as servants rush onto the scene. The illustration on the right shows Leporello beginning his "Catalogue Aria," singing to Donna Elvira from the long list of Don Giovanni's prior loves. The moment depicted here follows the escape from the scene of Don Giovanni, who is visible at the back, between the balcony with flowers and the statue of the god of love showing his disgust.

Source: Courtesy of the Library of Congress

watch Donna Elvira's astonishment turn to rage as Don Giovanni slips away, leaving Leporello to deal with her. In his ensuing aria, "Madamina! il catalogo è questo" ("Madam! Here is the catalogue"), Leporello tries to assuage Donna Elvira with evidence that she is "neither the first nor the last" of Don Giovanni's conquests. He shows her a catalogue he has kept of all of them. In the first part of the aria Leporello enumerates his master's seductions by country; in the second part he describes them by type (old or young, fair-haired or dark-haired, large or small). The music reflects this shift of focus. The first part is allegro; the second part, with its own theme, moves at a more leisurely tempo (Andante con moto).

Although we have no letters describing the creation of *Don Giovanni* in any detail, Mozart's comments on one of his earlier operas, *Idomeneo*, give us some idea of the

COMPOSER PROFILE   Wolfgang Amadeus Mozart *(1756–1791)*

Wolfgang's father Leopold was a competent composer in his own right and renowned in his day as the author of the most important treatise of his time on violin method. Wolfgang was a child prodigy who began composing before he was 5. When he was 6, Leopold began taking Wolfgang and his talented sister Anna (also a keyboard player) on concert tours throughout Europe. Posterity has not been kind to Leopold for this, condemning him, probably with some justification, for exploiting his children. These tours, however, took Wolfgang to almost every musically important city in Europe, providing him with the best education a young musician of the time could have received.

Mozart astonished audiences on these tours. One English witness recounted handing the 8-year-old prodigy

> a manuscript duet, which was composed by an English gentleman to some favourite words in Metastasio's opera of *Demofoonte*. The whole score was in five parts, viz. accompaniments for a first and second violin, the two vocal parts, and a base. I shall here likewise mention, that the parts for the first and second voice were written in what the Italians stile the *Contralto* cleff. My intention in carrying with me this manuscript composition was to have an irrefutable proof of his abilities, as a player at sight, it being absolutely impossible that he could have ever seen the music before. The score was no sooner put upon his desk, than he began to play the symphony in a most masterly manner, as well as in the time and stile which corresponded with the intention of the composer. I mention this circumstance, because the greatest masters often fail in these particulars on the first trial.[3]

In addition to performing, Mozart would also listen, attending whatever concerts he could. In Rome, for example, he heard Gregorio Allegri's *Miserere*, an early-17th-century work for double choir that had traditionally been reserved for exclusive performance by the papal choir. Afterward, Mozart wrote out the work from memory. In this way, city by city, country by country, the young Mozart absorbed almost everything Europe had to offer in the way of music. As a result, he could later write to his father, matter-of-factly and without boasting, that he "could write in any style" he chose.

Although we tend to regard Mozart as a figure of almost godlike stature, he was in fact extremely earthy at times. Letters to his cousin Bäsle are full of what might charitably be called bathroom humor. (Mozart maintained a lifelong obsession with bodily functions.) He made rude comments (in private) about the Archbishop of Salzburg, and after moving to Vienna in 1781 refused to engage in that city's musical politics. Indeed he seldom had anything good to say about contemporary composers (Haydn was an exception), and it must have been painful for him to see key appointments go to lesser composers.

Like many child movie stars today, Mozart had difficulty adjusting to adulthood. He had to teach composition to supplement his income, and his efforts to secure a steady position at the Habsburg court in Vienna did not bear fruit until the last years of his life, when he was given a minor, essentially part-time position that entailed little more than writing new dances for New Year's galas and other celebrations.

Why was Mozart not more popular in his own time? He was certainly well known, and some of his music—most notably his operas *Le Nozze di Figaro* and *Don Giovanni*—were tremendously successful. But much of his music was perceived to be too complicated, too full of artifice. "Too many notes," the Emperor Joseph II is said to have complained after hearing one of Mozart's operas. Other composers, although they held Mozart in high regard, agreed that the complexity of his music sometimes put it beyond the grasp of contemporary audiences. When the composer Carl von Dittersdorf offered a set of string quartets in 1781 to the same publishing firm that, three years earlier, had published some Mozart quartets, he predicted his quartets would earn the firm more money. Why? Because although Mozart's quartets "deserved the highest praise," their "overwhelming and unrelenting artfulness" made them unappealing to a wider public.

Ironically, Mozart's popularity seems to have been rising just before he died. His singspiel *Die Zauberflöte* (1791) was a great hit, and he was finally beginning to make inroads at the Habsburg court.

There is a myth about Mozart that composition was effortless for him. Like most myths, it is based on an element of truth. Mozart wrote an astonishing quantity of music, especially considering that he died just short of his 36th birthday. He often packed more melodies into a single movement than most of his contemporary composers used in an entire composition. From time to time in his letters, he mentions works he has already composed in his head but "not yet written down." He is said to have composed the overture to *Don Giovanni* the night before the first performance. And unlike Beethoven a generation later, he did not labor through multiple drafts of a single idea. However, he abandoned an enormous number of works before making very much progress on them. One recent scholar has estimated that for every work he completed he abandoned two. And although Mozart did have a remarkable ability to work out ideas in

---

3. Daines Barrington, "An Account of a Very Remarkable Young Musician," 28 September 1769 (published in Deutsch, *Mozart: A Documentary Biography*, p. 96).

his head before committing them to paper and a quick sense of what would and would not work once he actually began writing down a musical idea, he nonetheless did sometimes revise and re-revise. The autograph score of the "Dissonance" Quartet, K. 465, for example, includes scrapings and corrections indicating that he reworked the dissonant opening on more than one occasion.

PRINCIPAL WORKS

SYMPHONIES   Mozart wrote almost 50 symphonies, but even though the early ones are full of delightful surprise, it is mostly the later ones that are performed with any frequency today. Unlike Haydn, who had a standing orchestra at his disposal, Mozart had no incentive to compose symphonies regularly. He apparently composed his last three symphonies (nos. 39, 40, 41), all in 1788, with an eye toward the kind of trip to London that Haydn would undertake a few years later. In many respects, these

The Mozart family. This portrait of Mozart's family was painted around 1780, shortly before his departure from Salzburg to Vienna. The family would never again be together for more than brief visits thereafter. Leopold Mozart (1719–1787), holding the violin, presides. Mozart's sister Anna (1751–1829) sits with her brother at the piano. Nannerl, as her family called her, was also a noted keyboard performer. Mozart was the first composer to write music for four hands that required the performers to cross hands, as he and Nannerl are doing here. Maria Anna Mozart—Leopold's wife and Wolfgang and Nannerl's mother—died in 1778, but this painting reproduces a portrait of her hanging on the wall. A statue of Apollo holding a lyre occupies a place of prominence in an alcove in the wall.

Source: Johann Nepomuk della Croce, "The Mozart Family." Oil on canvas. 140 × 168 cm. Mozart House, Salzburg, Austria. Erich Lessing/ Art Resource, NY

last three symphonies are even larger and more ambitious than Haydn's "London" symphonies. Mozart was much quicker than Haydn to integrate the clarinet into the orchestra. With the finale of the Symphony no. 41 in C Major, K. 551 ("Jupiter"), he established the important precedent for later composers, most notably Beethoven, of placing a symphony's emotional and intellectual weight more in the finale than the first movement.

STRING QUARTETS AND QUINTETS   Mozart wrote 27 string quartets, including the 6 dedicated to Haydn and published in 1785. His late quartets are remarkable for their transparent textures. In them all four instruments participate as more or less equal partners to an extent that would not be equaled until Beethoven's middle- and late-period quartets. The cello part is especially prominent in Mozart's last three quartets (K. 575, 589, 590), which he apparently intended to dedicate to the king of Prussia, who was an accomplished cellist.

Mozart turned to the string quintet (a quartet with a second viola) relatively late in life. His two works in this genre, the Quintet in G minor (K. 515) and Quintet in C Major (K. 516), are worthy counterparts to his last two symphonies in the same keys (K. 550 and K. 551).

SOLO AND CHAMBER WORKS FOR PIANO   In addition to 19 sonatas for solo piano, Mozart also wrote several keyboard duets, variations, fantasias, rondos, and minuets. He also wrote 36 sonatas for violin and piano, 6 piano trios, 2 piano quartets, and a quintet for piano and winds.

CONCERTOS   Mozart's earliest piano concertos are not original works, but rather arrangements of existing sonatas or sonata movements by a variety of composers, both well known (J. C. Bach, C. P. E. Bach) and not so well known (H. F. Raupach, L. Honauer). He wrote the bulk of his 23 original piano concertos during his years in Vienna, where they provided a way to showcase his talents both as a composer and performer. His correspondence reveals that he was calculating about the effects of these works on his audience. After finishing a set of three concertos in Vienna, for example, Mozart wrote to his father in Salzburg that the works were "a happy medium between what is too easy and too difficult" for listeners. "They are very brilliant, pleasing to the ear, and natural, without being vapid. There are passages here and there from which connoisseurs alone can derive satisfaction; but these passages are written in such a way that the less learned cannot fail to be pleased, though without knowing why."[4] In addition to piano concertos, Mozart also wrote five concertos for violin, four for

4. Mozart, letter of 15 November 1780. Transl. MEB

horn, one for clarinet, one for bassoon, two for flute, and one for flute and harp.

OPERAS Mozart explored every subgenre of opera available to him in his time. *Idomeneo*, K. 366, written for the court at Munich in 1781 and later revived in Vienna, reflects the influence of Gluck's operas. *La Clemenza di Tito*, K. 621, written for the coronation of Emperor Leopold II in Prague in 1791, is in the tradition of opera seria; its text is an adaptation of a much earlier libretto by Metastasio (see Chapter 9). The male lead in both of these works featured a castrato. Mozart's *singspiele*—German-language plays with songs—include *Die Entführung aus dem Serail* ("The Abduction from the Seraglio"), K. 384, and *Die Zauberflöte* ("The Magic Flute"), K. 620. The latter is a fairy-tale opera that had a wide-reaching influence on 19th-century German opera. The three operas Mozart wrote in collaboration with the librettist Lorenzo da Ponte—*Le nozze di Figaro* ("The Marriage of Figaro"), K. 492, *Don Giovanni*, K. 527, and *Così fan tutte* ("All Women Do it Like That"), K. 588—represent an intriguing mixture of buffa and seria styles.

MASSES AND OTHER SACRED WORKS Mozart's duties in Salzburg in the 1760s and 1770s required him to write considerable quantities of sacred music: settings of the Mass and Vespers as well as shorter texts, such as psalms and offertories. But the 1780s were not hospitable to sacred music in Vienna. Emperor Joseph II, in an attempt to reduce the influence of the church, issued decrees limiting the performance of sacred music for voices and instruments together. In the last year of his life, Mozart received a private commission to write a Requiem but died before he could finish it. His widow, Constanze, approached several of Mozart's pupils to finish the work so she could receive payment, making it difficult to know who composed various parts of it. Most of it, however, is demonstrably by Mozart himself, and these sections include some of his most moving music.

KEY DATES IN THE LIFE OF MOZART

1756	Born in Salzburg (Austria) on January 27.
1763–1771	Undertakes a series of trips with his father to England, Holland, France, Germany, and especially Italy.
1769	Appointed concertmaster at the court in Salzburg.
1770s	Continues travels across the European continent but is unable to secure a satisfactory position.
1779	Returns to Salzburg to his previous position as concertmaster and becomes court organist as well, but he detests the provinciality of his native town.
1781	Against the protests of his father, moves to Vienna to seek a position there, earning money by giving concerts and lessons, and through sales of his published works.
1782	Marries Constanze Weber.
1785	Dedicates a set of six string quartets to his friend Joseph Haydn.
1791	Dies in Vienna on December 5.

kinds of considerations he took into account when setting a dramatic text to music. In a letter to his father dated November 15, 1780, for example, Mozart mused about the detrimental effect an aria would have during a particularly turbulent moment in the drama:

> In the last scene of Act II, [the character] Idomeneo has [in the libretto] an aria . . . between the choruses. It will be better to have just recitative here, of a kind in which the instruments can be put to work. For in this scene, which will be the finest in the whole opera . . . there will be such noise and confusion on the stage that an aria would cut a poor figure at this particular point. Beyond this, there is the thunderstorm, which is not likely to subside because of an aria being sung by Herr Raaf, is it?[5]

---

5. Mozart, letter of 26 September 1781. Transl. MEB

Mozart's concern for the careful ordering of tonal areas within larger scenes is evident in another letter to his father, written from Munich in 1781 while he was at work on *Die Entführung aus dem Serail* ("The Abduction from the Seraglio").

> In working out the aria I have . . . allowed Fischer's beautiful deep notes to glow. . . . And because Osmin's rage increases throughout, the allegro assai (which comes just at the moment when the aria seems to have reached its end) is of necessity in a totally different meter and key, thereby allowing it to make the best possible effect. For a man who finds himself in such a towering rage will overstep all bounds of order, moderation, and propriety and completely forget himself; and in just this manner, so must the music, too, forget itself. But because the passions, whether violent or not, must never be expressed to the point of arousing disgust, and as music, even in the most hair-raising situations, must never offend the ear, but must please the listener, or in other words must always remain *music*, so I have chosen a key that is not foreign to F (the key of the aria) but one related to it—not the nearest, D minor, but the more remote A minor.[6]

SACRED MUSIC

Almost every major composer of the Classical era wrote music for the church. Within the boundaries of the Holy Roman Empire, however, political factors limited the possible outlets for sacred music after 1780, when the Emperor Joseph II became the empire's sole ruler. Influenced by Enlightenment principles, the emperor instituted extensive reforms intended to limit the hereditary privileges of the nobility, strengthen the state bureaucracy, and restrict the influence of the church. His ecclesiastical reforms extended to music. Elaborate Masses requiring full orchestra, chorus, and soloists were no longer welcomed. Instead, the court encouraged simpler, more chordal settings of the liturgy. As a result, many composers—including Haydn and Mozart—abandoned the field of sacred music altogether until after Joseph II's death in 1790, when the restrictions were relaxed or dropped altogether. Even then, however, the church continued to struggle with the proper role of music in the liturgy. By the end of the 19th century, the Vatican was trying to steer its followers away from elaborate concert-style Masses on the grounds that they were overly secular.

In their orchestration, melodic style, and demand for vocal virtuosity, the sacred works of Haydn, Mozart, and others are indeed sometimes hard to distinguish from their secular theatrical works. On the whole, however, church music remained relatively conservative during the Classical era, retaining the basso continuo long after it had been abandoned in the concert hall, and well after it was still necessary from a strictly technical point of view. Sacred music also preserved more of the tradition of strict counterpoint than was customary in either the theater or the chamber. Certain sections of the Mass, such as the end of the Gloria and Credo, were often set as elaborate fugues in what was called the *stile antico*, the "old style," featuring subjects in long note values and written in *alla breve* meter.

The Introit of Mozart's unfinished *Requiem*, K. 626, is a good example of the synthesis of older and newer styles often found in the sacred music of the Classical era. For this movement, Mozart drew on the opening chorus from Handel's *Funeral Anthem for Queen Caroline*, written in 1737, and available to Mozart in Vienna through

CD8, Track 4
MOZART
Requiem, K. 626
Score Anthology II/112

---

6. Mozart, letter of 28 December 1782. Transl. MEB

Baron Gottfried van Swieten, a nobleman who took a special interest in the works of Handel and J. S. Bach. (Van Swieten had once commissioned from Mozart an arrangement of Handel's *Messiah* that includes clarinets and horns.) For the section beginning with the words "Te decet hymnus Deus in Sion" ("To thee, Lord in Zion, we sing a hymn"), Mozart brings in an even older source of sacred music, Gregorian chant. Here, in the soprano, he introduces the Ninth Psalm Tone (see Chapter 1), also associated in German-speaking lands with the Magnificat, another hymn of praise to God. The concluding "Dona eis pacem" ("Grant them peace") section brings back

Women as musical performers in the church. The priest is celebrating Mass at the high altar, but almost every eye in the (largely male) congregation is riveted on the female soloist. Even the musicians (especially the trumpeter in the opposite gallery) seem lost in admiration. The appeal is both physical and aural. This illustration first appeared in a Protestant tract in 1784 and reflects the view among at least some Protestant denominations that music in church, when performed by women, distracted the congregation from the liturgy. The Catholic church, in contrast, was more open to women performers, particularly in the Austrian Empire before 1790. The Empress Maria Theresa herself once sang the soprano part in a Mass written by Michael Haydn (Joseph's brother), and Mozart apparently wrote the virtuosic soprano line in his Mass in C minor, K. 427 (417a) for his wife, Constanze.

Source: Bildarchiv der Oesterreichischen Nationalbibliothek the opening theme ("Requiem aeternam") but now combines it with a new counter-subject. Mozart's *Requiem* has been surrounded in controversy since the time of its composition. It was known at the time that Mozart had died before he could complete the work, yet it was in his widow's interest to portray the efforts of the various collaborators who finished it—mostly students of her late husband—as inconsequential. Scholars have been trying to sort out Mozart's work from those of others since at least the 1820s. There is no dispute, however, about the authorship of the opening half of the work, including the Introit, because it has been preserved in manuscript in the composer's own hand.

SONG

If the sonata was the quintessential domestic instrumental genre in the Classical era, the song was the quintessential domestic vocal genre. Because songs were financially lucrative for composers and publishers alike, the Classical song repertory is enormous, but most of it remains unexplored today.

An 18th-century ballad singer.
Thomas Rowlandson's watercolor of a ballad singer (1789) captures the ease and naturalness of public singing in an earlier age. The woman holds in her hands the words of the latest ballad and is probably singing them to a well-known tune. Onlookers stop to listen, and some may give money at the end of the song.

Source: Thomas Rowlandson, "The Ballad Singer," 1789 © The National Library of Wales Picture Collection

Social song. This frontispiece to William Billings's *The New-England Psalm-Singer* (1770) was engraved by the silversmith Paul Revere (1735–1818), better known for his ride from Boston to Lexington on April 18, 1775. It shows a group around a table performing the canon "Wake Ev'ry Breath." Music was an important element in most social gatherings, both in Europe and in the colonies of North America. The performance here is not in a church, but in a home.

Source: Corbis/Bettmann

Johann Friedrich Reichardt's "Italien" (Italy) offers a good example of the kind of song writing that flourished throughout the Classical era. The setting is strophic and almost entirely syllabic. Both the vocal and piano parts are straightforward and technically undemanding. The range of the vocal line barely exceeds an octave, and is mostly doubled by the piano. The text, also known as "Kennst du das Land" (Do you know the land), is from Goethe's widely read novel *Wilhelm Meisters Lehrjahre* ("Wilhelm Meister's Years of Apprenticeship"), the story of a young man's coming of age. Wilhelm is an aspiring actor who falls in with an odd assortment of characters, one of whom is a mysterious young girl named Mignon. She has no family, and Wilhelm becomes something of a father figure to her, but there is a powerful erotic tension beneath the surface of their relationship. From time to time throughout the novel, Mignon sings songs, of which Goethe gives only the words. Reichardt (1752–1814) was one of the first composers to set these texts to music, and Goethe expressed his pleasure with these settings. (They even collaborated on some *Singspiele*.) But as we shall see (Chapter 16), many later composers were also drawn to this and other texts by Goethe that are not nearly so straightforward.

Composers could also use strophic songs as operatic arias to suggest characterization. InIn *Die Zauberflöte* (1791), Mozart had at his disposal two classes of characters to illustrate the serious and comic sides of opera. A fellow Mason, Emanuel Schikaneder (1751–1812), composer, librettist, and actor, offered the "fairy-tale opera" to Mozart, who responded with magnificent arias and duets for his "noble characters"—the future lovers, the benevolent father figure, the demonic mother figure—as they participate in a Masonic philosophical allegory. For the comic side, he focuses primarily on the bird-catcher Papageno (played originally by Schikaneder), who is given the folksiest German-sounding music imaginable, eminently hummable

CD8, Track 11
REICHARDT
Italien
Score Anthology II/114

CD8, Track 10
MOZART
Der Zauberflöte
Score Anthology II/113

and instantly memorable. Pagageno makes his Act I entrance with the strophic aria "Der Vogelfänger bin ich ja" (Yes, I am the bird-catcher), in which he describes his profession and his longing for a spouse. The orchestral accompaniment provides the lighthearted bounce to support the upbeat mood, and "covers" for him by including the panpipe incorporated into the aria (in the likelihood that having the singer do it himself would be impractical for any number of reasons).

William Billings (1746–1800), a native of Boston, was one of the first American-born composers to achieve international fame (albeit posthumously). He was largely self-taught, and his musical style, although indebted to English precedents, exhibits a certain roughness that gives it great energy. Billings's part-song *Chester* ("Let tyrants shake their iron rod/And slav'ry clank her galling Chains/we fear them not we trust in God/New England's God for ever reigns") became an unofficial anthem of the American Revolution. His hymn "Africa" was printed in his first collection, *The New-England Psalm-Singer* (1770), without text; he later added a text by the great English hymnodist Isaac Watts when "Africa" was republished in *The Singing Master's Assistant* (1778). As with other Billings choruses, the four-part texture is often expanded in performance to six parts by doubling the treble and tenor lines at the octave. Billings also composed many "social songs," intended to be sung at a social gathering like the one depicted on the frontispiece to his first collection, reproduced on p. 355. Social singing was a tradition brought to the American colonies from England, which had long cultivated part-songs of various kinds. In addition to anthems and hymns, lighter part-songs such as catches and glees were part of the repertoire, while the texts of canons usually addressed moral or religious subjects.

CD8, Track 12
BILLINGS
Africa
Score Anthology II/115

CONCLUSION

Vocal music—opera, sacred music, and song—maintained its traditional position of aesthetic superiority throughout the Classical era. Opera, in particular, was considered the highest of all musical genres and became increasingly accessible to a wider public, particularly in cities like London and Vienna. Although opera seria remained the favored subgenre at European courts, opera buffa appealed to a wider audience. Mozart, in particular, was able to integrate seria and buffa styles in a series of operas that fundamentally shaped the future of the genre.

DISCUSSION QUESTIONS

1. How has the idea of "naturalness" been evoked at various times in music history, up to and including the Classical era?

2. What distinguishes sonata form from binary form?

3. Many writers of the late 18th century compared the string quartet to a conversation among four rational individuals. Judging from a work like Haydn's String Quartet in C Major, op. 33, no. 3 (Anthology), how valid is this comparison?

4. How does double-exposition concerto form integrate sonata form and the ritornello principle?

5. How do Gluck's principles for the "reform" of opera compare to the efforts of the Florentine Camerata in the late 16th century to create a genre of sung drama?

6. What effect did Haydn's career—the circumstances of his employment as a composer—have on the genres in which he wrote?

7. In what ways does Mozart's *Don Giovanni* retain certain elements of *opera seria*?

8. Many writers of the late 18th century conceived of instrumental music as a language, with syntactic structures analogous to linguistic phrases and sentences. How valid is this analogy?

FRANCE

The celebrated Swiss-French philosopher and novelist **Jean-Jacques Rousseau** (1712–1778) devoted considerable energies to music. As an ardent advocate of Italian music, he was rather an outcast in France. He wrote most of the articles on music for the *Encyclopedia* and an important dictionary of musical terms (1768). His opera *Le devin du village* (The Village Soothsayer, 1752) enjoyed great popularity in France well into the 19th century. Rousseau advocated a natural style in music that excluded elements he considered artificial, such as counterpoint and overly elaborate harmony or dissonance.

François-Joseph Gossec (1734–1829) and **André-Ernest-Modeste Grétry** (1741–1813) both gained fame as composers of opera. Gossec, who was Belgian but spent most of his life in Paris, was also active in the establishment of the Paris Conservatory in the years after the French Revolution. Grétry was widely credited with establishing the tradition of French comic opera that would thrive in the 19th century under such composers as Auber, Adam, and Boieldieu.

GREAT BRITAIN

Charles Avison (1709–1770) is best remembered for his many concertos for a variety of instruments. **Thomas Arne** (1710–1788), the composer of the tune to "Rule, Britannia," also wrote many masques and operas. **William Boyce** (1711–1779) published *Cathedral Music*, a monumental collection of sacred works in three volumes, from 1760 to 1778. He also wrote symphonies, sonatas, operas, and songs.

ITALY

Although born in the same year as Handel and J. S. Bach, **Domenico Scarlatti** (1685–1757) wrote in a style that in many ways looks forward to the lighter textures of the Classical era. Only a small fraction of his nearly 600 sonatas were published during his lifetime. These single-movement works, mostly in binary form, range from the technically simple to the highly demanding. The son of Alessandro Scarlatti (see Chapter 9), he spent his last three decades in the service of the Spanish court in Madrid, were he wrote the bulk of his harpsichord music.

Baldassare Galuppi (1706–1785), **Niccolò Jommelli** (1714–1774), and **Tomasso Traetta** (1727–1779) were hailed in their time as masters of Italian opera. Galuppi has been called "the father of Italian comic opera"; Jommelli and Traetta preceded Gluck in the movement to reform opera (see Chapter 13). **Domenico Cimarosa** (1749–1801) composed almost 80 operas in the span of 29 years. He served for almost a decade as court composer in St. Petersburg, Russia.

Giovanni Battista Sammartini (1701–1775), his brother **Giuseppe Sammartini** (ca. 1693–ca. 1750), and **Luigi Boccherini** (1743–1805) are best remembered for their instrumental music. G. B. Sammartini was active in Milan and was one of Gluck's teachers. His most important works are his concert symphonies, some of which date from the 1730s, making them among the earliest works of this kind. Giuseppe Sammartini lived for many years in London, where he played oboe and conducted various ensembles. Boccherini, the leading cello virtuoso of his day, spent many years in the service of the Spanish court in Madrid. Among his many chamber works are 125 string quintets, works of great beauty and formal ingenuity.

Antonio Salieri (1750–1825) and **Muzio Clementi** (1752–1832), born in Italy, gained fame elsewhere. Salieri was court composer in Vienna and wrote many operas. Clementi spent most of his adult life in England, gaining renown as a piano virtuoso, composer, publisher, and piano manufacturer. His most celebrated compositions are the sonatas for piano.

THE AUSTRIAN EMPIRE

Christoph Willibald Gluck (see Composer Profile in Chapter 13), **Joseph Haydn** (see Composer Profile in Chapter 12), and **Wolfgang Amadeus Mozart** (see Composer Profile in Chapter 13) are the most prominent among a remarkable number of musicians born or raised in the Austrian empire during the 18th century. **Georg Matthias Monn** (1717–1750) wrote many instrumental works that fall stylistically somewhere between Baroque and Classical (see Chapter 10 and Anthology). Monn's Harpsichord Concerto would later be transcribed by Arnold Schoenberg for cello and orchestra (1933). **Johann Georg Albrechtsberger** (1736–1809) was a prolific composer of sacred music as well as chamber music; Beethoven studied counterpoint with him in the 1790s. **Carl Ditters von Dittersdorf** (1739–1799) was similarly prolific. His works include a series of 12 programmatic symphonies based on episodes from Ovid's *Metamorphoses*. **Michael Haydn** (1737–1806), the younger brother of Joseph Haydn, worked largely in Salzburg and was a close friend of the Mozart family. A symphony long attributed to Mozart (no. 37) was actually written by Michael Haydn. The Viennese composer **Johann Baptist Vanhal** (or Wanhal) (1739–1813) suffered a similar misattribution; until the 20th century several of his symphonies were wrongly thought to be by Joseph Haydn.

GERMANY

In Prussia, **Princess Anna Amalia** (1723–1787) and her brother, **Frederick II** ("The Great," 1712–1786), sponsored a remarkably active musical life at the court in Potsdam, just outside Berlin. The princess composed several instrumental works and chorales, but is best remembered for assembling an astonishing musical library that included many works by J. S. Bach. Frederick was an accomplished flutist and wrote a number of flute sonatas and concertos. His court flutist, **Johann Joachim Quantz** (1697–1773), contributed even more music for this instrument and wrote an important treatise on playing the flute. Another important court employee was **Carl Philipp Emanuel Bach**. His younger brother **Johann Christian Bach** enjoyed the favor of the English court in London. (See Chapter 11 for a Composer Profile on the Bach brothers.)

A native of Hamburg, **Johann Adolph Hasse** (1699–1783) gained renown as a composer of Italian operas that were popular throughout Europe. He also wrote many oratorios, Masses, and other sacred works. He spent his later years at the Saxon court at Dresden.

Johann Stamitz (1717–1757) was the most prominent composer for and musical director of the Mannheim orchestra, the remarkable musical establishment assembled and funded by the elector Carl Theodor from the 1740s into the 1780s (see Chapter 11). Stamitz was one of the first composers to write a symphony that used clarinets and among the first consistently to employ the four-movement format in his symphonies. His sons **Carl** (1745–1801) and **Anton** (1750–1796) were composers at the same court.

NORTH AMERICA

Musical life in England's American colonies, and later in the United States, during the Classical era was dominated by European music. **William Billings** (1746–1800) of Boston was one of the country's first native-born composers. He wrote and published a great deal of sacred music that was extremely popular in its time.

Part V

The 19th Century

Prelude

The 19th century was a period of unprecedented change in Western society. The population of the world's major powers increased by more than 150 percent, and the political boundaries of Europe were redrawn several times over. Many European nations established overseas empires, and the United States grew from an outpost at the edge of civilization to a world power reaching from the Atlantic to the Pacific. Technological developments fundamentally altered commerce, travel, and the exchange of information.

PROGRESS AND DISLOCATION

The Industrial Revolution that began in the 18th century accelerated rapidly in the 19th, with profound social, economic, and political consequences. Technological advances in transportation and communication—particularly the railroad and telegraph—changed daily life in basic ways. In 1825, it took a day and a half to travel the almost 200 miles between New York City and Boston by horse-drawn coach; by 1850, the same trip could be completed by rail in under six hours. By 1840, the British rail system was carrying some 18 million passengers a year. The American transcontinental railroad, opened in 1869, bound the newly acquired western territories of the United States firmly to the nation's northeastern urban-industrial core. The development of metal-hulled, coal-powered steamships produced a comparable revolution in maritime travel and commerce. In 1830, it cost the equivalent of about $800 in today's money to transport one ton of goods from Australia to England; by 1870, the same ton of freight could be transported for about $7.50.

The implications of the new communications technologies were equally profound. From the beginning of history until the invention of the telegraph in 1837, a message could travel no faster than the messenger who carried it. Now signals could be transmitted through wires almost instantaneously over great distances, even between Europe and the Americas, once the first transatlantic cable had been laid in 1866. The invention of the telephone in 1876 made it possible to transmit sound over comparably long distances, and the invention of the phonograph in 1877 made it possible to record, preserve, and reproduce sound for the first time in history. The consequences of recording technology on the ways music is produced and distributed continue to unfold today.

Science and technology combined to change daily life in other areas as well. New fertilizers and new machines like reapers and tractors increased agricultural yields. In medicine, Edward Jenner developed a vaccine for smallpox, and Louis Pasteur demonstrated that microorganisms could cause disease. Anesthesia and the sterilization of instruments became routine elements of surgery during the second half of the 19th century, and in the 1890s, Wilhelm Roentgen's work on X-rays opened up an entirely new approach to the diagnosis and treatment of diseases and injuries. Public health also improved, at least in certain locales. Major cities in Europe and the United States began constructing water and sewage systems, substantially reducing the spread of disease.

These and other technological advances—the invention of the sewing machine in the 1850s and the incandescent light bulb in 1879, for example—fed a growing belief in the inevitability of progress, the conviction that every passing year would bring new improvements to life. But for much of the population, this progress came at a heavy price. Industrialization produced disorienting social change. Europe's population increased dramatically

PRIMARY EVIDENCE   Twenty Miles an Hour

The railroad changed not only commerce and transportation but the very concept of speed itself, as suggested by Thomas Creevey's diary account of his first train ride, in November 1829. Creevey (1768–1838), a Member of Parliament who at first opposed the building of the Liverpool & Manchester Railroad, was invited to take his first rail trip on it; like others, he reported a range of responses.

I had the satisfaction, for I can't call it pleasure, of taking a trip of five miles on it, which we did in just a quarter of an hour—that is, 20 miles an hour. . . . But the quickest motion is to me frightful: The machine was really flying, and it is impossible to divest yourself of the notion of instant death to all upon the least accident happening. It gave me a headache which has not left me yet. . . . Altogether I am extremely glad indeed to have seen this miracle, and to have travelled in it. Had I thought worse of it than I do, I should have had the curiosity to try it, but having done so I am quite satisfied with my first achievement being my last.

"Stephenson's Rocket." This early steam locomotive won a major British competition for the most powerful and efficient engine of its kind in 1829.

Source: Private Collection/The Bridgeman Art Library

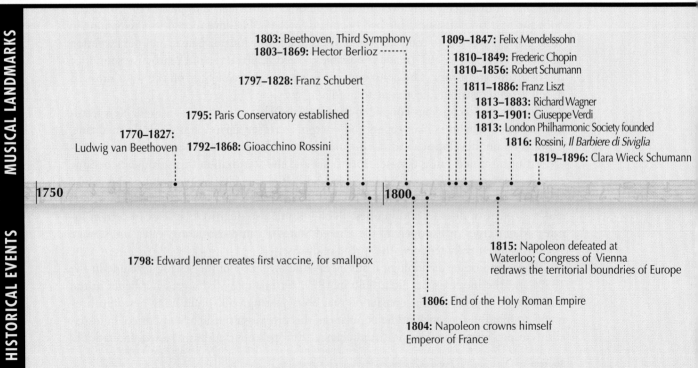

19TH CENTURY TIMELINE

MUSICAL LANDMARKS

1803: Beethoven, Third Symphony
1803–1869: Hector Berlioz
1797–1828: Franz Schubert
1795: Paris Conservatory established
1770–1827: Ludwig van Beethoven
1792–1868: Gioacchino Rossini

1809–1847: Felix Mendelssohn
1810–1849: Frederic Chopin
1810–1856: Robert Schumann
1811–1886: Franz Liszt
1813–1883: Richard Wagner
1813–1901: Giuseppe Verdi
1813: London Philharmonic Society founded
1816: Rossini, *Il Barbiere di Siviglia*
1819–1896: Clara Wieck Schumann

1750   1800

HISTORICAL EVENTS

1798: Edward Jenner creates first vaccine, for smallpox

1815: Napoleon defeated at Waterloo; Congress of Vienna redraws the territorial boundries of Europe

1806: End of the Holy Roman Empire

1804: Napoleon crowns himself Emperor of France

The 19th-Century Population Explosion in Europe and the United States

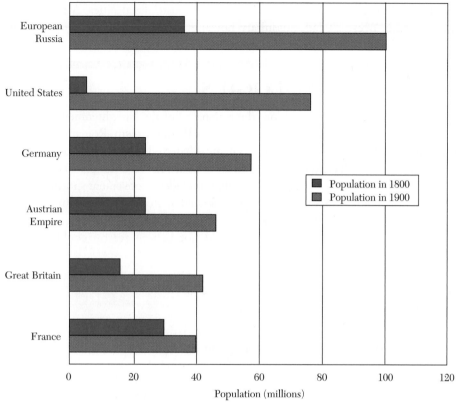

Legend:
- ■ Population in 1800
- ■ Population in 1900

Population (millions)

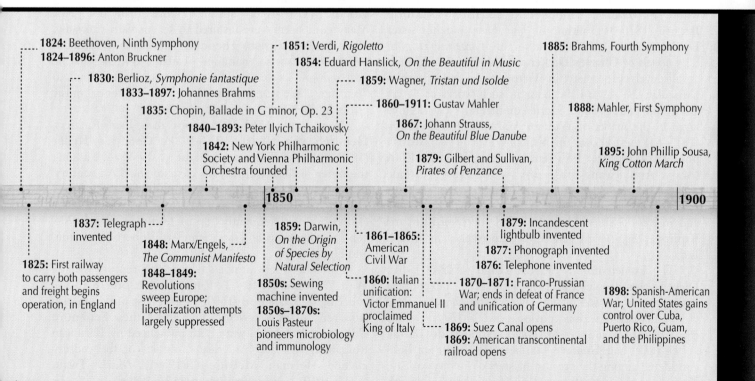

1824: Beethoven, Ninth Symphony
1824–1896: Anton Bruckner

1830: Berlioz, *Symphonie fantastique*
1833–1897: Johannes Brahms
1835: Chopin, Ballade in G minor, Op. 23
1840–1893: Peter Ilyich Tchaikovsky
1842: New York Philharmonic Society and Vienna Philharmonic Orchestra founded

1851: Verdi, *Rigoletto*
1854: Eduard Hanslick, *On the Beautiful in Music*
1859: Wagner, *Tristan und Isolde*
1860–1911: Gustav Mahler
1867: Johann Strauss, *On the Beautiful Blue Danube*
1879: Gilbert and Sullivan, *Pirates of Penzance*

1885: Brahms, Fourth Symphony

1888: Mahler, First Symphony

1895: John Phillip Sousa, *King Cotton March*

1850

1900

1837: Telegraph invented

1825: First railway to carry both passengers and freight begins operation, in England

1848: Marx/Engels, *The Communist Manifesto*
1848–1849: Revolutions sweep Europe; liberalization attempts largely suppressed

1859: Darwin, *On the Origin of Species by Natural Selection*
1850s: Sewing machine invented
1850s–1870s: Louis Pasteur pioneers microbiology and immunology

1861–1865: American Civil War
1860: Italian unification: Victor Emmanuel II proclaimed King of Italy

1879: Incandescent lightbulb invented
1877: Phonograph invented
1876: Telephone invented
1870–1871: Franco-Prussian War; ends in defeat of France and unification of Germany
1869: Suez Canal opens
1869: American transcontinental railroad opens

1898: Spanish-American War; United States gains control over Cuba, Puerto Rico, Guam, and the Philippines during the 19th century (see graph). Millions migrated from the countryside in search of work, swelling the populations of the newly industrialized cities. Many factory workers lived in overcrowded, unsanitary housing and worked in dangerous conditions for low wages and with tenuous job security.

IDEAS AND IDEOLOGIES

In the wake of the French Revolution, the rationality of the Enlightenment gradually gave way to a new mode of thought loosely known as **Romanticism.** Romanticism is one of those terms that has been used to mean so many different things—one scholar working in the middle of the 20th century counted no fewer than 11,396 definitions of the term—that a concise definition seems impossible. Still, it provides a convenient shorthand for a new aesthetic and philosophical outlook that took hold in the early 19th century.

In general, the Romantic outlook respected reason but, in contrast to the rationalism of the Enlightenment philosophes, did not believe reason could solve all

---

FOCUS   **Major Literary Figures of the 19th Century**

England was home to some of the most notable poets of the Romantic movement, including **William Blake** (1757–1827), **William Wordsworth** (1770–1850), **Samuel Taylor Coleridge** (1772–1834), **George Gordon, Lord Byron** (1788–1824), **Percy Bysshe Shelley** (1792–1822), **John Keats** (1795–1821), and **Alfred, Lord Tennyson** (1809–92). The 19th century was also an era of great English novelists, most notably **Jane Austen** (1775–1817), whose works include *Pride and Prejudice*, *Emma*, and *Persuasion*; **Mary Wollstonecraft Shelley** (1797–1851), whose *Frankenstein* continues to fascinate; **Charlotte Brontë** (1816–55), author of *Jane Eyre*; and her sister **Emily Brontë** (1818–48), author of *Wuthering Heights*. The novels of **Charles Dickens** (1812–70) chronicle life at all levels of society in Victorian England, with a particular eye toward the poor in such works as *Oliver Twist* and *Hard Times*. Social commentary also figures large in the works of **William Makepeace Thackeray** (1811–63), best known for his *Vanity Fair* (1847). British novelists of the later 19th century include **George Eliot** (**Mary Ann Evans**, 1819–80), whose works include *Adam Bede*, *Silas Marner*, and *Middlemarch*, and **Thomas Hardy** (1840–1928), author of *The Mayor of Casterbridge* and *Jude the Obscure*. The novels and poetry of **Rudyard Kipling** (1865–1936) reflect his experiences in British India.

The French novelist **Victor Hugo** (1802–85), like Dickens, was deeply concerned with social and political issues, as we can see in his novels *Notre Dame de Paris* (1831; the basis of various movies known as *The Hunchback of Notre Dame*) and *Les Misérables*. **Honoré de Balzac** (1799–1850) and **Gustave Flaubert** (1821–80) are both considered among the greatest masters of literary realism, characterized by the effort to show life in all its facets, both pleasant and unpleasant. Balzac wrote a long series of novels and stories loosely collected under the title *La comédie humaine* ("The Human Comedy"), a title chosen to contrast pointedly with Dante's *Divine Comedy* of the 14th century, which had dealt with such unworldly realms as hell, purgatory, and paradise. Flaubert's *Madame Bovary* created a scandal in its time for its portrait of the psychological and financial decline of a middle-class woman trapped in a loveless marriage.

In Germany, the career of **Johann Wolfgang Goethe** (1749–1832) spanned more than 60 years. Many composers were inspired to set his verses to song. The novelist **Ernst Theodor Amadeus Hoffmann** (1776–1822) was so enamored of Mozart's music that he changed one of his middle names from "Wilhelm" to "Amadeus." He was also one of the most influential music critics in the history of the art.

Jean Paul (1763–1825, born Jean Paul Richter), **Heinrich von Kleist** (1777–1811), **Gottfried Keller** (1819–90), and **Theodor Fontane** (1819–98) are among the other leading German novelists of the 19th century. The poetry of **Joseph von Eichendorff** (1788–1857), **Heinrich Heine** (1797–1856), and **Eduard Mörike** (1804–75) was frequently set to music by such 19th-century composers as Franz Schubert, Robert Schumann, and Hugo Wolf.

Notable American poets of the 19th century include **Walt Whitman** (1819–92), **Emily Dickinson** (1830–86), and **Edgar Allan Poe** (1809–49), the last of whom also won renown as a novelist. Poe and **James Fenimore Cooper** (1789–1851) were both influenced by European Romanticism. Later American novelists of the century include **Herman Melville** (1819–91), **Mark Twain** (1835–1910), and **Henry James** (1843–1916).

Dresden against the regime that employed him as a conductor at the Dresden Opera; a warrant was issued for his arrest, but he fled to Switzerland.

Although these revolutions had been quelled by 1849, pressure continued for more representative government. By the end of the 19th century, France, Germany, and Italy all enjoyed parliamentary democracies of one form or another. Great Britain, which was spared the trauma of revolution in 1848, had passed a reform act in 1832 (The Great Reform Act) that lowered the qualifications for voters to own property, thereby expanding the number of eligible voters by about 50 percent. Subsequent laws widened eligibility still further.

In Germany and Italy, the Revolutions of 1848–1849 also served as a catalyst for national unification. For centuries, both regions had been divided into many independent or semi-independent states, each with its own ruler, laws, and currency. Through sustained military and diplomatic campaigns, the Prussian chancellor Otto von Bismarck (1815–1898) engineered the political unification of most German states into a single entity, a task that was completed with the defeat of France in the Franco-Prussian War of 1870–1871 and the installation of Wilhelm I as emperor of a united Germany. In Italy, unification followed the defeat of the Austrian forces that had occupied much of the northern Italian peninsula for many decades. Victor Emmanuel was crowned king of Italy in 1860. The occupation of Rome by Italian troops in 1870 marked the end of the Papacy as a territorial power.

The early 19th century marked a decline in Europe's imperial expansion into other areas of the globe. Indeed, in the late 18th and early 19th centuries, Britain and Spain lost many of their American colonies to independence movements. In the late 19th century, however, European nations, including Belgium, Portugal, Spain, and Italy as well as Great Britain, France, and Germany, began again to stake claims throughout the world. This *new imperialism*, as it has been called, represented the high tide of European influence in the world. By the early 20th century, Great Britain alone controlled about one-fifth of the world's land area and 25 percent of the world's population. The United States, which had spread rapidly across the entire North American continent in the early 19th century, joined the ranks of the colonial powers with the acquisition of Alaska from Russia in 1867 and the acquisition of the Philippines, Puerto Rico, and other territories in the Pacific and Caribbean following the Spanish-American War of 1898.

In the late 19th century, economic hardship, religious persecution, and population growth combined to impel millions of Europeans, especially from southern and eastern Europe, to leave their homes and seek opportunity in other parts of the world. Most of the migrants went to the United States and other countries in the Western Hemisphere. The United States alone absorbed an influx of more than 20 million people between 1870 and 1910, drawn by the nation's open spaces and rapidly growing factories. In 1900, the second largest city in the nation, Chicago, boasted a population of almost 1.7 million, of whom 1.3 million were either immigrants or the children of immigrants. Within the United States people were likewise on the move, drawn from the countryside to opportunities in the cities.

THE MUSICAL WORLD OF THE 19TH CENTURY

The wide-ranging political, social, and economic changes that occurred during the 19th century had correspondingly wide-ranging consequences for the arts. From a strictly commercial point of view, music achieved a scale never before imagined, thanks

Europe in 1871, after Italian and German Unifications.

to advances in music printing, the manufacture of instruments, the growth of public concerts, music journalism, music education, transportation, and the enormous growth of the population in general.

Political change had a direct effect on the way composers made a living. The established order of Europe did not collapse with the French Revolution of 1789, but it did begin to totter. Over the next several decades, the power of the nobility gradually gave way to the power of the wealthy—some of whom were members of the old guard, but many of whom had created their own wealth through commerce and industry. By the middle of the 19th century, private orchestras had all but disappeared because aristocratic patrons, like those in whose palaces Haydn and Beethoven had given the premieres of various symphonies, could no longer maintain them. Concerts became

Farmer Giles & his Wife shewing off their daughter Betty to their Neighbours, on her return from School

The perils of domestic music making. Over the course of the 19th century, it became a social necessity for any household with aspirations to a higher social standing to own a piano. Daughters were routinely taught to play, and often sing, at a modest level of accomplishment. This cartoon, "drawn by an Amateur" in 1809, caricatures the feelings at this gathering, as exhibited by the family group, the audience with its different degrees of attentiveness (no doubt waiting for the liquid refreshment about to be served), and the bedraggled, perhaps bored dog.

Source: James Gillray, British (1757–1815), "Farmer Giles and his Wife showing off their daughter Betty to their neighbors on her return from School," 31.8 × 47.8 cm. Fine Arts Museums of San Francisco, Achenbach Foundaton for Graphic Arts, 1963.30.32811

increasingly public as more and more cities established civic orchestras. The salons of aristocrats and wealthy professionals and merchants remained an important venue for chamber music and song in the upper levels of society, but the middle-class family and home took on new importance in the early 19th century as a source of private music making. The ability to read and perform music, in the minds of many, was a sign of a well-rounded education. Middle-class families took pains to see that their children, especially their daughters, could play the piano and sing.

As aristocratic patronage declined, the sale of printed music became an increasingly important source of income for composers. Fortunately, technological advances in paper manufacturing and lithography substantially lowered the cost of music printing, and advances in communication and transportation further expanded the market for published music. Still, few composers could rely exclusively on music sales; most had to find additional work to make ends meet. Franz Schubert taught school, Hector Berlioz and Robert Schumann worked as music critics, and Frederic Chopin taught piano. Almost all composers performed or conducted as well. Gustav Mahler, for example, conducted nine months out of the year and was able to focus on his own compositions only during summer holidays. Among the handful of artists able to devote themselves more or less exclusively to their own compositions were Gioacchino Rossini (whose success was so great that he was able to retire at the age of 37), and Giuseppe Verdi and Johannes Brahms, both of whom also conducted, but not out of financial necessity.

No matter how they earned their living, composers benefited from the immense growth in the production and consumption of music across all levels of society. Public education became increasingly widespread over the course of the century, with a corresponding increase in musical literacy as well as general literacy. This helped make the 19th century the era of the amateur musical society. Even small cities that lacked a civic orchestra usually had a variety of amateur musical organizations. Brass bands were a source of considerable pride for many small villages, particularly in England and Wales. Choral societies became popular in Great Britain and Germany, spawning a vast repertory of choral music—most of it a cappella—by composers as diverse as Felix Mendelssohn, Schumann, Franz Liszt, and Brahms. Although this music is seldom performed today, it sold well in its time. Amateurs also gathered at music festivals to perform large-scale works, particularly symphonies and oratorios. These festivals were participatory events, not passive spectacles, and their success was measured not so much in terms of musical quality (which by all accounts varied greatly), but by the number and diversity of the participants, who often traveled a considerable distance to attend.

In addition to the intrinsic joy of performing, many amateur performers were motivated by the belief that music making is a wholesome and uplifting pursuit that strengthens social bonds. Indeed, many factory owners encouraged workers to form musical groups for precisely this purpose, as the following passage suggests:

> The Messrs. William, George and Joseph Strutt of Derby, men of great wealth and acquirements, employ nearly the whole population of Belper. . . . To give a higher taste to the work people at Belper, Mr. John Strutt (the son of George) has formed a musical society by selecting forty persons, or more, from his mills and workshops, making a band of instrumental performers and a choir of singers. These persons are regularly trained by masters and taught to play and sing in the best manner. Whatever time is consumed in their studies is reckoned into their working hours. On the night of a general muster, you may see five or six of the forgemen, in their leather aprons, blasting their terrific notes upon ophicleides [forerunners of the tuba] and trombones.[1]

The contrast with the workplace today is striking. Employers still sometimes use music to enhance productivity, but they pipe it in. For employees, it is something they listen to while at work, not a diversion from work.

National governments recognized the role of music in the politics of culture and began to assume responsibility for musical education. The establishment of the state-funded Paris Conservatory in the 1790s spawned dozens of imitators across the Continent over the next 50 years. Virtually every government recognized that it needed a body of civic-minded musicians, composers, and music educators, and that it should establish the institutions to educate such individuals. The most important conservatories of the time were established in Bologna (1804), Milan (1808), Naples (1808),

---

1. Henry Raynor, *Music and Society Since 1815* (New York: Schoken Books, 1976), p. 155; citing in turn William Gardiner, *Music and Friends* (London, 1838), vol. 2, pp. 511–13.

PRIMARY EVIDENCE — Music and the State

For most European governments, the identification and fostering of musical talent was a matter of national importance not to be left to the whims of economic circumstance. The Czech composer Antonín Dvořák (1841–1904) was one of many composers and musicians who benefited from this outlook. The government in his native Bohemia supported several outstanding conservatories, often providing promising students—Dvořák was one of them—with full scholarships. When Dvořák visited the United States in the 1890s, he was struck by the lack of state support for music education. In this extract from an article he wrote for *Harper's New Monthly Magazine* in 1895, he criticizes this lack of support as shortsighted, comparing it unfavorably to the system that nurtured him.

Not long ago a young man came to me and showed me his compositions. His talent seemed so promising that I at once offered him a scholarship in our school [the private National Conservatory of Music, in New York, where Dvořák was teaching at the time]; but he sorrowfully confessed that he could not afford to become my pupil, because he had to earn his living by keeping books in Brooklyn. Even if he came on but two afternoons in the week, or on Saturday afternoon only, he said, he would lose his employment, on which he and others had to depend. I urged him to arrange the matter with his employer, but he only received the answer: "If you want to play, you can't keep books. You will have to drop one or the other." He dropped his music.

In any other country the state would have made some provision for such a deserving scholar, so that he could have pursued his natural calling without having to starve. With us in Bohemia the Diet each year votes a special sum of money for just such purposes, and the imperial government in Vienna on occasion furnishes other funds for talented artists. Had it not been for such support I should not have been able to pursue my studies when I was a young man. Owing to the fact that, upon the kind recommendation of such men as Brahms, Hanslick, and Herbeck, the Minister of Public Education in Vienna on five successive years sent me sums ranging from four to six hundred florins, I was able to pursue my work and to get my compositions published, so that at the end of that time I was able to stand on my own feet. This has filled me with lasting gratitude towards my country.

Such an attitude of the state towards deserving artists is not only a kind but a wise one. For it cannot be emphasized too strongly that art, as such, does not "pay," to use an American expression—at least, not in the beginning—and that the art that has to pay its own way is apt to become vitiated and cheap.

Source: Antonín Dvořák, "Music in America," *Harper's New Monthly Magazine* 90 (1895): 429–34.

Prague (1811), London (1822), Brussels (1832), Berlin (1850), and St. Petersburg (1862). The conservatories of Vienna (1817) and Leipzig (1843) were private, as were all the earliest such institutions in the United States. Those that endured include the Peabody Conservatory of Music (Baltimore, 1857), the Oberlin Conservatory (Oberlin, Ohio, 1865), the New England Conservatory of Music (Boston, 1867), the Chicago Musical College (1867), and the Cincinnati Conservatory (1867). Colleges and universities first established schools and departments of music in the last three decades of the century. Not until 1892 did a state-supported institution of higher learning—the University of Michigan, in Ann Arbor—establish its own school of music. Unlike most European nations, the United States never embraced the idea of a national conservatory. This was due in part to the nation's decentralized system of higher education, in part to the perception that music is less important to national development than such disciplines as engineering, medicine, and the law (see Primary Evidence: Music and the State).

The Age of the Tone Poet

The greatest changes in music during the early decades of the 19th century were not primarily in matters of style but rather perception. Composers and audiences alike began to conceive of music and hear it—instrumental music in particular—in a radically new manner. Although respect had been growing for instrumental music before 1800, critics of the Classical era considered it inferior to vocal music (see Chapter 12). In their view, instrumental music was a language of the heart, with its own rules of syntax and rhetoric. It had the power to move the passions, but without a poetic or dramatic text, it was incapable of conveying concepts or reason. This assessment, however, began to change in the mid-1790s with a new generation of poets and critics, including Friedrich Schlegel (1772–1829), Ludwig Tieck (1773–1853), and E. T. A. Hoffmann (1776–1822). The abstract nature of music, they maintained, was an asset, not a liability. Instrumental music, *because* it was free from the confining strictures of language, was capable of conveying ideas and emotions too profound for mere words.

Composers, responding to this changing perception, began to see themselves as well in an entirely new way. Beethoven reflected this trend when he dubbed himself a "tone poet," an artist who creates poetry with notes rather than words. The public, in turn, began to see great composers as divinely inspired high priests of art who could provide glimpses into a loftier, more spiritual world. Eventually, the idolization of instrumental music triggered a backlash among composers and critics who favored vocal music. Echoing claims that date back to the early Baroque, they argued that opera in particular occupied a higher aesthetic plane than instrumental music alone because it represented a synthesis of all the arts.

ROMANTICISM AND THE NEW PRESTIGE OF INSTRUMENTAL MUSIC

The term *romantic* derives from the name of a literary genre—the romance—that first emerged in the medieval era. A romance tells a long story in verse or prose. (As such, the genre is a forerunner to the novel, and indeed the word for "novel" in both German and French is *roman*.) Unlike other literary forms, such as epic or lyric poetry, the romance is largely free of structural or narrative conventions. It was because of this association with relatively freer narrative expression that the genre gave its name to an artistic movement—Romanticism—that values imagination and personal expression.

With its stress on imagination, Romanticism was closely associated with the philosophical outlook known as **Idealism,** a system of thought based on the premise that objects in the physical world are a reflection of ideas in the mind. Idealists differ about the source of those ideas, whether they are inherent to the mind itself or derive from a higher, more abstract—ideal—world. In either case, Idealism allows for a realm that lies beyond reason and words (in contrast to the rationalism of the Enlightenment) and thus grants more room to the spiritual and even mystical. And for many 19th-century Idealist philosophers and critics, instrumental music—because it is intrinsically abstract—was the art form that most approximates the disembodied realm of ideas. Other art forms of the early 19th century, such as painting and poetry, consistently represent some identifiable object, setting, or event. Music does not, moving instead beyond the realm of the physical to the realm of the spiritual and infinite.

The novelist and playwright Ludwig Tieck was one of the first to give voice to this new outlook, arguing as early as 1799 that Johann Friedrich Reichardt's overture to *Macbeth* was superior to Shakespeare's original play (see Primary Evidence: The Perceived Superiority of Instrumental Music).

By 1810, E. T. A. Hoffmann proclaimed instrumental music to be "the most romantic of all the arts—one might almost say, the only genuinely romantic one—for its sole subject is the infinite." Hoffmann included Haydn and Mozart among the "Romantic composers" not on the basis of their style but because their music provided a glimpse into the realm of "the spirit world" (see Primary Evidence: E. T. A. Hoffmann's Review of Beethoven's Fifth Symphony in Chapter 15). Eight years later, the German philosopher Arthur Schopenhauer (1788–1860) was arguing that "if music is too closely united to the words, it is striving to speak a language which is not its own." For it is not in the nature of music to "express this or that particular and definite joy, this or that sorrow, or pain, or horror, or delight, or merriment, or peace of mind," but rather "joy, sorrow, pain, horror, delight, merriment, peace of mind *themselves*, to a certain extent in the abstract, their essential nature, without accessories, and therefore without their motives."[1] Music, in other words, should not descend to the level of words.

THE COMPOSER AS HIGH PRIEST

With art in general and music in particular now perceived as a window on the realm of the infinite and spiritual, the social status of composers rose enormously. In the Classical era, the composer had been viewed essentially as an artisan providing goods made to order. By the 1830s, the composer had taken on the aura of a divinely inspired creator, a demigod. There was much talk in the early 19th century about "Art-Religion."

---

1. Arthur Schopenhauer, *The World as Will and Idea*, vol. 1, trans. R. B. Haldane and J. Kemp (London: Kegan Paul, Trench, Trubner & Co., 1896), I, 338.

PRIMARY EVIDENCE   The Perceived Superiority of Instrumental Music

In a remarkable essay entitled "Symphonies," Ludwig Tieck (1773–1853) argued that Johann Friedrich Reichardt's overture to a German-language stage production of Shakespeare's *Macbeth* was superior to the drama itself. (*Symphony* and *overture* were still interchangeable terms in the late 18th century.) Tieck chose the Reichardt work because it was well known in its time, and it allowed him to draw a sharp contrast between the power of instrumental music (the overture) and the poetry of the subsequent play, which struck him as relatively pedestrian in comparison.

In instrumental music . . . the art is independent and free, it writes its own laws only for itself, it fantasizes freely and without purpose and nevertheless fulfills and attains the highest. It follows entirely its own dark drives and expresses the deepest, the most [unforeseen] miraculous with its [seeming] trivialities. The full choruses, polyphonic pieces that are elaborated with great art, are the triumph of vocal music. The highest victory, the most beautiful prize of instruments are the symphonies.

These symphonies can present a colorful, varied, complicated and so beautifully developed drama such as the poet can never produce, for they reveal in an enigmatic language that which is most enigmatic. They do not depend on any laws of probability, they do not need to be affiliated with any story or any character . . . they remain in their purely poetic world. They thereby avoid all means for transporting us, for delighting us. From beginning to end, the thing itself is their object. The goal itself is present at every moment, beginning and ending the artwork. . . .

I remember in particular one such pleasure given to me by music recently on a trip. I went to the theater; *Macbeth* was to be given. A famous musician [Johann Friedrich Reichardt] had created a particular symphony [i.e., overture] for this wonderful tragedy. It delighted and intoxicated me so much, that I still cannot forget the great impressions it made on my spirit. I cannot describe how wonderfully allegorical this great composition struck me, and yet full of highly individualized images, just as the true, highest allegory similarly loses cold universality through itself, and which we find only with poets who have not yet grown to a stature commensurate with their art. I saw in the music the dark, foggy moor, in whose twilight muddled circles of witches passed in and out of one another, with the ever-thickening clouds all the while sinking ever closer and more poisonously to the earth. Horrible voices cry and moan through the desolation, and like ghosts, there is a trembling throughout all this chaos; a laughing, gruesome *Schadenfreude* appears in the distance. The forms take on more definite outlines, horrifying shapes stride meaningfully across the heath, the clouds break. Now the eye sees a revolting fiend that lies in its black cave, bound with heavy chains. He strives with all his power, with all his strength, to rid himself of these chains, but he is still restrained. Around him begins the magic dance of all the ghosts, all the ghouls. With weeping melancholy, the eye trembles in the distance, hoping that the chains will restrain the terrible one, that they will not break. But the commotion grows louder and more horrible, and with a terrifying scream, with the innermost rage the monster breaks loose and jumps with a wild leap into the ghouls. There is a wailing and exultation intermixed. The victory is decided, hell triumphs. The chaos now becomes even more chaotic and becomes truly horrible. Everything flees in terror and returns. The triumphant song of the damned ends the [overture].

After this great phenomenon, many scenes of the drama struck me as tired and empty, for the most terrifying and revolting had already been announced in a grander and more poetic fashion. All I did was to keep thinking back to the music. The drama oppressed my spirit and disturbed my memories, for with the close of this symphony everything was completely finished for me. I know of no master and no work of music that would have aroused this in me, in that I could have perceived the restless, ever more enraged drive of all the soul's power, this terrible, dizzying shift of all musical pulses. The drama should have closed with this great artwork, and in one's fantasies, one could not conceive of or wish for anything higher. For this symphony was the more poetic incarnation of the drama, the most audacious presentation of a lost, lamentable human life that was stormed and conquered by all that is monstrous.

Source: Ludwig Tieck, "Symphonien" (1799), from Wilhelm Heinrich Wackenroder and Ludwig Tieck, *Phantasien über die Kunst für Freunde der Kunst*, in Wilhelm Heinrich Wackenroder, *Sämtliche Werke und Briefe: Historisch-kritische Ausgabe*, ed. Silvio Vietta and Richard Littlejohns, 2 vols. (Heidelberg: Carl Winter Universitätsverlag, 1991), I, 245–54. Transl. MEB

This referred not so much to the worship of art as to the revelation of the divine through the medium of art. Composers emerged as the high priests of this new religion, for they dealt with the most abstract (and thus the most revealing) of all the arts.

The composer, according to Schopenhauer, was like a clairvoyant or sleepwalker, someone who in a half-conscious, half-dreaming state "reveals the innermost nature of the world in a language his reasoning faculty does not understand." Critics and artists of the 18th century, as we saw in Chapter 11, drew a distinction between natural, divinely inspired genius and the teachable techniques—the art—through which that genius found expression. In the 19th century, the distinction between genius and technique became a chasm that only artistic geniuses could bridge—and even then they were not expected to understand the process. If music could provide a glimpse of the infinite, then the distance between inspiration and technique could be neither described nor measured.

This image of the composer as sleepwalker abounds in accounts of the Polish composer Frederic Chopin's performances of his own music. An English critic writing in 1848 described how "the performer seems to abandon himself to the impulses of his fancy and feeling, to indulge in a reverie and to pour out unconsciously, as it were, the thoughts and emotions that pass through his mind."[2] Robert Schumann described the "unforgettable picture" of Chopin "sitting at the piano like a dreamy clairvoyant," playing in such a way that "the dreams he had created seemed to appear before us."[3] Such accounts were not often written before the 19th century.

The listening public sought insight into the working methods of composers as never before. Beethoven's sketches commanded high prices in the marketplace. Autograph scores of his works sold well, too, but the sketches held a special fascination for critics and collectors because they offered a glimpse into the "half-conscious, half-dreaming" essence of the creative process. The German scholar Gustav Nottebohm (1817–1882), who studied composition with both Mendelssohn and Schumann in his youth, took it upon himself to gather and examine as many of Beethoven's sketches as he could lay his hands on, and his findings remain useful to scholars even today. The sketches show—sometimes in considerable detail—the sequence of steps by which Beethoven developed seemingly insignificant ideas into powerful, original works of art. Yet in a strange way, the publication of Beethoven's sketchbooks actually made the composer's creative process even more mysterious, for although the record of that process—the sketches—had been preserved, the process of composition itself remained unfathomable.

The public also wanted to know more about the composers themselves, and their biographies began to appear in great numbers. Book-length accounts of any composer's life were rare before 1800, but 19th-century writers produced a long series of biographies about such figures as J. S. Bach (by Johann Nikolaus Forkel in 1802, then by Philipp Spitta in 1873–1880), Handel (Friedrich Chrysander, 1858–1867), Mozart (Otto Jahn, 1856–1859), and Beethoven (Alexander Wheelock Thayer, 1866–1879).

Composers, too, were more likely to write about themselves and their art. Berlioz, Schumann, Liszt, and Wagner all wrote prose as well as music. In earlier eras, audiences had been too small and listeners on the whole not sufficiently curious enough to make such publications profitable. It had been assumed, moreover, that a composer was obligated to make his music sufficiently intelligible and accessible for listeners to

---

2. George Hogarth, *Daily News*, 19 July 1848, quoted in Jean-Jacques Eigeldinger, *Chopin, Pianist and Teacher as Seen by His Pupils*, trans. Krysia Osostowicz and Naomi Shohet, ed. Roy Howat (Cambridge: Cambridge University Press, 1987), p. 294.

3. Robert Schumann, *Gesammelte Schriften über Musik und Musiker*, 4th ed., 2 vols., ed. F. Gustav Jansen (Leipzig: Breitkopf & Härtel, 1891), II, 23. Transl. MEB

understand without the need of outside help. In the 19th century, however, the idea began to take hold that the composer, as a demigod or high priest, did not always "speak" in an immediately comprehensible manner—hence the need for explanatory texts. Beethoven's symphonies were among the first works to elicit this kind of attention. E. T. A. Hoffmann's lengthy review of the Fifth Symphony in 1810 is an early testament to the musical public's desire to understand a work of music at a deeper level (see Primary Evidence: E. T. A. Hoffmann's Review of Beethoven's Fifth Symphony in Chapter 15). A decade later, the Berlin music critic Adolf Bernhard Marx (1795–1866) would pen a series of essays on all of Beethoven's symphonies. Hector Berlioz's own essays on these works were eventually published in book form and sold widely. Later in the century, Wagner's music dramas also demanded, and received, book-length guides for the listening public.

Composers were also far more likely than ever before to incorporate autobiographical elements into their music. Robert Schumann encoded the names of at least two of the women in his life into his piano cycle *Carnaval* (1835; Anthology II/132, discussed in Chapter 16). Berlioz called his first symphony "Episode in the Life of an Artist." (The title by which it is known today—*Symphonie fantastique*—was for many years only its subtitle.) The very notion of writing a work of music *about* an artist is quintessentially Romantic, and although Berlioz never named the artist of the title, there can be no doubt it was he. He also wrote an elaborate prose program for the work that is transparently autobiographical (see Primary Evidence: The Program of Berlioz's *Symphonie fantastique* in Chapter 15).

Given the new perception of the composer as a divinely inspired creator, it is scarcely surprising that performers and listeners would begin to place more weight on the accuracy and authority of published scores. Performers began to question whether the edition from which they were performing actually represented the intentions of the composer. Publishers, taking note of this demand, represented their editions as the most reliable available—sometimes truthfully, sometimes not. Authoritative editions of composers' collected works began to appear for the first time in the 19th century, including the complete works of Beethoven, Schubert, Schumann, and Wagner.

The most revered composers became cultural heroes, bringing honor to their native cities, which, in turn, felt obligated to erect statues in their honor. Salzburg erected its statue of Mozart in 1842, Leipzig completed its monument to J. S. Bach in 1843, and Bonn unveiled its statue of Beethoven in 1845. The funerals of Haydn (1809) and Beethoven (1827) in Vienna were state occasions. Later in the century, Wagner became a cult figure whose influence extended far beyond music. His most devoted followers adopted not only his radical political views but even his vegetarian dietary practices.

ORIGINALITY AND HISTORICAL SELF-CONSCIOUSNESS

Artists and critics of the 19th century were obsessed with the idea of originality. They firmly believed that every work of art must be new and different. Whereas earlier composers had often recycled themes or even entire movements into new works (see Conceptions of the Compositional Process in Chapter 9), composers of the 19th century were far less inclined to engage in this practice. Critics began to condemn any work that bore too strong a resemblance to any other work, especially one by a different composer. To copy Haydn, Mozart, or even Beethoven was considered unacceptable for any composer who aspired to greatness. Earlier composers, in contrast, would have been pleased to have their style likened to that of an acknowledged master. Now composers sought to find their own distinctive voice and express it in music unlike any heard before.

Not surprisingly, composers who wrote about their own work tended to portray themselves as revolutionaries, as radicals who rejected the music of the past. Many critics took up this same approach, arguing that established conventions of form, genre, and harmony were restrictive in and of themselves. As we have seen in Chapter 11, earlier composers routinely integrated originality and convention. The Romantics nevertheless chose to interpret and portray their innovations as a rejection of convention, as an act of artistic liberation. Virtually every Romantic artist saw himself or herself blazing a unique path to truth.

In an odd way, however, the cult of originality made composers more aware of the musical past than their predecessors had been. One could not be original, after all, in a vacuum. Composers studied earlier music carefully with an eye toward doing something different. The music of the past also began to be heard in the concert hall and opera house with unprecedented frequency. Before the 19th century, it would have been unusual to hear the music of a composer from a previous generation. There were exceptions, of course. Lully's operas were still favorites in Paris a hundred years after his death and Handel's oratorios continued to be performed regularly in England throughout the Classical era and beyond. In the early 19th century, however, works by earlier composers became staples in the active repertoire, beginning with the later symphonies and quartets of Haydn and Mozart and the operas of Gluck and Mozart. By the end of the century, it would have been difficult to find a concert without at least one work from an

The virtuoso as idol. Throughout the 19th century, the great musical virtuosos and composers were perceived as endowed with divine, superhuman powers. This satirical drawing of the great Polish composer and pianist Ignace Jan Paderewski (1860–1941) from ca. 1895 also reminds us that the public's fascination with long-haired musicians began long before The Beatles. One newspaper of the time reported that "three New York ladies have embroidered musical phrases from [Paderewski's] Minuet on their stockings." In his 1892–1893 concert tour of the United States, Paderewski traveled in his own private railcar along with his secretary, valet, manager, chef, two porters, his Steinway piano, and his piano tuner. The grotesquely exaggerated hand stretch, covering the entire keyboard, betrays the mixture of awe and derision with which the public viewed its virtuosos: awe at their seemingly superhuman powers, derision at their "trained seal" status.

Source: Caricature of Ignace jan Paderewski from John Mansfield Thomsons "Musical Delights: A Cavalcade of Cartoon and Caricature" (London: Thames and Hudson, 1985) p. 35

earlier era. With newer and older works now on the same program, younger composers were inevitably compared not only to their contemporaries, but to masters of earlier generations as well. This could be discouraging. When the young Robert Schumann finally managed to get two movements of a never-to-be-finished symphony performed in the early 1830s, his music had to share the program with Beethoven's Seventh Symphony, a work written some twenty years before. Comparisons with the past made the drive for originality all the more compelling and all the more challenging.

By the middle of the 19th century, consciousness of the past took on a new form, that of **historicism,** in which composers openly embraced the forms and styles of earlier generations while presenting them in original ways. Anton Bruckner (1824–1896), for example, whose symphonies used some of the most advanced chromatic harmonies of his time, wrote a number of sacred choral works and Masses in an intentionally anachronistic idiom, one that the unsuspecting ear might mistake briefly for that of Palestrina (see Chapter 17, Anthology). Brahms, appropriating a theme from a cantata by J. S. Bach, openly incorporated the archaic form of the passacaglia into the finale of his Fourth Symphony (see Chapter 18).

Interest in early music led musicians and scholars to seek out forgotten repertories, leading to the recovery of quantities of music from the medieval era, the Renaissance, and the Baroque period. In 1828, Felix Mendelssohn became the first musician to conduct J. S. Bach's *Saint Matthew Passion* since Bach's death. Mendelssohn's rediscovery inspired the editing and publication of other works by Bach as well. By the end of the century, almost all of Bach's music had been carefully edited and published in a sumptuous edition. Handel, Schütz, and earlier composers such as Lassus and Palestrina enjoyed the same process of rediscovery in the 19th century.

THE NEW DICHOTOMY BETWEEN ABSOLUTE AND PROGRAM MUSIC

The growing prestige of instrumental music as an abstract art created a critical backlash around the middle of the 19th century. The composers and critics involved in this reaction maintained that music could achieve its highest potential only through a synthesis with other arts, including the arts of the word. Richard Wagner led the attack on what he derisively termed **absolute music,** meaning music that was cut off from the larger world of words and ideas. (The prefix *ab* in *absolute* derives from the Latin word for "separate" or "disconnected.") Wagner's criticism of absolute music echoed the view of 18th-century critics toward instrumental music: he valued its ability to move the passions but considered it too abstract to carry true meaning. Only with the "fertilizing seed" of the word, Wagner argued, could music realize its full potential. This could take the form of a program or programmatic text—like that which Berlioz wrote for his *Symphonie fantastique*—or better still, a text to be sung. Even Beethoven, Wagner argued, had recognized the limitations of purely instrumental music when he introduced voices into the finale of his Ninth Symphony (see Primary Evidence: Wagner on the End of the Symphony in Chapter 15). Franz Liszt similarly argued that, with the benefit of a written program outlining the "ideas that he [the composer] sought to embody in his work," the work would be "elevated to definite impressions" and not limited to the "vague impressions" provoked by absolute music (see Primary Evidence: Liszt on the Superiority of Program Music).

The term *absolute* was soon embraced as a label for purely instrumental music even by its proponents, but with a different, positive, interpretation. To them, pure instrumental music was absolute in its ability to transcend earthly life, rising above mundane,

PRIMARY EVIDENCE   Liszt on the Superiority of Program Music

Franz Liszt, along with Richard Wagner, was a leader in the battle to legitimize program music. In an essay he wrote in 1855 on Berlioz's symphony *Harold en Italie*, he identifies the key distinction between the "purely musical composer" (that is, one dedicated to the idea of absolute music) and the more engaged composer who wrestles with ideas extending beyond music.

―――――――――•―――――――――

The purely musical composer, who places value and emphasis only on the formal shaping of his material, does not have the capacity to derive new formulations from this [musical] material or to breathe new powers into it. For there is no spiritual necessity that compels him to discover new means, he is not driven and compelled by any glowing passion that wills itself toward the light! It is for this reason that those who are called upon to enrich form [i.e., composers of program music] are those who would extend it, make it adaptable, and use it as merely one medium of expression shaped according to the demands of those ideas which are to be expressed. The formalists [i.e., "purely musical" composers], by contrast, are capable of nothing better or cleverer than to use, propagate, rearrange, and occasionally rework that which has already been achieved by these others.

The purpose of the program is merely to indicate, in a preliminary sort of way, those spiritual states of mind that drove the composer to the creation of his work, the ideas that he sought to embody in his work. It is childishly pointless and usually impossible to draft programs after the fact in an attempt to clarify the emotional content of an instrumental poem, for to do so would necessarily destroy the magic and desecrate the feelings and tear apart the finest spun webs of the soul, precisely because such works assumed their shape according to their form and not through words, images, or ideas. At the same time, the master is master of his own work, which he may have created under the influence of distinct impression, which he then later wishes to bring into the complete and full consciousness of his listeners.

Altogether then, the pure symphonist takes his listeners into ideal regions and leaves it to each individual's fantasy just how to conceive of these regions and adorn them. In such instances it is very dangerous for us to impose on our neighbor the same scene and sequence of ideas into which our own imagination feels itself transported. Better to let each listener take silent joy in the revelations and visions for which there are no names and no designations. But the poeticizing symphonist, who takes it upon himself to convey clearly an image distinctly present in his own mind, a succession of spiritual states that appear unambiguously and distinctly within his consciousness—why should he not strive to be fully understood by the aid of a program? . . .

In so-called Classical music, the recurrence and thematic development of themes are determined by formal rules that are considered inviolable, even though its composers possessed no other prescription for these processes than their own fantasies. These composers arranged the formal layout of their works in a manner that some would now proclaim as law. In program music, by contrast, the recurrence, variation, and modification of motifs are determined by their relationship to a poetic idea. Here one theme does not beget another according to any formal laws; the motives are not a consequence of stereotypical similarities or contrasts of timbre; coloration in itself does not determine the grouping of ideas. Although certainly not ignored, all exclusively musical considerations are subordinated to the treatment of the subject at hand. Accordingly, the plot and subject of this symphonic genre demand an engagement that goes beyond the technical treatment of the musical material. The vague impressions of the soul are elevated to definite impressions through a defined plan, which is taken in by the ear in much the same manner in which a cycle of paintings is taken in by the eye. The artists who favor this kind of art work enjoy the advantage of being able to connect with a poetic process all those affects which an orchestra can express with such great power.

Source: Franz Liszt, *Gesammelte Schriften*, vol. 4, ed. L. Ramann (Leipzig, 1882), 49–50, 69. Transl. MEB

everyday existence. This usage reflected Idealist philosophy, in which *absolute* had been used as a noun to convey the idea of the infinite. The most influential advocate of this view of absolute music in the middle of the 19th century was the Viennese critic Eduard Hanslick (1825–1904). Hanslick argued that the content of music does not and cannot extend beyond the notes themselves but consists instead of "forms moving through sound." Music's independence from earthly life is the quality that makes it most moving (see Primary Evidence: Hanslick on the Superiority of Absolute Music).

PRIMARY EVIDENCE Hanslick on the Superiority of Absolute Music

Eduard Hanslick's *On the Beautiful in Music*, first published in 1854, was the manifesto of the musical conservatives who believed in the sanctity of absolute music. Hanslick (1825–1904) argued that music could not in its own right express emotions. By this he did not mean that music is incapable of moving the listener, but rather that beauty in music flows from its ability to project "forms animated through sound."

The nature of beauty in a musical composition is specifically musical. By this we understand a beauty that is independent and in no need of any external content. It is a beauty that lies entirely in the notes and in their artistic interweaving. The meaningful connections of inherently pleasing sounds, their concords and discords, their departure and arrival, their eruption and subsiding—this is what comes before our spiritual perception in free forms and pleases us as beautiful.

If we now ask what is to be expressed with this musical material, the answer is: Musical Ideas. A complete musical idea is already self-sufficient beauty; it is an end in itself and in no way merely a means or the material for the presentation of emotions or thoughts.

The sole and exclusive content and object of music are forms animated through sound.

The manner in which music can bring forth beautiful forms without any particular affective content can be illustrated in a general way by a branch of ornamentation in the visual arts: the arabesque. We take in sweeping lines; at times they dip gently, at times they strive boldly upward; they discover and leave one another; they correspond in their curves large and small, seemingly incommensurable yet always well proportioned. Everywhere there is a welcoming counterpart or pendant, a gathering of small details and yet a whole. Let us contemplate this arabesque not as if it were something dead and static, but rather as something constantly in the process of creating itself before our eyes. How the broad and fine lines surprise the eye at every moment, pursuing one another, raising themselves from small curves to a magnificent height, then sinking again, then expanding, coming together and in ingenious alternation of rest and tension! The image as a whole thus becomes higher and more noble. If we think of this living arabesque as the active emanation of an artistic spirit who ceaselessly pours into the arteries of this motion his fantasy—does not this impression approximate quite closely that of music? . . .

It is extraordinarily difficult to describe this self-sufficiently beautiful in music, this specifically musical beauty. Because music has no prototype in nature and expresses no conceptual content, it can be discussed only either in dry technical terms or through poetic fictions. Its kingdom is truly "not of this world." All the fantastic descriptions, characterizations, and paraphrases of a musical work are figurative or wrong. What in accounts of every other art is merely descriptive is already metaphorical in music. Music demands to be perceived simply as music; it can be understood and enjoyed only in terms of its own self. . . .

The concept of "form" is realized in music in an entirely distinctive manner. The forms created out of tones are not empty but full; they are not merely the outlines of a vacuum, but rather a spirit that creates itself from within. In contrast to the arabesque, music is nevertheless in fact an image, albeit one whose object we cannot express through words and comprehend through concepts. In music we find sense and order, but these are musical; music is a language that we speak and understand yet are incapable of translating. That one speaks of "thoughts" in musical works represents a profound insight, and as in speech, a trained judgement easily distinguishes genuine thoughts from empty phrases. In just this way, we recognize the rationally self-contained quality of a group of notes in that we call this grouping a "sentence." We feel precisely where its sense is completed, just as in a logical sentence, even though the truths of the two propositions are entirely incommensurable.

Source: Eduard Hanslick, *Vom musikalisch-Schönen* (Leipzig: R. Weigel, 1854). Transl. MEB

Unlike Wagner and Liszt, who wrote forcefully in favor of program music, none of the composers of stature who favored absolute music took pen to paper in its defense. Johannes Brahms, for example, one of the most prominent practitioners of absolute music, preferred, according to one of his close associates, "to polemicize with works of music rather than with words."[4] The debate itself was charged with political overtones. Wagner and Liszt claimed for themselves the mantle of progressivism, calling their

---

4. Max Kalbeck, *Johannes Brahms: Leben und Werk*, 4 vols. (Vienna, Leipzig, and Berlin, 1904–1914), IV, 109.

work "The Music of the Future," whereas Hanslick (and by association, composers like Brahms) were associated with the forces of conservatism.

As often happens in ideological battles, however, the basic issues in this one became murky over time. By the last quarter of the 19th century, both sides had begun to realize they were debating a distinction without a difference. To the question, "Does instrumental music have any meaning beyond itself?" both sides would answer "yes," although they differed on just how that meaning could manifest itself. A new generation of composers, critics, and audiences saw merit in both points of view. Many composers were ambivalent on the matter or changed their opinions gradually. Even Wagner began to realize that absolute music was really not so empty after all. And Liszt, the great champion of program music, issued one of his most significant works, the Sonata in B minor, with a generic title, refusing to provide his followers with indications about any extramusical "meaning" in spite of repeated requests. Berlioz tried (unsuccessfully) to suppress the detailed program of his *Symphonie fantastique*; Brahms, who remained aloof from open debate on the issue, incorporated certain programmatic elements into at least some of his works, although he never revealed these connections to a wider public.

The question of instrumental music's meaning nevertheless remained a central topic of debate throughout the 19th century. The literary critic Walter Pater (1839–1894) summed up the matter neatly when he declared that music's ability to embody form without the burden of specific content was the envy of poetry and painting, and that "all art constantly aspires towards the condition of music."[5] Such an attitude acknowledges music's unique ability to transcend the representation of objects or ideas while also allowing for the incorporation of nonmusical elements.

NATIONALISM

While composers and critics debated the relative merits of program and absolute music for conveying meaning, some noted that music's meaning could at times be political. Writing in 1898, for example, the American critic James Huneker declared that "the most profound truths, the most blasphemous things, the most terrible ideas, may be incorporated within the walls of a symphony, and the police may be none the wiser. It is its freedom from the meddlesome hand of the censor that makes of music a playground for great brave souls."[6]

Nationalist sentiments and aspirations in particular lent themselves to musical expression, notably in the work of composers from eastern Europe. Chopin, for example, whose native Poland was under Russian control, made a nationalistic statement with the mazurkas and polonaises—both traditional Polish dance forms—that he wrote while living in Paris as part of the Polish exile community. This nationalistic element was not lost on listeners. Schumann pointed out as early as 1837 that if the czar of Russia "knew what a dangerous enemy threatened him in Chopin's works, in the simple tunes of his mazurkas, he would forbid this music. Chopin's works are cannons buried in flowers."[7]

Russia itself was in the process of becoming a major European power, and with its vast empire straddling Europe and Asia was seeking to define a national identity that would both relate it to and distinguish it from its neighbors to the west. In response, many Russian composers sought to create a distinctively Russian musical idiom based on the melodic and harmonic inflections of Russian folk music. In 1836, Mikhail Glinka

---

5. Walter Pater, "The School of Giorgione," in his *Studies in the History of the Renaissance* (1873).
6. James Gibbons Huneker, *Mezzotints in Music* (New York: G. Scribner's Sons, 1899), p. 122.
7. Robert Schumann, *Gesammelte Schriften über Musik und Musiker*, 5th ed., 2 vols. (Leipzig: Breitkopf & Härtel, 1913), I, 167 (1837).

(1804–1857) wrote an opera—*A Life for the Tsar* (also known as *Ivan Susanin*)—that was an early landmark in this endeavor. Based on a story from Russian history, it has a Russian libretto, and the score, although following the conventions of contemporary Italian opera, incorporates elements from Russian folk music. Glinka's precedent inspired many later Russian composers, most notably Alexander Borodin (1833–1887) and Modeste Mussorgsky (1839–1881). Borodin's orchestral work *In the Steppes of Central Asia*, for example, incorporates two folk songs and employs such features of Asian music as the pentatonic whole-tone scale. Mussorgsky's opera *Boris Godunov* (1869; revised 1872), like Glinka's *A Life for the Tsar*, draws its story from Russian history and includes folk songs and folk-song-like elements in the music.

Throughout Europe and the Americas, many 19th-century composers cultivated styles of writing that in some way drew on the folk idioms of their respective nationalities: Verdi in Italy, Wagner in Germany, Dvořák in Bohemia (now part of the Czech Republic), and Gottschalk in the United States (see Chapter 16). Nationalist music was particularly strong among those peoples who had not yet achieved—or were in the process of achieving—a political unity. Germany and Italy remained fragmented politically until the second half of the 19th century, and the Czechs did not establish an independent state until the 20th.

Norway, which had been ruled by Denmark since the 14th century, accepted a union with Sweden in 1814 that allowed it constitutional and military independence at the price of Swedish hegemony. During the rest of the 19th century, a nationalist cultural movement began to flourish there. Its two most famous exponents, the playwright Henrik Ibsen (1828–1906) and the composer Edvard Grieg (1843–1907), collaborated on the verse drama *Peer Gynt* (1867), which premiered in Christiania (now Oslo), Norway, in 1876.

CD9, Track 1
GRIEG
Halling
Score Anthology II/116

Grieg's incidental music has survived, and the best known of the original 23 numbers are found in the two orchestral *Peer Gynt* suites of four excerpts each (opus 46, 1888; opus 55, 1891). While most of the score is composed in the composer's early manner, as yet barely touched by Norwegian folk music, there are two dance tunes played on the traditional Hardanger fiddle (*hardingfele*), a violin with sympathetic strings and a variety of cross-tunings. One of these dances, a "Halling" (a difficult, almost acrobatic dance in duple meter), was later made into a piano miniature by Grieg, in one of his many sets of *Lyrical Pieces* (opus 47, no. 4, 1885–88).

Composers sometimes used folk music from lands not their own to add an exotic flavor to their music, to pay homage to another nationality, or to indulge in the general Romantic interest in folk culture. The Italian composer Giuseppe Verdi, for example, incorporated what he thought to be Egyptian musical elements into his opera *Aida* (1871), which is set in ancient Egypt; the work was written to commemorate the opening of the Suez Canal and had its first performance in Cairo. Brahms, who came from the northern German city of Hamburg, used a Hungarian idiom in his various Hungarian Dances. Dvořák incorporated what he thought to be elements of Native American music into his Symphony no. 9, subtitled "From the New World." He did this in part to encourage American composers to forge their own national idiom (see Chapter 18).

THE GROWING DIVISION BETWEEN ART AND POPULAR MUSIC

It was during the 19th century that musicians, composers, and the music-consuming public began to draw a distinction between *art music* and *popular music*. The terms, it turns out, are misleading and impossible to define musically in any consistent way (see Appendix 4: The Concepts of Art and Popular Music). Still, their emergence reflects real changes in social attitudes toward music and the economics of the music business.

Before the 19th century, composers routinely wrote music to suit their immediate audiences. Mozart, for example, wrote two entirely different works for the stage in the final months of his life: *Die Zauberflöte* ("The Magic Flute"), a *Singspiel*, for a middle-class theater in Vienna, and *La Clemenza di Tito* ("The Clemency of Titus"), an opera seria commissioned for the celebrations surrounding the coronation in Prague of Emperor Leopold II as king of Bohemia. *La Clemenza di Tito*, although admired in its time and into the 19th century, never had a substantial audience. At least some numbers from *Die Zauberflöte*, however, became so popular that to this day many Germans believe they are folk songs and are surprised to discover they were actually written by Mozart. In Mozart's time, these two works would have been performed before audiences of different social levels in decidedly different kinds of theaters. By the end of the 19th century, however, an opera house would present both operas to the same audience. The works themselves had not changed, but rather the attitudes toward them.

This shift in attitudes can be traced to changing assumptions about the nature and purpose of music. Accepting their status in the Romantic imagination as high priests of the new religion of art, at least some 19th-century composers no longer felt obliged to take their audiences into account, at least not directly. Listeners, in turn, came increasingly to accept that it was their job to understand a composer's music, not the composer's job to make it accessible to them. At the same time, undemanding music was becoming increasingly accessible to the broad public. One audience, the audience for music as art, saw it as a means to spiritual enlightenment. The other audience, the audience for what was considered popular music, saw it as a source of entertainment.

Economic factors reinforced this division. With the decline of royal and aristocratic patronage and the growth of an educated middle class, orchestras and opera houses became increasingly reliant on income from ticket sales, which in turn drove them to stage music with broad popular appeal. Publishers, too, recognized there was serious money to be made in music that could be easily performed and readily absorbed, the kind of music that before the 19th century would have been part of the orally transmitted unwritten tradition. The development of recording technology in the 20th century would make this music ever more pervasive.

Concert manners—a revealing index of attitudes toward music—also changed considerably over the course of the 19th century. In earlier times, audiences felt free to respond openly at musical performances whenever moved to do so. Mozart, writing to his father from Paris in 1778, describes how he had marked a crescendo in an orchestral work in such a way as to solicit applause from the audience and how the audience had responded on cue. "What a fuss the oxen here make of this trick!" Mozart observed, half amused, half pleased with the effect. What is particularly revealing in his comment is the assumption that listeners would express their delight without inhibition in the middle of a performance. Such outbursts are still common today at jazz, rock, and country music concerts but not in the realm of the concert halls where Mozart's music is now performed.

By 1900, a little more than a hundred years after Mozart's death, outbursts in the middle of a concert performance had become rare, and even applause between movements was becoming the exception rather than the rule. The new behavior was certainly more respectful to fellow listeners and to the music itself, but it put a damper on the kind of spontaneity that so amused Mozart. For all practical purposes, the concert hall had become a temple, a sanctuary that fostered devotion and contemplation. But there was a price: the rituals of concert decorum that made

The expansion of musical literacy. With a look of weary resignation, the tavern keeper realizes that removing the music stands has not discouraged his clients from continuing with their music making. (The dog seems particularly distressed about this.) Instruction in basic music literacy became a standard part of school curricula in many European nations after 1800, and these amateurs are reading music, not performing from memory. The part-song for men's chorus, a now largely forgotten genre, was popular in the 19th century. Schubert, Schumann, and Brahms all contributed to it. The guitar was ubiquitous in domestic music making; its portability gave it an advantage over the piano. Transported to a comparable scene from today, this group would no doubt be listening to recorded music.

Source: Bildarchiv der Oesterreichischen Nationalbibliothek

music easier to hear by reducing distractions also made the listening experience more passive and self-conscious. In the dance hall and music hall, in contrast, audiences continued to respond to performances spontaneously and vocally; at homes, singing societies, and other establishments, amateurs played on the piano and sang choruses and songs.

The growing rift between art and popular repertories in the 19th century has revealing parallels in the world of drama. For most of the century, Shakespeare's plays were routinely altered to appeal to the widest possible public. No one paid much attention to the edition being used in performance, and scenes from different plays were often presented in quick succession (under such titles as "Gems from Shakespeare's Dramas"), with jugglers, dancers, and acrobats entertaining audiences between the unconnected scenes. In one form or another, Shakespeare's plays remained sufficiently popular to draw audiences from all levels of society. (The episode in Mark Twain's *Huckleberry Finn* in which two vagabonds stage hilariously inaccurate versions of various scenes from Shakespeare for a country audience willing to pay money to see them reflects this popularity.) By the end of the century, however, Shakespeare's plays were being performed from carefully edited, authentic versions before respectful audiences without supplementary entertainments. Shakespeare had become serious art, Culture with a capital C.

The distinction between art and entertainment was not yet firmly established in the concert hall in the early 19th century. At the premiere of Beethoven's Violin Concerto in Vienna on December 23, 1806, the first movement was followed by an intermission, which began only after the soloist had played a short piece of his own while holding his instrument upside down. By the end of the 19th century, such relaxed informality had disappeared. The mixed concert, blending songs, choruses, and instrumental works for orchestra, chamber ensemble, and soloists, had also fallen by the wayside. Programs became increasingly homogeneous and as a result appealed to an increasingly narrower audience.

Still, we should not underestimate the wide appeal through most of the century of what we now think of as serious genres. Some of Verdi's music achieved extraordinary popularity among people who probably never set foot in an opera house but who heard the music sung in the streets or performed in arrangements for any of a variety of instruments. Verdi's own account of a rehearsal for the premiere of his early *Nabucco* (1842) illustrates this phenomenon:

> The artists were singing as badly as they knew how, and the orchestra seemed to be bent only upon drowning the noise of the workmen who were busy making alterations in the building. Presently the chorus began to sing, as carelessly as before, the [chorus] "Va pensiero," but before they had got through half-a-dozen bars, the theatre was still as a church. The men had left off their work, one by one, and there they were, sitting about on the ladders and scaffolding, listening! When the number was finished they broke out into the noisiest applause I have ever heard, crying *Bravo, bravo, viva il maestro!* ["Long live the master!"], and beating on the woodwork with their tools. Then I knew what the future had in store for me.[8]

It is difficult to imagine a comparable reaction among stagehands at an opera house today preparing the set for any recently composed work.

MUSIC IN THE 19TH CENTURY: A STYLISTIC OVERVIEW

The growing drive toward originality opened up a wide variety of options in every element of music: texture, melody, harmony, rhythm, and form. Almost every major composer sought to cultivate a style that was uniquely his or her own.

Textures ranged from the simple homophony of a song like Schubert's *Wanderers Nachtlied* (Anthology, discussed in Chapter 16) to the extreme complexity of a Mahler symphony (Anthology, discussed in Chapter 18). Beethoven introduced a rich array of textures in his late quartets that later composers would explore further. In his String Quartet, op. 130, for example (Anthology, discussed in Chapter 16), all four voices contribute on an essentially equal basis to the fabric of the whole in a way that sounds more like an intimate conversation among friends—the metaphor 18th-century observers had used to characterize the ideal string quartet—than any previous work in the genre.

8. Marcello Conati, ed., *Encounters with Verdi*, transl. Richard Stokes (Ithaca and London: Cornell University Press and Victor Gollancz Ltd., 1984), p. 238. Used by permission of Cornell University Press.

Melodic structures similarly range from the simple to the complex. Periodic phrase structure persists but becomes increasingly less apparent and regular over the course of the century. The principal theme of the first movement of Berlioz's *Symphonie fantastique* (Example 14–1) reflects this trend. It begins with a clear antecedent-consequent structure based on units of 4 + 4 but then dissolves into a series of repeated fragments that enter at ever higher pitches, mirroring the obsessive mental state of the artist who is the subject of the symphony's program. The harmonic direction, rhythmic structure, and thematic content do not follow any conventional pattern after the first eight measures.

Over the course of the century, harmonies became increasingly chromatic, a trend that can be traced in settings of the same poem, Goethe's "Kennst du das Land," by four different composers: Johann Friedrich Reichardt (1795; Anthology II/114, discussed in Chapter 13), Franz Schubert (1815; Anthology II/124a), Robert Schumann (1849; Anthology II/124b), and Hugo Wolf (1888; Anthology II/124c; the l9th-century settings are discussed in Chapter 16). Reichardt's setting is almost purely diatonic, whereas those by Schubert and Schumann feature chromatic passages and unexpected key contrasts while staying within a diatonic idiom. Wolf's setting, however, changes key signature eight times within its 122 measures. By the end of the 19th century, chromaticism was no longer reserved for inflections between various points of stability, but had become a legitimate idiom in its own right—open ended, ambiguous, and unstable in the best sense of all these terms. Franz Liszt's *Nuages Gris* ("Gray Clouds") from 1881 (Anthology II/133, discussed in Chapter 16) exemplifies this new approach.

As harmonies became increasingly chromatic, rhythm became increasingly complex. Even the initially regular rhythm of the principal idea in the first movement of Berlioz's *Symphonie fantastique* (Example 14–1) is accompanied by a metrically irregular, impulsive figure. On the final page of his Ballade in G minor, op. 23 (Anthology II/130, discussed in Chapter 16), Chopin introduces passages in rhythmic groupings of 29 and 39 notes over the span of two measures each, followed by groupings of 21 and 28 notes within individual measures (measures 246–255). Such passages

Example 14–1 Berlioz, *Symphonie fantastique*, first movement, measures 72–111: the initial appearance of the principal melody.

cannot be played with rhythmic exactitude; instead, Chopin uses these large groupings to indicate that performers can present them freely and not in strict meter.

Composers continued to structure works according to such formal conventions of the Classical era as sonata form, scherzo (minuet), and rondo, but because of the demand for originality and innovation, they often downplayed or disguised their presence. How could a composer of genius, after all, write an original work whose formal outline could be found in a compositional textbook? Sonata form maintained its central importance in instrumental music, even for composers as disparate as Johannes Brahms and Gustav Mahler. Yet both composers were also inclined to alter the outlines of the form to make it at times unrecognizable, at least on the surface. Thus in many 19th-century sonata-form movements, particularly those written toward the end of the century, the distinctions between exposition and development or between development and recapitulation can be hard to hear.

Cyclical coherence became increasingly important to composers for multi-movement instrumental works. Compared to the subtle connections late-18th-century composers sometimes created between movements (see Chapter 12), the connections between movements in 19th-century works tend to be more overt. Probably the best known example of such an overt thematic link is the short-short-short-long rhythmic motif that opens Beethoven's Fifth Symphony and is repeated in various transformations in every movement. The idea that a multi-movement cycle should be built around a central thematic idea reflects the increasingly prevalent view that artworks should appear organic, as if they grew from a single seed. E. T. A. Hoffmann, for example, praised Beethoven's Fifth Symphony for the unity that underlies its seeming chaos. Only on closer examination, he pointed out, would listeners discover that the symphony, like a "beautiful tree" with all its "buds and leaves, blossoms and fruits" had grown "out of a single seed." Wagner's music dramas, with their interconnected network of thematic motifs (see Chapter 17), are a late-19th-century manifestation of this organic analogy.

Published music also became more technically demanding over the course of the 19th century. Much of the music from this period lies beyond the technical ability of all but the most skillful performers. Orchestral writing became so intricate that conductors became a necessity. Up until the 1820s, most orchestras were conducted by the concertmaster—the principal first violinist—or the keyboard player within the basso continuo. But the increasing complexities of orchestral textures, the tendency toward more fluid changes in tempo, and the growing intricacies of rhythm created a need for a single individual—someone not playing an instrument—to coordinate and direct the ensemble. The intricate textures of works such as the finale of Brahms's Fourth Symphony (Anthology II/146, discussed in Chapter 18), the opening wind and violin figures in Mendelssohn's *Overture to A Midsummer Night's Dream* (Anthology II/119, discussed in Chapter 16), and the constantly changing and elastic tempos of the slow movement from Mahler's First Symphony (Anthology II/148, discussed in Chapter 18) demand the kind of coordination possible only with a conductor.

Orchestral rehearsals, long an exception, also became the rule. Above one particularly demanding orchestral passage in the first movement of his *Symphonie fantastique* (1830), Berlioz entered this note: "The following eleven measures are extremely difficult. I cannot recommend strongly enough to conductors that this passage be rehearsed many times and with the greatest care. . . . It would be good to have the first and second violins study their parts alone at first, then with the rest of the orchestra."[9] Here, in effect, Berlioz has invented the sectional rehearsal.

---

9. Hector Berlioz, *Symphonie fantastique* (New York: Kalmus, n.d.). Transl. MEB

CONCLUSION

Stylistic changes between the music of the Classical era and the music of the early 19th century were neither sudden nor pronounced. Changing attitudes toward the nature and function of music in the early decades of the new century, however, exercised a profound long-term influence on the development of musical styles. Composers, seeking an original voice, developed idioms that were distinctively individual. The range of compositional choices expanded enormously in all elements of music.

Summary of Style Differences between Music of the Classical Era and 19th Century

	CLASSICAL	19TH CENTURY
Style	Sacred music tends to be somewhat more conservative, preserving basso continuo and much imitative writing, but most music is written in what was thought of at the time as the modern style.	Composers seek to develop a distinctly personal style; originality becomes paramount in all genres.
Text setting	Greater emphasis on sense of natural declamation, less focus on the projection of individual words.	A wide range of options from the simple to the ornate emerges.
Texture	Predominantly homophonic, especially in the early years of the Classical era, although with increasing use of nonimitative counterpoint (obbligato accompaniment) in later decades.	The polyphonic and homophonic coexist, with composers drawing on whichever approach best suits their immediate needs.
Rhythm	Periodic phrase structure predominates, but this supposedly natural symmetry is often inflected by subtle irregularities.	Periodic phrase structure continues in the works of certain repertories (dance, march), but on the whole becomes increasingly less obvious over the course of the century.
Melody	Predominantly lyrical, with emphasis on periodic phrase structure. Virtuosity remains an option, but an aesthetic of "naturalness" predominates.	Ranges from the simple to the complex.
Harmony	A relatively slower harmonic rhythm on the whole, with relatively limited and carefully controlled use of dissonance. The growing polarity of tonic and dominant allows composers to create movement-length forms on the basis of large-scale areas of harmonic stability.	Becomes increasingly chromatic over the course of the century, which makes harmonic simplicity unusual.
Form	Syntactic forms predominate, particularly binary form and its outgrowth, sonata form; rondo form becomes increasingly popular in finales from the 1780s onward. The only paratactic form of significance is the set of variations on a theme.	The large-scale formal conventions of the Classic era continue in use, but often in a manner that obscures their presence. Cyclical coherence becomes an increasingly important issue within multi-movement works.
Instrumentation	A clear distinction between vocal and instrumental parts becomes the norm. The nucleus of the modern orchestra (strings, winds, brass, percussion) emerges as the standard ensemble for large instrumental works.	The distinction between vocal and instrumental writing becomes even more pronounced. The orchestra grows in both size and instrumental variety.

Orchestral Music, 1800–1850

The growing prestige of instrumental music in the early decades of the 19th century created new demands for orchestral genres of all kinds. The symphony and concerto became increasingly substantial in length and tone, and the new genre of the concert overture provided an important new format for program music. Performed by a large body of musicians before a large audience, these genres distinguished themselves both in scope and content from the more private spheres of chamber music, song, and short pieces for solo piano.

BIGGER HALLS, BIGGER AUDIENCES, AND LOUDER INSTRUMENTS

With the decline of royal and aristocratic patronage in the first half of the 19th century, orchestral music became an increasingly public genre. Concert impresarios, dependent on ticket sales for revenue, sought bigger venues to boost profits. Audiences grew in size, and concert halls grew larger to accommodate them. Whereas most 18th-century symphony audiences had numbered around two to four hundred, many concert halls built during the 19th century could seat a thousand or more, and the audiences that filled them were more socially diverse than before.

These economic trends had important aesthetic implications for orchestral music. The larger halls required a new approach to orchestral sound. Ensembles grew substantially in size, particularly the string sections. The design of stringed instruments was also modified to increase the volume of sound they produced. The changes included raising the height of the bridge, lengthening the fingerboard, and increasing the angle at which it drops away from the body of the instrument. The effect of these was to increase the tension on the strings, resulting in a louder, more aggressive sound. Longer and heavier bows also contributed to an increase in dynamic potential. Between 1820 and 1850, most older violins, violas, and cellos were modified according to these new specifications.

Wind instruments also helped change the sound of the orchestra. The clarinet established itself as a standard orchestral instrument in the early years of the 19th century, and by the 1820s the trombone, long a fixture of the opera house, was becoming increasingly common in the concert hall. Technical developments in the flute created an instrument with a greater volume of sound and a more even tone. The "Boehm flute," named after its creator, Theobald Boehm (1794–1881), went into large-scale production in the 1840s and had become standard by the 1870s. Its all-metal design featured a cylindrical bore, larger holes, and a mechanism of padded keys, all of which helped to make the flute a more versatile instrument.

The development of valve technology for brass instruments beginning about 1815 further increased the possibilities for orchestration and texture. Keyed valves allowed players to adjust an instrument's tubing length easily, and thus its natural overtone sequence, permitting them to play chromatic intervals cleanly within the instrument's full range. Before valves, French horn players, for example, could not have played a line with nondiatonic notes without switching instruments, from, say, a horn in B to a horn in C, something not possible in a short space of time. With valves, in contrast, they could play a long melodic line with several nondiatonic notes evenly on a single instrument. By about 1850, valved instruments—including trumpets and tubas as well as French horns—had become standard. This technological change in turn allowed composers to integrate brass more fully into the texture of the orchestra.

THE SYMPHONY

By 1800, the symphony had established itself as the most prestigious of all instrumental genres, in part because of its size and length—four movements for a large orchestra—and in part because of its distinctly public nature.

Standard scoring around 1800, the year of Beethoven's First Symphony, consisted of double winds (flutes, oboes, clarinets, bassoons), two horns, two trumpets, timpani, and strings. New instruments were introduced into the genre steadily over the course of the century. Trombones, which had traditionally been restricted to the realms of church and theater, appear in the finale of Beethoven's Fifth Symphony, the "Storm" movement of his Sixth, and the finale of his Ninth. Instruments normally reserved for special effect, such as the piccolo, contrabassoon, bass drum, triangle, and cymbals (as, for example, in Haydn's Symphony no. 100 ("Military") and the finale of Beethoven's Ninth) became increasingly common. With so many timbral options, sonority itself became a distinctive feature of the genre, which made every major 19th-century symphonist feel compelled to some extent to create a distinctive orchestral sound.

Because the symphony required the more or less equal participation of many instruments in a large ensemble, critics came to view it metaphorically as an expression of communal spirit. The theorist Heinrich Cristoph Koch, for example, wrote in 1802 that the symphony had "as its goal, like the chorus, the expression of a sentiment of an entire multitude."[1] The critic Gottfried Wilhelm Fink, writing a generation later (1835), called the symphony "a story, developed within a psychological context, of some particular emotional state of a large body of people."[2] Shortly before his death in 1883, Wagner distinguished between Beethoven's sonatas and quartets, in which "Beethoven makes music," and his symphonies, in which "the entire world makes music through him."[3] And in 1907, Gustav Mahler declared that a symphony must "be like the universe" and "embrace everything."[4]

1. H. C. Koch, *Musikalisches Lexikon* (Frankfurt/Main: A. Hermann d. J., 1802), article "Sinfonie oder Symphonie." Transl. MEB

2. Gottfried Wilhelm Fink, "Ueber die Symphonie, als Beitrag zur Geschichte und Aesthetik derselben," *Allgemeine musikalische Zeitung* 37 (1835): 523. Transl. MEB

3. Cosima Wagner, *Die Tagebücher*, vol. 2, ed. Martin Gregor-Dellin and Dietrich Mack (Munich: Piper, 1976), p. 1103 (entry for January 30, 1883). Transl. MEB

4. Robert P. Morgan, *Twentieth-Century Music: A History of Musical Style in Modern Europe and America* (New York: Norton, 1991), p. 122.

The understanding of the symphony as a genre of universal import helps explain the readiness of 19th-century commentators to associate specific symphonies with extramusical ideas. Sometimes composers themselves provided these associations, with a title (like Beethoven, who called his third symphony *Eroica*, or "heroic") or a detailed program distributed at performances (like Berlioz for his *Symphonie fantastique*). But even works with no such explicit extramusical theme were presumed nonetheless to have some transcendent meaning. Beethoven, for example, gave no hint of any programmatic idea on the score for his Fifth Symphony. The public, however, was quick to accept what Anton Schindler, Beethoven's personal secretary, claimed was Beethoven's explanation for the symphony's famous opening—"Thus fate knocks at the door"—despite Schindler's questionable veracity. E. T. A. Hoffmann and others had already perceived in this symphony an allegory of struggle leading to victory, and Schindler's supposedly eyewitness account merely reinforced this perception.

Beethoven's Symphonies

Beethoven's nine symphonies encompass a wide range of compositional approaches. Indeed, his symphonies are so varied that it is impossible to single out any one of them as typical. Almost all of them explore some fundamentally new approach to the genre. With the Third Symphony, for example, he extended the reach of the genre into the moral, social, and philosophical realms for the first time. The work's title, *Eroica*, evokes the ethical and political ideals associated with the French Revolution. (Beethoven composed it in 1803 when Napoleon Bonaparte was beginning his conquest of Europe. The composer, who initially idealized Napoleon as an enlightened ruler, intended at one point to call the work "Grand Symphony Entitled Bonaparte"—see illustration—but changed his mind in a rage when he learned that Napoleon had crowned himself emperor in 1804.) In the second movement, labeled "Funeral March," Beethoven confronts death itself.

The Fifth Symphony (1808)—with its thematic transformation of a prominent rhythmic motive (the famous short-short-short-LONG of the work's opening), its blurring of movement boundaries (between the two final movements), and the return of an extended passage from one movement (the third) within the course of another (the fourth)—makes explicit strategies of cyclical coherence that had long been latent in earlier music. In the Sixth Symphony (*Pastoral*; 1808), Beethoven explores the potential of instrumental music to represent objects and ideas. Each of the work's five movements bears a programmatic title related to images and feelings inspired by the countryside. The verbal clues about the music's meaning range from the vague to the astonishingly specific. The first movement, for example, bears only the heading "Awakening of Happy Thoughts Upon Arriving in the Countryside," but the slow movement. "Scene by the Brook," ends with an evocation of birdcalls that Beethoven actually labels by species: nightingale, cuckoo, and quail. The Seventh Symphony (1812), perhaps the most popular of all Beethoven's symphonies in the 19th century, eschews programmatic headings but explores orchestral sonorities and rhythms with unparalleled intensity.

With the Ninth Symphony (1824), Beethoven fused vocal forces into a symphonic framework. The use of a chorus and soloists to sing a portion of Friedrich Schiller's poem *An die Freude* ("To Joy") in the last movement was unusual and controversial at the time. As we have seen, it suggested to some critics an acknowledgment of the expressive limits of purely instrumental, or absolute, music. But like the Third Symphony, it confirmed the status of the symphony as a vehicle for the expression of ideas extending well beyond music.

CD9, Track 3
BEETHOVEN
Symphony no. 3 (Eroica)
Score Anthology II/117

If most of Beethoven's symphonies are innovative, the *Eroica* nevertheless stands out as a work of singular historical significance. First performed in 1805 in the Viennese palace of its dedicatee, Prince Lobkowitz, the *Eroica* breaks new ground in many respects. The first movement, although it is in sonata form, is of an unprecedented length; at 691 measures it dwarfs any previous sonata-form first movement. In the slow movement, Beethoven became the first composer to make symphonic use of the **march,** a military form in duple meter characterized by a strong, repetitive beat for keeping soldiers in orderly formation. The third movement of the *Eroica* epitomizes the transformation of the 18th-century minuet—a courtly dance—into the **scherzo** (Italian for "joke"). Although the term had been used for dance-inspired movements before, the designation became standard in the 19th century. Like the *Eroica*'s third movement, scherzos tend to be faster and longer than minuets; this particular scherzo has a written-out return of the opening section, that is, it is not a straightforward da capo form after the middle-section trio. The finale, consisting of a series of variations on a theme, is proportionately substantial and complex yet at the same time readily accessible. The work as a whole, moreover, has an overarching musical trajectory,

Beethoven cancels the original title of the *Eroica* Symphony. Beethoven, who initially idealized Napoleon Bonaparte as an enlightened ruler, became enraged when he learned that Napoleon had accepted the title of emperor. From the title page of the autograph score of the *Eroica* Symphony, it is clear that Beethoven crossed out the words *intitolata Buonaparte* after *Sinfonia grande* ("Grand Symphony entitled Bonaparte"). In his typically sloppy fashion, though, Beethoven left just enough of the words around their edges to make the original still readable. The title page shows an odd mix of Italian (the title itself) and French ("Louis van Beethoven"). Both were more fashionable than German at the time. Only later in life would Beethoven begin to give titles, tempos, and expressive markings in his native language. This reflects the rise of German as a literary language as well as a growing German nationalism, which first emerged around 1810 in part as a response to Napoleon's invasion of German-speaking lands.

Source: Archiv der Gesellschaft der Musikfreunde in Wien

PRIMARY EVIDENCE

E. T. A. Hoffmann's Review of Beethoven's Fifth Symphony

Ernst Theodor Amadeus Hoffmann (1776–1822), better known as the author of the children's tale *The Nutcracker*, was also a composer whose works include several operas and a symphony. His critical writing, however, is his greatest legacy in music. His widely read review of Beethoven's Fifth Symphony, in particular, has been extraordinarily influential. Unusually long and detailed—more so than any earlier review—it combines technical analysis with descriptive accounts of the power of the music. The excerpt here is from the opening of the review. In it Hoffmann extols instrumental, that is, "pure" music, as the most romantic of all the arts.

When music is spoken of as an independent art, does not the term properly apply only to instrumental music, which scorns all aid, all admixture of other arts (poetry), and gives pure expression to its own peculiar artistic nature? It is the most romantic of all arts, one might almost say the only one that is genuinely romantic, since its only subject-matter is infinity. Orpheus's lyre opened the gates of Orcus. Music reveals to man an unknown realm, a world quite separate from the outer sensual world surrounding him, a world in which he leaves behind all precise feelings in order to embrace an inexpressible longing. . . .

In singing, where the poetry suggests precise moods through words, the magical power of music acts like the philosopher's miraculous elixir, a few drops of which make any drink so much more wonderfully delicious. Any passion—love, hate, anger, despair, etc.—presented to us in an opera is clothed by music in the purple shimmer of romanticism, so that even our mundane sensations take us out of the everyday into the realm of the infinite. Such is the power of music's spell that it grows ever stronger and can only burst the fetters of any other art.

It is certainly not merely an improvement in the means of expression (perfection of instruments, greater virtuosity of players), but also a deeper awareness of the peculiar nature of music, that has enabled great composers to raise instrumental music to its present level.

Mozart and Haydn, the creators of modern instrumental music, first showed us the art in its full glory; but the one who regarded it with total devotion and penetrated to its innermost nature is Beethoven. The instrumental compositions of all three masters breathe the same romantic spirit for the very reason that they all intimately grasp the essential nature of the art; yet the character of their compositions is markedly different. . . .

Haydn romantically apprehends the humanity in human life; he is more congenial, more comprehensible to the majority.

Mozart takes more as his province the superhuman, magical quality residing in the inner self.

Beethoven's music sets in motion the machinery of awe, of fear, of terror, of pain, and awakens that infinite yearning which is the essence of romanticism. He is therefore a purely romantic composer. Might this not explain why his vocal music is less successful, since it does not permit a mood of vague yearning but can only depict from the realm of the infinite those feelings capable of being described in words?

Source: *Allgemeine musikalische Zeitung* (Leipzig), 1810, trans. Martyn Clarke. In David Charlton, ed., *E.T.A. Hoffmann's Musical Writings* (Cambridge: Cambridge University Press, 1989), pp. 96–7, 98.

---

reflected in the similarity between the opening themes of the first movement and the finale. The finale, in other words, is more than the last movement of the work: it represents a culmination of the whole. Critics seeking to describe the effect of this musical trajectory have consistently described it as a passage from struggle (first movement) and death (second movement) to rebirth (third movement) and triumph (fourth movement). That this work could evoke such profound associations is both a tribute to the power of Beethoven's music and a reflection of the high regard for instrumental music as a vehicle for the expression of abstract ideas in the Romantic aesthetic.

The two loud tonic chords at the opening of the first movement (Allegro con brio) provide the briefest of introductions and serve a double function: to catch the audience's attention and to allow Beethoven to introduce the principal theme at a soft volume. The metrically regular triadic opening of this theme (measures 3–6) contrasts with its syncopated, chromatic continuation (measures 7–10). The transition section (measures 45–83) is unusually long, occupying roughly 25 percent of the exposition. It contains three distinct thematic ideas, each of which will be developed later in the movement. The first idea in this secondary key area (the dominant, B♭ Major), beginning in measure 83, offers a distinct but brief contrast to the turbulence of the opening and the transition. Momentum soon builds, however, culminating in a series of syncopated chords (measures 123–131) just before the end of the exposition.

Within the development, the **fugato**—a passage that begins like a fugue but does not sustain itself after a series of initial entries—starting at measure 236 leads to a thematic standstill in a series of loud repeated chords (measures 248–283). Syncopation is emphasized at the expense of melody. The theme beginning in measure 284 that follows these chords is one we have not heard before. The introduction of an entirely new theme in the development of a sonata-form movement was not without precedent. Haydn did this in his *Farewell* Symphony of 1772. Beethoven, however, expands on this device in an innovative way by working his new theme into the remainder of the movement and restating it prominently in the coda.

Beethoven has additional surprises in store before the recapitulation. The long passage on the dominant between measures 338 and 358 seems to signal the end of the development section and the beginning of the retransition to the tonic. But Beethoven avoids the tonic and instead extends the development still further. The true retransition begins at measure 382 with a thinning out of the orchestral texture over an extended V^9 harmony. Then, in a quiet yet deeply bizarre gesture, Beethoven has a solo horn enter with the opening theme in the tonic (measure 395) while the strings are still sounding a dominant harmony. In effect, Beethoven has deliberately written an apparent mistake into the score, making it seem to an unsuspecting listener that one of the hornists has come in too early.

The recapitulation itself, which begins at measure 398, is highly unstable at first, moving from the tonic to the supertonic (F Major) after only 11 measures. The harmony finally settles firmly on the tonic with the full orchestral passage that begins in measure 430. From this point onward, the recapitulation is fairly stable. The coda, which begins in measure 557, is substantial. It amounts, in effect, to a second development section, during which the new theme introduced in measure 284 is finally restated in the tonic (beginning at measure 589).

Beethoven's second movement—the "Funeral March"—bears all the characteristic features of that genre: minor mode, slow tempo (Adagio assai), the imitation of muffled drums in the double basses, dotted rhythms in the melody, and a subsequent alternation between minor- and major-mode themes. As the diagram here indicates, the movement is structured to feature the prominent return of the mournful opening figure (A) at key points between other ideas; in other words, this Marcia funebre is very rondo-like, albeit in a much slower tempo than most rondos (see Chapter 12).

The Structure of the Second Movement of Beethoven's *Eroica*

Section	A¹	B	A²	C	A³	Coda
Measure	1	69	105	114	173	209
Key	C minor	C Major	C minor	unstable	C minor	A♭ Major → C minor

The coda of the second movement begins with a ticktock-like figure in the violins that may well represent the passing of time, a reminder of human mortality. The highly syncopated music that follows has a dreamlike quality quite different from the turbulent syncopations of the first movement. In the closing bars the opening theme returns, but fragmented in a way that suggests the gasping breath of the dying.

PERFORMANCE PERSPECTIVE

Beethoven's Eroica *Symphony on Period Instruments*
CD9   Tracks 3–4

This recording of the first two movements from the *Eroica*, made in 1993 by the, Orchestre Révolutionnaire et Romantique, conducted by John Eliot Gardiner, is performed by an ensemble playing on instruments from Beethoven's own time, or on modern copies of such instruments. The sound is markedly different from that of a standard modern-day orchestra. The strings in this recording are fewer in number (10 first violins, 8 second violins, 5 violas, 6 cellos, 3 double basses) and less penetrating in tone by virtue of gut strings and a lower bridge (see p. 389); the performers also use rather less vibrato than is customary nowadays. By way of comparison, the leading orchestras of today normally use a string section of at least 12 first violins, 12 second violins, 10 violas, 10 cellos, and 8 double basses.

The winds, too, differ in structure and sound from their modern-day equivalents. The flutes are wooden rather than metal and feature a conical rather than cylindrical bore. The resulting sound is softer and less resonant but for many listeners more "pure." The oboes, clarinets, and bassoons likewise have a more rounded sound than their modern counterparts, and the wind players also use much less vibrato than their counterparts in a standard modern orchestra. The natural horns and trumpets, without valves, sound a bit rougher around the edges but offer a more open tone. The timpani (kettledrums) are smaller and played with wooden or leather-covered stick-heads, as opposed to the more common felt stick-heads of today. The 18th-century sound is more focused and penetrating.

Orchestral textures as a whole tend to be more transparent: it is generally easier to pick out individual lines and voices in performances by a period-instrument ensemble than in performances by a modern-day orchestra. The overall volume of sound is lower—there are fewer players, and their instruments are individually less powerful—yet it should be kept in mind that concert halls in the early 19th century were considerably smaller than those of today.

Are performances on period instruments superior to those on modern instruments? Most critics would agree that instruments alone do not ensure quality—musicianship remains an essential element to any performance. Beyond this, there is widespread disagreement. Those who advocate the use of period instruments argue that such performances allow the music to be heard with the kind of sound the composers themselves would have recognized. Others maintain that today's larger concert halls were not built for smaller ensembles: period ensembles in such a setting sound more feeble than they would have to Beethoven's contemporaries. An even more basic objection is that the very concept of "authenticity" is itself deeply problematic. Performance practices of earlier times varied widely even within a given locale and time, and making music involves the kind of imagination and originality that was rarely put down in writing, either in notation or in prose accounts of performance. Yet all would agree that the revival of period instruments, which grew gradually over the course of the 20th century and accelerated enormously after 1970, has increased the range of performance options available to performers and listeners alike.

Orchestre Révolutionnaire et Romantique. Established in 1989, the Orchestre Révolutionnaire et Romantique is one of several period-instrument ensembles that have flourished in recent decades, offering listeners new perspectives on the works of such composers as Beethoven, Weber, Schubert, Berlioz, Mendelssohn, Schumann, Verdi, Brahms, and Fauré. John Eliot Gardiner also founded the Monteverdi Choir in 1963 (with which he has recorded a Bach cantata cycle) and the English Baroque Soloists in 1978 (recordings of the mature Mozart operas, the piano concertos, and the Requiem) and has led major orchestras throughout Europe and the United States.

Source: Monteverdi Choir & Orchestra Ltd

COMPOSER PROFILE   Ludwig van Beethoven (1770–1827)

Beethoven's contemporaries were quick to note the striking contrast between the man and his music. "Whoever sees Beethoven for the first time and knows nothing about him." wrote an observer in 1797, "would surely take him for a malicious, ill-natured, quarrelsome drunkard who has no feeling for music. . . . On the other hand, he who sees him for the first time surrounded by his fame and his glory will surely see musical talent in every feature of an ugly face."[5]

Beethoven's tendency to isolate himself from society grew with his increasing deafness, the first signs of which he acknowledged privately around the age of 30. It is unclear exactly what caused this deafness, but in the remarkable document known as the "Heiligenstadt Testament"—which Beethoven wrote in 1802 and kept hidden until his death in 1827—he reveals the pain it caused him.

> Oh you men who think or say that I am malevolent, stubborn or misanthropic, how greatly do you wrong me. You do not know the secret cause which makes me seem that way to you. . . . But, think that for 6 years now I have been hopelessly afflicted, made worse by senseless physicians, from year to year deceived with hopes of improvement, finally compelled to face the prospect of *a lasting malady*. . . . If at times I tried to forget all this, oh how harshly was I flung back by the doubly sad experience of my bad hearing. Yet it was impossible for me to say to people, "Speak louder, shout, for I am deaf." Ah, how could I possibly admit an infirmity in the *one sense* which ought to be more perfect in me than in others, a sense which I once possessed in the highest perfection, a perfection such as few in my profession enjoy or ever have enjoyed.

His despair, he goes on, drove him almost to suicide. "It was only *my art* that held me back," he concedes. "Ah, it seemed to me impossible to leave the world until I had brought forth all that I felt was within me."[6]

Another document found with the Heiligenstadt Testament after Beethoven's death—a letter dated only July 6 to an unknown woman he addresses as "Immortal Beloved"—provides insight into a different side of the composer's character. The identity of the intended recipient, she either returned the letter or Beethoven never sent it, has been a matter of considerable contention. The American scholar Maynard Solomon has demonstrated convincingly that the letter dates to 1812 and the woman in question is Antonie Brentano (1780–1869). Unfortunately for Beethoven, Brentano was the wife of a prosperous Viennese merchant, hence the repeated references to the impossibility of a physical relationship. "Yes," he writes, "I am resolved to wander so long in distant lands from you until I can fly to your arms and say that I am really at home with you, and can send my soul enwrapped in you into the land of the spirits—Yes, unhappily it must be so."[7]

As if to compensate for the isolation his deafness forced on him, Beethoven's art engages life to the fullest. Some of his most famous works manifest a sense of struggle to overcome an adversity imposed by fate. The Third, Fifth, and Ninth Symphonies, in particular, follow a trajectory that has been compared to a journey from strife to victory, from darkness to light. A portrait commissioned by the composer a few years after the Heiligenstadt Testament certainly conveys this idea, showing Beethoven with his back to a scene of stormy darkness moving toward a sun-drenched field (see "Beethoven as Orpheus," page 397).

Born in Bonn in 1770, Beethoven grew up in a musical household. His father was a singer at the court there, and his grandfather had been Kapellmeister. But his father was alcoholic, and the young Beethoven had to take on adult responsibilities at an early age. He was appointed assistant organist at the court in 1782 and also played viola in the theater orchestra. Recognizing the young man's talent as a composer, the elector of Bonn (the city's ruler) arranged for him to go to Vienna to study with Haydn in 1792. Count Ferdinand Waldstein, another early supporter of the young composer, wrote prophetically in Beethoven's notebook before his departure for Vienna: "With the help of assiduous labor, you shall receive Mozart's spirit from Haydn's hands."[8] Mozart had died less than a year before (in December 1791).

Although the image of Beethoven receiving the spirit of Mozart from the hands of Haydn has become fixed in the public imagination, the composer himself did not create an immediate sensation when he arrived in Vienna, nor did he get along particularly well with Haydn. When Beethoven sent supposedly new works back to Bonn a few years later, these were exposed as compositions that he had mostly already written before he had left for Vienna. Beethoven nevertheless managed to attract the attention of an important group of aristocratic patrons in Vienna who would provide him financial support in various ways for most of the rest of

5. From the Diaries of Carl Friedrich Baron Kübeck von Kubau (1797), cited in H. C. Robbins Landon, *Beethoven: A Documentary Study* (New York: Macmillan, 1970), p. 71.

6. Alexander Wheelock Thayer, *Thayer's Life of Beethoven*, rev. and ed. Elliot Forbes (Princeton, NJ: Princeton University Press, 1967), pp. 304–6.

7. Maynard Solomon, *Beethoven*, 2nd ed. (New York: Schirmer, 1998), pp. 209–11.

8. Thayer, *Thayer's Life of Beethoven*, p. 115.

his life. When Jerome Bonaparte, Napoleon's brother, offered Beethoven a lucrative position as Kapellmeister in Kassel in 1808, a group of these aristocrats pooled their resources to keep the composer in Vienna by creating what amounted to a trust fund for him, a large sum of money that generated enough interest to provide a regular income. The last 15 years of Beethoven's life were not happy, however. Inflation ate into his income, he suffered from chronic poor health (his liver, pancreas, and intestines seem to have given him particular problems), his deafness became increasingly worse, and he became embroiled in a bitter custody battle with his sister-in-law over her son Karl, whose father was Beethoven's deceased brother. Beethoven held his sister-in-law in low regard, as did the courts, which awarded him custody of the boy in 1816. But Beethoven was not well prepared to become the single parent of a teenager, and constant struggles involving the boy over the next decade, both in and out of court, took their toll both emotionally and financially.

With so many physical ailments in his final decade, Beethoven was constantly in search of new doctors and new cures. Yet he seems to have maintained a healthy sense of ironic detachment and even humor in the face of all this. His letters and the records of his conversations (visitors wrote their comments in conversation books for the deaf composer to read) show him careening from expressions of deep physical and emotional pain to attention to the mundane details of daily life, like making sure he would have meat in the evening's soup. Most of his voluminous correspondence with publishers revolves around fees and printer's errors, yet in rare moments of openness, as in a letter of September 1824, he could also step back to survey his own output as a composer:

> All too burdened with work and poor health as I am, it is necessary to have a certain amount of patience with me. I am here [in Baden, a spa outside Vienna] because of my health, or more accurately because of my illnesses. But there is already improvement. Apollo and the Muses will not yet turn me over to the Grim Reaper, for I still owe them a great deal, and before I depart for the Elysian fields [home of the deceased Greek heroes] I must leave behind what the spirit provides me and commands me to finish. It really seems to me as if I had written hardly any music at all. I wish you all good success in your exertions on behalf of art, for it is art and science alone that point toward a higher life and give us the hope of attaining that life.[9]

It is commonly (but erroneously) believed that Beethoven's music was misunderstood in his own lifetime. On the contrary, his music was extremely popular. Some of his more unconventional works, such as the *Eroica* Symphony, were not well understood at first, but this may have been because they were poorly performed as much as anything else. By 1810, Beethoven was already recognized as the greatest living composer of instrumental music. When he died in 1827, he had become a national hero. Throngs of mourners attended his funeral hoping to catch a last glimpse of the great tone poet.

Beethoven as Orpheus. Anyone who sat for a portrait in Beethoven's time took great care in selecting and arranging the setting and surrounding objects. A portrait, after all, was one of the principal means by which one projected one's self to society as a whole. (People often pose for photographic portraits in the same way today.) This portrait, painted in 1804 or 1805, shows Beethoven with his back to a scene of darkness and turmoil moving toward green, sunlit fields. In his left hand he holds a lyre-guitar, a fashionable instrument of the day. The lyre is traditionally associated with Apollo and (especially) Orpheus, who had great musical powers, so the implication here is that Beethoven is a modern-day Orpheus. Only a few years later, E. T. A. Hoffmann would open his celebrated review of Beethoven's Fifth Symphony by reminding readers how the lyre of Orpheus—instrumental music—had opened up a spirit realm otherwise closed to mortals. Not coincidentally, this portrait presents a much more handsome-looking Beethoven than any other contemporary likeness.

Source: Willibrord Joseph Mahler (1778–1860), "Ludvig van Beethoven," 1804, oil on canvas/Historisches Museum der Stadt Wien, Vienna, Austria/ The Bridgeman Art Library

9. Beethoven to B. Schott's Sons, Mainz, September 17, 1824, in Ludwig van Beethoven, *Briefwechsel: Gesamtausgabe*, ed. Sieghard Brandenburg, vol. 5 (Munich: Henle, 1996). Transl. MEB

BEETHOVEN'S THREE STYLES

Around the middle of the 19th century, critics and historians began to divide Beethoven's musical works into three broad style periods: early (to about 1802), middle (from roughly 1802 until 1815), and late (1815–1827). Although some disagreement has arisen about just when each of these periods begins and where certain works fit, this division has proved remarkably useful over time because it does reflect certain broad changes in Beethoven's style.

EARLY PERIOD Like any aspiring composer, Beethoven took the works of acknowledged masters, especially Mozart and Haydn, as his model. Still, such early works as the Piano Sonatas op. 10 and op. 13 (*Pathétique*) or the Second Symphony are hardly mere imitations of earlier composers or styles. We hear in them an original voice that is unquestionably Beethoven's.

MIDDLE PERIOD On the whole, however, it is the works of the middle period that are generally recognized as quintessentially Beethovenian: the *Waldstein* and *Appassionata* Piano Sonatas, the *Razumovsky* String Quartets, the Third through Eighth Symphonies, the Third through Fifth Piano Concertos, the Violin Concerto, and the opera *Fidelio*. The middle period style is often called "heroic" because of its evocation of struggle and triumph, as in such works as the Third Symphony (subtitled *heroic*), the Fifth Symphony, and the Third *Leonore* Overture.

LATE PERIOD In the last 12 years of his life, Beethoven became increasingly withdrawn from society and his music became increasingly introspective. With only occasional exceptions (most notably the Ninth Symphony), he abandoned the heroic style for one that many subsequent critics have found to be more enigmatic yet no less moving. Above all, the late works are characterized by an exploration of musical extremes in such areas as form, proportion, texture, and harmony. The finale of the Ninth Symphony, for example, conforms to no conventional pattern at all, and with its unprecedented choral conclusion it incorporates voices into what had been a purely instrumental genre. Exploring extremes of length, Beethoven wrote some of his longest works—the Ninth Symphony, the *Hammerklavier* Piano Sonata op. 106—as well as some of his briefest, such as the almost cryptic piano works he (ironically) labeled *Bagatelles*, or "little bits of nothing." In the late style we also find extremes of texture, ranging from the simple to the extraordinarily complex. Many movements have the directness of song (such as the *Cavatina* from the String Quartet op. 130); others explore the intricacies of fugue at great length. Finally, in the late period, Beethoven exhibits an increasing sense of harmonic freedom and a kind of raw emotion in tone that is something new in music. In the middle of the *Cavatina* in the String Quartet op. 130, for example, Beethoven moves from E♭ to C♭ Major and tells the first violinist to play the lyrical melody in a manner that is *beklemmt*—literally, "caught in a vise." And indeed, the music sounds like an operatic heroine so emotionally devastated that she is gasping for breath. Beauty is no longer the primary consideration. What is primary now is psychological truth.

PRINCIPAL WORKS

SYMPHONIES Although the first two symphonies are distinctive in their own right, they operate within the traditions of the genre as transmitted by Haydn and Mozart. In contrast, the Third Symphony—the *Eroica*— is a truly revolutionary work, not only because of its size (almost twice as long as any symphony before) but also because of its structural complexity, its treatment of the orchestra, the weight of its finale, and what might be called its ethical dimension, its engagement with the idea of heroism. (Beethoven's symphonies are considered at length in this chapter.)

PIANO SONATAS Like the symphonies, Beethoven's 32 piano sonatas explore a remarkable variety of styles. Many of these works are known by nicknames that have no connection with the composer. Op. 27, no. 1, for example, became the *Moonlight* Sonata because it reminded one critic of moonlight on a lake. The designation *Appassionata* for op. 57 derives from the passionate tone of the outer movements of the work. The name of the *Tempest* Sonata (op. 31, no. 2) comes from Anton Schindler (1795–1864), Beethoven's personal secretary, who fabricated many stories about the composer. Schindler claimed that when he asked Beethoven about the poetic program behind this sonata, the composer growled, "Go read Shakespeare's *Tempest*." (Even if the report is true, did Beethoven mean it seriously?) Other nicknames have a more solid foundation. The *Waldstein* Sonata (op. 53; discussed in Chapter 16) is in fact dedicated to Count Waldstein. And Beethoven himself, in an indisputable example of the effect of events in his life on his work, named Sonata op. 81a *Les Adieux* ("The Farewell") to commemorate the departure, exile, and return of his pupil and patron,

Archduke Rudolph, who had been forced into exile by the arrival of French troops in Vienna. The late sonatas (opp. 101, 106, 109, 110, 111) enjoy a special place in the piano repertory. Op. 106 (the *Hammerklavier*) has been called the "Mount Everest of the Piano" because of its size and technical difficulty, particularly in the fugal finale. The last of these sonatas, op. 111, is in two movements, which prompted the original publisher to inquire whether or not the composer had neglected to send him the finale.

STRING QUARTETS AND OTHER CHAMBER WORKS

Beethoven wrote his first set of string quartets, op. 18, under the shadow of Haydn, the acknowledged master of the genre at the time. At least one of these works, however (op. 18, no. 5), takes a quartet by Mozart (K. 464) as its model. Beethoven's next set of quartets, published in 1808 as op. 59, is altogether different: larger, more difficult, and full of the heroic style associated with the Third and Fifth Symphonies. The three works as a whole are known as the *Razumovsky* Quartets by virtue of their dedicatee, the Russian ambassador to the Austrian Empire, who was also one of Beethoven's most important patrons in Vienna. All of the subsequent quartets were substantial enough to be issued individually. The *Harp* Quartet, op. 74 (so called because of its many arpeggiated pizzicato figures in the first movement) still belongs to the middle period, but op. 95 (1810) cannot be classified so easily. Many critics consider it one of the first works in the late style.

The five late quartets (opp. 127, 130, 131, 132, and 135) constitute some of the most demanding music of the 19th century, both technically and aesthetically. Indeed, for much of the 19th century, these works were seen as manifestations of Beethoven's extreme sense of isolation from the external world and were more respected than loved. In the 20th century they came to be appreciated as probing explorations of the human psyche, providing inspiration for such diverse composers as Schoenberg, Bartók, Stravinsky, and Carter.

In addition to the string quartets, Beethoven also wrote ten sonatas for violin and piano, five for cello and piano, six piano trios, five string trios, and various other chamber works in a variety of combinations for strings, winds, and piano. All of these were popular in their day and have endured as staples of the chamber repertoire.

VOCAL MUSIC Beethoven wrote a great deal more vocal music than most people realize. Several dozen songs, more than a hundred folk-song arrangements, two substantial settings of the Mass ordinary, several secular cantatas and miscellaneous works for chorus and orchestra, an oratorio (*Christ on the Mount of Olives*), an opera (*Fidelio*, originally entitled *Leonore* and revised several times), and almost fifty canons for various numbers of voices. Given this considerable output, it must have galled Beethoven that his contemporaries almost always qualified their praise by calling him the greatest living composer of *instrumental* music.

KEY DATES IN THE LIFE OF BEETHOVEN

1770	Born December 16 in Bonn (Germany).
1782	Appointed assistant organist at the court in Bonn.
1792	With financial support from the elector of Bonn and other benefactors, goes to Vienna to study with Haydn.
1801	Acknowledges to a few close friends the onset of deafness.
1802	Writes the Heiligenstadt Testament, revealing his tumultuous inner life and near suicidal despair over his growing deafness.
1809	Declines offer from the king of Westphalia to become music director to the court there; leverages the offer to secure a fixed annual income from the pooled resources of several Viennese patrons, on the condition that he stay in Vienna.
1812	Writes passionate love letter to the "Immortal Beloved," probably Antonie Brentano.
1815	With increasing deafness, withdraws into an ever-smaller circle of friends and assistants.
1816–1820s	Fights a bitter legal battle with his sister-in-law over the custody of his nephew Karl. The struggle occupies a great deal of the composer's time and energy.
1827	Dies in Vienna on March 26.

FOCUS   Notable Composers of Symphonies, 1800–1850

Beethoven and Berlioz were not the only composers of symphonies in the first half of the 19th century. Other prominent composers cultivated this genre as well.

FRANZ SCHUBERT (1797–1828), by his own admission, labored under Beethoven's shadow in the realm of the symphony yet managed to produce several remarkable works of his own, including the "Unfinished" in B minor and the "Great" C-Major Symphony (so-called to distinguish it from a smaller work by Schubert in the same key). Yet neither of these symphonies was known publicly during the composer's lifetime. Robert Schumann discovered the "Great" C-Major Symphony while visiting Schubert's brother in Vienna in 1839, and the "Unfinished" did not resurface until the mid-1860s.

FELIX MENDELSSOHN (1809–1849) wrote a series of string symphonies in his youth and reorchestrated one of them as his First Symphony in 1824. His Second Symphony, called *Lobgesang* ("Song of Praise"), follows the pattern of Beethoven's Ninth with three instrumental movements and a vocal finale for soloists and chorus. His Third and Fourth Symphonies, known as the "Scottish" and "Italian," reflect the impressions of his travels. His Fifth Symphony ("Reformation") is actually a much earlier work

than its number would imply. It features Luther's hymn *Ein feste Burg ist unser Gott* (A Mighty Fortress Is Our God) in its instrumental female.

ROBERT SCHUMANN (1810–1856) composed four symphonies, all of them purely instrumental, between 1841 and 1850. While none has an explicit program, Schumann gave descriptive titles to the first ("Spring") and third ("Rhenish"—that is, having to do with the Rhine region). The "Rhenish" includes a folk-like dance in its third movement and a wonderfully dark, contrapuntal slow movement in which the low brass and strings predominate. Its finale, like the finale of the Second Symphony, recalls and transforms musical ideas from earlier movements.

LUDWIG SPOHR (1784–1859) enjoyed wide renown during his lifetime as a symphonist. He cultivated the programmatic symphony more than any other major composer of his generation. Most notable among these is his "Historical Symphony," with the first movement reflecting the style of "The Bach-Handel Period (1720)," the slow second movement "The Haydn-Mozart Period (1780)," the scherzo "The Beethoven Period (1810)," and the finale "The Latest Period (1840)."

The Symphony after Beethoven

With its vocal finale, Beethoven's Ninth Symphony provoked a crisis of confidence among composers. How, they wondered, could anyone surpass Beethoven's accomplishments in this genre? By 1830, the future of instrumental music—the symphony in particular—had become a topic of intense debate. In 1835, Robert Schumann wrote that after Beethoven's Ninth, there was reason to believe the dimensions and goals of the symphony had been exhausted. Schumann declared Felix Mendelssohn to have won "crown and scepter over all other instrumental composers of the day," but noted that even Mendelssohn had "apparently realized that there was nothing more to be gained" in the symphony and was now working principally within the realm of the concert overture, "in which the idea of the symphony is confined to a smaller orbit."[10] (The *Overture to a Midsummer Night's Dream*, discussed in the next section, is the kind of work Schumann had in mind here.)

Richard Wagner maintained that the Ninth Symphony effectively marked the end of the genre. With it Beethoven had demonstrated what Wagner considered the "futility" of absolute music. Any composer tempted to write a symphony now would have no choice but to copy Beethoven by including voices and text, thereby committing the sin of unoriginality, or retreat to the inadequacy of a purely instrumental format. In contrast to Wagner, other composers saw the Ninth as an aberration, a onetime experiment, and indeed, the surviving sketches for the symphony Beethoven was working on when he died suggest it would have been purely instrumental.

---

10. Robert Schumann, "A Symphony by Berlioz" (1835), trans. Edward T. Cone, in Hector Berlioz, *Fantastic Symphony*, ed. Edward T. Cone (New York: Norton, 1971), pp. 227–8.

Beethoven's sketches for the Ninth Symphony. Because so many of Beethoven's composition sketchbooks have survived, we know more about his working methods than those of almost any other composer before the 20th century. Some of these sketchbooks are small enough to fit in one's pocket, which is where Beethoven liked to keep them. He would jot down ideas as they came to him on walks, in coffee houses, or wherever he might find himself. Larger sketchbooks record the composer's efforts to shape thematic ideas into more promising form. Beethoven wrestled with dozens of different versions of the "Ode to Joy" theme from the finale of his Ninth Symphony before finally arriving at the tune that seems so simple and natural. Still other sketchbooks preserve Beethoven's struggle to shape a work or movement in its larger form.

Source: Art Resource/Bildarchiv Preussischer Kulturbesitz

CD9, Track 5
BERLIOZ
Symphonie fantastique
Score Anthology II/118

As it turned out, it was the French composer Hector Berlioz (1803–1869) who would be most widely acclaimed as Beethoven's true heir, not because he imitated Beethoven, but because each of his three symphonies was so strikingly original and different from anything heard before. With his brilliant and original orchestration, his fresh approach to the grand scale of the genre, and his ability to blend music and narrative, he demonstrated for subsequent composers that it was possible to follow Beethoven's spirit of originality without directly imitating him. The symphonies of Liszt and Mahler, in particular, are deeply indebted to the legacy of Berlioz.

All three of Berlioz's symphonies are programmatic to varying degrees. The first of them, the *Symphonie fantastique* of 1830, as already mentioned, is based on a detailed program of Berlioz's own invention. Inspired by the composer's infatuation with an actress named Harriet Smithson, the program relates the increasing emotional turmoil of a young musician as he realizes the woman he loves is spurning him (see Primary Evidence: Berlioz's Program for the *Symphonie fantastique*). The emotional trajectory of the symphony is thus almost the reverse of Beethoven's Ninth. Beethoven's symphony moves from a turbulent first movement to a joyous finale; the *Symphonie fantastique*, in contrast, moves from a joyous first movement, which evokes of the young musician's first infatuation, to a dark finale, labeled "Dream of a Witches' Sabbath," which evokes the image of the musician's beloved dancing demonically at his funeral. The sounding of the *Dies irae* ("Day of Wrath") from the well-known plainchant Mass for the Dead within the finale serves as a dark counterpoint to Beethoven's theme for the vocal setting of Schiller's "Ode to Joy" in the finale of the Ninth. Instead of a vision of heaven, we are given a vision of hell and the triumph of evil.

Not everyone found Berlioz's program for his *Symphonie fantastique* helpful. Robert Schumann, in an otherwise favorable review of the work, argued that the movement titles alone would have been sufficient, and that "word of mouth would have served to hand down the more circumstantial account, which would certainly arouse interest because of the personality of the composer, who lived through the events of the symphony himself." German listeners in particular, Schumann argued, disliked having their thoughts "so rudely directed," all the more so given their "delicacy of feeling and aversion to personal revelation." But Berlioz, Schumann rationalized, "was writing primarily for his French compatriots, who are not greatly impressed by refinements of modesty. I can imagine them, leaflet in hand, reading and applauding their countryman who has depicted it all so well; the music by itself does not interest them."[11]

PRIMARY EVIDENCE — Berlioz's Program for the *Symphonie fantastique*

Berlioz was for many years adamant about the importance of the program: "At concerts where this symphony is to be performed," he once declared, "it is essential that this program be distributed in advance in order to provide an overview of the dramatic structure of this work." The program exists in two versions. The one given here is from the published score of 1845; a later edition presents the entire story as an opium-inspired dream that is part of an unsuccessful suicide attempt. In the end, however, Berlioz rejected both programs, wearied no doubt by the lavish attention given his prose at the expense of his music. The frequent ellipses in the program are Berlioz's own. The *ranz des vaches* (Example 14–1) is a shepherd's call, frequently associated with reed instruments in orchestral compositions of this era. The *Dies irae* in the last movement is a chant sung during the Mass for the Dead. The text is apocalyptic. It is safe to say that every member of Berlioz's original audience would have recognized this melody (and its implicit text) at once.

---

(1) Dreams—Passions. The author imagines that a young musician, afflicted with that malady of the spirit called the *vague des passions* by one well-known writer, sees for the first time a woman who embodies all the charms of the ideal being of his dreams, and he falls hopelessly in love with her. By bizarre peculiarity, the image of the beloved always presents itself to the soul of the artist united with a musical idea that incorporates a certain character he bestows to her, passionate but at the same time noble and shy.

This melodic image and its source pursue him ceaselessly as a double *idée fixe*. This is the reason for the persistent appearance, in every movement of the symphony, of the melody that begins the opening Allegro. The transition from this state of melancholic reverie, interrupted by a few spasms of unfounded joy, to one of delirious passion, with its animations of fury, jealousy, its return to tenderness, its tears, its religious consolations—this is the subjection of the first movement.

(2) A Ball. The artist finds himself in the most varied situations in the middle of the tumult of a party, in the peaceful contemplation of the beauties of nature. But everywhere—in the city, in the countryside—the cherished image of his beloved presents itself to him and troubles his spirit.

(3) Scene in the Countryside. Finding himself in the countryside one evening, he hears in the distance two shepherds conversing with each other through a *ranz des vaches*. The pastoral duet, the scenic setting, the light rustling of the trees sweetly swayed by the wind, some reasons for hope that have lately come to his knowledge—all unite to fill his heart with unaccustomed tranquility and lend a brighter color to his fancies. He reflects upon his isolation; he hopes that he will not be lonely too much longer. . . . But if she should be deceiving him! . . . This mixture of hope and fear, these thoughts of happiness troubled by certain dark presentiments constitute the subject of the Adagio movement. At the end, one of the shepherds resumes the *ranz des vaches*; the other no longer responds. . . . Distant noise of thunder . . . solitude . . . silence. . . .

(4) March to the Scaffold. Convinced that his love has been ignored, the artist poisons himself with opium. The dose of the narcotic is too weak to kill him and plunges him into a sleep accompanied by the most horrible visions. He dreams that he has killed the woman he loved, that he is condemned, led to the scaffold, and is to witness his own execution. The procession moves to the sound of a march at times somber and fierce, at times brilliant and solemn, in which the muffled noise of the heavy footsteps is followed without any transition by the noisiest outbursts. At the end of the march, the first four measures of the *idée fixe* reappear like a final thought of love interrupted by the fatal blow [of the guillotine].

(5) Dream of a Witches' Sabbath. He sees himself at the Sabbath, in the middle of a frightening troupe of ghosts, sorcerers, monsters of every kind, all gathered for his funeral rites. Strange noises, groans, bursts of laughter, distant cries to which other cries seem to respond. The beloved melody reappears, but it has lost its noble and shy character. It is nothing more than the melody of a common dance, trivial and grotesque; it is she who comes to join the Sabbath. . . . A roar of joy at her arrival. . . . She throws herself into the diabolical orgy. . . . Funeral knell, burlesque parody of the *Dies irae*. Witches' Round Dance. The dance and *Dies irae* combined.

---

11. Ibid.

PRIMARY EVIDENCE

Heinrich Heine on Berlioz, Harriet Smithson, and the *Symphonie fantastique*

The German poet Heinrich Heine (1797–1856) spent most of his adult life in self-imposed exile in Paris. His "Letters on the French Stage" (1837) include an intriguing anecdote about Berlioz. The account probably doctors the truth—no evidence indicates that Berlioz ever played the timpani in the Conservatory orchestra, for example—but it captures the spirit of the *Symphonie fantastique* and Berlioz's passion for the young woman who inspired it.

———◆———

It is a shame he has had his hair cut. I will always remember him the way I saw him for the first time, six years ago, with his antediluvian hair style, his hair standing on end, over his forehead like a forest growing on the edge of a steep cliff. The setting was the Conservatory of Music, during a performance of a great symphony by him. . . . The best part of the work was a Witches' Sabbath, in which the Devil said Mass and Catholic church music was parodied with the most terrifying, bloodiest foolery. It is a farce in which all the secret serpents that we carry in our hearts come gladly hissing up to the surface. The fellow sitting next to me, a talkative young man, pointed out to me the composer, who was sitting at the far end of the concert hall in a corner of the orchestra, playing the timpani. For the timpani is his instrument. "Do you see there in the stage-box," my neighbor said to me, "that fat Englishwoman? That is Miss Smithson; Monsieur Berlioz has been madly in love with her for three years, and it is this passion we have to thank for the symphony we are now hearing." And in fact, Miss Smithson, the famous actress from Covent Garden, was sitting in the stage-box. Berlioz kept looking directly at her, and every time their gazes met, he would pound away on his drum as if possessed. Miss Smithson has since become Madame Berlioz, and her husband has gotten his hair cut. When I heard the Symphony once again at the Conservatory this past winter, Berlioz was sitting there again as the timpanist in the back of the orchestra, the fat Englishwoman was again sitting in the stage-box, their gazes met once again . . . but this time he no longer beat the drum so furiously.

Source: Heinrich Heine, "Über die französische Bühne" (1837). Transl. MEB

Whatever their response to the program, listeners were universally impressed by the work's orchestration. More than any composer before or since, Berlioz expanded the sound of the orchestra. The instruments called for in the *Symphonie fantastique* of 1830 were extraordinary in both number and variety:

2 Flutes (one doubling on piccolo)	Timpani
2 Oboes (one doubling on English horn)	Bass drum
2 Clarinets in B♭, A, C, E♭	Snare drum
4 Bassoons	Cymbals
4 Horns in E♭, E, F, B♭, C	Bells
2 Cornets in B♭, A, G	2 Harps
2 Trumpets in C, B♭, E♭	Strings (at least 15 first violins and
3 Trombones	15 second violins, 10 violas, 11 cellos,
2 Ophicleides [a forerunner of the tuba]	and 9 double basses, according to the composer)

Berlioz's handling of the orchestra was also unusually forward looking for 1830. At the beginning of the *Symphonie fantastique*, for example, he calls for the high winds to play *pp*, then *ppp*, and then to decrescendo, presumably to an inaudible level. And in the fourth movement, the "March to the Scaffold," he introduces a brass sound never before heard in the concert hall: massive, forceful, and rhythmically charged. Berlioz also peppers his scores with instructions of a hitherto unknown specificity. In the *Symphonie fantastique*, for example, he marked exactly what kind of stick head—wood,

Harriet Smithson, the inspiration for the *idée fixe* in Berlioz's *Symphonie fantastique*. Harriet Smithson (1800–1854) was an Irish actress and a member of a theatrical troupe that performed Shakespeare's plays in English in Paris in the late 1820s. Berlioz fell in love with her and worshipped her from afar for several years before actually meeting her. They married in 1833 but separated definitively in 1844. The day after her death, Berlioz remarried.

Source: Portrait of Harriet Smithson (1800–54) (oil on canvas), French School, (19th century)/Private Collection, Lauros/ Giraudon/The Bridgeman Art Library International

leather, or felt—percussionists should use in any given passage. Previously this kind of choice would have been up to the individual performer.

The *Symphonie fantastique* is also notable for its realism: Berlioz avoids prettifying ugly or grotesque themes, representing them instead with what were, for the time, harsh-sounding musical devices. The last movement, "Dream of a Witches' Sabbath," for example, opens with an extended diminished seventh chord, a dissonance that may seem rather tame (even clichéd) today, but that would have sounded jarring at the time, conjuring for listeners a world of dark spirits. In measure 11, Berlioz briefly dispenses almost completely with triadic harmony in his effort to conjure the chaos and depravity of the imagined gathering of witches. The strings play a series of fourths mediated by an occasional third (C-F-B-E/G-C-F-B/D-G-C), rather like the tuning of a guitar, the only instrument Berlioz himself ever mastered. The moment is fleeting, but it signals the beginning of an assault on what had been the foundation of Western harmony for at least two centuries. The return of the *idée fixe*, the theme associated with the beloved, in measure 40 on the E♭ clarinet is also fittingly grotesque. The beloved, according to the program, has lost her noble and shy character and assumed the form of a witch.

THE CONCERT OVERTURE

The **concert overture** grew out of the 18th-century tradition of performing opera overtures in the concert hall, independently of the operas for which they had been written. Mozart, for example, wrote an alternate ending to his overture to *Don Giovanni* so it could be performed outside the theater. But because most listeners of the time would have known the plot of *Don Giovanni*, they associated the drama with the overture; these connections were further reinforced by the overture's use of music that appears within the opera itself.

By the early 19th century, then, the overture had emerged as a work of instrumental music in a single movement connected in some way with a known plot. Overtures themselves became increasingly dramatic, none more so than Beethoven's *Leonore* Overture no. 3 (op. 72a, 1806), one of four different overtures Beethoven wrote for his opera *Fidelio* (entitled *Leonore* in its original version). The plot of *Fidelio* involves faithful love and political injustice. Florestan, imprisoned for his political beliefs by Don Pizarro, a wicked governor, languishes in jail. To free him, his wife, Leonore, disguises herself as a man, takes the name Fidelio ("Faithful One"), and gains the confidence of Florestan's jailer. After long months of menial work, she is finally allowed to take a few scraps of bread and some water to the dungeon that houses the "most dangerous" of all the jail's prisoners, Florestan. But just as she is about to spring her husband free, Don Pizarro appears, intent on killing Florestan. Leonore intervenes and reveals her true identity. Just then an enlightened state minister arrives, saves the couple, frees the rest of the prisoners, and punishes Pizarro.

Beethoven's *Leonore* Overture no. 3 wordlessly encapsulates this drama. It opens with a darkly chromatic slow introduction in C minor before moving to a buoyant Allegro in C Major. The end of the turbulent development reenacts the arrival of the minister with an offstage trumpet fanfare, and the recapitulation provides the climactic moment of triumph. The blaze of C Major at the end of the overture reflects the release of all the political prisoners.

Why did Beethoven reject this overture? It is certainly one of his most dramatic instrumental works, but this was precisely the problem. By synthesizing the emotional unfolding of the entire story—gloom, hope, despair, rescue, jubilation—Beethoven had created an overture that made the opera itself something of an anticlimax, rather like a performance of Shakespeare's *Macbeth* seemed to Ludwig Tieck after he had heard Reichardt's overture to the drama (see Primary Evidence: The Perceived Superiority of Instrumental Music in Chapter 14). The instrumental overture had outgrown its function, and Beethoven wisely published it as a separate work. In its place, he composed a much shorter, less dramatic, but effective overture for *Fidelio*, the one played before the opera in performances today.

Functionally, then, the *Leonore* Overture no. 3 had been transformed from an introduction to a dramatic work intended for performance in the opera house to a drama in its own right intended for performance in the concert hall. And it was this transformation that gave rise to a new genre: the concert overture, a single-movement work that is in some way associated with a drama, poem, place, event, or mood.

Inspired by Beethoven's example, other composers began writing overtures expressly for the concert hall. Felix Mendelssohn wrote his *Overture to A Midsummer Night's Dream* when he was 17 years old as a stand-alone work; only later did he compose additional movements to make the work suitable as incidental music for a theatrical production of Shakespeare's play. Unlike Beethoven's *Leonore* Overture no. 3, the piece does not recount the drama in brief. Instead, Mendelssohn presents a succession of themes representing the play's main characters. The opening five measures, given entirely to the winds, draw us into the enchanted forest that is the setting for much of the play. The scurrying high-pitched figure in the strings that begins in measure 5 conjures up the kingdom of the fairies, led by Oberon and Titania, whereas the pompous theme that begins at measure 62 suits Theseus, the human ruler. The first theme in the secondary key area (beginning at measure 130) corresponds to the young humans—two women and two men—who over the course of the play, through magic, will fall in and out of love with one another in various combinations. Finally, the exposition's closing theme (beginning at measure 195) is clearly associated with the "rude mechanicals," the artisans who present a play-within-a-play. One of these artisans, Bottom the weaver, at one point in the play appears with the head of an ass, a transformation reflected in the music by an unmistakable braying sound at measure 200 and elsewhere. In the development section (beginning at measure 250), the scurrying theme associated with fairies predominates. One of the ways Mendelssohn captures the sometimes chaotic magical spirit of the midsummer night's forest here is through the simultaneous use of disparate dynamics. At measure 294, for example, he brings in the horns *fortissimo, con tutta la forza* ("with all possible force"), even as the strings and high winds maintain their elfin *pianissimo* figures.

Mendelssohn himself outlined the work's thematic associations in a remarkable letter of February 15, 1833, to his publisher. The composer is reluctant to equate the music and the stage action directly, yet he cannot deny they are connected. He coyly explains his music by altering the sequence of events in the drama to correspond with the sequence of events in his composition. Shakespeare's drama does not open with the fairies, for example, but rather with a scene at the court of Theseus.

CD9, Track 6
MENDELSSOHN
*Overture to A Midsummer
Night's Dream*
Score Anthology II/119

> It is not possible for me to indicate the course of ideas in this composition for the printed concert program, for this course of ideas *is* my overture. The piece is nevertheless closely associated with the play, and thus it might perhaps be quite appropriate to indicate to the public the main events of the drama, to remind them of Shakespeare's play. . . . I believe it would suffice to recall how the elf-royalty, Oberon and Titania, appear with all their train throughout the play, at one moment here, at another there; then comes Duke Theseus of Athens, who goes hunting in the forest with his bride-to-be; then the two pairs of tender lovers, who lose and find one another; and finally the troop of clumsy, coarse tradesmen, who pursue their heavy-handed amusements; then the elves once again, who tease all of them—it is precisely out of all this that the work is constructed. When at the end everything is resolved and the main characters depart fortunate and happy, the elves follow them, bless the house, and disappear as the morning dawns. So ends the play, and my overture too. I would prefer it if on the printed program you would summarize only this content and said nothing further about my music, so that it can simply speak for itself, if it is good; and if it is not good, then no explanation will help at all.[12]

Mendelssohn, in other words, admits to broad parallels between his music and the play, but not to explicit thematic connections. His ambivalence reflects the feelings of many composers about the question of "meaning" in their music. Clearly, Mendelssohn wanted his listeners to associate his overture with Shakespeare's play, but he also wanted them to accept his composition on its own terms, as music. Whatever Mendelssohn felt, audiences liked to hear explicit thematic connections of the kind he tried to play down. An *Overture to A Midsummer Night's Dream*, it seems, is easier to focus on than the same work with an abstract title like Overture in E Major.

Mendelssohn wrote many other popular concert overtures in addition to the *Overture to A Midsummer Night's Dream*. These include *The Hebrides* (also known as *Fingal's Cave*), which conjures up a landscape off the Scottish coast; *Calm Seas and a Prosperous Voyage*, which is based on a poem of the same title by Goethe; and *The Fair Melusine*, which reflects a folktale about a mermaid who takes on human form.

---

12. Felix Mendelssohn Bartholdy, *Reisebriefe aus den Jahren 1830 bis 1832*, ed. Paul Mendelssohn Bartholdy (Leipzig: Hermann Mendelssohn, 1869), p. 136, letter to his family of March 29, 1831. Transl. MEB

COMPOSER PROFILE   Hector Berlioz *(1803–1869)*

Berlioz, admired today as one of the most original of 19th-century composers, was an outsider almost all of his life. Born in a rural province of southern France, he had to fight to make his way in the bitterly partisan world of Parisian musical politics. By the time he won the grudging admiration of his countrymen, he was nearing the end of his life, and he was never embraced in his native France the way he was in Germany.

Berlioz's father, a physician, sent his son to Paris to study medicine. The young Hector wrote home regularly to report on the progress of his course work and just as regularly to ask for more money. In fact, however, the youth had largely given up attending classes and was busy immersing himself in the local musical scene. This charade could not continue indefinitely, of course, and Berlioz eventually found himself on his own. In 1826, he enrolled in the Paris Conservatory, whose teachers considered him talented but willful and undisciplined. Every year the Conservatory held a contest among its composition students for an award—the coveted Prix de Rome—that automatically opened doors of opportunity for the winner. Berlioz yearned for the prize but failed to win it several years in a row. Finally, in desperation, he resigned himself to writing in a style he knew the judges would like, and he won in 1830.

During this same period, Berlioz was composing the stunningly original *Symphonie fantastique*. The woman who inspired this work, the subject of its thematic *idée fixe* and the object of Berlioz's infatuation, was the Irish actress Harriet Smithson, whom he first saw in a performance of Shakespeare's *Hamlet* in 1827. He eventually met and married her, but the marriage did not last.

The Prix de Rome required winners to spend two years in Italy, and shortly after the premiere of the *Symphonie fantastique* in December 1830, Berlioz left for what he called his "exile" there. He no longer wanted to go, for it meant being away from his beloved Harriet, not to mention such important musical events as the Parisian premiere of Beethoven's Ninth Symphony. Felix Mendelssohn, also in Rome at the time, wrote home with this amusing impression of his French colleague:

> Berlioz consumes himself without a spark of talent; he gropes in the dark, thinking himself the creator of a new world. All the while he writes the most grotesque things, dreaming and thinking of nothing but Beethoven, Schiller, and Goethe. At the same time, he is possessed of boundless vanity and looks down grandly on Mozart and Haydn. . . . But just as I am about to strangle him, he waxes enthusiastic about Gluck, and on that point I must agree with him.[13]

After his return to Paris in 1832, Berlioz struggled to get a commission from the Opéra, the city's most prestigious musical institution, but the politics of artistic patronage conspired against him on repeated occasions. He turned to music journalism to supplement his income, and his reviews still make fascinating reading.

In later decades, Berlioz received greater acclaim from abroad, particularly from Germany and Russia, than at home in France. In 1843, he published a groundbreaking textbook on orchestration that took into account the new possibilities of the orchestra's changing instruments. The text would later be revised by that

The shock of the loud: Berlioz conducts (1846). Like any caricature, this one builds on an element of truth. Audiences in the 19th century found Berlioz's orchestras enormous, his music staggeringly loud. Berlioz was also among the first virtuoso conductors. Until roughly 1830, ensembles had been led by the principal first violinist, the concertmaster, or by a keyboard player seated at the piano or harpsichord. By 1850, the conductor had come to be seen as a true interpreter of the music at hand, not merely as someone who kept the ensemble together. Weber, Mendelssohn, and Ludwig Spohr, like Berlioz, were esteemed as both conductors and composers.

Source: Andreas Geiger (1765–1856), A Concert of Hector Berlioz (1803–1869) in 1846, engraving/Musée de l'Opéra, Paris, France/ The Bridgeman Art Library.

---

13. Mendelssohn, *Briefe an deutsche Verleger* (Berlin: de Gruyter, 1968), pp. 25–6, letter of 15 February 1833. Transl. MEB

other 19th-century master of orchestration, Richard Strauss, and is still in use in many music conservatories.

PRINCIPAL WORKS

SYMPHONIES AND CONCERT OVERTURES Berlioz's three major symphonies rank among the greatest works of their kind in the 19th century. Each is utterly different from the other, but all have a literary foundation: The *Symphonie fantastique* (1830) follows a prose program of Berlioz's own invention. *Harold en Italie* (1834) draws on Byron's epic poem *Childe Harold's Pilgrimage*, and *Roméo et Juliette* (1839) is based on Shakespeare's *Romeo and Juliet*. It was the novelty and variety of these various approaches to the genre that led Berlioz's German contemporaries to hail him as Beethoven's true successor.

The works of a variety of authors, from Shakespeare to Sir Walter Scott, inspired Berlioz's concert overtures. These include *Waverly* (1828), *Les francs-juges* (1828), *King Lear* (1831), *Rob Roy* (1832), and *Le Corsaire* (1844). Building on Beethoven's accomplishments in this genre, Berlioz's overtures are important forerunners to the symphonic poems that Liszt and Richard Strauss would compose later in the century.

OPERAS Although admired, Berlioz's two operas have never achieved widespread popularity. *Benvenuto Cellini* (1838) traces the life of the celebrated Renaissance sculptor. *Les Troyens* (The Trojans, 1859) is based on the story of the Trojan War. Only the second half of this work was ever performed during Berlioz's lifetime; the complete opera was not produced in its original French until 1920, and then not in Paris, but in Rouen.

VOCAL MUSIC Berlioz wrote several unstaged vocal works that are difficult to classify but always dramatic in spirit. These include the massive *Requiem* (1837), which calls for antiphonal orchestras and choruses; *L'Enfance du Christ* (The Infancy of Christ, 1854), a "sacred trilogy"; and *La Damnation de Faust* (1846), an *opéra en concert* (concert opera). *Lélio, or the Return to Life* (1831), a sequel to the *Symphonie fantastique*, is a unique mixture of orchestral music, chorus, song, and melodrama. In 1841, building on the tradition of the French chanson, Berlioz invented a new genre with his song cycle for voice and orchestra, *Les nuits d'été* (Summer Nights, 1841).

KEY DATES IN THE LIFE OF BERLIOZ

1803	Born at Côte-Saint-André (southern France) on December 11.
1821	Goes to Paris to study medicine so he might follow in the footsteps of his father, a physician.
1826	Abandons medicine and enrolls in the Paris Conservatory, where he is as unhappy with the instructors as they are with him.
1826–1829	Applies unsuccessfully for the coveted Prix de Rome; all three of his compositions for this competition are rejected.
1830	Wins the Prix de Rome with a more conventional composition.
1833	Marries Harriet Smithson, an Irish actress whom he has worshipped from a safe distance for many years and who was the inspiration for his *Symphonie fantastique* (1830). The marriage is a disaster, however, and ends in separation in 1844. He remarries after her death in 1854.
1842	Makes the first of several successful tours of Germany, where his symphonies are greeted with greater enthusiasm than in France.
1843	Publishes his *Treatise on Instrumentation and Orchestration*, a work that would subsequently go through many editions and be translated into many languages.
1852	Appointed librarian of the Paris Conservatory, an honorary post but one that acknowledges his place in the musical world of France.
1869	Dies in Paris on March 8.

Over the course of the 19th century, a great many commentators created programs for instrumental works that had none, often in an attempt to make the difficult and highly abstract art of instrumental music more approachable to untrained listeners. The need for such clues was driven at least in part by the growing formal, harmonic, and rhythmic complexity of the music. Listeners perplexed by Mahler's First Symphony in the last decade of the 19th century, for example, accused the composer of having suppressed the work's program (which in fact is precisely what he had done). The work would have been far more intelligible, they insisted, had its story been revealed to them.

COMPOSER PROFILE   Felix Mendelssohn *(1809–1847)*

Mendelssohn was born into a prominent family whose fame was unconnected to music. His grandfather, Moses Mendelssohn, was one of the leading philosophers of his day, and his father, Abraham Mendelssohn, was a very successful banker in Berlin. Abraham converted to Christianity and added "Bartholdy" to the family's name, hence the designation Felix Mendelssohn Bartholdy (often with an erroneous hyphen).

Felix was the greatest child prodigy of his age, both as a composer and as a pianist. The prestigious Singakademie of Berlin performed his setting of the 19th Psalm in 1819, and the young child traveled across Europe in much the same way as Mozart had half a century before. By the time he was 17, he had already written the Octet for strings op. 20 and the *Overture to a Midsummer Night's Dream*, op. 21. He also excelled as a conductor. In 1828, on the hundredth anniversary of its premiere, he led a hugely successful performance of J. S. Bach's *Saint Matthew Passion*, a then-forgotten work he had helped rediscover.

Mendelssohn was closely attached to his sister, Fanny (1805–1847), who was a talented pianist and composer in her own right. After her marriage in 1829, she published several books of songs and many short piano pieces under the name Fanny Mendelssohn Hensel. She shared her brother's interest in the music of J. S. Bach and remained his closest musical confidante until her sudden death at the age of 41. Biographers have speculated, in fact, that her brother's intense grief hastened his own sudden demise later that same year.

Mendelssohn's death occasioned prolonged public mourning across Europe, and numerous writers speculated on the bleak future of music without him. Within a decade, however, he had become the favorite target of ridicule by musicians who thought of themselves as progressive. To these figures, particularly Wagner, Mendelssohn represented the most conservative elements of music. In the 1930s and 1940s, Mendelssohn became the object of vicious attacks from Germany's Nazi regime because of his Jewish ancestry.

Mendelssohn's music can seem almost too beautiful at times, too effortless. And against the paradigm of Beethoven and other 19th-century composers, Mendelssohn might appear more a member of the establishment, both personally and professionally. He never rebelled against anything and was the darling of both Prussian and English royalty, and in this respect he does not fit the popular image of the Romantic composer. Yet his private letters reveal a far more complex personality than is generally recognized.

PRINCIPAL WORKS

SYMPHONIES AND OTHER ORCHESTRAL WORKS

Mendelssohn wrote several symphonies for strings in his youth and arranged one of them for full orchestra in 1824 as his First Symphony, op. 11. Later, however, he repudiated this and several other works in the genre, including his *Reformation* Symphony (1832), whose finale includes the melody from Martin Luther's famous hymn "A Mighty Fortress Is Our God." Mendelssohn allowed only a few performances of the *Italian* Symphony in the mid-1830s, which has since become his most popular,

Felix Mendelssohn. In contrast to the many likenesses of Beethoven that portray him as a fiery individualist, this image of Mendelssohn done by J. W. Childe in 1829 portrays the composer as a gentleman. Mendelssohn's lack of personal rebelliousness has contributed to his image as a conservative, not willing to assault tradition in the manner of his near-contemporaries Berlioz, Liszt, and Wagner. Mendelssohn is shown here on the first of his ten trips to England, where he was idolized both as a composer and as a conductor.

Source: Ruth Schacht/Art Resource/Bildarchiv Preussischer Kulturbesitz and appears never to have been completely satisfied with it. The *Scottish* Symphony, op. 56 (1842), was the one work in the genre Mendelssohn allowed to be published. (Although first performed as a symphony, the *Lobgesang* of 1840 was later redesignated a symphony-cantata.)

The concert overtures have fared even better with audiences than the symphonies. Three of them—*The Hebrides* (also known as *Fingal's Cave*), *A Midsummer Night's Dream*, and *The Fair Melusine*—are staples of the orchestral repertory today. In these works, Mendelssohn combined programmatic elements with symphonic writing on a smaller scale, and his contributions in this area exercised a profound influence on later composers of symphonic poems. The Violin Concerto in E minor, op. 64, remains a touchstone of the repertory. The two piano concertos, widely performed in their time, have not fared as well.

CHAMBER WORKS   Aside from the youthful Octet op. 20, Mendelssohn's chamber music—piano trios, string quartets, and string quintets—is not performed as much as it deserves. The early string quartets, opp. 12 and 13, are among the few works of their kind written under the direct influence of Beethoven's late quartets. The later chamber music, in particular, features a distinctly personal idiom that integrates counterpoint and lyricism.

PIANO WORKS   The 48 *Lieder ohne Worte* ("Songs without Words"), published in eight separate books, were enormously successful in their time. The piano sonatas and various other miniatures combine brilliance with substance.

VOCAL MUSIC   The oratorios *Paulus* (1836) and *Elijah* (1846) enjoyed extraordinary popularity in the 19th century, particularly in England. Choral societies there were quick to add these works to their repertories alongside the oratorios of Handel, which served as Mendelssohn's principal model in the genre. The choral writing, inspired by Bach as well as Handel, is among the most powerful and moving of the entire 19th-century repertory. Mendelssohn also wrote many works for a cappella chorus, some of them in a deliberately archaic style, evoking the music of earlier composers such as Palestrina and Bach.

KEY DATES IN THE LIFE OF MENDELSSOHN

1809	Born February 3 in Hamburg.
1819	Becomes a member of the Berlin Singakademie; its director, Carl Friedrich Zelter, introduces the young Mendelssohn to Goethe in 1821, initiating a friendship that would continue until the poet's death in 1832.
1826	Composes his *Overture to A Midsummer Night's Dream*.
1828	Conducts Bach's *Saint Matthew Passion* with the Berlin Singakademie on March 11, almost exactly a hundred years after the work's premiere; the work, essentially unknown to 19th-century audiences, sparks renewed interest in Bach's music.
1829	Makes the first of ten trips to England, where he becomes the most beloved composer of his generation, helped in part by the favor and patronage of Queen Victoria and Prince Albert.
1836	Becomes conductor of the Leipzig Gewandhaus Orchestra, which he builds into the leading orchestra of Europe. Also initiates a series of "historical concerts" with music by composers of previous generations.
1843	Helps establish the Leipzig Conservatory, which soon becomes the leading institution of its kind in Germany and second in prestige only to the Paris Conservatory.
1847	Dies in Leipzig after a brief illness on November 4.

THE CONCERTO

The 19th century was the age of the great instrumental composer-virtuoso. The violinist Niccolò Paganini (1782–1840), Joseph Joachim (1831–1907), and Pablo de Sarasate (1844–1908) all wrote concertos for themselves, as did the pianists Beethoven, Chopin, Mendelssohn, Clara Schumann, Brahms, Liszt, and Grieg. As with Vivaldi and Mozart, the concerto provided the ideal vehicle for a composer-performer to show off his or her talents in both fields at once.

Most 19th-century concertos maintained the three-movement fast-slow-fast format of the Classical era. With the decline of basso continuo in the late 18th century, however, the role of the soloist in the concerto changed significantly. No longer obligated to support or play along with the ensemble during tutti sections, the soloist instead waited in silence before making a grand entrance. Unlike the symphony and concert overture, the concerto remained a mostly nonprogrammatic genre, at least on the surface. Few composers openly associated their concertos with extramusical ideas, yet audiences could not help but hear drama in the interplay between soloist and orchestra.

The interplay between soloist and orchestra in the second movement of Beethoven's Fourth Piano Concerto, op. 58, illustrates this kind of drama quite vividly. The soloist and the orchestra—limited in this movement to the strings—engage in an extended dialogue that moves from confrontation to resolution. The strings open with a loud unison figure characterized by dotted rhythms and staccato articulation. The piano responds with an utterly different kind of statement, a lyrical, hymnlike theme that Beethoven marks *molto cantabile*. To underscore the timbral difference between soloist and orchestra, Beethoven calls on the pianist to play the entire movement *una corda* ("one string")—that is, using one of the foot pedals to shift the entire keyboard action so the hammers strike only a single string. Orchestra and soloist alternately present their respective ideas. Neither gives ground at first, but the tutti eventually diminishes in volume. At measure 47, the soloist moves on to a new idea, a soaring melody that sounds very much like a singer's aria. This gives way to a dramatic series of simultaneous runs and trills in an extended (and written-out) cadenza. Beethoven asks the soloist to increase the sound first to two strings, then to the full complement of three, before receding back to the original una corda sound. (This effect is no longer possible on the modern piano, so that the performer must simulate the changes in tone.)

CD10, Track 1
BEETHOVEN
Piano Concerto no. 4, op. 58
Score Anthology II/120

PRIMARY EVIDENCE   Mendelssohn in London

Thanks in part to the patronage of the royal family, Mendelssohn enjoyed immediate and great success in England. Indeed, the popularity of his music endured there long after it had begun to wane on the Continent. Mendelssohn's letters, which have yet to be published in their entirety, offer fascinating insights into the composer's thoughts and 19th-century musical life in general. Here, in a letter to his mother, written from London in 1842, Mendelssohn describes his hectic but exhilarating life in the British capital.

◆━━━━━━◆━━━━━━◆

If today's letter seems rather tired and creaky, then it reflects my feelings. They really have been driving me a little too hard here. When I was playing the organ the other day in Christ Church in Newgate Street, I thought for a moment I was going to suffocate, so great was the commotion and pressing of the crowd around the organ bench. And a few days after that, when I had to play before an audience of 3,000 in Exeter Hall, they cheered me with "Hurrahs" and waved their handkerchiefs and stamped their feet until the whole place rang with it. I didn't notice any problems at the time, but the next morning my head felt dizzy, as though I had not slept. And then there is the pretty and charming Queen Victoria, who is so girlishly and shyly friendly and polite, who speaks German so well, and who knows all my things so well—the four books of *Songs without Words*, and those with words, and the Symphony, and the *Song of Praise*. Yesterday evening I was at the Palace, where the Queen and Prince Albert were almost entirely alone by themselves. She sat down beside the piano while I played to her seven *Songs without Words*, then the Serenade, then two fantasias on *Rule Britannia* and on Lützow's *wilde Jagd* and *Gaudeamus igitur*. The last was a bit difficult, but I could hardly decline, and because she had given me these themes I could therefore play them. There is also a beautiful, magnificent gallery in Buckingham Palace, where she drank tea and where there is a picture of two pigs by Paul Potter, and several others that struck me as not bad at all. Also, the people here like my A-minor Symphony [the *Italian*] very much. They welcomed us with a pleasant friendliness and thoughtfulness that surpassed anything I have ever experienced in the way of hospitality. At times all this makes my head spin and makes me a bit giddy, and I have to take myself firmly in hand so as not to lose my composure.

Source: Mendelssohn, letter to his mother, London, June 21, 1842. Transl. MEB

At least some listeners have interpreted this movement as a musical reenactment of part of the myth of Orpheus and Euridice. According to this idea, measures 1–5 and 14–18 represent Orpheus descending into the underworld and confronting Charon; measures 19–46 represent him charming Charon with music; measures 47–54 represent him crossing the river Styx to the underworld to retrieve Euridice; measures 55–63 (the solo cadenza) represent his doubts about whether Euridice is still behind him as he ascends back to the world of the living; and finally, the empty-sounding final cadence reflects his despair at the second loss of his beloved. Although Beethoven himself left no direct evidence to support this interpretation, accounts by friends and acquaintances suggest that it is at least plausible. And as a painting he commissioned of himself suggests (see "Beethoven as Orpheus"), Beethoven apparently did think of himself as a modern-day Orpheus.

In its breadth of sound and susceptibility to programmatic interpretation, this movement also illustrates the growing influence of the symphony on the concerto in the 19th century. A result of this trend was to increase the role of the orchestra without diminishing the demand for soloistic virtuosity. This is evident in Beethoven's four other piano concertos, his Violin Concerto, op. 61, and his "Triple Concerto" for cello, violin, and piano, op. 56. The trend toward symphonic scale and tone would continue throughout the first half of the 19th century in the concertos of Felix Mendelssohn (two for piano, one for violin), Robert Schumann (one each for piano, violin, and cello), and Johannes Brahms (two for piano, one for violin, one for violin and cello together). Indeed, Brahms's First Piano Concerto, op. 15 (1854) started life as a symphony; only after he began to expand on its basic ideas did Brahms decide to fashion it into a concerto. Less symphonic in tone but no less impressive in scope and scale are the concertos by Frédéric Chopin (two for piano), Niccolò Paganini (four for violin), and Ignaz Moscheles (eight for piano), which on the whole tend to distinguish more clearly between the roles of the soloist as virtuoso and the orchestra as an accompanimental ensemble.

CONCLUSION

The dimensions of orchestral music expanded in almost every conceivable respect in the first half of the 19th century. Orchestras grew in size and volume, symphonies and concertos became longer, and instrumental music in general took on the task of transcending the realm of mere sound. Beethoven's symphonies, in particular, served as a catalyst in transforming attitudes toward the scope of instrumental music, demonstrating to the listening public the ability of music to convey ideas and images without a text. Following Beethoven's lead, later composers like Mendelssohn also developed the emerging genre of the concert overture, a programmatic orchestral work in a single movement. Before 1800, vocal music had always been considered aesthetically superior to instrumental music. By the 1830s, this was no longer the case. Precisely because of its independence from words, instrumental music—above all, the symphony—was increasingly perceived as the highest form of the musical art.

Piano Music, Chamber Music, Song

In contrast to orchestral genres, the repertories of piano music, chamber music, and song occupied a more private sphere. These smaller-scale genres were performed largely in social gatherings in homes or salons rather than in public concerts. The phenomenon of the solo piano recital before a paying public did not begin to emerge until the end of the 1830s.

BEETHOVEN'S PIANO SONATAS AND STRING QUARTETS

The gulf between music written for amateurs and for professionals expanded greatly during the 19th century. Beethoven's piano sonatas, although widely admired, were repeatedly criticized during his lifetime for their technical difficulty. His Sonata in C Major, op. 53, completed in 1804 and dedicated to Count Waldstein, an early patron from Bonn, may seem relatively undemanding compared to later works, but its rapid passagework and broken octave scales put it beyond the reach of most amateurs at the time it was written. In a break with what had become standard practice in the Classical era, the exposition of the first movement modulates to the mediant (E Major, which later becomes E minor) instead of the dominant (G Major). This kind of modulation reflects the increasing chromaticism of 19th-century harmonic practice and the consequent erosion of the polarity between tonic and dominant that had characterized the formal structures of the mid- to late 18th century. Later composers working within the conventions of sonata form would often modulate to keys other than the dominant or relative major.

While looking forward in terms of its technical demands and harmonic structure, the *Waldstein* also looks back for thematic inspiration, illustrating Beethoven's ability to transform a predecessor's idea into an entirely new creation. The opening bears striking parallels to Haydn's String Quartet op. 33, no. 3 (Anthology II/105, discussed in Chapter 12). Like Haydn's quartet, Beethoven's sonata is in the key of C Major, begins with a series of repeated notes, introduces its thematic idea in fragments, and repeats this idea on a series of unusual scale degrees before finally reestablishing the tonic (measure 14). We do not know if Beethoven was conscious of these underlying connections, but we do know that he studied the works of Haydn and Mozart carefully, even copying out entire quartets or quartet movements on occasion to better understand their craft of composition.

CD9, Track 7
BEETHOVEN
Piano Sonata in C Major, op. 53
("Waldstein")
Score Anthology II/121

CD10, Track 2
BEETHOVEN
String Quartet in B♭ Major, op. 130
Score Anthology II/122

Like his piano sonatas, Beethoven's string quartets also reflect the trend toward increasing technical difficulty. Good amateurs could readily have performed the six quartets he published as op. 18 in 1801, but not the three substantially longer quartets he published as op. 59 in 1808. Beethoven's late quartets—opp. 127, 130, 132, and 135, composed between 1824 and 1826—are among the most challenging works he wrote in any genre, for performers and listeners alike. Contemporary listeners had never heard anything quite like the opening of the Quartet in B♭ Major, op. 130. The music is full of unexpected starts and stops. What appears at first to be a slow introduction, for example, turns out to be an integral part of the sonata-form exposition. And instead of modulating to the expected dominant (F) in the exposition, Beethoven dramatically overshoots it (measure 51) and lands instead in the unlikely key of G♭ (♭VI, measure 55).

Subsequent movements are similarly full of formal and technical surprises. The second movement scherzo, marked Presto, runs less than two minutes in many performances, even those that observe all of Beethoven's repeat signs. (The first movement, in contrast, usually runs between 12 and 13 minutes.) The third movement, marked Andante con moto, ma non troppo, is a study in equal-voiced texture. In the opening measures, for example, melody and accompaniment are nearly indistinguishable. The fourth movement, a German dance (Alla danza tedesca), also features unusual textures, especially toward the end (measures 129–140). Here the melodic line bounces from instrument to instrument, each playing solo but completing together a continuous line of melody. Some later writers have compared this technique to pointillism, a painting technique developed in the late 19th century in which recognizable images are created from a pattern of tiny, discrete dots of color.

The fifth movement of this quartet, labeled "Cavatina," is of particular interest. In Italian opera, **cavatina** designated any introductory aria sung by a main character. In Germany, however, the term was reserved largely for simple arias of an introspective quality, free of virtuosic display, and it is clearly this kind of cavatina that Beethoven had in mind. It is in effect an aria without words, with the first violin openly imitating a solo voice. Many composers had written arialike string quartet movements before; what makes this one different is the interplay of the ensemble as a whole. The other three voices create a texture that is at once homophonic and contrapuntal. The soloist, moreover, "sings" in a voice that is almost sobbing, choking—as Beethoven marks it, *beklemmt* ("as if caught in a vise"). Violinists produce this effect by reducing pressure on the bow, letting it ride lightly across the string. The resulting tone is neither full nor beautiful, but nonetheless dramatically moving.

The original finale of op. 130 was an enormous fugue that Beethoven later published as a separate work with its own opus number, the *Grosse Fuge* ("Great Fugue," op. 133). This work has justly been called Beethoven's equivalent to *The Art of Fugue*, Johann Sebastian Bach's compilation of fugues on a single theme. It is no coincidence that it should have originally been intended to provide the capstone to a work so thoroughly occupied with issues of texture. In its place, Beethoven wrote a shorter finale in which an apparently simple opening, based on a kind of folklike dance, becomes increasingly complex, with a remarkable multiplicity of textures.

SONG

Like many of his later compositions, Beethoven's String Quartet op. 130 was not particularly well received at first. Most contemporary performers and listeners preferred less demanding music. This explains in part the enormous popularity of the genre of song for solo voice and piano in the first half of the 19th century.

German composers cultivated this genre with such intensity that it is often designated by its German name, the **Lied** (pronounced "leet"; the plural, **Lieder,** is pronounced like the English word "leader"). Several important factors converged to give the Lied its newfound prominence:

- The rise of German poetry
- The growing availability of the piano
- The idealization of domesticity and the family

For much of the 18th century, German was not widely considered a literary or cultured language, not even in Germany itself. Frederick II ("The Great"), king of Prussia from 1740 until 1786, conducted official business in French, not German. Beginning around 1750, however, the works of several remarkable poets and playwrights began to change attitudes toward the German language. These writers included Gotthold Ephraim Lessing (1729–1781), Friedrich Klopstock (1724–1803), Johann Wolfgang Goethe (1749–1832), and Friedrich Schiller (1759–1805). Goethe, who has been called the Shakespeare of the German language, played an especially important role in establishing German as a literary language. Schiller was almost as prominent an influence, and the works of the two together galvanized German letters. Composers were drawn to their poetry as a source of texts to be set to music.

The second factor, the growing availability of the piano, reflects advances in piano design and production in the early decades of the 19th century. These advances substantially reduced manufacturing costs, making the instrument increasingly affordable to middle-class families (see Focus: The Piano). With its varied shades of dynamics, wide register, and resonant tone, the piano was the ideal instrument to accompany the voice.

The idealization of domesticity and the family, in turn, provided the perfect context in which songs for a single voice and piano could be performed and heard. The period of European history between 1815 and 1848—that is, between the Congress of Vienna and the Revolutions of 1848—was one of relative stability. After the upheavals of the Napoleonic Wars, European society seemed happy to turn away from heroic, revolutionary ideologies and withdraw into itself. The family became a new center of attention, idealized as a sort of miniature society in its own right. Aesthetic emphasis in the late 1810s and 1820s shifted from the grandiose to the intimate, increasing the appeal of domestic genres of music like the Lied, which lent itself to performance at home. The result was a growing demand for new songs.

Performed by only two musicians in a room of modest size before a select audience, the song is a genre in which the slightest inflections of harmony, dynamics, and register can have great effect. In contrast to a monumental genre like the symphony, the song calls for heightened sensitivity from composers, performers, and listeners. Its popularity reflects a belief that simplicity can be profound, that a universe of emotions can be encapsulated within a work of small dimensions.

From the perspective of form, songs generally fall into one of three categories: strophic, modified strophic, or through composed. In *strophic form*, the simplest of the three, each verse (strophe) of a poem is set to the same music. In **modified strophic form,** as in a variation on a theme, the music varies from strophe to strophe—with melodic embellishment, for example, or alteration of texture or harmony—but remains otherwise recognizably the same. A *through-composed* song, in contrast, has no recognizable pattern of repetition, and often no repetition at all.

Song composers in the 19th century were judged according to the extent to which their music enhanced the words of the poems they set. The repetitive rhythmic

FOCUS   The Piano

The piano grew in almost every respect over the course of the 19th century. By 1900, its compass had increased from five octaves to the now-standard 88 keys. A substantial increase in the size of the frame and various improvements in escapement action made it possible for a single instrument to combine both lightness and power. Leather hammer coverings were eventually replaced with felt, producing a thicker, heavier sound. Improvements in damper pedals and the addition of a shifting pedal to allow hammers to strike only one string for each note (una corda) increased timbral variety. The introduction of a one-piece cast-iron frame increased both durability and sound volume.

When pianos began to be mass produced in the second quarter of the 19th century, their cost dropped, and by the 1850s they had become standard fixtures in middle- and upper-class homes. Every home with any pretensions to culture had one, and every daughter in such a home was almost certain to have been subjected to piano lessons at some point in her upbringing. As a result, the market for piano teachers and piano music was enormous. The popularity of the instrument also made it feasible for composers (and publishers) to disseminate music in other genres—operas, symphonies, concertos, and even string quartets—in the form of piano reductions.

Piano manufacturing. The mass manufacture of pianos in the 19th century made the instruments considerably more affordable. The upright models being assembled here in the Parisian piano factory of Pleyel around 1845 were designed to fit into the smaller spaces of middle-class homes. The contrast of scale with 18th-century methods of instrument production is striking (see illustration, "Interior of a brass instrument workshop in Paris, ca. 1760," in Chapter 12).
Source: Image Works/Mary Evans Picture Library Ltd.

CD10, Tracks 5–7
SCHUBERT
Erlkönig, Prometheus,
and Wanderers Nachtlied
Score Anthology II/123

insistence of Franz Schubert's *Erlkönig* ("Elf-king") reflects the content and iambic meter of Goethe's strophic poem. Schubert, however, goes beyond this rhythmic device to magnify the poem's emotional force in a setting that hovers somewhere between through-composed and modified-strophic form. *Erlkönig* tells a chilling tale of a father riding home with his feverish son in his arms. The boy hears the Elf-king calling to him with seductive blandishments and cries out in fear as his father tries vainly to calm him. When they arrive, the boy is dead in his father's arms. The poem has four voices—a narrator, the Elf-king, the boy, and the father—and Schubert gives each of them a distinctive character through the strategic use of key, mode, texture, and register.

Free verse, as is found in a poem like Goethe's *Prometheus*, calls for a flexible musical structure. Schubert's through-composed setting emphasizes the declamatory tone and irregular rhythms of the poetry. The music and the text are equally dramatic. In Greek myth it was Prometheus who, against the will of Zeus, gave fire to humanity.

Music in the home. The private home was ideally suited for piano music and song. Two technological factors combined to foster domestic music making: the declining cost of pianos and the declining cost of printed music. This illustration, from the title page to Wilhelm Heinrich Riehl's anthology entitled *Hausmusik* ("House Music") of 1856, exemplifies the culture of domestic music making in this era. The grandmother prefers the warmth of the tile oven, but everyone else (including the dogs) gathers around the piano. Music— represented by the piano—is as much a focal point of family activity as the hearth or the dinner table visible in the background. Buoyed by the demand this cultural phenomenon created, the publishers of accompanied songs and short, easy piano pieces flourished.

Source: Courtesy of the Library of Congress

As punishment for this transgression, Prometheus was chained to a rock, where every day an eagle came to eat out his liver, which grew back every night. In the poem the unrepentant Prometheus hurls scorn and defiance on Zeus. Schubert's setting conveys this defiance with the dotted rhythms of the piano introduction. The passages marked "Recit." (for recitative) are to be sung in the relatively free, declamatory style characteristic of operatic recitative.

A brief poem of a single strophe like Goethe's *Wanderers Nachtlied* ("Wanderer's Night Song") elicited from Schubert an intense attention to detail. The limited melodic motion and straightforward rhythms of the opening capture the sense of calm that pervades the text ("Above all summits is calm . . .") and make the subsequent syncopation (measures 5–8) all the more pronounced. The repeated horn call-like figures in measures 9–13 take on added importance through repetition. In so brief a setting, every gesture carries added weight. Even the one-measure epilogue in the piano (measure 14) resonates with significance, given the remarkably small scale of this work.

Schubert also helped establish the genre of the **song cycle,** a collection of songs ordered in such a way as to convey at least the outline of a story or idea. His *Die schöne Müllerin* ("The Beautiful Daughter of the Miller"), to texts by Wilhelm Müller, is a series of 20 songs that tell the story of a journeyman miller who falls in love with his master's daughter but is spurned and eventually commits suicide. Other cycles, such as Robert Schumann's *Dichterliebe,* op. 48, a setting of poems by Heinrich Heine, are more loosely structured in terms of text but carefully organized in terms of tonality and other musical parameters.

Different composers were often drawn to the same text, bringing to it a variety of interpretations that reflect changing styles and expanding musical options. For example, Johann Friedrich Reichardt's late-18th-century setting of Goethe's poem "Kennst du das Land?" ("Do You Know the Land?) under the title "Italien" (Anthology II/114, discussed in Chapter 13) is relatively straightforward, with a limited melodic range and folklike diatonicism. Later settings—like those by Schubert, Schumann, and Hugo Wolf—have more intricate vocal lines, richer textures, and increasingly

CD10, Tracks 8–10
SCHUBERT, ROBERT SCHUMANN, AND WOLF
Settings of Goethe's Kennst du das Land?
Score Anthology II/124

chromatic harmonies that reflect the 19th century's ever-expanding harmonic vocabulary. Wolf's setting, in particular, illustrates the move away from the aesthetic of simplicity among composers of the latter part of the 19th century. His "Mignon," composed in 1888, focuses on the second part of each strophe ("Kennst du es [ihn] wohl? Dahin!"), initiated by the accompaniment (marked *Belebt*, in measures 21, 58, and 99), to provide structural background through repetition and melodic climax. The first half of each strophe is more freely composed, with multiple changes of tempo, key, and dynamic level, building in intensity until the final strophe, in which Mignon pleads with Wilhelm, "Dahin! Dahin geht unser Weg! o Vater, lass uns ziehn!" (The version included on the CD set is Wolf's second of two orchestrations [1893] of "Mignon.")

This genre was also popular in the United States, where songs for voice and piano were cultivated with special intensity. Particularly in the first half of the 19th century, Americans had relatively little opportunity to hear large professional musical ensembles, increasing the appeal of music that could be performed in a domestic setting. By far the most important 19th-century American songwriter was Stephen Foster (1826–1864). Born in Pennsylvania, he initially worked as a bookkeeper but eventually supported himself entirely from the sale of his music, the first American composer to do so. Although he spent most of his adult life in Cincinnati, Pittsburgh, and New York City, he is indelibly associated with the pre–Civil War South because of his contribution to the subgenre of the **minstrel song.** Typically performed by white performers in blackface, minstrel songs purported to represent African American slave life. There were black troupes, but most of these formed after the Civil War. A minstrel ensemble generally included a tambourine, castanets ("bones"), banjo, and fiddle. The shows often portrayed African Americans with demeaning caricatures and exaggerated dialect, helping reinforce and perpetuate racial stereotypes. Foster's songs, although sentimental (in the modern sense), usually portrayed his subjects with compassion and dignity. At least some of these songs have been performed by such 20th-century African-American singers as Paul Robeson and Roland Hayes. The minstrel tradition, moreover, to the extent that it indeed featured and popularized music with characteristically African-American syncopations, was one of the roots of ragtime, a genre that became immensely popular in the early 20th century (see Chapter 20). Among Foster's

African-American minstrels, ca. 1860s. A rare photograph of four African-American musicians from some time around the 1860s, playing the tambourine, violin, banjo, and castanets ("bones").

Source: James Bollman

COMPOSER PROFILE   Franz Schubert *(1797–1828)*

Schubert was born into a musical family and received his early training from his father (a schoolmaster), his brother, and the organist of his parish church. In 1808, he gained a place in the Imperial court choir, and with it, admission to the prestigious Imperial and Royal City College. While there, he studied composition with Antonio Salieri, the court Kapellmeister.

As a composer, Schubert followed very much in the footsteps of Mozart in Vienna: he never managed to secure a position as a composer at the court in spite of his talent; he was forced to give music lessons to make ends meet; and he died young, at the age of 31. Unlike Mozart, however, Schubert never achieved operatic success, in spite of repeated efforts to write a theater hit. His greatest talents lay in the realm of song, where he had an extraordinary ability to match texts with melodies ranging from the lyrical to the dramatic, the simple to the intricate. He found ample opportunity to perform his songs within his circle of friends, which included many poets and singers. His reputation as a songwriter attracted the attention of Beethoven and helped secure him a more or less open arrangement with the Viennese publisher Cappi and Diabelli to publish any new songs he might compose. Unfortunately, this fame and the potential for financial security it promised came only a few years before the composer's untimely death.

Schubert was incredibly prolific. In the year 1815 alone, he composed no fewer than 144 songs. In the 1820s, he turned more and more toward instrumental music, particularly piano sonatas, quartets, piano trios, and symphonies. He composed more songs toward the end of his life, however, and the publisher Haslinger issued a posthumous set under the title of *Schwanengesang* ("Swansong").

For almost a century and a half, the predominant image of Schubert was that of a dreamy, introverted Romantic who was more or less indifferent to events and persons around him and who lived only for his music. The recent work of several musicologists, however, has given us a far more complex image of the composer. Schubert was apparently an intensely sensual man of uncertain sexual orientation. He belonged to a group of artists who called themselves "The Nonsense Society" and who enjoyed playing practical jokes and creating enigmatic images of one another. One of these, a watercolor titled *Der Sündenfall* ("The Original Sin"), is reproduced here.

PRINCIPAL WORKS

SYMPHONIES   Schubert took Haydn, Mozart, and, later, Beethoven, as models for his instrumental music,

Schubert in his circle of friends. This curious watercolor—*The Original Sin* ("Der Sündenfall"), by Leopold Kupelwieser (1821)—shows a gathering of Schubert's circle of friends engaged in a pantomime. Kupelwieser, the artist, stands by the door, posing as the "Tree of Knowledge," while the poet Franz von Schober plays the part of a serpent. The couple in front of him represents Adam and Eve, who are about to be driven from the Garden of Eden. Schubert, seated at the keyboard in the foreground, has interrupted his playing to look on. But why are so few members of the audience actually looking at the pantomime? The figure opposite Schubert is the poet Joseph Spaun, who gazes intently over the piano's music stand at the composer, seemingly oblivious to the pantomime. The similarity in posture between Schubert and the dog behind him is too obvious to be coincidental, but what is its significance? On the whole, this watercolor gives a sense of the kind of obscure symbolism favored by Schubert's circle, many of whom belonged to a group that called itself the "Nonsense Society."

Source: Leopold Kupelwieser, (1796–1862) "The Family of Franz Peter Schubert (1797–1828) playing games"/Historiches Museum Der Stadt, Vienna/The Bridgeman Art Library

confessing to a friend in 1824 that he was working his way toward a large-scale symphony by composing string quartets. At the time, in fact, he had already completed the two remarkable movements of his so-called *Unfinished* Symphony in B minor (D. 759) and sketched portions of a third. In the last year of his life, he completed his Symphony in C Major (D. 944, "the *Great*"), a masterpiece that points toward a remarkably distinctive approach based less on principles of thematic manipulation and counterpoint than on melody, color, and large-scale harmonic design. Both the *Great* and the *Unfinished* remained essentially unknown, however, until their rediscovery and first public performances in 1839 and 1865, respectively. As with Mozart, we can only speculate about the kinds of works Schubert might have written had he lived longer.

STRING QUARTETS AND OTHER CHAMBER WORKS
Two of Schubert's best known chamber works incorporate slow movements related to his songs. The 12th of the 15 string quartets, D. 810, is known as *Death and the Maiden* because its slow movement is a set of variations on Schubert's own song of the same name. The *Trout* Quintet, D. 667, for violin, viola, cello, double bass, and piano, features a set of variations on his song *Die Forelle* ("The Trout"). The two late piano trios are remarkably expansive works that point toward the scope of his Symphony in C Major, "the Great."

PIANO SONATAS AND MISCELLANEOUS WORKS FOR PIANO As a composer of instrumental music, Schubert is inevitably compared to Beethoven, but Schubert's distinctive voice is abundantly evident in his works. By his late 20s—which is to say, toward the end of his life—he had even managed to achieve a distinctive approach toward sonata form, based on the large-scale juxtaposition of broad harmonic areas, as opposed to Beethoven's characteristic intensive manipulation and fragmentation of thematic ideas. The *Wanderer* Fantasy, D. 760, consists of four movements played without interruption, all of them based on a theme derived from Schubert's song of the same name. Miscellaneous works for solo piano include marches and dances, as well as the *Impromptus* and *Moments musicaux*, both of which bear a certain resemblance to song in both tone and form. Performers of four-hand piano music particularly prize Schubert's contributions to that repertory.

SONGS Had Schubert written only a handful of the hundreds of songs he did, he would still be honored as the greatest composer of all time in this genre. His choice of poetry varies widely from some of the best ever written in the German language (by Goethe and Schiller) to some that is mediocre at best. Whatever their quality, however, Schubert always managed to elevate the texts he set. A few dozen songs have emerged as perennial favorites, such as *Gretchen am Spinnrade* (set to a text from Goethe's *Faust*), *Der Lindenbaum*, *An Schwager Kronos*, and *Die Forelle*. The two song cycles, *Die schöne Müllerin* ("The Beautiful Daughter of the Miller") and *Die Wintereise* ("The Winter Journey"), have also achieved enduring popularity, in part because they combine the miniature essence of the genre with a larger scale plot. His less well-known songs and many part-songs deserve greater exposure than they have had. Recordings today group many songs together, encouraging listeners to play through many at a time. Schubert, however, intended them, like all miniatures, to be savored individually.

KEY DATES IN THE LIFE OF SCHUBERT	
1797	Born January 31 in Lichtenthal (now a part of Vienna).
1808	Becomes a singer in the Imperial court choir at Vienna; later receives composition lessons from Antonio Salieri, the court Kapellmeister.
1813	Becomes an elementary school teacher in the school his father directs.
1815	Composes the song *Erlkönig*, later published in 1821 as his op. 1. Prepublication performances establish a reputation that leads to the sale of a remarkable 300 copies within the first 18 months.
1820s	Tries repeatedly, without success, to secure a position at the court in Vienna. Meager income from private lessons and sales of his songs leaves him always on the edge of poverty.
1828	Dies in Vienna on November 19 and is buried near Beethoven, testifying to the belated recognition of his enormous talent.

CD10, Track 11
FOSTER
Beautiful Dreamer
Score Anthology II/125

most famous minstrel songs are *Oh! Susanna*, *My Old Kentucky Home*, *Camptown Races*, *Old Folks at Home*, and *Massa's in the Cold, Cold Ground*.

Foster also wrote many **parlor songs** (so called because of their place of performance, the 19th-century equivalent of today's living room). The texts are invariably strophic and sentimental, as in Foster's *Beautiful Dreamer*. The simplicity and melodic straightforwardness of these songs is very much in keeping with the aesthetic of the German Lied in the first half of the century, with its emphasis on naturalness and directness. Although billed as his last song on early editions—the work was first published after the composer's death—*Beautiful Dreamer* was in fact written in 1862, when Foster was still turning out songs at the rate of about two a month.

The ***mélodie,*** as the song was known in France, was cultivated by such composers as Berlioz, Charles Gounod (1818–1893), Jules Massenet (1842–1912), Ernest Chausson (1855–1899), and above all Gabriel Fauré (1845–1924). Berlioz's *Nuits d'été* ("Summer Nights") of 1840–1841 is the earliest French song cycle, and when the composer orchestrated the set in 1856, it marked the beginning of a new genre, the orchestral song. This type of composition would later be cultivated by the Austrian composers Gustav Mahler and Hugo Wolf, both of whom orchestrated their Lieder with piano accompaniment (as had Berlioz with *Nuits d'été*); see the discussion of Wolf's Mignon earlier).

In Russia, the most important composers of song included Mikhail Glinka (1804–1857), Alexander Dargomyzhsky (1813–1869), and Modeste Mussorgsky (1839–1881). Russian composers often incorporated folklike elements into their songs, repeating or varying slightly a folklike melody, for example, or using characteristically Russian chromatic and modal inflections. Mussorgsky's *V chetyrjokh stenakh* ("In Four Walls"), from the song cycle *Bez solnca* (1874, "Sunless"), illustrates the ever-expanding presence of chromaticism in music from the later decades of the 19th century, as well as Mussorgsky's penchant for a naturalistic kind of declamation

CD10, Track 12
MUSSORGSKY
V chetyrjokh stenakh
Score Anthology II/126

A raucous crowd at a Jenny Lind song recital, 1845. Jenny Lind (1820–1887) was widely regarded as the greatest singer of her generation. She toured the United States from 1850 to 1852, under the sponsorship of P. T. Barnum, who is better remembered today for his circuses than his concerts. Barnum billed Lind as "The Swedish Nightingale" and was undoubtedly inspired by the circuslike atmosphere of scenes like the one caricatured here, which depicts Lind in Hamburg five years before her first American tour. The few women in the audience are pointedly not applauding, whereas the men, in a frenzy not unlike that seen at rock concerts today, clamber over the seats to get closer to the stage. The caption reads: "We are blessed! We are transported! Madame Lind has made our heads spin!" According to his contract with Lind for her American tour, Barnum was to pay her $1,000 for every performance, plus expenses. But when Lind discovered the first concert grossed $28,000, she demanded $1,000 per concert, plus half the receipts over $3,000, plus expenses, and Barnum capitulated. The tour ultimately grossed more than $712,000, earning Lind $175,000. At the time, the president of the United States earned $25,000 a year.

Source: Museum of Hamburg History

that fits well with his often dark and brooding texts. (Performers who are native speakers of Russian can add an extra bite to the text with clear pronunciation of its frequently complex consonants and consonant combinations.) The recitative-like declamation elicits a chordal piano part, sprinkled with brief parallel countermelodies.

THE CHARACTER PIECE

The **character piece,** a new genre associated almost exclusively with the piano, is the instrumental counterpart to the song. A work of relatively small dimension, it seeks to portray and explore the mood or "character" of a particular person, idea, situation, or emotion. Sometimes these are specified, sometimes not. The character piece tends to be brief, sectional, and fairly simple in construction. Many follow an ABA, AAB, or ABB pattern.

By its very nature, the character piece operates on the border between programmatic and absolute music. Mendelssohn's provocatively titled *Lieder ohne Worte* ("Songs

---

PRIMARY EVIDENCE   The Salon

The salon was a vital forum for music making in the 19th century, particularly chamber music, piano music, and song. The setting—the residence of a wealthy host or hostess—was small enough to be intimate yet large enough to exercise influence on a city's broader musical life. On occasion, a host or hostess might engage a single artist to perform for the assembled guests: many contemporary accounts of Chopin's playing derive from performances he gave in salons. Countess Marie d'Agoult, Liszt's longtime companion, recalls the more common system for arranging the musical entertainment in a Parisian salon in the mid-1820s. Anyone throwing a party catered the artists, in effect, along with the food. In this case, the musical caterer was Rossini.

◆——————◆

Composers and singers still had their place apart; in spite of the eagerness to have them, they appeared in the salons only on the footing of inferiors. If someone wanted to give a fine concert, he sent to Rossini, who, for a recognized fee—it was small enough, only 1,500 francs if I recollect rightly—undertook to arrange the program and to see to its carrying out, thus relieving the master of the house of all embarrassments in the way of choice of artists, of rehearsals, and so on. The great maestro himself sat at the piano all evening accompanying the singers. Generally he added an instrumental virtuoso—Herz or Moscheles, Lafont or Bériot, Nadermann (the leading Paris harpist), Tulou (the king's first flute), or the wonder of the musical world, the little Liszt. At the appointed hour they arrived

A Parisian salon. The pianist Henri Herz (1803–1888) in a Parisian salon of the 1840s. Music (center), drawing (far left), and conversation (far right) were staples of salon gatherings.

Source: Bibliothèque nationale de France

in a body, entering by a side door; in a body they sat near the piano; and in a body they departed, after having received the compliments of the master of the house and of a few professed dilettantes. The next day the master sent Rossini his fee and believed he had discharged his obligations toward them and him.

Source: Marie d'Agoult, *Mes Souvenirs*, quoted in Arthur Loesser, *Men, Women, and Pianos: A Social History* (New York: Simon & Schuster, 1954), p. 344.

without Words,") invite—indeed challenge—performers and listeners to imagine the nature of the words that the composer so pointedly omits. Mendelssohn himself was reluctant to elaborate on these works, letting them suggest the possibility of concrete interpretation while remaining abstract. In an eloquent answer to a friend who had asked for descriptive titles for several of these pieces, Mendelssohn emphasized the inadequacy of words to capture the spirit of music:

> There is so much talk about music, and so little is said. I believe that words are not at all up to it, and if I should find that they were adequate I would stop making music altogether. People usually complain that music is so ambiguous, and what they are supposed to think when they hear it is so unclear, while words are understood by everyone. But for me it is exactly the opposite—and not just with entire discourses, but also with individual words; these, too, seem to be so ambiguous, so indefinite, in comparison with good music, which fills one's soul with a thousand better things than words. What the music I love expresses to me are thoughts not too *indefinite* for words, but rather too *definite*.
>
> Thus, I find in all attempts to put these thoughts into words something correct, but also always something insufficient, something not universal; and this is also how I feel about your suggestions [to provide titles for the individual "Songs without Words"]. This is not your fault, but rather the fault of the words, which simply cannot do any better. So if you ask me what I was thinking of, I will say: just the song as it stands there. And if I happen to have had a specific word or specific words in mind for one or another of these songs, I can never divulge them to anyone, because the same word means one thing to one person and something else to another, because only the song can say the same thing, can arouse the same feelings in one person as in another—a feeling which is not, however, expressed by the same words. . . .
>
> Will you accept this as my answer to your question? It is at any rate the only one I know how to give—though these, too, are nothing but ambiguous words.[1]

Felix's sister Fanny Mendelssohn Hensel (her married name from 1829) composed numerous character piano pieces as well, including sets of *Lieder ohne Worte*. Fanny extends the notion a step further in her Piano Trio in D minor, op. 11: she labels the third movement *Lied*, that is, a "Song without Words" for piano, violin, and cello. The single melody is treated strophically, but the composer skillfully alters it each time it returns: changing the notes (and harmonies) slightly, allowing each instrument to have a turn at it, or changing the nature of the accompaniment. This creates a satisfying, almost Classical sense of both variety and unity. The 19th-century element is the intimacy of music written for salon rather than concert hall use, to be shared among participants and a small audience in tune with the domestic spirit of the era.

Chopin's Mazurka op. 17, no. 4 (1833), is one of many 19th-century character pieces modeled on a particular dance—in this case, the mazurka, a Polish peasant dance in triple meter, often with an accent on the second or third beat. The work is harmonically ambiguous in several ways. It opens with three three-note chords that do not follow a harmonic progression in any conventional sense. The focus, instead,

CD10, Track 13
FANNY MENDELSSOHN HENSEL
Piano Trio in D minor, op. 11, Lied
Score Anthology II/127

CD10, Track 14
CHOPIN
Mazurka in A minor, op. 17, no. 4
Score Anthology II/128

1. Quotation from letter to Gerard Souchay, 15 October 1842, trans. In Oliver Strunk, *Source Readings in Music History*, rev. ed., ed. Leo Treitler (New York: Norton, 1998), pp. 120–1. Copyright 1998 W. W. Norton & Company, inc. Used by permission.

FOCUS   Overcoming Obstacles: Fanny Mendelssohn Hensel

As a composer, Fanny Mendelssohn Hensel (1805–1847) faced two major obstacles. The first was the immense fame of her younger brother, an international celebrity as both a performer and composer while still in his teens. In spite of her considerable accomplishments as a pianist (she could play Bach's *Well-Tempered Clavier* from memory by age 13) and composer, Fanny was inevitably known as "Felix's sister." The second obstacle was her sex. Fanny grew up in an era when musical composition was not considered an appropriate profession for women, and she grew up in a family in which women were not expected to pursue a vocation of any kind. Her father, Abraham Mendelssohn, wrote to her in 1820—she was 15 at the time—that while Felix might pursue a musical career, music "for you will always remain but an ornament; never can or should it become the foundation of your existence." This helps explain why for most of her life, Fanny published her music under her brother's name. Only later—just a year before her death, as it turned out—did she begin issuing compositions under her own name.

Only recently have critics and historians begun to discover the full range of Fanny's talents as a composer of more than 200 songs, over 100 works for piano (including *Das Jahr* a cycle commemorating the months of the year), more than two dozen works for chorus (among them biblical cantatas), and works for a variety of chamber ensembles (including the Piano Trio in D minor, op. 11, and two string quartets).

Fanny Mendelssohn Hensel.
Source: Lebrecht Music & Arts Photo Library

appears to be the motion of the middle note in each chord, the only one of the three to change. The progression B-C-D within the framework of the F and A in the outer voices prefigures a harmony that will prove repeatedly elusive. The cadence at the end of measure 4 can be read as an F-major chord in first inversion (A-C-F), but the absence of B♭ gives the work more a modal sound, either Lydian (a scale on F without the B♭) or Aeolian (a scale on A with no accidentals). The chromatic descent of linked thirds beginning in measure 9 (F♯–D♯ followed by F♮–D♮) further undermines the sense of a strong tonal center. Chopin creates the expectation of a strong cadence on A minor at the downbeat to measure 13, but delays it until measure 20. And even then, he gives us just enough stability in A minor to make us think we know where we are going and the piece has a tonal center. The middle section of this work, by contrast (measures 61–92), hammers away at A-Major triads so relentlessly that it seems to take all the energy it can muster to move to a dominant harmony even briefly. But with the return of the opening section at measure 93, we are thrust back into the realm of harmonic ambiguity. At the end of the piece, Chopin repeats the opening sequence of harmonically ambiguous chords followed by an A-C-F triad, giving us a conclusion but no harmonic closure. A harmonically ambiguous opening had many distinguished precedents. One need think only of such works as Mozart's 'Dissonant' Quartet, K. 465, or Haydn's Symphony no. 103 ("Drumroll"; Anthology). But a harmonically ambiguous close like this one was a phenomenon essentially new to the 19th century.

As a work for solo instrument, this mazurka and other character pieces like it allowed for considerable rhythmic freedom in performance. By all accounts, Chopin himself took many rhythmic liberties when playing his own music, so many that Berlioz accused him of not being able to play in time. The noted conductor Sir Charles Hallé (1819–1895) described in greater detail what it was that so aroused the ire of Berlioz:

> I once ventured to observe to him [Chopin] that most of his Mazurkas (those dainty jewels), when played by himself, appeared to be written not in 3/4 but in 4/4 time, the result of his dwelling so much longer on the first note in the bar. He denied it strenuously, until I made him play one of them and counted audibly four in the bar, which fitted perfectly. Then he laughed and explained that it was the national character of the dance which created the oddity. The more remarkable fact was that you received the impression of a 3/4 rhythm whilst listening to common time. Of course this was not the case with every mazurka, but with many.[2]

Chopin and other pianists of the day also made considerable use of **tempo rubato** (literally, "robbed time"), a performance tradition that involved subtle accelerations and decelerations in tempo and at times complete independence of the hands, with the "singing" hand moving in a freer rhythm against the steady beat of the accompaniment. Carl Mikuli, one of Chopin's students, described his teacher's playing in this way:

> In keeping time Chopin was inexorable, and some readers will be surprised to learn that the metronome never left his piano. Even in his much ma- ligned *tempo rubato*, the hand responsible for the accompaniment would keep strict time while the other hand, singing the melody, would free the essence of the musical thought from all rhythmic fetters, either by lingering hesitantly or by eagerly anticipating the movement with a certain impatient vehemence akin to passionate speech.[3]

Character pieces were usually too brief to be published separately, and so works like Chopin's nocturnes, polonaises, and waltzes, or Mendelssohn's *Songs without Words* were issued typically in collections of three, four, or more individual pieces. Occasionally, however, composers organized a set of character pieces as a coherent cycle. Chopin's 24 preludes, for example, follow the circle of fifths to move systemati- cally through the 24 major and their relative minor keys of the 12-note scale (from C Major and A minor to G Major and E minor, and so forth). The homage to J. S. Bach's *Well-Tempered Clavier* is unmistakable (Anthology; see Chapter 10), although Chopin's ordering differs from Bach's. The first prelude, in C Major, imitates the broken chordal writing in the corresponding prelude of the first book of Bach's collection and uses harmonic progressions to create a sense of overall shape. And even though Chopin's preludes lack fugues, many of them explore unusual possibilities of voice leading. In the A-minor Prelude, for example, a back-and-forth half-step motion in one voice is framed by another voice making leaps of a tenth.

Although composers in the generations after Beethoven never abandoned the multimovement sonata entirely, it gradually gave way to larger scale forms in a single movement such as the ballade, cultivated by Chopin, Liszt, Brahms, and Fauré, and the scherzo, cultivated by Chopin and Brahms. At least some of these longer character pieces were substantial enough to be published separately. Chopin's Ballade in

CD11, Track 1
CHOPIN
Preludes, op. 28
Score Anthology II/129

---

2. Sir Charles Hallé, *Life and Letters of Sir Charles Hallé* (London: Smith, Elder & Co., 1896), p. 34.

3. Jean-Jacques Eigeldinger, *Chopin: Pianist and Teacher as Seen by his Pupils*, trans. Krysia Osostowicz and Naomi Shohet, ed. Roy Howat (Cambridge: Cambridge University Press, 1987), p. 276, quoting in turn Carl Mikuli, Preface to *Chopin's Pianoforte-Werke*, ed. Mikuli (Leipzig: Kistner, 1880).

COMPOSER PROFILE   Frédéric Chopin *(1810–1849)*

The son of a French father and a Polish mother, Chopin never felt quite at home anywhere. Poland had lost its always precarious independence in the late 18th century and during Chopin's youth was mostly under Russian domination. After early training in his homeland, Chopin set out on a European tour in 1830. Kept abroad by an ultimately abortive nationalist uprising in Poland, Chopin settled in France, never to return to his homeland. Polish nationalism continued to smolder after the uprising, particularly among the nation's exile community. Chopin's own deep affection for his native land is reflected in his cultivation of such national dances as the polonaise and mazurka.

Thanks in part to the large number of Polish expatriates in Paris, Chopin was able to circulate in the highest levels of Parisian society. He made a good living from teaching and the sale of his music, as well as from the occasional public concert, although he avoided these as much as he could, especially in his later years. His fame allowed him to charge far more than the going rate for piano lessons. In 1837, he began a decade-long liaison with the novelist Amandine-Aurore Lucile Dudevant (1801–1876), better known by her pen name, George Sand. The relationship eventually went sour, but for a time at least, Sand helped provide Chopin more freedom and time to compose than he would have had otherwise. In 1838–1839, the two wintered on the island of Majorca, off the Spanish coast in the Mediterranean. During their stay, Chopin took ill and was diagnosed with tuberculosis by local doctors. Chopin refused to believe them. In a letter to a friend, he wrote:

> I have been sick as a dog these last two weeks; I caught cold in spite of 18 degrees of heat [65 degrees Fahrenheit], roses, oranges, palms, figs, and three most famous doctors of the island. One sniffed at what I spat up, the second tapped where I spat it from, the third poked around and listened how I spat. One said I had died, the second that I am dying, the third that I shall die. . . . I could scarcely keep them from bleeding me. . . . All this has affected the Preludes [op. 24], and God knows when you will get them. . . . Don't tell people that I've been ill; or they'll make up a tale.[4]

Despite his poor health, Chopin continued to compose steadily until the last months of his life. On tour in England and Scotland during the early fall of 1848, he described what would prove to be his final decline:

> Things are getting worse with me every day. I feel weaker; I cannot compose, not for want of inclination, but for physical reasons, and because I am every week in a different place. . . . I am all morning unable to do anything, and when I have dressed myself I feel again so fatigued that I must rest. After dinner, I must sit for two hours with the gentlemen, hear what they say in French, and see how much they can drink. Meanwhile I feel bored to death. I think of something totally different, and then go to the drawing room, where I require all my strength to revive, for all are anxious to hear me [play the piano]. Afterwards my good Daniel [his servant] carries me upstairs to my bedroom, undresses me, puts me to bed, leaves the candle burning, and then I am again at liberty to sigh and dream until morning, to pass the next day just like the preceding one.[5]

PRINCIPAL WORKS

SOLO PIANO   The bulk of Chopin's output consists of works for solo piano. In addition to the mazurkas and preludes already discussed, these include the following:

- *Nocturnes.* These "night pieces," characterized by lyrical melody and a relatively clear homophonic texture, follow no particular fixed form. The genre itself was relatively new, related to the tradition of the serenade, an "evening song" performed outside a loved one's window. The nocturne as a character piece was first introduced into the piano repertory by the Irish composer John Field (1782–1837).

- *Etudes.* Chopin's two books of "Studies," op. 10 and op. 25, each consisting of 12 numbers, reflect the composer's devotion to strict technique and his abhorrence of the standard finger exercises that were so common in his time. Each of the etudes addresses a particular technical challenge—such as scalar runs, three-against-two rhythms, or rapid broken arpeggiations—but presents that challenge in a form that sounds like anything but a mechanical exercise.

- *Polonaises.* Chopin created many highly stylized versions of this Polish dance. The polonaises have generally heavier textures than those of Chopin's other music.

4. Quotation from letter from Frédéric Chopin ca. 1838–1839, in *Chopin's Letters*, ed. Henryk Opienski, trans. E. L. Voynich (New York: [no publisher]: 1931; reprinted New York: Vienna House 1971; and 1988: Dover Publications), p. 186. Used by permission of Dover Publications.

5. Quotation from letter from Frédéric Chopin, October 1848, in Tad Szulc, *Chopin in Paris* (Scribner, 1998), p. 381. Used by permission of Janklow & Nesbit Associates, agents for Tad Szulc.

■ *Waltzes.* These, too, are stylized pieces, not meant for dancing. They vary widely in character, tempo, and dimension.

■ *Sonatas.* The earliest, op. 4, is a youthful work, but the two later ones are substantial four-movement works. Robert Schumann, in an otherwise favorable review of these later works shortly after their publication, questioned their cyclical coherence and accused Chopin of having smuggled "four of his dearest children" into a single work under the guise of composing a "sonata." With their uncharacteristically dense textures, these show Beethoven's influence more than any of Chopin's other works.

■ *Ballades.* The four ballades are among the most celebrated works of the 19th-century piano repertory. Technically demanding and inherently dramatic, each gives the impression of telling a different kind of story. Long thought to be associated with the ballads of the Polish poet Adam Mickiewicz (1798–1855), these works adopt a distinctly narrative approach with clearly delineated episodes of contrasting character.

■ *Scherzos.* The four scherzos are large-scale works, like the ballades, but without their narrative qualities. The scherzos also feature more repetition of extended sections. As is characteristic of the scherzo form, they are in triple meter and approximately ABA form. But although *scherzo* many mean "joke" in Italian, these works are not particularly joking.

■ *Impromptus.* These few works (there are only three) are lighter in tone, as their name suggests, than those in the other genres Chopin cultivated. The *Fantasie-Impromptu* of 1835 remained unpublished during the composer's lifetime but has become a perennial favorite since then.

■ *Individual piano pieces.* In addition to pieces in the genres just listed, Chopin also wrote several independent works of substantial proportion. These include the *Barcarolle*, the *Berceuse* ("Cradle Song," a fascinating compositional study on a gently rocking ostinato bass figure, in keeping with the title), the *Bolero* (inspired by Spanish music), and the *Fantasie*.

OTHER WORKS All of Chopin's other works involve the piano with other forces. These include two piano concertos, the Sonata for Cello (op. 65), The Piano Trio (op. 8), and some posthumously published songs on Polish texts.

Chopin. One of the earliest known photographic images of any composer, this daguerreotype, made in 1849, reveals weariness from the tuberculosis that had sickened Chopin for so long and that would kill him a few months later.

Source: Corbis/Bettmann

KEY DATES IN THE LIFE OF CHOPIN

1810	Born near Warsaw on February 22.
1825	Publishes first piano works.
1831	After touring central Europe, gives first concert in Paris and soon afterward settles there, living off lessons, performances, and the publication of his works.
1837	Meets the novelist George Sand and begins a decade-long relationship with her.
1838	Suffering from tuberculosis, spends the winter with Sand on the island of Majorca in the Mediterranean.
1849	Dies in Paris on October 17 and is buried between Cherubini and Bellini.

CD11, Track 5
CHOPIN
Ballade in G minor, op. 23
Score Anthology II/130

G minor, op. 23, written between 1831 and 1835, is an extended work with many elements of sonata form. After a brief introduction (measures 1–7), Chopin establishes two main key areas, G minor (measures 8–44) and E♭ major (measures 68–93), connected by a transition section (measures 45–67). Although the modulation here is from i to VI rather than the more typical i to III, the form of this opening corresponds to the conventions of a sonata-form exposition. Then, as in the development section of a sonata-form movement, Chopin takes the two main ideas through a variety of new key areas and manipulates them thematically before introducing a new idea (measure 138). The recapitulation deviates from the conventions of sonata form in that the theme originally presented in E♭ major returns in that same key (measure 166) rather than in the tonic. Only later does the first theme finally return to reestablish the tonic (measure 194). A coda (measures 208–264) introduces yet another new theme. Given so many deviations from the conventions of sonata form, it would be misleading to say that Chopin's G-minor Ballade is "in sonata form." At the same time, it would be wrong to deny altogether that it reflects the influence of sonata form. Many 19th-century instrumental works share this kind of formal ambiguity, simultaneously operating within and pushing beyond the conventions of established forms.

It was long believed that Chopin based each of his four ballades on one of the poetic ballads of the 19th-century Polish poet Adam Mickiewicz, but no evidence supports this belief. The G-minor Ballade nevertheless projects a strong sense of narrative direction. The powerful unison opening is a call to attention, and the rhythmic regularity of the subsequent moderato (measures 8–32) conveys a sense of metered verse. Each section of the work embodies a particular affect, moving from the resigned (measures 8–32) to lyrical (measures 68–93), to ecstatic (measures 106–124), to agitated (measures 124–137), to waltzlike (measures 138–154), to furious (measures 208–242). The catastrophic conclusion (measures 244 to the end), with its abrupt finish, brings to mind the abrupt and tragic end of Goethe's well-known poetic ballad *Erlkönig* (see Anthology II/123a for Schubert's setting). Indeed, the work as a whole conveys a strong sense of the kind of creative improvisation associated with the ballad. Like the singer of ballads as described by Goethe, Chopin "has so thoroughly internalized his pregnant subject—his characters, their actions, their emotions—that he does not know how he will bring it to light. . . . He can begin lyrically, epically, dramatically and proceed, changing the forms of presentation at will, either hastening to the end or delaying it at length."[6]

Ambiguity and complexity were not the only interests of 19th-century composers; there was an ever-increasing number of good amateur players for whom to write music. Franz Liszt evokes a fashionable dance of the period with his *Galop de bal* (ca. 1840). It places relatively limited demands on the performer and with its relentless accents captures the physical frenzy of the ballroom (see "Dance fever, 1839," in this chapter). Other composers also wrote music in a disarmingly simple style. Robert Schumann's cycle of character pieces entitled *Kinderszenen* ("Scenes from Childhood"), op. 15 (1838), evoke the ancient idea that truth is to be found in the unspoiled innocence of childhood. *Träumerei* ("Reveries") and *Der Dichter spricht* ("The Poet Speaks") are two well-known works from this set: they are technically quite straightforward yet every bit as profound as the more openly virtuosic and sophisticated character pieces of their time.

Schumann's *Carnaval*, op. 9 (1835), is a cycle of character pieces ranging from the simple to the complex, linked by the common theme of Carnival, the brief season of revelry immediately preceding the penitential season Lent. During Carnival, whose

CD11, Track 6
FRANZ LISZT
Galop de bal
Score Anthology II/131

CD11, *Track 7*
ROBERT SCHUMANN
Carnaval, op. 9
Score Anthology II/132

---

6. Goethe, "Ballade," in Johann Wolfgang Goethe, *Sämtliche Werke*, XIII/1 (Munich: Hanser, 1985), p. 505.

Der große Galop. von Joh. Strauß.

Dance fever, 1839. *The Grand Galop of Johann Strauss*, engraving by A. Geiger after J. C. Schöller. The "Grand Galop" was a favorite finale of dance events, a group activity in which partners could hold one another tightly while moving at dizzying speeds. The pace was clearly too much for the couple in the left foreground of this illustration. A pileup looms behind them as they stumble to the ground. (Is she more upset to have fallen or to have discovered her partner was wearing a toupee?) The single young men clustered in the middle look on with envy. The orchestra, conducted by Johann Strauss the elder (1804–1849, father of the "Waltz King"), plays on the balcony, with the bass drum occupying a place of special prominence.

Source: Austrian Nationalbibliothek Bildarchiv, Picture Archive: Pk3626

only high-profile manifestation in the United States today is the Mardi Gras celebration in New Orleans, conventional social standards are set aside. In Schumann's time it was perfectly acceptable—and indeed expected—for people to go about in costume and do behind masks what they could only dream of doing openly.

Like the season for which it is named, many of the movements of Schumann's *Carnaval* contain elements of intrigue, impersonation, excess, and downright nonsense. Why Schumann chose the French form of the word for the title, rather than his native German, is one of the many mysteries of this work that have never been adequately explained. Indeed, the entire cycle is based on a riddle, whose key is given in the movement entitled "Sphinxes." In Greek mythology, the sphinx was a creature who posed a riddle to passersby, killing those who couldn't solve it. Here, Schumann presents a series of brief motivic ideas in archaic breves. The key to the riddle is to be found in the German names for the notes of each motivic idea. Adding "s" to any note name in German designates it as flat. Thus E♭ is "Es" and A♭ is "As." In addition, German designates B♮ with the letter "H." With this in mind, we can see that one of the sequences (E♭-C-B-A) spells "Schumann" in an abbreviated form, and the other two (A♮-C-B and A-E♭-C-B) spell "Asch":

E♭	C	B	A		A♭	C	B
Es	C	H	A		As	C	H
S	**C**	**h(um)**	**a(nn)**		**As**	**c**	**h**

			A	E♭	C	B
			A	Es	C	H
			A	**s**	**c**	**h**

"Asch" was the hometown of Ernestine von Fricken, who was Schumann's fiancée when he wrote *Carnaval*. The use of notes in this way to spell names or other words has a long tradition in Western music. Josquin, for example, did it in the 16th century with the cantus firmus of his *Missa Hercule Dux Ferrariae* (see Chapter 5), and J. S. Bach did it in the 18th century when he spelled his name in a countersubject in his *The Art of Fugue* (see Chapter 9).

COMPOSER PROFILE   Robert Schumann *(1810–1856)*

A pianist by training, Schumann quite naturally began his compositional career with a series of piano works. But in 1840, he shifted almost exclusively to song and in 1841, to orchestral music; chamber music followed in 1842, oratorio in 1843. These successive pursuits of a single genre have sometimes been interpreted as evidence of a manic-depressive personality and a foreshadowing of the debilitating mental illness of his last years. It seems equally plausible that these periods of intense engagement with a particular genre were the result of Schumann's systematic effort to broaden his scope as a composer.

Schumann was also one of the most influential critics in the history of music. His collected journalistic writings fill two thick volumes and have shaped the way we think and write about music today. He founded and edited for a decade the *Neue Zeitschrift für Musik* ("New Journal of Music"), which quickly established itself as the most important journal of its kind and is still published today. Schumann and his colleagues took on the more conservative elements of the musical establishment with an "us versus them" attitude, dubbing themselves the *Davidsbund*, the "Band of David," because they saw themselves fighting the numerically superior but aesthetically deficient "Philistines." Schumann was one of the first to extol Berlioz's *Symphonie fantastique*, and he was the first major critic to recognize publicly the compositional genius of both Chopin and Brahms.

To give voice to different points of view in his reviews, and in general to represent different aspects of his own persona, Schumann invented several fictional characters: the exuberant, extroverted Florestan; the more circumspect and introverted Eusebius; and the sagacious Magister Raro, who sometimes mediates between the other two. Schumann attributes the opening of his review of *the Symphonie fantastique*, for example, to Florestan, and its detailed account of the work's technical structure to Eusebius. All three characters are drawn from the fiction of Schumann's favorite novelist, Jean Paul (Johann Paul Friedrich Richter, 1763–1825).

Schumann's last years were turbulent. He accepted the directorship of the municipal orchestra at Düsseldorf in 1850, but the arrangement was mutually unsatisfactory. Advancing signs of mental instability forced him to resign in 1853, and thereafter his condition deteriorated rapidly. In 1854, he attempted suicide by throwing himself into the Rhine and was confined to an institution. In his last months he rarely recognized visitors.

Robert and Clara Schumann (1850). Schumann married Clara Wieck (1819–96), the daughter of his piano teacher, in 1840. (For a profile of Clara Wieck Schumann, see Chapter 17.) By the time this photograph was made ten years later, she had become on of the most renowned piano virtuosos of her time. She sacrificed much of her early career to help raise their children but was able to concertize more extensively from about 1845 onward. Clara's innate grace and Robert's innate awkwardness are amply evident in this revealing dual portrait. Even before his final illness, Robert was a notoriously uncomfortable conversationalist, whereas Clara, by all accounts, could captivate any gathering. Upright pianos like the one in this picture were a 19th-century innovation that lowered costs and made it possible to fit pianos into small spaces.

Source: Art Resource/Reunion des Musees Nationaux

PRINCIPAL WORKS

SYMPHONIES AND OTHER ORCHESTRAL WORKS   Like almost every other composer of his generation, Robert Schumann struggled against Beethoven's legacy in the symphony, eventually opting for a smaller scale, less monumental approach to the genre. His four numbered symphonies have gained in prestige over the years. The myth that Schumann was an incompetent orchestrator is also beginning to disappear, thanks to recent performances on period instruments, which reveal a clarity of texture and counterpoint that had been obscured by later transformations of the orchestra, not to mention numerous retouchings at the hands of conductors like Felix Weingartner and Gustav Mahler. Schumann's other works for orchestra include the *Overture, Scherzo, and Finale*, op. 52, several concert overtures, and the ever-popular Piano Concerto in A minor, op. 54, written for and widely performed by his wife, Clara Wieck Schumann. The Cello Concerto in A minor, op. 129, is one of the few late works to have gained general acclaim.

CHAMBER MUSIC   In 1842, his "year of chamber music," Schumann wrote three string quartets, op. 41, the Piano Quartet, op. 47, and the Piano Quintet, op. 44. To this remarkably intensive output, he later added three piano trios and various other works for combinations of piano and strings or winds.

PIANO MUSIC   Schumann's piano music, particularly the early works from the 1830s, established his reputation as a composer, and these works remain central to the piano repertory. Outstanding among them are *Papillons* ("Butterflies"), op. 2; the *Davidsbündlertänze* ("Dances for the Brotherhood of David"), op. 7; *Carnaval*, op. 9 (discussed in this chapter); the *Symphonic Etudes*, op. 13, a set of etude-variations on an original theme; and *Kreisleriana*, op. 16, evoking the mystical world of E. T. A. Hoffmann's fictional Kapellmeister, Johannes Kreisler. Perhaps surpassing even these in greatness, however, is the monumental *Fantasie*, op. 17, the proceeds from which Schumann donated to the erection of a statue of Beethoven in Bonn.

SONGS   Marriage to Clara in 1840 coincided with a remarkable outpouring of song, including the cycles *Liederkreis*, op. 24, and *Dichterliebe* ("Poet's Love"), op. 48, both to texts by Heinrich Heine; another *Liederkreis*, op. 39 (to texts by Joseph von Eichendorff); and *Frauenliebe und -leben* ("Woman's Love and Life"), op. 42, to texts by Adelbert von Chamisso. *Dichterliebe*, in particular, explores the many subtle techniques by which a series of miniatures can be linked in a larger cycle. Stylistically, Schumann's songs continue the tradition cultivated by Schubert, albeit with the more pronounced chromaticism we would expect from a later composer. Schumann also gave the piano a more prominent role. Although instrumental preludes had long been a common feature in songs, Schumann cultivated the idea of allowing the piano to continue after the voice has stopped, providing a kind of wordless commentary on the text that has gone before.

VOCAL MUSIC   Most of Schumann's choral music is forgotten today, but in its time, the oratorio *Das Paradies und die Peri* was hugely popular, as were a number of compositions for men's, women's, and mixed choruses, both with and without orchestra. The decline in the reputation of these works is in part social, for Schumann's music provided important repertory for the widespread choral societies of his time. He himself founded and conducted one such group in Dresden in the late 1840s. With the decline of such choral societies in the 20th century, this and similar music by Schubert, Mendelssohn, and even Brahms has unfortunately fallen into obscurity.

KEY DATES IN THE LIFE OF ROBERT SCHUMANN

1810	Born in Zwickau (Saxony, in central Germany) on June 8.
1828	Studies law at Leipzig, later at Heidelberg, but eventually abandons law for music.
1830	Moves to Leipzig and lives with his piano teacher, Friedrich Wieck.
1832	Injures his hands through a device intended to promote independence of the fingers; forced to abandon a performance career, he turns increasingly to journalism and composition.
1834	Co-founds the *Neue Zeitschrift für Musik*.
1840	Marries Clara Wieck.
1841	Produces or begins five major works for orchestra.
1842	Writes three string quartets, a piano quartet, and a piano quintet.
1850	Moves to Düsseldorf to become the city's musical director.
1853	Meets the 20-year-old Johannes Brahms and proclaims the young composer's talent to the world in the celebrated essay "New Paths." First signs of growing mental instability.
1854	Attempts suicide and is confined to an asylum at Endenich, near Bonn.
1856	Dies at Endenich on July 2.

Among the riddles Schumann poses with these Sphinxes is to find all the ways in which he embeds them within the individual pieces in *Carnaval*. The opening notes in the upper part of "Papillons," for example, are A, E♭, C, and C♭ (= B♯ = H). The opening of "Chiarina" is A♭, C, B♯ (= H). It turns out—and this presents another riddle—that Schumann never uses the first Sphinx, the one derived from his own name. And in still another riddle, he leaves unstated whether or not the Sphinxes themselves are to be played in performances of the work.

As the Sphinxes suggest, *Carnaval* is an autobiographical work, rather like Berlioz's *Symphonie fantastique*. Schumann uses the mask of music to say things he would not otherwise have ventured to acknowledge openly. Consider, for example, the trio of movements labeled "Chiarina," "Chopin," and "Estrella." Chiarina was the nickname of the 15-year-old Clara Wieck, the daughter of his own piano teacher. Schumann would later marry Clara, but when he wrote *Carnaval* he was engaged to Ernestine, whose nickname was Estrella. In a gesture clearly anticipating the inevitable end of his engagement to Ernestine, Schumann marks "Estrella" to be played *con affetto* ("with affection") and, in pointed contrast, marks "Chiarina" to be played *passionate* ("passionately"). The two women in question surely grasped the significance of these indications. The two movements are mediated by one named after Chopin, a composer Schumann greatly admired, who had paid personal visits to both Clara and Robert in September 1835. The admiration was mutual: Chopin dedicated his Second Ballade for piano to Schumann in 1840. In an imitation of Chopin's style, the piece titled "Chopin" has a graceful and soaring melodic line, an elaborately arpeggiated

The title page to Louis Moreau Gottschalk's *The Banjo* (1855). The fanciful artwork, with its rustic lettering, conjures up images of the American backwoods, in keeping with the work's subtitle, "An American Sketch." Note the international distribution of this seemingly provincial work: France, Spain, England, Germany, Italy, and Portugal.

Source: Dover Publications, Inc.

accompaniment, and a clear homophonic texture, and it offers plenty of opportunity for *tempo rubato* in performance.

Like the song, the character piece became increasingly chromatic in the latter part of the 19th century. Liszt's *Nuages gris* ("Gray Clouds"), written in 1881 but unpublished at the composer's death five years later, opens with a rising fourth, followed by a rising augmented fourth and a descending G-minor triad in measure 2. In its context, this triad sounds neither particularly triadic nor like a triad in the tonic; but is it? Liszt inserts chromatic passages (chords, with tremolo octaves) that question the tonal identity; in measures 21–32, the opening figure returns in the left hand as the melody cadences on notes of the G minor triad. Immediately thereafter, the left hand figure turns into an unstable ostinato, and a chromatic ascent in octaves leaves off with on the leading tone, F♯, unresolves (measure.44). Even the final chords fail to confirm any tonality; the leading-tone resolution undermined is by the harmony, notably the G-B♮ dyad with an open A₉ chord in the lower voices that concludes the piece. The music seems to float like the clouds evoked in its title, with little sense of any forward motion. In this respect, it anticipates the Impressionist style of the late 19th and early 20th centuries (see Chapter 20).

CD11, Track 12
LISZT
Nuages gris
Score Anthology II/133

THE VIRTUOSO SHOWPIECE

Virtuosity was not a new phenomenon in the 19th century: singers and instrumentalists had long been dazzling audiences through improvisation and the performance of notated music far beyond the technical range of average musicians. During the middle third of the century, however, more and more composers began writing music of this kind. The **etude** (the French word for "study") became a public genre, to be performed and heard outside the practice studio, and a number of character pieces of the time display an increasing tendency toward musical showmanship. One cannot hear such pieces without being aware of the immense technical abilities involved in bringing them to life.

The composers who wrote these virtuoso showpieces were usually performers themselves, and many of them cultivated an aura of mystique, encouraging audiences to view them as superhuman, endowed with unearthly talents. Rumor had it that the Italian composer and violinist Niccolò Paganini (1782–1840) had made a pact with the devil to win his extraordinary skills as a virtuoso. Paganini did nothing to dispel this story. His 24 Caprices, op. 1 (published in 1820 but probably written at least a decade before) are themselves homage to a set of 24 caprices published by Pietro Locatelli, an earlier violin virtuoso, in 1733. The last of Paganini's 24 Caprices makes an unusually wide array of technical demands on the violinist. Formally, it is a set of variations on a theme, with each variation highlighting a particular technique:

CD11, Track 13
PAGANINI
Caprice in A minor Op. 1, no. 24
Score Anthology II/134

- **Variation 1:** Spiccato arpeggiation (bouncing the bow lightly on the string).

- **Variation 2:** Bariolage, the rapid and repeated alternation between two adjacent strings, one open, the other fingered.

- **Variation 3:** Octaves. Because the violin does not feature fixed pitches, like a piano, octaves require absolutely perfect placement of two fingers in relation to each other.

- **Variation 4:** High chromatic passages. The higher the hand moves on the fingerboard, the smaller the physical space between the finger placements of the individual notes.

COMPOSER PROFILE Franz Liszt (1811–1886)

Liszt is a figure who seems to pop up everywhere. He crossed paths with virtually every major musician in the generations from Beethoven through Brahms and played an important role in the careers of such diverse personalities as Berlioz, Paganini, Chopin, and Wagner. He was extraordinarily generous with his time and energy toward younger composers and performers. He was also a man of enormous contradictions. Liszt cultivated his image as a Hungarian composer (his *Hungarian Rhapsodies* for piano are perennial favorites), but his native language was German, and he learned Hungarian only toward the end of his life. After living a life full of earthly pleasures, he took holy orders in his mid-50s and assumed a new identity as Abbé Liszt.

Physical appearance was part of his mystique: the imposing height, aquiline nose, swept back hair, and graceful hands all contributed to an air of suavity and mystery that captivated audiences. The Countess Marie d'Agoult (1805–1876, better known by her pen name, Daniel Stern) was Liszt's mistress in the late 1830s and the mother of his three children. She recalled her first impressions of the young artist in this way:

A tall figure, excessively thin, a pale face with large sea-green eyes in which glistened swift flashes of light like waves catching the sunlight, features at once suffering and powerful, a hesitant step which seemed less to tread the floor than glide over it, an absent-minded and uneasy look, like that of a ghostly visitant for whom the hour of returning to the shades is about to sound—that was how I saw before me this young genius. . . .

In politics as in religion Franz detested moderation and boldly embraced extreme opinions. He despised bourgeois royalty and middle-of-the-road government, and prayed for the reign of justice; which, he explained to me, meant the Republic. With the same restiveness he turned to innovations in the arts and letters which threatened the old disciplines. . . . All the proud or desperate revolutionaries of romantic poetry were the companions of his sleepless nights. With them he enthused in proud disdain of the conventions; like them he shuddered under the hated yoke of those aristocracies which had no foundation in genius or virtue.[7]

Liszt revolutionized the art of the recital and indeed gave the phenomenon its very name. *Recitals* had previously been confined to the sphere of oratory (as in a "recital of facts"). Playing on the image of music as a language in its own right, Liszt transferred the term to musical performance. He also turned the piano sideways on the stage so the audience could see his dramatic profile. When possible, he even placed two pianos on stage facing one another and alternated between them so all of the audience could see his hands (and profile) at some point. Liszt also developed the idea of putting selected members of the audience, usually aristocratic women, in a semicircle around him at the back of the stage, occasionally chatting with them between numbers. His audiences, men and women alike, consistently spoke of being "transported" by his playing. So great were the passions generated by Liszt's playing that the poet Heinrich Heine coined the term "Lisztomania" to describe a condition having "every resemblance to an infectious disease."[8] (For a portrayal of a Liszt recital, see "Liszt at the piano," on page 435.)

For all this solitary splendor on the stage, Liszt was actively involved in the broader musical world of his day. Through his composing, conducting, and writing, he became one of the two central figures (along with his eventual son-in-law, Richard Wagner) on what many saw as the "progressive" side of the struggle against musical "conservatives."

PRINCIPAL WORKS

SYMPHONIES AND SYMPHONIC POEMS Liszt's two symphonies represent a synthesis of symphony and symphonic poem. The *Faust-Symphonie* of 1854 (revised 1857) consists of what he called three "character pieces" reflecting the three central figures in Goethe's *Faust*: Faust, Gretchen, and Mephistopheles. In this work, Liszt used what would later come to be known through Wagner's music dramas as *Leitmotivs*, a network of interrelated musical ideas that convey some sort of extramusical idea. The motives associated with Faust in the first movement, for example, become palpably softer and gentler in Gretchen's movement, mirroring Faust's own emotional transformation through love; Mephistopheles, in turn, has no significant theme of his own but instead consistently distorts and disfigures themes heard in earlier movements. The symphony concludes with a brief section for tenor and chorus based on the closing scene from Part II of Goethe's *Faust*. The *Symphonie zu Dantes Divina commedia* of 1856, also in three movements, similarly concludes with a brief vocal section that culminates a trajectory leading from struggle (*Inferno, Purgatorio*) to paradise. The text is taken from the Magnificat.

---

7. Adrian Williams, *Portrait of Liszt: By Himself and His Contemporaries* (Oxford: Clarendon Press, 1990), pp. 55, 58.
8. Alan Walker, *Franz Liszt*, vol. 1 (New York: Knopf, 1983), p. 371.

Liszt called his early one-movement works for orchestra *overtures* because at the time of their composition there was no better designation by which to describe them. In the mid-1850s, however, he coined the terms *symphonic poem* and *tone poem* to convey their alliance with some kind of literary program or idea.

Liszt at the piano. A number of celebrated figures listen to Liszt perform in this idealized scene painted in 1840 by Josef Danhauser. On the far left is Alexandre Dumas, the author of *The Three Musketeers* and *The Count of Monte Cristo*. To his left is the novelist George Sand, who was Chopin's mistress at the time. In keeping with the male persona of her pseudonym (her real name was Amandine-Aurore-Lucile Dudevant) she often dressed in men's clothing and smoked cigars. Standing behind Sand and Dumas is Victor Hugo, best known as the author of *Notre Dame de Paris* and *Les Misérables*. His drama *Le roi s'amuse* was the basis for the libretto to Verdi's *Rigoletto* (see Chapter 17). Standing against the wall, in front of a portrait of Lord Byron, the quintessential Romantic poet, are Niccolò Paganini (left) and Giaocchino Rossini (right). Paganini was to the violin what Liszt was to the piano, both as a composer and as a performer. Rossini had retired from opera by the time this painting was done, but his Parisian salon continued to attract the leading figures in all the arts. On the floor leaning her head against the piano is Liszt's mistress, Marie d'Agoult (1805–1876). Like her friend George Sand she was a writer, and she also wrote under a male pseudonym (Daniel Stern). She bore three children by Liszt, including a daughter, Cosima, who married Richard Wagner. With her back turned to us, Marie d'Agoult alone is focused on Liszt. The others gaze into space. Liszt himself seems to be looking past the bust of Beethoven on the piano to the infinite sky beyond. The painting as a whole, by showing literary and musical figures together, wonderfully represents music's ability to unite the arts. But it also illustrates music's ability to transcend the word—Dumas, Hugo, and Sand, the three literary figures, have all been interrupted in their reading—and to direct attention to a higher realm.

Source: Juergen Liepe/Art Resource/Bildarchiv Preussischer Kulturbesitz

PIANO WORKS   Liszt's piano music covers an enormous range, from large-scale works like the Sonata in B minor to miniatures, most of it beyond the technical reach of amateurs. Many of the character pieces relate to texts, like the *Sonnets after Petrarch*, or to places, like the *Années des pèlerinages* ("Years of Pilgrimage"), which take the listener on a series of wide-ranging journeys. Programmatic ideas behind Liszt's piano music are as likely to be sacred ("Saint Francis of Assisi Preaches to the Birds") as demonic (the various "Mephisto" Waltzes). The *Transcendental etudes* are even more technically difficult than Chopin's *Etudes*. Liszt also transcribed for solo piano all of Beethoven's symphonies and numerous songs by Schubert. His paraphrases on contemporary operas were in great demand during his lifetime.

VOCAL MUSIC   The four Masses, Requiem, three oratorios, and numerous works for chorus and orchestra, although they constitute an important portion of the composer's output, are for the most part forgotten today. Liszt's more than 60 songs for voice and piano occasionally find their way into performances but largely await rediscovery.

KEY DATES IN THE LIFE OF LISZT

1811	Born near Ödenburg (Hungary), in what was then part of the Austrian Empire.
1821	Moves with family to Vienna and begins study of the piano with Carl Czerny, one of the leading virtuosos of his day and a friend of Beethoven.
1827	Moves to Paris and continues to amaze audiences with his dazzling performances on the piano.
1830s	Concertizes extensively and publishes many works for piano.
1848	Becomes music director at the court of Weimar and turns more and more to writing for the orchestra.
1861	Moves to Rome but continues extensive travels.
1865	Receives minor holy orders by decree of Pope Pius IX and becomes an abbot.
1870	Daughter Cosima marries Richard Wagner, further intensifying his already well-established support of that composer.
1886	Dies in Bayreuth on July 31.

- **Variation 5:** String crossing. This variation requires the player to move quite rapidly across strings.

- **Variation 6:** Thirds and octaves. Again, both pitches must be perfectly fingered.

- **Variation 7:** Bowing. The player must pick up and replace the bow in a downstroke rapidly in succession while playing a triplet figure that moves through all registers of the instrument.

- **Variation 8:** Triple stopping. The performer rolls a series of chords on three different notes, each played on a different string.

- **Variation 9:** Left-hand pizzicato. The player must alternate rapidly between notes played with the bow and notes plucked with the left hand (not the right hand, as in normal pizzicato).

- **Variation 10:** High position. The performer must execute rapid runs in a very high register.

- **Variation 11:** Successive double stops.

- **Finale:** Long runs and successive double stops.

This particular caprice was so appealing that a long list of composers would draw on it in one form or another: Franz Liszt made a piano transcription of it; Robert Schumann added a piano accompaniment to Paganini's violin line; and Johannes Brahms wrote a set of variations on it. In the 20th century Sergei Rachmaninoff used it as the basis for his *Rhapsody on a Theme of Paganini* (1934) for piano and orchestra. More recently still, the Polish composer Witold Lutoslawski made this theme the centerpiece of his *Paganini Variations* for piano and orchestra (1978).

Paganini weaves his magic.
Paganini never did anything to contradict the rumors that he had made a pact with the devil to gain his extraordinary skills as a violin virtuoso; the story only added to the artist's mystique. The orchestra players here look on in amazement. Note the high hand position on the fingerboard: part of Paganini's virtuosity lay in his ability to play fluently in the uppermost range of the instrument.

Source: Daniel Maclise (1806–1870). *Niccolo Paganini at the King's Theater, Haymarket.* Victoria & Albert Museum, Lond/Art Resource, NY

Paganini's counterpart on the piano was Franz Liszt, whose technical prowess was unrivalled even in an age of great virtuosos. Chopin is said to have expressed envy at Liszt's ability to play his own—Chopin's—etudes with such facility. Liszt wrote a good many etudes of his own, including a set entitled *Etudes d'exécution transcendante* (1838; revised 1851), that is, etudes requiring a technique transcending the ordinary. The first of these, in C Major, clearly fits into the tradition of C Major works that open large, systematically ordered sets, such as Bach's C Major Prelude in the *Well-Tempered Clavier* (Anthology I/95), Chopin's C Major Prelude in his Preludes, op. 24 (Anthology II/129), and the opening C Major Etude in Chopin's Etudes for piano, op. 10. Liszt follows the same organizational pattern in these etudes that Chopin had used in his Preludes: a circle of descending fifths in the major keys, with each major-mode work followed by one in the relative minor. But from the perspective of technical demands, Liszt's opening salvo in these "Transcendental" Etudes leaves all earlier works in its wake. Robert Schumann, reviewing an earlier version of Liszt's set, called them "studies in storm and dread, fit for ten or twelve players in the world." Weaker players, Schumann added, "would arouse only laughter with these works."

A similar spirit of extreme virtuosity is evident in Louis Moreau Gottschalk's *The Banjo*, a character piece for piano bearing the subtitle "An American Sketch." Gottschalk (1829–1869) was born in New Orleans but toured throughout Europe and Latin America as a pianist, often performing his own music. A showman as well as a musician, he always made a ceremony of taking off his white gloves before he played in public.

The banjo was probably African-American in origin, but minstrelsy had made it popular among all Americans. "The piano may do for love-sick girls who lace themselves to skeletons, and lunch on chalk, pickles, and slate pencils," Mark Twain wrote in a 1865 article for the *San Francisco Dramatic Chronicle*. "But give me the banjo. . . . When you want *genuine music*—music that will come right home to you like a bad

CD11, Track 14
LISZT
*Etudes d'exécution transcendante,
no. 1*
Score Anthology II/135

CD11, Track 15
GOTTSCHALK
The Banjo
Score Anthology II/136

Franz Liszt, 1858. Photograph by Franz Hanfstägl.

Louis Moreau Gottschalk.
Gottschalk's artistry and good looks were a source of constant commentary in the American press wherever he performed. A showman as well as a musician, he always made a ceremony of taking off his white gloves before he played in public.

Beethoven—in the form of a bust—looms over all. The conspicuous placement of the piano's brand name is no coincidence: Gottschalk was paid to endorse this particular brand of piano. Chickering was one of hundreds of American piano firms that thrived in the 19th and early 20th centuries but eventually went out of business or were absorbed by larger companies.

Source: Art Resource/The New York Public Library

quarter, suffuse your system like strychnine whisky, go right through you like Brandreth's pills, ramify your whole constitution like the measles, and break out on your hide like the pin-feather pimples on a pickled goose—when you want all this, just smash your piano, and invoke the glory-beaming banjo!"

The Banjo replicates the sounds of this quintessentially American instrument. The music's constant strumming rhythms and jaunty syncopations anticipate the ragtime style that would become popular in the United States a few decades later (see Chapter 20). In a concession to public sales, Gottschalk at various points offers alternative, slightly easier ways of performing some of the work's more difficult passages; these are marked "Facilité" in the score and notated above the standard line of music.

Virtuosity of this kind provoked both wonderment and scorn in the 19th century. Many critics dismissed such bravura works on the grounds that they were "merely" virtuosic, as if virtuosity were somehow not a musical quality. But audiences clearly responded (and continue to respond) to this repertory, especially when performed by a musician in complete command of the required skills.

CONCLUSION

Chamber music, song, and music for solo piano found a ready market in 19th-century households. The growing affordability of the piano made this instrument the new focus of music making in the home. Sonatas and other works for solo piano, as well as songs for voice and piano, became a staple of the domestic repertory. The emergence of German as a literary language gave composers new texts to set by such prestigious poets as Goethe and Schiller. The character piece for piano, in turn, provided an instrumental counterpart to song, a miniature genre with strong suggestions of programmatic content but without an explicit text. Virtuoso showpieces highlighted the performer's ability to play works whose technical demands lay far beyond the capacities of the average player.

Dramatic and Choral Music

In spite of the growing significance of instrumental music in the 19th century, the large-scale genres of vocal music—opera, operetta, and sacred music—maintained their long-standing aesthetic prestige. Opera, in particular, was still considered by many critics and listeners to be the pinnacle of the musical art, for it combined drama (the libretto), music (the score), and the visual arts (scenery, costume) in a single genre. It continued to attract the finest singers and many of the most talented composers of the day, and it was by far the most financially lucrative of all genres. Through ticket sales, printed scores, and the prospect of future commissions, a hit opera was a composer's surest path to fame and success. Operetta, a lighter form of musical drama, usually featuring spoken dialogue as well as singing, commanded an even wider following among the public. Sacred music, in turn, became increasingly varied in scope, ranging from monumental settings of the Mass and Requiem in the most modern style to smaller scale motets strongly influenced by the idiom of the late Renaissance.

OPERA

Since its emergence in the early 17th century, opera had been periodically rocked by controversies that pitted the demands of music against the demands of drama. Melodic structure and vocal virtuosity had rarely meshed with dramatic realism or the clear declamation of texts, and over the course of the 19th century, particularly from the 1840s onward, composers of all nationalities pursued new approaches to reconciling these conflicting agendas. By the end of the century, their efforts had fundamentally changed the genre of opera, but in ways that were different in Italy, France, and Germany.

Italy in the Early 19th Century: Rossini

The first three decades of the 19th century are often referred to as the "Age of Beethoven," but it would be more accurate to call this period the "Age of Rossini and

CD12, Track 1
ROSSINI
Il Barbiere di Siviglia
Score Anthology II/137

Beethoven." Like Beethoven in the realm of instrumental music, Gioacchino Rossini (1792–1868) enjoyed unquestioned preeminence in the world of opera in the first half of the 19th century. Rossini helped establish a style of Italian opera known as **bel canto**—literally, "beautiful singing." The term refers to a vocal technique that emphasizes lyrical melodic lines, legato phrasing, and a seemingly effortless vocal technique, even in passages of great technical difficulty. Orchestral accompaniment in 19th-century bel canto opera is typically discreet, limited to harmonic underpinning with little or no counterpoint. The emphasis throughout is on the voice. Although not every aria or every role in a bel canto opera conforms to this style, the ideal of beautiful production lies at the aesthetic core of all these works.

Rossini's *Il Barbiere di Siviglia* ("The Barber of Seville," 1816), the most popular of his many operas, integrates the traditions of opera buffa into the style of bel canto. The barber of the title is Figaro, a buffa-like character whose profession brings him into contact with people at the highest levels of Seville's society, making him an ideal go-between—a "factotum," as he calls himself. Over the course of the opera, Count Almaviva (disguised as a student) uses Figaro to help him win the hand of Rosina, who is also being pursued by a certain Doctor Bartolo. The drama unfolds in a series of madcap antics full of mistaken identities, disguises, and secret notes.

In this opera the music illustrates the essential nature of the characters in ways that the text alone cannot do. Figaro's opening number, for example, *Largo al factotum* ("Make way for the factotum"), does a marvelous job introducing the title character. He half complains, half boasts that his services are in such demand among people of quality that he is always busy. Constantly repeating the same lines of text, Figaro works himself into a frenzy, imitating people calling "him—"Figaro! Figaro!"—in that famous three-note melody (beginning at measure 187) that has come to be indelibly associated with his character. "One at a time!" he half shouts to himself in response.

Rosina's *Una voce poco fa* ("A voice a short while ago") is very much in the bel canto tradition and draws an equally sharp characterization. Like many arias of this period, it consists of two sections, a slow opening and a lively conclusion, known as the **cabaletta.** Rosina sings while writing a letter to Lindoro, who is in fact Count Almaviva in disguise. After declaring Lindoro her chosen suitor, she professes to be "docile, respectful, and obedient." The music, however, gives the lie to this claim, changing from reserved to lively and spontaneous in the cabaletta as she goes on to sing, "But if you push me the wrong way, I'll be a viper, and the last laugh will be on you." By the time she returns to her profession of docility, the feistiness of the music has infected the orchestra, leaving no doubt that the music, not the words, represents Rosina's true character.

Italy at Midcentury: Verdi

In the generations after Rossini, composers devoted increasing attention to issues of dramatic integrity. Giuseppe Verdi (1813–1901) was the leading composer of Italian opera in the generation in the middle of the 19th century, and his *Rigoletto* exemplifies several key characteristics of the new approach to the genre: dramatic realism, the use of the *scena* (scene) as the unit of dramatic organization, and dramatically justified virtuosity.

CD11, Track 16
VERDI
Rigoletto
Score Anthology II/138

Dramatic Realism. Verdi was fiercely committed to the idea of realism on the stage and struggled throughout his life to find librettos of high literary quality. For *Rigoletto*, he used an adaptation of the play *Le roi s'amuse* ("The King Amuses Himself") by the French writer Victor Hugo (1802–1885), one of the greatest playwrights of his age. Verdi worked closely with the Italian dramatist Francesco Piave (1810–1876) to

COMPOSER PROFILE   Gioacchino Rossini *(1792–1868)*

Born into a family of musicians—his father was a town trumpeter, his mother a soprano on the stage—Rossini was internationally famous as an opera composer by the age of 21. Between 1815 and 1823, he composed 20 new operas, including a critically acclaimed setting of Shakespeare's *Othello* in 1816. He toured the Continent extensively, scoring successes in Vienna, Paris, and London. In 1829, he won renewed acclaim with his opera *Guillaume Tell* ("William Tell"). For reasons that remain unclear, he then abruptly retired from the world of opera at the age of 37, composing only a few nonoperatic pieces thereafter. He spent the remainder of his life in Florence, Bologna, and Paris, where he became a fixture in the salons. The painting of Liszt at the piano reproduced on page 435 shows Rossini in just such a salon in the company of other literary and musical notables.

PRINCIPAL WORKS

Except for works written during his student years, Rossini's output consists almost entirely of operas and cantatas. He wrote opere serie (*Tancredi, Otello, Semiramide*) as well as opere buffe (*Il Barbiere di Siviglia, La Cenerentola*, the latter based on the story of Cinderella). *Guillaume Tell*, regarded by many as Rossini's masterpiece, fuses Italian lyricism into the tradition of French grand opera. He is among the admirers in Josef Danhauser's painting of Liszt at the piano (see Composer Profile, "Franz Liszt," in Chapter 16).

KEY DATES IN THE LIFE OF ROSSINI

1792	Born in Pesaro (northern Italy) on February 29.
1813	Achieves his first major operatic success with *Tancredi*, an opera seria.
1816	Premiere of *Il Barbiere di Siviglia*, his most famous work.
1829	Premiere of *Guillaume Tell*, his last opera, after which he abruptly retires from the world of opera.
1868	Dies in Paris on November 13.

adapt Hugo's stage play into a suitable libretto. The opera's plot revolves around the Duke of Mantua, a notorious womanizer; his humpbacked court jester, Rigoletto; Rigoletto's daughter and only child, Gilda; and a wronged father's curse. The Duke's courtiers resent Rigoletto's malicious wit and plot to humiliate him. Rigoletto has been keeping Gilda in seclusion, allowing her out only on Sunday to attend church. The courtiers discover her, but mistake her for Rigoletto's mistress, and plot to abduct her for the Duke's pleasure. But the Duke, disguised as a young student, has already approached her on her Sunday outings and has determined that she will be his next conquest. In the opening sequence, Rigoletto belittles Count Monterone, who has come to denounce the Duke for seducing his daughter. As he is led off to prison, Monterone turns on Rigoletto and the courtiers and hurls a curse at them all, but singling out Rigoletto in particular. When the courtiers abduct Gilda and bring her to the Duke, Rigoletto attributes his misfortune to Monterone's curse. Discovering the Duke has had his way with Gilda, Rigoletto hires an assassin to kill his master. But Gilda, in love with the Duke despite his faithlessness, saves his life by sacrificing herself at the last moment to the assassin's knife. When Rigoletto realizes what has happened, he cries out in despair, "Ah, the curse!"

Verdi and Piave encountered serious obstacles from government censors in their effort to bring *Rigoletto* to the stage in Venice. Both Hugo's play and Piave's adaptation present royalty in an unflattering light, featuring, as they do, a philandering ruler who hides behind the protection of his lofty position in society. Almost as problematic was the character of Rigoletto himself. In an age when the physically disabled were thought unsuitable subjects for a drama, it was daring indeed to feature a hunchback in an opera's title role.

Larger Units of Dramatic Organization.   Although Verdi uses many of the traditional elements of Italian opera (such as arias, duets, choruses, and accompanied

PRIMARY EVIDENCE — Stendhal Describes a Performance of an Opera by Rossini

The novelist Stendhal (Marie-Henri Beyle; 1783–1842) was a keen observer of contemporary manners, including the world of music. His description of this unnamed opera by Rossini captures the spirit of the Paris Opéra in the 1820s.

———————◆◆◆———————

As the overture begins, you could hear a pin drop; as it bangs its way triumphantly to an end, the din bursts with unbelievable violence. It is extolled to high heaven; or alternately, it is whistled, nay rather *howled* into eternity with merciless shrieks and ululations. There is no parallel in Paris, where cautious vanity anxiously eyes a neighboring vanity beside it; these are men possessed of seven devils, determined at all costs, by dint of shrieking, stamping, and battering with their canes against the backs of the seats in front, to enforce the triumph of *their* opinion, and above all, to prove that, come what may, *none but their opinion is*

correct—for, in all the world, there is no intolerance like that of a man of artistic sensibility. . . .

Each *aria* of the new opera, in its turn, is listened to in perfect silence; after which, the cataclysm is let loose once more; and the bellowing of a storm-tormented sea is nothing but the feeblest comparison. The audience makes its opinion of the singers on the one hand, and of the composer on the other, distinctly audible. There are cries of *Bravo Davide! Bravo Pisaroni!*, or on other occasions, the whole theatre will echo with demonic shrieks of *Bravo maestro!* Rossini rises from his seat at the piano, his handsome face assuming an unwonted expression of gravity. He bows thrice, submitting to storms of applause, and deafened by a most unlikely variety of acclamations, for whole sentences of adulation may be flung at his unresisting head; after which, the company proceeds to the next item.

Source: Stendhal, *The Life of Rossini;* trans. Richard N. Coa (London: Calder, 1956). p. 118–19.

recitative), he consistently incorporates these into a larger dramatic unit of multiple elements. Verdi was not the first to take this approach to dramatic organization. It was already being used by Gluck and Mozart in the 18th century and was particularly prominent, as we saw in Chapter 13, in the opening sequence of Mozart's *Don Giovanni* (Anthology). It is also found in works by Rossini and his contemporaries, such as Gaetano Donizetti (1797–1848) and Vincenzo Bellini (1801–1835). But Verdi and other midcentury composers expanded on this approach to create increasingly extended spans of music and drama uninterrupted by scenery changes or obvious opportunities for applause.

In *Rigoletto* this practice results in greater dramatic realism. Verdi's means of expression are remarkably economical. Avoiding an extended overture, he opens instead with a brief, somber instrumental Prelude that sets the tone of this deeply tragic opera. The opening bars introduce the motif associated with Monterone's curse. Although we do not yet know its meaning, we recognize at once the dark character of the music. The effect is similar to that of the theme that begins the overture to Mozart's *Don Giovanni*, a theme later associated with the Commendatore's death and subsequent vengeance. Indeed, *Rigoletto* is in many ways Verdi's homage to Mozart's opera. Both concern the fate of a libertine and his victims.

The curtain rises to reveal a scene of dancing, drinking, and revelry in the ballroom of the Duke's palace, labeled simply "N[umber] 2. Introduction." This extended opening unit of music unfolds continuously, yet consists of eight discrete yet interconnected subsections, in each of which the music underscores the dramatic action:

1. The opening dance, although not given a label in the score, has the same kind of frenzied beat associated with the *galop* (see Anthology). The incessant accentuation on every note conjures up a sense of intense physical activity.

INTERIOR OF CASTLE GARDEN AT THE TIME OF MAX MARETZEK'S BENEFIT.

Interior view of Castle Garden, New York. Originally constructed between 1807 and 1811 as a fort to guard New York harbor, Castle Garden was converted into a theater and dance hall in the 1820s. A second major renovation in 1844 turned it into one of the most desirable performance venues in the entire country, and it was here that Beethoven's Ninth Symphony received its American premiere in 1846. The entire facility was converted into a reception station for immigrants in 1855, then altered yet again in 1896 to become an aquarium. Only the foundation is still visible today. The domed theater in the round could seat 5,000 people. Jenny Lind (see Chapter 16) made her American debut here to a sellout crowd on September 11, 1850. The pillars in front of the stage were necessary to support the structure's domed roof.

Source: Corbis/Bettmann

2. When the Duke and one of his courtiers enter, the music shifts to a dance that has a lighter texture with emphasis only on beats 1 and 3 of a four-beat measure. This change allows the recitative-like patter of the voices to emerge clearly over the orchestra.

3. The Duke's first aria (*Questa o quella*) is also the first moment in the opera in which the voice carries the melody completely. The texture here is utterly homophonic, with the orchestra providing a demure accompaniment. Verdi's critics carped that this kind of accompaniment was "organ barrel grinder music," a complaint that, even if true, is irrelevant given the extraordinary beauty of Verdi's melodies. Verdi, moreover, used this style only when it was dramatically justified. Here, the Duke is bragging about his sexual prowess: why should he share the spotlight with the orchestra or anyone else? The dramatic setting demands a straightforward aria, and it is precisely the compelling simplicity of this number that makes it so powerful. The Duke sings two musically identical strophes, ending with a vocal cadenza that matches perfectly the boastful nature of his words.

4. With the entrance of the Countess of Ceprano—a woman the Duke has set his eyes on—the music changes to a minuet played by an onstage string ensemble. This decidedly old-fashioned dance fits perfectly with the Countess's traditional character. She resists the Duke's advances and insists she must remain with her husband.

5. When the Duke leaves with the reluctant Countess, Rigoletto and the courtiers ridicule her husband, who anxiously follows after his wife and the Duke. One of the festive dance melodies from the opening returns briefly here. Rigoletto exits and the onstage ensemble strikes up a new melody, which Verdi labels a *perigordino*, an Italian dance in 6/8 meter whose frenzied character is very different from that of the preceding minuet. This purely instrumental passage allows for a brief ballet.

6. The opening galoplike dance resumes briefly with the entrance of Marullo, a courtier who brings "great news." Rigoletto, he reports, has a secret lover. As in segment 2, Marullo's recitativelike delivery is accompanied by a lighter texture and a less insistent rhythm.

PRIMARY EVIDENCE   Verdi Reacts to the Censors' Proposed Changes to the Libretto of *Rigoletto*

Verdi had to fight many battles with censors throughout his artistic career. Government officials were quick to realize the political potential of the genre of opera, and various state offices kept close watch over the librettos, the music, and the staging of new works. Venice, like most of Italy, was at the time under the direct or indirect control of the Austrian Empire, and an opera like *Rigoletto*, depicting a dissolute monarch, was inevitably subjected to intense scrutiny. Censors demanded that many elements of the plot be altered: among other changes, the character of the Duke was to be made more sympathetic, and Rigoletto was to lose his humpback. In this letter of December 14, 1850, to Carlo Marzari, president of La Fenice (the Venetian theater that had commissioned Verdi's new work), Verdi reacts angrily to the proposed changes.

I have taken very little time to re-examine the new libretto: but I have seen enough to realize that, reduced to the present condition, it lacks character and importance; further, the dramatic moments have become very cool indeed. . . . In the fifth scene of Act I, all that anger vented by the courtiers against Triboletto [the original name of the jester, later changed to Rigoletto] makes no sense. The old man's malediction [curse], so terrible and sublime in the original, becomes ridiculous here, because the motive for his malediction is not so important any more, and because this is no longer a subject speaking so boldly to his king. Without this malediction what purpose, what significance does the play have? The Duke is a nonentity: the Duke must absolutely be a libertine; otherwise, Triboletto's fear that his daughter might leave her hiding place is ungrounded: and the play impossible. How does it happen

that the Duke, in the last act, goes to a remote tavern all alone, without an invitation, without an appointment? I don't understand why the sack was taken out! Of what consequence was the sack to the police? Are they afraid of its effect? Forgive me, but what makes them think they know more about the subject than I do? Who is entitled to be a Maestro? Who is entitled to say, this will be effective, that won't? A difficulty of that kind arose on account of the horn in *Ernani* [one of Verdi's earlier operas]. Well then, did anyone laugh at the sound of that horn? Take away that sack, and it becomes improbable that Triboletto should speak to a corpse for half an hour, till a flash of lightning reveals it to be that of his daughter. Finally, I note that they have avoided making Triboletto ugly and humpbacked!! A singing humpback? Why not! . . . Will it be effective? I don't know; but if I don't know, neither does, I repeat, the person who suggested the change. As a matter of fact, I think it is a very fine thing to depict this extremely deformed and ridiculous character who is inwardly impassioned and full of love. I chose the subject expressly because of these qualities, and if these original traits are removed, I can no longer set it to music. If I'm told that my notes will suit the present drama just as well, I answer that I have no understanding for these arguments, and I frankly state that, good or bad, I never write music at random and I always manage to give it character.

In short, what was an original, powerful play has been turned into something very common and cold. I very much regret that the Board of Directors has not answered my last letter. I can only repeat and request that what I wrote in it should be carried out, for upon my artist's conscience I cannot set this libretto to music.

Source: *Letters of Composers through Six Centuries,* ed. Piero Weiss (Philadelphia, Chilton, 1967), pp. 217–18.

7. The Duke, Rigoletto, and Count Ceprano return, and with them the opening galop-like theme. The Duke rebukes Rigoletto for his excessive jesting about the Count. The chorus of courtiers joins in, and in a general frenzy all agree to get their revenge on Rigoletto.

8. The choral frenzy ends abruptly with the entrance of Monterone. He has come to find his daughter, who at some earlier point had been abducted by the Duke. The music now shifts ominously to accompanied recitative: Monterone lays down his accusation and Rigoletto taunts him. Monterone, in response, lays a curse on the entire court, particularly on Rigoletto. The curtain closes on a scene of general confusion and distress.

FIGURINI dell' Opera **RIGOLETTO** del Maestro G. **VERDI**

Costume designs for the premiere of Verdi's *Rigoletto* (1851). Stage and costume design were matters of great importance to 19th-century opera producers and audiences. The costume designs shown here give some idea of the variety available to each major character in Verdi's *Rigoletto* at its world premiere in Venice in 1851. Gilda's first costume is actually that from the end of Act III, when she appears at the tavern disguised as a man. Rigoletto is shown in his two guises, with and without his jester's costume. Note that the jester's hunchback is played down in this setting; many subsequent productions have emphasized this characteristic feature far more strongly, but Verdi had already gone through considerable difficulties in persuading the censors to accept the very idea of a hunchback appearing on the stage (see Primary Evidence, p. 444).

Source: Embassy of Italy

Every dramatic turn on the stage, every arrival or departure of a main character, is articulated through a change in the music. The action continues without interruption from the beginning to the end of the entire scene. The next unit of action (Act I, scene 7; not in Anthology), a dialogue between Rigoletto and the assassin Sparafucile, functions as a transition to the subsequent "Scene and Duet" (Act I, Scene 8), which is far more complicated. The "scene" is a monologue in which Rigoletto muses on his deformity, his malicious wit, and his contempt for the Duke and his courtiers. In his extended duet with Gilda, Rigoletto reveals another, more compassionate side to his character (see Table: Structure of *Rigoletto*, Act I, Scene 8).

The final duet within the duet has its own internal structure (see Table: Structure of the Closing Duet in *Rigoletto*, Act I, Scene 8). It is, in effect, a series of variations on a single theme and follows the traditional pattern of love duets: he sings, she sings, and then finally they both sing, and in this respect, Verdi adheres to convention. But he also slips in important plot developments within the duet. At measure 279, Rigoletto hears a prowler—the Duke, it turns out—and interrupts himself to launch into an agitated inquisition of Gilda's nursemaid, Giovanna. Thus we have a dramatic dialogue in the middle of the duet (Rigoletto: "No one has followed her from church?" Giovanna, lying: "Never!" and so on). Meanwhile, the Duke himself has been listening in on all this and realizes the woman he has been pursuing (Gilda) is the daughter of his court jester (Rigoletto) and interjects a few asides to express his astonishment at this revelation. With his fears calmed, Rigoletto resumes his duet with Gilda, who sings a glorious descant to his original melody (measure 303). The protracted farewell provides the traditional cabaletta, an extended concluding section that accelerates as it nears the end of this very long unit of music.

Structure of Verdi's *Rigoletto,* Act I, Scene 8

	MEASURE	TEMPO	TEXT	DRAMATIC ACTION
Scene	1–11	Adagio	"Pari siamo . . ."	Rigoletto muses on the similarities between himself and Sparafucile, the assassin.
	12–14	Adagio	"Quel vecchio maledivami!"	Rigoletto: "That old man has laid a curse on me!" Return of the "curse" motif.
	15–29	Allegro/ Adagio	"O uomini! o natura!"	Curses his deformity and fate.
	30–40	Moderato	"Questo padrone mio . . ."	Rigoletto thinks of the Duke, who is "young, powerful, and handsome."
	41–51	Allegro	"Oh dannazione!"	Curses the Duke and all the members of his court. "If I am evil, it is only because of you!"
	52–57	Andante	"Ma in altr' uomo qui mi cangio . . ."	"But here I change into another man." Rigoletto arrives home.
	58–68	Andante/ Allegro	"Quel vecchio . . ."	Unwelcome memory of Monterone's curse.
Duet	69–116	Allegro	"Figlia!"	Gilda enters, and Rigoletto embraces her.
	117–124	Adagio	"Se mi volete . . ."	Rigoletto reminds Gilda never to leave the house; he has never revealed to her his true identity as jester; she knows him only as her father.
	125–202	Andante	"Deh non parlare"	Rigoletto tells Gilda that she is his sole consolation in life; Gilda is moved by his suffering.
	203–242	Andante	"Già da tre lune"	Gilda asks why she must always remain at home, allowed to leave only to attend church on Sunday. Rigoletto, constantly fearful that she will be abducted, thinks he hears a prowler; it is Giovanna, the family's servant.
	243–343	Allegro	"Ah! veglia, o donna . . ."	Rigoletto implores Giovanna to protect Gilda.

Dramatically Justified Virtuosity. The music in *Rigoletto* requires virtuoso singing, but Verdi never introduces virtuosity for its own sake. Arias never interrupt the flow of the drama and always reflect the character of the singer. The Duke's brilliant vocal displays, for example, reflect his pompous strutting, just as Gilda's soaring yet delicate and airy lines reflect her fragile innocence and key moments of emotional ecstasy.

The celebrated Quartet from Act III of *Rigoletto, Bella figlia dell'amore* (Beautiful daughter of love), illustrates Verdi's remarkable ability to convey contrasting emotions simultaneously. Verdi is the only composer ever to have rivaled Mozart in this regard. Scene 2 has just concluded with one of the most famous arias in all of opera, the Duke's *La donn' è mobile*, yet another self-justification for his philandering ("Women are always changing," he sings, "like a feather in the wind"). The subsequent Quartet

Structure of the Closing Duet in *Rigoletto*, Act 1, Scene 8, measures 243–343

Tempo	Allegro moderato assai			Allegro Più mosso	Tempo 1	Più mosso
Voices	Rigoletto (solo)	Gilda (solo)	Rigoletto (solo)	Rigoletto, Gilda, Duke, Giovanna; free material, quasi recitative	Rigoletto and Gilda (duet)	Cabaletta to the duet
Measure	243	259	274	278	303	318
Harmony	E♭ Major	A♭ Major	E♭ Major	D♭ minor/B♭ Major	E♭ Major	E♭ Major
Dramatic action	Rigoletto implores Giovanna to protect Gilda.	Gilda: "What love, what affection."	Rigoletto resumes but is interrupted.	Rigoletto hears someone prowling (the Duke), who in turn now realizes that Gilda, the object of his latest adventure, is the daughter of his jester, Rigoletto.	Rigoletto and Gilda resume Gilda's "lassù in ciel" is a premonition of her dying words in Act III.	Rigoletto and Gilda bid farewell.

(Anthology II/138b) presents two scenes simultaneously. One is inside the inn where Sparafucile plans to murder the Duke; the other is outside. Inside, the Duke tries to seduce Maddalena, Sparafucile's sister. She resists but finds him charming nonetheless. Outside, Gilda and Rigoletto witness the goings on inside. Rigoletto asks his daughter if she does not finally realize what a scoundrel the Duke is; she watches in stunned disbelief and anguish. Verdi meshes the contrasting emotions of these four characters in a manner that is astonishingly intricate without sounding complex. The music seems to fall into place simply.

The power of this quartet, one of the most contrapuntally sophisticated passages in all opera, made it also one of its most popular. In 1860, Liszt published a concert paraphrase for piano that itself gained popular renown.

Opera and Politics

As in previous eras, the influence of opera extended beyond the purely musical into the realm of social and political expression. The opera house was a meeting place for socialites and businesspeople and a forum for the often symbolic dramatization of political and moral ideas. State censors scrutinized *Rigoletto* for subversive ideas because they knew that composers, librettists, and audiences all were prone to interpret events on the stage as a kind of allegorical commentary on current events. Early in the century, Beethoven struggled with Viennese authorities over his politically charged *Fidelio*, which advocated freedom of political speech. Daniel-François-Esprit Auber's *La muette de Portici* ("The Deaf Girl of Portici") was the likely catalyst for a popular uprising that erupted in Brussels when it was performed there in 1830. The plot, about a peasant revolt in Naples in 1647, was apparently enough to ignite the smoldering passions of the populace. Verdi's *Un ballo in maschera* ("A Masked Ball") in 1859 encountered more resistance from the censors in Naples than *Rigoletto* had received from the censors in Venice. The Neapolitan censors prohibited the performance of the opera because it was based on the real-life assassination of King Gustavus III of Sweden. Only when Verdi and his librettist changed the time and place of the opera's setting to remote colonial

Massachusetts and the victim to a fictitious Earl of Warwick did the censors relent. And when George Bernard Shaw interpreted Wagner's *Der Ring des Nibelungen* as an allegory for the struggles during the 19th century among the competing forces of capitalism, socialism, and anarchy, his views were taken very seriously indeed.

France: Grand Opéra and Opéra Comique

French opera of the 19th century divides into two broad categories, each with its own tradition. **Grand opéra** emphasized story lines drawn from historical subjects and typically featured lavishly expensive stage designs, ballets, and large choral numbers. Works written in the tradition of grand opéra tend to be long and are almost invariably in five acts. Although always sung in French, they were written by composers from across the Continent: the Italians Rossini and Gaspare Spontini (1774–1851), the German Giacomo Meyerbeer (1791–1864, born Jakob Beer), and the French Daniel-François-Esprit Auber (1782–1871) and Jacques-François-Fromental-Elie Halévy (1799–1862). Meyerbeer was acknowledged as the unrivaled master of the genre. A protégé of Rossini, he wrote works that appealed to the public love of spectacle combined with frequent evocations of the supernatural, especially in his most popular work, *Robert le diable* ("Robert the Devil," 1831). Grand opéra was a true institution of the political establishment. Commissions were given as much on the basis of personal contacts as on talent; intrigue was rampant.

The city's other two leading opera houses, the Opéra Comique and the Théâtre Lyrique, offered alternatives to the grand style. In spite of its name, the genre known as **opéra comique** was not always comic. But it allowed for spoken dialogue and placed far less emphasis on ballet, stage design, and crowd scenes. Composers like Charles Gounod (1818–1893), Bizet, and Jules Massenet (1842–1912) all contributed to this genre. Among the works still performed today are Gounod's *Faust*, Bizet's *Carmen*, and Massenet's *Manon*. The fate of Bizet's *Carmen* illustrates the gulf between the two worlds of French opera. In its original form, the work could not be presented at the prestigious Opéra. But shortly after Bizet's death, his friend Ernest Guiraud set

The quartet from Act III of Verdi's *Rigoletto*. This ensemble manifests one of the powers of opera to do what spoken drama cannot: convey contrasting emotions simultaneously. Inside the tavern, the Duke is seducing Maddalena (the sister of and co-conspirator with the assassin Sparafucile); outside, Gilda watches and listens in horror while her father, Rigoletto, asks if she is not now convinced that the man she loves (the Duke) is in fact a libertine. The room above (only the bottom of the window is visible here) is where the Duke will retire for the night and sing the reprise of his famous aria *La donn' è mobile*. Near the end of the opera, when Rigoletto hears the Duke singing again, he thinks at first it is a dream; but he quickly discovers it is in fact his daughter who has been murdered and not the Duke.

Source: Corbis/Bettmann

the spoken dialogues to music in the form of recitative and added a ballet scene to Act IV, drawing on music from other works by Bizet. In this guise—and still translated into Italian—*Carmen* became one of the most popular operas of all time.

Germany: Weber to Wagner

German opera had been slow to develop before the 19th century. Italians and French had dominated the German stage, both as composers and as performers. Most of the dramatic works even of the German-speaking composers Haydn and Mozart had Italian texts. The most important exceptions were Mozart's *Die Entführung aus dem Serail* ("The Abduction from the Seraglio") and *Die Zauberflöte* ("The Magic Flute"). Like Beethoven's later *Fidelio*, these works were *Singspiele*—that is, written in German, with spoken dialogue and only occasional accompanied recitatives.

Carl Maria von Weber (1786–1826) caused a sensation in 1821 with yet another work of this kind, *Der Freischütz*, the story of a hunter who strikes a bargain with the devil to win a shooting contest that in turn will allow him to marry the woman he loves. *Freischütz* is something of a Faust story with a happy ending, and Weber's setting captured the imagination of his contemporaries. The "Wolf's Glen Scene" at the end of Act II won special praise, with its electrifying combination of music and special effects, including diminished sevenths played on low tremolo strings, an offstage chorus, shadowy figures, and a burning wagon wheel careening across the stage. The use of spoken dialogue accompanied by the orchestra was known as **melodrama** (that is, dramatic speech with musical underpinning); already in the 18th century, opera-length works were written in this genre. Audiences also responded to the folklike arias, choruses, and dance scenes elsewhere in *Freischütz*. Weber's sudden death at the age of 39 cut short what would have certainly been a brilliant career, but his works inspired the next generation of German composers to write stage works in their native tongue.

The most important of Weber's successors was Richard Wagner (1813–1883). Like so many composers of his generation, Wagner was committed to making opera more dramatically realistic, but the approach he eventually settled on differed radically from that of Weber, Verdi, or for that matter any other figure in the history of the genre.

Wagner rejected traditional opera on the grounds that in it the libretto, the drama, served as little more than a pretext for the music, and more specifically, for virtuosic singing. Traditional opera, according to Wagner, suffered from a fatal flaw: neither of its constituent elements—text and music—could stand on its own, without the other. In other words, a staged, spoken performance of a typical opera libretto would be dramatically unsatisfactory, whereas a performance of an opera's score, without its text, would be musically incoherent. Even a composer as great as Mozart, Wagner maintained, could not overcome this fundamental problem. The "error of opera," declared Wagner, was that "a means of expression"—the music—had become an end in its own right while the goal of that expression—the drama—"had been made a means." The challenge for composers, Wagner maintained, was to integrate drama and music in a way that would work to the advantage of both.

The Elements of Wagnerian Music Drama

Accomplishing this integration, correcting the "error of opera," was easier said than done. Wagner struggled with this problem for decades but eventually arrived at a solution he considered so revolutionary that it represented not merely a new kind of opera, but an entirely new genre altogether, the **music drama.** In spite of its outward similarity to opera, Wagnerian music drama rests on premises and elements not ordinarily found in earlier forms of opera.

COMPOSER PROFILE   Giuseppe Verdi *(1813–1901)*

Little in Verdi's early life suggests his later greatness. He showed musical talent as a child but failed the entrance examination for the Milan Conservatory. He turned instead to private teachers and immersed himself in the study of harmony and counterpoint. Verdi then secured a series of conducting posts in his native Busseto, a relatively small community. His first opera, *Oberto*, scored a success at one of Europe's leading opera houses, La Scala in Milan, in 1840, opening further opportunities in the theater. Two years later, Verdi enjoyed even greater success with *Nabucco* (1842). The opera's chorus of the captive Israelites in Babylon (*Va, pensiero*) became one of the unofficial anthems of the simmering Italian uprising against the occupying Austrian forces, helping secure Verdi's place, at age 30, within the great tradition of Italian opera.

Several of Verdi's operas constituted thinly veiled appeals for the unification of Italy, which at the time was still a loose confederation of small states, many of them under the domination of the Austrians. Italian patriots seeking independence from the Austrians and unity for the Italian people used Verdi's name as an acronym for "**V**ittorio **E**manuele, **R**e **d'I**talia" ("Victor Emanuel, King of Italy"). This slogan, innocent enough on the surface ("We are only celebrating our favorite composer of opera!"), was in fact a deeply subversive rallying cry for Italian nationalists. Verdi himself became swept up in the political struggles of the day when he was voted into the newly constituted Italian parliament in 1860. He served until 1865 but by his own admission did not take an active role:

> For two long years I was absent from the Chamber and afterwards I attended only rarely. Several times I was about to hand in my resignation but some obstacle always came up at the last moment and I'm still a deputy against every wish and every desire, without having the slightest inclination nor aptitude nor talent. There you have it. Anyone who wishes or who has to write my biography as Member of Parliament has only to print in large letters in the middle on a blank sheet of paper: "The 450 are really only 449 because Verdi as a deputy doesn't exist."[1]

The remainder of Verdi's long life revolved around a series of commissions. He was at home in both Italy and France but spent the majority of his time in Milan. In addition to his Italian works for the stage, he produced two grand operas in French, *Les Vêpres siciliennes* (1855) and *Don Carlos* (1867). The influence of French grand opera is also evident in *Aïda* (1871, in Italian), commissioned to celebrate the opening of the Suez Canal. After being coaxed out of retirement, Verdi produced two operas that many consider his finest: *Otello* (1887) and

Falstaff (1893), the latter produced when Verdi was 80. Visitors who recorded their impressions of Verdi almost invariably spoke of the man's modesty and self-effacing nature. A few years before his death, he established a home for retired musicians unable to support themselves and consigned all his royalties for 30 years after his death to this institution.

PRINCIPAL WORKS

OPERAS The operas fall roughly into three periods. The works through the 1840s (including *Oberto*, *Nabucco*, *Ernani*, *Macbeth*, and *Luisa Miller*) build on traditions established by his predecessors. The middle-period works, beginning with *Rigoletto* (1851), include some of the composer's most popular operas—*Il Trovatore*, *La Traviata*, *Un ballo in maschera*, *La forza del destino*, and *Aïda*—which all remain staples of the operatic repertory. But Verdi was

Verdi. When preparing a new opera for production, Verdi's attention to detail was legendary. He coached the singers, kept or had made copious notes on staging and scenery, and devoted great care to historical detail. Although he could not attend the premiere of *Aïda* in Cairo in 1871, he made sure the stage designs were supervised by August Mariette, a renowned Egyptologist of the day.

Source: Library of Congress

---

1. Quoted in Julian Budden, *Verdi* (London: J. M. Dent, 1985), pp. 84–5, citing in turn *I copialettere di Giuseppe Verdi*, Milan, 1913, pp. 601–2. Used by permission of Oxford University Press, Oxford, U.K.

never content to remain within established formulas, and he was consistently able to make the operatic conventions of his day sound fresh and original. His style ranged from the utterly straightforward (homophonic texture, strophic form) to the astonishingly complex (polyphonic textures, through-composed forms). In his late works—*Otello* (1887) and *Falstaff* (1893)—he integrated the orchestra into the vocal texture to an unprecedented degree and at the same time developed a formal approach that considerably reduced the number of such recognizable units as arias and duets. Many contemporaries saw this change as a concession to Wagner's principles of music drama (discussed later). But anyone familiar with Verdi's earlier works can recognize the continuing development of tendencies already present in his earlier works.

SACRED MUSIC   After writing a few small sacred pieces in his early years, Verdi turned almost exclusively to opera. But after his initial retirement from the stage with *Aïda* in 1871, he returned to choral music on sacred themes. When Rossini died in 1868, Verdi conceived of asking 13 different Italian composers to contribute one movement each to a setting of the Requiem Mass. Verdi wrote the last movement, "Libera me," but the plan did not otherwise bear fruit. When he learned of the death of Alessandro Manzoni (1785–1873), poet and novelist, Verdi resolved to complete the Requiem himself. The result, his *Messa da Requiem*, premiered one year to the day after Manzoni's death. Its theatricality—the furor of the "Dies irae" is particularly famous—has led more than one wit to term it "Verdi's best opera." The *Four Sacred Pieces* were published in 1898; the first of these, *Ave Maria*,

is composed on what the composer called the "enigmatic scale"—of C-D♭-E-F♯-G♯-A♯-B-C—which is neither major nor minor nor even wholly diatonic, given the interval of three half steps between D♭ and E. Even the 85-year-old Verdi was open to chromatic experimentation.

KEY DATES IN LIFE OF VERDI	
1813	Born near Busseto (northern Italy) on October 10.
1832	Applies to the Milan Conservatory but is rejected for lack of technical knowledge; studies privately instead.
1839	His first opera, *Oberto*, is greeted warmly at La Scala in Milan, one of Italy's leading opera houses.
1840s	Establishes his reputation in Italy with a series of operatic successes, most notably *Nabucco*, *Macbeth*, and *Luisa Miller*.
1850s and 1860s	Achieves international fame with *Rigoletto* (1851), *Il Trovatore* (1853), *La Traviata* (1853), *Un ballo in maschera* (1859), and *Don Carlos* (1867, in French).
1871	Premiere of *Aïda*, commissioned for the opening of the Suez Canal and first performed in Cairo.
1887	Persuaded to come out of retirement to write two last operas on Shakespearean themes: *Otello* (1887) and *Falstaff* (1893).
1901	Dies in Milan on January 27.

The Ideal of the *Gesamtkunstwerk*.   Wagner summarized his approach to his art with an imposing term—*Gesamtkunstwerk*—a compound based on three German words:

- *Gesamt*, meaning "synthesized, unified, whole, complete, self-contained"

- *Kunst*, meaning "art" (that is, the arts in general, including music, poetry, and gesture or movement)

- *Werk*, meaning "work" (of art)

For Wagner, the *Gesamtkunstwerk* was a work that synthesized all the arts. It could be argued, of course, that opera had all along been integrating music, drama, poetry, gesture, architecture, and painting—the latter two through stage design. Wagner anticipated this charge by arguing that these various arts merely coexisted in the opera house, and not even very well. A true *Gesamtkunstwerk* was one in which all the requisite elements were at once both self-sufficient yet inextricable from one another. Thus

The "Wolf's Glen Scene" from Weber's *Der Freischütz*.
This illustration from the 1820s depicts the opera's central moment, when Max, the unlucky hunter, casts seven magic bullets under the guidance of the evil spirit Samiel. The scene was renowned for its combination of scenic and musical effects, most notably its extensive use of unharmonized chromaticism and diminished seventh chords, both of which filled contemporary listeners with a sense of mystery, horror, and the supernatural.

Source: Image Works/Mary Evans Picture Library Ltd.

the music should cohere as in a symphony by Beethoven, the drama should be as compelling as a drama by Goethe, and these two elements, music and drama, should be mutually motivating.

Drama as "Deeds of Music Made Visible." Wagner's breakthrough came with his realization that the drama being acted out on the stage could be treated as a visible and verbal manifestation of the drama being acted out by the instruments of the orchestra. He recognized that purely instrumental music was inherently dramatic but only in an abstract way. Inspired by such works as Beethoven's Third and Fifth Symphonies, and particularly the *Leonore* Overture no. 3 (see Chapter 15), Wagner sought to transfer the power of instrumental music into the theater by establishing "genuine drama on the basis of absolute music." In music drama, the music alone, separate from the text, should have its own dramatic coherence and trajectory. In a particularly memorable turn of phrase, Wagner called the drama—the events transpiring on the stage—"deeds of music made visible." What happens on the stage, in other words, is a tangible reflection of what is going on in the orchestra pit. By the same token, what happens in the orchestra pit is the musical manifestation of the actions on stage. Ideally, then, we should be able to follow the course of a Wagnerian music drama through the music alone, by tracing the fate of its various musical ideas. These musical ideas would eventually come to be known as *Leitmotivs*.

PRIMARY EVIDENCE

George Bernard Shaw on the Advantages of Opera over Drama

The playwright George Bernard Shaw (1856–1950) worked for many years as a music critic. His writings are always witty and often insightful. This passage, from an essay written in 1894, goes to the heart of Wagner's ability to integrate music and words and the advantages of music drama over traditional spoken drama; Shaw seems at odds with Johann Matheson's opinions concerning Baroque text setting (see Chapter 11).

—————✦✦✦—————

Wagner regarded all Beethoven's important instrumental works as tone poems; and he himself, though he wrote so much for the orchestra alone in the course of his music dramas, never wrote, or could write, a note of absolute music. The fact is, there is a great deal of feeling, highly poetic and highly dramatic, which cannot be expressed by mere words—because words are the counters of thinking, not of feeling—but which can be supremely expressed by music. The poet tries to make words serve his purpose by arranging them musically, but is hampered by the certainty of becoming absurd if he does not make his musically arranged words mean something to the intellect as well as to the feeling.

For example, the unfortunate Shakespeare could not make Juliet say:

> O Romeo, Romeo, Romeo, Romeo, Romeo;

and so on for twenty lines. He had to make her, in an extremity of unnaturalness, begin to argue the case in a sort of amatory legal fashion, thus:

> O Romeo, Romeo, wherefore art thou Romeo?
> Deny thy father and refuse thy name,
> Or, if thou wilt not, etc., etc., etc.

It is verbally decorative; but it is not love. And again:

> Parting is such sweet sorrow
> That I shall say goodnight till it be morrow;

which is a most ingenious conceit, but one which a woman would no more utter at such a moment than she would prove the rope ladder to be the shortest way out because any two sides of a triangle are together greater than the third.

Now these difficulties do not exist for the tone poet. He can make Isolde say nothing but "Tristan, Tristan, Tristan, Tristan, Tristan," and Tristan nothing but "Isolde, Isolde, Isolde, Isolde, Isolde," to their hearts' content without creating the smallest demand for more definite explanations; and as for the number of times a tenor and soprano can repeat "Addio, addio, addio," there is no limit to it.

Source: Reproduced in *Shaw on Music*, ed. Eric Bentley, pp. 114–15, which in turn quotes *The World*, January 17, 1894.

The Leitmotiv.   Literally, a "leading motive," a **Leitmotiv** is a brief musical idea connected to some person, event, or idea in a music drama. Opera composers had long used specific musical motifs as tags for specific dramatic themes, bringing them in repeatedly at appropriate points in a plot. The curse motif in Verdi's *Rigoletto* is a perfect example of this well-established practice of musical reminiscence. We hear it at the beginning of the Prelude as a kind of premonition, ominous and important but as yet unspecific; we realize its meaning when it accompanies the moment Monterone curses the jester; and we hear it again every time Rigoletto thinks about that fateful moment.

The occasional return of an isolated idea or two, however, cannot ensure the musical coherence of a work as sizable as an opera. To do that, Wagner expanded on the technique of reminiscence to create complex webs of musically interrelated and constantly changing motifs. What distinguishes Leitmotiv from reminiscence in Wagner's music dramas is (1) the musical metamorphosis of these ideas over time according to the dramatic situation, and (2) the musical and dramatic interrelationship of these motifs within a broad network of thematic ideas. A Leitmotiv, then, is a musical figure capable of growth, development, and transformation.

CD12, Track 3
WAGNER
Tristan und Isolde
Score Anthology II/139

The network of Leitmotivs in Wagner's *Tristan und Isolde* illustrates the way these thematic ideas work. Based on an ancient legend that had circulated in various forms throughout northern Europe, *Tristan und Isolde* tells a story of ill-fated love. Tristan, a knight in the service of King Mark, has been given the task of bringing the Irish princess Isolde back to Cornwall, on the western coast of England, where she is to marry Mark, against her will. But Tristan and Isolde have already met: she had nursed him back to health some years before, and Tristan now feels torn between his debt to her and his allegiance to King Mark. The two vow to drink poison and kill themselves before their ship lands in Cornwall, but Brangaene, Isolde's maidservant, substitutes a love potion for the poison. Tristan and Isolde fall madly in love, yet they must hide their passion from all others, especially King Mark. In Act II, the lovers contrive a pretext to meet alone: Tristan drops back from a hunting party and returns to the castle under cover of night. But their deception is revealed, a fight ensues, and in the closing Act III, Tristan dies of the new wounds he has suffered. Isolde, overcome with grief, sinks lifeless upon his corpse, uniting the two lovers in death.

In their simplest forms, the motifs in this opera have a one-to-one relationship with corresponding onstage actions. Wagner makes sure, for example, that we will associate the motif in Example 17–1 with the potion that causes Tristan and Isolde to fall in love. We hear it first at the beginning of the Prelude, but as with the curse motif that begins the Prelude to *Rigoletto*, we do not yet know its implications. But the symbolic associations of the motif become clear when the theme recurs in Act I at the moment when Tristan and Isolde (thinking they are about to die) drink the love potion. They do not die, of course, but are instead seized by passionate feelings for one another. Wagner has thereby established a direct connection between the music and the drama. What happens on stage—the drinking of the potion—is a visible manifestation of the music, which captures the sense of longing that seizes lovers at that inexplicable moment when they fall in love.

What conveys that sense of longing in this Leitmotiv is its celebrated dissonance, beginning with what has come to be known as the "Tristan chord" (F-B-D♯-G♯ on the downbeat of measure 2 in Example 17–1). Commentators have often cited the progression from this chord to the end of the motif as signaling the beginning of the end of traditional harmony. Although the progression can be described, technically, as a movement from an augmented ("French") sixth (F-B-D♯-A) to V^7 in the key of A minor (E-G♯-D-B), such an account scarcely captures the sense of harmonic instability this opening chord creates. The rhythmic emphasis on the dissonant G♯, which is held for almost an entire measure before resolving upward to A, was especially grating to contemporary ears. That this should be the very first harmony heard in the entire work made the dissonance all the more striking: although the unison opening of measure 1, played by the cellos, had suggested the key of A minor, it had not really established any firm sense of a tonal center. That the downbeat of the succeeding measure (measure 3) should also be dissonant compounded the perception of harmonic groundlessness. The concluding V^7 chord itself, moreover, remains unresolved, leading to a long silence,

Example 17–1 The "love potion" motif, with the "Tristan chord" highlighted

"Tristan" chord

followed by a series of upwardly moving chromatic progressions that similarly fail to resolve. This absence of harmonic resolution caused a sensation in Wagner's time, giving the "Tristan chord" its well-deserved notoriety.

Within the course of the Prelude, Wagner goes on to fragment, extend, transpose, invert, and otherwise manipulate this basic idea over and over again. The rising minor chromatic third first heard in measures 2–3 assumes special importance. Following the model of thematic elaboration provided by the instrumental music of Beethoven, Wagner manipulates a fragment of this theme (Example 17–2a, first measure; Example 17–2b) by using repetition, harmonic and melodic variation, and silence to enrich each successive statement. The Prelude as a whole follows no established convention of large-scale form. Instead, the music seems to propel itself forward through a series of constant transformations. The rising three-note figure that first appears in the cellos in measure 17, for example (Example 17–2, measure 2), represents a metamorphosis of the rising minor chromatic third from measures 2–3. This new idea, in turn, is further fragmented and manipulated (measures 36–37). The orchestra, all the while, builds gradually in size and volume, reaching a high point of sorts with the fortissimo statement of yet another version of the cello's theme at measure 74. But a crashing dissonance (measure 83) turns out to be the true climax, for it ushers in a return to the quiet tension of the opening (measure 85). There is no sense of resolution here: the music closes pianissimo and leads without a pause into the opening scene of Act I.

Having developed at least some of the intrinsically musical potential of the Prelude's central thematic idea, Wagner establishes its dramatic significance by bringing it back toward the end of Act I, at the crucial moment when Tristan and Isolde drink what they believe is a death potion. But what makes the technique of Leitmotiv different from the convention of isolated reminiscences is the manner in which the thematic transformations of these motifs relate to the events of the drama. When we listen to

Example 17-2 Subsequent transformations of the "love potion" motif

(a)

(b)

Act II more closely, we realize the distinctive chromatic rise in the "love potion" motif has actually been present for quite some time in a variety of guises—sometimes rising, sometimes falling—going all the way back to the Prelude to Act I. We hear these kinds of transformations in Act II, for example, when Brangaene laments having switched potions (measures 351–353), and then again even more tellingly shortly afterward (measures 380–382), when Isolde explains it was the power of love that caused the potion to transform itself. Here, underneath Isolde's declamation (beginning at measure 385), the orchestra spins out a series of thematic variants based on the characteristic rising chromatic third we first heard in the work's opening measures. Isolde now views the love potion quite differently, and the orchestra reflects this by presenting the motif within the guise of a softer, more lyrical tone. In Wagnerian terms, Isolde gives voice to what the orchestra is already expressing through music alone.

The motif known as "love's longing" (Example 17–3) represents yet another manipulation of the rising chromatic third. Here, the melodic trajectory is reversed: the chromatic line moves downward and is supported by a clearly outlined triadic base. The feeling here is more confident, more directional, as befits the dramatic situation. This motif dominates the tension that builds toward an event Isolde knows will happen: Tristan's return. Still another metamorphosis of this motif (Example 17–4) emerges when Tristan finally arrives: the theme becomes ecstatic in mood, rising in its opening to a high note before descending, rather than descending from the very start. Such changes, subtle but effective, have led more than one commentator to accord this idea a separate identity, associating it with the idea of "bliss," which is of course the desired consequence of longing. The musical and dramatic parallels function in tandem.

Example 17-3 "Love's longing"

Example 17–4 "Bliss"

Another prominent Leitmotiv in *Tristan und Isolde* is associated with death (*Tod* in the German text). Like the "love potion" motif, the "death" motif (Example 17–5) is chromatic and harmonically unusual. (Wagner often used chromatic themes or unusual harmonic progressions to evoke conditions of pain, such as love and death.) Although the "death" motif manifests itself in many different ways, its characteristic harmonic feature is the juxtaposition of two otherwise distant chords (such as Ab major and A major, as in Example 17–5, or C major and Ab major in Example 17–6), combined with a distinctive dotted rhythm.

Example 17–5 "Death"

Death-destined head! Death-destined heart!

Example 17–6 Transformation of the "death" motif

Life and death are subordinate [to love]

Example 17–7 "Hero's call"

Hail to our hero, Tristan, who knows how to exact tribute!

Having established these and other motifs in the listener's mind, Wagner is free to use them in any number of ways, some of them obvious, some of them not. Near the end of Act II, Scene 1, for example, when Isolde extinguishes her torch, signaling Tristan to leave the hunting party and return to the castle, Wagner embeds the "death" motif in the orchestra, beginning at measure 485; the texture is so thick at this point that the motif is not evident in the piano reduction of the score in the anthology. What is the connection between this moment and death? Once Tristan returns, the lovers will consummate their passion, which in turn will lead to their deaths. By linking the extinguishing of the torch to the "death" motif, Wagner is telling us, in musical terms, that the act carries ultimately fatal consequences.

More mundane elements of the plot receive appropriately mundane music. The "hero's call" motif with which Tristan's crew acclaims him in Act I (Example 17–7) is based on pointedly conventional harmonic and melodic progressions. The phrase is intentionally trite, and when Tristan hears it, he remains unmoved. His men literally sing his praises, but he himself is torn between loyalty to King Mark (to whom he is delivering Isolde) and a mixture of love and guilt toward Isolde. This "hero's call" motif, then, means nothing to Tristan, because it concerns only his public persona: it is associated with crowds, daylight, and the realm of reason. Its musical squareness provides an effective contrast with the private world of Tristan and Isolde's passion, which occupies the spheres of darkness and intimacy.

When the lovers are finally reunited in Act II, Isolde reminds Tristan in jest of how he had once loved the day, and the mock-heroic tone she briefly assumes (measure 776) recalls the music of this "hero's call" motif. After so much chromaticism, the music seems trite and distant from the passion of the moment. At an even more subtle level, Wagner transforms the very opening of this motif (a fifth down, then up a third stepwise) into a very different kind of idea used throughout much of Act II and associated with the idea of day. When the characters on stage speak of the day (*Tag*) or daylight (*Tageslicht*), we hear variants of this "hero's call" motif so consistently and repeatedly (particularly from measure 809 onward) that we might well label this manifestation of the motif the "day" motif.

The labels we have been using to identify these Leitmotivs, although useful for analyzing Wagner's music, can lead us to think of them (incorrectly) as fixed entities, both musically and in terms of their dramatic associations. Probably for this reason, Wagner himself almost never explicitly identified any of these themes. It would be tedious, pointless, and ultimately impossible to ascribe an individual name to every different manifestation of every motif, in any event. More important is to recognize how Wagner works his Leitmotivs into an ever-evolving web of complementary and contrasting musical and dramatic relationships that can sustain a work lasting many hours in performance.

The Relationship of Voice and Orchestra.   Wagner's Leitmotivs are sometimes sung, but more often they appear in the orchestra alone. In traditional opera, in

Cross-section of the Bayreuth Festspielhaus. In addition to writing his own librettos and music, Wagner designed his own theater, the "Festival Drama House," in Bayreuth, a small municipality halfway between Munich and Berlin. The design puts most of the orchestra beneath the stage. This ingenious device brings the audience closer to the stage and also projects the sound of the orchestra more directly toward the audience, creating a better blend of voices and the orchestra within the hall. The acoustics in Bayreuth have long been considered ideal for the integration of orchestral and vocal lines so characteristic of Wagner's music dramas.

Source: © 2003 Yale University Press/Spotts, *Bayreuth: A History of the Wagner Festival* (1994), image p. 9.

contrast, the voice carries the melody while the orchestra provides the accompaniment. Constant repetition of text is likewise common in traditional opera. Indeed text set to ornate vocal lines often has to be repeated if it is to be understood. Wagner abhorred this practice, and it was his desire to make the text intelligible that prompted him to shift the melodic element from the voice to the orchestra. Doing so allowed him to have the characters on stage sing in a declamatory manner lying between aria and recitative. A typical Wagnerian vocal line, considered without any accompaniment at all, is not nearly as lyrical as a vocal line by Verdi, but the texture of Wagner's writing allows the words to come through with remarkable clarity. His design for the opera house in Bayreuth (illustrated on p. 459) also helps the vocal line to project through and above a large orchestra.

The Structure of the Dramatic Text. Unlike most composers of opera, Wagner wrote his own librettos, developing in his mind (and occasionally committing to paper) the musical motifs to be associated with particular moments of the drama. Wagner was also careful to avoid distinctions between verse and prose in his librettos. Traditionally, arias had been written in metrical verse, recitative in prose. In his effort to eliminate what he considered the arbitrary and disturbing disjunction between recitative and aria, Wagner wrote his librettos in a consistently free poetic style that avoided any suggestion of metrical (and thus also melodic and musical) regularity. He did not, however, turn to entirely free verse, employing instead an alliterative poetic device called *Stabrheim* start here that had been cultivated in certain repertoires of German poetry of the Middle Ages. *Stabrheim* literally means "staff rhyme"—staff in the sense of a shepherd's crook, something that gathers together loose elements. What it gathers, though, is not rhyme (which typically occurs within an established metrical pattern) but rather the initial or internal sounds of two or more different words. For example, here are the words Isolde uses to command her servant to extinguish the light in Act II of *Tristan und Isolde* (beginning at measure 304):

> Lösche des Lichtes letzten Schein!
> Dass ganz sie sich neige, winke der Nacht!
> Schon goss sie ihr Schweigen durch Hain und Haus,
> schon füllt sie das Herz mit wonnigem Graus.

O lösche das Licht nun aus,
lösche den scheuchenden Schein!
Lass' meinen Liebsten ein!

(Extinguish the last glow of the light!
So that night might approach fully, give her [the night] a signal!
She has already poured her silence on field and house,
She already fills the heart with blissful horror.
Oh, extinguish the light,
Put out the frightening glow!
Let my lover in!)

This passage is typical of Wagner's texts, in that it rhymes at certain points (Haus/Graus/aus; Schein/mein) and, although it avoids any fixed, predictable rhythm, does verge at times on metrical regularity. As is characteristic of *Stabrheim*, its rhyme and meter are fluid, which is precisely the quality Wagner sought to bring out in the music to which these words would be declaimed. While the internal alliteration has its (intentional) bumps along the way, Anglo-Saxon and early English poetry made use of a similar approach.

Endless Melody.   Another concept central to Wagner's theory of music drama is what he called "endless melody." By "endless," Wagner meant fluidly continuous. His music dramas include units comparable to arias, but at least until the end of an act, these elide smoothly into subsequent material. Wagner thus keeps his music moving from the beginning to the end of an act, leaving the audience no opportunity to applaud in between. Indeed in two instances—the original version of *Der fliegende Holländer* (1841) and *Das Rheingold* (1854)—an entire work moves continuously from beginning to end without a break. "Endless" does not, as some of Wagner's critics suggested, mean interminable. His music dramas are no longer than the typical grand operas of his time.

By "melody," Wagner had in mind something different from what the term is commonly understood to mean. He differentiated "true melody" from what might be called filler. He abhorred the empty figuration that played such an important role in the Italian opera of his time and even in the instrumental music of Mozart. He sought to avoid virtuosity for virtuosity's sake, stressing the need for true melody at all times in both orchestral and vocal parts.

In practice, Wagner was not always entirely rigorous in applying his theories of music drama. There are recognizable numbers—arias, even strophic songs—woven into the fabric of his music from time to time. Once he had demonstrated the viability of his new approach, he seems to have felt free to use more traditional forms in his later music dramas. Wotan's farewell to Brünnhilde at the end of *Die Walküre*, the soaring love duet between Siegfried and Brünnhilde at the end of *Siegfried*, and the trio of revenge in Act II of *Götterdämmerung* are all in the tradition of 19th-century Italian and French opera. The playwright George Bernard Shaw (1856–1950), an ardent Wagnerite, placed the whole of *Götterdämmerung* with its vast sets, large choral numbers, and extended ensembles, squarely within the tradition of grand opera.

On the whole, however, Wagner's method of integrating music and text opened important new vistas for opera. His influence extended well beyond his lifetime, leaving a deep imprint on the operas of Richard Strauss, Arnold Schoenberg, Alban Berg, and even Giaccomo Puccini (see Chapter 21).

OPERETTA

Around the middle of the 19th century, the lighter genre of **operetta** began to establish itself. As the diminutive suffix suggests, this form of musical theater operated on a smaller scale than opera. It usually mixed spoken dialogue with sung numbers and dealt invariably with humorous and lighthearted subjects. Operetta was also more likely than opera to be composed or at least performed in the vernacular. Thus separate traditions of operetta developed in France, Germany, Italy, and even England, scarcely a bastion of operatic composition in the 19th century.

Operetta grew out of the long tradition of songs with plays. In 18th-century Germany, these were known as *Singspiele* (literally, "song plays") and included such works as Mozart's *Die Entführung aus dem Seraglio* and *Die Zauberflöte*, both of which were written to German texts. This tradition continued with later works like Johann Strauss's *Die Fledermaus* ("The Bat," 1874) and Franz Lehár's *Die lustige Witwe* ("The Merry Widow," 1905). In France, the operettas of Jacques Offenbach (1819–1880) were enormously popular. A transplanted German, Offenbach wrote more than ninety works of this kind, the most famous of which is *Orphée aux enfers* ("Orpheus in the Underworld," 1858), a farce on the ancient Greek legend in which Eurydice is quite happy to be in Hades. The work includes the famous "can-can" music danced by spirits of the underworld.

No English composer for the stage has achieved the enduring renown of Sir Arthur Sullivan (1842–1900), who, in partnership with the librettist Sir William S. Gilbert (1836–1911), created a long string of box office successes that continue to fill theaters today. Gilbert and Sullivan's *Pirates of Penzance* (1879) illustrates both the similarities and differences between 19th-century opera and operetta. It draws heavily on the principal forms of opera, with numbers that are easily recognizable as arias, duets, ensembles, and even accompanied recitatives. At the same time, the work manages to poke fun at almost every one of these very same conventions. The General's famous patter song ("I am the Very Model of a Modern Major General") is entertaining enough in its own right and even more so when we realize it is a parody of a model established by Rossini. In addition to the humor inherent in the song's rapid declamation, it is also incongruous to see a supposedly noble figure of authority like a general performing in a manner usually reserved for servants like Leporello in Mozart's *Don Giovanni* or Rossini's *Figaro*.

Still, the distinction between opera and operetta was not always clear, even in the 19th century. The New York orchestra rehearsing the world premiere of *The Pirates of Penzance* threatened to go on strike on the grounds that the new work was an opera rather than an operetta and the musicians should therefore be paid on a higher scale. But a strike was averted and *Pirates* opened to great acclaim. Within 18 months it had been performed not only in such major cities as Boston, Philadelphia, Chicago, St. Louis, and New Orleans, but also in smaller cities in New Jersey, Pennsylvania, Ohio, Indiana, Michigan, Missouri, Tennessee, Kentucky, Kansas, Nebraska, Iowa, Minnesota, and Wisconsin.

CD12, Track 5
GILBERT AND SULLIVAN
Pirates of Penzance
Score Anthology II/140

CHORAL MUSIC

Choral music was a genre by which art music composers could reach an audience away from the operatic world. Musical literacy had become even more a part of the educational curriculum throughout Europe than ever before. Singing had always been part of religious observance; now a new repertoire of a cappella, four-part songs

COMPOSER PROFILE   Richard Wagner *(1813–1883)*

"Wagner," one historian recently observed, "is the most controversial artistic figure of all time." Such a claim might well seem like an exaggeration at first, but it is difficult to think of any other artist who has aroused such powerful feelings of support and opposition over such a long period of time. Musically, politically, and personally, Wagner has been worshiped by some, reviled by others. Indeed it is often said there are only two other figures in the history of the world about whom more has been written: Jesus Christ and Napoleon. This probably *is* an exaggeration, but the frequency with which this claim is repeated reflects the never-ending fascination with the figure of Wagner, whose cultural importance goes far beyond the world of music.

Born in Leipzig, Wagner aspired early to a career as a composer and conductor. He immersed himself in the music of Beethoven and put bread on his table by writing music criticism. A series of increasingly prestigious positions as a conductor of opera in Germany culminated in his appointment as Kapellmeister in Dresden in 1843. Wagner would have been assured success had he stayed in this prestigious position the rest of his life, for he had outstanding resources at his disposal there.

The Revolution of 1848 changed everything. Wagner fought on the barricades, in effect seeking to overthrow the very regime that employed him. A warrant was issued for his arrest and he fled to Switzerland, where he lived in exile for the next decade, composing, among other works, *Tristan und Isolde*. He eventually won the support of King Ludwig II of Bavaria, who spared no expense to support the composer and his art. It was around this time, in the mid-1860s, that Wagner became intimate with Cosima Liszt von Bülow, the daughter of Franz Liszt and the wife of the conductor Hans von Bülow. Wagner, Cosima, and von Bülow lived for a time in a bizarre ménage à trois, with all three devoted to Wagner's art. Eventually, Cosima divorced von Bülow and married Wagner, by whom she had already borne three children.

The final phase of Wagner's life centered around Bayreuth, a small city roughly halfway between Munich and Berlin, the respective capitals of Bavaria and Prussia. "Germany" had only recently become a political reality, and it was Wagner's aim to build in Bayreuth a *Festspielhaus*—a "festival drama house"—that would unify Germany culturally as well. Wagner oversaw every detail of the building and the performances to be held within it. Thus, when the *Ring* received its premiere there in 1876, Wagner could legitimately claim not only to have written the libretto and the music, but to have built the opera house as well. He died in Venice in 1883.

As a critic, Wagner was one of the most prolific and influential of all composers who have also written about music. In addition to his early reviews, he wrote program notes, pamphlets, numerous essays, an autobiography, and an especially important (if long-winded) three-volume treatise entitled *Opera and Drama* (1850).

As an individual, Wagner is one of the least appealing composers in the history of music. He was vain and selfish, almost never paid his debts on time, and was deeply anti-Semitic. During the Third Reich, Hitler gave Wagner special prominence in the pantheon of German

Richard Wagner at his home in Bayreuth. This richly symbolic scene shows Wagner in the last year of his life at the center of an admiring circle of intimates, all eyes on him. The composer, standing, is reading from the libretto of his latest (and last) work, *Parsifal*, which received its premiere in Bayreuth in 1882, the same year in which this group portrait was executed. On the wall above his left shoulder is a portrait of the great German philosopher Arthur Schopenhauer, who had singled out music as the greatest of all the arts because it alone could capture the essence of the universe. Wagner's position suggests that he and his works embody Schopenhauer's ideas. Sitting to the composer's right is his wife, Cosima Liszt Bülow Wagner. A portrait of Cosima leans against the back wall, above her head. On the floor behind her is a painting of one of the sets from *Parsifal*, the Temple of the Grail. The first figure to Wagner's left is his father-in-law, Franz Liszt, who seems to be conducting an imaginary orchestra from a manuscript, probably the score of *Parsifal*, in his lap. Wagner's hands overlap Liszt's, symbolizing the important links—both familial and artistic—between these two musical giants of the 19th century. The third seated figure, Hans von Wolzogen, was a disciple of Wagner who wrote many pamphlets identifying the Leitmotivs in Wagner's music dramas.

Source: Anonymous, "Wagner with Liszt, and Liszt's daughter, Cosima"/ Wagner Museum, Bayreuth, Germany/The Bridgeman Art Library composers. The composer's virulent nationalism and anti-Semitism meshed well with the ideals of Nazi Germany, and to this day, performances of Wagner's music are for all practical purposes banned in Israel. The posthumous use of any composer's work remains problematic, however. In Germany, almost every political faction from the far left to the far right has appropriated the music of Beethoven at one time or another. Whether or not this has or should change our opinion of Beethoven and his works remains an open question.

The painting by W. Beckmann reproduced here shows Wagner at home in Bayreuth surrounded by family and other intimates.

PRINCIPAL WORKS

In his early years, Wagner wrote in a variety of genres, including song, sonata, and quartet; he even tried his hand at the symphony on more than one occasion. But the young composer soon recognized that his talents and interests lay in the realm of theater music, and from the 1840s onward, almost all his most significant works are operas—or, as he called his later works, "music dramas." Dates in parentheses here represent the date of first performances.

EARLY OPERAS Wagner used a number of models for his early operas, drawing particularly on the works of Rossini, Donizetti, Weber, and Heinrich Marschner for *Die Feen*, a fairy-tale opera; *Das Liebesverbot*, a comic opera based on Shakespeare's *Measure for Measure*; and *Rienzi*, a grand opera based on a contemporary novel about a tribune of the Roman Empire.

THE ROMANTIC OPERAS *Der fliegende Holländer* ("The Flying Dutchman," 1843) is based on the Norse legend of the sea captain who is condemned to eternal wandering and who will find rest, and death, only through the love of a woman. Every seven years, the Dutchman lands ashore to seek his salvation, which he ultimately finds in a woman named Senta. The most famous number in the opera is Senta's ballad in Act II, in which she tells the story of the Dutchman and becomes transported by her own narrative.

Tannhäuser (1845) is an opera about the minnesingers, medieval Germany's equivalent of the French troubadours and trouvères (see Chapter 1). Once again, Wagner deals with the redemptive power of a woman's love and the title character's struggle between sensual pleasure and religious faith.

Lohengrin (1850) also draws on Germanic legend. Lohengrin, a knight of mysterious origins, makes a dramatic appearance just in time to defend the honor of

Elizabeth, who has been falsely accused of murdering her brother. Lohengrin makes only one demand of Elizabeth: that she accept him for who he is and not demand to know his name or his lineage. Elizabeth accepts this condition, and Lohengrin defeats her accuser in a duel, thereby winning her hand in marriage. But plotting by the defeated accuser and his sister eventually drives Elizabeth mad with curiosity, and she puts the fateful question to Lohengrin just before they are to be married. (The famous wedding march known as *Here Comes the Bride* is from this opera.) In *Lohengrin*, we sense that Wagner is on the edge of making the breakthrough from traditional opera to the music drama.

THE MUSIC DRAMAS *Tristan und Isolde* (1859) draws on a medieval legend to tell the story of the tragic love triangle of Tristan, Isolde, and King Mark. As in so many of Wagner's works, redemption comes only through death.

Die Meistersinger von Nürnberg (1868), like *Tannhäuser*, deals with the minnesingers of medieval Germany, but in a much more lighthearted vein. In this thinly veiled account of Wagner's own battle with his critics, Beckmesser, a pedant, insists that songs must always be written according to the rules while other characters show him just how dry and stale such an approach is. Wagner weaves a love story around all of this, but for once no one dies in the end.

Wagner worked on the libretto for *Der Ring des Nibelungen* ("The Ring of the Nibelungs," 1876) from the late 1840s through the mid-1850s before setting the text to music. He interrupted his work for some seven years in the late 1850s and early 1860s to compose *Tristan* and *Meistersinger*. Although some of the works in the *Ring* cycle were premiered individually, the cycle as a whole received its debut at the newly opened Festspielhaus in Bayreuth in 1876. The plot, based on various legends from Norse mythology, is intricate and highly symbolic, revolving around a web of conflicts that pits love against both power and duty. The *Ring* consists of four separate works performed ideally on four successive days: *Das Rheingold*, *Die Walküre*, *Siegfried*, and *Götterdämmerung*.

In *Parsifal* (1882), Wagner turned again to medieval legend. The title character is the "perfect" fool, an innocent who discovers the truths of life, self-denial, and love (both sacred and profane) through the Fellowship of the Grail. It was Wagner's wish that *Parsifal* never be performed anywhere except at Bayreuth. Fortunately, this wish has been disregarded.

KEY DATES IN THE LIFE OF WAGNER

1813	Born in Leipzig (Germany) on May 22.
1831	Studies composition with Theodor Weinlig, cantor of the *Thomasschule* and thus an indirect successor to J. S. Bach.
1832	Publishes first composition, a piano sonata, and writes a symphony, both strongly influenced by the music of Beethoven.
1833–1843	Takes on a series of increasingly responsible positions in German opera houses (Würzburg, Königsberg, Riga), with a three-week stint in debtors' prison (1840).
1843	Appointed music director at the Royal Opera House in Dresden, one of the most coveted positions of its kind in Germany.
1848–1849	Participates actively in the Revolution; a warrant is issued for his arrest, and he flees to Switzerland.
1850s	While in exile, writes *Tristan und Isolde*, begins composing *Der Ring des Nibelungen*, and writes several important treatises on music.
1864	Receives support from the new king of Bavaria, Ludwig II ("Mad Ludwig"), who supports Wagner financially with public funds, much to the dismay of the Bavarians and the members of Ludwig's court.
1868	First contact with the philosopher Friedrich Nietzsche, who at first supports Wagner and later turns against him.
1870	Marries Cosima Liszt von Bülow, who keeps a detailed diary that records the remainder of the composer's life in astonishing detail.
1872	Cornerstone laid for the Festspielhaus in Bayreuth. The central work on the dedicatory concert is Beethoven's Ninth Symphony, the work Wagner considered the cornerstone for the "Music of the Future."
1876	The Bayreuth Festspielhaus opens with the first complete performance of the *Ring* cycle.
1883	Dies in Venice on February 13.

CD12, Track 7
CLARA WIECK SCHUMANN
Vorwärts!
Score Anthology II/141

was written expressly for amateur small choruses (often, but not always all men or women), which gathered on a regular basis to perform. If this practice's *raison d'être* was primarily social at first (as portrayed in "The expansion of musical literacy" in Chapter 14), it was soon taken far more seriously by others, who formed singing clubs (*Singverein*) with strong community ties, performing in concerts and competitions and opening a new market for publishers.

It was for such a group that Clara Wieck Schumann (see Composer Profile) wrote *Drei gemischte Chöre* (Three Mixed Choruses, to texts by Emanuel Geibel, 1848), from which "Vorwärts" (Forwards) is taken. ("Vorwärts" is the universal German cry into battle, whatever the mission and whenever and wherever it might take place.) The text was written in 1840, when stirrings against autocratic post-Napoleonic governments were being felt. Schumann's setting, composed as the 1848–49 revolutions were on the verge of breaking out, is full of fervor; does not simply repeat the music for all five strophes. The composer structures the music as $ABA^1B^1A^2$; the repeated final phrase ("Wer den Himmel will gewinnen, /Muss ein rechter Kämpfer sein!"—Who would win the heavens must be a true fighter!) features a climactic high note on "Himmel" (heavens) and a brief staggered entry for further emphasis prior to the close of the piece. It should be noted that the choruses remained in manuscript and were not published until 1988, which certainly kept Schumann out of political difficulty at the time.

COMPOSER PROFILE   Clara Wieck Schumann *(1819–1896)*

Clara Wieck Schumann was one of the most celebrated piano virtuosos of the 19th century, and her work as a composer has been recognized more and more in recent decades. Her partnership with Robert Schumann reflects the evolving pattern of relationships between men and women in 19th-century society. The two married out of love, against her father's wishes, and they forged a musical partnership throughout their 16 years of marriage, which ended only with Robert's death in 1856. They concertized widely—Robert conducting, Clara performing on the piano—throughout Europe. Indeed in many respects Clara was more famous as a virtuoso than Robert was as a composer.

Clara was the daughter of Robert's piano instructor, Friedrich Wieck, but the courtship was not an easy one. Wieck did not want his daughter to marry a composer and journalist, particularly one of such limited financial means as Schumann. In the middle of an extended series of legal battles with her father, the couple eloped. Until her father eventually reconciled himself to the marriage, Clara found herself in often heartbreaking conflict with him. At one point she had to go to court to get back from him a piano she herself had paid for. She nevertheless concertized widely, and her performances of Beethoven's sonatas and concertos, Chopin's piano pieces, and her husband's compositions were legendary in their time. She developed a close relationship with Johannes Brahms, 14 years younger, who helped her manage her affairs during the difficult last years of her husband's life. After his death, she resumed her concert touring; later in life, she edited the first complete edition of her husband's works.

For a photo of Clara Schumann with her husband Robert, see page 430.

PRINCIPAL WORKS OF CLARA WIECK SCHUMANN

Clara Schumann worked in many of the same genres as Robert Schumann, even before their marriage. She composed songs, part-songs, and several works of chamber music, the most notable of which is the Piano Trio in G minor, op. 17 (1846). She also wrote a Piano Concerto in A minor in 1836, ten years before her future husband's piano concerto in the same key.

KEY DATES IN THE LIFE OF CLARA WIECK SCHUMANN

1819	Born in Leipzig on September 13.
1828	After studying piano with her father, gives her first public recital.
1832–1839	Gives concert tours throughout Germany, Austria, and France.
1840	Against her father's wishes, marries Schumann; concertizing over the next 16 years includes an extended tour of Russia.
1856	Moves to Berlin with her children after her husband's death; continues concertizing.
1878–1882	Directs the piano division of the Hoch Conservatory of Music in Frankfurt.
1896	Dies in Frankfurt on May 20.

The growing importance of instrumental music and the fierce debate about the nature of opera during the 19th century have tended to obscure the many important works of sacred music written during this time. As with other genres, settings of the Mass grew considerably in length: Beethoven's *Missa solemnis*, op. 123, and Bruckner's Mass in F minor both run well over an hour in performance. Schubert, Weber, Mendelssohn, Schumann, and Liszt also contributed to this repertory. Settings of the Requiem enjoyed special favor in the 19th century, most notably at the hands of Berlioz, Verdi, and Fauré. The first two are particularly theatrical, combining chorus and orchestra (and in Berlioz's work, multiple orchestras) to great effect.

The oratorio also flourished, allowing composers a chance to write sacred vocal music to librettos of their own choosing. The oratorios of Handel remained the model for virtually all 19th-century composers, including Beethoven (*Christ on the Mount of Olives*), Mendelssohn (*Elijah, Paulus*), Berlioz (*L'enfance du Christ*), and Brahms (*A German Requiem*, set to biblical texts). These works combine large choruses (almost always with at least one extended fugue), solo arias, and solo ensembles, mixed with recitative.

CD12, Track 8
BRUCKNER
Virga Jesse floruit
Score Anthology II/142

Over the course of the 19th century, the Catholic church became increasingly uncomfortable with what it perceived to be the overly virtuosic and operatic nature of music written for the liturgy. These misgivings are reminiscent of the objections raised at the Council of Trent in the mid-16th century about the "profane" nature of sacred music (see Chapter 6). A number of 19th-century composers allied themselves to what came to be known as the **Caecilian movement,** named after the patron saint of music, which sought to restore Gregorian chant and the style of 16th-century a cappella polyphony as the ideals of church music. During the 1830s, the Benedictine monks of Solesmes, France, began to prepare critical editions of Gregorian chant, and a number of composers cultivated a self-consciously archaic style modeled on the polyphonic sacred works of the late Renaissance. Bruckner's motet *Virga Jesse floruit,* for example, is indebted to what was broadly known as the "Palestrina style" in its rhythms and textures, even if its harmonies are highly chromatic from time to time. No one would mistake this for a work by Palestrina, yet Palestrina's influence is undeniably evident in this and many other sacred works of the period.

CONCLUSION

In spite of the growing prestige of instrumental music, vocal music more than maintained its hold on the musical world of the 19th century. In Italy, Giuseppe Verdi developed an approach to opera that strove to create a greater sense of dramatic realism by integrating text and music to an unprecedented degree. In Germany, Richard Wagner sought to fuse operatic and symphonic idioms in a new genre he called the music drama, in which the dramatic coherence of the music coming from the orchestral pit was as important as the dramatic coherence of the words and gestures unfolding on the stage. Operetta, a lighter form of opera with spoken dialogue between the musical numbers, attracted even wider audiences. And although the importance of the church as a patron of new music declined somewhat in the 19th century, composers of this era produced a remarkable range and quantity of sacred music, from monumental works in the most advanced idiom to small-scale compositions reflecting the influence of Renaissance masters.

Orchestral Music, 1850–1900

The civic orchestra, a permanent ensemble located in a single city and giving a regular schedule of public concerts season after season, became the predominant musical institution for orchestral music in the second half of the 19th century. Few such ensembles had existed before this time. The orchestra Haydn conducted in England in the 1790s was assembled expressly for him and disbanded after he left; London had no organization providing regular concerts until the establishment of the Philharmonic Society in 1813. Vienna—home to Mozart, Beethoven, and other prominent composers—offered only occasional concerts performed by mostly ad hoc ensembles until the establishment of the Vienna Philharmonic in 1842. The New York Philharmonic was likewise established in 1842. The leading orchestra of Paris in the 1820s and 1830s was that of the Conservatory. By the end of the century, however, every city with any claim to cultural significance could boast its own opera company and civic orchestra. Smaller cities housed both in a single building, whereas larger, more affluent cities built separate structures for each.

MUSIC FOR DANCING AND MARCHING

The concert hall was not the only important venue for orchestral music in the 19th century. Others included the dance hall, music hall, and parade ground. Dance halls and music halls served up food, drink, and music in varying proportions to clients from all classes of society. Dance, which offered unmarried couples the opportunity for physical contact at a time when it was otherwise frowned on, was a vital element in the rituals of courtship, and music was indispensable for dance. The most popular dances in the 19th century were the quadrille (a type of square dance), the polka (a lively dance in duple meter), and, above all, the waltz, which originated in Vienna in the last decades of the 18th century and swept all Europe in the first decades of the 19th. Much of its popularity was due to the nature of the dance itself. It was one of the first socially acceptable dances that allowed partners to hold each other in a relatively close embrace, with the man's hand on his partner's back. George Gordon,

Lord Byron, captured the mania for the dance in 1812 in these lines from his "The Waltz: An Apostrophic Hymn":

> Endearing Waltz!—to thy more melting tune
> Bow Irish jig and ancient rigadoon.
> Scotch reels, avaunt! And country-dance, forego
> Your future claims to each fantastic toe!
> Waltz—Waltz alone—both legs and arms demands,
> Liberal of feet and lavish of her hands;
> Hands which may freely range in public sight
> Where ne'er before—but—pray "put out the light." . . .

"How uneasy an English mother would be to see her daughter so familiarly treated," Charles Burney remarked in an entry on the "Waltz" for an English encyclopedia that appeared in 1819, "and still more so to witness the obliging matter in which the freedom is returned by the females."

The popularity of the waltz was boosted by the memorable music written for it by such composers as Joseph Lanner (1801–1843) and the two Johann Strausses, father (1804–1849) and son (1825–1899). All three hailed from Vienna, a city that became inextricably linked in the public mind with the waltz. The younger Strauss's *On the Beautiful Blue Danube* (1867) is representative of the genre. It consists of an extended introduction followed by a series of individual waltzes (numbered 1, 2, 3, etc.), most in binary form, each with its own thematic idea, and some with their own introductions (marked *Intrada* ["entry"] in the score). This modular structure allowed ensembles to repeat any individual waltz as often as needed. At the same time, Strauss was careful to integrate the sequence of dances into a coherent whole. The introduction (notated in A major but heard as the dominant of D) establishes the tonic key of D major for most of the waltzes. The fourth waltz modulates to F major for the sake of harmonic variety, and an extended coda brings the work to a close in the tonic and reprises the theme of the opening waltz.

Typically for dance music, each of the individual waltzes within *An der schönen blauen Donau* is built on units of 4 or 8 measures, which join to create larger units of 16 or 32 measures, and most of the waltzes follow a simple ABA pattern. This kind of rhythmic and structural predictability was essential for the function of social dance and would become the basis for many forms of dance or dance-related genres in the 20th century, including ragtime, the blues, and even rock and roll.

Music halls offered a mixture of instrumental and vocal works together with comedy, vaudeville routines, and animal acts. *Ta-Ra-Ra-Boom-de-ay*, still used in circuses today, is a typical music hall song of the 1890s. It was described by one critic of the time as

> a senseless ditty with a dismal yet fascinating melody. . . . "Ta-Ra-Ra-Boom-de-ay" drove all London mad, and the rest of the world marveled at its madness. It became an epidemic. Babies lisped it, school children sang it, tottering old men and staid old ladies hummed it, and street boys whistled and shrieked it. Costers [street vendors] . . . stamped, kicked, and yelled it until they were hoarse and feeble from sheer exhaustion. Street organs and German bands played nothing else: it was taken up and echoed from town to village, and the cry throughout the land from cockcrow till midnight was "Ta-Ra-Ra-Boom-de-ay."[1]

CD12, Track 9
STRAUSS
An der schönen blauen Donau
Score Anthology II/143

---

1. Anonymous source of the 1890s, quoted in Archibald Haddon, *The Story of the Music Hall* (London: Fleetway Press, 1935), p. 96.

Music and industry. In 19th- and early-20th-century America, businesses routinely commissioned musical works to commemorate special events. John Philip Sousa's *King Cotton March* (1895) was commissioned by an industrial trade fair, the Cotton States and International Exposition, held in Atlanta in 1895. Note the enormous variety of instruments for which the work has been arranged: two mandolins and piano, two mandolins and guitar, zither solo, etc.

Source: Hartman Center for Sales, Advertising & Marketing History

CD12, Track 10

SOUSA
King Cotton
Score Anthology II/144

The march, like dance music, was written to coordinate physical movement—in this case, of soldiers. In the hands of such masters as the American composer John Philip Sousa (1854–1932), however, the march became a genre for the bandstand as well as the parade ground. Like Strauss's waltzes, Sousa's marches are invariably modular in structure and build on units of 4, 8, 16, and 32 measures. But Sousa's marches are less concerned with issues of tonal closure; in fact, he often ends his marches in the subdominant. *King Cotton*, for example, begins in E♭ major but closes in A♭ Major. While the 6/8 time signature may seem odd for a march (usually in a duple or quadruple meter), the effect is that each beat equals a triplet in eighth notes; the modular measure groupings further subdivide into (2 + 2 triplets) = 12/8, conducted as 4/4.

A women's banjo, mandolin, and guitar ensemble, ca. 1890. Every American high school and college has its musical organizations, but few can boast of an ensemble like this particular group, probably from a college toward the end of the nineteenth century. This group might well have included in its repertory one of the many arrangements of John Philip Sousa's *King Cotton March*.

Source: James Bollman

FOCUS — Music Periodicals of the 19th Century

With rare exceptions, the relatively few music periodicals established in the 18th century were short lived. The 19th century, by contrast, witnessed an explosion in the number of journals devoted exclusively to music. Many of these survived for a decade or more, and a few remain in publication today. These are some of the more important journals of the 19th century:

- *Allgemeine musikalische Zeitung* (Leipzig, 1798–1848; 1863–1865; 1866–1882). The "General Musical News," originally published by the firm Breitkopf & Härtel, reported musical events from across Europe and also printed many important reviews and essays, including E. T. A. Hoffmann's famous review of Beethoven's Fifth Symphony (see Primary Evidence feature, Chapter 15).

- *Neue Zeitschrift für Musik* (also Leipzig, 1834–). Founded and first edited by Robert Schumann, the "New Journal of Music" offered direct competition to the *Allgemeine musikalische Zeitung*, which Schumann

and his circle perceived as stuffy and old-fashioned. The *Neue Zeitschrift für Musik*, which has continued under various different names to the present day, was the forum for most of Schumann's writings on music, including his celebrated review of Berlioz's *Symphonie fantastique* and his essay of extravagant praise for the young Johannes Brahms (see Primary Evidence: Schumann Proclaims the Young Brahms a Musical Messiah, later in this chapter).

- *The Musical Times* (London, 1844–) provides a fascinating mirror of musical life in Great Britain. The advertisements alone reveal much about the changing nature of music from the mid-19th century to the present day.

- *Dwight's Journal of Music* (Boston, 1852–1881), founded and edited by John Sullivan Dwight, provides an important record of the growth of music in the United States.

THE BALLET

Accounts of theatrical dance go back as far as the Renaissance, and ballet had played an important role in opera since the very beginnings of that genre around 1600. Ballet nevertheless assumed unprecedented importance in the 19th century. It began to provide the main attraction for entire evenings of public entertainment in Paris in the 1870s. Ballet offered yet another approach to that enduring artistic dilemma: how to reconcile the abstract with the concrete. Ballet is less abstract than purely instrumental music, but without words, it avoids the specificity of opera. Audiences are free to interpret the dancers' movements as direct representations of emotions or actions, or they can view these gestures abstractly, as movements that are beautiful in their own right.

The 19th century witnessed many technical innovations in ballet, including a more athletic kind of movement, as well as dancing *en pointe* (on the tips of the toes). Costumes became shorter, and eventually skintight, showcasing the human form. On the whole, choreography avoided realism, combining massive formations of dancers (as in Hollywood musicals of the 1930s and 1940s) with a focus on a principal female soloist, the *prima ballerina*. Male dancers remained secondary until the early 20th century. In their time, the ballerinas Marie Taglioni, Fanny Elssler, Fanny Cerrito, Carolotta Frisi, and Lucille Grahn were as admired as the most celebrated singers and instrumental virtuosos.

France, which had always been preeminent in the field of dance, continued to lead the way in the 19th century, as ballet became an increasingly public genre, moving outside the patronage of the courts. The most prominent French ballet composers of the period were Adolphe Adam (1803–1856) and Léo Delibes (1836–1891). Adam's *Giselle* (1841) and Delibes's *Coppélia* (1870) remain staples of the ballet repertoire.

In the last third of the century, the Russian composer Peter Ilyich Tchaikovsky (1840–1893) emerged as the preeminent ballet composer. Tchaikovsky's lyrical melodies and rich orchestrations combined to make his *Swan Lake* (1876), *Sleeping*

CD12, Track 11
TCHAIKOVSKY
The Nutcracker
Score Anthology II/145

COMPOSER PROFILE   Peter Ilyich Tchaikovsky *(1840–1893)*

Tchaikovsky was a late bloomer. He did not enter a musical conservatory until the age of 21, having already secured a position as a government clerk. Within five years, however, he was teaching harmony at the Moscow Conservatory. A wealthy widow, Nadezhda von Meck, provided him with a long series of generous commissions that allowed him to resign his teaching position in 1878 and devote himself entirely to composition. Remarkably, Tchaikovsky never met his patroness, preferring instead to keep the relationship on an idealized plane through an extensive correspondence. By the time Madame von Meck withdrew her support in the late 1880s, Tchaikovsky had achieved wealth and fame on his own.

As a conductor, Tchaikovsky traveled widely across Europe and even made a brief tour of the United States in 1891. His highly popular Piano Concerto no. 1, through a series of odd circumstances, had received its premiere in Boston in 1875. He was an intensely private individual who acknowledged his homosexuality privately but otherwise kept it concealed for fear of public condemnation. The strain of this concealment, some have speculated, contributed to his repeated bouts of depression.

Tchaikovsky embraced his Russian heritage but did not make a display of it, unlike some of his contemporaries, who made a point of writing explicitly nationalistic music. Stylistically, Tchaikovsky was an internationalist, blending Russian, French, Italian, and German traditions with his remarkable gift for melody.

The circumstances surrounding his death have long been controversial. He died apparently of cholera during an epidemic of the disease in St. Petersburg. Some maintain that he knowingly drank contaminated water, effectively committing suicide, but nothing in his correspondence suggests he was unusually depressed at the time.

PRINCIPAL WORKS

BALLETS AND OPERAS Even had he written nothing else, Tchaikovsky's ballets would be enough to justify his fame as a composer. *Swan Lake* (1876), *Sleeping Beauty* (1889), and *The Nutcracker* (1892) all became immediate staples of the repertory. Nineteenth-century Russia looked westward to France as its principal cultural model, but Russian achievements in the realm of ballet eventually surpassed those of France. Tchaikovsky also wrote many operas, only a few of which are well known today, most notably *Eugene Onegin* (1879) and *Queen of Spades* (1890).

SYMPHONIES, OVERTURES, CONCERTOS Tchaikovsky's six completed symphonies are remarkable for their lyricism, orchestration, and dramatic tone. Formally, they broke little new ground, although the last, the *Pathétique*, has a waltzlike second movement in 5/4 and ends with a long slow movement full of heroic resignation rather than triumph. Tchaikovsky also cultivated the symphonic poem, preferring the more traditional designation of "overture" for these works. The celebrated *1812 Overture*, written to commemorate the Russian victory over Napoleon's invading army, incorporates the French and Russian national anthems and concludes with a blast of cannons. The First Piano Concerto and the Violin Concerto are among the most enduringly popular works of their kind.

Tchaikovsky. When the composer toured the United States in 1891, he helped inaugurate the newly built Carnegie Hall in New York City. His tour was sponsored, in part, by the Knabe & Co. Piano Manufactory of Baltimore, at the time the third largest piano manufacturer in the world.

Source: Library of Congress

Beauty (1889), and *The Nutcracker* (1892) among the most enduringly popular works of their kind. *The Nutcracker*, based on the well-known story by E. T. A. Hoffmann, combines a real-life plot with fairy-tale fantasy. In Act I, a mysterious inventor named Drosselmeyer gives a young girl, Clara, a magical nutcracker as a present. At night the nutcracker comes to life and leads an army of toy soldiers into battle with an army of mice. When Clara saves the Nutcracker's life, he transforms into a handsome young man. In Act II, the transformed Nutcracker takes Clara on a magical journey that ends in the Land of Flowers where they meet the Sugar Plum Fairy. The divertissements of Act II allow Tchaikovsky to construct a series of loosely connected vignettes, each of which presents the characteristic sound (or what at least was believed at the time to be the characteristic sound) of a variety of exotic lands. In "Le café" ("Coffee"), Tchaikovsky uses a drone-like bass beneath a trio of single-reed instruments (English horn and two clarinets), muted strings, and tambourine to evoke images of Arabia. "Le thé" ("Tea") takes us to China, for which Tchaikovsky creates a very different kind of sound based on the contrast of flutes and piccolo against pizzicato strings, all inflected melodies based on a pentatonic or quasi-pentatonic scale, traditionally associated (at least in the Western mind) with the music of China. The initial statement of the pizzicato figure in the strings, for example, is constructed solely on the pitches F-A-B♭-C-D. The ensuing "Trépak" takes up the rhythms of this characteristically Russian dance. The musical exoticism of all these dances held particular appeal for audiences of the late 19th century at a time when the European world was claiming dominion over vast portions of the earth.

THE SYMPHONIC POEM

By 1850, Berlioz, Mendelssohn, and Schumann had all contributed important works to the symphonic repertory. Yet widespread skepticism remained about the continuing viability of the genre. Richard Wagner had proclaimed the death of the symphony (see Primary Evidence: Wagner on the End of the Symphony, in Chapter 15) and many composers, like him, avoided the genre altogether. Others, like Brahms, as we will see, took it on despite its historical freight. Still others negotiated a middle ground in the genre of the symphonic poem.

Liszt coined the term **symphonic poem** (*Symphonische Dichtung*) in 1854 as a new name for what had traditionally been called a concert overture (see Chapter 15). By the 1830s, the traditional designation had become a misnomer because works in this genre were no longer overtures in any meaningful sense of the word. Although usually programmatic and only one movement long, they were written for the concert hall, not as an opening for a play or opera. The new term caught on quickly because it captured the main characteristics of the genre: symphonic and poetic. The programmatic source for a symphonic poem could range from the vague to the specific and might be reflected in the music in anything from a very general to a very particular way. A list of the extramusical associations for Liszt's 13 symphonic poems (see Focus: The Programmatic Sources for Liszt's Symphonic Poems) gives some idea of the variety of programmatic sources composers turned to for inspiration.

Richard Strauss (1864–1949) succeeded Liszt as the acknowledged master of the symphonic poem, combining his gifts as an orchestrator with his genius for joining symphonic forms and story lines. Strauss's symphonic poems include *Also sprach Zarathustra* (loosely based on a treatise of the same name by the poet and philosopher Friedrich Nietzsche), *Don Juan* (based on a poem by Nicholaus Lenau), *Don Quixote* (based on the novel by Cervantes), and the quasi-autobiographical *Ein Heldenleben* ("A Hero's Life").

These expansive, opulent works epitomize the late 19th century's love of grandeur, particularly in their exploitation of the ever-expanding resources of the modern orchestra. It was Strauss who revised Berlioz's influential treatise on orchestration (see Composer Profile: Hector Berlioz, in Chapter 15) and he did so in part to

FOCUS   The Programmatic Sources for Liszt's Symphonic Poems

Liszt drew on a variety of extramusical sources for his symphonic poems, from specific poems to historical events to general ideas.

TITLE	EXTRAMUSICAL ASSOCIATIONS
Ce qu'on entend sur la montagne (1849)	Poem by Victor Hugo ("That Which is Heard on the Mountain")
Tasso (1849)	Poem by Johann Wolfgang Goethe
Heroïde funèbre (1850)	Funeral march
Prometheus (1850)	The myth of Prometheus
Mazeppa (1851)	Poem by Victor Hugo
Festklänge (1853)	Marriage celebration ("Festival Sounds")
Orpheus (1854)	The myth of Orpheus
Les préludes (1848; revised 1854)	Poem by Alphonse de Lamartine
Hungaria (1854)	The dream of an independent Hungary
Die Ideale (1857)	Poem by Friedrich Schiller ("The Ideals")
Die Hunnenschlacht (1857)	Painting by Wilhelm von Kaulbach ("The Battle of the Huns")
Hamlet (1857)	Shakespeare's play
Von der Wiege bis zum Grabe (1882)	Painting by Mihály Zichy ("From Cradle to Grave")

account for the expanded size of the orchestra and the new instruments (such as the tuba and saxophone) that had been added to it since Berlioz's day. The forces Strauss calls for in his symphonic poems represent the orchestra at its peak—or, as some critics would have it, at its most overblown. In *Don Juan* (1889), for example, he called for the following:

3 Flutes (one doubling on piccolo)	3 Trombones
2 Oboes	Tuba
English horn	3 Timpani
2 Clarinets	Triangle
2 Bassoons	Cymbals
Contrabassoon	Glockenspiel
4 Horns	Harp
3 Trumpets	Strings

Strauss was careful to use these forces judiciously, frequently dividing them into smaller units and reserving the full ensemble for special effect.

THE SYMPHONY

The symphony enjoyed renewed vigor in the second half of the 19th century. Many of the most prominent composers of instrumental music turned to this genre, creating works of unparalleled breadth and scope. The growing size of the orchestra, the increasing number of civic orchestras and standing concert series, and the inherently public nature of the genre all helped reinforce the symphony's standing as the largest, most ambitious, and most prestigious of all instrumental genres.

In an effort to take the genre of the symphony in new directions, several prominent composers created works that draw on elements from other genres. Outstanding examples include hybrids with the concerto (Berlioz's *Harold en Italie*, Lalo's *Symphonie espagnole*); cantata (Mendelssohn's *Lobgesang*, Félicien David's *Le Desert* and *Christophe Colombe*, the latter two bearing the designation *ode-symphonie*); opera (Berlioz's *Roméo et Juliette*); and even the symphonic poem (Liszt's *Faust-Symphonie*, each of whose three movements the composer called a "Character Sketch," the first for Faust, the second for Gretchen, the third for Mephistopheles).

The symphonic character of many pieces lying nominally outside the genre is also evident in works such as Rimsky-Korsakov's *Sadko* (1867; revised 1869 and 1891), subtitled "Symphonic Pictures," and Debussy's *La Mer* (1898), subtitled "Three Symphonic Sketches," in which the remnants of symphonic form are clearly discernible: a slow introduction to a fast opening movement, followed by a scherzo and a fast culminating finale. Symphonic form and breadth are also frequently evident in concertos. The concertos of Schumann, Brahms, and Dvořák, for example, all display a symphonic tone, avoiding virtuosity for its own sake and more fully integrating soloist and orchestra than earlier concertos.

The Challenge of the Past: Brahms

Still other composers, most notably Johannes Brahms and Antonín Dvořák, continued to write symphonies in the traditional four-movement pattern. Brahms in particular embraced his musical heritage, openly aligning himself with the traditions of composers like Bach, Haydn, Mozart, Beethoven, Schubert, and Schumann. But he did so with considerable ambivalence, for like all 19th-century composers, he felt compelled to demonstrate creative originality. Approaching the age of 40, Brahms despaired of ever writing a symphony. When asked whether he would, he confided to a friend, "You have no idea how it feels . . . when one always hears such a giant marching along behind." The "giant" was of course Beethoven. In his First Symphony, Brahms introduced a triumphant lyrical theme in the finale that closely resembles the "Ode to Joy" in the finale of Beethoven's Ninth. When someone pointed this resemblance out to the composer, Brahms is said to have replied, "Yes indeed, and what's really remarkable is that every jackass notices it at once."

Despite the inhibiting effect of Beethoven's long shadow, Brahms was able to write four symphonies that each bear his own distinct stamp. As with Beethoven, his symphonies have no common formula; each takes a different conceptual approach to the genre. In general, Brahms sought to avoid making the symphony even more monumental than it had already become. The relatively diminutive inner movements of his First Symphony, for example, serve almost as interludes to the outer movements, and the last movement of the Second Symphony breaks with the tradition of the finale as a grandiose symphonic culmination.

CD13, Track 1
BRAHMS
Symphony no. 4
Score Anthology II/146

The imposing set of variations in the finale of his Fourth Symphony, however, stands well within a tradition set down in the last movement of Beethoven's *Eroica*. But here, Brahms reaches past Beethoven to an even earlier tradition, that of J. S. Bach. On one level, the structure of this finale is quite simple: it is a series of 30 variations, each eight measures long and based on the same eight-measure theme. Within this relatively simple, potentially restrictive, framework, Brahms introduces a stunning variety of thematic ideas, textures, harmonies, and colors. The theme is based on the ostinato subject of the finale of Bach's Cantata no. 150, a work that Brahms knew well. (Bach used the ostinato technique in a similar fashion in the first movement of Cantata no. 78, Anthology, discussed in Chapter 9).

Bach's ostinato theme (Example 18–1) is not particularly distinctive; it fills in the interval of a fifth and ends with an octave leap on the dominant, which in turn sets up the repetition of the theme. Brahms (Example 18–2) extends the theme to eight measures (one note per measure), moves the melodic idea to the uppermost voice, and adds a striking dissonance by sharpening the second iteration of the fourth scale degree (A♯). He further deviates from Bach's theme by ending on the first scale degree. The resulting harmonic closure increases the challenge of composing a continuous movement from a string of such sequences, but it is a challenge Brahms confronts with zeal. By the time we reach the middle of this movement, we have to remind ourselves that it is in fact a set of variations on a theme. The division between Variations 6 and 7 (measures 49–56 and 57–64) is almost imperceptible even when we listen for it. The

Example 18–1 Ostinato theme of Bach, Cantata no. 150, finale (transposed)

Example 18–2 Brahms's ostinato theme for the finale of his Symphony no. 4

Schumann Proclaims the Young Brahms a Musical Messiah (1853)

In what would turn out to be his last published piece of musical criticism, Robert Schumann introduced the musical world to a still unknown 20-year-old composer named Johannes Brahms. Schumann begins by reviewing the most promising young composers of the age and then poses the question of who might follow in the steps of Beethoven.

———————◆—◆—◆———————

After such an antecedent there would and must appear quite suddenly one who was called to articulate the highest expression of the age in an ideal manner, one who would bring us mastery not in a process of step-by-step development, but would instead spring fully-armored, like Minerva, from the head of Cronus. And he has come, a new blood at whose cradle the graces and heroes stood guard. His name is Johannes Brahms; he came from Hamburg, where, working in dark stillness, he was nevertheless educated by an excellent and enthusiastic teacher [Eduard Marxsen] in the most difficult elements of the art, and he was recently recommended to me by a venerated and well-known master [Joseph Joachim]. Even in his external appearance, he carried with him all the characteristics that proclaimed to us: This is One who has been called. Sitting at the piano, he began to reveal the most wonderful regions. We were drawn into an increasingly

magic circle. There we heard the most genial playing, which made an orchestra out of the piano, with lamenting and jubilant voices. There were sonatas, more like disguised symphonies; songs, whose poetry one would understand without knowing the words, although there was through all of them a profound vocal line; individual piano pieces, some of a demonic nature in the most daring form; then sonatas for violin and piano; quartets for stringed instruments; and each so different from the other that they all seemed to flow out of different sources. . . .

If he lowers his magic staff where the massed forces of chorus and orchestra give their powers, then we shall yet have even more wondrous glimpses into the secrets of the spiritual world. May the highest spirit of genius strengthen him for this. The prospect for this exists, given that another spirit of genius already lives within him, the spirit of modesty. His colleagues greet him on his first journey through the world, where wounds, perhaps, await him, but also laurels and palms. We welcome him as a strong combatant. There dwells in every age a secret society of kindred souls. Close the circle tighter, ye who belong to it, so that the truth of art might glow ever more clearly, spreading joy and blessings everywhere!

Source: Robert Schumann "Neue Bahnen" ("New Paths"), *Neue Zeitschrift für Musik* (1853). Transl. MEB

movement nevertheless holds consistently to the repeating eight-measure structure all the way through Variation 30. Only the coda, beginning in measure 253 after a few introductory measures, is freely composed.

Within this self-imposed structure of variations on a theme, Brahms integrates another formal principle, that of tripartite (ABA[1]) form (variations 1–15; 16–23; 24–coda). There is an unmistakable sense of transition in Variations 10 and 11 (measures 81–88, 89–96) and a clear change of mood with Variation 12 (measures 97–104); then the meter changes, the music is marked *dolce* for the first time, and the timbre of the solo flute dominates the substantially thinned texture. The impression of change is reinforced in Variation 13 (measures 105–112) with a shift to E Major. Variation 16 marks the onset of what corresponds to the B section, and Variation 24 sounds very much like the beginning of a recomposed A section. The material after Variation 30, as already noted, constitutes a freely composed coda.

With this finale of his last symphony, Brahms seems to be reminding the musical world that old forms are capable of rejuvenation, that it is possible to search for the new without abandoning tradition entirely. The Baroque technique of basing a set of variations on an ostinato (which Brahms labeled a chaconne) provides a most compelling structure for the composer; in its ostensibly simple construction, this movement is firmly rooted in tradition, but in its harmony, orchestration, and sense of flow, it is distinctly progressive.

COMPOSER PROFILE   Johannes Brahms *(1833–1897)*

Brahms was once caricatured in silhouette walking next to a hedgehog, an image that captures the composer's personality perfectly. Brahms was an intensely private man. Among his close friends, he was known for his warmth and dry sense of humor, but to the public, he remained reclusive and cold. He zealously collected sketches by Beethoven and other composers, but he wanted no one to pry into his own workshop. When he realized he was dying of cancer, he destroyed his remaining sketches and drafts. He wanted his art to speak for itself.

Like Beethoven, Brahms was from the northern part of Germany—Hamburg—and chose to spend most of his adult life in Vienna. The decisive moment of his career came at the age of 20, when Robert Schumann declared him the new messiah of music (see Primary Evidence: Schumann Proclaims the Young Brahms a Musical Messiah). This pronouncement proved both a blessing and a curse. Thanks to Schumann's stature, it gave Brahms immediate recognition, but its extraordinary language burdened him with unrealistic expectations. Critics predisposed to dislike his music (that is, the followers of Liszt and Wagner) were quick to belittle Brahms's first works for falling short of those expectations.

Stung by these early assaults, Brahms soon developed a thick skin. For the rest of his life, he more or less ignored his critics and moved forward as he alone saw fit. His music cannot be easily classified as either "progressive" or "conservative." In many ways, it was both at the same time. In the 20th century, Arnold Schoenberg, one of the most radical composers of his generation, hailed Brahms as one of the most progressive composers of the late 19th century, primarily because of Brahms's ability to reveal the rich potential of a seemingly simple germinal idea. Many critics in Brahms's own lifetime found his music texturally and harmonically complicated, structurally intricate, and difficult to comprehend.

Brahms was nevertheless deeply committed to building on and rejuvenating the works of the great composers of the past, from the recent Schumann, Beethoven, Mozart, and Haydn to the more distant Bach, Handel, and Schütz of the Baroque era, and the even more distant Palestrina of the Renaissance. In an era remarkable for its emphasis on novelty and originality, Brahms thus embraced the musical past. In contrast to Liszt and Wagner, he refused to accept that music could or should be subordinate to any other art.

In keeping with these beliefs, Brahms composed numerous works in the traditional genres of instrumental music. He also applied the principles of sonata form more openly than almost any other composer of the late 19th century. This is not to say that Brahms's sonata-form movements are predictable—he manipulated the conventions of the form in the same spirit as had Haydn and Beethoven.

Brahms found another outlet for his historicism as a music editor. He prepared many new editions (often without credit or payment) of music by Couperin, Handel, Bach, Mozart, Schubert, and Schumann. His friends included many prominent music scholars who were helping launch the first substantial effort to publish critical editions of past composers. Among these scholars were Philipp Spitta, who wrote the first full-scale biography of J. S. Bach and was a driving force in the first complete edition of Bach's music; Friedrich Chrysander, Handel's biographer and editor of his music; and Gustav Nottebohm, renowned for his work on Beethoven's sketches. (Brahms once created a fake sketch by Beethoven and surreptitiously paid a Viennese street

Brahms (right) and Johann Strauss, Jr. (1894). Brahms admired the art of the "Waltz King" deeply. He once wrote the opening theme of the *Blue Danube Waltz* on a lady's fan and underneath it added the words "Leider nicht von Brahms" ("Not by Brahms, unfortunately"). The contrast between these two men in appearance and style of dress is striking, especially when we realize the dapper Strauss was almost eight years older than Brahms. When this photograph was taken, Strauss was 69, Brahms 61.

Source: Corbis/Bettmann

vendor to use the sheet as a wrapper for some cheese Nottebohm was buying.)

PRINCIPAL WORKS

SYMPHONIES AND OTHER ORCHESTRAL WORKS Brahms struggled off and on for more than twenty years to write a first symphony. Throughout the 1860s and early 1870s he produced a small but steady stream of orchestral works. These include the two Serenades (1858, 1860), and the *Variations on a Theme of Haydn* (1873; more recent scholarship has revealed that the tune is in fact probably not by Haydn, although Brahms had every reason to think it was). After finally finishing his First Symphony in 1876, he produced three more in relatively quick order: no. 2 in D Major (1877), no. 3 in F Major (1883), and no. 4 in E minor (1885). Each is different from the others, yet all four fall squarely within the symphonic tradition.

Brahms's later orchestral works include two overtures: the *Academic Festival Overture* (1880), written as a thankful gift to the University of Breslau for conferring an honorary doctorate on him, and the *Tragic Overture* (1881), a work for the concert hall. "One laughs, one cries," Brahms noted of these two works.

CONCERTOS Although few in number, Brahms's concertos helped define the genre in the second half of the 19th century. The two piano concertos (1854, 1881), the Violin Concerto (1878), and the "Double" Concerto for violin and cello (1887) are all symphonic in scope and tone. These works demand great virtuosity on the part of the soloist, yet the solo part never seems arbitrarily difficult.

CHAMBER WORKS Brahms cultivated chamber music with an intensity unmatched by any other composer of his generation. His output includes three violin sonatas, two cello sonatas, two clarinet sonatas, three piano trios, trios for horn, cello, and piano and for clarinet, cello, and piano, three string quartets, three piano quartets, a piano quintet, a clarinet quintet, and two string sextets. All of these works are technically demanding and lie well beyond the range of the average amateur musician.

PIANO MUSIC Brahms established his early reputation both as a pianist and as a composer. His op. 1, in fact, is a piano sonata with strong echoes of Beethoven's *Hammerklavier* Sonata, op. 106. But with op. 5, he abandoned the solo piano sonata and turned instead to variations, producing sets based on themes by Schumann, by Handel, and by Paganini. Later in life, he cultivated the character piece, even though he gave these generic names such as Capriccio, Rhapsody, Intermezzo, or the utterly neutral designation of *Klavierstück* ("Piano Piece"). Brahms pointedly avoided references to external ideas or objects in these works, presumably to distance himself from other 19th-century composers for the piano like Gottschalk and Liszt, who applied programmatic ideas to otherwise straightforward etudes. Brahms's late piano pieces include some of his most beautiful and moving compositions.

SONGS Considering how many songs Brahms wrote, it is surprising that so relatively few remain in the active repertory today. In addition to the standard settings for voice and piano, there are also a number of vocal duets and quartets. Brahms also arranged a number of German folk songs for publication.

VOCAL MUSIC The *German Requiem* (1868), written to texts selected from the Bible, is a staple of the choral repertory. Less well known but every bit as appealing are such works as the *Alto Rhapsody* (1869) and *Nänie* (1881). Brahms also wrote music for men's, women's, and mixed choruses that is little known but deserves wider exposure. He also wrote his share of occasional music, such as the *Triumphlied* of 1871 to celebrate the German victory in the Franco-Prussian War of 1870–1871.

KEY DATES IN THE LIFE OF BRAHMS

1833	Born in Hamburg (Germany), May 7.
1847	Gives first public concert as a pianist.
1853	On tour with the violin virtuoso Joseph Joachim, meets both Liszt and Schumann. Schumann introduces the young Brahms to the world as the new messiah of music.
1862	Moves to Vienna, where he spends most of the remaining years of his life. Makes his living subsequently almost exclusively from conducting and from sales of his own compositions.
1876	Finishes First Symphony; declines an honorary doctorate from Cambridge University but accepts one from Breslau University.
1897	Dies in Vienna on April 3 and is buried alongside Beethoven and Schubert in Vienna's Central Cemetery.

Nationalism: Dvořák

With its perceived ability to give voice to communal feeling (see Chapter 15), the symphony proved itself a particularly fertile genre for composers seeking to introduce nationalistic elements into their music. In Russia, such composers as Nikolai Rimsky-Korsakov, Peter Ilyich Tchaikovsky, Dmitri Balakirev, and Aleksandr Borodin were quick to incorporate into their symphonies such nationalistic elements as modal inflections, folk-inspired rhythms, and the rich tradition of the Russian brass ensemble.

Several important American composers also used the symphony as a vehicle for nationalistic expression. Anthony Philip Heinrich, who emigrated to the United States from Bohemia in the first decade of the 19th century, incorporated such tunes as *Yankee Doodle* and *Hail, Columbia* into his *Columbiad: Grand American National Chivalrous Symphony* (1837). Like Dvořák many decades later, Heinrich was fascinated with the music of Native Americans, as is reflected in his *Manitou Mysteries, or The Voice of the Great Spirit*, subtitled *Gran sinfonia misteriosa-indiana* (1845). Despite its unusual title, the work follows a traditional four-movement format, with a rondo finale. Louis Moreau Gottschalk's *La Nuit des tropiques: Symphony No. 1* (1859), in contrast, is a two-movement work that integrates rumba and fugue toward the end of its finale. The *Gaelic* Symphony by Amy Beach (1896) uses Irish melodies, in keeping with the fin-de-siècle cultural revival known as the "Celtic twilight." These and other American symphonies of the 19th century remain little known but are well worth investigating.

Ironically, the best-known "American" symphony from the second half of the 19th century was written by a Czech, Antonín Dvořák (1841–1904). During an extended sojourn in the United States (1892–1895), he composed his Symphony no. 9 in E minor and subtitled it "From the New World." Its themes are supposedly based on or inspired by Native American ("Indian") and African-American ("Negro") musical idioms. Dvořák's motivations here seem to have been in part didactic: he hoped to show American composers how they might use indigenous musical materials to create a distinctively American style, thereby weaning themselves from the European tradition.

CD12, Track 14
DVOŘÁK
*Symphony no. 9
(From the New World)*
Score Anthology II/147

Dvořák urged American composers to model orchestral music on the music of African Americans and Native Americans. "These are the folk songs of America," he wrote, "and your composers must turn to them. All the great musicians have borrowed from the songs of the common people. . . . In the Negro melodies of America I discover all that is needed for a great and noble school of music. . . . It is music that suits itself to any mood or any purpose. There is nothing in the whole range of composition that cannot be supplied with themes from this source. The American musician understands these tunes and they move sentiment in him. They appeal to his imagination because of their associations."[2]

In his Symphony no. 9, Dvořák synthesizes the traditions of both the Old and New Worlds. Structurally, the work follows the standard pattern of four movements: a sonata-form first movement with an extended slow introduction; a pastoral slow movement (the Largo); a fast, dance-like third movement in triple meter; and a rousing finale that breaks through from minor to major. Within each of these individual movements, however, Dvořák incorporates what he considered to be characteristic elements of indigenous American music. The principal theme of the Largo, for example (beginning at measure 7), is largely **pentatonic**—that is, based on a scale of only five notes. Although frequently associated with the music of East Asia, pentatonic scales

---

2. Antonín Dvořák, "On the Real Value of Negro Music," *New York Herald*, 21 May 1893; quoted in Michael Beckerman, "The Master's Little Joke: Antonín Dvořák and the Mask of the Nation," in *Dvořák and His World*, ed. Michael Beckerman (Princeton, NJ: Princeton University Press, 1993), p. 138.

COMPOSER PROFILE   Antonín Dvořák *(1841–1904)*

In 1857, Antonín Dvořák moved to Prague to focus on composition studies. He began to gain recognition, first with the help of his fellow Bohemian, Bedřich Smetana, who performed his music in Prague, and later through the support of Johannes Brahms, who had been introduced to Dvořák's work while serving on a panel that awarded governmental stipends for music. Emulating his own experience with Schumann, Brahms recommended Dvořák to the German publisher Simrock, who issued the first set of *Slavonic Dances* (1878), Dvořák's first major success, which led to international attention and performances. Although he was advised to move to Vienna and write an opera in German; Dvořák, a Czech nationalist who resented the Habsburg view of his native land's culture as parochial, did neither.

To build his reputation, Dvořák spent the next years touring throughout Europe, especially England, and had an audience with the emperor in Vienna. By the time his popular *Carnival Overture* was premiered in 1891, he had been appointed professor of composition at the Prague Conservatory. But Dvořák soon accepted the directorship of the National Conservatory of Music of America in New York, where he remained from 1892 to 1895. He conducted at Chicago's World Columbian Exposition, and vacationed with his family at a Czech-speaking colony in Spillville, Iowa. Back in New York, he was apparently introduced to the African-American spiritual by his composition student Harry Thacker Burleigh; contact with this music and that of Native Americans, combined with his personal experiences as a musical nationalist, led him to urge American composers to develop a distinctly national style by drawing on these indigenous idioms. Upon the premiere of his Symphony no. 9 by the New York Philharmonic in 1893, he chose to argue his point in a letter to the *New York Herald*:

> [T]he new American school of music must strike its roots deeply into its own soil. There is no longer any reason why young Americans who have talent should go to Europe for their education. . . . The country [i.e., the United States] is full of melody, original, sympathetic and varying in mood, color and character to suit every phase of composition. It is a rich field. America can have great and noble music of her own, growing out of the very soil and partaking of its nature—the natural voice of a free and vigorous race.[3]

The success of the "New World" Symphony as "American music" testified to Dvořák's ability to capture a national spirit that by rights was not "natural" to him.

Dvořák returned to Prague, where he resumed his duties at the Prague Conservatory and composed successful operas, symphonic poems, and his most popular work after the Ninth Symphony, the Cello Concerto in B minor (1895), given its premiere in London in 1896; Brahms said of this work, "Had I known that one could write a cello concerto like this, I would have written one long ago!" Dvořák served as the conservatory's director from 1901 until his death.

PRINCIPAL WORKS

SYMPHONIES AND OTHER ORCHESTRAL WORKS   Until quite recently, Dvořák was considered to have written five symphonies, which were published accordingly. After the four earlier works were "rediscovered" after his death, the symphonies originally numbered 1 through 5 were renumbered nos. 6, 7, 5, 8, and 9, respectively. As in other genres, the early works reflect various influences—Schubert, Beethoven, Wagner, Liszt—that he gradually integrated into a Czech nationalist style, akin to but more easygoing and fluid than Brahms, and by no means superficially "folksy": there are many darker passages in

Antonín Dvořák.

---

3. Antonín Dvořák, letter to the editor, *New York Herald*, 28 May 1893; quoted in Michael Beckerman, "The Master's Little Joke: Antonín Dvořák and the Mask of the Nation," in *Dvořák and His World*, ed. Michael Beckerman (Princeton, NJ: Princeton University Press, 1993), p. 137.

these works. He also composed a cycle of symphonic poems based primarily on Czech folklore (1896–97), concert overtures, the Symphonic Variations, the String Serenade, and the two series of *Slavonic Dances*. Concertos for violin and piano solo preceded the cello concerto; he also orchestrated a number of his piano and chamber pieces, including the "American Suite" for piano and *Silent Woods* for cello and piano.

CHAMBER WORKS AND PIANO MUSIC Dvořák wrote a considerable amount of chamber music, demonstrating a considerable melodic gift. In addition to 14 string quartets, he composed 4 piano trios, 2 piano quartets, and 2 piano quintets, and smaller pieces. His solo and duet piano works were often based on familiar genres (minuet, Scottish, march, humoresque, impromptu) as well as Czech idioms (dumka, furiant, polka); he also published two solo piano cycles.

OPERAS Unlike Brahms, Dvořák ventured into musical theater, the most lucrative venue for a composer at the time. Like so many others, he was caught up in the Wagnerian music drama as a young composer, but soon put that influence to rest, looking to Russian models. His two major successes, *The Devil and Kate* and *Rusalka*, came late in his career, as did a major failure, *Armida* (1903–04, based on the same source that Gluck used; see Chapter 13).

SONGS Dvořák's song cycles range from the early *Cypresses* (an unsuccessful wooing present to the sister of the woman he would eventually marry), *Evening Songs*, *Gypsy Melodies* (which he set in German), and the *Biblical Songs*, written after the deaths of his friends Tchaikovsky and Hans von Bülow. Almost all his other songs were based on folk poetry or written in a folk music style. As with any song written in a less common language, performances of Dvořák's songs are rare outside his native land.

VOCAL MUSIC Modern choral ensembles are more likely to encounter Dvořák's works. As with other foreign composers (including Handel and Mendelssohn), he found England to be receptive to him; even more significant is that his best-known choral works are Latin settings: the *Stabat Mater*, the Mass in D Major, the Requiem Mass, and the *Te Deum*.

KEY DATES IN THE LIFE OF DVOŘÁK

1841	Born in Nelahozeves, near Kralupy (Austrian Empire; now Czech Republic), September 8.
1857	Moves to Prague, where he studies music, joins the Provisional Theatre orchestra, and receives his first important performances.
1878	Brahms introduces him to the Berlin publisher Simrock, who publishes Dvořák's music until 1890, when Dvořák ends relationship.
1884–1891	Tours throughout Europe and especially England as composer and conductor.
1892–1895	Based in New York as director of the National Conservatory of Music in America; becomes acquainted with the music of Native Americans and African Americans.
1893	Begins his campaign to encourage American composers to draw from the traditional music of their own country as a resource; Symphony no. 9 ("From the New World") is premiered on December 16 in New York.
1895	Returns to Prague, where he resumes teaching at the Conservatory, becoming its director in 1901.
1904	Dies in Prague on May 1 after becoming ill at the first performance of his *Armida* and is buried in the city's Vyšehrad Castle cemetery.

figure large in many traditional ("folk") idioms of the West as well, and when Europeans like Dvořák heard Native Americans making music, they tended to hear the melodies as characteristically pentatonic. The opening phrase on the English horn (which sounds a fifth lower than notated) uses primarily the pitches D♭, E♭, F, A♭, and B♭. The C♮ that first appears in measure 11 functions as a leading tone to the tonic, but the scale of the melody pointedly avoids the fourth scale degree in the key of D♭ (that is, G♭), thereby lending a strongly pentatonic coloring to the theme. The melody of the contrasting section in C♯ minor (beginning at measure 46), played on flutes and oboes, is also constructed on a pentatonic scale (C♯-D♯-E-G♯-B), again omitting the fourth scale degree (F♯).

The orchestration and harmonization of both these melodies contribute to the pastoral tone of the movement. The English horn and oboe are both reed instruments and thus connected, at least indirectly, to the shepherd's reed pipe; the flute, too, is an instrument associated with the idealized serenity of the countryside. The drone bass underneath both melodies, reminiscent of a bagpipe, further contributes to this air of calm. But pastoral scenes are almost inevitably disrupted at some point, and Dvořák's Largo holds true to form: the C♯ minor section introduces a dark and at times threatening tone to the whole. The extended section over a "walking bass" (beginning at measure 54) includes still more pentatonically inflected melodies. The idea in the flute incorporates the so-called "Scotch snap," a short note on the accented beat followed by a longer note. In measure 60, for example, the sixteenth note in the flute is followed by a dotted quarter tied to a half, emphasizing rhythmically the melodic absence of the fourth scale degree in the melodic fragment E-F♯-G♯-B-C♯. Yet another interruption, a lively major-mode section (beginning at measure 90) leads to a portentous reference back to the main theme of the first movement (measure 96)—Dvořák carefully integrates all four movements of the symphony—before the original mood of calm is restored with the return of the English horn theme in the tonic (measure 101).

Dvořák himself pointed to Henry Wadsworth Longfellow's *The Song of Hiawatha* as the source of inspiration for this movement, though it is not altogether clear whether Dvořák meant a particular passage in this long poem or the mood of the poem as a whole. The composer denied from the outset that the work was primarily based on what were called "Negro melodies." As one critic of the time noted, "The composer has not taken the external forms of plantation music, but has used his own themes suggested by the southern music. Now and then the motifs and the rhythms strongly suggest the origin of the symphony."[4] But the association with a genuine spiritual was reinforced in the public mind in 1922, when the American composer William Arms Fisher, a Dvořák student, set the Largo's English horn theme to a text he had written in the style of a Negro spiritual ("Goin' home, goin' home, I'm a-goin' home/Quiet like, some still day, I jes' goin' home"). This "neo-spiritual" and its many arrangements continue to fuel the still widely held belief that Dvořák did use an old spiritual as the basis for the Largo.

Dvořák's "New World" Symphony evoked an ongoing debate about the identity of "American music" at the end of the 19th century. It was widely assumed that composers of the United States were obligated to develop a distinctively national style, but what form would that style take? Many of these composers had learned their craft in Europe or at the very least looked to European composers as models. The idea that music of the disenfranchised—African Americans and Native Americans—might provide the basis of a national musical style unleashed a stream of controversy. Many critics thought this music unworthy of the concert hall, and they often expressed their opinions with elements of undisguised racism. But the debate about what constitutes "American music" was on, and it would continue for some time. Perhaps the critic of the *New York Daily Tribune* summed it up best in 1894 when he observed that the "New World" Symphony, along with several other recent compositions by Dvořák, had captured "something which sounds native in a style which is pleasant and natural in the ears of the people, the vast, vague, varied people of America."[5]

4. James Creelman, "Dvořák's Negro Symphony," *Pall Mall Budget*, 21 June 1894; reproduced in *Dvořák and His World*, ed. Michael Beckerman (Princeton, NJ: Princeton University Press, 1993), p. 179.
5. Henry Krehbiel, "Dvořák's American Compositions," *New York Herald*, 31 January 1894, anthologized in *Dvořák and His World*, ed. Michael Beckerman (Princeton University Press, 1993), p. 171.

The world turned upside down. Gustav Mahler once revealed that this well-known woodcut had inspired the slow movement of his First Symphony. The image is one of a world turned upside down: animals bury the hunter. The weeping and mourning are of course deeply ironic and provide an important clue to the nature of the third movement's funeral march, which is at times sincere, at times sardonic.

Source: Moritz von Schwind. *How Animals Bury the Hunter* (Wie die Tiere den Jäger begraben). Woodcut 1850. Reproduced in Gerhard Pommeranz-Leidtke, *Moritz von Schwind, Mahler und Poet* (Vienna and Munich: Anton Schroll, 1974), Ill. no. 24.

The Collision of High and Low: Mahler

Straddling the 19th and 20th centuries are the symphonies of Gustav Mahler (1860–1911). Although his later symphonies, particularly the Ninth (1910) and unfinished Tenth, anticipate 20th-century idioms and approaches to the genre, his First Symphony (1888) is a decidedly 19th-century work. Like many of Beethoven's symphonies, it follows a trajectory from struggle to triumph.

The funereal third movement of Mahler's First Symphony careens wildly from the beautiful to the grotesque, the sincere to the ironic. Mahler himself once suggested that the entire movement was inspired by a well-known illustration, reproduced here, showing wild animals bearing a hunter to his grave. By writing a funeral march into his symphony, Mahler is of course directly linking it to the funeral march in the second movement of Beethoven's *Eroica*. But the ironic tone of this music, inspired by a grotesque ceremony in which the hunted bury the hunter, mocks the somberness of the earlier work. The solemn tread of the timpani in the opening measures of the movement, combined with its slow tempo, low register, and minor mode, all announce that this will be a funeral march befitting the slow movement of a symphony. The instrument playing the melody is a solo double bass, and it is playing in a torturously high range for that instrument. The tone is not deep and resonant, but pinched and forced. Odder still, the melody turns out be a minor-mode variant of the children's tune *Frère Jacques* (or *Bruder Martin*, as it is known in German-speaking lands). A children's play song in minor in the slow movement of a symphony? We can begin to understand why so many contemporary critics found Mahler's music perplexing and at times exasperating.

Still other critics (many of them motivated by anti-Semitism) criticized the passage immediately following the funeral march for its "Jewish" or "eastern" qualities. The sound world evoked here (beginning in measure 39) is that of the *klezmorim*, the professional Jewish musicians of eastern Europe, who performed what we refer to today as **klezmer** music, characterized by a steady oompah sound in the bass (here, in

CD13, Track 2
MAHLER
Symphony no. 1
Score Anthology II/148

COMPOSER PROFILE   Gustav Mahler *(1860–1911)*

When Gustav Mahler was a child, he was reportedly asked what he wanted to be when he grew up. "A martyr" was the young boy's reply. Mahler certainly got his wish. In spite of his acknowledged brilliance as a conductor, he would eventually be driven from his post as music director of the Vienna Opera, and his contemporaries would dismiss his compositions, mostly symphonies and songs, as little more than a harmless sideshow. "My time will yet come," Mahler predicted, and again correctly. For almost five decades after his death, the composer's symphonies were considered monstrous curiosities, championed only by a small group of devoted followers. Thanks to the advent of long-playing records and such outstanding conductors as Jascha Horenstein, John Barbirolli, and above all Leonard Bernstein, Mahler's music began to gain a huge following in the early 1960s. Today he is acknowledged as one of the towering figures of late-19th- and early-20th-century music.

This belated recognition has much to do with the nature of Mahler's music, which most of his contemporaries found to be a confused mixture of incompatible styles and idioms. But it is precisely this juxtaposition of the serious and comic, the sublime and the banal that seems so appealing today. This deep sense of conflict is very much an extension of Mahler's own personality: he struggled throughout his life with the question of life after death, and in one way or another translated this issue into all of his symphonies. He was also torn between his Jewish heritage and the Catholic faith, to which he converted in 1897. There has been considerable debate about the sincerity of this conversion. Anti-Semitism was so rampant in Austria that Mahler would not, as a Jew, have been able to assume the directorship of so prestigious an institution as the Vienna Opera. At the same time, the theological promise of life after death made Christianity deeply appealing to Mahler. He ended his life as a pantheist, finding manifestations of God and eternal life in all things.

Mahler's extended tours of the United States in the years 1907 to 1911 reflect the growing cultural power of the United States in the late 19th and early 20th centuries. Organizations like the Metropolitan Opera and the New York Philharmonic now had the financial resources to attract musicians of the highest stature from across the Atlantic. Although Mahler struggled constantly with the management of both institutions, he helped raise the artistic standards of American musical life immeasurably.

PRINCIPAL WORKS

SYMPHONIES Like Beethoven, Mahler consistently rethought the nature of the genre every time he began a new symphony. These works nevertheless fall into several broad categories:

- The *Wunderhorn* Symphonies (nos. 1–4). Each of these incorporates thematic material from at least one of his *Wunderhorn* songs (see later), and three of the four incorporate voices as well. The First, the only purely instrumental work of the group, follows the pattern of struggle to triumph established in Beethoven's Fifth and Ninth Symphonies, as does the second (*Resurrection*), which includes a grandiose choral finale. The fourth and fifth movements of the Third Symphony are vocal, but the slow finale is instrumental. The Fourth Symphony's finale is a *Wunderhorn* song for voice and orchestra, but the entire work operates on a smaller scale than any of the previous three.

Working holiday. Mahler is shown here on holiday in the Austrian Alps in the summer of 1908 with the younger of his two daughters, Anna (1904–1988), who would go on to become an accomplished sculptor. Because he devoted most of the year to conducting, Mahler could focus on composing only during the summer. He typically wrote new works while on holiday and left matters of revision and orchestration for fall, winter, and spring.

Source: Gustav Mahler and his daughter Anna, 1909 (sign.: NB 609.393-B). Austrian National Library, picture archives.

- The Middle-Period Symphonies (nos. 5–7). These are strictly instrumental works, independent of earlier songs. The Fifth follows a trajectory from struggle to triumph; the Sixth (*Tragic*) is equally heroic but ends in the minor mode. The Seventh ends with an almost maniacally joyful rondo in C Major, but only after working its way through an inner movement that Mahler marks *schattenhaft* ("shadowy").

"Noise" invades the symphony. Mahler's use of cowbells, an anvil, and bunched twigs (applied to the timpani) in his Sixth Symphony of 1905 evoked howls of derision in many critical circles. (The sleigh bells had been used in the Fourth Symphony; the ratchet is fictional.) The caption reads, "Heavens, I've forgotten the automobile horn! I'll have to write another symphony."

Source: Courtesy Henry-Louis de la Grange.

- The "Symphony of a Thousand" (no. 8). So-called (with some exaggeration) because of its large performance forces, this work is unique within Mahler's output. The symphony is in two movements, each with soloists and chorus. The first is a setting of the Latin hymn *Veni creator spiritus* ("Come creator spirit"), the second a setting of scenes from the end of Part II of Goethe's *Faust*, concluding with the celebrated line "The eternal-feminine draws us ever onward" (*Das Ewig-Weiblich zieht uns hinan*). These seemingly disparate texts are in fact closely related, as are the musical themes of these two enormous movements.

- The Late Symphonies (nos. 9 and 10 and *Das Lied von der Erde*). These works mark a turn away from the triumphalism of most earlier works. An air of quiet resignation dominates all of these late works, including even their finales. Mahler had a fear of writing a Ninth Symphony, knowing that Beethoven, Schubert, and Bruckner had all died without completing a Tenth. Mahler thought to avoid this by not numbering what would have been his ninth symphony, calling it instead *Das Lied von der Erde* ("The Song of the Earth"), a "Symphonic Song Cycle for Tenor and Alto" based on a German translation of Chinese poetry. His subsequent Ninth Symphony, however, would indeed prove to be his last finished work. Both *Das Lied* and the Ninth end with long, slow elegiac movements, and the last measure of *Das Lied* remains harmonically open, a C-Major triad juxtaposed with the note A. Several subsequent composer-scholars have produced their own completions of the Tenth, left unfinished at the composer's death.

SONGS   Mahler stands at the end of the entire 19th-century tradition of song, integrating Schubert's lyricism with the chromaticism of Wagner and Wolf. In addition to numerous miscellaneous songs for voice and piano, Mahler wrote three major cycles for voice and orchestra: *Des Knaben Wunderhorn* ("Youth's Magic Horn") and *Lieder eines fahrenden Gesellen* ("Songs of a Wayfarer") are settings of German folk poetry, whereas the *Kindertotenlieder* ("Songs on the Death of Children") are based on texts by the poet Friedrich Rückert.

KEY DATES IN THE LIFE OF MAHLER

1860	Born in Kalischt, Bohemia (then part of Austrian Empire; now in the Czech Republic) on July 7.
1880–1888	Obtains increasingly responsible conducting positions in a number of opera houses, including Ljubliana, Olmütz, Kassel, and Leipzig.
1888	Appointed music director at the Royal Opera in Budapest. Conducts from fall through spring and devotes summer vacations to composing.
1897	Appointed music director of the Vienna Court Opera, the most prestigious institution of its kind in the Austrian Empire and arguably in all of Europe.
1901	Marries Alma Schindler (1879–1964), an aspiring composer of songs; Mahler at first prohibits her from composing, then relents and promotes her music enthusiastically.
1907	Forced out of his position as music director of the Vienna Court Opera in spite of critical acclaim for his artistic accomplishments; accepts offer to become principal conductor of the Metropolitan Opera in New York.
1908	Appointed principal conductor of the New York Philharmonic Society.
1911	After several years of slowly declining health, dies in Vienna.

low strings, bass drum, and cymbals) and rhythmically free winds above. Chromatic passages in thirds, exaggerated accents, repeated half steps back and forth, and the prominence of the shrill-sounding E♭ clarinet all contribute to what many critics dismissed as the music of peasants, not suited to the lofty realm of the symphony. After a brief return of the *Bruder Martin* theme (measure 71), the mood shifts yet again, introducing a passage of lyrical beauty accompanied now by the harp (beginning in measure 83). Mahler uses here a melody from a song he himself had written several years before entitled *The Two Blue Eyes of My Beloved*, and the tone is decidedly sincere: the composer indicates this section is to be played "very simply and unadorned, like a folk melody," in contrast to the klezmer-like passages, which he directs at one point to be played "like a parody" (measure 45).

All these contrasts are intentionally jarring, and Mahler uses them to drive home his belief that a symphony can and should encompass the banal and mundane as well as the beautiful. The contrast between the funeral marches of Beethoven's Third Symphony and Mahler's First manifests the enormous changes music had experienced in less than a century. Beethoven's music is earnest, sincere, unselfconscious; Mahler's, by contrast, combines hauntingly beautiful melodies with passages that fairly drip with irony. Mahler's subsequent symphonies manifest similar contrasts of tone, at times deadly serious, at times lighthearted and remote. All of his symphonies are large-scale works: unlike Mendelssohn, Schumann, and Brahms, he built on the monumental aspect of the genre as embodied above all in Beethoven's Ninth Symphony, but also in Schubert's *Great* C-Major Symphony, D. 944, and the symphonies of Bruckner.

CONCLUSION

Music for the orchestra assumed many forms in the second half of the 19th century: functional music for dancing and marching, the stylized dance of the ballet, the programmatic symphonic poem, and—in its most expansive manifestation—the symphony, a genre capable of being presented or interpreted with or without programmatic associations. Civic orchestras proliferated toward the end of the century, further strengthening the importance of the symphony and symphonic poem within the social network of music.

DISCUSSION QUESTIONS

1. What factors account for the sudden rise in the prestige of instrumental music in the early 19th century?

2. Why did Beethoven refer to himself as a "tone poet" (*Tondichter*)?

3. What elements distinguish Beethoven's Symphony no. 3 (*Eroica*) from all earlier symphonies?

4. What kinds of new musical institutions emerged in the 19th century and why?

5. What musical features distinguish *public* genres like the symphony, concerto, and symphonic poem from the more *private* genres of song, character piece, and chamber music?

6. How did Wagner's theory of the music drama differ from previous approaches to opera?

7. How did the orchestra change over the course of the 19th century?

8. In what ways did historicism manifest itself musically in the 19th century?

9. Why did the concept of absolute music first arise in the 19th century?

10. Why did critical editions of composers' complete works first begin to appear in large quantities in the 19th century and not earlier?

Major Composers of the 19th Century

FRANCE

Berlioz (see Composer Profile, Chapter 15) and the Polish expatriate **Chopin** (see Composer Profile, Chapter 16) were the most prominent of many illustrious French composers in the 19th century. **Luigi Cherubini** (1760–1842) was highly esteemed for his operas and sacred music. **Charles Gounod** (1818–1893), **Georges Bizet** (1838–1875), and **Jules Massenet** (1842–1912) were among the leading theatrical composers of France in the second half of the century. Gounod's best known work is *Faust;* Bizet's fame rests largely on *Carmen*, one of the most popular operas of all time. Massenet's *Manon* and *Werther* continue to be staged today.

    César Franck (1822–1890) was born in Liège (now a part of Belgium) but became a French citizen in 1873. He was one of the great organ virtuosos of his century. His one symphony, in D minor, is a staple of the concert repertory. **Camille Saint-Saëns** (1835–1921) worked in virtually every genre of his era and was immensely prolific. He lived such a long life that, despite the immense vitality of his work, he eventually came to be identified with musical conservatism in France. His Symphony no. 3, which includes a prominent part for the organ, remains popular, as does his opera *Samson et Dalila*.

    Eduard Lalo (1823–1892) is best remembered today as the composer of the *Symphonie espagnole*, for violin and orchestra; his opera *Le Roi d'Ys* is occasionally performed as well. **Gabriel Fauré** (1845–1924) ranks as one of the great song composers of the 19th century; his chamber music and choral music, especially the Requiem, are also significant. **Vincent d'Indy** (1851–1931) and **Ernest Chausson** (1855–1899) both wrote masterfully for the orchestra. Like many of their French contemporaries, they also fell under the spell of Wagner, succumbing to what came to be known in France as *Wagnerisme*. D'Indy is best remembered for his *Symphony on a French Mountain Air*, which incorporates a French folk song. He also wrote an important composition manual and founded the Schola Cantorum in 1896 in an attempt to revive the plainchant repertory. Chausson's most frequently performed works are his *Poème* for violin and orchestra and his one symphony.

GREAT BRITAIN

The piano virtuoso and composer **John Field** (1782–1837) was born in Dublin but spent most of his adult life on the Continent. His nocturnes influenced the young Chopin. **Charles Villiers Stanford** (1852–1924), also born in Ireland, and **Charles H. H. Parry** (1848–1918) contributed much to the repertory of sacred music. **Sir Arthur Sullivan** (1842–1900) is best known for his collaborations with the lyricist William Schwenk Gilbert (1836–1911). Together, Gilbert and Sullivan wrote a string of enormously successful operettas, the most beloved of which are *H.M.S. Pinafore, The Pirates of Penzance, Iolanthe, The Mikado, The Yeomen of the Guard*, and *The Gondoliers*. Sullivan also wrote the music to the hymn *Onward, Christian Soldiers*.

ITALY

Only slightly younger than **Rossini** (see Composer Profile, Chapter 17), **Gaetano Donizetti** (1797–1848) and **Vincenzo Bellini** (1801–1835) also worked largely in the field of opera, emerging from Rossini's shadow after his abrupt retirement in 1829. Donizetti's most celebrated operas include *L'Elisir d'amore, Lucrezia Borgia, Lucia di Lammermoor,* and *Don Pasquale*. Bellini's most frequently performed works for the stage are *Il Pirata, La Straniera, La Sonnambula,* and above all, *Norma*. Italian opera composers working in the wake of **Verdi** (see Composer Profile, Chapter 17) include **Pietro Mascagni** (1863–1945) and **Ruggiero Leoncavallo** (1858–1919). They are inseparably linked in the mind of the musical public by two one-act operas that are frequently performed on the same bill: Mascagni's *Cavalleria rusticana* and Leoncavallo's *I Pagliacci*.

SPAIN

Fernando Sor (1778–1839), the most celebrated guitar virtuoso of the 19th century, wrote many short pieces for that instrument. **Pablo de Sarasate** (1844–1908) was to the violin what Sor was to the guitar; his most popular work is *Zigeunerweisen*, on gypsy-style themes. **Isaac Albéniz** (1860–1909) and **Enrique Granados** (1867–1916) count among Spain's first nationalistically inclined composers; both also won fame as pianists. Albéniz's best known work is *Iberia*, a suite for piano. Granados's most popular composition is his piano suite *Goyescas*, each of whose movements is associated with a specific painting or etching by the Spanish artist Francisco Goya.

GERMANY AND AUSTRIA

Beethoven (see Composer Profile, Chapter 15) cast a long shadow over his contemporaries. Most prominent among these are two who are best known today for their work in opera: **Carl Maria von Weber** (1786–1826) and **Heinrich Marschner** (1795–1861). Both created works rich in special effects and fairytale atmospheres. In addition to *Der Freischütz* (see Chapter 17), Weber also wrote *Euryanthe* and *Oberon*. Marschner gained fame through such works as *Der Vampyr* ("The Vampire") and *Hans Heiling*. Both composers exercised considerable influence on **Wagner** (see Composer Profile, Chapter 17).

    Ludwig Spohr (1784–1859) worked in a variety of genres, composing six symphonies, ten operas, and four oratorios. He was regarded as one of the leading musicians of his day, excelling as violinist, conductor, and composer. Like **Mendelssohn** (see Composer Profile, Chapter 15), **Schumann** (see Composer Profile, Chapter 16), and **Brahms** (see Composer Profile, Chapter 18), Spohr wrote a number of important symphonies, as did the Austrian **Anton Bruckner** (1824–1896). Bruckner was associated in the public mind with Wagner because of his penchant for large orchestras and advanced chromaticism, but Bruckner devoted himself largely to symphonies (nine of them numbered) and sacred music. **Carl Loewe** (1796–1869) and **Hugo Wolf** (1860–1903) are best known for their songs. Loewe, a near contemporary of **Schubert** (see Composer Profile, Chapter 16), cultivated the ballad with particular intensity.

    Richard Strauss (1864–1949) belongs equally to the 19th and 20th centuries. Along with **Mahler** (see Composer Profile, Chapter 18), Strauss was deeply influenced by the works of **Liszt** (see Composer Profile, Chapter 16), Wagner, and Bruckner. Strauss was also one of the great conductors of his generation. He favored the genres of opera and symphonic poem in particular. His works for the stage include *Elektra*, *Salome*, and *Der Rosenkavalier*. At the time of its premiere in 1907, *Salome* was considered particularly daring, not only because of its advanced chromaticism but also its erotically charged subject matter. Most of Strauss's symphonic poems date from the earlier decades of his career: among the most often performed are *Till Eulenspiegel's Merry Pranks*, *Don Juan*, *Death and Transfiguration*, *Thus Spake Zarathustra*, and *Don Quixote*, the last a series of "variations on a knightly theme" for solo cello and orchestra. Even Strauss's most bitter critics conceded that he was one of the greatest orchestrators of all time, and it is only fitting that he should have produced a new edition of Berlioz's *Treatise on Orchestration*, bringing it up to date to reflect more recent developments in the orchestra.

SCANDINAVIA

Niels Gade (1817–1890) was a protégé of Felix Mendelssohn, who conducted Gade's First Symphony in Leipzig in 1843. Gade went on to become a leading figure in Denmark's musical life. The Norwegian **Edvard Grieg** (1841–1907), one of the celebrated piano virtuosos of his day, achieved renown not only through his performances, but also through his own compositions. His Piano Concerto remains a favorite in the repertory of 19th-century concertos.

BOHEMIA

Dvořák (Composer Profile, Chapter 18) and **Bedřich Smetana** (1824–1884), both natives of Bohemia (now part of the Czech Republic), grew up in what at the time was part of the Austrian Empire. Smetana's *The Bartered Bride* was the first Czech opera to register international success; his cycle of symphonic poems, *Má Vlast* ("My Country"), continues to enjoy great popularity.

RUSSIA

Mikhail Glinka (1804–1857) was one of the first Russian composers to gain international fame. While studying in Italy as a young man, he experienced "musical homesickness," the desire to hear music that was distinctively Russian. His two great operas, *A Life for the Czar* and *Ruslan and Ludmila*, inspired several subsequent generations of Russian composers, including the group known as "The Five": **Mily Balakirev** (1836–1910), **César Cui** (1835–1919), **Alexander Borodin** (1833–1887), **Modeste Mussorgsky** (1839–1881), and **Nikolai Rimsky-Korsakov** (1844–1908). Many Russian composers considered **Tchaikovsky** (see Composer Profile, Chapter 18) too foreign in training and outlook to belong to this group of nationalists. Russian musical idioms are especially evident in such works as Balakirev's symphonic poem *Islamey*; Borodin's *In the Steppes of Central Asia* (also a symphonic poem) and his opera *Prince Igor*; and Mussorgsky's operatic masterpiece *Boris Godunov* and his celebrated piano suite *Pictures at an Exhibition* (later orchestrated by Maurice Ravel). Rimsky-Korsakov, the dean of Russian composers at the end of the century, won renown with such orchestral works as *Scheherezade* and the *Le Coq d'or* suite, and also wrote an important treatise on orchestration. As an educator, he lent guidance and support to a great many younger Russian composers, including Igor Stravinsky.

UNITED STATES

Lowell Mason (1792–1872) wrote many hymns and sacred works still in use today, but his greatest legacy is as an educator. Mason worked tirelessly to ensure that children be taught to read music in the schools; his efforts paralleled a similar movement in Europe. Mason himself eventually became superintendent of music in the Boston public school system, but his impact extended far beyond New England.

Dan Emmett (1815–1904) played in minstrel bands and wrote both the words and music to *Dixie*, the unofficial anthem of the Confederate States of America during the Civil War. **Stephen Foster** (1826–1864) was unquestionably the greatest of all 19th-century songwriters in America. He earned his early reputation as a composer of minstrel songs (discussed in Chapter 16). Foster's first great hit, *Old Folks at Home* ("Way Down upon the Swanee River . . .") sold some forty thousand copies in its first year. Several of his songs became so popular that many people still believe them to be folk songs.

Anton Philipp Heinrich (1781–1861), Bohemian by birth, was one of the first composers to write in a self-consciously American idiom, often drawing on Native-American themes. He wrote hugely ambitious works with such titles as *Complaint of Logan the Mingo Chief*, *Last of His Race* and *The Mastodon: A Grand Symphony in Three Parts for Full Orchestra*, whose finale bears the title "Shenandoah, a Celebrated Oneida Chief." **Louis Moreau Gottschalk** (1829–1869) also worked American inflections into many of his works, including *The Banjo* (Anthology). A showman as well as a musician, he always made a ceremony of taking off his white gloves before he played in public.

Many composers born in the United States went to Europe for their training, among them **John Knowles Paine** (1839–1906), who taught at Harvard, and **Horatio Parker** (1863–1919), whose pupils at Yale included the young Charles Ives (see Composer Profile, Chapter 20). Another New Englander, **Amy Beach** (1867–1944), was the first American woman to gain recognition as a significant composer of large-scale orchestral works. Her compositions include the *Gaelic Symphony*, based on Irish folk melodies, and a Mass in E♭.

The 20th Century

Prelude

The most striking aspect of music in the 20th century is its stylistic diversity. By the end of the century, composers, performers, and listeners had more access to more different kinds of music than ever before, thanks largely to technological advances in travel and communication. Either firsthand or through recordings, people could experience entire repertories of music that in previous eras would have remained unknown to them. Musical styles that had once existed only in the form of unwritten folk traditions could now be disseminated through recordings and broadcasts. These in turn expanded the musical vocabulary of composers working within the written tradition. The spirit of the age was one of innovation, and in pursuit of innovation many composers rejected—or at least tried to reject—tonality, up until this time one of the most basic elements in all of Western music. Still other composers embraced tradition. The result, by the end of the century, was a musical landscape that was either hopelessly fragmented or abundantly diverse, depending on one's point of view.

This diversity reflects 20th-century society as a whole, which was itself far more inclusive in its approach to previously marginalized groups than any society had been in the past. In the United States, women gained the right to vote in 1920, and the civil rights movement of the 1950s and 1960s ended the legal segregation that had relegated African Americans to second-class citizenship.

The world itself was far more diverse in 2000 than it had been 100 years earlier. The sprawling overseas empires of the United Kingdom, France, Spain, Portugal, Belgium, and the Netherlands disappeared almost completely in the years between 1945 and 1970. Even in Europe, new states asserted their independence from traditional rulers: Norway (from Sweden, 1905), Finland (from Russia, in 1917), and Ireland (from the United Kingdom, in 1921). The right of self-determination was one of the guiding forces behind the Treaty of Versailles after World War I, leading to the establishment of such nations as Czechoslovakia (which later split into two separate states, the Czech Republic and Slovakia), Poland (reestablished after World I, with new boundaries pushed westward after World War II), and the Baltic republics of Estonia, Latvia, and Lithuania (annexed by the Soviet Union in 1940 but reestablished as independent nations in the early 1990s). The number of sovereign nations in the world as a whole grew from 55 in 1900 to 192 in 2000.[1]

Wars, revolutions, and long-term international conflicts changed the political landscape of the globe at several junctures during the 20th century. In 1914, the growing territorial rivalries among the European powers—France and Great Britain in western Europe, Germany and Austria-Hungary in central Europe, and Russia to the east—culminated in World War I, which would leave some 10 million dead in its wake. The United States joined the conflict against Germany and Austria-Hungary in 1917 and helped turn the tide of battle. The Treaty of Versailles (1919) redrew the map of Europe, based on the principles of self-determination, and laid the groundwork for the League of Nations, headquartered in Geneva.

---

1. http://www.fordemocracy.net/electoral.shtml.

◀ Roy Lichtenstein (1923–1997), "Reverie", from the portfolio 11 Pop Artists, Volume II, 1965, color serigraph on paper, 27 1/8 × 23 in/Smithsonian American Art Museum, Washington, D.C./Art Resource, NY./© Estate of Roy Lichtenstein

World War I also helped precipitate the Russian Revolution. In March 1917, after teetering on the edge of dissolution for more than a decade, the Russian monarchy collapsed. The provisional government that replaced it was in turn overthrown by Nikolai Lenin's Bolshevik party in October of that same year. Lenin thereby succeeded in establishing the renamed Soviet Union as the first communist state, ruled in theory by the people themselves—the proletariat—but in fact controlled by a handful of party bureaucrats.

By the mid-1920s, most of the world had entered what would become a long-term economic depression. Economic uncertainty in Germany undermined that nation's fledgling attempt at democratic rule and contributed to Adolf Hitler's rise to power in the early 1930s. The United States, which enjoyed an economic boom during the 1920s, plunged into the Great Depression following a precipitous collapse in prices on the New York Stock Exchange in October 1929. By 1932, one-third of the American work force was unemployed.

War broke out again in 1939 when Hitler's Germany invaded Poland. World War II (1939–1945), which pitted the Axis powers (Germany, Italy, Japan) against the Allies (Great Britain, France, and, from 1941, the Soviet Union and the United States), was the bloodiest and most far-flung conflict in history. It left an estimated 50 million dead, provided cover for the attempted extermination of all the Jews by the German Nazi regime, and ended with the detonation of two atomic bombs over Japan in August 1945. The United Nations was founded that same year to help avoid international conflicts.

Although the United States and the Soviet Union fought as allies against Germany, they rapidly became enemies after the end of World War II. The Soviet Union translated its battlefield victories in eastern Europe into a sphere of influence that gave it control over the satellite states of Poland, East Germany, Czechoslovakia, Hungary,

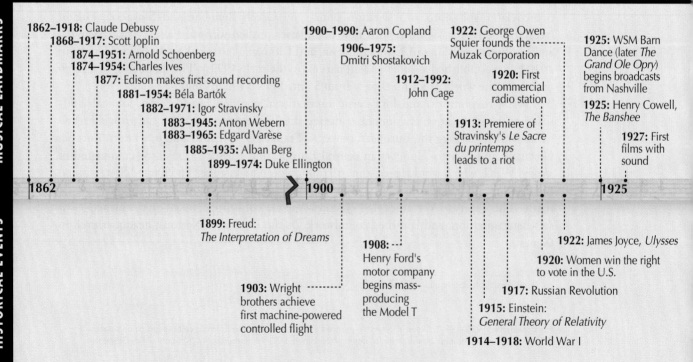

20TH CENTURY TIMELINE

MUSICAL LANDMARKS

- **1862–1918:** Claude Debussy
- **1868–1917:** Scott Joplin
- **1874–1951:** Arnold Schoenberg
- **1874–1954:** Charles Ives
- **1877:** Edison makes first sound recording
- **1881–1954:** Béla Bartók
- **1882–1971:** Igor Stravinsky
- **1883–1945:** Anton Webern
- **1883–1965:** Edgard Varèse
- **1885–1935:** Alban Berg
- **1899–1974:** Duke Ellington
- **1900–1990:** Aaron Copland
- **1906–1975:** Dmitri Shostakovich
- **1912–1992:** John Cage
- **1922:** George Owen Squier founds the Muzak Corporation
- **1920:** First commercial radio station
- **1913:** Premiere of Stravinsky's *Le Sacre du printemps* leads to a riot
- **1925:** WSM Barn Dance (later *The Grand Ole Opry*) begins broadcasts from Nashville
- **1925:** Henry Cowell, *The Banshee*
- **1927:** First films with sound

1862 | **1900** | **1925**

HISTORICAL EVENTS

- **1899:** Freud: *The Interpretation of Dreams*
- **1903:** Wright brothers achieve first machine-powered controlled flight
- **1908:** Henry Ford's motor company begins mass-producing the Model T
- **1915:** Einstein: *General Theory of Relativity*
- **1914–1918:** World War I
- **1917:** Russian Revolution
- **1920:** Women win the right to vote in the U.S.
- **1922:** James Joyce, *Ulysses*

Romania, and Bulgaria (Yugoslavia broke with the Soviet Union in 1948, and Albania turned to communist China for support in 1961). Tensions between the communist nations of this "Eastern bloc" (led by the Soviet Union) and the "Western bloc" (led by the United States) threatened to explode into war at many points in the four decades after World War II. However, the threat of mutual annihilation through nuclear weapons helped prevent a third world war. Because the two superpowers—the United States and the Soviet Union—never confronted one another directly on the battlefield, this period came to be known as the cold war. One of the most striking symbols of this era was the Berlin Wall, erected by East German authorities in 1961 to prevent the mass exodus of their population to the West.

The cold war featured many indirect confrontations between the two superpowers. Among the most significant of these were the Korean War (1950–1953) and Vietnam War (1964–1973), in both of which the United States and its allies fought proxies of the Soviet Union. Both wars reflected the American strategy of containment, by which Western nations sought to limit the global spread of communism.

Confronted with a collapsing economy in the mid-1980s, Premier Mikhail Gorbachev (b. 1931) sought to promote economic reform (*perestroika*) and greater political openness in the Soviet Union. By the late 1980s, however, the Soviet Union was losing control of its satellite states in eastern Europe. The dismantling of the Berlin Wall in 1989 and the reunification of Germany a year later signified the end of Communist Party domination of the Soviet Union and most other communist states in eastern Europe, and with it the end of the cold war. In late 1991, the Soviet Union officially disbanded into a loose Commonwealth of Independent States (CIS), the largest of which were Russia, Ukraine, Belarus, Georgia, Armenia, and Kazakhstan. The Baltic states of Estonia, Latvia, and Lithuania reemerged as independent nations.

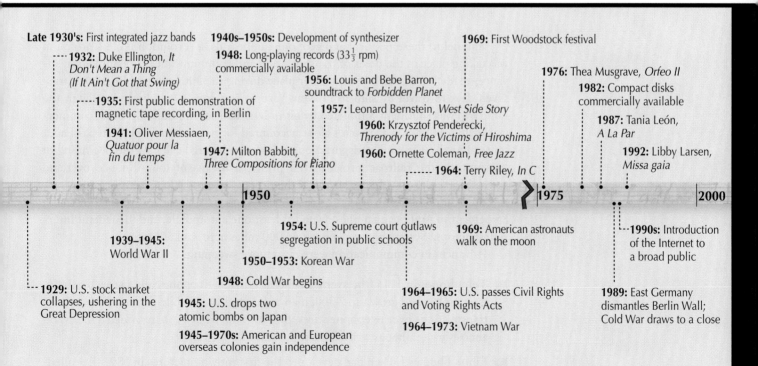

Late 1930's: First integrated jazz bands

1932: Duke Ellington, *It Don't Mean a Thing (If It Ain't Got that Swing)*

1935: First public demonstration of magnetic tape recording, in Berlin

1941: Oliver Messiaen, *Quatuor pour la fin du temps*

1940s–1950s: Development of synthesizer

1948: Long-playing records (33⅓ rpm) commercially available

1956: Louis and Bebe Barron, soundtrack to *Forbidden Planet*

1957: Leonard Bernstein, *West Side Story*

1960: Krzysztof Penderecki, *Threnody for the Victims of Hiroshima*

1960: Ornette Coleman, *Free Jazz*

1947: Milton Babbitt, *Three Compositions for Piano*

1964: Terry Riley, *In C*

1969: First Woodstock festival

1976: Thea Musgrave, *Orfeo II*

1982: Compact disks commercially available

1987: Tania León, *A La Par*

1992: Libby Larsen, *Missa gaia*

1950   1975   2000

1939–1945: World War II

1954: U.S. Supreme court outlaws segregation in public schools

1950–1953: Korean War

1948: Cold War begins

1929: U.S. stock market collapses, ushering in the Great Depression

1945: U.S. drops two atomic bombs on Japan

1945–1970s: American and European overseas colonies gain independence

1964–1965: U.S. passes Civil Rights and Voting Rights Acts

1964–1973: Vietnam War

1969: American astronauts walk on the moon

1990s: Introduction of the Internet to a broad public

1989: East Germany dismantles Berlin Wall; Cold War draws to a close

Europe in 2000.

Parallel to these political and economic upheavals, a revolution no less profound was taking place in the fields of transportation and communication. Technological advances made the world an ever smaller place during the 20th century. In 1900, it took seven days to travel by ship from New York to London. A hundred years later, the same trip was routinely completed by air in less than seven hours. By 2000, commercial airlines in the United States alone accounted for more than 600 billion passenger miles annually. Ground transportation changed no less radically. At the beginning of the century, the railroad provided the principal means of long-distance overland travel. Horse-drawn vehicles were still the primary means of local travel; the recently invented automobile was only for the wealthy and paved roads were few. By 2000, 85 percent of American families owned at least one automobile, and the federal Interstate Highway System covered almost 43,000 miles across all 50 states.

Advances in communication were even more sweeping:

■ **Telephone:** In 1915, the average American made 40 phone calls a year; by 2000, the number had grown to 2,300, many of them from mobile phones. Facsimile transmissions over telephone wires, first introduced in 1966, provided a means of almost instantaneous written communication.

■ **Film:** Thomas Edison had developed the first moving pictures in 1891 (he called his device a "projecting kinetoscope"), but the first commercially marketed films were not released until 1902. Films with sound ("talkies") arrived in 1927, and the first major feature films in color were produced in the late 1930s.

- **Radio:** Invented by the Italian Guglielmo Marconi in 1894, the radio was used in the early decades of the 20th century mainly for voice broadcasting by the military, ships, businesses, and private citizens. After the first commercial radio broadcasting license was issued in the United States in 1920, the industry began two decades of exponential growth. FM radio began commercial broadcasting in 1939. In 2000, there were some 10,300 commercial radio stations nationwide, and 99 percent of American households owned at least one radio. Satellite radio became a viable option, and stations began broadcasting on the Internet.

- **Television:** The television, invented in 1927, proliferated in the second half of the century. In 1950, 9 percent of households in the United States owned a television; by 1955, this figure had increased to 64.5 percent, and by 1965, it was 92.6 percent. Cable television, widely available by the early 1980s, expanded the number of available channels from a mere handful to dozens; satellite technology in the 1990s pushed the number into the hundreds.

- **Computer:** First developed during World War II, computers were used almost exclusively in business and industry through the 1960s. In 1981, the personal computer was introduced to the general public and soon became a common amenity. The Internet and e-mail became widely available to the public in the early 1990s.

THE IMPACT OF RECORDED SOUND

The emergence of sound recording in the late 19th century marks the most important development in the transmission of music since the introduction of music printing by movable type in the early 16th century. Thomas Edison created the first viable recording—his recitation of "Mary Had a Little Lamb"—in his laboratory in Menlo Park, New Jersey, in 1877. Edison's metal (later, wax) cylinders eventually gave way to the shellac disk, played on a turntable moving at the rate of 78 revolutions per minute

Little Nipper. Recorded sound is so common today that we can scarcely imagine how astonishing it must have been to hear disembodied voices and music for the first time. The 1896 logo for the Victor Talking Machine Company, "His Master's Voice," captures the combined sense of bafflement and fascination that humans shared with dogs.

Source: US Patent & Trademark Office

The technology of early sound recording. Until the development of useful microphones in the mid-1920s, amplification remained a fundamental obstacle to making recordings. Orchestras had to work in cramped settings and rely on megaphone-like devices to convey the music directly onto disk. Tapes and the possibilities of editing would not emerge until the 1940s. In this image from 1919, the English composer Edward Elgar conducts his Cello Concerto; the soloist is his compatriot Beatrice Harrison (1892–1965), the first woman cellist ever to give a solo performance at Carnegie Hall in New York.

Source: © Hulton-Deutsch Collection/CORBIS

(rpm). By 1910, these 78 rpm disks had become standard features of well-to-do households. In retrospect, the format seems bulky and cumbersome, with each disk holding less than five minutes of music per side. And in an era before the invention of the microphone, the challenges of recording a large ensemble were considerable. Still, the very notion of being able to listen to an orchestral rendition of a complete symphony by Beethoven or an aria by Verdi in one's home at a time of one's own choosing represented a stunning advance. The great Italian tenor Enrico Caruso (1873–1921) was one of the recording industry's first superstars: at the peak of his career, he was earning $115,000 a year from recordings alone, the equivalent of almost $2 million today. His success on the stage fueled sales of his recordings, and the popularity of his recordings further boosted his success on the stage.

Recordings had an enormous impact on composers as well, shrinking the distance between musical cultures. Lacking access to recordings, the only way Claude Debussy could hear a Javanese gamelan in Paris in the late 19th century was to witness a performance of an ensemble specially organized for the world's fair that took place there in 1889 (and which also gave us the Eiffel Tower). A hundred years later, a composer in Paris could place an order through the Internet for compact disk recordings of three dozen different gamelan ensembles and have them delivered to her door within a few days. Recording technology also changed the very notion of what constitutes a work of music. By the 1960s, composers as diverse as Milton Babbitt and John Lennon and Paul McCartney of the Beatles were creating works that could not be performed by musicians in a live setting but existed solely in recorded form.

MODERNISM: THE SHOCK OF THE NEW

Modernism was a phenomenon that affected all the arts in the 20th century, including literature and painting as well as music. It is not a style in its own right but rather an attitude, one that gave rise to a variety of important styles. Modernism is the self-conscious striving for novelty at almost any cost, based on a conviction that the new

Milestones of Sound Recording and Broadcast Technology

1877	Recording on cylinders invented by Thomas Edison.
1897	Shellac disk recordings, rotating on a turntable at 78 revolutions per minute (rpm) begin to enjoy wide distribution, driving Edison's cylinders out of the market.
1920	Radio station KDKA in Pittsburgh begins operation as the nation's first commercial radio station.
1927	The first commercial film with spoken dialogue—*The Jazz Singer*, starring Al Jolson—is released, signaling the end of the silent film era. Recorded music soon becomes an integral part of the film industry.
1935	Magnetic tape recording is introduced publicly in Berlin; part of the Nazi secret war effort, it is uncovered by the Allies at war's end.
1948	The 12-inch $33\frac{1}{3}$ rpm long-playing record is introduced; the LP holds 23 minutes per side, in contrast to the 5-minute capacity of the 12-inch 78 rpm record.
1949	The first 7-inch 45 rpm record is introduced; each side of the disk holds up to five minutes of music, making this format an ideal medium for the distribution of popular songs.
1958	Stereo recordings enter the commercial market.
1963	Cassette tape, a format offering unprecedented portability, becomes available commercially.
1982	Compact disks become commercially available and within six years surpass sales of LPs. They have a capacity of 80 minutes.
1990s	The Internet becomes a major vehicle for transmitting music.

must be as different as possible from the old. Since at least the Renaissance, artists have consciously sought to create new kinds of art, and in this sense modernism has long been a driving force in the creative process. But in the 20th century, the quest for novelty took on unprecedented centrality, involving the outright rejection of what had long been fundamental elements: rhyme and meter in poetry, linear narrative in literature (see Primary Evidence: "Literary Modernism"), representation and perspective in painting, and ornament in architecture. Each generation had what it thought of as its **avant-garde.** The term is French for "vanguard," the first troops to engage the enemy in battle. As such it conjures the image of a small band of artists waging war against the conservative tastes of resistant audiences. In all the arts in the 20th century, the avant-gardists (modernists) considered it their duty to lead art in new directions.

In music, the most obvious manifestations of modernism were the abandonment of conventional forms and of tonality. Musical modernism produced a succession of new approaches—impressionism, expressionism, atonality, serial composition, aleatory music—that confronted listeners with the challenge of the New. Even the less overtly confrontational idioms of neoclassicism, minimalism, and postmodernism can be understood as manifestations of modernism, insisting on a distinction between new and old even while accepting certain elements of the old. The most extreme forms of modernism sought to erase all links to the past. "Creators must look straight ahead," the composer and conductor Pierre Boulez (b. 1925) once declared. "It is not enough to deface the Mona Lisa because that does not kill the Mona Lisa. All the art of the past must be destroyed." On another occasion, and in a more conciliatory mood, Boulez maintained that "history as it is made by great composers is not a history of conservation but of destruction—even while cherishing what is being destroyed."

In the process of destroying the past, cherished or not, composers had to confront the music of that past at every turn. Novelty, after all, could only be measured

FOCUS   Major Literary Figures of the 20th Century

One of the most influential figures in all of 20th-century literature was not a novelist or poet at all, but rather a psychologist: **Sigmund Freud** (1856–1939). Freud developed a radical new theory of the mind that posits the existence of the unconscious and a therapeutic technique, psychoanalysis, in which patients reveal their unconscious motivations by free association.

Many of the most important literary figures of Freud's generation expanded on the idea of free association. The Irish novelist **James Joyce** (1882–1941) developed a technique known as "stream of consciousness," which tries to mimic in prose a character's unedited, internal thought processes. His *Ulysses* (1922) is a landmark of modernist literature. The American poets **Ezra Pound** (1885–1972) and **T. S. Eliot** (1888–1965), the latter of whom spent most of his life in England, are both known as pioneers of modernist poetry: dense, challenging to the reader, and full of allusions.

Marcel Proust (1871–1922) was the leading literary modernist in France. His multivolume *Remembrance of Things Past* (1913–1927) explores the realm of the unconscious through a series of extended interior monologues. **Jean-Paul Sartre** (1905–1980) and **Simone de Beauvoir** (1908–1986) wrote novels that espoused a philosophy known as existentialism, which viewed humankind as isolated and free within a universe whose meaning cannot be defined in conventional terms. De Beauvoir's nonfictional *The Second Sex* (1950) is an early landmark in the growing movement toward equal social and legal status for women. **Samuel Beckett** (1906–1989), although born in Dublin, wrote most of his works in French. He is associated most closely with the so-called theater of the absurd, in which events often fail to unfold in a logical fashion, running counter to the conventions of plot and time. **Marguerite Duras** (1914–1996), born in French Indochina (now Vietnam), was one of many French writers who sought to create a new kind of novel that incorporated many different genres in addition to narrative.

A number of German poets and novelists rose to prominence in the first half of the 20th century. **Franz Kafka** (1883–1924) is best known for his surrealistic yet moving explorations of the darker corners of the human psyche. In *The Metamorphosis*, the central character wakes up one morning to discover he has turned into a gigantic insect. **Hermann Hesse** (1877–1962) wrote novels of a decidedly mystical bent; he was strongly influenced by Eastern religions, especially Hinduism. **Thomas Mann** (1875–1955) is known for his novels that combine psychology and philosophy; the central character of *Doktor Faustus* (1947) is loosely based on the composer Arnold Schoenberg, who like Mann lived in exile in Los Angeles. A number of composers set to music poetry by 20th-century German poets such as **Stefan George** (1868–1933), **Rainer Maria von Rilke** (1875–1926), and **Georg Trakl** (1887–1914). In the realm of opera, the playwrights **Hugo von Hofmannsthal** (1874–1929) and **Bertolt Brecht** (1898–1956) collaborated with the composers Richard Strauss and Kurt Weill, respectively. In the period after World War II, the most prominent German-language literary figures were **Max Frisch** (1911–1991), **Heinrich Böll** (1917–1985), and **Günter Grass** (b. 1927).

Latin America produced a number of distinguished writers during the 20th century. The most notable of these were the Argentine **Jorge Luis Borges** (1899–1986), who wrote poetry, short stories, and criticism; the Chilean poet **Pablo Neruda** (1904–1973); and the Colombian **Gabriel García Márquez** (b. 1928), whose novels *One Hundred Years of Solitude* (1967) and *Love in the Time of Cholera* (1985) became international best-sellers. All three writers received the Nobel Prize in Literature.

Gertrude Stein (1874–1946) was one of many American writers who lived and worked in Paris, where she encouraged the work of her compatriots, the novelists **Ernest Hemingway** (1899–1961) and **F. Scott Fitzgerald** (1896–1940). Stein's work is decidedly modern in the way it challenges readers to decipher its many intrigues. Hemingway, by contrast, is noted for his terse and direct prose. Fitzgerald's novels depict the essence of the Jazz Age, the 1920s. Another American in Paris, **Henry Miller** (1891–1980), won both fame and notoriety for the frankness of novels like *Tropic of Cancer* (1931), tame by today's standards but scandalous in its time. **William Faulkner** (1887–1962) chronicled the American South in his novels, many of which show the influence of Joyce's stream of consciousness technique.

Prominent American writers from the second half of the century include **John Steinbeck** (1902–1968), **John Hersey** (1914–1993), **Arthur Miller** (b. 1915–2005), **Norman Mailer** (b. 1923–2007), **John Updike** (b. 1932), and **Joyce Carol Oates** (b. 1938). Prominent African-American writers include **Zora Neale Hurston** (1901–1960), **Langston Hughes** (1902–1967), **Richard Wright** (1908–1960), **Ralph Ellison** (1914–1994), **James Baldwin** (1924–1987), **Maya Angelou** (b. 1928), and **Toni Morrison** (b. 1931).

PRIMARY EVIDENCE — Literary Modernism: The Stream of Consciousness

In the early decades of the 20th century, modernist writers abandoned the idea of a logical, directed narrative. Several of them, including James Joyce (1882–1941), Ezra Pound (1885–1972), and T. S. Eliot (1888–1965), opted for what came to be known as a stream of consciousness style, in which the prose resembles the fragmented manner in which most people think their private thoughts. Although carefully crafted, this style sometimes gives the impression of randomness. The selection here, from Joyce's *Ulysses* (1922), is from the "Sirens" episode, which bears strong parallels to the account of Odysseus and the sirens in Homer's *Odyssey*. Joyce's character Leopold Bloom, eating his lunch in a Dublin bar, listens to Simon Daedalus sing an aria from Friedrich von Flotow's opera *Martha* (sung in English as "When first I saw that form endearing"). Bloom is moved by the music for it evokes multiple complications in his own life, and toward the end of this passage he wraps his fingers in an elastic band. The act faintly echoes Odysseus's command to his men that they bind him to the mast of their ship so he might hear the song of the sirens without being lured to his death (see p. 13).

The harping chords of prelude closed. A chord longdrawn, expectant drew a voice away.

—*When first I saw that form endearing.*
Richie turned.
—Si Dedalus' voice, he said.
Braintipped, cheek touched with flame, they listened feeling that flow endearing flow over skin limbs human heart soul spine. Bloom signed to Pat, bald Pat is a waiter hard of hearing, to set ajar the door of the bar. The door of the bar. So. That will do. Pat, waiter, waited, waiting to hear, for he was hard of hear by the door.
—*Sorrow from me seemed to depart.*
Through the hush of air a voice sang to them, low, not rain, not leaves in murmur, like no voice of strings of reeds or what doyoucallthem dulcimers, touching their still ears with words, still hearts of their each his remembered lives. Good, good to hear: sorrow from them each seemed to from both depart when first they heard. When first they saw, lost Richie, Poldy, mercy of beauty, heard from a person wouldn't expect it in the least, her first merciful lovesoft oftloved word.

Love that is singing: love's old sweet song. Bloom unwound slowly the elastic band of his packet. Love's old sweet *sonnez la* gold. Bloom wound a skein round four forkfingers, stretched it, relaxed, and wound it round his troubled double, fourfold, in octave, gyved them fast.

Source: James Joyce, *Ulysses* (New York: Vintage, 1961), pp. 273–4.

against what had already been done. John Cage, perhaps the most quintessentially modernist of all 20th-century composers, summed up this paradox neatly in the form of an anecdote:

> Once in Amsterdam, a Dutch musician said to me, "It must be very difficult for you in America to write music, for you are so far away from the centers of tradition." I had to say, "It must be very difficult for you in Europe to write music, for you are so close to centers of tradition."[2]

The gulf between new and old became wider and wider as the century progressed. To be sure, audiences had confronted so-called difficult music before the 20th century, but in the early decades of the century a number of younger composers posed an unprecedented challenge when they started writing music without a tonal center. Most listeners found the new idiom difficult to follow, and many reacted with overt hostility. Arnold Schoenberg and his followers in Vienna, weary of having their concerts disrupted, formed their own Society for Private Musical Performances, withdrawing themselves from public scrutiny altogether. Audiences became less confrontational after World War II as the rage of earlier listeners eventually cooled, partly through

2. John Cage, "History of Experimental Music in the United States" (1959), in Cage, *Silence* (Boston: M.I.T. Press, 1966), p. 73.

FOCUS   Major Visual Artists of the 20th Century

Modernism found many forms of expression in the visual arts, beginning with the impressionists of the late 19th century (see Chapter 20). The most important impressionist painters were **Edouard Manet** (1832–1883), **Edgar Degas** (1834–1917), **Claude Monet** (1840–1926), **Berthe Morisot** (1841–1895), and **Pierre Auguste Renoir** (1841–1919). These artists used an accumulation of short brush strokes instead of a continuous line to produce not so much a representation of an object as a sensation—an impression—of it. Monet's painting "Impression: Sunrise" (see page 519) gave this artistic movement its name. The Spanish-born **Pablo Picasso** (1881–1973) is widely acknowledged as the most influential artist of the entire century. He appropriated an astonishing array of styles and techniques throughout his long career and was a leading proponent of such movements as cubism and primitivism.

Expressionist artists, known for their bold brush strokes and unflinching eye toward the darker sides of life, include the Germans **Franz Marc** (1880–1916) and **Max Beckmann** (1884–1950), the Austrians **Oskar Kokoschka** (1886–1980) and **Egon Schiele** (1890–1918), the Russian **Wassily Kandinsky** (1866–1944), and the Norwegian **Edvard Munch** (1863–1944).

Realism and surrealism were two other important movements in 20th-century art. Realism attempted to capture photographic-like images of the world, whereas surrealism mixed partially realistic representations with fantasy-like elements. The Spanish artist **Salvador Dali** (1904–1989) is the best known exponent of surrealism; the American **Norman Rockwell** (1894–1978) epitomizes realism. Dali's *The Persistence of Memory*, with its melting clocks, was painted in the same year (1931) as Norman Rockwell's cover art for the *Boy Scout Handbook*.

The leading masters of abstract art—art based solely on form and color, conspicuously avoiding all references to recognizable objects—were the Americans **Jackson Pollock** (1912–1956) and **Willem de Koonig** (1904–1997). The movement flourished in the middle decades of the century. Postmodernism (see Chapter 23), a reaction against abstraction and modernism, entered the scene in the 1950s and 1960s with the work of such artists as **Andy Warhol** (1928–1987), whose work openly appropriates a wide variety of styles and genres, including icons of pop culture.

acceptance of new sounds but also partly through indifference. More and more people began to think of so-called classical music as music by dead composers. It is a sad but undeniable fact that by the end of the 20th century, Béla Bartók's *Concerto for Orchestra* (1944) remained the most recent major orchestral work to have entered the standard concert hall repertory.

For much of the 20th century, what came to be known as "difficult" music, while not particularly popular with the general listening public, nevertheless enjoyed a certain prestige within the community of musical artists. A great many composers took comfort in Ralph Waldo Emerson's pronouncement that "To be great is to be misunderstood." Popular success, in fact, became suspect in certain circles. This is especially evident in the case of a composer like Leonard Bernstein, who wrote so-called difficult music as well as music of wide appeal, most notably his Broadway musicals *Candide* and *West Side Story*. Even when criticizing the isolation of difficult music in the mid-1960s, Bernstein felt compelled to adopt an apologetic tone:

> As of this writing, God forgive me, I have far more pleasure in following the musical adventures of Simon & Garfunkel or of The Association singing "Along Comes Mary" than I have in most of what is being written now by the whole community of "avant garde" composers. . . . Pop music seems to be the only area where there is to be found unabashed vitality, the fun of invention, the feeling of fresh air. Everything else suddenly seems old-fashioned: electronic music, serialism, chance music—they have already acquired the musty odor of academicism.[3]

---

3. Leonard Bernstein, *The Infinite Variety of Music* (New York: Simon & Schuster, 1966), p. 10.

Modernism in painting: Cubism.
Modernist developments in music in the first decade of the 20th century have striking parallels in other arts. Atonality, for example, has often been compared to cubism, an artistic movement of the same period that went out of its way to violate the conventions of representation, especially perspective. Cubism emerged between 1907 and 1914 in the work of Pablo Picasso (1881–1973) and Georges Bracque (1882–1963), contemporary with the earliest atonal works by Schoenberg and his pupils. In cubism, objects that are often only barely recognizable appear disassembled and reassembled with all sides of an object showing at once, as if on a flat plane. As in this 1911 painting by Picasso—*Man with a Violin*—no one perspective has priority, just as no key has priority in atonal music. The effect can be disturbing or refreshing—or both at the same time.

Source: Pablo Picasso (Spanish) "Man with a Violin" c. 1911–12, oil on canvas 39 3/8 × 29 7/8 in. Philadelphia Museum of Art: Louise and Walter Arensberg Collection. ©1998 Estate of Pablo Picasso/Artists Rights Society (ARS), New York.

Bernstein's remark is deeply revealing. Although open as a conductor to new music of many different styles, he had experienced a certain degree of disdain from composer colleagues who accused him of selling out to popular tastes; he was well aware that his comments were likely to antagonize a good many of his peers. To be popular, in the view of these avant-gardists, was to be shallow. Compositional complexity was a correlative of quality, and if the public didn't "get it," the fault lay with the public. "I can't be responsible for the audience," the British composer Harrison Birtwistle (b. 1934) pointed out late in the 20th century. "I'm not running a restaurant."[4]

The widespread acceptance of such a perspective was new in the 20th century. Earlier composers—Haydn and Verdi, for example—had seen little if any conflict between popularity and musical integrity. But in the end it is pointless to blame either composers or listeners for this state of affairs. Audiences have always listened to the music that moves them, and at no point in history were there ever so many listeners, or so large a menu of musical styles from which to choose, as at the end of the 20th century.

---

4. Nicholas Cook, *Music* (New York: Oxford University Press, 1998), p. 40.

The Growth of Pluralism

The diversity of 20th-century musical styles was a source of both pleasure and anxiety for composers and listeners alike. The proliferation of styles during this era can be viewed from several different perspectives, all of which reflect broader trends in society as a whole.

FROM HOMOGENEITY TO DIVERSITY

At the beginning of the 20th century, Western nations dominated much of the globe, and Western peoples presumed for themselves a corresponding cultural superiority. The United States proudly proclaimed itself a social melting pot in which people from all over the world could blend into an already established homogeneous society. By the end of the century, the melting pot metaphor had changed to that of a mosaic—that is, many individually distinct units combining to create a larger whole. The shift in imagery is revealing, for the mosaic metaphor rejects the idea that diverse cultures can (or should) be homogenized into a single mainstream. What had previously been seen as fragmentation, a source of weakness, was now recognized as diversity, a source of strength.

Attitudes toward music in Western culture of the 20th century reflect a similar transformation in outlook. In the early and middle decades of the century, music that did not conform to the mainstream idiom of tonal music was widely condemned. The tonally unconventional works of Arnold Schoenberg and the rhythmically unconventional works of Igor Stravinsky were seen in part as a rebellion against the social status quo (which in a sense they were); performances of this music occasionally led to riots in the concert hall, as the cartoon on the next page illustrates. Rhythmically charged music like ragtime (in the 1900s and 1910s), jazz (1920s and 1930s), and rock and roll (1950s and 1960s) also touched off their share of controversy. Part of this animosity was motivated by racial prejudices and generational conflicts, but, as in the case of Schoenberg and Stravinsky, the music offended listeners because it was perceived to threaten the existing social order, a concern that cultural observers have expressed at many times throughout history. Plato, for example, had warned more than two thousand years before that "a new type of music is something to beware of as a hazard of all our fortunes. For the modes of music are never disturbed without unsettling of the most fundamental political and social conventions." This mistrust of new music was still common in the first half of the 20th century.

"The next concert by Schoenberg in Vienna."
Schoenberg continues to conduct even though pandemonium has broken out. The figure on the floor at the bottom center appears to be Schubert, suggesting that Schoenberg's music is an affront not only to his contemporaries but to Viennese composers of the past as well. The image caricatures an actual event, the Viennese "Scandal Concert" of March 31, 1913, in which a performance of Alban Berg's *Altenberg Lieder,* op. 4, led to an open revolt of the audience. One of the organizers of the concert was arrested for striking the operetta composer Oscar Straus, who at the trial glibly remarked that the punch to his head "seemed to be the most harmonious sound of the entire evening."

Source: Phaidon Press Limited

In the later decades of the century, however, audiences became more and more inclined to take a pluralistic, live-and-let-live attitude, embracing the music they liked and simply ignoring any they found objectionable. Performances of innovative music stopped being a matter of controversy. Indeed, it became increasingly difficult for composers to shock listeners at all. Aside from lyrics and stage antics, there seemed to be very little that would move listeners to disrupt a performance or call for a ban on sales of recordings. Rap music came under fire in the 1990s primarily for its words, not its musical style. Just as the image of the melting pot had given way to that of a mosaic, the illusion of a musical mainstream had evaporated to leave a sense of tolerance toward many varied musical styles. By the 1980s, Western society as a whole was embracing a greater diversity of musical idioms than at any point in its past: country music (including bluegrass) and rock (the two most popular), rhythm & blues (encompassing soul, hip-hop, and traditional blues), jazz and big band, classical, gospel and hymns, songs from musicals and operettas, easy listening ("mood music"), ethnic or world music (particularly Latin), and folk (American traditional).

Technology such as television—an invention of the mid-20th century—offers a key to understanding the transformation of attitudes toward music. In the 1950s, most Americans could tune in only two or three national networks; any additional channels they could receive were likely to be local ones. When Elvis Presley and the Beatles appeared on *The Ed Sullivan Show*, their audiences included viewers of all ages, from children to adults. This weekly show was designed to offer something for everyone: comedians, acrobats, magicians, and musicians of all kinds, from Maria Callas's performing Puccini's *Tosca* to Bo Diddley singing "Bo Diddley." The shows with Elvis in 1956 were seen by one out of every three Americans, and one of the Beatles's three 1964 broadcasts garnered the largest single audience in television history up to that point. Not everyone approved of the latest developments in music, but almost everyone knew what they were.

By the mid-1980s, this was no longer the case. Much as radio stations were already developing highly focused niche audiences before World War II, the rise of cable television now made the concept of the network variety show obsolete. With so many channels to choose from, viewers could focus not only on specific shows but entire networks devoted to specialized interests: sports, cooking, comedy, and so on. While such diversity is, of course, advantageous to individual viewers, who gain a far greater freedom of choice, this diversity has eroded a sense of shared culture. In the 1950s and 1960s, it was almost impossible for adults of all ages to avoid seeing Elvis and the Beatles because so many of them watched *The Ed Sullivan Show* every Sunday night, no matter who the guests on any given broadcast happened to be. By the 1980s, viewers who wanted to watch the latest music videos chose MTV or VH1. With so many television and radio broadcasts available, musical groups were no longer competing for a common audience, and listeners were content to leave one another more or less alone; it became relatively easy for listeners of one generation to be wholly unaware of the music of another. A dominant culture with a dominant set of norms was replaced by cultural pluralism. By the year 2000, the World Wide Web had pushed traditional notions of shared culture even further to the brink; individuals were now able to offer their work directly to a global audience (see Epilogue).

The multiplicity of musical styles in the 20th century can be found even within the works of individual composers. Here are some examples:

■ **Scott Joplin** (1868–1917), known during his life as the "King of Ragtime" because of his enormously popular piano rags (see Chapter 20), integrated the style of ragtime into the classical genre of opera. Although a concert production of his *Treemonisha* (1911) failed to arouse great interest during Joplin's lifetime, the work was successfully revived in a staged performance in 1972 and won a special posthumous Pulitzer Prize in 1976.

■ **George Gershwin** (1898–1937) moved easily between popular song ("Swanee," "Let's Call the Whole Thing Off") and the traditional genres of the opera house and concert hall with works that frequently incorporate jazz idioms (see Chapter 22). *Rhapsody in Blue* (1924) is in effect a one-movement concerto for piano and jazz orchestra, and the opera *Porgy and Bess* (1935) draws on African American sources.

■ **Duke Ellington** (1899–1974) defies categorization (see Chapter 20). He wrote popular songs, dance numbers for big bands, sacred music, and works for orchestra. Songs like "Sophisticated Lady" and "It Don't Mean a Thing (If It Ain't Got That Swing)" stand side by side in his output with works like *Harlem*, commissioned by Arturo Toscanini for the NBC Symphony Orchestra, and *Black, Brown, and Beige*, a symphonic poem that runs some 45 minutes in performance.

■ **Frank Zappa** (1940–1993) pursued an astonishing variety of musical styles, writing for rock bands as well as for orchestras. His "Dog Breath Variations," for example, began life on *Uncle Meat* (1969), an album recorded with his rock group The Mothers of Invention; Zappa subsequently refashioned the work on two occasions, once for orchestra and once for a smaller wind ensemble.

■ **Jim Morrison** (1943–1971) crossed many boundaries both as a performer and as a composer. His 1967 recording of the "Alabama Song" from Kurt Weill's *Aufstieg und Fall der Stadt Mahagonny* (Anthology, discussed in Chapter 22) introduced an entire generation of rock aficionados to a German opera written in the 1920s. Morrison's eleven-minute "The End," released on the same album

(*The Doors*), extended both the textual and musical expectations of what a rock group could do.

■ **Wynton Marsalis** (b. 1961) has used his virtuosic trumpet skills to accompany Sarah Vaughan and Dizzy Gillespie and collaborate with soprano Kathleen Battle, country singer Willie Nelson, and poet Maya Angelou. He has led the Lincoln Center Jazz Orchestra, recorded classical trumpet concertos, and composed music for several modern dance companies. He has written two major oratorios—*Blood on the Fields* (1994; Pulitzer Prize in Music, 1997) and *All Rise* (1999)—and recorded numerous albums, including the provocative *The Majesty of the Blues*, with its strong stance favoring early jazz. Marsalis heads Jazz at Lincoln Center, which since 1995 has held equal status with the Center's New York Philharmonic, Metropolitan Opera, and New York City Ballet.

In spite of such personal diversity, marketing dictated that musical works—specifically, recordings—be packaged in such a way as to target specific audiences and tastes. The Grammy Awards, presented annually by the National Academy of Recording Arts and Sciences, provide a good index of how the music industry promotes its products. The proliferation of award categories for the Grammys in recent years suggests that almost every category of music eventually breeds its own subcategories; for example, gospel music, generally viewed as a "single" genre, is divided by the academy into no fewer than seven different categories: traditional, pop/contemporary, Southern/country/bluegrass, traditional soul, contemporary soul, contemporary rhythm and blues (that is, hip-hop), and rock. There is now even a separate evening of Latin Grammy awards. Such distinctions inevitably shape the way we hear these and other kinds of music.

Marketing also plays a basic role in what kinds of music listeners hear in the first place. Laurie Anderson's (b. 1947) minimalist "O Superman (For Massenet)" became a number two hit in the United Kingdom in 1981. Polish composer Henryk Gorecki (b. 1933) rocketed to fame in the mid-1990s when his neo-modal Third Symphony (with soprano, 1976) was marketed in England as a pop recording in 1992; it rose to number six on the charts. When Samuel Barber's highly chromatic *Adagio for Strings* (originally composed in 1936) appeared on Hollywood film soundtracks—*Elephant Man* (1980) and *Platoon* (1986), among others—it became a worldwide hit with listeners who had never before heard of Barber.

THE PAST CONFRONTS THE PRESENT

The listening public's interest in new idioms was not confined to new music. The rediscovery of what has come to be known as early music—generally speaking, music written before 1700—opened up an entirely new section of the musical menu. Earlier repertories that had for all practical purposes been inaccessible to the music public became readily available through scores, performances, and above all recordings. The works of Du Fay, Josquin, and Monteverdi, for example, had all languished in obscurity for centuries and were virtually unknown in 1900; by 2000, some of them had become very well known indeed.

Arnold Dolmetsch (1858–1940) was in many respects the father of what in his time was called the early music movement. He was one of the first and certainly the most visible of a number of musicians in the late 19th and early 20th centuries who began performing on instruments that had remained essentially dormant for a century or more, such as the harpsichord, clavichord, spinet, viola da gamba, viola d'amore, and a variety of wind and percussion instruments. Although amateurish by today's standards, Dolmetsch's work was profoundly important in laying the foundation for the post–World War II revival of interest in music of the medieval, Renaissance, and Baroque eras. In the years between 1950 and 1980, a number of outstanding groups sprang up that specialized in what came to be known as period instruments, either originals or accurate copies of instruments contemporary to the repertory being performed. At first the music and instruments were so strange and novel to audiences that they often required commentary from the performers. But before long, the work of musicians like Nikolaus Harnoncourt, David Munrow, and Roger Norrington had become so well known that explanations were no longer necessary. Indeed, Norrington extended the concept of period instruments into the repertory of the mid- and even late-19th century with the symphonies of Brahms.

By the late 1970s, Josquin, Du Fay, and Machaut had joined Bach, Beethoven, and Brahms in the record (and later CD) stores. Even Gregorian chant hit the charts in the mid-1990s. In a sense, then, a great deal of supposedly new music in the 20th century was in fact extremely old, but the style of it was new to listeners. Composers of the late 20th century thus had to struggle for recognition not only within the realm of contemporary music and the standard repertory (from Bach onward), but against extremely old works as well. To a certain extent, the early music movement has satisfied the desire of listeners for new repertories without recourse to newly composed music.

Some composers found new sounds in instruments of the past. Although the harpsichord had never disappeared entirely, it enjoyed a renaissance in the early

---

PRIMARY EVIDENCE — "This Ugly Game of Idolizing the Past"

In response to a questionnaire distributed in 1984 by the International Music Council, the eminent German avant-garde composer Karlheinz Stockhausen (1928–2007) railed against the preoccupation of artists and the recording industry with music of the past to the exclusion of music of the present. At no time before the present, Stockhausen argued, has the public ever been so absorbed with music of prior generations and so unconcerned with new music. Here he proposes a program of change, supporting "musical evolution" rather than "idolizing the past."

———◆———

What can be done: Shake up the leading interpreters in the world, ask them to refuse to serve any longer the machinery of composer-stripping, financial exploitation of dead composers through established gangs of cultural manipulation and "music marketing"; insist that they serve musical evolution: help vulnerable new musical organisms rather than living from a 300-year-old bank account of musical literature; spend at least 50 percent of their time rehearsing and performing new works; fight for progress and refuse to continue this ugly game of idolizing the past.

Source: Karlheinz Stockhausen, "To the International Music Council," *Perspectives of New Music*, 24 (1985): 44.

Karlheinz Stockhausen in the recording studio, ca. 1965.

Source: © Hulton-Deutsch Collection/CORBIS. All Rights Reserved.

20th century through works like Manuel da Falla's Harpsichord Concerto. Many popular recording artists, among them the Beatles and singer Tori Amos, also made use of the instrument in their recordings. Paul Hindemith, in turn, wrote several pieces for the viola d'amore, an instrument that had not been in general use since the Baroque era. Sonorities, forms, and styles of earlier times inspired still other composers of the 20th century. Many works by the Estonian composer Arvo Pärt (b. 1935), for example, are indebted to the textures and sonorities of 13th-century polyphony. The American composer Ellen Taaffe Zwillich (b. 1939), in turn, has written works from time to time that openly evoke the forms and styles of the Baroque, such as her *Concerto Grosso* (1985) and *Partita* for violin and string orchestra (2000).

RECORDED VERSUS LIVE MUSIC

Until the late 19th century, music had always been a quintessentially social art, one that brought people together in the same space to share the experience of performing and hearing music. A person could read a novel or contemplate a painting in solitude, but listening to anyone other than one's own self was possible only in places where others were making music. People who wanted to appreciate and enjoy music played an instrument or sang, and they often learned to read musical notation. In 1900, almost every village of any size had a community band, chorus, or both; music lessons were a standard feature of a middle-class childhood, and the typical middle-class family owned a piano.

Some middle-class families also owned what was then a new invention: a phonograph. With this device, for the first time in history, a single performance could be preserved and repeated almost indefinitely, and a work of music could be heard outside the presence of a performing musician. Over the course of the 20th century, the phonograph was supplemented by radio, television, video- and audiotape, the compact disc, and other recording technologies that the inventors of the first phonograph could scarcely have dreamed of. Recording technology transformed the manner in which music was both produced and consumed. As a result, today a greater selection of music is more readily available to more people in more places than ever before.

This technological evolution had the unintended consequence of turning music into an increasingly less social experience. Whereas in 1900, the phonograph's megaphone filled a room with sound, making listeners of everyone present, in 2000, the preferred music source of millions was the earphone-equipped personal playback device. The availability of recorded music in general also made music a more passive experience. Making music for oneself and one's friends became a far less common activity than it once was, and the number of community choruses and bands declined markedly.

We are so accustomed to sound recordings today that it is difficult to recapture the sense of alienation this technology created when it was new. In the early 20th century, many believed something intangible was lost, that recordings changed the very nature of the musical experience for the worse. The absence of a performer, some felt, robbed music of its expressive and emotional power. The opportunity to hear a given piece as often as desired, whenever desired, was thought to reduce the immediacy of the musical experience. In 1929, the American Federation of Musicians issued a plea against "Canned Music" (see illustration "Canned Music on Trial"), which today may strike us as self-serving and quaint. Nevertheless, the experience of listening to live music is different from that of listening to recorded music in ways that cannot be measured or identified, at least not yet.

"Canned Music on Trial" (1929). The introduction of recorded sound caused enormous anxiety for musicians. Although some profited from the new technology, many more were driven from their jobs. In the era of silent films, for example, a pianist or organist or even a small orchestra might provide live music to accompany the images on screen. After 1927, such opportunities became increasingly rare. The American Federation of Musicians appealed to the public to resist "canned" music on the grounds that mechanization destroys the soul of art. The objection seems slightly odd today, accustomed as we are to recorded sound, but this advertisement reminds us that the fundamental perception of music has changed radically since the beginning of the 20th century.

Source: Hartman Center for Sales, Advertising & Marketing History

An outspoken advocate of recorded music, the Canadian pianist Glenn Gould (1932–1982) shunned public performances for most of his mature career, arguing that he "could better serve music in a recording studio than in a concert hall."[1] Although Gould's stance may have been extreme, his point remains an important one. The musical possibilities of the recording studio are in many respects considerably greater than those of the live stage. In the studio it is possible to overdub tracks and modify sounds in myriad ways. It is even possible to make music without any performer at

---

1. http://www.sonyclassical.com/artists/gould/bio.html. Accessed April 17, 2008.

all—at least in the traditional sense—by using prerecorded sounds such as the singing of birds or whales, or with a preprogrammed electronic synthesizer, or by sampling snippets of other recordings.

The ready availability of recordings also altered listener expectations, making many listeners less tolerant of wrong notes, flawed tuning, or other imperfections in live performances. By the end of the century, more and more live performances were integrating recorded sounds, even to the point of overdubbing the lead singers themselves. The distinctions between recorded and live music became increasingly fuzzy in the last decades of the 20th century.

AUTHENTICITY

The tendency to view music not as a source of entertainment, but as a source of insight into a higher, more spiritual realm, grew throughout the 19th century and reached new extremes in the 20th, particularly in the repertory of the concert hall. The idea of performing a work of music in a manner that reflected the composer's original intentions became more important than ever. Reasonably good editions prepared in the 19th century were replaced with scrupulously prepared editions in the 20th (see Appendix 2: A Guide to Musical Editions). Editorial techniques rose to a level worthy of biblical scholars, and indeed the output of Bach (or Mozart, or Beethoven, among others) was treated for all intents and purposes as if it were holy writ. Many performers took up the cause of historical authenticity as well, not only by using period instruments, but by performing them in a manner consistent with practices that were current in the composer's own time. These techniques included different kinds of vibrato, articulation, and attack, as well as various approaches to tempo, dynamics, and phrasing. These historically informed performances were a revelation to listeners. The way Bach's cantatas and Handel's oratorios were performed at the end of the 20th century was substantially different from the way they had been presented in 1900, or even 1950—and, most would agree, far more representative of what the composers originally intended.

But historical authenticity exacted a price. Repertories shrank in scope. Large orchestras were less inclined to play Bach's Brandenburg Concertos and Orchestral Suites in the second half of the 20th century than they had been in the first because these works were not written for modern instruments or such large ensembles. Pianists were less likely to perform the music of Bach, or even Haydn and Mozart, in their recitals in 2000 than 50 years before because the modern piano is not authentic to the period of those composers. Except for encore pieces, instrumentalists of all kinds dropped most arrangements of works not originally composed for their instruments from their repertories. Concerts and recordings became far less heterogeneous in the second half of the 20th century. Orchestras differentiated more and more between "standard" and "pops" concerts, with increasingly little repertory crossing boundaries. This kind of division discouraged breadth of taste. The exigencies of marketing to specific audiences dictated that recordings and concerts contain, in effect, only a single type of music rather than a variety.

In other repertories, authenticity took on a different form. Many jazz and rock vocalists cultivated a sound considered emotionally authentic precisely because it ran counter to the standards of cultivated voice production. Voices that might have judged strained, distorted, or out of tune in an earlier era were no longer automatically criticized as defective. To the contrary, a "realistic" sound, unvarnished by training and practice, was taken to be a reflection of the performer's emotional authenticity. The emotional ideal of most rock music demanded a correspondingly authentic, or at least seemingly authentic, style of singing (see Primary Evidence: Authentic Spontaneity).

Many critics have dismissed much of the popular repertory as trivial and shallow because of its supposed simplicity. But equating complexity with quality and simplicity with cheapness denies the driving force that ultimately gives music its ability to move the human spirit. Rock music, for example, is often deprecated for its harmonic, rhythmic, textural, and textual simplicity and for its unrefined directness of emotion. Yet these are the very same qualities valued in the song repertory of the late 18th and early 19th centuries. With its loud volume, insistent rhythms, and glorification of the sensuous, rock music often generates an experience that can overwhelm the listener. As the music critic and journalist Robert Palmer (1945–1997) reminds us, however, the rock concert is in many respects the closest thing we have nowadays to the Dionysian frenzies of ancient Greece, wild celebrations of physical and spiritual ecstasy in the name of Dionysus, the god of wine.

survivors can go on practicing and perfecting their craft while the younger generation's best and brightest assume the Dionysian mantle and get on with the main program, which is liberation through ecstasy. Somewhere, in some sleazy bar or grimy practice room or suburban garage, young musicians wielding guitars or turntables, drum kits or beat boxes, sequencers or samplers, are creating the music for tomorrow's rock and roll revelry. Now that women have belatedly been accepted as guitarists, bassists, drummers, songwriter-auteurs, and "not just another pretty face," we're witnessing the birth of a whole new style of rock and roll frenzy and transcendence. Even the media overkill surrounding the much-hyped "riot grrrls" can't rob the term of its Dionysiac import. Don't let the faux-Apollonians fool you. As rockers, we are heirs to one of our civilization's richest, most time-honored spiritual traditions.

We must never forget our glorious Dionysian heritage.

And that's the beauty of rock and roll. The lifestyle can be perilous, the rate of attrition remains high, but the

Source: Robert Palmer, *Rock & Roll: An Unruly History* (New York: Harmony Books, 1995), p. 155.

THE USES OF MUSIC IN 20TH-CENTURY SOCIETY

Technological advances in the reproduction and dissemination of sound created a wealth of new potentials—and pitfalls—for music in 20th-century society. Music was used on a scale and in places that could not have been imagined a century before. Indeed, the largest single event in human history, the Live Aid concert held July 13, 1985, to raise money for famine relief in Ethiopia, was focused on music. The concert featured almost a hundred different artists and groups, including Bob Dylan, Joan Baez, Phil Collins, U2, Mick Jagger, Eric Clapton, Neil Young, David Bowie, Paul McCartney, Elton John, the Beach Boys, The Who, Sting, and the Four Tops. It was staged simultaneously in London (Wembley Stadium) and Philadelphia (John F. Kennedy Stadium) and broadcast live over 14 satellites to an estimated 1.6 billion people in 160 countries. Music was a powerful unifying force in this global undertaking: "Maybe for the first time since Man left the African Rift Valley we began to talk in a common language, and that language, bizarrely, turned out to be pop music," proclaimed organizer Bob Geldof a decade after the event.[2]

In truth, there was nothing at all bizarre about the idea of music uniting people of different nationalities or of using music to raise money for worthy charities. Haydn had conducted a number of performances in London in the 1790s to support needy

2. http://www.herald.co.uk/local_info/live_aid.html. Accessed April 17, 2008.

musicians in their old age, and Liszt had given recitals in 1838 to benefit victims of a recent flood on the Danube River. But 20th-century technology made it possible to disseminate music, and raise money, on an unprecedented scale.

Music and the State

Since the time of Plato (see Prologue), governments have recognized the ability of music to move the emotions of entire populations, and with the increased reach the new technologies of amplification, recording, and broadcasting made possible, music took on an even more significant role in political life in the 20th century. Instrumental music was particularly susceptible to varied political interpretation. The fate of Beethoven's symphonies in 20th-century Europe offers a good case in point. They were used by every element of the German political spectrum, from the extreme right (Nazis) to the extreme left (communists) and every party in between, before, during, and after World War II. Ironically, they were even used by Germany's enemies: the opening motif of the Fifth Symphony served as a sonic icon of Allied resistance throughout World War II, and was used in coded messages. German troops found it difficult to suppress this use among partisan resisters, who could rightly claim they were just "whistling a little Beethoven." Nazi Germany was quick to suppress jazz, because of its African-American origins; all music by Jewish composers (including Mendelssohn); and virtually all 12-tone composition (see Chapter 21); none of these styles, it was said, belonged to the "natural" idioms of the Aryan nations.[3]

The Soviet Union also struggled with nontraditional musical styles. In the decade or so after the revolution of 1917, the communist government encouraged experimentation, and the avant-garde flourished. But by the early 1930s, the regime had changed its stance. Josef Stalin encouraged native composers to produce music that was accessible to the masses, and that was informed, at least to some degree, by folk music. Absolute music—particularly abstract, complex music—came under special censure as "formalist" on the grounds that it was seemingly written without an eye toward its emotional effect on average citizens. At one time or another during the period 1930 to 1970, Dimitri Shostakovich, Serge Prokofiev, and many other composers came under attack from the government for writing overly formalist music. Serial composition (see Chapter 21), without a tonal center, was discouraged and openly derided by political leaders. As late as the 1960s, the premier of the Soviet Union, Nikita Khrushchev, condemned it as a threat to the "wholesomeness" of socialist ideals, declaring, "Our people can't use this garbage as a tool of their ideology."

Others, however, continued the long tradition of using music to assert their opposition to the status quo. Kurt Weill and his librettist Bertolt Brecht collaborated to produce a series of stage works ridiculing capitalism and middle-class values; Alban Berg took up the cause of society's outcasts with his opera *Wozzeck* (Anthology, discussed in Chapter 21).

The American government never became embroiled in musical politics to the same degree as in western Europe. No president ever offered an opinion one way or the other about serial composition, and the government as a whole never invested very heavily in any of the arts. There have been at times congressional attempts to censor or otherwise pressure the music industry, most recently via the 1985 hearings held by the Parents Music Resource Center to bring about labeling of recorded media as to

---

3. For an examination of modernism during the German occupation of Vichy France in World War II, see Jane F. Fulcher, "French Identity in Flux: Vichy's Collaboration, and Antigone's Operatic Triumph," paper read at the American Philosophical Society Annual General Meeting, Philadelphia, November 12, 2004; online at http://www.apspub.com/proceedings/1502/1500203.pdf. Accessed May 5, 2008.

FOCUS   Songs about the Atom Bomb

Almost every major event in human history has inspired songs—the beginnings or ends of wars, the death of great leaders, or new inventions like the telephone, airplane, the automobile. As the following list suggests, the atomic bomb inspired many songs:

Karl and Harty, *When the Atom Bomb Fell* (1945)

Slim Gaillard Quartette, *Atomic Cocktail* (1945)

The Buchanan Brothers, *Atomic Power* (1946)

The Golden Gate Quartet, *Atom and Evil* (1946)

The Sons of the Pioneers, *Old Man Atom* (1947)

Jackie Doll and his Pickled Peppers, *When They Drop the Atomic Bomb* (1951)

Billy Hughes and the Rhythm Buckaroos, *Atomic Sermon* (1953)

Sonny Russell, *50 Megatons* (1956)

The Commodores, *Uranium* (1957)

The Five Stars, *Atom Bomb Baby* (1957)

Skip Stanley, *Satellite Baby* (1957)

Bob Dylan, *A Hard Rain's A-Gonna Fall* (1963)

Barry McGuire, *Eve of Destruction* (1965)

Tom Lehrer, *So Long, Mom (A Song for World War III)* (1966)

Using humor and pathos, some songwriters took a approach that entertained but also helped listeners cope with the terrifying prospect of nuclear war; other songwriters (Dylan, McGuire) took a more sober approach.

their lyrical content. (The most powerful witness against this proposal was Frank Zappa.) Efforts to establish a national conservatory of music in the 1920s failed for lack of funds and were never seriously revived. The founding of the National Endowment for the Arts in the early 1960s represented a modest step in the direction of government patronage of the arts. Yet while this agency helped many programs and individuals, its funding for music was never substantial enough to provoke a national political debate over any music it did fund.

Music nevertheless played a potent role in the American political landscape. A politician's choice of music revealed much about his or her identity. Harry Truman's campaign for the presidency in 1948 was accompanied by the Eubie Blake song, "I'm Just Wild about Harry." When Bill Clinton accepted the presidential nomination of the Democratic Party in 1992, the loudspeakers blared out Fleetwood Mac's 1977 hit "Don't Stop (Thinking about Tomorrow)." The moment was revealing in more than one respect. The traditional music played at every recent Democratic Party convention had been a Depression-era song, "Happy Days Are Here Again," performed by a band of brass and woodwinds. By embracing a rock song, the (recorded) music of a new generation, Clinton helped define himself as a New Democrat. Candidate Clinton used music again later in the campaign when he played a jazz number on the saxophone on a late-night talk show. Had he sat at the piano and played Schoenberg's Piano Suite, op. 25, he would have sent a very different message to viewers.

Music and Race

Music played a vital role in the ongoing struggle for racial justice throughout the world, particularly in the United States. Ragtime, jazz, and rhythm and blues (the basis for rock and roll, which evolved into rock) were closely associated with African-American culture when they first arrived on the musical scene, yet all were embraced and cultivated by white people as well. All three genres still had to overcome considerable resistance, much of it blatantly or subtly racist. Yet the appeal of this music ultimately transcended racial lines, even if the process was slow.

A 1938 jam session. Jazz, more than any other kind of music, promoted racial integration for audiences as well as performers, although the process was subtle. Here the celebrated clarinetist Artie Shaw jams with Duke Ellington and drummer Chick Webb in 1938. At the time, most American institutions, including the military and schools—not to mention housing, restaurants, and hotels—were segregated either by law or in practice.

Source: Photograph by Charles Peterson, courtesy of Don Peterson

There can be no doubt that Elvis Presley's enormous success was helped by his being white and therefore vastly more marketable to a white public in the middle 1950s than the black artists of the time who performed in much the same style (Little Richard, James Brown, Richard Berry). Presley's remake of a rhythm and blues hit like "Hound Dog" by Big Mama Thornton received greater exposure and higher sales; a less provocative white singer, Pat Boone, did the same with Fats Domino's "Ain't That a Shame" and "I'll Be Home" by the Flamingos. African-American artists such as Chuck Berry had to adapt their music and stage presentation to be accepted by white audiences; Chubby Checker recorded "dance craze" songs that crossed racial lines, but were more successful in the white-dominated Top 40 charts than in the black-dominated rhythm and blues charts.

From the 1920s through the 1940s, all African-American popular artists were relegated by major labels to the less widely distributed category of "race records," without serious attempts to reach a wider market. Beginning in the 1950s black musicians were being marketed aggressively in the economic mainstream, no longer labeled or segregated (officially, at least) as race records. Black musicians had to wait for greater support until the 1960s, when well-run record labels owned by African Americans came into being.

Ragtime, jazz, rock—all of these increasingly brought black and white performers and audiences together at a time when American society and most of its institutions were racially segregated. Integrated ensembles were almost unknown in the 1920s and still rare in the 1930s. The African-American singer Billie Holiday, appearing in Detroit with Count Basie's jazz band in 1936, recalled that she had been compelled to apply what she called "dark grease paint" to her face because the theater's management was afraid her light complexion might cause her to appear "too yellow to sing with all the black men in the band."[4] By the late 1930s, however, the white clarinetist Benny Goodman's bands were featuring four African-American musicians: pianist Teddy Wilson, vibraphonist Lionel Hampton, guitarist Charlie Christian, and arranger

---

4. W. Peretti, *The Creation of Jazz* (Urbana: University of Illinois Press, 1992), p. 187.

Fletcher Henderson. Other white jazzmen like Artie Shaw, Charlie Barnet, and Woody Herman soon followed Goodman's lead in hiring African Americans. The African-American composer and bandleader Duke Ellington likewise began integrating white musicians into his group in the late 1930s.

With the progress of the civil rights movement beginning in the 1940s and the end of legal segregation in the 1960s, the black-white divide in jazz and rock, although it remained present, became less pronounced. When rap music, a new idiom rooted in the black experience, emerged in the 1990s, it encountered, like its predecessors, a round of racially tinged criticism. And like its predecessors, it too was soon adopted by white musicians.

Music and Protest

The protest music of three movements in the 20th century stands out in particular: that of the labor movement, especially in the decades 1910 to 1950; that of the civil rights movement of the 1950s and 1960s; and that associated with the opposition to the Vietnam War from the mid-1960s through the early 1970s.

Group song helped labor unions create and sustain a sense of solidarity. The International Workers of the World (IWW, also known as the "Wobblies") issued its first songbook in 1909. Over the next 70 years, the *Little Red Song Book: Songs to Fan the Flames of Discontent* would go through 35 editions.

It is difficult to imagine the civil rights movement of the 1950s and 1960s without the songs that were a basic tool for protesters who were marching for racial equality. "We Shall Overcome," a hymn transformed into a striker's song by the 1940s, became an unofficial anthem of the movement and was sung at almost every rally, protest, or meeting. The text alone is fairly straightforward; it is the music that gives this song its true power. The low, confident beginning, the soaring rise in the middle, the return to the opening register at the close—all these combine to make a powerful musical statement. Other modern folk songs came to be associated with the movement as well: "If I Had a Hammer" (by Pete Seeger and Lee Hays of the Weavers), "The Times They Are A-Changin'" (by Bob Dylan), and "We'll Never Turn Back" (by Bertha Gober).

Protesters against American military involvement in Vietnam in the 1960s and early 1970s used music as a means of galvanizing support for their cause. Some of the more notable songs of this kind included "I Feel Like I'm Fixin' to Die Rag" (1965) by Country Joe [McDonald] and the Fish; "War" (1970) by Edwin Starr; and "What's Going On" (1971) by Marvin Gaye. Less well remembered are the songs supporting the war, such as Barry Sadler's "Ballad of the Green Berets" (1966). With its minimal amplification and snare drum accompaniment, this strophic song topped the U.S. sales charts for five weeks, sold more than 9 million copies, and became the theme song for a movie starring John Wayne.

Protest messages did not depend on texts alone. Jimi Hendrix's distorted rendition of "The Star-Spangled Banner" on an electric guitar at the Woodstock Festival in 1969, although wordless, was universally understood as an act of protest. The melodic distortions, heavy electro-acoustic feedback, and the free flights of improvisation helped turn the national anthem into a statement of dissent.

Music Therapy

Music has been used to cure illnesses since ancient times, as suggested by the biblical story of David curing Saul of his melancholy by playing the harp (see p. 7). It was not until the 20th century, however, that music therapy established itself as an acknowledged protocol for the treatment of psychological, physical, and cognitive problems. Doctors treating wounded and traumatized soldiers after World War I noticed that patients exposed to music or given a chance to make music tended to recover more rapidly and more fully than those who were not. The first professional association of music therapists in the United States was established in 1950, the outgrowth of an expanding body of scientific literature that had substantiated the positive effects of music on the physical and mental health of individuals.

In clinical settings, music therapy has proved particularly important in helping patients suffering from neurological disorders like Alzheimer's and Parkinson's diseases. Scientists believe that music's therapeutic effects relate to its ability to enhance the processes by which the brain reorganizes cerebral functions that have been damaged by disease or injury. By the 1990s, music therapy workshops were also being used as agents of social change, as at the Pavarotti Music Center, a grammar school in Mostar, Bosnia-Herzegovina. Initially funded by the singer Luciano Pavarotti (1915–2007), the Center applied music making to the bridging of divides, both ethnic and religious, between longtime antagonists (1997–2003).

Ambient Music

Ambient music—background music—is the sonic equivalent of architecture in that its primary purpose is to shape actions and attitudes rather than to be a focus of attention. Music had been used to create moods and influence human behavior long before the 20th century, but the idea of placing it in the background, and not as the immediate focus of listeners' attention, was first introduced by Erik Satie (1866–1925) in the form of **musique d'ameublement** (furnishing music). He wrote a small number of pieces thus designated for various ensembles, with descriptions referring to "arrival of the guests . . . to be played in a vestibule"; "phonic tiling—can be played during lunch or a civil marriage"; and "wallpaper in a prefect's office."

George Owen Squier (1865–1934) saw the commercial applications of ambient music. In 1922 he founded what eventually became the Muzak Corporation, marketing the service to private homes; but Squier soon discovered that carefully programmed music—mostly soft-edged arrangements of well-known tunes—could increase productivity in the workplace and make customers spend more time in retail outlets or less time in restaurants, thereby boosting sales or increasing turnover. Audio architects became adept at designing playlists to meet the needs of any given business. Although few listeners were aware of the presence of ambient music at any given moment, by the end of the century it had become the most widely heard source of music in the world, with more than 100 million listeners daily. And almost none of them, as its critics pointed out, could turn this music off.

Satie's idea of creating new works designed to function specifically as ambient music caught the imagination of a number of talented composers in the last quarter of the 20th century. This kind of ambient music is characterized by widely spaced textures, consistently soft dynamics, and an extremely subdued sense of rhythm or pulse. The English composer Brian Eno (b. 1948) maintained that his *Music for Airports* (1978) was "intended to induce calm and a space to think. Ambient music must be able to accommodate many levels of listening attention without enforcing one in particular; it must be as ignorable as it is interesting."[5] Eno's half-joking, half-serious title reflects the ways in which the use of ambient music has altered the tacit assumptions

5. Brian Eno, liner notes to *Music for Airports/Ambient 1*, PVC 7908 (AMB 001), 1978.

about conventional ways of listening, whether in a concert hall or in the privacy of one's home through a recording. In recent years, ambient music in the style of Eno's *Music for Airports* has actually been used in airports.

MUSIC IN THE 20TH CENTURY: A STYLISTIC OVERVIEW

The history of Western music in this era follows a trajectory of ever-expanding possibilities. Anyone who composes music today can choose from an unprecedented array of options in every element of the art. Indeed, styles vary so markedly from genre to genre, within genres, and even within the work of many individual composers that it is no longer possible to identify a lowest common denominator of style.

Textures in 20th-century music ranged from the extremely simple to complex. No single genre or style can be associated exclusively with any particular texture.

Rhythm, like other musical elements, manifested itself in a variety of possibilities. Dance music, as in all previous eras, relied on a steady beat. Ragtime, jazz, country

Summary of Style Differences between Music of the 19th Century and 20th Century

	19TH CENTURY	20TH CENTURY
Style	Composers seek to develop a distinctly personal style; originality becomes paramount in all genres.	An even greater variety of compositional styles; originality remains paramount in most genres.
Texture	The polyphonic and homophonic coexist, with composers drawing on whichever approach best suits their immediate needs.	A wide range of options, from monophony to complex polyphony.
Rhythm	Periodic phrase structure continues in the works of certain repertories (dance, march), but on the whole becomes increasingly less obvious over the course of the century.	A continuation and intensification of 19th-century tendencies; post–World War II extremes range from repetitive music to the conceptual use of silence.
Melody	Ranges from the simple to the complex.	From the simple to the complex, with added possibilities derived from nondiatonic scales, such as whole tone, pentatonic, and microtonal.
Harmony	Becomes increasingly chromatic over the course of the century, which in turn makes harmonic simplicity a potentially unusual feature.	In addition to inherited idioms, atonality—the absence of a tonal center—emerges as one of many compositional options.
Form	The large-scale formal conventions of the Classical era continue in use, but often in a manner that obscures their presence. Cyclical coherence becomes an increasingly important issue within multimovement works.	Conventional forms remain important in the work of some composers; others avoid these forms at all costs.
Instrumentation	The distinction between vocal and instrumental writing becomes even more pronounced. The orchestra grows in both size and instrumental variety.	Along with new and previously excluded acoustic instruments, amplification and the electronic production of sound open new dimensions in timbre; through the use of a synthesizer, any audible wave length can be reproduced precisely.

music, and rock all evolved from dance idioms and accordingly built on a steady rhythm. Ragtime and jazz tended toward syncopated rhythms, sometimes quite intricate. In contrast, some art music consciously avoided the steady meters of dance-related music.

Like melody, musical textures in the 20th century ranged from the extremely simple to complex. No single genre or style can be associated exclusively with any particular texture. Melody varied greatly according to genre, the intended audience, and the function of the work at hand. The melodic variety evident in much music of the late 19th century continued to grow, supplemented by increasing use of nondiatonic scales such as whole tone, pentatonic, and octatonic. At the same time, many composers at the end of the century were still writing in a diatonic idiom not terribly different from that of Mozart and Haydn. But this was a choice made consciously and not for lack of options.

Harmony was widely perceived in the first two-thirds of the 20th century as the defining element of style, in spite of important developments in other areas, such as rhythm, timbre, and form. Harmony emerged as the chief battleground in the debate over musical modernism, by which critics tended to categorize composers according to their preferred harmonic idiom; when a new piece was performed, accounts invariably mentioned its place on the spectrum between tonality and atonality. (Atonal music, discussed in Chapter 21, is characterized by the lack of any tonal center. It emerged early in the century in the works of several innovative composers.) Indeed, the controversy over harmony in the early decades of the 20th century bears many remarkable similarities to the debate over the merits of the *prima prattica* and the *seconda prattica* in the years around 1600 (see Chapter 8). In both instances, new and old styles continued to flourish side by side. Harmony based on the whole-tone scale and quartal harmonies expanded tonal possibilities even further.

Form also ranged from the simple to the complex. Composers who chose to work within the tonal idiom were generally more inclined to use such traditional forms as sonata form, rondo, and ABA. Those working outside the tonal idiom typically preferred to use dynamics, texture, and orchestration rather than harmony and thematic ideas as the basis of large-scale structures. Serial composition (see Chapter 21), based on the manipulation of a basic series of notes (and, later, rhythmic and other elements) throughout a work, provided important structural alternatives for composers working outside the tonal idiom. Minimalism (see Chapter 23) and aleatoric music (see Chapter 23) offered some of the more radical new approaches to form.

Instrumentation featured the greater use of a variety of percussion. Beyond the realm of acoustic instruments, electronically generated sounds through such instruments as the electric guitar, the synthesizer, and the computer were added (see Chapter 23). The synthesizer and computer provided composers the opportunity to control with precision the basic elements of pitch, vibrato, and timbre.

CONCLUSION

As in the early decades of the Baroque era, composers working at the end of the 19th century and the beginning of the 20th had the option of writing in both "old" and "new" styles. However, thanks to the rapid emergence and evolution of new technologies in sound recording, radio and television broadcasting, and computers, the range of idioms available to composers expanded dramatically over the course of the 20th century. The result, by the end of the century, was a stylistic pluralism that made it impossible to identify anything resembling a musical mainstream.

The Search for New Sounds, 1890–1945

The two generations of composers working between approximately 1890 and 1945 confronted and challenged many of the most basic stylistic premises of Western music, including triadic harmony, traditional forms, and conventional timbres. The result of these challenges was a variety of new approaches to self-expression through sound.

IMPRESSIONISM

The movement known as **impressionism** represents one of the earliest attempts to explore fundamentally new approaches to music. The term was first used in painting to designate the style of a group of painters, among them Claude Monet, Edouard Manet, Pierre-Auguste Renoir, and Edgar Degas, who used an accumulation of short brush strokes instead of a continuous line to produce not so much a representation of an object as a sensation—an impression—of it. (See Monet's painting *Impression: Sunrise* on page 519. The name of the movement derived from the title of this painting.)

In impressionist painting, color takes precedence over line. Similarly, the impressionist style in music is based on a blurring of distinct harmonies, rhythms, and forms. It also makes greater use of color (timbre) than any previous style of music. The number of composers thought of today as impressionists is relatively small—the most prominent are Claude Debussy (1862–1918) and Maurice Ravel (1875–1937)—but their influence on later composers and later styles was considerable.

Musical impressionism can be broadly characterized as follows:

- *Form:* Impressionist music for the most part avoids the kind of goal-oriented structures that had dominated music of the preceding century or more. These works flow instead from one moment to the next, building and receding in tension but without the same sense of striving toward resolution. They tend to be structured less around harmony and thematic ideas than around masses of sound.

- *Harmony:* Although impressionist composers never abandon tonality, they use ninth, eleventh, and thirteenth chords to an unprecedented degree. They also draw occasionally on nondiatonic scales such as the whole tone and pentatonic, creating sounds evocative of East Asia.

Impressionism. Impressionist paintings command big money in the auction house nowadays, but the style was widely rejected when it first came onto the scene in Paris in the mid-1870s. One critic, writing of an exhibition in which this 1872 painting—Claude Monet's *Impression: soleil levant* (Impression: Sunrise)—appeared, complained that Monet, Renoir, Cezanne, and others were "impressionists in that they do not render a landscape, but the sensation produced by the landscape. The word itself has passed into their language: in the catalogue, the *Sunrise* by Monet is called not landscape, but *Impression.* Thus they take leave of reality and enter the realms of idealism." Another critic of the time was even less charitable: "Wallpaper in its embryonic state is more finished than that seascape." Musical impressionism, similarly concerned more with color than with line, also met with resistance for a time; one critic declared that Debussy's *Prélude à l'Après-midi d'un faune* was "to a work of music what an artist's palette is to a finished painting."

Source: Corbis/Bettmann

■ *Voice leading:* Individual voices often move more or less independently of one another, without strict regard to the traditional rules of voice leading. Parallel fourths, fifths, and octaves contribute to the distinctive sound of impressionism.

■ *Rhythm:* The rhythms of impressionist music tend to be fluid, often avoiding any definite sense of meter and preferring instead an elusive sense of motion that at times moves forward and at times seems to hang in suspension.

■ *Timbre:* Impressionist composers drew new sounds out of the piano and orchestra alike. Debussy once declared that Beethoven had written in an overly percussive style for the piano; he advocated a style that treats the piano as an "instrument without hammers," with a tone that is more lyrical, intimate, and sensuous.[1] Debussy and Ravel were both renowned for their orchestrations, which rely frequently on techniques that distribute thematic ideas throughout the entire fabric of the orchestra.

Debussy hated the term impressionism, particularly when used to describe his music. He insisted he was more concerned with making "something new—realities—as it were: what imbeciles call 'impressionism.'"[2] His objection rests on the belief that our sensory perceptions, our impressions of the world, in fact construct their own kind of reality, an alternative to a conscious and supposedly objective, external reality that may not even exist in the first place. This attitude was not a new one: the Romantics of the early 19th century had embraced the idea of music as a means of conveying an alternate reality, but the impressionists extended the inward turn of the eye (and ear) still further.

---

1. Harold C. Schonberg, *The Great Pianists*, rev. ed. (New York: Simon & Schuster, 1987), p. 477.
2. William W. Austin, *Music in the 20th Century* (New York: Norton, 1966), p. 25.

CD13, Track 3
DEBUSSY
Prélude à l'Après-midi d'un faune
Score Anthology II/149

Debussy's music also resonates with the French poetry of his day. Poets like Charles Baudelaire (1821–1867), Stéphane Mallarmé (1842–1898), Paul Verlaine (1844–1896), and Arthur Rimbaud (1854–1891) relished the sound of language for sound's sake and were not constrained by syntax or logic. These poets, who became known as symbolists, envied music's ability to suggest without stating, to construct forms without the burden of representation, and they sought to recreate this in their poetry. In place of narrative in their works—a linear progression of ideas—we find a succession of images, often connected only loosely. In place of description, we find symbols, allusions, suggestions.

Debussy's music takes a comparable approach to sound. His *Prélude à l'Après-midi d'un faune* ("Prelude to an Afternoon of a Faun," 1894) was actually inspired by a symbolist poem, Stéphane Mallarmé's *L'Après-midi d'un faune* (1876). Evocative and at times obscure, Mallarmé's poem captures the ruminations of a mythological faun, a half man, half goat who remembers—or did he only dream about?—his erotically charged encounter with a pair of wood nymphs. The opening line reads, "Those nymphs, I want to make them permanent," and the rest of the poem floats between dream and consciousness. Illusion and reality are indistinguishable.

Critics have drawn many indirect and a few direct connections between Mallarmé's poetry and Debussy's music. The faun's instrument is traditionally the flute, and it is this instrument that opens Debussy's work. The languorous chromatic line falls and rises like the faun's own fantasy. Debussy himself was evasive about further particulars, however, stating merely that his piece conveyed "a general impression of the poem, because if music were to follow more closely it would run out of breath, like a dray horse competing for the Grand Prize with a thoroughbred."[3] Yet the consistent opposition between flute and strings and the points of structural articulation (measures 30–31, 37, 55, 79, 94) resonates subtly with both the design and content of Mallarmé's poem.

It is also unclear why Debussy called this the "Prelude" to the faun's afternoon. At one point he had announced a forthcoming work entitled *Prélude, interludes et paraphrase finale pour l'Après-midi d'un faune*, and it would seem that the first of these, the prelude, was the only movement the composer actually completed. In a way, though, the title fits the poetry, which holds many mysteries that cannot be explained rationally.

For traditionally minded listeners of the late 19th century, Debussy's *Prélude à l'Après-midi d'un faune* was an enigma. They found the lack of clearly defined themes, the successions of seventh chords (measures 48–49), and the parallel fifths (measure 102) primitive in the worst sense of the word. Almost thirty years after the work's premiere, Camille Saint-Saëns (1835–1921), one of the leading French composers of his generation, wrote privately to a friend that he could make little sense of the work:

> The need to be new at any price is an illness of our era. In earlier times, in all the arts, even in the industrial arts, all artists used the same formulas, yet none of this prevented those artists of the first order from affirming their personalities. . . . But if one has no personality, then the quest for originality can lead only to the baroque, to twaddle, to clatter. . . . True, one can adjust to anything, to obscenity, even to crime itself; but it is precisely these kinds of things that one should not get used to. It has now gone well beyond accommodation. The public . . . now applauds a work in which the trumpets violently present to your ears a succession of fourths and fifths. It is a return to the earliest attempts at harmony. This is no longer music.

---

3. Glenn Watkins, *Soundings: Music in the Twentieth Century* (New York: Schirmer, 1995), p. 13.

The *Prelude to the Afternoon of a Faun* has a pleasing sonority, but one finds in it scarcely anything that could properly be called a musical idea. It is to a work of music what an artist's palette is to a finished painting. Debussy has not created a style; he has cultivated an absence of style, of logic, and of common sense.[4]

But others found in this "absence of style" an inspiration, a new approach to music that opened the door to writing in a manner that was decidedly modern. Although no single work can be said to represent the birth of modernism, Debussy's *Prélude à l'Après-midi d'un faune* epitomizes the assault on traditional elements and attitudes that characterizes a great deal of music written at the end of the 19th century and the beginning of the 20th.

CHALLENGES TO TONALITY

For all its chromaticism and harmonic ambiguities, Debussy's *Prélude à l'Après-midi d'un faune* stands well within the tonal tradition: it ends squarely in the key of E Major. But his later *Voiles*, published in the first book of *Preludes for the Piano* in 1910, goes beyond the traditions of even advanced chromatic harmony. *Voiles* is full of parallel octaves and fifths, and its harmonies are obstinately nondirectional. Its supple rhythms add to a sensation of constant fluidity, as does its form. Although the work seems to follow a general ABA outline, we hear no clear delineation for the beginning of the middle section (measure 22 or 42?) or the return of A (measure 48 or 58?). Here as elsewhere, Debussy's music is delightfully ambiguous. Even the title has two possible meanings: "sails" or "veils."

More importantly, *Voiles* also illustrates the increasing use of nontraditional scale forms in the early decades of the 20th century. Debussy constructs the melodic ideas of this work primarily from **whole-tone** and **pentatonic scales**:

CD13, Track 4
DEBUSSY
Voiles
Score Anthology II/150

- Based on six notes, each a whole tone apart (Example 20–1), the whole-tone scale subverts some of the most basic elements of diatonic harmony: it cannot be used to construct major and minor triads, and it permits a few seventh chords. In *Voiles*, Debussy uses a whole-tone scale. Here again, the effect is one of a freely floating tonality with no clear center, very much in keeping with the work's evocative title. The opening figure is based on a scale without half steps.

Example 20–1 Whole-tone scale

- Although frequently associated with East Asian music, pentatonic scales (Example 20–2)—scales based on five notes—are found in many traditional ("folk") idioms of the West as well. Debussy uses one such scale in the inner section of *Voiles*, beginning toward the end of measure 42.

Example 20–2 Pentatonic scale

4. Letter to Maurice Emmanuel, August 4, 1920, published in *La Revue musicale*, 1947. Transl. MEB.

COMPOSER PROFILE   Claude Debussy *(1862–1918)*

Debussy's life straddled two centuries—he was born during the American Civil War and died a few months before the end of World War I—yet he is widely regarded as the first great composer of the 20th century. The inevitable association with the label of impressionism tends to obscure the genuine novelties of his music: no other single figure of his era did more to expand the possibilities of form, harmony, voice leading, and timbre.

In all this, Debussy developed a style of writing that provided a model for countless subsequent composers seeking to overthrow the cultural domination of 19th-century German music, particularly that of Beethoven, Brahms, and Wagner. Yet he remained curiously aloof from the musical scene of his day. He held no formal posts after his youth, appeared in public only sporadically as a pianist or conductor, and left behind no direct pupils. He nevertheless had many imitators (*Debussyistes*, as they were known), and his death was widely mourned throughout the musical world. Prominent composers, including Igor Stravinsky, Béla Bartók, Paul Dukas, Manuel de Falla, Maurice Ravel, and Erik Satie, contributed short pieces to the commemorative volume issued as *Le tombeau de Claude Debussy* in 1920.

PRINCIPAL WORKS

PIANO MUSIC The *Suite bergamasque* (1890–1905) includes the celebrated *Claire de lune*. Debussy wrote *The Children's Corner* (1908) in a deceptively simple style: like all great works for children, it offers something to young and old alike. Its title and the titles of its individual movements are all in English, a nod to the propensity of affluent French families to hire English nannies. Each of the 24 *Préludes* (in two books, 1910 and 1913) bears a

Debussy and Stravinsky. This photo, taken around 1912 by the composer Erik Satie, documents a meeting of two of the greatest composers of the 20th century. Stravinsky, 20 years younger than his French colleague, owed much to Debussy's style, particularly in matters of form and timbre. Debussy, in turn, consulted Stravinsky about the orchestration of his ballet *Jeux*, which, like Stravinsky's *Le Sacre du printemps*, was produced for the Ballets Russes of the Russian impresario Sergei Diaghilev. Debussy acknowledged Stravinsky's present of a score of *Le Sacre* with these words: "It is a special satisfaction to tell you how much you have enlarged the boundaries of the permissible in the empire of sound."

Source: Corbis/Bettmann

A growing number of composers in the early 20th century also turned—or perhaps more appropriately, returned—to modal scales. Since about the end of the 17th century, modal scales—Dorian, Lydian, Phrygian, and so on (see Chapters 4, 6, and 7)—had been used relatively little, especially outside the realm of sacred music. But composers of Debussy's generation began to draw on these modes in an attempt to break away from conventional major and minor scales. Ironically, the music derived a distinctly new sound from these archaic modes. English composers particularly fond of modal writing included Ralph Vaughan Williams, Benjamin Britten, and the songwriting team of John Lennon and Paul McCartney, whose *Norwegian Wood* (1966) uses the Mixolydian mode.

The **octatonic** scale was another important source of new sounds for composers of the early 20th century. It alternates between half and whole steps and contains within itself all possible intervals, from the minor second to the major seventh. Although the octatonic scale had been used on occasion in the 19th century for coloristic effect descriptive title that appears at the end of each piece: *The Sunken Cathedral* and *The Girl with the Flaxen Hair* are two of many well-known works in this set. Each of the twelve *Etudes* (1915), implicit homages to Chopin, addresses a particular technical challenge (repeated notes, arpeggios, octaves, etc.) without sounding like an exercise.

ORCHESTRAL MUSIC Debussy was a master of orchestration from the very beginning. His *Prélude à l'Après-midi d'un faune* (1894), *Nocturnes* (1899), *La Mer* ("The Sea," 1905), and *Images* (1908) are all staples of the orchestral repertory. He avoided the symphony as a genre, even though traces of the form are evident in the three-movement cycle *La Mer*.

DRAMATIC MUSIC Although *Pelléas et Mélisande* (1902) is the only opera Debussy actually completed, he labored on several others throughout his life, including settings of two stories by Edgar Allan Poe, *The Devil in the Belfry* and *The Fall of the House of Usher. Jeux* (1913), a ballet with a scenario that takes place on a tennis court, was written for Diaghilev's Ballets Russes (see Focus: Sergei Diaghilev) and performed in the same year as Stravinsky's *Le Sacre du printemps.*

CHAMBER MUSIC Debussy's String Quartet (1893) is the most frequently performed of all French quartets. Toward the end of his life, Debussy set out to write a series of six sonatas for different combinations of instruments. Unfortunately, by the time of his death he had completed only three of these works: the Sonata for Flute, Viola, and Harp (1915); the Cello Sonata (1915); and the Violin Sonata (1917).

SONGS Debussy's songs continue the rich tradition of the French *mélodie* fostered before him by Berlioz, Fauré,

Gounod, Franck, and Massenet, among others. Debussy was particularly drawn to the texts of such symbolist poets as Charles Baudelaire, Paul Verlaine, and Stéphane Mallarmé. He cultivated melodic lines that combine sinuous melody with a declamatory style; the piano is an equal partner throughout.

KEY DATES IN THE LIFE OF DEBUSSY

1862	Born in the Parisian suburb of St.-Germain-en-Laye, August 22.
1872	Admitted to the Paris Conservatory at the age of 10.
1880	Becomes the piano teacher for the children of Nadezhda von Meck, the pa-troness of Tchaikovsky; travels through Switzerland, Italy, and Russia, where he becomes familiar with the works of Mussorgsky.
1884	Wins the Prix de Rome, the highest compositional prize of the Paris Con-servatory.
1888	Visits Bayreuth and falls briefly under the spell of Wagner's music, but struggles against this tradition over the decade, even though its influ-ences remain evident in Debussy's only completed opera, *Pelléas et Mélisande.*
1889	Hears Javanese gamelan at the Paris Exposition and begins to experiment with new, non-Western approaches to timbre, form, and harmony.
1901	Begins writing music criticism for a Parisian journal in an attempt to pay debts.
1907	Begins a series of tours throughout Europe as a conductor and pianist.
1918	Dies in Paris on March 25.

CD13, Track 5
BARTÓK
Diminished Fifth
Score Anthology II/151

(by Liszt, Mussorgsky, and Rimsky-Korsakov, among others), it became an important element for such later composers as Alexander Scriabin, Debussy, Stravinsky, Maurice Ravel, and Béla Bartók. Because of its symmetrical construction and strict alternation between half and whole steps, this scale, too, tends to subvert the idea of a tonal center. Bartók's short piano piece *Diminished Fifth*, from Book 4 of his *Mikrokosmos*, repeatedly juxtaposes two **tetrachords** (four-note units) that together make up the octatonic scale outlined in Example 20–3.

Example 20–3 Octatonic scale used in measures 1–5 of Béla Bartók, *Diminished Fifth*

The possibilities of harmonies based on unconventional scales were almost limitless. In 1947, the composer and critic Nicolas Slonimsky published a systematic list of more than a thousand different kinds of scales, some based on as few as two notes, others containing as many as twelve. Relatively few of the scales in Slonimsky's *Thesaurus of Scales and Melodic Patterns* were used in practice, but the exercise of compiling so many different possibilities in a single source exemplifies the attitude of experimentation that characterizes so much of the 20th century's music.

In Russia, Alexander Scriabin (1872–1915) promoted the possibilities of what he called his "mystic chord," which he believed would give his music an unusually ethereal tone. The chord (Example 20–4) consists of augmented and diminished fourths.

Example 20–4 Scriabin's "mystic chord"

CD13, Track 6

IVES

The Cage

Score Anthology II/152

In the United States, Charles Ives (1874–1954), independently of Scriabin, was also experimenting with the idea of **quartal harmonies,** chords built on the interval of a fourth rather than a third. His song *The Cage* (1906) is based entirely on such chords. The unsettling text, about a leopard pacing in his cage, receives an appropriately repetitive and unsettling melody whose relentless up-and-down progression creates a kind of cage in its own right. The accompaniment provides little sense of direction, at least not within the expected conventions of triadic harmony. This brief song, in effect, is in no key at all.

Ives's *The Things Our Fathers Loved* (1917), a song written to a text by the composer himself, plays with traditional harmony in a different way by stringing together a series of tunes from popular songs but joining and harmonizing them in an extremely unusual manner, often in the "wrong" key. *Dixie*, at the very beginning, merges imperceptibly into *My Old Kentucky Home*, followed by *On the Banks of the Wabash* (at the words "I hear the organ on the Main Street corner"), the hymn tune *Nettleton* ("Aunt Sarah humming Gospels"), *The Battle Cry of Freedom* ("The village cornet band, playing in the square. The town's Red, White and Blue"), *In the Sweet Bye and Bye* ("Now! Hear the songs!") through the end of the text. The harmonizations of these tunes, all of them familiar to Ives's contemporaries, create a strange sense of distance. The familiar becomes unfamiliar, and the way in which one melodic fragment flows into the next, always to words from a different source, seems very much in keeping with the literary technique of the stream of consciousness developed by the modernist author James Joyce. The net result is a song that insists on its modernity even while celebrating (and quoting from) songs of the past.

CD13, Track 7

IVES

The Things Our Fathers Loved

Score Anthology II/153

The conflict between traditional and nontraditional harmonies is particularly acute in Ives's *The Unanswered Question* (1908), in which the solo trumpet and the small ensemble of flutes seem to occupy an entirely different sphere from the strings, which speak in slow, measured, choralelike tones, using the tonal language of conventional triads. Dissonance in the strings is carefully controlled and resolved: the entire string part, in fact, looks and sounds almost like a student essay in species counterpoint, not terribly different from the kind of exercises Beethoven had worked out under the critical eye of Haydn (see Chapter 12). The solo trumpet, by contrast, repeatedly poses a five-note figure that implies no harmonic center at all (B♭-C♯-E-E♭-C, or, in some instances, ending with a B♮ instead of a C). The winds, in turn, are even more

CD13, Track 8

IVES

The Unanswered Question

Score Anthology II/154

tonally diffuse and grow rhythmically more independent. The work ends with a serene, perfect authentic G-Major triad, yet the sensation it creates is not one of resolution.

In his foreword to the score of *The Unanswered Question*, Ives gave some hint as to the symbolism behind these contrasting elements:

> The strings play *ppp* throughout with no change in tempo. They are to represent "The Silence of the Druids—Who Know, See and Hear Nothing." The trumpet intones "The Perennial Question of Existence," and states it in the same tone of voice each time. But the hunt for "The Invisible Answer" undertaken by the flutes, and other human beings, becomes gradually more active, faster and louder through an *animando* [animatedly] to a *con fuoco* [with fire]. This part need not be played in the exact time position indicated. It is played in somewhat of an impromptu way; if there be no conductor, one of the flute players may direct their playing. "The Fighting Answerers," as the time goes on, and after a "secret conference," seem to realize a futility, and begin to mock "The Question"—the strife is over for the moment. After they disappear, "The Question" is asked for the last time, and "The Silences" are heard beyond in "Undisturbed Solitude."[5]

It is revealing that Ives should choose to represent this metaphysical debate through a simultaneous contrast of the musical old (conventional harmony and regular rhythms within a single tempo) and the musical new (unconventional harmony and irregular rhythms within shifting tempos). Like other modernist composers of the early 20th century, Ives felt the need to challenge listeners out of what he perceived to be their all-too-comfortable habit of listening to "beautiful" music—listeners who, like the Druids of *The Unanswered Question*, are content within themselves and oblivious to all that is around them. Ives elsewhere wrote:

> [B]eauty in music is too often confused with something that lets the ear lie back in an easy chair. Many sounds that we are used to do not bother us, and for that reason we are inclined to call them beautiful. Frequently— possibly almost invariably—analytical and impersonal tests will show, we believe, that when a new or unfamiliar work is accepted as beautiful on its first hearing, its fundamental quality is one that tends to put the mind to sleep. A narcotic is not always unnecessary, but it is seldom a basis of progress—that is, wholesome evolution in any creative experience.[6]

Ives was profoundly disturbed by what he perceived as the tendency of most music to take the easy path of sentimentality and convention. After hearing a performance by the Kneisel Quartet, one of the premier chamber ensembles of the early 20th century, he declared, "[They] played so exquisitely 'nice' that I lost some respect for those four instruments. A whole evening of mellifluous sounds, perfect cadences, perfect ladies, perfect programs, and not a dissonant cuss word to stop the anemia and beauty during the whole evening." In his own Second String Quartet, Ives said he wanted to make "those men fiddlers get up and do something like men," and he peppered the score with such half-facetious indications as "Largo sweetota" and "Allegro con fisto swato."

As is so often the case with "nationalist" composers, Ives's music is considered so quintessentially American that the nationalist surface of his work has often deflected

---

5. Quotation from Charles Ives, Foreword to the score of *The Unanswered Question* (New York: Southern Music Publishing, 1953), p. 2. Published by Southern Music for Peer International. Used by permission.

6. Charles Ives, "Essays before a Sonata" (1920), in *Essays before a Sonata and Other Writings*, ed. Howard Boatwright (New York: Norton, 1962), pp. 97–8.

COMPOSER PROFILE Charles Ives *(1874–1954)*

I ves was a true American original whose music incorporates many of the idioms blended in the melting pot of late-19th-century American society. As a youth in Danbury, Connecticut, he absorbed a wide variety of musical traditions: the orchestral repertory of the concert hall, hymns in church, band music at community gatherings like the Fourth of July, and popular songs in the parlors of the town's homes. Ives worked all of these styles into his own music at various times, often in the same work. And all this was merely a part-time hobby, for Ives's real profession was in the insurance business.

George Ives, the composer's father and first teacher, was a bandmaster in the Civil War and a musical eccentric in his own right who at times experimented with polytonality and quarter-tone tuning. At Yale, Charles Ives studied with a very different kind of teacher, Horatio Parker, one of the leading American composers of his era but for all intents and purposes a European composer in outlook and idiom. German trained, Parker wrote in the style of Mendelssohn, Schumann, and Brahms, and Ives absorbed the finer points of this tradition. But Ives's String Quartet no. 1, written as an undergraduate, shows his interest in other idioms as well. Subtitled *A Revival Service*, it is full of references to popular hymns of the day. The first movement is based on the hymn tune *From Greenland's Icy Mountains* by another American composer, Lowell Mason.

After graduation, Ives entered the insurance business but continued to write music in his spare time. If a composer "has a nice wife and some nice children," he once asked, "how can he let them starve on his dissonances?"[7] But he more or less stopped composing in his early to mid-40s after his health began to fail, writing only a small number of songs after his heart attack. Ives achieved only modest fame as a composer during his lifetime, in part because of the advanced idiom of his

Ives the Revolutionary: graduation portrait, Yale University, 1898. Beneath the conventional clothing and demeanor lay an undergraduate seething at the strictures of musical convention. Ives had studied music at Yale with Horatio Parker, who was only 11 years older than Ives but already one of the most celebrated American composers of his generation. Parker was of the Old School—which is to say, the school of German tradition; Ives, in turn, came to Yale having already experimented with polytonality and quarter-tone tunings. The relationship of pupil and teacher was predictably strained.

Source: Courtesy of Yale University Music Library

---

7. Quoted in Jan Swafford, *Charles Ives: A Life with Music* (New York: Norton, 1996), p. 143.

attention from more fundamental elements of his approach to music. At least one European contemporary, however, Arnold Schoenberg (see Chapter 20), understood Ives's attitude. Writing as an exile in Los Angeles in 1945, Schoenberg noted that "There is a great man living in this country—a composer. He has solved the problem of how to preserve one's self and to learn. He responds to negligence by contempt. He is not forced to accept praise or blame. His name is Ives."[8]

---

8. Arnold Schoenberg, ca. 1945, in a note found by his widow after his death. Quoted in "Ives the Innovator," Time, August 22, 1960, online at http://www.time.com/time/magazine/article/0,9171,869817,00.html?promoid=googlep. Accessed May 7, 2008.

style, in part because he never really promoted himself. Many of his more important works were not performed publicly until long after they had been composed. The String Quartet no. 2, for example, was written in 1913 but not performed in public until 1946, and his Symphony no. 2 (1902) had to wait almost fifty years for its premiere in 1951. He won the 1947 Pulitzer Prize for his Symphony no. 3 (1904), a year after its long-awaited premiere. But Ives's fame and influence have grown steadily since the 1950s, and in many ways his music was an inspiration to later composers, in part for his readiness to combine contrasting idioms, and in part because of his irreverence toward the seriousness of "high art."

PRINCIPAL WORKS

ORCHESTRAL MUSIC In spite of their eccentricities, the five symphonies (four with numbers, one titled *Holidays*) stand well within the tradition of the genre as an expression of broad, communal sentiment. The first dates from Ives's college years, the last from 1916; each differs from the others in style and the balance between philosophical depth and the familiar reference, sometimes poignant, at other times comic. Even in the final years of his life he talked of writing an enormously ambitious "Universe Symphony," which Ives described as "a striving to . . . contemplate in tones rather than in music . . . to paint the creation, the mysterious beginnings of all things, known through God to man, to trace with tonal imprints the vastness, the evolution of all life, in nature of humanity from the great roots of life to the spiritual eternities, from the great unknown to the great unknown."[9] Ives also wrote a number of programmatic works for orchestra, including *Three Places in New England* and *The Unanswered Question*.

PIANO AND CHAMBER MUSIC Ives wrote a *Three-Page Sonata* for piano in 1905 and his Sonata no. 1 in 1909. His Sonata no. 2—subtitled *Concord, Mass., 1840–1860* and inspired by the writings of fellow New Englanders Emerson, Hawthorne, the Alcotts, and Thoreau—is widely regarded as one of his finest works in any genre. Ives published the work at his own expense in 1919. In addition to two string quartets, Ives also wrote four violin sonatas, a trio for violin, clarinet, and piano, and a piano trio.

VOCAL MUSIC In 1922 Ives collected and published at his own expense a volume entitled *114 Songs* for distribution to friends free of charge. These works, like his many compositions for chorus, range from exceedingly simple to exceedingly complex, spanning his entire career.

KEY DATES IN THE LIFE OF IVES

1874	Born October 20 in Danbury, Connecticut.
1894	Enters Yale University, where he studies composition with Horatio Parker, one of the leading American composers of the day.
1898	Graduates from Yale and enters the insurance business.
1907	Establishes an insurance firm of his own in partnership with George Myrick and plays an important role in developing the modern industry of life insurance.
1918	Suffers heart attack and begins a long period of ill health that will last until his death.
1922	Publishes and distributes to friends, at his own expense, *114 Songs*.
1947	Receives the Pulitzer Prize for his Third Symphony, written in 1911.
1954	Dies May 19 in New York City.

9. Ralph Kirkpatrick, *A Temporary Mimeographed Catalogue of the Music Manuscripts and Related Materials of Charles Edward Ives* (New Haven: Yale University, 1955), p. 27.

RADICAL PRIMITIVISM

Modernism's rejection of tradition assumed many forms in the early 20th century. One of the most powerful of these was **primitivism,** sometimes referred to more specifically as radical primitivism. *Primitive* is often used as a derogatory term, but as an aesthetic movement in the early 20th century, primitivism was considered a positive, purifying force in all the arts. The impetus behind primitivism was a rejection of the self-imposed, arbitrary conventions of Western culture. Primitive peoples, what the Enlightenment philosopher Jean-Jacques Rousseau had called "noble savages,"

Primitivism in painting. Musical primitivism had parallels in the visual arts. Henri Rousseau (1844–1910) painted fantastical visions that often juxtapose humans and nature. Here, in *Femme se promenant dans une forêt exotique* (Woman Walking in an Exotic Forest), completed in 1905, the exotic nature of the subject, the simplicity of line, and the bold colors of the flowers all suggest that true power resides not in the civilized woman—a relatively small figure in this painting—but in the tropical forest with its improbably oversized plants. Like Stravinsky's music for *Le Sacre du printemps*, Rousseau's art is sophisticated, even while conveying a sense of raw power, unrefined and elemental.

Source: Henri J. F. Rousseau (1844–1910), "Woman Walking in an Exotic Forest," 1905, oil on canvas/The Barnes Foundation, Merion, Pennsylvania, USA/The Bridgeman Art Library

CD13, Track 9
STRAVINSKY
Le Sacre du printemps
Score Anthology II/155

were uneducated and unrefined but for that very reason all the more genuine and pure. The primitive was regarded as a source of both beauty and strength, representing a stage of civilization unthreatened by decadence and self-consciousness. In painting, primitivism manifested itself in the work of the group of artists known as the *fauves*—the "wild beasts"—who used a seemingly crude kind of draftsmanship, coupled with bold, unrealistic colors. These artists owed much to Paul Gauguin (1848–1903), who had abandoned his career as a Parisian stockbroker to move to Tahiti in the South Pacific, where he devoted his life to painting; and to Henri Rousseau (1844–1910), another Frenchman who painted in a style critics initially derided as childlike and simplistic. But Rousseau's striking use of line and color—as in his *Femme se promenant dans une forêt exotique (Woman Walking in an Exotic Forest)*, see page 528—was soon recognized for its boldness.

Musical primitivism manifested itself in many ways over the course of the 20th century, particularly in the work of composers who sought to elevate rhythm to a level of unprecedented importance. Rhythm, after all, is the most basic of all musical elements, for music can exist without harmony and even without melody, but not without rhythm. Composers associated with primitivism also tended to abandon or substantially alter such "civilized"—arbitrary—concepts as voice leading, triadic harmony, and the major and minor forms of the diatonic scale.

All of these traits are evident in Igor Stravinsky's ballet *Le Sacre du printemps* ("The Rite of Spring," 1913), subtitled "Pictures from Pagan Russia." By rejecting traditional harmonic progressions, timbres, and above all rhythms, Stravinsky was able to create a score that reflected the same kind of raw, elemental relationship between humans and nature that is represented on stage through the story of the dance. The ballet's story centers on a pre-Christian ritual that welcomes the coming of spring and offers in thanks to the gods a human sacrifice—primitive and uncivilized to be

Example 20-5 Stravinsky, *Le Sacre du printemps*, Sacrificial Dance (rhythm only)

Source: Passage mm. 1–12 (1913 edition, rhythm only), Stravinsky *Le Sacre du printemps*, Sacrificial Dances, in *Aspects of Twentieth-Century Music* by Richard DeLone et al.; coordinating editor, Gary E. Wittlich (Englewood Cliffs, NJ: Prentice-Hall, 1975), p. 220. *The Rite of Spring* (1913), Copyright 1921 by Edition Russe de Musique. Copyright assigned 1947 to Boosey & Hawkes for all countries of the world. Reprinted by permission.

sure, but consequently all the more elemental and powerful. Stravinsky elevated the role of rhythm in this ritual in a number of ways, sometimes through complexity, sometimes through simplicity. Just before the moment of sacrifice at the end of the piece, audiences hear a passage in which the meter shifts no fewer than eight times in the span of only 12 measures (Example 20–5).

In Part I (Adoration of the Earth), the passage beginning at measure 88 is equally unpredictable, even though it is based on a series of repeating eighth-note chords. Stravinsky strips the music of all harmonic and melodic variety. The orchestra, in effect, functions as a kind of giant, polychordal drum, repeating the same chord 32 times in succession (Example 20–6). By marking each iteration with a down bow, Stravinsky

Example 20-6 Measures 1–8 after no. 13

Source: Passage mm. 1–8 after No. 13 from Stravinsky, *Le Sacre du printemps*, "Danse des Adolescentes" from *Twentieth-Century Music: A History of Musical Style in Modern Europe and America* by Robert P. Morgan (New York: W. W. Norton, 1991), p. 98. *The Rite of Spring* (1913), Copyright 1921 by Edition Russe de Musique. Copyright assigned 1947 to Boosey & Hawkes for all countries of the world. Reprinted by permission.

Example 20–7 Measures 1–4 after no. 14

Source: Igor Stravinsky, *Le Sacre du printemps*, "Danse des Adolescentes," English horns, bassoon, & cello, mm. 1–4 after No. 14. *The Rite of Spring* (1913), Copyright 1921 by Edition Russe de Musique. Copyright assigned 1947 to Boosey & Hawkes for all countries of the world. Reprinted by permission.

eliminates the slight alternation of strong and weak that is often perceptible from standard back-and-forth (down-up) bowing, and by placing accents at irregular intervals, he eradicates any sense of a rhythmic pattern.

The **polytonal** harmony of this same passage posed further challenges to early listeners. Contrasting triads are juxtaposed simultaneously, with each of four instrumental groups—two sets of horns, high strings, low strings—playing its own chord:

Violins, violas, horns 1–4	E♭^{7} chord (E♭-G-B♭-D♭)
Cellos, basses, horns 5–8	E Major chord (F♭-A♭-C♭ = E-G♯-B)

Stravinsky juxtaposes arpeggiated chords in an even more jarring fashion: an implied B♭^{7} arpeggio in the English horn, against C major in the bassoons, against an alternation of E major and E minor in the cellos (Example 20–7). Each chord is perfectly tonal within itself, but the simultaneous sounding of these chords rubbed many ears the wrong way, at least on first hearing in 1913. Within a decade, however, the elemental power of the score had won over a large following of critics and listeners alike.

For all its aesthetic primitivism, Stravinsky's *Le Sacre du printemps* is extremely intricate. The orchestra used to create its so-called primitive sounds is enormous, even by the standards of the early 20th century, and is in fact the product of hundreds of years of development and innovation:

Woodwinds

1 piccolo

3 flutes, 1 doubling on second piccolo

1 alto flute

1 English horn

4 oboes, 1 doubling on second English horn

1 E♭ clarinet

3 clarinets, 1 doubling on second bass clarinet

1 bass clarinet

4 bassoons, 1 doubling on second contrabassoon

1 contrabassoon

Brass

8 French horns, 2 doubling on tenor tubas

1 high trumpet (D trumpet)

4 trumpets

1 bass trumpet

3 trombones

2 bass tubas

Percussion

Timpani, bass drum, cymbals, gong, güiro, tambourine, triangle

Strings

First violins, second violins, violas, cellos, double bass

But Stravinsky often uses these instruments in unconventional ways to create an *impression* of rawness. The very opening of the ballet illustrates this point quite well. The high range of the bassoon makes the instrument sound strained, and the disconnected entrances of the other winds contribute to a sensation of hearing the orchestra in an inarticulate, almost chaotic state. We do not hear the traditions of Bach, Beethoven, or Brahms in these measures, but a more elemental, unrefined means of expression.

Textures in *Le Sacre du printemps* are correspondingly complex. The passage beginning at figure 11, for example, presents no fewer than 18 distinct and rhythmically unique ideas all at the same time:

- Flutes and piccolos (five rhythmically independent ideas)
- Oboes and English horn (two)
- Clarinets (four)
- Bassoons (one)
- Horns (one)
- Piccolo trumpet (one)
- Solo violin (one)
- Violas (one)
- Cellos (one)
- Double basses (one)

Although layered textures were certainly cultivated in the 19th century, nothing had ever approached this degree of intricacy. For most orchestras, the challenge of performing passages like this lies not in the notes themselves, but in the rhythms and the coordination of so many independent parts.

The audience rioted at the premiere of *Le Sacre du printemps*, in Paris in May 1913. As the composer himself later recalled:

> The complexity of my score had demanded a great number of rehearsals, which [Pierre] Monteux had conducted with his usual skill and attention. As for the actual performance, I am not in a position to judge, as I left the auditorium [to stand backstage in the wings] at the first bars of the prelude, which had at once evoked derisive laughter. I was disgusted. These demonstrations, at first isolated, soon became general, provoking counter-demonstrations and very quickly developing into a terrific uproar. During the whole performance I was at [the choreographer Vaslav] Nijinsky's side in the wings. He was standing on a chair, screaming "sixteen, seventeen,

COMPOSER PROFILE   Igor Stravinsky *(1882–1971)*

Stravinsky occupies a central place in the history of 20th-century music not only because of the quality of his works but also because of their remarkable range and variety. He was a true cosmopolitan who at various times called Russia, France, Switzerland, and the United States home. Like almost every composer of his generation, he absorbed the chromaticism and bombast of late Romanticism, but he went on to explore other idioms as well, including primitivism, Neoclassicism and, in the last 15 years of his life, even serial composition. His detractors called him a "musical chameleon," but the epithet does not give due credit to his remarkable ability to assimilate new styles and approaches to music. The phases of his career break down roughly in this way:

■ *Russian period.* Like almost every other composer of his generation, Stravinsky began writing in a style of advanced chromaticism. The early ballets written for Diaghilev—*L'oiseau de feu* ("The Firebird"), *Petrouchka*—belong very much to the traditions of the 19th century. *Le Sacre du printemps* and *Les Noces* ("The Wedding") both mark a turn to primitivism; in their modal inflections, polytonality, and impulsive rhythmic vitality, both capture the spirit of what Stravinsky called "Pagan Russia."

■ *Neoclassical period.* In the period after World War I, Stravinsky changed styles, moving toward a greater economy of both means and expression (see Chapter 22). The intensity of *Le Sacre* gave way to the cool detachment ("objectivity") of the Octet, the Concerto for Piano and Winds, *Pulcinella* (another Diaghilev ballet, based on preexistent 18th-century material), the *Symphony in C*, the *Symphony in Three Movements*,

the *Symphony of Psalms*, and the opera *The Rake's Progress*.

■ *Serialist period.* Prompted in part by his personal assistant, Robert Craft, Stravinsky began studying serial music in the early 1950s and was drawn to the works of Anton Webern in particular. His own serial compositions using this technique include the ballet *Agon* (1957, only partly serial), *Threni* (1958), and the *Requiem Canticles* (1966).

Even during his lifetime Stravinsky was widely considered one of the century's two greatest composers (the other was Schoenberg). He always seemed to stay one step ahead of everyone else, reinventing himself at various points along the way. In spite of his avowed modernism (more than one critic dubbed him "Modernsky"), his music found a relatively wide following among concertgoers. Although he had no direct students, his influence on subsequent generations of composers was profound.

For a photo of Stravinsky, see p. 522.

PRINCIPAL WORKS

BALLETS AND OTHER ORCHESTRAL WORKS   Stravinsky made his early mark in the world through his ballets, particularly *L'oiseau de feu* (1910), *Petrouchka* (1911), *Le Sacre du printemps* (1913), and *Les Noces* (1920), all produced for Sergei Diaghilev's Ballets Russes in Paris. All three use striking orchestral effects, and the combined brilliance of their music and choreography soon propelled Stravinsky into the forefront of modernist composers. His later ballets include *Apollon Musagète* (1928), commissioned by the Elizabeth Sprague Coolidge Foundation

eighteen"—they had their own method of counting to keep time. Naturally, the poor dancers could hear nothing by reason of the row in the auditorium and the sound of their own dance steps. I had to hold Nijinsky by his clothes, for he was furious, and ready to dash on to the stage at any moment and create a scandal. [The impresario Sergei] Diaghilev kept ordering the electricians to turn the lights on or off, hoping in that way to put a stop to the noise. That is all I can remember about that first performance. Oddly enough, at the dress rehearsal, to which we had, as usual, invited a number of actors, painters, musicians, writers, and the most cultured representatives of society, everything had gone off peacefully, and I was very far from expecting such an outburst.[10]

---

10. Igor Stravinsky, Stravinsky: *An Autobiography* (New York: Simon & Schuster, 1936), pp. 72–3.

and premiered in Washington, DC, at the Library of Congress; *Perséphone* (1934), with recitation and chorus, to a text by André Gide; *Jeu de cartes* ("Card Game," 1937); and *Orpheus* (1948).

The reputation of the ballets tends to overshadow that of the symphonies, all of which are significant works in the history of the genre: the *Symphony for Winds* (1920, written in memory of Debussy), the *Symphony in C* (1940), the *Symphony in Three Movements* (1945), and above all the *Symphony of Psalms* (1930) for chorus and orchestra, commissioned by the Boston Symphony Orchestra. Stravinsky also wrote several significant (and quite individual) concertos: for piano and winds (1924), for violin (1931), for clarinet and swing band (the *Ebony Concerto*, 1946), for chamber orchestra (the Dumbarton Oaks Concerto, 1938), and for string orchestra (the Concerto in D, 1947).

VOCAL AND DRAMATIC WORKS *L'Histoire du soldat* ("The Soldier's Tale," 1918) is scored for narrator and seven instrumentalists and written in Stravinsky's Neo-classical style, as is the "opera-oratorio" *Oedipus Rex* (1927), based on Sophocles' drama, which can be performed either in concert or as a theatrical piece. *The Rake's Progress* (1951), acknowledged by most to be Stravinsky's greatest opera, set to an English-language libretto by W. H. Auden and Chester Kallman, was inspired by a series of engravings by the 18th-century English artist William Hogarth; the work traces the decline and fall of a libertine.

CHAMBER WORKS In addition to the Octet (1923), Stravinsky wrote a number of small-scale works for chamber ensembles: the *Duo concertante* for violin and piano, The Septet for piano, strings, and winds (1954), and an instrumental arrangement of three madrigals by the Renaissance composer Gesualdo (1960).

KEY DATES IN THE LIFE OF STRAVINSKY

1882	Born June 17, son of the famous bassist Feodor Stravinsky, in Oranieneburg, near St. Petersburg.
1903	While studying law, begins private lessons with Nikolai Rimsky-Korsakov, the leading Russian composer of his day.
1910	Premiere of the ballet *L'oiseau de feu* in Paris, commissioned by the Russian impresario Sergei Diaghilev.
1911	Moves to Paris and produces a string of stunningly successful ballets for Diaghilev: *Petrouchka* (1911), *Le Sacre du printemps* (1913), *Le Rossignol* (1914), *Pulcinella* (1920), *Les Noces* (1923)
1925	First American tour; he receives many commissions from American patrons and institutions from this point onward.
1934	Becomes a French citizen.
1939	Leaves France, settles in Hollywood, and becomes an American citizen in 1945.
1939–1940	Delivers (in French) the Charles Eliot Norton Lectures at Harvard University, largely ghostwritten by the composer Roland-Alexis Manuel Lévy.
1950–1962	Tours and conducts widely, including a return to the Soviet Union in 1962, where he is welcomed warmly.
1971	Dies in New York on April 6 and is buried in Venice, near Diaghilev.

The noted Parisian critic Pierre Lalo spoke for many of his contemporaries when he characterized the work in these terms:

> The essential characteristic of *Le Sacre du printemps* is that it is the most dissonant and the most discordant composition that has ever been written. . . . Never before has the system and cult of the wrong note been applied with such industry, zeal, and obstinacy. From the first measure of the work to the last, whatever note one expects is never the note that follows; instead, we get the note next to it, that is, the note that should not come. Whatever the previous chord, the chord one actually hears, and this chord and this note are used expressly to produce the impression of falseness that is acute and almost excruciating. When two themes are superimposed, the composer

The art of noises. One of the more curious manifestations of musical modernism was the movement known as Futurism, led by the Italian composer Luigi Russolo (1885–1947). Russolo, shown here on the left, was determined to break down what he considered the artificial barriers between music and noise. To this end, he designed a great many "Noise-Makers" (*Intonarumori*—in Italian, *rumor* is the word for "noise"). During the 1910s and 1920s Russolo mounted a series of concerts using these instruments in works with such colorful titles as *The Gathering of Automobiles and Airplanes* and *The Awakening of a City.*

Source: Art Resource/The New York Public Library Photographic Services

scarcely uses themes that might work together; quite to the contrary, he chooses themes whose superimposition produces the most irritating friction and grating that can be imagined.[11]

But the riot soon turned to Stravinsky's advantage. Within a few short months, audiences across Europe were greeting *Le Sacre du printemps* with great enthusiasm, and the initial rejection of the work served to rally all artists of modernist tendencies. They saw in this incident a vindication of artistic vision in the face of conservative public tastes. Audiences, in turn, became less likely to express their opinions in quite such a physical fashion and began to become increasingly tolerant of modernism in general.

Meanwhile, radical primitivism in music became more prevalent. Composers who wrote pieces emphasizing **motoric rhythm,** speed, extreme dynamics, repetitive patterns, and dissonant harmony include Béla Bartók, Paul Hindemith, Henry Cowell, Leo Ornstein (1893–2002), and George Antheil (1900–1959, best known for his 1924 *Ballet Mécanique,* scored for player and regular pianos, xylophones, electric bells, airplane propellers, siren, and percussion). Many of these composers were also pianists who performed their works and those of others in solo recitals. Prior to *Sacre du Printemps,* Stravinsky's 1911 ballet *Petrushka* (originally conceived as a piano concerto) had explored similar territory. He rescored his new ballet *Les noces* (begun 1914) several times before its final (1923) version for pitched and unpitched percussion and four pianos, accompanying rapidly singing choruses and four soloists. By this time, however, Stravinsky had transformed from radical primitivism to Neoclassicism, as other former "enfants terribles" had done or would do shortly.

Sergei Prokofiev (1891–1953) was an excellent pianist who toured throughout Europe and the United States before World War II; he wrote nine sonatas, five concertos, and several sets of pieces (including *Sarcasms, Visions Fugitives,* and *Tales of an Old Grandmother* for his instrument. The Toccata, opus 11 (1912), is based on a symmetrical structure surrounding the tonic (D minor), to which the music returns constantly. A more intricate and satisfying work of this type is the finale of his Piano

CD13, Track 11
PROKOFIEV
Piano Sonata no. 7 in B Major
Score Anthology II/157

---

11. *Le Temps,* Paris, June 3, 1913. Transl. MEB

FOCUS   Sergei Diaghilev

Few nonmusicians exerted such an enormous effect on 20th-century music. As a producer, an impresario, Sergei Diaghilev (1872–1929) assembled teams of artists that included painters, dancers, choreographers, conductors, and composers. Finding just the right mix of talent could yield impressive results, and Diaghilev scored success after success in the first three decades of the 20th century. The "Russian Ballet" did in fact consist largely (but not exclusively) of Russian dancers, but the list of other artists Diaghilev engaged at various times includes many of the early 20th century's most distinguished figures:

■ **Composers** Erik Satie, Igor Stravinsky, Sergei Prokofiev, Claude Debussy, Maurice Ravel, Darius Milhaud, Francis Poulenc, Manuel de Falla

■ **Artists and stage designers** Pablo Picasso, Léon Bakst, Juan Gris, Georges Braque, Max Ernst, Juan Miró, Giorgio de Chirico

■ **Dancers** Vaslav Nijinsky, Tamara Karsavina, Léonide Massine, George Balanchine, Anna Pavlova, Serge Lifar

Diaghilev's troupe cultivated many different styles of dance, but he is best remembered for his abandonment of the classical traditions of dance, moving away from graceful movements and women dancing *en pointe* (on the point of their toes) and toward a more vigorous, athletic kind of dance. The choreography for Stravinsky's *Le Sacre du printemps* exemplifies this new approach to ballet.

Sergei Diaghilev, ca. 1916. The Russian impresario found great success in Paris through his collaborations with Stravinsky and other artists, including composers, poets, painters, and choreographers.

Source: Lebrecht Music & Arts/Lebrecht Music & Arts Photo Library

Sonata no. 7 in B♭ Major, opus 83 (1939–1942). Prokofiev labels this movement *Precipitato*, and the performer has to play at a sufficient tempo to achieve the desired effect. With the cascading octaves and leaps around the keyboard, Prokofiev provides a three-note bass figure in octaves that anchors the piece as it poses a question: Is Prokofiev parodying (or honoring) a popular musical style he would have heard during his years in the West? Or is the figure intended to be objective, the result of pure composition, so that the listener should discount her or his assumptions (if there are any)? Either approach can produce different results, and both are valid, even if one decides that one is more satisfying.

NATIONALISM

Musical nationalism, like primitivism, was driven by a desire to return to cultural roots through a musical idiom connected to the people. Already evident in the 19th century (see Chapters 14 and 18), musical nationalism took on new importance in the 20th with the growing political and cultural aspirations of ethnic groups throughout Europe and the Americas. The Austro-Hungarian Empire, ruled by the Habsburg dynasty from its German-speaking capital of Vienna, provides a good example of the ethnic diversity within a single political entity. In 1900, the Habsburgs governed an empire that encompassed portions or all of what are now Austria, Hungary, the

Czech Republic, Slovakia, Croatia, Slovenia, Bosnia, Herzegovina, Serbia, Romania, Poland, and even Italy. Yet each of these regions had its own language and culture, and music was an important means of asserting ethnic identity.

When Béla Bartók set out into the field to record the melodies sung and played by peasants (see the photograph in Composer Profile: Béla Bartók), he was thus attempting to capture not only a repertory of songs but also the very identity of the ethnic groups singing them. Bartók and others like him were driven in part by the belief that folk song represents the untarnished purity of preindustrial society. "Folk music," the English folk song collector Cecil Sharp declared, "is the ungarbled and ingenuous expression of the human mind, and on that account it must reflect the essential and basic qualities of the human mind." After collecting folk songs throughout the British Isles for several decades, Sharp (1859–1924) transferred his base of operations to the Appalachian region of the United States in the belief that only in the backwoods and mountains of a former colony could he find what he considered to be the true spirit of the English peoples.

For modernist composers, folk music offered important stylistic alternatives to the traditions of conventional melody and harmony. Bartók and his colleague Zoltán Kodály (1882–1967) found an altogether different set of melodic possibilities in the folk music of various ethnic groups they collected throughout central and eastern Europe. The two made frequent use of distinctively ethnic characteristics in their own music. They often incorporated irregular rhythms and meters and generally avoided the conventions of functional harmony, preferring instead to substitute intervals of the second, fourth, and seventh in favor of the traditional triad. They also drew on a variety of nondiatonic scales, including whole tone and pentatonic.

Bartók in particular favored the kind of irregular meters that characterize a good deal of the folk music of eastern Europe. The first of his *Six Dances in Bulgarian Rhythm* from his *Mikrokosmos*, Book 6, for example, is built on a metrical pattern notated as follows:

$$\frac{4+2+3}{8}$$

This kind of meter is sometimes referred to as complex meter, and although it ostensibly had its origins in folk music, it found its way into much modernist music as well.

Nor were Bartók and Kodaly alone in such ventures. Charles Ives worked many traditional American melodies not only into his songs, but also his symphonies and string quartets. George Gershwin, in turn, regarded jazz as "an American folk music; not the only one but a very powerful one which is probably in the blood and feeling of the American people more than any other style." Gershwin's *Rhapsody in Blue* (1924), for piano and orchestra, was one of the earliest of many works by American composers to integrate the jazz idiom into the repertory of the concert hall. Igor Stravinsky, drawing on recent Russian scholarship of the time, adapted several published folk melodies to great effect in *Le Sacre du printemps*. The English composer Ralph Vaughan Williams (1872–1958) made his own intensive study of English folk song and frequently incorporated such melodies into his own music.

Composers could, of course, also freely adapt the music of cultures not their own. The French composer Darius Milhaud (1892–1974) drew on Latin American tunes and dance rhythms in his *Saudades do Brasil* ("Nostalgia for Brazil," 1921). These dances integrate popular dance rhythms into a harmonic idiom that is delightfully unpredictable. Milhaud's use of polytonality distinguishes his music from the sounds we would be likely to hear in the streets of, say, Rio de Janeiro; yet the rhythms are true to life enough to provide the music with a decidedly Brazilian flavor.

CD13, Track 10
BARTÓK
Six Dances in Bulgarian Rhythm
Score Anthology II/156

CD13, Track 12
MILHAUD
Saudades do Brasil
Score Anthology II/158

COMPOSER PROFILE   Béla Bartók *(1881–1945)*

Alongside his conventional training as a pianist and composer, Béla Bartók developed an intense interest in the folk musics of central and eastern Europe. He took advantage of recent developments in recording technology to make what we would now call field recordings, and his published transcriptions attempt to capture nuances of singing and playing not normally notated in concert repertory. Bartók had a keen ear for the more fluid sense of pitch and meter in the unwritten tradition, along with its flexible rhythms and distinctive timbres.

This kind of music eventually worked its influence on Bartók's own compositions. He wrote his earliest works in the style of Brahms, but from about 1905 onward most of his music incorporates at least some elements that give it an ethnic sound. For Bartók, the idioms of the people offered a source of inspiration and tradition that was at once genuine and a departure from the established (and predominantly German) tradition of Bach, Haydn, Mozart, Beethoven, and Brahms. Bartók sometimes used folk tunes more or less directly, adding harmonies; on other occasions he created original tunes with folklike inflections.

Bartók emigrated to the United States in 1940, but his music did not at first generate much interest in North America beyond a small group of dedicated enthusiasts. His *Concerto for Orchestra* (1944), however, commissioned by Serge Koussevitsky, the conductor of the Boston Symphony Orchestra, soon established itself as one of the most popular of all 20th-century orchestral works. Already ill, the composer died of leukemia less than a year after its premiere.

PRINCIPAL WORKS

ORCHESTRAL WORKS The *Music for Strings, Percussion, and Celesta* (1937) and *Concerto for Orchestra* (1944) are two of the most popular of all 20th-century orchestral works. The Violin Concerto (1939) and the Third Piano Concerto (1945) have also established themselves in the repertory. Other works for orchestra include the Concerto for Two Pianos and Orchestra (1942, an arrangement of his own Sonata for Two Pianos and Percussion) and the Viola Concerto (1945, completed by his pupil Tibor Serly).

VOCAL AND DRAMATIC WORKS *Bluebeard's Castle* (1911), an opera in one act, and especially the ballets *The Wooden Prince* (1917) and *The Miraculous Mandarin*

(1919) are admired but have not achieved the popularity of some of the orchestral works.

CHAMBER MUSIC The six string quartets rank among the greatest in the literature. As in the case of Beethoven, we can trace the composer's development from early to late styles in these works, which explore an astonishing variety of forms, tones, and instrumental techniques. Bartók's two sonatas for violin and piano, as well as a sonata for solo violin, are also significant additions to the repertory.

PIANO MUSIC In the tradition of J. S. Bach, Bartók wrote many pedagogical works for his own children and pupils, most notably *Mikrokosmos*, a set of 153 progressive works, many of them influenced by his work as a collector of traditional musics. His *Allegro barbaro* and his many Hungarian and Romanian dances for piano also incorporate folklike elements.

Bartók records in the field (1908). Bartók was one of the first researchers to make field recordings of folk musicians. His recordings and transcriptions of music from across eastern Europe remain a valuable source of information for ethnographers. In Bartók's day, the musical traditions of the remote villages he visited were still relatively untouched by the growing influence of urbanization, radio, and recorded sound. The villagers are dressed in their Sunday finest: this is, after all, a memorable day in the life of the village. But their garb manifests a more subtle problem faced by field workers who go out to collect "authentic" data. The formality of the occasion might well affect the nature of the performance. Would a villager dressed in his Sunday finest sing for an outsider with a strange recording device in exactly the same way as when dressed in ordinary work clothes singing in an everyday setting?

Source: Corbis/Bettmann

KEY DATES IN THE LIFE OF BARTÓK

1881	Born March 25 in Nagyszentmiklós, in the Transylvania region of Hungary (now Romania).
1899	Enters the Royal Academy of Music in Budapest and studies both piano and composition.
1905	Begins collaboration with the composer Zoltán Kodály to collect folk music of central and eastern Europe; continues to travel to remote regions to record and transcribe the songs and instrumental music of many different ethnic groups.
1907	Appointed piano instructor at Royal Academy of Music, Budapest.
1922	Tours London and Paris, performing his own music and accompanying a number of noted violinists.
1927–1928	Makes his first tours of the United States and the Soviet Union
1934	Commissioned by the Hungarian Academy of Sciences to prepare an edition of some thirteen thousand Hungarian folk songs; the work would be completed and published posthumously.
1940	Emigrates to the United States and settles in New York; receives an honorary degree from Columbia University.
1941	Takes position as research fellow at Columbia to pursue folk song studies; receives several major commissions for new compositions.
1945	Dies in New York on September 26.

NEW TIMBRES

In addition to rhythm and pitch, many modernist composers of the early 20th century sought novelty in timbre, through new instruments or new ways of playing old instruments.

CD13, Track 14

COWELL
The Banshee
Score Anthology II/159

Although the 20th century brought relatively few technical changes to the piano itself, composers developed many novel ways of using the existing instrument. One such group involved direct contact with the piano strings, rather than by striking the keys; the piano top would be open or removed altogether. Henry Cowell (1897–1965) called such actions "string piano"; the current, more generic, term is "extended techniques." In *The Banshee* (1925), Cowell calls on the performer to manipulate directly by hand the strings inside the instrument. *The Banshee* actually requires two performers, although the only responsibility of the one at the keyboard is to keep the damper pedal down throughout the entire work. The other player stands in the crook of the instrument and touches the strings with his or her fingers. Cowell's explanation of the special performance symbols for the work takes up almost as much space as the score itself. The opening of the piece calls for the standing player to "sweep with the flesh of the finger from the lowest string up to the note given," ending with another lengthwise sweep of the finger on the string of that highest note. Different sounds are gradually introduced: the sweep concludes with a pluck of strings, then with a sweep along the strings of three notes together, then sweeping with the back of the fingernails instead of the fleshy part of the finger, and so on. The unearthly effect is unlike anything anyone had heard before this time. The eerie quality of the sound fits with the work's title. In Cowell's own words, a banshee is "a woman of the Inner World . . . who is charged with the duty of taking your soul into the Inner World when you die. . . . She has to come to the outer plane for this purpose, and she finds the outer plane very

Henry Cowell. Cowell's innovative piano techniques were not limited to those found in *The Banshee* (Anthology II/160). Here, he demonstrates his method for playing "tone clusters"—note the position of his left arm on the black keys. The physical force of the image captures the radical attitude of the self-styled "ultramodern" composers of the 1920s. In addition to composing and performing, Cowell was also a renowned writer on music and made important recordings of music from outside the Western art tradition. He was an early champion of the music of Charles Ives and later held teaching positions at Peabody Conservatory (1951–1956) and Columbia University (1949–1965). In the opinion of John Cage, Cowell provided the "open sesame" for new music in the America.

Source: Frank Driggs Collection

uncomfortable and unpleasant, so you will hear her wailing at the time of a death in your family."[12]

In some of his other works for piano, like *Advertisement* (1914), Cowell pioneered the use of tone clusters, directing that adjacent keys be struck with the forearm, flat of the hand, or some object of an appropriate shape, such as a block of wood. This technique foreshadowed the sounds of the "prepared piano" devised by one of Cowell's pupils, John Cage (see Chapter 23), who in the 1940s began placing objects like paper clips and pieces of rubber and wood on the strings to produce unusual sounds.

Edgard Varèse's *Ionisation* (1931) is another seminal work reflecting the growing range of sounds available to 20th-century composers. The title comes from the world of particle physics, and the timbre is appropriately abstract and challenging. *Ionisation* is the first major composition to have been written entirely for percussion. Most of the 37 instruments have no definite pitch at all: four tam-tams, gong, cymbals, three different sizes of bass drum, bongos, snare drums, güiro ("scraper"), slapsticks, Chinese blocks, claves ("rhythm sticks"), triangle, maracas ("shakers"), sleigh bells, castanets, tambourine, anvils, and two sirens. Previously, these sounds would have been used for special effects and ethnic references: church bells (Berlioz), working anvils (Verdi and Wagner operas), castanets and tambourines for Hispanic-flavored music (Bizet), or cowbells (Mahler symphonies). The entrance of pitched instruments (piano, celesta, chimes) toward the end of *Ionisation* creates a strange sensation, for by this point listeners have somehow grown accustomed to the sound of no pitches of any kind.

12. Interview with Cowell recorded on *Henry Cowell: Piano Music* (Washington, DC: Smithsonian Folkways, CD SF40801).

Much as happens with the "Tristan chord" in pieces discussed earlier, the familiar is made unfamiliar, or at least awkward, in context.

When analysts speak of the different "themes" and "subjects" in this work, then, they are talking almost exclusively about rhythms and timbres, not pitch. We are so accustomed to hearing musical structures on the basis of pitch and harmony that the formal element of repetition in this particular work is often not readily apparent on first hearing. The first subject, for example, which appears after an eight-measure introduction, returns in modified form, then again in fragmentary form toward the very end.

Like a good many modernist pieces, *Ionisation* alienated its share of critics. One of them—writing anonymously—had this to say about the work's premiere, in New York's Carnegie Hall, in 1933:

> Varèse's latest effort, played twice, contains almost nothing of traditional tonal quality, being scored for various gatling-gun species of percussion, a dolorous and quaintly modulated siren, sleigh bells and an ingenious instrument that imitated the voice of an anguished bull. Toward the end of this strange work, which moved even earnest devotees of the musically esoteric to smiles, there was a slight undercurrent of the lyrical in some muted tones of a piano and a celesta.[13]

Although such reviews make for entertaining reading today, we should not lose sight of the genuine difficulties posed by a work like *Ionisation*. No one had ever heard a work of this size written almost entirely without fixed pitches, and it conformed to no established convention of form or genre.

In an interview given in 1924, almost a decade before writing *Ionisation*, Varèse explained the motivation behind his search for new musical timbres:

> Stringed instruments are still the kings of orchestras, despite the fact that the violin reached its zenith in the early part of the eighteenth century. Why should we expect this instrument, typical of its period, to be able to carry the main burden of the expression of today? The rest of the conventional orchestra of today precludes the exploitation of the possibilities of different tone colors and range. . . . In order to exploit the art of sound (i.e. music) we shall require an entirely new medium of expression. We certainly should forget forthwith the pianoforte and all the arbitrary mechanical restrictions which it has imposed.[14]

In his ongoing research in the possibilities of new timbres, including percussion, Varèse also worked with Bell Laboratories at various times to develop the possibilities of electronic music; his 1958 *Poème électronique*, put together with the aid of Iannis Xenakis (see Chapter 23), was written specifically for the striking World's Fair building in Brussels designed by Le Corbusier. Heard on 11 channels over 425 loudspeakers in the Philips Pavilion, the combination represents a unique blend of music and architecture. "I refuse to submit myself only to sounds that have already been heard," he once declared.[15] "I do not write experimental music. My experimenting is done before I make the music. Afterwards, it is the listener who must experiment."[16]

---

13. Review of the Pan-American Association of Composers Concert, March 6, 1933, Carnegie Hall. *Musical Courier*, vol. 106, no. 11 (1933): 12.

14. Quotation from Edgard Varèse in *The Evening Standard* (London), July 31, 1924. Reprinted by permission of *The Evening Standard*.

15. Joseph Machlis, *Introduction to Contemporary Music*, 2nd ed. (New York: Norton, 1979), p. 353.

16. From *Music of Edgar Varèse* (Albany, NY: One Way Records, 1996).

Edgard Varèse. Earlier composers had often portrayed themselves seated at the keyboard, surrounded by their most recent works. For this photographic portrait from the 1950s, Varèse gave strategic prominence to the metronome, immediately identifying himself as a musician even while setting himself apart from composers of previous generations.

Source: Photo by Roy Hyrkin. Courtesy Ann McMillian archives at Electronic Music Foundation

Varèse wrote relatively little music, yet his influence on 20th-century composition was enormous. During his lifetime, he was highly regarded by avant-garde composers but little known outside this circle until the 1950s, when his contributions to the art of music first began to gain widespread recognition, particularly from such younger composers as Pierre Boulez, Karlheinz Stockhausen, and Frank Zappa.

CONCLUSION

The early decades of the 20th century witnessed a series of radical challenges to established musical conventions. Claude Debussy, Igor Stravinsky, and Charles Ives, each in his own way, developed strikingly original approaches to such basic elements of music as melody, harmony, rhythm, and form. Primitivism emerged as a driving force in all the arts, but nowhere more strongly than in music, which embraced the elemental rhythms of Stravinsky's ballets and the motoric rhythms of works by Prokofiev and others. The musical idioms of eastern European peoples recorded by Béla Bartók and others provided an important source of inspiration to composers looking for new sounds. Still other composers, like Henry Cowell and Edgard Varèse, extended the range of timbres inherited from the 19th century, either through performing on old instruments in new ways or through the cultivation of instruments that had not previously been used in the concert hall. The sound of the early 20th century, in short, was decidedly new.

Beyond Tonality

Atonality

Serial Composition

Around the turn of the 20th century, as we have seen, several prominent composers were exploring extended chromaticism as an alternative to triadic harmony based on the major and minor diatonic scales. Among these composers were Gustav Mahler (particularly in his later works, such as the Ninth and unfinished Tenth Symphonies and *Das Lied von der Erde*), Hugo Wolf, and Richard Strauss (especially in the operas *Elektra* and *Salome*), as well as Claude Debussy. Indeed, the chromatic harmonies of Wagner's *Tristan und Isolde* (see Chapter 17) no longer seemed so radical by 1908 when Debussy poked fun at the celebrated "Tristan" chord by quoting it—quite out of context—in his own *Children's Corner Suite* (see Chapter 24). And when Alban Berg slipped a similar reference into the finale of his decidedly nontonal *Lyric Suite* of 1926, the effect was shocking, but for quite a different reason: what had once seemed daring now sounded positively tame if not downright banal. Berg could not more eloquently have made his point that dissonance and consonance are relative concepts, changing from generation to generation.

None of the elements characteristic of early-20th-century extended chromatic harmony was new, after all. Augmented triads, extended sonorities built on thirds (9th, 11th, and 13th chords), unresolved dissonances, nonharmonic tones, nonfunctional bass lines, enharmonicism, fleeting or merely implied tonicization, parallel voice leading—all of these can be found in the music of the mid- to late 19th century. What *was* new at this time was the substantially greater prominence given to all these kinds of features.

The opening of Schoenberg's Chamber Symphony in E Major, op. 9 (1906) provides a good illustration of the limits of traditional chromatic tonality (Example 21–1). The initial chord builds up gradually out of a series of fourths rather than thirds (G-C-F-B♭-E♭-A♭). This sonority resolves to an F-major chord in measure 4 through an augmented sixth chord on G♭ (a French sixth) that includes an additional A♭. The goal of this progression is clearly tonal: there is nothing ambiguous about the second chord in measure 4. But the manner in which the music arrives at this harmony makes the triadic sonority seem all the more isolated and out of place, as if it is the consonance that is dissonant. The tonal basis of the work is further confused by the following four measures, which open with a different series of fourths (D-G-C-F-B♭-E♭) that then moves through a series of whole-tone chords in descending parallel motion. The sense of a goal-oriented functional harmony is so remote here that its very presence is called into doubt. Once again, the resolution (vii⁷/E with an added D♮, moving to E Major first inversion) sounds almost out of place, even though it is technically correct according to the standards of traditional harmony and voice leading. The resolutions seems to echo the "Tristan" chord while at the same time they outshine its effect, which is by this time a half-century in the past.

ATONALITY

The boundary between extreme chromaticism and **atonality**—the absence of a tonal center altogether—is often difficult to identify. By the time he had completed his Chamber Symphony, op. 9, Schoenberg was beginning to recognize that chromatic harmony was approaching the point at which distinctions between dissonance and consonance had become almost meaningless. At some point, logically, the extended avoidance of a tonal center becomes the absence of a tonal center.

Schoenberg knew he was in the process of saying farewell to tonality: the third movement of his earlier Second String Quartet, op. 10 (1908) had incorporated a lengthy quotation from the children's song *Ach, Du lieber Augustin* (better known in English as "Did you ever see a lassie go this way and that way?"), in which the relentless repetition of tonic and dominant harmonies dissolves into banality. Schoenberg wanted to wean the public from its entrenched familiarity with tonality and explore, in the words sung by the solo soprano who enters in the finale to the Second String Quartet, the "air of other planets." The public, for the most part, was reluctant to travel with him.

Partly independently, partly in conjunction with his pupil-colleagues Anton Webern and Alban Berg, Schoenberg persisted in advancing what he called "the emancipation of the dissonance." In a truly atonal idiom, Schoenberg argued, dissonances would no longer be considered a "spicy addition to dull sounds" but instead the "natural and logical outgrowths" of a musical "organism."[1] Schoenberg hated the term *atonality*, on the grounds that it defined an idiom in terms of what it was not. "I am a musician," Schoenberg declared, "and I have nothing to do with the atonal. Atonal might well mean simply: something that corresponds in no way to the essential nature of tones. . . . A piece of music will always be tonal, at least in the sense that there must be some kind of a relationship from one tone to the next."[2] He advocated calling such music *pantonal*, but the term never caught on.

The impetus toward atonality was more than merely technical. Schoenberg, Webern, and Berg were searching for a new way of writing music whose emotional impact would be more direct and immediate than anything available in the vocabulary

---

1. Arnold Schoenberg, "My Evolution (1949)," in *Style and Idea*, ed. Leonard Stein, trans. Leo Black (Berkeley and Los Angeles: University of California Press, 1984), p. 91.
2. Arnold Schoenberg, *Harmonielehre*, 3rd ed. (Vienna: Universal Edition, 1922), pp. 487–8.

Example 21-1 Schoenberg, Chamber Symphony in E Major, op. 9 (1906), measures 1–10

of extended chromaticism. Atonality, as it turned out, was particularly well suited to the aesthetics of **expressionism,** a broad artistic movement of the time that sought to give voice (expression) to the unconscious, to make manifest humanity's deepest and often darkest emotions. Expressionism is related to primitivism in that both attempt to strip away the veneer of so-called civilized behavior and reveal the darkest recesses of human emotion. In Freudian terms, expressionist art bypasses the ego, the conscious self, and aims straight for the id, the unconscious repository of basic instincts and drives. Expressionism in all its forms—in literature, painting, cinema, and music—rejects conventional techniques of representation, favoring instead devices that exaggerate and distort. It is driven by an attempt to confront the innermost corners of the human psyche, including its more unpleasant elements. Psychological truth becomes the object of art, not beauty, at least not beauty in the conventional sense. Inner emotion takes precedence over any sense of external reality.

Expressionist art is not a means of escaping the human condition, but rather of confronting it. The quintessential act of expressionism is the scream (see "The Scream," page 547), an utterance that is not a word, a product of civilization, but rather an intense, spontaneous reaction to something that has caused pain or fear. Indeed, the Austrian poet and critic Hermann Bahr (1863–1934) defined expressionism precisely in terms of this act: "Man screams from the depths of his soul; the whole era becomes a single, piercing shriek. Art also screams, into the deep darkness, screams for help, screams for the spirit. This is expressionism."[3]

Schoenberg, who was deeply sympathetic to expressionist art, and whose own paintings are very much within the expressionist idiom (see the self-portraits in the

---

3. Hermann Bahr, quoted in *Art in Theory, 1900–1990: An Anthology of Changing Ideas,* ed. Charles Harrison and Paul Wood (Oxford: Blackwell, 1993), p. 119.

CD13, Track 15
SCHOENBERG
Pierrot lunaire
Score Anthology II/160

Composer Profile), was drawn to the surreal, violent, and eerie imagery in Albert Giraud's *Pierrot lunaire* (1883), a poetic cycle that had recently been translated from their original French into German; he was especially pleased to receive a commission from the actress-singer artist Albertine Zehme (1857–1946) to set a group of 21 ("three times seven") poems taken from the larger selection that she had already used in spoken recitals accompanied by piano music. Schoenberg enjoyed the composition process immensely, aided by Zehme's willingness to allow for more than piano accompaniment; the resulting 1912 setting of this cycle for soprano and instrumental ensemble is one of the most widely admired works of musical expressionism and one of the earliest works of atonal music to achieve a wide following.

Pierrot is one of the stock masked characters from the commedia dell'arte, and *Pierrot lunaire* draws on the mask as a metaphor for the human manners that conceal deeper emotions. Pierrot himself is the melancholy, moonstruck clown who lives in a state of constant longing. The atonality of no. 7 ("The Sick Moon") makes the moon seem far more ill than any tonal idiom could. Schoenberg projects the violence of the text in no. 14 ("The Cross")—whose first line reads "Holy crosses are the verses on which poets bleed to death"—by having the voice make leaps of ninths, diminished and augmented octaves, and other nontriadic intervals, thereby undermining any sense of a tonal center.

By setting a series of relatively short poems in *Pierrot lunaire*, Schoenberg was able to circumvent one of the more pressing challenges of writing within the new atonal idiom: how to construct large-scale musical forms in the absence of tonality. The tonal system, after all, had provided the basic framework for most musical forms for several centuries. It is no coincidence, then, that most of the atonal works from the early decades of the century are relatively brief, and that many of them are vocal. The texts of these works provide a certain degree of structural coherence in the absence of traditional tonality.

PRIMARY EVIDENCE   "The Last Word in Musical Anarchy"

Schoenberg's *Pierrot lunaire* (1912) posed a challenge to many if not most of its first listeners. The American music critic Arthur M. Abell (1868–1958) filed this review from the work's London premiere.

To arouse any kind of a sensation in these days of such enormous overproduction in every branch of music is of itself an extraordinary feat. Arnold Schoenberg may be either crazy as a loon, in which case we may assume that his efforts are prompted by honest conviction, or he may be a very clever trickster who is apparently determined to cause a sensation at any cost, finding, seemingly, the cheapest and surest way to be by writing music that in its hideousness and illogical, ear splitting ugliness defies description. At any rate, he is just at present the most talked of musical personality of the day, not excepting Richard Strauss. And he has succeeded in twice filling Choralion Hall and each time the audiences were made up chiefly of professional musicians and critics. His music to Albert Giraud's fantastical poems entitled "The Songs of Pierrot Lunaire," is the last word in cacophony and musical anarchy. Some day it may be pointed out as of historical interest, because representing the turning point, for the outraged muse surely can endure no more of this; such noise must drive even the moonstruck Pierrot back to the realm of real music. Albertine Zehme, a well known Berlin actress, dressed in a Pierrot costume, recited the "Three Times Seven" poems, as the program announced, while a musical, or rather unmusical, ensemble consisting of a piano, violin, viola, cello, piccolo and clarinet, stationed behind a black screen and invisible to the audience, discoursed the most ear splitting combinations of tones that ever desecrated the walls of a Berlin music hall. Schoenberg has thrown overboard all of the sheet anchors of the art of music. Melody he eschews in every form; tonality he knows not and such a word as harmony is not in his vocabulary. He purposely and habitually takes false basses and the screeching of the fiddle, piccolo and clarinet baffled description. The remarkable part of this whole farce is that Schoenberg is taken seriously. A musically cultured audience sits through such an atrocity with hardly a protest. The grotesque sounds which emerged from behind the black screen occasionally called forth outbursts of merriment, but the audience was as a whole very well behaved. The critics have written columns about Schoenberg. To be sure, they condemn him almost to a man, but they give him space—from four to five times the space that other more deserving composers get and they do this for the same reason that I am now doing it, because there is an element of interest for the readers of their papers in the whole scheme. As I said before, Schoenberg has succeeded in causing a veritable sensation. He even has adherents who rally round his standard and swear by his muse, declaring that this is music of the future. Otto Taubmann, the critic of the *Börsen Courier*, expressed the feelings of all sane musicians when he wrote, "If this is music of the future, then I pray my Creator not to let me live to hear it again."

Source: Arthur M. Abell, review in *The Musical Courier*, November 6, 1912.

The first interpreters. In this photograph of the performers of the 1912 premiere of *Pierrot lunaire*, Albertine Zehme (center) is flanked on her right by Arnold Schoenberg and on her left by Eduard Steuermann, pianist and Schoenberg pupil.

Source: Arnold Schoenberg and Pierrot Lunaire Ensemble. Berlin 1912. © Arnold Schoenberg Center

Sprechstimme, the style of singing called for throughout *Pierrot lunaire,* reinforces the surreal quality of the text and music. *Sprechstimme* (literally, "speech-voice," with "voice" understood here in the sense of "singing") is neither speech nor song, but a means of declamation somewhere between the two. Unlike speech, in *Sprechstimme* the vocalist must articulate specified pitches and rhythms. Instead of sustaining a pitch as in the conventional method of singing, however, the performer allows the pitch to drop rather in the same way one's voice drops with the enunciation of a spoken word.

Sprechstimme is indicated by means of standard notes with a small "x" through the stem. The effect is unique: as song, it falls short of lyricism, and intentionally so; as speech, it constitutes a purposefully exaggerated, overblown kind of delivery. It occupies a kind of twilight zone between speech and song that calls attention to the essentially artificial distinction between the two.

Schoenberg did not invent *Sprechstimme*. It had been in use in the theater since at least the 1890s, cabaret singers had long cultivated a style of singing that was half spoken and half sung, and he himself used it in his oratorio *Gurrelieder* (1900–01). But in *Pierrot lunaire*, Schoenberg used this device to create a heightened sense of surrealism, a feeling that the speaker-singer is somehow distanced from the text she is delivering. Many commentators have in fact detected a certain degree of irony in the work, arguing, in effect, that its extreme emotionalism is in the end a parody of extreme emotionalism. This kind of irony would be fitting in a work that draws so deeply on the traditions of the *commedia dell'arte*, a style of performance in which the performers are constantly calling attention to the fact that they are performers.

The atonal idiom of *Pierrot lunaire* also provided Schoenberg with an effective foil for the limited use of tonality. The final number of the cycle (no. 21, "O Ancient Scent") speaks of the intoxicating "ancient scent" that comes "from the time of fairy tales," and throughout this finale, the composer's music is more nearly tonal for longer stretches than at any other point in the entire cycle. At the very end of *Pierrot*, the moonstruck clown wistfully longs for the age of tonality, the age of childhood and fairy tales, but seems to realize this is only a dream, that there is no turning back now. The voice descends so low at the very end that the final words—half spoken, half sung in *Sprechstimme*—are almost inaudible. The contrast with the closing numbers of the previous two parts, the eeriness of no. 7 and the violent expressionism of no. 14, could not be greater. The dream is over, the nightmare and screams of expressionism exhausted, a return to the past impossible.

Early composers writing atonal works without a text had to find other means to structure them. Anton Webern's *Five Pieces for String Quartet*, op. 5 (1908), is a series of miniatures that concentrates its resources into a remarkably intense form of expression. Like most atonal works, it uses a limited number of building blocks that usually consist of four or five notes—sometimes fewer, sometimes more, but rarely very many more. These units tend to avoid triads, both in their linear (melodic) and vertical (harmonic) alignments. Webern, like Schoenberg and Berg, saw himself as a traditionalist who continued in the manner of Beethoven and Brahms by manipulating motivic ideas in a process that Schoenberg called "developing variation." Although the extreme brevity of the movements in Webern's op. 5 makes it difficult to hear this process, at least on first listening, this music does in fact rest on the manipulation of a few thematic ideas that are laid out at the beginning and sustained through to the end. The work's unusual voicings and textures, and Webern's avoidance of any strong sense of meter over extended periods, make it all the more difficult to discern order in a work in which no one pitch emerges as more important than any other. Fortunately, set theory, which was developed in the third quarter of the 20th century by the American scholar Allen Forte, provides us with a framework for identifying the constituent elements that go into most atonal music and helps us realize that in spite of its surface challenges, this music is in many respects quite traditional (see Focus: Set Theory and the Analysis of Atonal Music).

By far the most successful atonal work of the early 20th century—both critically and commercially—was Alban Berg's opera *Wozzeck*, completed in 1922 and premiered in Berlin in 1925. The libretto, drawn from selected scenes of the drama *Woyzeck* by the Austrian playwright Georg Büchner (1813–1837), traces the mental and physical deterioration of a simple army soldier, who is treated abysmally by everyone: his captain,

CD13, Track 18
WEBERN
*Five Pieces for String Quartet,
op. 5, no. 4*
Score Anthology II/161

CD14, Track 1
BERG
Wozzeck
Score Anthology II/162

COMPOSER PROFILE   Arnold Schoenberg *(1874–1951)*

Schoenberg was a tortured soul, an outsider who longed to be accepted yet never felt comfortable within the establishment. Widely perceived as a radical, he saw himself as a traditionalist extending the heritage of Bach, Beethoven, and Brahms. Born Jewish, he converted to Christianity, then later back to Judaism. An Austrian by birth, he moved back and forth between Vienna and Berlin, finally emigrating to the United States when the Nazis assumed power in Germany. (It was in the United States that he changed the spelling of his name from Schönberg to Schoenberg.)

His work falls into three broad periods:

■ *Early (advanced chromaticism).* Schoenberg's early works explore the outer limits and reaches of chromaticism. Lush harmonies, thick textures, and an almost constant avoidance of cadences characterize such works as *Verklärte Nacht* ("Transfigured Night"), a tone poem for string sextet; *Gurrelieder*, an oratorio of enormous proportions; the Quartet in D minor, in one large movement; the Chamber Symphony no. 1 in E Major, op. 9; and many songs.

■ *Middle (atonal).* Around 1908, Schoenberg abandoned tonality altogether and declared the "emancipation of the dissonance." Principal works of the atonal period include the String Quartet no. 2 (whose finale features a solo soprano singing the words "I breathe the air of other planets"); the Piano Pieces op. 11 and op. 19; *Pierrot lunaire*; the monodrama *Erwartung* ("Expectation," for soprano and orchestra); the unfinished oratorio *Jakobsleiter* ("Jacob's Ladder"); and the *Five Orchestral Pieces*, op. 16.

■ *Late (serial).* Dissatisfied with the lack of a more structured formal principle by which to organize his atonal works, Schoenberg eventually developed the method of 12-tone serial composition (discussed later) in which no note is repeated until all other 11 pitches of the scale have been stated. His earliest attempts at serial composition date from around 1920, and within a few years he was applying this method in almost all his music. The principal serial works include the String Quartets nos. 3 and 4; the *Variations for Orchestra*; the opera *Moses und Aron*; and the String Trio.

A portrait of Schoenberg by the Viennese painter Richard Gerstl (1883–1908). Around or shortly after the time he made this portrait, Gerstl began having an affair with Schoenberg's wife. When their liaison ended and Mathilde Schoenberg returned to her husband in 1908, Gerstl committed suicide. The events bear strong similarities to the plot of Schoenberg's opera *Die glückliche Hand* ("The Magic Touch") of 1913.

Source: © Wien Museum Karlsplatz, Vienna, Austria/The Bridgeman Art Library.

With Stravinsky, Schoenberg was widely regarded as one of the two great composers of the 20th century. No one, however, ever accused him of being a "musical chameleon," as Stravinsky had been called. Even those who did not care for his music respected his uncompromising pursuit of artistic principles. His influence, moreover, extended well beyond his two most famous pupils, Anton Webern and Alban Berg. Every subsequent generation of composers has studied Schoenberg's music carefully, and in this sense he stands as one of—and arguably *the*—most influential composers of the entire century.

PRINCIPAL WORKS

DRAMATIC WORKS   The unfinished opera *Moses und Aron*, based on the book of Exodus, is in many respects Schoenberg's masterpiece; it is also a veiled autobiography of the composer himself. Moses, the lawgiver, strives to elevate the people of Israel by transmitting the word of God. But Moses (a *Sprechstimme* role in the opera) cannot persuade with the fluency and eloquence of the young Aaron (a lyric tenor). Many critics have seen in this constellation a parallel with Schoenberg and his pupil Berg, whose atonal and 12-tone music was for most listeners more lyrical and accessible than Schoenberg's. Late in his life, Schoenberg also turned to the genre of the monologue with orchestra in such works as *Kol nidre*, the *Ode to Napoleon*, and *A Survivor from Warsaw*.

ORCHESTRAL MUSIC   The *Five Orchestral Pieces* and the *Variations for Orchestra* are atonal and serial, respectively. The Violin Concerto and Piano Concerto are later compositions.

PIANO MUSIC   The *Three Piano Pieces*, op. 11, and *Six Piano Pieces*, op. 19, are brief but important works in the development of the atonal idiom. Schoenberg turned to the piano again in developing his 12-tone method of composition, most notably in the Piano Suite, op. 25, which openly adopts the forms, but not the style, of a Baroque dance suite (see Chapter 10). The Piano Pieces op. 33a and 33b use combinatoriality (see Chapter 23).

CHAMBER MUSIC   *Verklärte Nacht*, for string sextet (later arranged for string orchestra), is a tone poem based on the story of a woman's confession of infidelity. Written in a lush, post-Wagnerian style, it is the most frequently performed of all Schoenberg's works. The five string quartets (1897, 1905, 1908, 1927, 1936; the first is not numbered) offer a good way to trace the various periods of Schoenberg's compositional career, as do the two chamber symphonies (1906, 1939).

WRITINGS   Schoenberg's writings are among the most important in the field of 20th-century theory. He wrote a massive treatise on harmony, and through his lectures, teaching, and analytical essays he exerted considerable influence on subsequent generations of composers, theorists, and listeners. Several of these essays were collected and published in English as *Style and Idea* (1950; expanded edition, 1975, reprinted 1984).

KEY DATES IN THE LIFE OF SCHOENBERG

1874	Born in Vienna on September 13.
1894	Begins private composition lessons with Alexander Zemlinsky; performs in local music halls to earn money.
1910	Appointed teacher of composition at the Vienna Academy.
1911	Finishes his *Harmonielehre*, dedicated to the recently deceased Gustav Mahler, one of his early supporters; moves to Berlin, where he teaches at the Stern Conservatory.
1912	Premiere of *Pierrot lunaire*, which causes a sensation.
1918	After serving in the Austrian military during World War I, settles once again in Vienna and organizes the Society for Private Musical Performances, to which only selected listeners are invited.
1925	Appointed professor at the Prussian Academy of Arts in Berlin.
1933	Dismissed from his position in Berlin because of his Jewish ancestry and emigrates to France and then the United States, where, after a year in Boston, he settles in Los Angeles.
1935	Appointed professor of music at the University of Southern California; begins teaching a year later at the University of California at Los Angeles; becomes an American citizen in 1941.
1951	Dies on July 13 in Los Angeles.

FOCUS   Set Theory and the Analysis of Atonal Music

Atonal music—works like Webern's *Five Pieces for String Quartet*, neither tonal nor 12-tone—seemed for a long time resistant to anything approaching systematic analysis. The American theorist Allen Forte (b. 1926) was the most prominent among a number of critics working in the 1950s and 1960s to develop a method for examining this kind of music. In what came to be called *set theory*, Forte proposed a system for identifying and clarifying the relationship of the relatively small units (*cells* or *sets*) that together provide the building blocks for a typical atonal composition. These sets can consist of anywhere between two and ten pitch classes (a pitch class is any manifestation of a particular pitch, regardless of register; thus the pitch class A–F can be used for units that go either down a major third or up a minor sixth—or down a tenth, and so on). A finite number of set types—220 to be exact—can be created out of all the various combinations of pitch classes (see table).

In analysis, these combinations of differing size are identified by a series of numbers reflecting the prime form of the set, beginning with 0 (the lowest note of the set) and moving upward by half step, in much the same way that 12-tone rows are identified numerically. Another important principle of the prime set form is that the pitch class numbers are ordered with smallest interval first (that is, are "packed" to the left); thus, the tetrachord set C-D♯-F-G would be reinterpreted as D♯-F-G-C, then transposed to C-D-E-A. This prime set form is designated 0–2–4–9 because D is two half steps above C, E is four half steps above C, and A is nine half steps above C. Sets can be presented either simultaneously (as a "chord") or successively (as a "melody"). Example 21–2 shows the two tetrachords of the opening set of Webern's op. 5, no. 4 (without transposition).

Looking at the score, we can see that set A is presented in the two upper voices in measure 1, set B at the beginning of measure 2. The pitches of set A recur on the final half beat of measure 2; set B appears as a melodic line in the first violin in measures 3–4, then again in the second violin (measure 4) transposed down a fifth. Identifying pitch-class sets can be a hit-or-miss process at times: some sets occur only once or twice in a piece and cannot really be considered to have structural importance. The identification of sets can nevertheless be extremely helpful for making audibly coherent a work of music that might otherwise seem shapeless, even after repeated hearings.

NUMBER OF PITCHES IN SET	NAME OF TYPE OF SET	NUMBER OF POSSIBLE COMBINATIONS
2	Dyad	6
3	Trichord	12
4	Tetrachord	29
5	Pentachord	38
6	Hexachord	50
7	Septachord	38
8	Octachord	29
9	Nonachord	12
10	Decachord	6
		Total: 220

Example 21–2 Two tetrachords from the opening of Webern's *Five Pieces for String Quartet*, op. 5, no. 4

his doctor, and the woman by whom he has fathered a child. In the end, he goes mad and murders Marie, the mother of his young son.

Berg used a series of traditional instrumental forms to structure his opera. He identified them himself as follows:

ACT I: FIVE CHARACTER PIECES (EXPOSITION)

Scene 1: Wozzeck and the Captain—Suite

Scene 2: Wozzeck and Andres—Rhapsody on three chords

Scene 3: Wozzeck and Marie—March (Drum Major) and Lullaby (Marie's Child)

Scene 4: Wozzeck and the Doctor—Passacaglia

Scene 5: Marie and the Drum Major—Quasi Rondo

ACT II: SYMPHONY IN FIVE MOVEMENTS (PERIPETEIA OR DEVELOPMENT)

Scene 1: Marie alone—Sonata-form Movement

Scene 2: Captain, Doctor, Wozzeck—Invention and Fugue on Three Themes

Scene 3: Marie and Wozzeck—Largo in the Instrumentation of Schoenberg's Chamber Symphony, op. 9

Scene 4: Wozzeck and Others in the Tavern—Scherzo

Scene 5: Wozzeck and Drum Major in the Barracks—Rondo Marziale

ACT III: SIX INVENTIONS (CATASTROPHE OR DENOUEMENT)

Scene 1: Marie and Child—Inventions on a Theme

Scene 2: Wozzeck and Marie by the Pond—Invention on One Note

Scene 3: Wozzeck and Others in the Tavern—Inventions on a Rhythm

Scene 4: Wozzeck, Later the Doctor and Captain—Invention on a Six-note Chord

Scene 5: Child, Other Children—Invention on an Eighth-note Rhythm (Perpetuum Mobile)

Berg insisted, however, that "there must not be anyone in the audience who . . . notices anything about these various fugues, inventions, suites and sonata movements, variations and passacaglias. Nobody must be filled with anything except the idea of the opera." The congruence of musical and dramatic form within each scene and across each act is extremely effective.

The opening scene of Act I, a suite, provides a good illustration of the manner in which the character of individual dances is matched to the dramatic dialogue. Berg uses here exactly the same device used by Verdi in the opening scene of *Rigoletto* (see Chapter 17): a series of dances, each with a particular symbolic meaning. The curtain goes up on a scene that is at once both mundane and chilling. We see Wozzeck shaving the Captain. With a flick of the wrist Wozzeck could kill him, and indeed the thought occurs to him as, in the process of trying to engage the laconic soldier in conversation, the Captain crosses the line by reminding Wozzeck of his illegitimate child. The scene is constructed as a suite, a series of dances (or rather, dance rhythms) that relate precisely to the nature of the conversation.

■ *Prelude (measure 1):* The Captain, who, as we later realize, is obsessed with the passage of time, reminds Wozzeck to proceed slowly, "one step at a time."[4] In the course of urging calm, the Captain himself becomes quite agitated.

■ *Pavane (measure 30):* The Captain broods on eternity and mortality. This section ends with a cadenza for the viola.

■ *Gigue (measure 65):* The Captain has not been able to engage Wozzeck in a conversation on morality, so he turns instead to the weather ("I believe the wind is from South-North"), but even these absurdities fail to capture Wozzeck's attention. The music ends with a cadenza for bassoon.

■ *Gavotte (measure 115):* Returns to the idea of morality and scores a hit when he declares that Wozzeck's child was born out of wedlock, "without the blessings of the church."

COMPOSER PROFILE Anton Webern *(1883–1945)*

Webern's music tends to be extremely concentrated and brief. The orchestral *Passacaglia*, op. 1, lasts about ten minutes in performance, but no subsequent work has more than five minutes of continuous music. A set of his complete works issued on long-playing records in the 1960s took up only four disks. This aphoristic quality strips music to its bare essentials. In much of his work, Webern never calls for a dynamic level louder than *piano*, and he uses silence more often and more effectively than any composer before him. Listening to this music is like listening to a brilliant speaker who wastes no words and speaks in a whisper: we strain to hear every detail, every nuance.

Born into an aristocratic family, the future composer completed a doctoral degree in historical musicology at the University of Vienna in 1906. His dissertation was on the second volume (1555) of the *Choralis Constantius* by the Renaissance composer Heinrich Isaac (see Chapters 5 and 6). Webern was fascinated by the constructive techniques of Renaissance music, particularly its elaborate canons. During this time, he also studied composition privately with Arnold Schoenberg, and together teacher and pupil explored the possibilities of atonal composition and, later, serial composition.

Webern's death is shrouded in mystery. While visiting his daughter and son-in-law in a small Austrian village shortly after the end of World War II, he stepped outside to enjoy his first cigar in months, only to be shot and killed by an American sentry who was part of the Allied force

Anton Webern and Alban Berg. Anton Webern (right) and Alban Berg were Arnold Schoenberg's two most prominent students and colleagues. At the time this photograph was taken in 1912, both had essentially broken their musical ties with tonality and had begun to explore the possibilities of the atonal idiom.

Source: © Universal Edition

- *Double I (measure 127):* Wozzeck finally responds and quotes Christ's words "Let the little children come unto me." At Double II (measure 133), the Captain's erratic rhythm takes over when he insists he had not been talking about Wozzeck at all. Suddenly it is the Captain who does not want to talk.

- *Air (measure 136):* Wozzeck erupts in a passion of genuine emotion, a lyrical outburst. "We poor people," he sings, and the music to these words will return often in the course of the opera. Morality, he proclaims, is a function of affluence.

- *Prelude (reprise) (measure 154):* The Captain, quite shaken, tries to regain his original air of calm. The music of the opening returns, and he resumes his verbal harassment of Wozzeck as if nothing had happened in the meantime.

In addition to introducing the opera's central character, this opening scene also introduces one of the work's principal ideas: the consequences of emotional repression. At first, Wozzeck assumes the guise of an automaton, answering each of the Captain's provocative questions with a monotonous and unthinking "Yes, Captain." Only when the Captain touches on the question of Wozzeck's child do we begin to see the soldier's true feelings emerge, but because they are so raw and powerful, the Captain quickly occupying Austria at the time. The soldier claimed self-defense and pointed out that Webern was outside after curfew, but it seems unlikely that the diminutive, middle-aged Webern could have posed any threat.

PRINCIPAL WORKS

ORCHESTRAL MUSIC The *Passacaglia*, op. 1, reveals Webern's early interest in strict forms and his gift for orchestration. His *Variations*, op. 30, reward careful analysis for the elaborate application of 12-tone devices. Webern's scoring for orchestra is extraordinarily transparent; he once said the sound of a full orchestra caused him physical pain.

CHAMBER MUSIC Webern preferred to work within the smaller scale genres of string quartet and song; even his one symphony is scored for a chamber ensemble and is quite brief. The Five Movements for String Quartet, op. 5, are celebrated for their conciseness and economy of expression, as are the Six Bagatelles, op. 9. The String Quartet, op. 28, is a 12-tone work.

VOCAL MUSIC Webern, along with his teacher Schoenberg, worked through many of the problems of atonality within the genre of song. He favored contemporary poets such as Stefan George, Georg Trakl, and Rainer Maria Rilke; he wrote several texts of his own as well. From 1926 onward, however, he set exclusively the texts of Hildegard Jone (1891–1963), a fellow Austrian whose texts greatly appealed to Webern's sense of an inherent connection between nature and art. Jone's poetry also provided the texts for the two cantatas.

KEY DATES IN THE LIFE OF WEBERN

1883	Born December 3 in Vienna.
1906	Receives Ph.D. in musicology from the University of Vienna with a dissertation on the Renaissance composer Heinrich Isaac.
1908–1914	Conducts theater orchestras in various cities in Austria and Germany.
1915–1916	Serves as a volunteer in the Austrian Army in World War I but is discharged because of poor eyesight.
1918	Helps run the Society for Private Musical Performance until its demise in 1921; begins giving private lessons in composition.
1926	Meets the poet Hildegard Jone and from this point on sets only her texts to music.
1933	The Nazis prohibit performances of Webern's music, and he is forced to lecture in secret and work as a proofreader for his Viennese publisher, Universal Edition.
1945	Dies September 15 in Mittersill, Austria, shot by an American soldier.

seeks to put them back in place, insisting (quite absurdly) that he had not even been talking to Wozzeck at all during this time.

Some critics, predictably, lambasted Berg's *Wozzeck*. Paul Zschorlich, writing in the *Deutsche Zeitung* of Berlin on December 15, 1925, commented:

> As I left the opera house last night I had the feeling that I was coming out of a public institution dedicated not to art, but rather out of a public asylum for the insane. On the stage, in the orchestra, in the hall, nothing but crazies. Among them were tightly-knit units in defiant cadres: the shock troops of atonalists, the dervishes of Arnold Schoenberg. . . . Alban Berg's *Wozzeck* was the battlecry. The work of a Chinaman from Vienna. For these massive onslaughts of instruments have nothing to do with European music and its development. . . . In Berg's music there is not even a trace of melody. There are only crumbs, scraps, hiccups, and burps. The work cannot be discussed from a harmonic perspective, because everything sounds wrong. . . . The perpetrator of this work . . . relies firmly on the stupidity and wretchedness of his fellow beings, and for the rest relies on God Almighty and Universal Edition [the publisher of *Wozzeck*]. I consider

FOCUS   Opera in the Early 20th Century

In the early decades of the 20th century, opera continued to thrive in the hands of such composers as Richard Strauss, Alban Berg, Giaccomo Puccini, and Leoš Janáček. From the perspective of form, most of these composers were descendants of Wagner in one way or another, emphasizing musicodramatic continuity even while preserving (in most cases) units still recognizable as arias, duets, and so on. Stylistically, opera was as diverse as the music of the 20th century itself, ranging from the atonal expressionism of Schoenberg's *Die glückliche Hand* (1913), to the tonal lyricism of Puccini's *Turandot* (1926), to the jazz-inspired harmonies and rhythms of Gershwin's *Porgy and Bess* (1935).

Among the more notable operatic composers of this period are the following:

Giaccomo Puccini—*La bohème* (1896), *Tosca* (1900), *Madama Butterfly* (1904), *La fanciulla del West* (1910), *Turandot* (1926)

Leoš Janáček—*Jenůfa* (1904); *Kátya Kabanová* (1921), *The Makropoulos Affair* (1926), *From the House of the Dead* (1928)

Richard Strauss—*Salome* (1905), *Elektra* (1909), *Der Rosenkavalier* (1911)

Arnold Schoenberg—*Erwartung* (1909), *Die glückliche Hand* (1913), *Moses und Aron* (1932)

Alban Berg—*Wozzeck* (1925), *Lulu* (1937)

Paul Hindemith—*Cardillac* (1926, rev. 1952), *Mathis der Maler* (1935)

Kurt Weill—*Die Dreigroschenoper* (1928), *Aufstieg und Fall der Stadt Mahagonny* (1929–30)

George Gershwin—*Porgy and Bess* (1935)

Igor Stravinsky—*Oedipus Rex* (1927), *The Rake's Progress* (1951)

Alban Berg a musical swindler and a composer who poses a threat to the public at large. Indeed, one must go still further than this. Unheard-of events demand new methods. The question we must seriously consider is this: Is it possible to treat music in a criminal manner, and if so, to what extent? For in the realm of music, we are dealing here with a capital offense.[5]

Wozzeck nevertheless became a critical and commercial success almost overnight, opening to great acclaim in 17 cities in Germany between 1926 and 1933. Audiences in Prague, Petrograd (St. Petersburg), Paris, Philadelphia, and New York welcomed the work enthusiastically. When the National Socialists under Adolf Hitler came to power in Germany in 1933, however, Berg's music—along with all other atonal and serial music—was repressed and eventually banned from public performance. In the years after World War II, *Wozzeck* quickly reestablished itself as a staple of the operatic repertory.

SERIAL COMPOSITION

For more than a decade, between roughly 1908 and the early 1920s, Schoenberg, Webern, Berg, and others struggled to find a means of creating large-scale atonal structures. Berg's use of traditional instrumental forms in *Wozzeck* was part of this effort, but the new idiom of atonality required a correspondingly new approach to form as well.

In response to this need, Schoenberg developed the technique of **serial composition** in the early 1920s. Serial composition is based on the premise that an established unit of music—most often a **row**, or **series** (hence the term "serial"), of 12 different pitches—can be varied repeatedly in such a way as to provide the structural basis for an entire work. A composer using this approach could integrate the row and any of its many possible permutations into established formal conventions—variations, sonata-form movements, rondos, and so on—but such forms were not essential to the

---

5. Quotation from review of *Wozzeck* by Paul Zschorlich, *Deutsche Zeitung* (Berlin, December 15, 1925). Transl. MEB

structural integrity of the work, which was ensured by the constant presence of the row in one guise or another. Serial composition provided composers seeking to break away from traditional tonality with the means to construct large-scale forms that were structurally coherent despite the absence of a tonal center.

Twelve-tone serial composition, also known as **dodecaphony** (from the Greek *dodeca*, meaning "12"), uses as its basic unit a row of 12 different pitches drawn from the 12 pitches of the chromatic octave (C, C♯, D, D♯, etc., up through B). Schoenberg identified three principal functions of the 12-tone row: (1) to avoid creating the impression of a principal note, which in turn might suggest a "tonic" key area; (2) to unify the composition motivically; and (3) to "emancipate" the dissonance, that is, to eradicate any distinction between consonance and dissonance (see Primary Evidence: "Schoenberg on the Three Functions of the 12-Tone Row"). It is important to distinguish between the theory and practice of 12-tone composition. In theory, 479,001,600 different basic rows are possible (this number is 12! or $12 \times 11 \times 10 \times 9 \times 8 \times 7 \times 6 \times 5 \times 4 \times 3 \times 2 \times 1$). In practice, composers pay careful attention to the musical qualities of the row, generally avoiding intervals or sequences of intervals that might suggest a key area, such as a succession of thirds or of pitches in a diatonic scale. In the strictest applications of 12-tone composition, no pitch is repeated until all other 11 pitches have been stated in that particular iteration of the row. In practice, composers applied this system with considerable flexibility, often repeating a particular pitch before moving on to another one.

There are four basic forms of any given row, each of which can be transposed to start on any of the 12 chromatic pitches in the diatonic scale:

- Prime (P) is the basic form of the row.

- Inversion (I) is the row played upside down: a rise of a major third in the prime form of the row becomes a fall of a major third; a fall of a minor second in the prime form becomes a rise of a minor second, and so on.

- Retrograde (R) is the row played backward, beginning with the last note and ending with the first.

- Retrograde Inversion (RI) is the inverted form of the row's retrograde, in other words, the inverted form played backward.

These different permutations of a single row are readily evident in Schoenberg's *Piano Suite*, op. 25, an early serial work, written in 1923. The prime form of the row consists of the pitches E-F-G-C♯-F♯-D♯-G♯-D-B-C-A-B♭. A **matrix** shows at a glance all the 48 possibilities of this row in the transposed versions of P, I, R, and RI (Example 21–3).

By convention, the **pitch class** on which each form of the row begins is designated by a number. (Theorists use the term *pitch class* to designate any set of notes—any A, any B, any C, and so on—regardless of its register.) The prime form of the row would thus be P-0 (no matter which pitch class the actual row begins with); the Inverted form beginning on 4 (that is, four half steps above the original note of P-0) would be I-4; the Retrograde Inverted form beginning on 8 would be RI-8; and so on. By the same token, the pitches of the rows themselves can also be designated numerically. Thus the basic row of Schoenberg's op. 25 (P-0) can be identified as 0–1–3–9–2–11–4–10–7–8–5–6; each of these numbers can in turn represent a transposition of the basic row and its permutations. (Some analysts use the series of numbers 1 through 12, but most American writers on music have tended toward the system using 0 through 11, as atonal set theory does, and it is this latter system that is used here.)

At first glance, such a compositional system might seem like little more than the equivalent of a musical crossword puzzle. But it is important to remember that all forms of composition, and especially the so-called strict forms such as canon and

CD14, Track 2
SCHOENBERG
Piano Suite, op. 25
Score Anthology II/163

Example 21–3 The matrix of the row for Schoenberg's *Piano Suite*, op. 25. The prime form in its original transposition (P-0) reads from left to right across the top row.

INVERSIONS

	0	1	3	9	2	11	4	10	7	8	5	6	
0	E	F	G	C#	F#	D#	G#	D	B	C	A	Bb	0
11	D#	E	F#	C	F	D	G	C#	A#	B	G#	A	11
9	C#	D	E	A#	D#	C	F	B	G#	A	F#	G	9
3	G	G#	A#	E	A	F#	B	F	D	D#	C	C#	3
10	D	D#	F	B	E	C#	F#	C	A	A#	G	G#	10
1	F	F#	G#	D	G	E	A	D#	C	C#	A#	B	1
8	C	C#	D#	A	D	B	E	A#	G	G#	F	F#	8
2	F#	G	A	D#	G#	F	A#	E	C#	D	B	C	2
5	A	A#	C	F#	B	G#	C#	G	E	F	D	D#	5
4	G#	A	B	F	A#	G	C	F#	D#	E	C#	D	4
7	B	C	D	G#	C#	A#	D#	A	F#	G	E	F	7
6	A#	B	C#	G	C	A	D	G#	F	F#	D#	E	6
	0	1	3	9	2	11	4	10	7	8	5	6	

PRIMES · RETROGRADES

RETROGRADE INVERSIONS

Source: Arnold Schoenberg, *Piano Suite*, op. 25 (Vienna: Universal Edition © 1926, renewed 1953). From *Materials and Techniques of Twentieth-Century Music* by Stefan Kostka, 2nd ed., Prentice Hall, © 1999, p. 201. Reprinted by permission of Pearson Education, Inc., Upper Saddle River, NJ.

fugue, involve self-imposed limitations. Such limitations, moreover, have nothing to do with the inherent quality of a work. There are good fugues and bad fugues, and the same is true of 12-tone compositions.

It is equally important to remember that in spite of all these limitations, the composer retains enormous control over the course of a serial work, because the number of ways in which the row can be permuted and combined with other iterations of the same row is virtually infinite. In fact, the matrix of any given row is far more than most composers ever need or use. Typically, only a small fraction of the 48 possible combinations of a row will actually come into play. In his *Piano Suite*, op. 25, to remain with the previous example, Schoenberg limited himself to just eight different versions of the row, as outlined in Example 21–4.

Schoenberg's *Piano Suite* offers a particularly clear example of how serial music works, in part because it is one of the composer's earliest attempts at a large-scale serial work. All six movements—Prelude, Gavotte, Musette, Intermezzo, Minuet, Gigue—are based on different manifestations of the same row. The prime form of the row (P-0) is presented in the upper voice (right hand) of the Prelude's first three measures. But what is going on in the left hand? Careful scrutiny of the first four pitches there (Bb, Cb, Db, G) reveals they are the first four notes of the same series transposed up a

PRIMARY EVIDENCE

Schoenberg on the Three Functions of the 12-Tone Row

In addition to composing, Schoenberg wrote a good deal about his own music and the music of others. He was a teacher at heart, and he tried throughout his life to make the logic of his music as accessible as possible. Here he identifies the three basic functions of the 12-tone row.

———◆———

The construction of a basic set of 12 tones derives from the intention to postpone the repetition of every tone as long as possible. I have stated in my *Harmonielehre* that the emphasis given to a tone by a premature repetition is capable of heightening it to the rank of a tonic. But the regular application of a set of twelve tones emphasizes all the other tones in the same manner, thus depriving one single tone of the privilege of supremacy. It seemed in the first stages immensely important to avoid a similarity with tonality. The feeling was correct that those free combinations of simultaneously sounding tones—those "chords"—would fit into a tonality. Today's ear has become as tolerant to these dissonances as musicians were to Mozart's dissonances. It is in fact correct to contend that the emancipation of the dissonance is at present accomplished and that twelve-tone music in the near future will no longer be rejected because of "discords."

The other function is the unifying effect of the set. Through the necessity of using besides the basic set, its retrograde, its inversion, and its retrograde inversion, the repetition of tones will occur oftener than expected. But every tone appears always in the neighbourhood of two other tones in an unchanging combination which produces an intimate relationship most similar to the relationship of a third and a fifth to its root. It is, of course, a mere relation, but its recurrence can produce psychological effects of a great resemblance to those closer relations.

Such features will appear in every motif, in every theme, in every melody and, though rhythm and phrasing might make it distinctly another melody, it will still have some relationship with all the rest. The unification is here also the result of the relation to a common factor.

The third advantage of composition with a set of twelve tones is that the appearance of dissonances is regulated. Dissonances are not used here as in many other contemporary compositions as an addition to make consonances more "spicy." For the appearance of such dissonant tones there is no conceivable rule, no logic, and no other justification than the dictatorship of taste. If dissonances other than the catalogued ones are admitted at all in music, it seems that the way of referring them all to the order of the basic set is the most logical and controllable procedure toward this end.

Source: Arnold Schoenberg, "Composition with Twelve Tones (2)," ca. 1948, in *Style and Idea: Selected Writings of Arnold Schoenberg*, ed. Leonard Stein, trans. Leo Black. (Berkeley and Los Angeles: University of California Press, 1984), pp. 246–7.

Example 21–4 Forms of the row actually used in Schoenberg's *Piano Suite*, op. 25

Source: Arnold Schoenberg, *Piano Suite,* op. 25 (Vienna: Universal Edition © 1926, renewed 1953). Reprinted with permission.

tritone (P-6) to begin on the note B♭ (= A♯). The relationship of the pitches is identical to that of the upper voice: up a half step (B♭-C♭ = A♯-B), then up a whole step (C♭-D♭ = B-C♯; the disposition of register is of no importance in identifying rows), then a tritone leap (D♭-G = C♯-G). The relationship is not audible on the surface (at least not to most people), yet the structure is every bit as present as the harmony of a I–IV–V progression in tonal work.

Matters become slightly more complicated in measures 2–3 in the left hand, where we see multiple pitches sounded simultaneously within the same row. Here, Schoenberg in effect divides the row in two: the "middle voice" (the upper line in the left hand) continues with the fifth through eighth pitches of the P-6 form of the row (C-A-D-G♯ = 2–11–4–10 (see the bottom line of the matrix on p. 556); the left hand at the same time is playing the ninth through twelfth pitches of this same form of the row (F-F♯-D♯-E = 7–8–5–6). The repetition of the B♭ in measure 3 is "permitted" because no other pitches have sounded in that particular voice. Once that voice leaves B♭, that pitch does not return until all other 11 have sounded in that particular voice. ("Permitted" is in quotation marks here because composers can of course do whatever they like, including bending or breaking their own self-imposed limitations.)

The distribution of material between right and left hands in the opening of the Minuet is fairly complicated, but if we pay close attention to the voice leading, we can see how consistently Schoenberg applies the serial process (Example 21–5). The presentation of rows in the Trio of this same movement is more straightforward, but this portion of the movement is also canonic, which provides us with a healthy reminder that serial composition does not by any means dictate all aspects of musical form. Indeed, the canonic element of this Trio is more clearly audible on the surface (through the agency of rhythm) than is the 12-tone construction itself. The analysis of 12-tone music may begin with an identification of rows but it does not end there. Other elements, such as rhythm, register, dynamics, and timbre, must also be taken into account.

For Schoenberg, the idea behind serial composition was deeply rooted in tradition. He maintained that every worthy piece of music, regardless of idiom, was a "working out" of a basic musical idea. This idea was more than just a theme: it could incorporate harmonic, contrapuntal, rhythmic, registral, timbral, and dynamic elements as well. All of Schoenberg's music manifests this basic process of what he called "developing variation," the process by which an idea grows and evolves over the course of a movement or entire work. It was in this sense that Schoenberg saw himself as the heir to the traditions of Beethoven and Brahms, who had also created large-scale musical structures through the unfolding of relatively simple motives and ideas.

What Schoenberg felt was necessary in new music, however, was the cultivation of what he called "musical prose," a style of writing in which musical ideas proceed in

Example 21–5 Schoenberg, *Piano Suite*, op. 25, opening of Minuet

Source: Arnold Schoenberg, *Piano Suite,* op. 25 (Vienna: Universal Edition © 1926, renewed 1953). Reprinted with permission. From Glenn Watkins, *Soundings: Music in the Twentieth Century* (Schirmer Books, 1988), p. 331. Used by permission of Belmont Music Publishers, Pacific Palisades, CA 90272.

a style analogous to prose, as opposed to rhymed, metered poetry. Using Johann Strauss's *The Blue Danube Waltz* (Anthology) as an example, Schoenberg showed how Strauss's melody was immediately comprehensible and memorable because of its regular rhythmical patterns (its phrase structure) and its sense of musical "rhyme" (consequent phrases satisfying the expectations of antecedent phrases). Schoenberg argued that in developing variation, little if anything should be repeated exactly or within a readily predictable pattern; instead the composer should "jump quickly to the remoter stages of development" and take for granted that "the educated listener is able to discover the intervening stages for himself."[6] Schoenberg's own 12-tone music exemplifies this approach: the multiple permutations of the prime form of the row are always present even if they are not easy to hear at first. In one of his most widely read essays, "Brahms the Progressive," Schoenberg sought to demonstrate that Brahms was already moving toward the idea of musical prose before Schoenberg himself had even begun to compose.

Schoenberg's premise of the musical idea and its unfolding continues the 19th-century tradition of **organicism,** which lies at the heart of an enormous amount of theoretical and analytical work in the 20th century. The primary goal of organicist analysis is to demonstrate the manner in which the many different elements immediately audible on the musical surface—contrasts in theme, timbre, harmony, rhythm, and so on—manifest a deeper coherence. The musical work was often seen as a living form, an organism, and many analysts perceived the challenge to be that of identifying what might be called the DNA of the work at hand, the blueprint behind the finished composition.

Dodecaphony was more a principle than a style. Schoenberg, Webern, and Berg each developed their own personal ways of applying the technique of serial composition, even though their followers lumped them together under the rubric of the "Second Viennese School" (following the earlier triumvirate of Haydn, Mozart, and Beethoven, who also worked in Vienna). As with any school of composers, common interests and differences exist side by side. Their interrelationships could be complex at times: respect and even love mingled with a palpable sense of rivalry. Schoenberg, for example, once accused Webern of stealing his ideas. Schoenberg, as the father figure of the group, was convinced his innovations would assure the continued supremacy of German music in the tradition of Bach, Beethoven, and Brahms. For all his revolutionary innovations in the realm of music, he saw himself as a profoundly traditional composer.

Webern's application of serial technique was the most complex and concentrated of the three. Many listeners perceive his music as cryptic and aphoristic; it has been said his compositions are to music what haiku is to poetry. He tended to work with subunits of the 12-tone row, small motifs of three or four notes. Very often, the first few notes of a row will be transformed in some way to create the remainder of the row. The row of his String Quartet, for example, consists of three different statements of the same pitch-class set, one of which spells out the notes "B-A-C-H." He relished the challenge of synthesizing serial technique with such contrapuntal and constructivist devices as canons, mirror canons, and passacaglias.

Berg tended to take a more liberal approach to serial composition than either Schoenberg or Webern. The first movement of his *Lyric Suite* for string quartet, for example, uses three different (yet related) rows, and not all of its six movements are serial: only the outer movements are entirely dodecaphonic. The third movement is serial in its outer sections but not in its trio, and only the trios of the fifth movement

CD14, Track 4
BERG
Lyric Suite
Score Anthology II/164

---

6. Arnold Schoenberg, "The Orchestral Variations, op. 31: A Radio Talk," *The Score* 27 (July 1960), p. 39.

Example 21–6 Berg, *Lyric Suite*, the row (a) and three derivations (b, c, and d)

Source: From *Twentieth-Century Music: A History of Musical Style in Modern Europe and America* by Robert P. Morgan. (New York: W. W. Norton. 1991), p. 215. Alban Berg, *Lyric Suite*. (© 1927 Universal Edition A.G., Vienna. © renewed. All Rights Reserved. Used by permission of European American Music Distributors LLC, sole U.S. and Canadian agent for Universal Edition A.G., Vienna.

are written using the 12-tone method. Berg manipulates the basic row of the work (Example 21–6a) in ingenious ways. He divides it into two **hexachords** (groups of six notes, Example 21–6b) and derives two "new" rows from these notes by rearranging their order (Examples 21–6c and d).

The tonal implications of Example 21–6b are particularly clear; this is the kind of row that Schoenberg and Webern avoided. For the third movement, Berg exchanges

FOCUS   The "Secret Program" of Berg's *Lyric Suite*

On a purely musical level, the quotation of the opening of Wagner's *Tristan und Isolde* in the finale of Berg's *Lyric Suite* is at once surprising, amusing, and revealing about the relationship between tonality and atonality: what had represented the extremes of chromatic harmony in 1859 now sounded positively tame. But there is yet another level of meaning at work here, for the entire *Lyric Suite* is a coded love letter from Berg to his mistress, Hanna Fuchs-Robettin.

The headings of the six movements trace the progression of the affair:

1. Allegretto gioviale   "Jovial"

2. Andante amoroso   "Amorous"

3. Allegro misterioso/Trio estatico   "Mysterious, ecstatic"

4. Adagio appassionato   "Passionate"

5. Presto delirando/Tenebroso   "Delirious, gloomy"

6. Largo desolato   "Desolate"

But the programmatic elements go even further in shaping the music. Berg used the notes A-B♭ (in German, A-B, for "Alban Berg") and B-F (in German, H-F, for "Hanna Fuchs") in much the same way that Schumann had used notes spelling the names of significant people in his life in *Carnaval* almost a hundred years before (see Chapter 16). The opening motif of the third movement plays on these four notes, which appear for the first time together in this movement. The formal proportions and metronome markings of the entire work revolve around the numbers 23 and 10, which Berg associated with himself and his lover. The third movement consists of a scherzolike A section of 69 measures (23 × 3) and a B section (trio) of 23 measures. The written-out return of the A section presents the music in shortened form (46 measures = 23 × 2) and in retrograde, as if to negate the declaration of love in the "Ecstatic Trio."

How do we know all this? In 1977, the American composer and Berg scholar George Perle uncovered Berg's annotated score in Mifflinburg, Pennsylvania, in the possession of Hanna Fuchs-Robettin's daughter. There, Perle found a first edition of the *Lyric Suite* that Berg himself had annotated as a "key" to the program. In this context, the *Tristan* reference toward the end of the work—the musical emblem of another ill-fated love affair—begins to make even more sense. The *Lyric Suite*, moreover, is not alone in its secret program. Similar encryptions are also found in Berg's Violin Concerto, his Chamber Concerto, and his second and final opera, *Lulu*.

COMPOSER PROFILE   Alban Berg *(1885–1935)*

Of the three members of the Second Viennese School, Berg stands out as the composer whose music is in many ways the most accessible. In spite of early opposition, his atonal opera *Wozzeck* has established itself as one of the only operas of its kind that can draw audiences in the same way as the operas of Verdi and Wagner. Berg's lyrical gifts and his uncanny ability to capture the dramatic moment with just the right sound contribute to his stature as one of the great opera composers of music history. As did Schoenberg and Webern, Berg began composing in a lush, post-Wagnerian style of extreme chromaticism, broke with the principles of tonality more or less completely around 1909, and then adopted the serial method in the mid-1920s. In his application of 12-tone technique, Berg tended to be rather more free than Schoenberg and especially Webern, yet he was particularly attracted to the idea of retrograding large sections of music, as in the return of the A section of the third movement of the *Lyric Suite*. This kind of large-scale retrograde structure is often associated in his music with some kind of emotional negation or reversal. Indeed, his music is full of secret programs and encrypted messages (see Focus: The "Secret Program" of Berg's *Lyric Suite*).

Berg was not a prolific composer. He suffered from ill health for much of his life, yet the works he left behind are more than sufficient in quality to ensure his place as one of the great masters of the atonal and serial idioms.

(See Composer Profile: Anton Webern for a photograph of Berg with Webern.)

PRINCIPAL WORKS

DRAMATIC WORKS   *Wozzeck* remains the most frequently performed of all atonal operas, indeed perhaps of all atonal works of any kind. Its ability to draw even listeners otherwise hostile to this idiom has proven extraordinary. *Lulu*, Berg's other 12-tone opera, is even more ambitious but remained unfinished at the composer's death. It was completed by the Austrian composer and scholar Friedrich Cerha and premiered in its full form in 1979.

ORCHESTRAL MUSIC   The 12-tone Violin Concerto is one of the few works of its kind that have thrived in the concert hall. Berg also made several arrangements of music from his *Lyric Suite*, *Wozzeck*, and *Lulu* that helped expose these larger works to a greater number of listeners.

CHAMBER MUSIC   In addition to one string quartet (op. 3) and the *Lyric Suite*, Berg wrote an important Chamber Concerto for piano, violin, and 13 wind instruments, based in part on serial principles and featuring a middle movement (*Adagio*) in "perfect" arch form, or palindrome—120 measures followed by the mirror image of those same 120 measures.

SONGS   Most of Berg's songs are early works for piano and voice. The *Five Orchestra Songs on Postcard Text by Peter Altenberg* (1912) display the composer's uncanny ability to shape texts and orchestral colors with melodic lines.

Alban Berg, ca. 1910. A portrait of the composer as a young man, by Arnold Schoenberg.

Source: Arnold Schoenberg (1874–1951), "Portrait of Alban Berg (1885–1935)." 1910. © Heeresgeschichtliches Museum, Vienna, Austria/ The Bridgeman Art Library.

KEY DATES IN THE LIFE OF BERG

1885	Born in Vienna on February 9.
1904	Begins compositional studies with Arnold Schoenberg.
1913	The premiere of Berg's *Altenberg Lieder*, op. 4, creates an uproar in the concert hall.
1915	Drafted into the Austrian army but declared unfit for active service because of severe and chronic asthma.
1918	Helps establish, with Schoenberg and Webern, the Society for Private Musical Performances.
1925	Premiere of *Wozzeck* in Berlin; in spite of many scathing reviews, the work soon gains acceptance and assures Berg's financial security for his remaining years.
1930	Appointed to the Prussian Academy of Arts, a testimony to the impact of *Wozzeck* on his contemporaries.
1935	Dies December 24 in Vienna from blood poisoning induced by an infected bee sting.

the pitches 3 (A) and 9 (G♭) in P-0 (Example 21–6a) and transposes the whole up a fourth to create a "new" primary row for this movement. The importance of this change is that it creates a row (Example 21–6d) in which the notes A-B♭-B-F appear in succession: this tetrachord held intense personal meaning for the composer because its notes spelled out the initials of his lover and himself (see Focus: The "Secret Program" of Berg's *Lyric Suite*). By rotating this newly derived row, that is, by beginning it on a pitch other than 0, Berg makes this tetrachord particularly clear. Every voice in the third movement's opening, for example, plays some version of this grouping:

- First violin—P-0 (beginning on 0). The first full statement of P-0 occurs in measures 2–3.

- Second violin—P-7 (rotated, beginning on 9). The first full statement of P-7 occurs in measures 3–4.

- Viola—P-10 (rotated, beginning on 3). The first full statement of P-10 occurs in measure 3.

These three forms of the row, along with I-5, are the only ones Berg uses in this section. The *Trio estatico* ("ecstatic trio") is freely composed; the return of the opening section at measure 93 presents the opening section in a large-scale retrograde. The inverse relationship of opening and closing becomes especially clear when we compare the first and last few measures of the movement.

CONCLUSION

The boundaries between extreme chromaticism and atonality became blurred in the music of certain composers working in the early decades of the 20th century, most notably Arnold Schoenberg, Anton Webern, and Alban Berg. Dissatisfied with the difficulties of creating coherent large-scale works in the absence of tonality, Schoenberg developed the idea of serial composition in the early 1920s, based on transpositions and permutations of a basic row or series of notes. Webern and Berg developed serial composition in their own individual ways. Although many composers and listeners refused to embrace these new idioms, the abandonment of tonality introduced a new range of musical options that would be widely explored in subsequent decades.

The Tonal Tradition

For all the importance of atonality and serial composition in the 20th century, many of the era's leading composers continued to work within the tonal tradition. Stravinsky, Bartók, Prokofiev, Shostakovich, Copland, and others all extended the bounds of the traditional harmonic idiom but retained the idea of a tonal center. For some composers, this was almost a matter of faith. The noted German composer Paul Hindemith (1895–1963) believed:

> Music, as long as it exists, will always take its departure from the major triad and return to it. The musician cannot escape it any more than the painter his primary colors or the architect his three dimensions. In composition, the triad or its direct extensions can never be avoided for more than a short time without completely confusing the listener. If the whim of an architect should produce a building in which all those parts which are normally vertical and horizontal (the floors, the walls, and the ceilings) were at an oblique angle, a visitor would not tarry long in this perhaps "interesting" but useless structure. It is the force of gravity, and no will of ours, that makes us adjust ourselves horizontally and vertically. In the world of tones, the triad corresponds to the force of gravity. It serves as our constant guiding point, our unit of measure, and our goal, even in those sections of compositions which avoid it.[1]

Others were even more blunt in their rejection of atonality. The American composer Alan Hovhaness (1911–2000) argued, "[A]tonality is against nature. There is a center to everything that exists. The planets have the sun, the moon, the earth. . . . All music with a center is tonal. Music without a center is fine for a moment or two, but it soon sounds all the same."[2]

1. Paul Hindemith, *The Craft of Musical Composition* (1937), trans. Arthur Mendel (New York: Associated Music Publishers, 1941), p. 4.
2. Alan Hovhaness, quoted in David Ewen, *American Composers: A Biographical Dictionary* (New York: G. P. Putnam's Sons, 1982), p. 342.

NEOCLASSICISM AND THE "NEW OBJECTIVITY"

Atonality, primitivism, and expressionism fostered their own counterreactions in the early decades of the 20th century. The most important of these was an aesthetic movement known as **Neoclassicism,** the deliberate imitation of an earlier style within a contemporary context. ("Classic" in this sense refers to anything from the distant past, not specifically to the Classical era or to so-called classical music in general.) The idea of writing in a deliberately old-fashioned style, or in a manner openly influenced by a much earlier style, was not an invention of the 20th century. Still, the movement known as Neoclassicism took on a special significance by virtue of its pointed rejection of such modernist developments. Neoclassicism is characterized by the following:

- a return to the tonal idiom, often chromatically inflected but not nearly to the extent found in the music of Wagner, Hugo Wolf, or Richard Strauss.

- a return to conventional genres and forms, particularly those of the Baroque and Classical eras, such as suite, sonata, concerto, and concerto grosso, along with their commensurate conventions of large-scale structure, such as the ritornello principle, sonata form, rondo, and theme and variations.

- a return to the ideal of absolute music—that is, music not connected with a text or program of any kind.

- a general tendency toward transparent textures, lighter orchestration, and smaller ensembles in general.

- conciseness of expression, avoiding grandiose or bombastic gestures.

Neoclassicism reached its height in the 1920s and 1930s, in the wake of World War I. Disillusioned by this devastating conflict, many artists and audiences took pleasure in the vaguely nostalgic sense evoked by Neoclassical music. "Back to Bach" and "The New Simplicity" became slogans. The new music did not sound like Bach, of course, nor was it necessarily harmonically simple; but it certainly sounded more like Bach (or other earlier composers) than the works of the day that attempted to overthrow the centrality of triadic harmony.

The Gavotta from the *Classical Symphony*, op. 25 (1917), by Sergei Prokofiev offers a good example of Neoclassicism. Prokofiev preserves the characteristic form and rhythms of the gavotte but transforms the melody and harmony in ways that are distinctively 20th century. The movement is essentially in D Major, yet the harmony consistently avoids any strong cadence in this key. When a cadence in the tonic finally arrives at the end of the second reprise, there is a strong sense of rhythmic arrival, but the harmony has been so skewed as to make the tonic sound unexpected at this point. The section that follows provides the thematic and textural contrast we would expect in the trio of such a dance: the droning open fifths evoke the sound of a bagpipe, hurdy-gurdy, or other similar folk instrument. And when the opening reprise returns in measure 29, it is now reorchestrated, with the winds taking the lead. The piece ends not with a bang but a whimper: *pianissimo*, understated, tongue in cheek.

Stravinsky is another prominent composer associated with Neoclassicism. As with Prokofiev, Neoclassicism was one of many styles he embraced over a long career. Stravinsky's ballet *Pulcinella* (1920) is based on themes from early-18th-century works attributed to Pergolesi (see Chapters 9 and 13); it was later discovered the music had in fact been written by a lesser-known composer of the day, but the important point is

CD14, Track 5
PROKOFIEV
Classical Symphony
Score Anthology II/165

that Stravinsky drew on material from a much earlier era. Other Neoclassical works by Stravinsky include the Concerto for Piano and Winds (1924) and the *Symphony in C* (1940; note the designation of key). Like *Pulcinella*, these works embrace pointedly old-fashioned idioms even while incorporating features that make them unmistakable products of their time. Other composers associated with Neoclassicism include Paul Hindemith and Aaron Copland (1900–1990), whose ballet *Appalachian Spring* includes an elaborate and decidedly tonal fantasy on a Shaker hymn tune.

Related to Neoclassicism is an outlook known as the "new objectivity." Today, we might think of it as the aesthetic of "cool"—music that is detached, unsentimental, and perhaps even slightly surreal. Part of Neoclassicism's appeal lay in its tendency toward understatement: if the quintessential act of expressionism is the scream, then the quintessential act of the "new objectivity" is the raised eyebrow. To view something objectively, we must step outside ourselves and consider it as—an object. This is precisely how Stravinsky described his Octet for Winds of 1923 (see Primary Evidence: Stravinsky on Musical "Objectivity"). The style of the explanatory prose itself is clinical, with clipped rhythms and a quasi-scientific tone. Stravinsky even goes so far as to deny the presence of emotional content within the work, although this may be meant ironically—irony being a favorite device of Neoclassicism in all the arts.

PRIMARY EVIDENCE   Stravinsky on Musical "Objectivity"

The clinical, almost robotic tone of Stravinsky's description of his Octet for Winds (1923) parallels his argument that the work is not "emotive," but is based instead on self-contained "objective elements." This music, according to the composer, has no room for "nuances" that cannot be notated precisely. How seriously can we take all this? Is it really possible to have music that can be performed without expressive nuance? Or is Stravinsky pulling our collective leg? Did such thinking anticipate the zealously detailed markings on scores written later in the century and their composers' heightened expectations of their realization?

⬦

My *Octuor* is a musical object. . . .

My *Octuor* is not an "emotive" work but a musical composition based on objective elements which are sufficient in themselves. . . .

I have excluded from this work all sorts of nuances, which I have replaced by the play of these volumes.

I have excluded all nuances between the *forte* and the *piano*; I have left only the *forte* and the *piano*.

Therefore the *forte* and the *piano* are in my work only the dynamic limit which determines the function of the volumes in play. . . .

To interpret a piece is to realize its portrait, and what I demand is the realization of the piece itself and not of its portrait.

It is a fact that all music suffers, in time, a deformation through its execution; this fact would not be regretted if that deformation were done in a manner that would not be in contradiction to the spirit of the work.

A work created with a spirit in which the emotive basis is the nuance is soon deformed in all directions; it soon becomes amorphous, its future is anarchic and its executants become its interpreters. The nuance is a very uncertain basis for a musical composition because its limitations cannot be, even in particular cases, established in a fixed manner.

On the other hand, a musical composition in which the emotive basis resides not in the nuance but in the very form of the composition will risk little in the hand of its executants.

I admit the commercial exploitation of a musical composition, but I do not admit its emotive exploitation. To the author belongs the emotive exploitation of his ideas, the result of which is the composition; to the executant belongs the presentation of that composition in the way designated to him by its own form. . . .

This sort of music has no other aim than to be sufficient in itself. In general, I consider that music is only able to solve musical problems; and nothing else, neither the literary nor the picturesque, can be in music of any real interest. The play of the musical elements is the thing.

Source: Igor Stravinsky, "Some Ideas about My Octuor" (1923), in Eric Walter White, *Stravinsky: The Composer and His Works* (Berkeley: University of California Press, 1966), pp. 528–31.

A similar attitude of detachment is evident in many of the works of the German composer Kurt Weill (1900–1950), who collaborated with the playwright Bertolt Brecht (1898–1956) on several stage works in the late 1920s and early 1930s. These productions often emphasized the distance between characters, their words, their music, and the audience. Speaking in the third person (a verbal technique of distancing), the composer announced, "Brecht and Weill have investigated the question of music's role in the theater. They have concluded that music cannot further the action of a play or create its background. Instead, it achieves its proper value when it interrupts the action at the right moments."[3]

CD14, Track 6
WEILL
Aufstieg und Fall der Stadt Mahagonny
Score Anthology II/166

Weill's second substantial collaboration with Brecht (the first, *Der Dreigroschenoper* of 1927, updated John Gay's *The Beggar's Opera*) was *Aufstieg und Fall der Stadt Mahagonny* ("Rise and Fall of the City of Mahagonny," 1928–29), a satire on capitalism that takes place in a fictional city (Mahagonny) in which the only crime is poverty. Everything is legal as long as it can be paid for. The "Alabama Song," sung by Jenny (a prostitute) and her six cohorts, assumes the outward form of a traditional aria, with a declamatory introduction and a soaring conclusion, but the words are surreal, a parody of pidgin English ("Oh! Moon of Alabama we now must say goodbye, / We've lost our good old mama and must have whisky oh you know why,")[4] and, oddly enough for a German opera, the text of this number is in English. All this creates a sense of distance—objectivity—that is magnified by the discordant sound of the honky-tonk–style accompaniment, using the American foxtrot rhythms that Europeans lovingly made their own after World War I.

ORCHESTRAL MUSIC

The genres of symphony and symphonic poem continued to flourish in the 20th century. The symphony retained its essential character as a large-scale work in multiple movements, and many of the most prominent composers of the century turned to this genre at one time or another. The symphony proved an especially important vehicle for musical nationalism. Prokofiev and another Russian composer, Dmitri Shostakovich (1906–1975), used folk or folk-like inflections in many of their symphonies, as did the Finnish composer Jan Sibelius, the English composer Ralph Vaughan Williams (1872–1958), the Americans Charles Ives, Roy Harris (1898–1979), and Aaron Copland (1900–1990), and the Mexican composer Carlos Chavez (1899–1978). Neoclassicists were also attracted to the symphony. Examples include Prokofiev's openly retrospective *Classical Symphony*, op. 25 (discussed earlier), and Stravinsky's *Symphony in C* (1940) and *Symphony in Three Movements* (1945), which are among the composer's most important orchestral works.

Despite this continued vitality, however, the symphony no longer occupied the position of central importance it had in the 19th century. The idea of musical pluralism extended to genres as well as styles, and composers of instrumental music in the 20th century were no longer expected to prove their abilities and accomplishments by writing a symphony. Atonal and serial composers, focused as they were on breaking with the past, largely avoided the genre, in part because it carried with it such an imposing tradition. The use of atonality, moreover, posed problems of large-scale formal organization that were difficult to solve at first; most early atonal works, as we have

---

3. Bryan Simms, ed., *Composers on Modern Musical Culture* (New York: Schirmer, 1999), p. 85.

4. Quotation from lyrics by Bertolt Brecht, "Alabama Song" from Kurt Weill & Bertolt Brecht, *Aufstieg und Fall der Stadt Mahagonny*, © 1929 by European American Music Corporation. © renewed. All Rights Reserved. Used by permission of European American Music Distributors LLC, sole US and Canadian agent for European American Music Corporation.

already seen, operated on a fairly small scale. Anton Webern's Symphony, op. 21 (1928), a 12-tone work, is really more an anti-symphony, written for chamber ensemble (one player to a part) rather than orchestra, and in two movements rather than the customary four. Like nearly all of Webern's music, the work is quite brief: the entire symphony takes less than ten minutes to perform.

The symphonic poem, like the symphony, appealed primarily to composers whose style remained within the tonal idiom. Debussy, after completing the *Prélude à l'Après-midi d'un faune* (see Chapter 19), would go on to *Nocturnes* and *La mer* ("The Sea"), a three-movement work that resembles a symphony in all but name but whose programmatic movement headings evoke specific images of the sea. His last orchestral triptych was *Images* (1912). Other composers who cultivated the symphonic poem include the following:

Paul Dukas—*The Sorcerer's Apprentice* (1897)

Arnold Schoenberg—*Pelleas und Melisande* (1903)

Alexander Scriabin—*Poem of Ecstasy* (1908), *Prometheus* (1910)

Jean Sibelius—*Finlandia* (1899), *Tapiola* (1926)

Charles Ives—*Holidays* (1904, 1909–1913), *Three Places in New England* (1911–1914)

Gustav Holst—*The Planets* (1917)

Sergei Rachmaninoff—*The Isle of the Dead* (1909)

Arthur Honegger—*Pacific 231* (1923), *Rugby* (1928)

Ottorino Respighi—*The Fountains of Rome* (1917), *The Pines of Rome* (1924)

Darius Milhaud—*The Ox on the Roof* (1919), *The Creation of the World* (1923)

George Gershwin—*An American in Paris* (1928)

Still other composers wrote large-scale works for orchestra that avoided programmatic and generic associations altogether. Béla Bartók's *Music for Strings, Percussion, and Celesta* (1936) suggests no programmatic elements and avoids aligning itself with the tradition of the symphony, even though its four movements follow an essentially symphonic format. The work is written for an unusual combination of instruments: a double string orchestra (including harp), celesta (a keyboard instrument that mimics the sound of small bells), and a battery of percussion instruments (timpani, piano, xylophone, bass drum, side drum, cymbals, tam-tam).

The work is tightly integrated, with all four movements deriving their principal thematic ideas from the fugue subject of the opening movement. This theme (Example 22-1) is built on the eight chromatic pitches between A and E, with three different meters over the course of its four measures.

The work is tonally centered, but not always within the framework of triadic harmony. Bartók frequently uses themes that employ all the chromatic pitches within a limited range. The opening phrase of the first movement's fugue touches on every

CD14, Track 7
BARTÓK
Music for Strings, Percussion,
and Celesta
Score Anthology II/167

Example 22-1 Opening subject of the first-movement fugue in Bartók's *Music for Strings, Percussion, and Celesta*; viola part chromatic note between A and E in a way that avoids any sense of triadic harmony, even while grounding the theme itself on A. The theme that enters at measure 6 of the third movement, to take another example, is similarly chromatic within a narrow range; its rhythms and articulations reflect the quasi-improvisatory performance style of much eastern European folk song without actually quoting from a recorded folk song. The underlying drone to this melody (measures 6–16) is not a perfect fifth but rather a tritone on C and F♯, the same pitches on which the work as a whole will end. Once again, Bartók has provided his music with a tonal center, but not one based on a triad.

The third movement of *Music for Strings, Percussion, and Celesta* is full of unusual sonorities. It opens with an extended solo on a single note in the upper reaches of the xylophone—a note so high, in fact, that its pitch (f^3, that is, F above the treble clef) can scarcely be perceived as a pitch at all. The repetitions of this echo follow the Fibonacci series,[5] after the initial sounding: {1, 1, 2, 3, 5, 8}, followed by the palindromic completion {5, 3, 2, 1, 1}. The xylophone is soon joined by timpani playing glissando rolls. The movement as a whole is structured around the principle of a symmetrical or **arch form,** by which the music progresses toward a midpoint and then more or less retraces its steps. This particular movement centers on measures 49–50, which present an essentially retrograde form of measures 47–48. The music "turns" this moment. On the whole, the movement can be broken down as follows:

	A	B	C	D	E	D	C	B	A
Measure	1	6	20	35	45	65	75	77	80

The proportions are not strict—Bartók was seldom pedantic about such matters—but the overall impression is one of growth, development, climax, and return to an original state. A glance at the opening and closing measures shows the gradual addition of instruments from xylophone to timpani and cello; the movement ends with instruments dropping out: first the violas, then xylophone, then timpani. The idea of symmetry operates at various points throughout this movement on a smaller scale as well. The opening rhythm of the xylophone gesture, for example, is symmetrical in its own right, with its midpoint at the downbeat of measure 3.

There is sufficient evidence that Bartók and other composers knew and applied theories of proportion and symmetry to their work. In *Music for Strings, Percussion, and Celesta*, for example, the Euclidean concept of the golden ratio (or section), a proportion that occurs naturally as well as unconsciously in the artifice of humanity, was first applied as an analytical tool to Bartók's music in the 1950s by Hungarian theorist Ernö Lendvai. By definition, if two parts of differing size within a whole section or composition are related so that part A is to part B as part B is to the whole, the resulting ratio of the parts would be the golden section, or approximately .618. In the third movement, the "turn" at measure 49 alluded to above should fall around that ratio: based on Bartok's own approximations of duration, the golden ratio occurs at the 4:04 mark, around measure 54, *quasi a tempo*, ♩ = ca. 80. How close to the "turn" does this fall? The *Allegretto* immediately following (measure 55) falls halfway between the beginning of section E and the return of section D in the arch form (see table above). Does this reinforce the climax's being a few seconds later than the "turn"? The issue may

<hr />

5. The Fibonacci series comprises an infinite set of integers "of which the first two terms are 1 and 1 and each succeeding term is the sum of the two immediately preceding" ("Fibonacci number," *Merriam-Webster's Collegiate Dictionary*, 11th ed. Springfield, MA: Merriam-Webster, 2003).

seem purely theoretical and overly analytical; but there seems to be a legitimate connection to the listening experience: the piece should simply "feel right," with the climactic structural moment coming at the place represented by the golden ratio. This analytical concept has been applied to music as far back as the Renaissance and beyond, not without controversy.[6]

FILM MUSIC

Film music was a new genre altogether in the 20th century. Although motion pictures were invented in 1891 by Thomas Edison, they did not begin to feature sound until 1927. Dialogue in silent movies was limited to what could be displayed in writing on the screen, with live music provided in the theater by an organist, pianist, small instrumental ensemble, or even (for especially important showings) an orchestra. Published anthologies from the early decades of the 20th century provided these musicians with a series of musical excerpts tied to general moods; much of the music is drawn from the classical repertory, particularly Beethoven, Liszt, and Wagner. With the advent of talkies, however, recorded music could be incorporated directly into the film itself, and producers soon discovered it was cheaper and more effective to commission music that would correspond precisely to the events and emotions being portrayed on the screen than to provide live music for every showing.

The challenge of writing for film was similar to that of writing for opera, with the key difference that composers were almost always asked to write music to fit a scene that had already been shot and whose timing was thus fixed. But by the middle of the 1930s a number of highly skilled composers were taking on this challenge. Among the more prominent who ventured into the world of cinema were the English composers Ralph Vaughan Williams, William Walton, and Benjamin Britten; the Frenchmen Darius Milhaud and Georges Auric; and the Americans Bernard Herrmann (1911–1975), Elmer Bernstein (1922–2004), Henry Mancini (1924–1994), and John Williams (b. 1932). From the 1930s onward, émigré composers from central and eastern Europe were particularly successful in this field—in fact, some of the most seemingly American films were set to music by artists who had spent relatively little time in the United States. The music for the Civil War epic *Gone with the Wind* (1939), for example, is by the Austrian Max Steiner (1888–1971); Russian-born Dimitri Tiomkin (1899–1979) created the score for one of the most famous of all Westerns, *High Noon* (1952). Erich Wolfgang Korngold (1897–1957), a brilliant child prodigy and a composer of symphonies and operas in his native Vienna, spent much of his life after 1934 in Hollywood, where he produced the music for such films as *The Adventures of Robin Hood* (1938) and *The Sea Hawk* (1940). Arnold Schoenberg even composed an *Accompaniment to a Cinematographic Scene* for orchestra (1929–1930), which has yet to have a film made for it.

Film music also provided the basis for a number of larger, independent works: Ralph Vaughan Williams reworked his music from the film *Scott of the Antarctic* (1948) into his Seventh Symphony (*Sinfonia antarctica*); Benjamin Britten originally wrote the music that would become *The Young Person's Guide to the Orchestra* for an instructional film entitled *The Instruments of the Orchestra* (1945); and Sergei Prokofiev's cantata *Alexander Nevsky* uses music from the original film of that name (1938).

The film *Alexander Nevsky*, directed by Sergei Eisenstein, is based on the true story of Grand Duke Alexander of Novgorod, who defeated the Swedes on the River

CD14, Track 8
PROKOFIEV
Alexander Nevsky
Score Anthology II/168

---

6. For a more detailed explanation of the Golden Section and Bartók's use of it, see Larry J. Solomon, *Symmetry as a Compositional Determinant*, chapter 7, "Analysis of Works with Intensive Applications," 1993, revised 2002; online at http://solomonsmusic.net/diss7.htm. Accessed April 16, 2008.

Alexander Nevsky. Prokofiev's music for Sergei Eisenstein's 1938 film *Alexander Nevsky* includes an extended number accompanying the central battle between the Russian troops and the invading Teutonic Knights. At the climax of this 13th-century battle, fought on a frozen lake, the icy surface opens and swallows the invaders. The film reflects the growing tensions of the late 1930s between the Soviet Union and Germany. With the Hitler-Stalin Non-Aggression Pact of 1939, Stalin ordered that the film be shelved; when Germany invaded the Soviet Union in 1940, he ordered the film to be rereleased to rouse popular support against this invasion from the west.

Source: Corbis/Bettmann

ALEXANDER NEVSKY Directed by Sergei Eisenstein
Produced by Mosfilm, Moscow, U.S.S.R.
Distributed by Amkino Corp.   printed in U.S.A.

Neva (hence "Nevsky" is his popular name) in the year 1240 and went on to repel an army of Teutonic knights in 1242 in a battle that took place on the frozen surface of Lake Chudskoye. In the film's climactic scene, the ice breaks and swallows the invaders. In 1939, Prokofiev turned his brilliant score for this movie into a cantata for mezzo-soprano, chorus, and large orchestra. The rousing fourth movement of this work ("Arise, People of Russia") represents the hopes of those people before the battle. Like much of the rest of the score, it integrates folksong-like melodies (of Prokofiev's own invention) with a harmonic idiom that is essentially triadic. The occasional modal and chromatic inflections are extremely limited, for this was music written to appeal to mass audiences and their spirit of patriotism. This kind of writing was actively promoted by Soviet authorities as **socialist realism,** a readily accessible style that evokes the music of the people in an overwhelmingly optimistic tone (see Primary Evidence: Socialist Realism)

The Soviet government was quick to recognize the potential of film and film music to galvanize patriotic fervor. The state itself financed Eisenstein's *Alexander Nevsky* in the late 1930s at a time when German invasion appeared imminent: the film's plot is deeply nationalistic and transparently anti-German. Soldiers of the Red Army were actually used as extras in the movie. But after signing the Non-Aggression Pact with Hitler in 1939 (the same agreement whose secret appendix also spelled out the later dismemberment of Poland by both Germany and the Soviet Union), Stalin had the film removed from circulation, only to have it rushed back into theaters after Germany's surprise invasion of the Soviet Union in June 1941. The film's powerful images were made all the more evocative by Prokofiev's stirring score.

Since 1945, two other approaches have changed the way in which some musical soundtracks are put together. The perceived need for a "hit" song had become an obsession with the marketing departments of film producers by the 1960s. A dispute between Bernard Herrmann and Alfred Hitchcock over this and others issues in the film *Torn Curtain* (1966) led to the end of a very successful partnership. Most contemporary film soundtracks consist of a potpourri of songs in the latest popular styles.

PRIMARY EVIDENCE   Socialist Realism

The leadership of the Soviet Union worked for decades to encourage composers to write in a style accessible to a wide audience. Socialist realism involved writing in a fundamentally tonal idiom, using folk song or folk-song-like melodies whenever possible and employing programmatic music favorable to the ideals of communism. Conversely, the authorities discouraged what they called "formalism"—abstract, nonprogrammatic music, particularly in an atonal or serial idiom—on the grounds that these techniques were not rooted in the arts of the people. In the pronouncement here, Tikhon Khrennikov (1913–2007), a prominent Russian composer who served as musical adviser to the Red Army during World War II and was secretary general of the Union of Soviet Composers during the late 1940s and early 1950s, denounces the "decadent" tendencies of Western music. Khrennikov reserves special scorn for his own countrymen who have turned away from writing music for "the people" in favor of a more intellectual style.

———◆———

It was established that repeated directives of the Party on the problems of art were not carried out by the majority of Soviet composers. All the conversations about "reconstruction," about switching of composers to folkways, to realism, remained empty declarations. Almost all composers who worked in the field of large forms kept aloof from the people, and did not enjoy popularity with the broad audiences. The people knew only songs, marches and film music, but remained indifferent towards most symphonic and chamber music. . . .

The Central Committee of the All-Union Communist Party (Bolsheviks) points out in its Resolution that formalistic distortions and anti-democratic tendencies have found their fullest expression in the works of such composers as Shostakovich, Prokofiev, Khachaturian, Popov, Miaskovsky, Shebalin, and others. In the music of these composers we witness a revival of anti-realistic decadent influences calculated to destroy the principles of classical music. These tendencies are peculiar to the bourgeois movement of the era of imperialism: the rejection of melodiousness in music, neglect of vocal forms, infatuation with rhythmic and orchestral effects, the piling-up of noisy ear-splitting harmonies, intentional illogicality and unemotionality of music. All these tendencies lead in actual fact to the liquidation of music as one of the strongest expressions of human feelings and thoughts. . . .

When occasionally [these composers] turned toward folk melodies they arranged them in an overcomplex decadent manner alien to folk art. . . .

All these creative faults are typical expressions of formalism.

Formalism is a revelation of emptiness and lack of ideas in art. The rejection of ideas in art leads to the preachment of "art for art's sake," to a cult of "pure" form, a cult of technical devices as a goal in itself, a hypertrophy of certain elements of the musical speech at the price of a loss of integrity and harmoniousness of art.

Source: Tikhon Khrennikov, quoted in Nicolas Slonimsky, *Music Since 1900*, 4th ed. Macmillan Reference U.S.A., © 1971. Reprinted by permission of The Gale Group.

The other was the introduction of electronic synthesis, which was seen not only as an appropriate medium for the newly popular genre of post-atomic outer space film—for example, MGM's *Forbidden Planet* (1956), discussed in Chapter 23)—but also as an expense-saving method of concocting scores. By 1968 and Stanley Kubrick's *2001: A Space Odyssey*, the taste for "far-out sounds" exhausted itself as gimmickry, and fully orchestrated European music of the previous 150 years was once again the model.

BALLET

Ballet enjoyed two "golden ages" in the 20th century. The first came in Paris in the years before World War I through the work of Sergei Diaghilev's Ballets Russes (see Chapter 20) and the American Isadora Duncan (1877–1927), another pioneer of modern dance. The second took place in the middle of the century in New York City through the work of choreographers like the émigré George Balanchine (1904–1983), who had choreographed for Serge Diaghilev (see Chapter 20); Martha Graham

CD14, Track 9

TRADITIONAL
Bonaparte's Retreat
Score Anthology II/169a

CD14, Track 10

COPLAND
Hoe-down
Score Anthology II/169b

(1893–1991) and Agnes de Mille (1909–1993), both of whom worked with Aaron Copland; Merce Cunningham (b. 1919), who danced for Graham and then collaborated for many decades with John Cage; and Jerome Robbins (1918–1998), who choreographed the original stage and film versions of Leonard Bernstein's *West Side Story* (see later) and who worked alongside Balanchine in the New York City Ballet.

Copland's first performed ballet, *Billy the Kid*, was premiered in 1938 by Ballet Caravan (one of Balanchine's first American companies) to choreography by Eugene Loring. Its tragic Western theme is reinforced by Copland's use of several folk songs in the score, and his open-fifth chords and wide spacing of timbres and orchestral voices became the signatures for his most "accessible" style. His next "American" ballet, *Rodeo*, was commissioned and danced by Agnes de Mille and the Ballet Russe de Monte Carlo in 1942. The scenario is far more lighthearted than its predecessor: a cowgirl refuses to "dress like a girl" simply to gain the attention of a champion wrangler; when a more traditional rancher's daughter seems to be winning the young man's heart, the cowgirl shows up in a dress for the square dance finale, "Hoe-down," and gets the guy. (The discomfort of the cowgirl with traditional gender roles was said to be autobiographical for de Mille.)

De Mille choreographed the entire ballet before Copland had written a note, and requested that the composer incorporate traditional tunes into the score. In the case of "Hoe-down," Copland turned to an anthology of American folk music edited by Alan and John Lomax called *Our Singing Country* (1941). This collection included a fiddle tune, "Bonaparte's Retreat" (or simply "Bonyparte"), transcribed by Ruth Crawford Seeger (see Chapter 23) from a recorded performance by "Fiddler Bill" Stepp in eastern Kentucky in 1937. Copland makes the melody his own, thanks to colorful elements such as the "tuning up" at the beginning, the tension between conjunct and disjunct melodic lines, Stravinsky-like accents applied to the principal tune in the violins (which sound like "fiddles" in cross-tuning), and the beautiful depiction of (temporary) technological breakdown after measure 207. When the next opportunity for a ballet came along, Copland wrote a *Ballet for Martha*, which Graham fit to her own American style and theme as *Appalachian Spring* (1944).

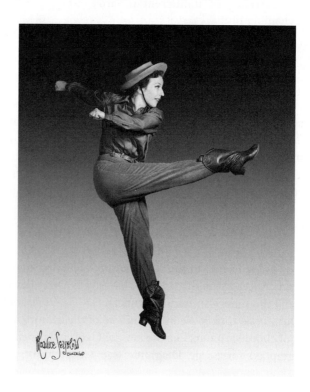

The American dancer Agnes de Mille in the role of the Cowgirl in the premiere of Copland's *Rodeo* (1942). De Mille (1905–93) was also the choreographer for this production, which blended modern ballet with square dancing. She later choreographed Broadway musicals, including *Oklahoma!* (1943), *Carousel* (1945), *Brigadoon* (1947), *Gentlemen Prefer Blondes* (1949), and *Paint Your Wagon* (1951). Together with her friend Martha Graham, de Mille is widely regarded as one of the most influential figures in 20th-century American ballet.

Source: © 2008. Ronald Seymour, Inc. Photo: Maurice Seymour

COMPOSER PROFILE   Aaron Copland *(1900–1990)*

Copland belonged to the generation of American composers that came of age in the 1920s and 1930s, a generation consumed with the idea of American music. Like so many of his contemporary colleagues, he was trained in the European tradition, studying composition with Nadia Boulanger in Paris and analyzing, under her guidance, a wide range of music by such composers as Monteverdi, Bach, Mahler, and Stravinsky. Some of Copland's music is extremely demanding for listeners and performers alike. Examples include the *Piano Variations* (1930), the freely serial Piano Quartet (1950), and the *Piano Fantasy* (1957). Yet he never lost what might be called a populist touch, more evident in such works as *Appalachian Spring, Billy the Kid, Rodeo, Lincoln Portrait*, and *Fanfare for the Common Man*. He also wrote music for a number of Hollywood films, including *Our Town* and *Of Mice and Men*. The appeal of Copland's music transcends generations. The filmmaker Spike Lee used several of his works in the soundtrack to *He Got Game* (1998). "When I listen to Copland's music," Lee explained, "I hear America, and basketball is America. It's like he wrote the score for this film."[7]

Over the last 40 years of his life, Copland was showered with a string of honors and awards: a Pulitzer Prize for *Appalachian Spring*, an Oscar for the score of the movie *The Heiress* (1950), the Presidential Medal of Freedom (1964), and a long series of honorary degrees from American universities. His unwillingness to "name names" of supposed Communists at the McCarthy hearings in 1953 led to personal difficulties for a number of years, but his reputation was fully restored by the 1960s.[8]

In addition to his work as a composer, Copland was also a superb lecturer and writer on music. His *What to Listen for in Music* remains a model of its kind, and his many essays for the journal *Modern Music* from the 1920s and 1930s have admirably withstood the test of time.

PRINCIPAL WORKS

BALLETS AND OTHER ORCHESTRAL WORKS   Copland's best known works are his ballets, particularly *Billy the Kid*

(1938, for the choreographer Lincoln Kirstein), *Rodeo* (1942, for Agnes de Mille), and *Appalachian Spring* (1944, for Martha Graham). His *Lincoln Portrait* (1942), for narrator and orchestra, is also frequently performed, as is his *Fanfare for the Common Man* (1942).

SONGS   The *Twelve Poems of Emily Dickinson* (1950) are widely admired. The *Old American Songs* (1950, 1952) are arrangements of American folk songs and as such another manifestation of Copland's populist side.

CHAMBER MUSIC   *Vitebsk* (1929), for piano trio, is a "Study on a Jewish Theme." The Piano Quartet (1950) and Nonet for Strings (1960) reflect the more demanding aspects of Copland's musical personality, as do the *Piano Variations* of 1930.

For a photo of Copland, see p. 577.

KEY DATES IN THE LIFE OF COPLAND

1900	Born November 14 in Brooklyn, New York.
1921–1924	Studies in Paris with Nadia Boulanger.
1924	Returns to New York and becomes a leading member of what was known as the "New Music" scene.
1940	Becomes head of the composition department at the Berkshire Music Center at Tanglewood in Lenox, Massachusetts, a position he would hold every summer through 1965.
1951–1952	Delivers the Charles Eliot Norton lectures at Harvard, later published as *Music and Imagination*.
1960s	Tours, conducts, and lectures extensively throughout the United States and Europe.
1990	Dies December 2 in North Tarrytown, New York.

---

7. http://www.sonyclassical.com/music/60593.

8. Copland testified in Washington, DC, on May 26, 1953, before the U.S. Senate Permanent Subcommittee on Investigations of the Committee on Government Operations, chaired by Senator Joseph McCarthy (R-Wisconsin). For a transcript of this "executive session," go to www.overgrownpath.com/2004/08/aaron-coplands-mccarthy-hearing.html. Accessed on April 16, 2008.

CHAMBER MUSIC

Chamber music appealed to composers working in a broad variety of styles. The string quartet maintained its traditional status as the most prestigious of all chamber genres: Schoenberg, Webern, and Berg all wrote atonal and serial works for this medium; Bartók and Shostakovich produced an impressive body of quartets within an essentially tonal idiom.

CD14, Track 11
MESSIAEN
Quatuor pour la fin du temps
Score Anthology II/170

Other composers explored less conventional groupings of instruments, sometimes out of necessity. The French composer Olivier Messiaen (1908–1992) wrote his *Quatuor pour la fin du temps* ("Quartet for the End of Time") to be performed by fellow inmates in a prisoner-of-war camp in Germany during the early years of World War II; the only instruments at his disposal were a clarinet, a violin, a cello, and a rickety piano. Although many inmates interpreted its title as an allusion to the end of their time in prison, the composer himself insisted the true inspiration for the work came from Chapter 10 of the New Testament book of Revelation, in which an angel causes time to cease at the end of the world. Messiaen compared the opening movement, "Liturgy of Crystal," to "the harmonious silence of the firmament." The **harmonics** in the cello help create a particularly light, ethereal timbre: by touching the string lightly wherever a lozenge-shaped note is indicated, the cellist creates a pitch—a harmonic overtone—that actually sounds two octaves higher than the notated pitch.

But the "End of Time" in the work's title is most directly evident in its organization of rhythm. The four voices operate on entirely different rhythmic levels: the violin and clarinet, which by the composer's own account reflect the songs of a nightingale and blackbird, respectively, are free, random, unpredictable. The cello and piano, in contrast, adhere to strict rhythmic and melodic patterns. The cello presents a 15-note melody eight and a half times over the course of the movement (Example 22–2). But because the melody begins before the downbeat and ends after it, these repetitions are rhythmically different with every iteration of the theme.

The rhythmic pattern of the melody is palindromic—the same forward as backward—or as Messiaen himself called it, **nonretrogradable rhythm.** This is not obvious at first because the note values begin in the middle of the rhythmic sequence: time, after all, has been going on before the piece begins. There are several ways to construct a palindromic sequence out of this line. If we count eighth-note values beginning six notes from the end of Example 22–2, for example, we find the following pattern, which is identical forward and backward:

1 1 3 1 1 4 4 3 4 4 1 1 3 1 1

Hearing such rhythms as palindromes seems far more difficult than apprehending the manipulations of a 12-tone row, especially a rhythmic pattern of this length; rhythm in music is always perceived as moving ahead (forward) in time. Messiaen establishes an overall pattern of repetition with this rhythm, in tandem with the repeating pitch content.

The piano's rhythm of 17 note values, although not palindromic, is also repeated many times. As in the case of the cello, the rhythmic pattern begins and ends in the middle of two different measures and thus shifts constantly in relation to the bar line. Thematically, the piano repeats a sequence of 29 chords throughout, but the thematic and rhythmic patterns do not coincide. This structure resembles that of the medieval isorhythm (see Chapter 3), in which a melodic pattern (*color*) is played against an independent rhythmic pattern (*talea*). Although Messiaen himself was well aware of

Example 22–2 Messiaen, *Quatuor pour la fin du temps*, first movement, cello line (sounding pitch), measures 2–8

Source: Olivier Messiaen, *Quatuor pour la fin du temps*. In Anthony Pople, *Messiaen: Quatuor pour la fin du temps* (Cambridge University Press, 1998), p. 21. Reprinted by permission of BMG Music Publishing Ltd./Durand.

Example 22–3 Messiaen, *Quatuor pour la fin du temps*, first movement, sequence of 29 chords in the piano part

Source: Olivier Messiaen, *Quatuor pour la fin du temps.* In Anthony Pople, *Messiaen: Quatuor pour la fin du temps* (Cambridge University Press, 1998), Ex. 1.3 p. 22. Reprinted with permission of Cambridge University Press.

isorhythm, he maintained that his more immediate sources were the rhythmic structures of certain Hindu modes.

This movement also reminds us just how remote a work can be removed from the framework of triadic harmony. Although many of the piano's 29 chords (see Example 22–3) incorporate triadic harmonies, they also have multiple additional nonharmonic tones. The inner voices of chords 9 through 12, for example, present a series of first-inversion harmonies on G♭ Major, G major, A♭ Major, and A Major, but the nonharmonic notes of the outer voices mask the sound of these triads. At the same time, the insistent F in the bass, which has been present since the very first chord, grounds the music around a semblance of a tonal center. Messiaen himself described the opening sonority as a "chord on the dominant"—in this case, of B♭ major, the tonality implied by the key signature—even though it does not function as such in the traditional sense.

The String Quartet no. 8 of the Russian composer Dmitri Shostakovich is also heavily autobiographical. "When I die," Shostakovich wrote to a friend, "it's hardly likely that someone will write a quartet dedicated to my memory. So I decided to write it myself." The work is saturated with a musical motif the composer himself identified as his musical monogram: the notes D-E♭-C-B, which in the German system of notation (see Chapter 16) spell D-S (or Es = E♭)-C-H (= B♮), shorthand for **D**mitri **Sch**ostakovich, the German transliteration of the composer's name. The piece as a whole is full of quotations from Shostakovich's operas, symphonies, and chamber works; it also includes snippets from Siegfried's funeral music in Wagner's *Götterdämmerung* and the first movement of Tchaikovsky's Sixth Symphony. The latter two are directly associated with the idea of death, as is the recurring *Dies irae* plainchant melody, the same tune used by Berlioz in the finale of his *Symphonie fantastique* (see Chapter 14).

Shostakovich dedicated his Eighth Quartet "to the memory of the victims of fascism and war"—that is, to the victims of the struggle against Nazi Germany in World War II—a sentiment wholly acceptable to Soviet authorities. But several of the composer's friends have since asserted the work was Shostakovich's "suicide note," that the composer planned to swallow an overdose of sleeping pills after finishing this work, so depressed was he at having been forced to join the Communist Party (and after being diagnosed with myelitis, an illness affecting the spinal cord). As is so often the case with Shostakovich, truth and fiction are difficult to separate. Eyewitness accounts of events in his life are not always reliable, many of them never having been committed

CD14, Track 12
SHOSTAKOVICH
String Quartet no. 8
Score Anthology II/171

Olivier Messiaen. A gifted performer as well as a composer, Messiaen served for more than 60 years as principal organist at a major Parisian church. He also found time to collect birdsongs from many parts of the world and incorporated some of them into his music, including his *Quatuor pour la fin du temps* (Anthology). "I have a passion for ornithology," Messiaen once declared. "Just as Bartók scoured Hungary for folk songs, so have I traveled for many years throughout the provinces of France transcribing the songs of the birds. It is an immense and endless labor. But it has given me the right to be a musician. What joy to hear a new melody, a new style, in a new landscape!"

Source: Haags Gemeentemuseum/ The Bridgeman Art Library, New York

to paper until after the composer's death. The music itself, however, clearly connects the images of Shostakovich (through the many quotations of his own music and of his musical monogram) and death (through the quotation of death-related music by other composers). In the final movement, the DSCH motif appears as a counterpoint to a quotation from the last scene of Shostakovich's opera *Lady Macbeth of the Mtsensk District* (1934, banned by the Soviet government) in which prisoners are being transported to Siberia. This could easily have been Shostakovich's own fate had he not agreed to join the Communist Party. Shostakovich used the ambiguity of the music as a shield for his own self-expression.

The third movement functions as a scherzo and assumes the form of a waltz, but it is a macabre kind of dance. The introduction begins with the DSCH theme in the first violin (D-E♭-C-B♮), which soon (measure 20) reenters as the main motive, now jarringly discordant with the simple G-minor accompaniment. Formally, the movement follows the standard scherzo-trio-scherzo pattern. It leads without a break into the finale.

OPERA AND MUSICAL THEATER

In the second half of the 20th century, although most opera houses relied principally on works of the past, a group of composers, including Benjamin Britten, Michael Tippett, Gian Carlo Menotti, Philip Glass, John Adams, Jack Beeson, and Harrison Birtwistle—produced new English-language works that attracted wide followings. Elsewhere, the works of Luigi Dallapiccola, Hans Werner Henze, Einojuhani Rautavaara, Alberto Ginastera, Aulis Sallinen, Krzysztof Penderecki, and Alfred Schnittke continued and expanded the range of topics and styles in opera. The revival of even earlier repertories, particularly the operas of Monteverdi and Handel, offered another kind of novelty to the public as well.

The most vital form of musical drama throughout the 20th century, however, was the Broadway musical, a genre that took its name from the New York City street on

COMPOSER PROFILE   Dmitri Shostakovich *(1906–1975)*

Shostakovich remains one of the great enigmas of 20th-century music. He labored for most of his life under the repressive regime of the Soviet Union and had to be extremely careful about what he said and wrote, both in words and in music. We are not even sure if he wrote the book that claims to be his memoir. The key question about *Testimony*, first published in the West in 1979 is the degree to which the composer differed with the communist regime. Like other citizens of the Soviet Union, he could not voice negative opinions openly without risking punishment, and this makes it difficult to distinguish between what he believed and what he was compelled to say. Shostakovich himself acknowledged the "validity" of Soviet attacks on his "decadence" and "formalism," for example, and dubbed his Fifth Symphony his "creative answer to justified criticism." But are we to take all this at face value? Historians continue to debate the point, often quite heatedly. Indeed, the furor over biography has lately tended to overshadow discussions of the music, most of which has yet to be discovered by the wider music-loving public.

Perhaps no other major composer of the 20th century was as indebted to Beethoven. Shostakovich was attracted to the same genres—symphony, sonata, concerto, quartet, opera—and much of his music follows the same emotional trajectory characteristic of much of Beethoven's music: struggle leading either to triumph or resignation. Shostakovich never abandoned tonality, yet his idiom is distinctly innovative for its time.

PRINCIPAL WORKS

ORCHESTRAL MUSIC The 15 symphonies are among the most impressive body of works of their kind by any 20th-century composer. They range from the heroic (nos. 5 and 7) to the resigned (nos. 13, 14, 15). The concertos (two each for piano, for violin, and for cello) are among Shostakovich's most popular compositions.

CHAMBER MUSIC The 15 quartets, written between 1938 and 1974, exhibit a remarkable range of styles, tones, structures, and instrumental techniques. They are becoming better known to audiences over time. The Piano Trio and Piano Quintet are already widely performed.

PIANO MUSIC The *24 Preludes and Fugues* are modeled in certain respects on Bach's *Well-Tempered Clavier* and deserve wider performance, as do the many miscellaneous works for solo piano, such as the Preludes, the two sonatas, and the *Aphorisms*.

OPERAS *Lady Macbeth of the Mtsensk District* (1934) drew the ire of Soviet authorities, not only because of its dissonant musical idiom, but also because it presented such dramatic themes as murder, suicide, and adultery, behaviors inconsistent with what the regime perceived to be the ideals of Soviet art. Shostakovich's earlier opera, *The Nose* (1930), reveals the composer's deep sense of the humorous and grotesque.

Dmitri Shostakovich and Aaron Copland. Shostakovich (left) and Copland meet at the Cultural and Scientific Conference for World Peace, held at the Waldorf-Astoria Hotel in New York City in March, 1949. This gathering of some 800 artists and scientists, known as the Waldorf Conference, sought to defuse the rapidly escalating tensions between the United States and the Soviet Union. In different ways, both Shostakovich and Copland were caught up in the politics of the Cold War. Shostakovich was allowed to travel to the United States for this conference with the understanding that he would deliver a speech condemning Western "warmongers." Just how much he believed personally in the content of this speech remains a matter of debate among scholars. Copland would later be compelled to testify before a Senate subcommittee headed by Senator Joseph McCarthy about his activities in organizations sympathetic to the political left and about his presence at events like the Waldorf Conference.

Source: Frank Driggs Collection

KEY DATES IN THE LIFE OF SHOSTAKOVICH

1906	Born September 25 in St. Petersburg (Russia).
1919	Enters the conservatory in his native city and studies piano and composition.
1926	Achieves international reputation with the premiere of his First Symphony.
1936	The opera *Lady Macbeth of the Mtsensk District* elicits a furious assault from Soviet authorities, who condemn the work as decadent, a "bedlam of noise." Rehabilitates himself with Soviet authorities with his Fifth Symphony and later (1942) with his Seventh Symphony, which supposedly depicts the defeat of the German army at the hands of the Soviets.
1949	Serves as a delegate to the Cultural and Scientific Congress for World Peace, in New York, but the U.S. State Department forces the entire Soviet delegation to leave the country prematurely.
1957	Elected as a secretary of the Union of Soviet Composers.
1959	Tours the United States and attends the world premiere of his Cello Concerto in Philadelphia.
1962	Pressured by the Soviet government to alter the text of his Symphony no. 13, commemorating the death of Jews in Kiev during World War II.
1966	Awarded two of the Soviet Union's highest honors, the Hero of Socialist Labor and the Order of Lenin.
1975	Dies August 9 in Moscow.

which many of the most prominent musical theaters are located. A direct descendant of the singspiel or operetta—a play with songs—the Broadway musical is a commercial venture that requires considerable capital. A hit show can bring handsome returns to investors, driving theaters to produce musicals that can attract audiences willing to pay high prices for good seats. Some shows have had runs that would be the envy of any opera: Andrew Lloyd Webber's *Cats* ran for some 7,485 performances between 1982 and 2000; revivals of earlier musicals like Richard Rodgers's *Oklahoma!* and Jerome Kern's *Show Boat* testify to the continuing appeal of older repertory.

The plots of many early musicals were no more than a framework for a **revue,** a successor to music hall and vaudeville performances in which a potpourri of acts followed in quick succession; song and dance were the dominant components of these shows. Although theatrical presentations continued to segregate performers and audiences, African Americans at the turn of the 20th century began to produce musical comedies on Broadway that drew white audiences (and on occasion integrated casts). Many of the offensive stereotyped images perpetrated by the minstrel shows were retained, but African-American musical and dance idioms were combined with more standard Broadway fare to produce a successful synthesis. Many stars emerged from these shows, including Ernest Hogan, Will Marion Cook, Bob Cole, George Walker, and Bert Williams (who later starred in *Ziegfeld's Follies*). After a hiatus of African-American shows in the 1910s, the genre was revived in *Shuffle Along* (1921, by Sissle and Blake, featuring Josephine Baker, Paul Robeson, and "I'm Just Wild about Harry"); *Blackbirds of 1928* (by Fields and McHugh, featuring Adelaide Hall, Bill "Bojangles" Robinson," and "I Can't Give You Anything but Love"), and *Hot Chocolates* (1929), a collaboration between Andy Razaf, Harry Brooks, and Thomas "Fats" Waller (1904–1943), a brilliant songwriter, pianist, and entertainer who played an jazz-inflected style of ragtime known as "stride piano." (Ragtime and jazz are discussed in Chapter 24.)

Hot Chocolates, which started life as a Harlem nightclub revue, is now best known for the song "Ain't Misbehavin'," later the eponymous title of a successful Broadway revue of Waller songs in 1978. Among the original cast of *Hot Chocolates* were the multitalented Cab Calloway and the trumpeter and bandleader Louis Armstrong (1901–1971). Although Calloway sang "Ain't Misbehavin'" in the show, Armstrong made his own recording with his "orchestra" (11 players) the same year the show opened. In Armstrong's version, the song (in the standard AABA song form) is played through three times; first as an ensemble, then sung by Armstrong in the improvisational style he was famous for, then as a platform for an skillful Armstrong solo. At one point he unexpectedly quotes a famous melody for humorous effect; this technique recalls similar references to the "Tristan chord" in works by Berg (see Chapter 21) and Debussy (see Chapter 24).

Many of the most successful musicals of the 20th century, like their operatic counterparts in the 19th, combined entertainment with social commentary. Here are some outstanding examples:

- *South Pacific* (1948, music by Richard Rodgers, lyrics by Oscar Hammerstein II), which addresses interracial love against the backdrop of World War II.

- *My Fair Lady* (1956, music by Frederick Loewe, lyrics by Alan Jay Lerner), based on George Bernard Shaw's play *Pygmalion*, which deals with class warfare as waged through the weapon of language.

- *Miss Saigon* (1989, music by Claude-Michel Schönberg, lyrics by Richard Maltby, Jr., and Alain Boublil), based loosely on Puccini's *Madame Butterfly*, which considers the aftermath of the American military involvement in Vietnam.

- *Rent* (1996, music and lyrics by Jonathan Larson), a reinterpretation of Puccini's *La Bohème* that confronts the problem of AIDS.

Leonard Bernstein's *West Side Story* (1957) focuses on the problem of gang warfare between Puerto Ricans (the Sharks) and whites (the Jets) in New York City. The libretto, by Stephen Sondheim (who would go on to compose many hit musicals of his own), was unusually gritty and realistic by the standards of its time. It draws liberally on Shakespeare's *Romeo and Juliet*, featuring a pair of lovers from rival groups and ending in the death of one of them.

The *Quintet* is an ensemble very much in the tradition of *Bella figlia dell'amore* from Act III of Verdi's *Rigoletto* (see Chapter 17). Dramatically, both revolve around the feeling of anticipation: the Sharks and Jets await their climactic conflict, while the sultry Anita knows she will get "her kicks" that night ("He'll walk in hot and tired, so what? Don't matter if he's tired, as long as he's hot.");[9] the music of the two gangs and Anita are closely related thematically. At the same time, the two lovers, Tony and Maria, await their meeting ("Tonight, tonight won't be just any night."). The number builds gradually and becomes increasingly contrapuntal as it progresses, with a lyrical love duet between Tony and Maria that unfolds above the animosity of the rival choruses. Bernstein uses a jazzlike orchestration, a rapid alternation of duple and triple meters, and even *Sprechstimme* at one point to give the music a decidedly modern sound. But the overall shape of the movement—contrasting emotions expressed simultaneously—owes much to the traditions of 19th-century opera.

CD14, Track 13
WALLER
Ain't Misbehavin'
Score Anthology II/172

CD14, Track 14
BERNSTEIN
West Side Story
Score Anthology II/173

---

9. Quotation from lyrics, "Tonight" from *West Side Story*. Music by Leonard Bernstein, Lyrics by Stephen Sondheim. Copyright © 1956, 1957, 1958, 1959 by Amberson Holdings LLC and Stephen Sondheim. Copyright Renewed. Leonard Bernstein Music Publishing Company LLC, Publisher. Boosey & Hawkes, Inc., Sole Agent. Reprinted by permission.

FOCUS	Notable Musicals of the 20th Century

1927	*Show Boat* (Jerome Kern)	1966	*Cabaret* (John Kander)
1931	*Of Thee I Sing* (George Gershwin)	1968	*Hair* (Galt MacDermott)
1934	*Anything Goes* (Cole Porter)	1971	*Jesus Christ Superstar* (Andrew Lloyd Webber)
1943	*Oklahoma!* (Richard Rodgers)	1975	*A Chorus Line* (Marvin Hamlisch)
1945	*Carousel* (Richard Rodgers)	1976	*Annie* (Charles Strouse)
1946	*Annie Get Your Gun* (Irving Berlin)	1979	*Sweeney Todd* (Stephen Sondheim)
1948	*Kiss Me Kate* (Cole Porter)	1979	*Evita* (Andrew Lloyd Webber)
1948	*South Pacific* (Richard Rodgers)	1982	*Cats* (Andrew Lloyd Webber)
1950	*Guys and Dolls* (Frank Loesser)	1987	*Les Misérables* (Claude-Michel Schönberg)
1951	*The King and I* (Richard Rodgers)	1988	*Phantom of the Opera* (Andrew Lloyd Webber)
1955	*My Fair Lady* (Frederick Loewe)		
1957	*West Side Story* (Leonard Bernstein)	1991	*Miss Saigon* (Claude-Michel Schönberg)
1957	*The Music Man* (Meredith Willson)	1996	*Rent* (Jonathan Larson)
1959	*The Sound of Music* (Richard Rodgers)	2001	*The Producers* (Mel Brooks and Glen Kelly)
1960	*The Fantasticks* (Harvey Schmidt)	2003	*Avenue Q* (Robert Lopez and Jeff Marx)
1964	*Hello, Dolly!* (Jerry Herman)	2003	*Wicked* (Stephen Schwartz)
1964	*Fiddler on the Roof* (Jerry Bock)	2005	*The 25th Annual Putnam County Spelling Bee* (William Finn)
1965	*Man of La Mancha* (Mitch Leigh)		

THE ORATORIO

Traditionally scored for vocal soloists, chorus, and orchestra, the oratorio remained the largest of all vocal genres outside of opera throughout the 20th century; Schoenberg (*Gurrelieder*, 1901–1911), Debussy (*Le Martyre de Saint Sébastien*, 1911), and Stravinsky (*Oedipus Rex*, 1927) all contributed to the genre.

It was in England, however, that composers cultivated the oratorio with greatest intensity. This was largely due to the local tradition of civic choral societies, amateur groups that had welcomed new repertory since the enormous successes of Mendelssohn's *Elijah* and *St. Paul* in Victorian England. By the turn of the 20th century, Edward Elgar (1857–1934) was the most important English contributor to the oratorio and related genres; *The Dream of Gerontius* (1899–1900) is generally regarded as his choral masterpiece. William Walton (1902–1983), a composer of orchestral and film music, won widespread acclaim for *Belshazzar's Feast* (1931), an oratorio on an Old Testament subject that used an advanced chromatic idiom with modal inflections. Michael Tippett (1905–1998), a leftist and pacifist who served time in prison as a conscientious objector during World War II, crafted his own libretto to *A Child of Our Time* (1939–1941), a work of protest inspired by events in Europe. Like a Baroque oratorio, *A Child of Our Time* is built on recitatives (the Narrator), arias and duets, and choruses; but Tippett set five African-American spirituals to replace the chorales used by Bach used as the framework in his Passions.

The culmination of the 20th-century English oratorio, is the *War Requiem* by Benjamin Britten (1913–1976), premiered in 1962 at the reconsecration of Coventry Cathedral, which had been bombed in 1940. A versatile and prolific composer in most genres, Britten's vocal writing in English was considered by many the best since Purcell;

CD14, Track 15

BRITTEN
War Requiem
Score Anthology II/580

he had already established that reputation with operas (*Peter Grimes, Billy Budd, Turn of the Screw*), short dramatic works (*Noye's Fludde, Curlew River*), works for young performers (*A Ceremony of Carols, Rejoice in the Lamb, The Little Sweep, Missa Brevis*), song cycles, and choral works.

In addition to setting the Latin text for the Requiem, Britten created a telling context by adding several poems by Wilfred Owen (1893–1918), a soldier who had led a rifle company in France and was killed just before the Armistice that ended World War I. Owen's remarkably modern and darkly ironic poems proved to be the perfect foil for the ancient Latin text. To intensify the sense of postwar disorientation, Britten scored the work for three separate groups: a full orchestra with chorus and solo soprano, a chamber ensemble accompanying a solo tenor and bass, and a portative organ–led boys' choir. The three groups are separated spatially: in one performance, the orchestral group took center stage, the chamber ensemble stood on the right apron, and the boys' choir sang from the first tier, above and behind the audience, projecting an eerie, ill-defined sound.

There are precedents for Britten's divided forces: the massive antiphonal choirs of brass for the "Tuba mirum" section of the Dies Irae in Hector Berlioz's *Grande messe des morts* (1837), or the antiphonal works written for San Marco in Venice during the late Renaissance (see Chapter 6). However, Britten was not seeking orchestral or antiphonal effects for their own sake. The power of the *War Requiem* resides in the tripartite divide between three groups, which emphasizes the universality and particularity of Owen's message: on the title page, Britten quotes from a preface the poet wrote to a collection he did not live to see in print: "My subject is War, and the pity of War/The Poetry is in the pity . . . /All a poet can do today is warn."

The closing "Libera me" is interrupted by the final Owen setting ("It seemed that out of battle I escaped . . ."), in which two soldiers meet "down some profound dull tunnel." "Strange friend," one addresses the other, "here is no cause to mourn." Toward the end of the poem, they realize "I am the enemy you killed, my friend." The two male soloists conclude singing "Let us sleep now . . ." to each other as a lullaby, while the chorus, boys' choir, organ, soprano soloist, and full orchestra gradually reenter for the first and only tutti in the entire oratorio ("In paradisum"). The effect is spellbinding, and the bells take up the F♯/C♮ tritone with which the work began (and which has dominated much of the harmony throughout). The boys' choir ("Amen, amen") seems to resolve the dissonance to the open fifth F♯/C♯, but then shifts to an F Major triad, a surprising but highly effective close to one of the 20th century's great choral works.

CONCLUSION

The tonal idiom thrived throughout the whole of the 20th century in every genre of music, particularly the symphony and symphonic poem, the new genre of film music, ballet, song, and musical theater. Some composers were content to remain within the idiom of extended chromaticism inherited from the late 19th century. Others expanded the limits of tonality beyond triadic harmonies and the diatonic scale. Yet all these composers remained committed to the principle of writing works with a tonal center of some kind. Tonal and atonal music thus coexisted in much the same way that the *prima prattica* and *seconda prattica* had flourished side by side in the 17th century.

The end of World War II marked a decisive turning point not only in world history but in music as well. The war had been a catastrophic experience: the majority of the 50 million killed in the conflict were civilians and included the estimated 6 million Jewish victims of the Nazi Holocaust. (The total population systematically murdered in Europe by the Axis powers was between 9 million and 11 million persons.) The atomic bombs dropped on Japan in 1945 opened an era in which humans became capable of destroying virtually all life on earth. People everywhere sought to turn away from these horrors and make a fresh start; artists in all fields were no exception. In the light of the recent past, the New became all the more appealing, setting off what amounted to a second, postwar wave of modernism.

THE QUEST FOR INNOVATION

One stylistic response involved dividing large ensembles into individual parts, so that the sonority could shift from one kind of mass (saturation) to another (unison). Iannis Xenakis (1922–2001), a Greek composer trained as an architect with Le Corbusier, helped Varèse with the latter's *Poème électronique*, written for the Philips Pavilion at the 1958 Brussels World's Fair (see Chapter 20). In 1953–1954, Xenakis composed *Metastasis* ("Dialectical Transformations"), premiered a year after its completion. Composed for 61 *obbligato* instruments (that is, without doubling), the work applies Einstein's theory of relativity, the Fibonacci number series (as Bartók had in the *Music for Strings, Percussion, and Celesta*; see Chapter 22); and stochastic theory, which evaluates the role of probability in a state of flux. For Xenakis, this symbolized the overhead flight of bullets during his wartime activities: the mass of sound remained constant, no matter when an individual gun was fired. Yet the score is absolutely precise. In keeping with Xenakis's theory of **meta-art** (the mathematical application of artistic expression in any medium), the hyperbolic results of his calculations for *Metastasis* were also applied to the architecture of the Philips Pavilion.

The Polish composer Krzysztof Penderecki (b. 1933) used a more intuitive approach to the *obbligato* texture en masse in his *Threnody for the Victims of Hiroshima* (1960). Using conventional contrapuntal techniques, Penderecki transforms this material with unique combinations of sounds from an orchestra consisting of 52 stringed instruments (24 violins, 10 violas, 10 cellos, 8 double basses). At times the string players are asked to create sharp, percussive sounds by snapping strings against the fingerboard; at other times they strike the body of the instrument with the finger-tips. At times Penderecki's score grants considerable freedom to the performers. At several points, individual players are to play "the highest note possible"; in other passages he directs different groups of instruments to play with vibrato at different rates of speed, indicated only generally by the size of the wavy line in the score; the precise speed is left up to individual players. On still other occasions, individual performers may choose from a group of four different notational sequences and perform the chosen group "as rapidly as possible." There are neither meter indications nor bar lines: durations are indicated by timings that run underneath the bottom of each system of the score (the score was initially named *8′ 37″*).

Other elements of the score, however, are extremely precise. Penderecki uses **microtones**—intervals smaller than a half step in the diatonic scale—at many points in the score. Western musicians had long been aware of microtones, but principally as a theoretical idea (see Prologue: Antiquity). It was not until the 20th century that composers like Ives, Bartók, Berg, Copland, and Ligeti began to use microtones in their works. Penderecki's *Threnody* explores these possibilities to an unprecedented degree, concluding with a massive quarter-tone cluster of tones and microtones spanning two octaves and played by all 52 instruments.

Structurally, *Threnody* offers a mixture of precision and imprecision. Like Varèse's *Ionisation* (see Chapter 20), the work is organized around sonorities, dynamics, and textures rather than themes or key areas. Although it resists ready-made formal analysis, *Threnody*'s ever-changing surface suggests a division into five large sections:

1. measures 1–5   High register, varying vibrato
2. measures 6–9   Pizzicato and bowed passages played on the tailpiece
3. measures 10–25   Expanding and contracting tone clusters
4. measures 26–62   Percussive, pointilistic sounds, with much tremolo
5. measures 63–end   Gradual return of tone clusters

After he heard the first performances of *this work*, Penderecki felt that, despite the abstract origins of its composition, the piece had proved emotionally powerful in realization. He decided to dedicate the work to the victims of Hiroshima. In 1964, he wrote, "Let the *Threnody* express my firm belief that the sacrifice of Hiroshima will never be forgotten and lost."[1] He was by no means the first to change his mind about a work's title (recall the dedication to Napoleon on the title page of Beethoven's Symphony no. 3 in Chapter 15).

COMBINATORIALITY

In the late 1920s, Arnold Schoenberg had discovered that certain 12-tone rows embody special features. He pointed out that a limited number of rows were **combinatorial**. A row is said to be combinatorial if one of its hexachords—its first six or last six notes, commonly referred to as hexachords A and B—can be combined with one of the hexachords of an inverted, retrograde, or retrograde inverted form of the same row without producing any duplication of pitches.

CD14, Track 16
PENDERECKI
Threnody for the Victims of Hiroshima
Score Anthology II/175

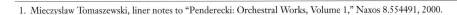

1. Mieczyslaw Tomaszewski, liner notes to "Penderecki: Orchestral Works, Volume 1," Naxos 8.554491, 2000.

Example 23-1 Row forms used in Babbitt's *Three Compositions for Piano*, no. 1

Source: © Copyright 1957 by Boelke Bomart, Inc. Used by permission.

CD15, Track 2
BABBITT
Three Compositions for Piano
Score Anthology II/177

The row for the first of Milton Babbitt's *Three Compositions for Piano* (1947) illustrates this property (see Example 23–1). Here, P-0 is combinatorial with R-6. In other words, hexachord A of P-0 combines with hexachord B of R-6 to produce all 12 pitches. The order of the pitches is different than in P-0, but combinatoriality is concerned only with the content of the individual (and combined) hexachords, not the actual sequence of the pitches. The complementary hexachords of the two forms (hexachord B of P-0 and hexachord A of R-6) are also combinatorial.

Schoenberg first developed the use of combinatorial rows in his *Variations for Orchestra*, op. 31 (1928), and in his *Piano Pieces*, op. 33a (1929). Combinatoriality eventually became his preferred method of 12-tone composition, but Berg and Webern never really embraced the technique.

Schoenberg's students and followers in the United States took up the idea with special fervor in the years after World War II. Combinatoriality allowed these composers to align different set forms to sound at the same time without risking simultaneous or nearly simultaneous iterations of the same pitch class. By exploiting the combinatorial properties of this row, Babbitt and others were able to create multiple statements of the 12-tone row not only horizontally (in individual voices) but also vertically through the alignment of two different forms of the row sounding simultaneously. In the opening measures of the *Three Compositions for Piano*, no. 1, for example, we find the basic row both horizontally and vertically:

■ Horizontally—the left hand in measures 1–2 presents P-0 in its entirety; the right hand presents P-6 in its entirety.

■ Vertically—taking both voices together, all 12 pitches appear in measure 1; all 12 appear again in measure 2, in measure 3, and so on.

DISSONANT COUNTERPOINT

As the Second Viennese School ploughed a path from chromatic consonance to serialism, a less widely publicized but distinctly American solution lay in the theories of Charles Seeger (1886–1979). Seeger, a professor who lost his first academic job because of his opposition to World War I, continued at other institutions, including the Roosevelt-era Works Project Administration.

In its classroom application, **dissonant counterpoint** was the reverse of tonal counterpoint: in this new system, first species counterpoint was exclusively dissonant, and consonances were resolved by skip, not step. There was also a premium on interval symmetry, mathematical rather than harmonic in nature. The result of such discipline, according to Seeger, was one of "purification." It would also be used to "dissonate" rhythm and other musical elements.[2]

Many of the works Seeger composed using his system were destroyed in a fire. More important to his legacy were those who became aware of his approach and applied it in their individual ways, especially Henry Cowell, Carl Ruggles (1876–1971), Henry Brant (b. 1913), and Dane Rudhyar (1895–1985). A Seeger student who helped him develop his system (and in fact married him in 1932) was Ruth Crawford (1901–1953). She broke several barriers as a woman, winning two Guggenheim awards and having the only American work played at the 1933 ISCM (International Society for Contemporary Music) Festival in Amsterdam. But Crawford seems to have been less concerned with the politics of feminism (she refused to join a women composers' alliance whose members she considered old-fashioned) than with the future of music. Crawford saw dissonant counterpoint as a viable alternative to developments in the Second Viennese School, and hoped that dissonant counterpoint would compete successfully in a "race" to organize atonality universally. But with the end of her modernist composing in 1933, she had to concede the atonal field to the Europeans.

First published in Henry Cowell's *New Music Quarterly* and recorded in full in 1960, Crawford's *String Quartet 1931* comprising four movements played *attacca* (without pause). The quartet displays features specifically associated with Seeger's theories, and exhibits Crawford's more personal compositional traits: simultaneous parts at different "speeds," alternation between stepwise and displaced passages, extreme textural contrasts (for example, one solo line supported by three trills or held notes), sustained overlapping dissonances, close canonic writing, and the lack of vertically displayed chords amid a primarily contrapuntal texture.

Answering Edgard Varèse's request for an analysis of one of her pieces for a 1948 seminar at Columbia University, Crawford provided notes on the third and fourth movements of the quartet.[3] Anticipating Bartók's procedure in the third movement of *Music for Strings*, Crawford structures the finale (*Allegro possibile*) as a virtual palindrome. In a dialogue between first violin (which she labels "Voice 1") and the rest of the quartet ("Voice 2"), Voice 1 slowly accumulates additional notes in its phrases, while the answering octave phrases in Voice 2 remove notes at the same rate. Crawford employs a ten-note row; every 20 measures or so, she employs rotation, in which the prime form of the row simply "picks up" somewhere after its first note, without transposition. In measure 58, the four parts reach the midpoint, hold a C first-inversion chord, sounding anything but "consonant" here. The process of "dissonation" now begins: the preceding music is played in reverse a half-step higher until the opening texture is restored, closing with the three fortissimo notes in Voice 1's lowest register (a half-step higher than originally). Even if the pitch content is (intentionally) dissociative and difficult to hear palindromically, the overall arch of the rhythmic palindrome is clearly audible, even with the ever-changing surface rhythm; compare Crawford's approach with Messiaen's nonretrogradable rhythm in *Quatuor pou la fin du temps* (see Chapter 22).

CD15, Track 1
CRAWFORD
String Quartet 1931
Score Anthology II/176

2. Charles Seeger, "On Dissonant Counterpoint," *Modern Music* 7, no. 4 (June–July 1930), pp. 25–26). A manuscript, "Tradition and Experiment in (the New) Music," reflects not only Seeger's basic premises but contributions by Crawford as well. (Judith Tick, "Ruth Crawford Seeger's Different Tunes," *ISAM Newsletter* 30, no. 2 [Spring 2001]; online at http://depthome.brooklyn.cuny.edu/isam/tick.html. Accessed on April 24, 2008.)

3. Published as Appendix A in Judith Tick, *Ruth Crawford Seeger: A Composer's Search for American Music* (New York and Oxford: Oxford University Press, 1997), pp. 357–60.

In the 1930s, Crawford shifted her focus away from composition in part as a response to national and international events, working instead with her husband to aid victims of the Depression. In the 1940s, she transcribed, added piano accompaniment, and published large numbers of American folksongs that had been collected by the Works Progress Administration in the 1930s (see the discussion of Aaron Copland's *Rodeo* in Chapter 22). The resulting collections had a tremendous impact on the repertory of American folksong; as Kodály and Bartók had done for Hungary, Crawford played a crucial role in preserving American folksong, providing a basis for the folk revival to come. However, Crawford's intention to resume her compositional career led to only one piece (the Suite for Wind Quintet, 1952) before her death from cancer. Had she continued to live and compose, the system of dissonant counterpoint she used might have been become better known; if she had been the beneficiary of feminist views concerning equal opportunity in the musical world, her music might have received greater attention sooner.

INTEGRAL SERIALISM

In the years immediately after World War II, Olivier Messiaen and Milton Babbitt, working independently of each other, developed ways of extending the parameters of serial composition beyond pitch to include such elements as rhythm and dynamics as well. This approach soon became known as **integral serialism** or **total serialism.**

Babbitt's *Three Compositions for Piano* (1947) is one of the earliest and most celebrated of all works to use integral serialism. In addition to manipulating the combinatorial properties of the row, Babbitt serializes the elements of rhythm, dynamics, and register as well. Using the sixteenth note as the unit of measure, he establishes a basic pattern of 5, 1, 4, 2 (that is, five sixteenth notes, followed by one sixteenth note, and so on) and "inverts" the rhythmic structure by subtracting these values from 6. Thus the rhythmic matrix of the work looks like this:

P = 5, 1, 4, 2
I = 1, 5, 2, 4
RI = 4, 2, 5, 1
R = 2, 4, 1, 5

Prime forms of the pitch row, regardless of the transposition, are always presented in the P rhythm (5, 1, 4, 2), inverted forms of the pitch row in the I rhythm (1, 5, 2, 4), retrograde inverted forms in the RI rhythm, and retrograde forms in the R rhythm. Rhythmic durations are articulated by disrupting the pattern of continuous sixteenth notes, either through rests or through slurred notes that create rhythms of longer duration. The grouping of 5 in the left hand in measure 1, for example, is created by the added duration on the fifth note after the four initial sixteenths, whereas the subsequent "1" is articulated through the eighth-note rest at the end of measure 1.

Dynamics are also determined by precompositional choices.

P = *mp* (*pp* in measures 49–56)
I = *f* (*mp* in measures 49–56)
RI = *p* (*ppp* in measures 49–56)
R = *mf* (*p* in measures 49–56)

The structure of the work as a whole is highly symmetrical. This is most immediately evident in a comparison of its opening and closing sections:

Section 1 (measures 1–8):

R.H.	P-6	R-0	RI-7	I-1
L.H.	P-0	RI-1	I-7	R-6

Section 6 (measures 49–56):

R.H.	P-0	RI-1	I-7	R-6
L.H.	RI-7	I-1	P-6	R-0

Close examination reveals comparable (and more intricate) symmetries between sections 2 (measures 9–18) and 5 (measures 39–48) and between sections 3 (measures 19–28) and 4 (measures 29–38).

Messiaen's *Mode de valeurs et d'intensités* ("Mode of Durations and Intensities"), published in 1949, is not quite as systematic, but it treats both pitch and rhythm in a quasi-serial fashion. He uses three different 12-tone rows, each in its own register (high, medium, low), spanning a total of 36 different notes. Each of these 36 notes, in turn, is assigned a unique rhythmic value, from a thirty-second note to a dotted whole note. Dynamic markings (from *ppp* to *fff*) and articulation (accent, staccato, a short vertical line, a wedge, or no marking at all) are aligned with specific notes as well, although not in a unique one-to-one correspondence.

Messiaen himself did not pursue integral serialism or even serialism itself much further in subsequent years, but his work in this area exercised great influence on a generation of younger composers, most notably Pierre Boulez (b. 1925) and Karlheinz Stockhausen (1928–2007). In the end, however, integral serialism proved more important as a concept than as an application. In later years, Boulez considered this approach as part of a larger attempt to work through the burdens of tradition: tonal as well as atonal, serial as well as nonserial:

> After the war [World War II], we felt that music, like the world around us, was in a state of chaos. Our problem was to make a new musical language, seeking out what was good from the past, and rejecting what was bad. Around 1950, and for the following three years, we went through a period of seeking out total control over music. The serial process, which originated with Schoenberg and was refined in Webern, pointed out the way. What we were doing, by total serialization, was to annihilate the will of the composer in favor of a predetermining system. . . . But total control, like the total lack of control, can lead to chaos. Gaining this control was a necessary step in our development, because of our need to transubstantiate our musical heritage. But once there, we were at the zero point as composers. Now we could begin. Our process since about 1955 has been to enlarge and generalize what we had acquired through the period of atomization. In that way, we could gain a freedom through conquest, not merely through *laissez-faire*.[4]

Advocates of serialism originally hailed it as the salvation of music, a way out of the perceived dead ends of tonality, extreme chromaticism, and atonality. In retrospect, it is

---

4. Quotation from Pierre Boulez to an unidentified New York journalist, 1963, quoted in Robert Jacobson, *Reverberations: Interviews with the World's Leading Musicians*, pp. 25–26. Copyright © 1974 by Robert Jacobson. Reprinted by permission of HarperCollins Publishers Inc.

easy to see that serialism was in fact only one of many alternatives that emerged for composers in the 20th century. In the decades immediately after 1945, however, its significance seemed far more central, and today it is difficult to appreciate just how vital the idea of serialism was in the minds of mid-20th-century composers. Even Stravinsky—long perceived as the polar opposite of Schoenberg—turned to 12-tone techniques in the mid-1950s and early 1960s, applying the kind of serial rotation Crawford had used in the *String Quartet 1931*. In the minds of many, Stravinsky's use validated the triumph of serial composition in 20th-century music.

By the end of the 20th century, however, serialism's prestige had declined greatly. Composition students might continue to learn it as a technique, but only as one of many; at best, it had become the 20th-century equivalent of species counterpoint. By the 1980s, serial composition was being perceived as outmoded. Once again, what had been radical at the time of its first appearance had become old fashioned within only a generation or two.

Still, our appreciation of this music will be enhanced if we understand that its aesthetic principles supported attempts of composers to construct coherent, large-scale forms without recourse to tonality, to move beyond the exigencies of advanced chromaticism, and to create a new kind of sound as satisfying as it is demanding.

ALEATORY MUSIC

Whereas integral serialism stressed a high degree of structure and control, **aleatory music** took precisely the opposite approach, with chance playing a leading role. The term *aleatory* comes from the Latin *alea* meaning "die" (the singular of "dice"), and aleatory music involves (at least metaphorically) a "roll of the dice"—that is, chance. The idea of writing music by chance, even by a literal throw of the dice, was by no means new in the 20th century. Mozart and other composers of the Classical era were fascinated by the possibility of creating works based on modular units chosen at random from an extensive array of possibilities. The idea of aleatory (or aleatoric) music enjoyed a healthy revival in the 1950s and 1960s through such composers as John Cage, Karlheinz Stockhausen, and Pauline Oliveros.

Aleatory music typically fixes one or more elements of the musical experience and leaves others to what might be called chance operations or events. In Terry Riley's *In C* (1964; Anthology II/180, discussed later in this chapter), for example, a group of musicians play written-out melodic gestures in a specific sequence within an ongoing pulse, but each performer is free to move on to the next gesture as he or she sees fit. Thus the composer determines the pitches to be played, but the instrumentation, rhythm, dynamics, and large-scale form are left to the performers. John Cage, in the score of his *Imaginary Landscape No. 4* (1951), for 12 radios, 24 players, and a conductor, specifies rhythm and dynamics with great precision but leaves the sound content entirely to chance. Cage calls for two performers on each radio, one controlling the frequency, the other the volume, with the conductor giving cues for each. The duration of the work, the volume, and the points of entry are all fixed, but what is actually heard at any given moment from any of the 12 radios is entirely unpredictable, from rock to talk to classical to static.

Even more celebrated is a work that essentially lies beyond chance operations: Cage's *4′33″*, first performed by Cage's longtime collaborator, the pianist David Tudor, on August 29, 1952, at the appropriately named Maverick Concert Hall in Woodstock, New York (near the site of the celebrated 1969 rock festival). The work,

PRIMARY EVIDENCE   John Cage on *4'33"*

When the composer and writer William Duckworth interviewed John Cage in the late 1980s, the conversation turned, almost inevitably, to Cage's best known work.

DUCKWORTH: Let me ask you a few questions about *4'33"*. Is it true that it was actually conceived of in the late forties and just not presented until the fifties?

CAGE: Yes. I knew about it, and had spoken about the possibility of doing it, for about four years before I did it. . . . I knew that it would be taken as a joke and a renunciation of work, whereas I also knew that if it was done it would be the highest form of work. Or this form of work: an art without work. I doubt whether many people understand it yet.

DUCKWORTH: Well, the traditional understanding is that it opens you up to the sounds that exist around you and . . .

CAGE: . . . to the acceptance of anything, even when you have something as the basis. And that's how it's misunderstood.

DUCKWORTH: What's a better understanding of it?

CAGE: It opens you up to any possibility *only* when nothing is taken as the basis. But most people don't understand that, as far as I can tell.

DUCKWORTH: Is it possible that instead of being taken as too foolish, it's now taken too seriously?

CAGE: No. I don't think it can be taken too seriously.

DUCKWORTH: What I mean is that it's approached too intellectually. My own feeling is that it's not a piece to approach intellectually, maybe not even a piece to approach, in the traditional sense.

CAGE: Well, I use it constantly in my life experience. No day goes by without my making use of that piece in my life and in my work. I listen to it every day. Yes I do.

DUCKWORTH: Can you give me an example?

CAGE: I don't sit down to do it; I turn my attention toward it. I realize that it's going on continuously. So, more and more, my attention, as now, is on it. More than anything else, it's the source of my enjoyment of life.

DUCKWORTH: But it seems to me that when you focus on that piece it becomes art silence rather than real silence. And that the understanding of real silence is what that piece is about. But that the only way you can get to real silence is through artistic silence. Is that accurate?

CAGE: Thoreau came to this same attitude of mind and use of his faculties without my being anywhere around.

DUCKWORTH: Yes, but you'd be hard-pressed to name another one who came to that attitude, wouldn't you?

CAGE: Well, I would think quite a lot of people in India feel that music is continuous, it is only we who turn away. This is a cliché in Indian thinking and, surely, in Indian experience. My affirmation of this is within the context of twentieth-century art music. But the important thing, surely, about having done it, finally, is that it leads out of the world of art into the whole of life. . . .

which consists of three movements in which the pianist plays no notes, was inspired in part by the "white paintings" by one of Cage's friends, the artist Robert Rauschenberg. These so-called blank canvases are by their very nature never truly blank, of course. Every canvas has its own unique colors and textures, and each canvas is constantly changing because of the way it reflects the light of its surroundings. In much the same way, Cage's *4'33"* challenges the notion that there is such a thing as silence—the musical equivalent of a blank canvas—and by extension, the very idea of music itself. By listening to a supposedly silent work, we become acutely aware of the sounds around us: breathing, coughing, a room's ventilation system, a dog barking in the distance. We are listening to a work that is not silent at all and changes constantly and differs from performance to performance. These kinds of sounds, moreover, are always a part of the listening experience: if we choose to shut them out, it is because we have been conditioned to do so. As Cage suggests in his interview with William Duckworth (see Primary Evidence: John Cage on *4′33″*), "[This piece] opens you up to any possibility *only* when nothing is taken as the basis."

Many interpreted Cage's work as the epitome of the modernist composer's contempt for the audience. Other listeners reveled in the work's profoundly provocative absurdity. The piece is in some respects even more absurd than most people realize, for its score (and it does have a score) directs that the work "may be performed and last any length of time by any instrumentalist or combination of instrumentalists" (the original durations were chosen using the *I Ching*, also called the *Book of Changes*). Thus the most famous aspect of the piece—its meticulously precise duration—is optional.

CD15, Track 3

CAGE

Our Spring Will Come
Score Anthology II/178

Cage was among several composers who wrote percussion or percussive works in the wake of the success of Varèse's *Ionisation* (see Chapter 20); others include Lou Harrison (who collaborated with Cage on *Double Music*), William Russell, Henry Cowell, and the Cuban composer Amadeo Roldàn (whose *Ritmicas* nos. 5 and 6 anticipated *Ionisation* by a year). When commissioned for a dance score for percussion, Cage found the intended performance space too small for such a ensemble, but large enough for a grand piano. Inspired by Henry Cowell's "string piano" (see Chapter 20), Cage used a **prepared piano** to solve the problem. In the resulting work, *Bacchanale* (1940), he directed that bolts and weather stripping be attached to the strings connected to 12 different notes; in later works, he incorporated screws, wool, bamboo, and coins into the preparation.

Our Spring Will Come was written for choreographer Pearl Primus and premiered in New York in 1944. There are three types of preparation: bamboo strips weaving in and out of adjacent strings (from $C\flat$ to $C\flat^1$), a combination of screws (with two nuts to hold them in place) and bolts (for F^1, $A\flat^1$, and E^2), and a combination of a single screw with two other types (G^2, C^3). The score thus comprises 20 prepared notes, plus two unprepared pitches (A_3, A^1). Reading the score while listening to the piece reveals everything but the actual timbres (except for the unprepared A's), which run the gamut from the sound of a dampered piece of metal being struck and a gamelanlike ring. A prepared piano score is more a tablature (telling a performer how to play) rather than a score (telling a listener what will be heard), much like a Renaissance lute tablature. At tempos between $\quarternote$ = 152 and 184, this mostly duple meter piece goes by very quickly (notwithstanding the occasional accelerando and closing ritardando!). It may seem incongruous now that the score was set to what was then radical choreography (Primus "grunted and hummed, whispered, sang, and spoke as she gave herself to movement") while actor Gordon Heath read the eponymous poem by Langston Hughes on the condition of African Americans. But in Heath's opinion, Cage's music proved "an uncannily percussive equivalent of Pearl's dialogue with herself. I marveled and enunciated my narration warily."[5]

ELECTRONIC MUSIC

Electronic music was a fundamentally new phenomenon in the 20th century. In its purest form, it requires no performer: the sounds are produced by a machine, and the recorded version *is* the work. The ideal apparatus allows composers to manipulate

---

5. Gordon Heath, Doris Abramson, and Ekwueme Mike Thelwell, *Deep Are the Roots: Memoirs of a Black Expatriate* (Amherst: University of Massachusetts Press, 1996), p. 60.

all possible frequencies at all possible amplitudes with all possible durations. No sound—including those inaudible to the human ear—is impossible.

Electronic instruments first emerged in the 1920s. The theremin, named after its Russian-born inventor, Léon Theremin (Lev Termen, 1896–1993), was one of the first such instruments to attract widespread attention. It produced a single tone whose pitch and volume could be controlled by the motion of the player's hands around its antenna. Its eerie, other-worldly sound made it a favorite instrument of composers writing scores for science fiction movies, such as *The Day the Earth Stood Still* (1951) and *It Came from Outer Space* (1953), not to mention the television cartoon series *The Jetsons* (1962) and the Beach Boys' 1966 hit *Good Vibrations*.

Far more significant was the development of electronic music synthesizers in the late 1940s and 1950s. These instruments made it possible for composers to create, modify, and control the entire spectrum of sound for the first time in history. The only real variants in a purely electronic composition are the quality of the sound system on which a work is reproduced and the acoustics of the space in which the work is presented. Milton Babbitt, one of the first major composers to exploit the possibilities of this new technology, praised the ability of these machines to realize complex rhythms to a degree not possible in most live performances. "The composer would do himself and his music an immediate and eventual service by total, resolute, and voluntary withdrawal from this public world to one of private performance and electronic media, with its very real possibility of complete elimination of the public and social aspects of musical composition," Babbitt declared in 1958 (see Primary Evidence: "Who Cares If You Listen?"). Although Babbitt's assertion may seem startling today, it reflects the ideals of many midcentury composers who sought a purity of expression they felt could not be achieved through the inconsistent and unpredictable agency of performers.

Electronic music can be categorized into three major subcategories: musique concrète, synthesized electronic music, and computer music. Any and all of the three can be combined with live performers.

Musique concrète (also called "electroacoustic music") is a French term used to denote music in which the sonic material to be manipulated is a recorded sound taken from everyday life (the sounds are thus real, or "concrete"). The "sources" themselves might include a passing train, speaking voices, or burning charcoal. These concrete sounds are manipulated by tape splicing, mixing, and superimposing to create a larger whole.

Musique concrète was first developed in the late 1940s by the French composer Pierre Schaeffer (1910–1995) and has since been explored by a variety of others, including Karlheinz Stockhausen (1928–2007, who composed the powerful *Gesang der Jünglinge*, 1956), John Cage, Luciano Berio, and Steve Reich. In *Different Trains* (1988), Reich incorporates recordings of railway sounds and the voices of his wartime governess, a railway porter, and three Holocaust survivors into a work for string quartet that reflects on the different implications of train travel during World War II.

The Canadian composer Hugh Le Caine's *Dripsody* (1955) derives entirely from the briefest moment of sound: a single falling drop of water. By running this single recorded sound over and over again through a variable-speed tape recorder, Le Caine (1914–1977) was able to create an astonishing variety of sounds never before heard. But the work is far more than interesting sonic effects: it has a definite shape, a trajectory that projects a sense of drama and development. The ending of the work, playing on the sound of the proverbial dripping faucet, is eerily reminiscent of Haydn's String Quartet op. 33, no. 2, which leaves the unsuspecting listener uncertain just when the work has ended.

CD15, Track 4
LE CAINE
Dripsody
Score Anthology II/179

PRIMARY EVIDENCE   "Who Cares If You Listen?"

When Milton Babbitt's essay "Who Cares If You Listen?" first appeared in 1958 it soon became the flashpoint of a larger debate about the difficulties audiences were experiencing with modern music. The provocative title—imposed on the author by the editors of *High Fidelity*—suggests that Babbitt and his colleagues had no concern for listeners. But Babbitt's real argument is that some composers need to be able to work in an environment that allows them to explore new ideas the same way scientists conduct experiments in their laboratories. Such an environment, Babbitt argued, is to be found in the university. There, free from commercial pressures, composers would be able to help music develop beyond its current state.

—————◆◆◆—————

This article might have been entitled "The Composer as Specialist" or, alternatively, and perhaps less contentiously, "The Composer as Anachronism." For I am concerned with stating an attitude towards the indisputable facts of the status and condition of the composer of what we will, for the moment, designate as "serious," "advanced," contemporary music. This composer expends an enormous amount of time and energy—and, usually, considerable money—on the creation of a commodity which has little, no, or negative commodity value. He is, in essence, a "vanity" composer. The general public is largely unaware of and uninterested in his music. The majority of performers

shuns and resents it. Consequently, the music is little performed, and then primarily at poorly attended concerts before an audience consisting in the main of fellow professionals. At best, the music would appear to be for, of, and by specialists. . . .

Nor do I see how or why the situation should be otherwise. Why should the layman be other than bored and puzzled by what he is unable to understand, music or anything else? It is only the translation of this boredom and puzzlement into resentment and denunciation that seems to me indefensible. After all, the public does have its own music, its ubiquitous music: music to eat by, to read by, to dance by, and to be impressed by. Why refuse to recognize the possibility that contemporary music has reached a stage long since attained by other forms of activity? The time has passed when the normally well-educated man without special preparation could understand the most advanced work in, for example, mathematics, philosophy, and physics. Advanced music, to the extent that it reflects the knowledge and originality of the informed composer, scarcely can be expected to appear more intelligible than these arts and sciences to the person whose musical education usually has been even less extensive than his background in other fields. But to this, a double standard is invoked, with the words "music is music," implying also that "music is *just* music." Why not, then, equate the activities of the radio repairman with those of the theoretical physicist, on the basis of the dictum that "physics is physics"? It is not difficult to find statements like the following, from the

---

Musique concrète raises provocative questions about distinctions between music and sound in general, and between music and speech. In an earlier era, music was tacitly understood to be a special type of sound, created for its own sake either with the voice or musical instruments (or both) and distinctly different from sounds that are mere by-products of daily life. But the composers who have manipulated everyday sounds have called into question this basic assumption.

Synthesized electronic music consists of sounds generated and manipulated entirely by electronic means, through an electronic oscillator or a modifying device like a synthesizer. Basic sine waves can be modified by modulators, filters, and reverberators, all of which in one way or another change the color of a tone by altering its overtones. Babbitt, Stockhausen, Le Caine, and Morton Subotnick (b. 1933) are three prominent composers associated with this kind of electronic music. As a member of the faculty at Princeton University, Babbitt had access to the RCA Mark II Sound Synthesizer in the Columbia-Princeton Electronic Music Center in New York City in the late 1950s and early 1960s. The machine, although expensive, slow, and cumbersome to operate by today's standards, was in its time a breakthrough that allowed

New York Times of September 8, 1957: "The scientific level of the conference is so high . . . that there are in the world only 120 mathematicians specializing in the field who could contribute." Specialized music, on the other hand, far from signifying "height" of musical level, has been charged with "decadence," even as evidence of an insidious "conspiracy."

It often has been remarked that only in politics and the "arts" does the layman regard himself as an expert, with the right to have his opinion heard. In the realm of politics he knows that this right, in the form of a vote, is guaranteed by fiat. Comparably, in the realm of public music, the concertgoer is secure in the knowledge that the amenities of concertgoing protect his firmly stated "I didn't like it" from further scrutiny. Imagine, if you can, a layman chancing upon a lecture on "Pointwise Periodic Homeomorphisms." At the conclusion, he announces: "I didn't like it." Social conventions being what they are in such circles, someone might dare inquire: "Why not?" Under duress, our layman discloses precise reasons for his failure to enjoy himself; he found the hall chilly, the lecturer's voice unpleasant, and he was suffering the digestive aftermath of a poor dinner. His interlocutor understandably disqualifies these reasons as irrelevant to the content and value of the lecture, and the development of mathematics is left undisturbed. If the concertgoer is at all versed in the ways of musical lifesmanship, he also will offer reasons for his "I didn't like it"—in the form of assertions that the work in question is "inexpressive," "undramatic," "lacking in poetry," etc., etc., tapping that store of vacuous equivalents hallowed by time for: "I don't like it, and I cannot or will not state why." The concertgoer's critical authority is established beyond the possibility of further inquiry.

I say all this not to present a picture of a virtuous music in a sinful world, but to point up the problems of a special music in an alien and inapposite world. And so, I dare suggest that the composer would do himself and his music an immediate and eventual service by total, resolute, and voluntary withdrawal from this public world to one of private performance and electronic media, with its very real possibility of complete elimination of the public and social aspects of musical composition. By so doing, the separation between the domains would be defined beyond any possibility of confusion of categories, and the composer would be free to pursue a private life of professional achievement, as opposed to a public life of unprofessional compromise and exhibitionism. . . .

Granting to music the position accorded other arts and sciences promises the sole substantial means of survival for the music I have been describing. Admittedly, if this music is not supported, the whistling repertory of the man in the street will be little affected, the concert-going activity of the conspicuous consumer of musical culture will be little disturbed. But music will cease to evolve, and, in that important sense, will cease to live.

Source: Milton Babbitt, "Who Cares If You Listen?" *High Fidelity*, vol. 8, no. 2 (1958): 38–40. Copyright Hachette Filipacchi Magazines, Inc. Reprinted by permission of the author.

Babbitt to produce a new kind of music. The introduction of portable synthesizers in the mid-1960s and the rise of the personal computer in the 1980s allowed virtually anyone to pursue this kind of composition. MIDI (Musical Instrument Digital Interface) emerged in the early 1980s as the standard computer language for driving electronic synthesizers, which in turn produce sound. MIDI allows composers to control pitch, rhythm, dynamics, vibrato, and timbre in a remarkably sophisticated manner. Acoustic instruments may also be adapted for use as MIDI controllers, and interactive works involving live performers and electronic equipment have become a staple of this repertory (see discussion below). MIDI has eliminated the need for much (but not all) programming associated with electronic and computer music.

One of the earliest and still best known works of synthesized electronic music is the soundtrack to the MGM film *Forbidden Planet* (1956), composed by the husband-and-wife team of Louis Barron (1920–1989) and Bebe Barron (b. 1927). A science fiction adaptation of Shakespeare's *The Tempest*, this was the first commercially released film to feature an entirely electronic soundtrack. The eerie soundscape resonated with the story's setting on a bleak and distant planet. Instead of a lushly orchestrated score,

COMPOSER PROFILE John Cage *(1912–1992)*

"Everything we do is music," Cage once declared, and in many respects his music was devoted to making life itself an art form. He did not see himself as a high priest of art but rather as a facilitator between listeners and sounds. Profoundly influenced by Zen Buddhism and its renunciation of striving and the will, Cage maintained his "purpose is to eliminate purpose," and many of his works from the late 1940s on seem to avoid or challenge the traditional stance of the composer as an omnipotent creator of a small musical world.

Cage's output falls into several broad categories:

■ *Works for percussion, including prepared piano.* The composer's early output includes a number of works for standard and nonstandard percussion instruments. A student of Henry Cowell (see Chapter 20), Cage extended his teacher's novel approach to the piano by calling for fitting the instrument's strings with such objects as screws, rubber bands, and coins, producing a range of timbres as oddly familiar as they are strange.

■ *Aleatory works.* In addition to *4′33″*, Cage wrote many works based on the element of chance. Several relate directly to the *I Ching*, also known as the *Book of Changes*, a system of interpreting the interplay of strong and weak forces based on the throw of dice. Cage's *Imaginary Landscape no. 4* (1951) calls for 12 radios tuned to 12 different stations playing simultaneously. The instructions to the performers are precise, but the results are naturally unpredictable. *0′00″* (1962) consists of an amplified projection of a

John Cage. Many of Cage's works from the 1960s and 1970s were multimedia productions created with other artists. Two of his longtime collaborators were the dancer and choreographer Merce Cunningham (b. 1919) and the pianist and composer David Tudor (1926–1996). In this live performance of Cage's *Variations V*, Cage is seated at the far left in the foreground, manipulating electronic sound equipment along with Tudor (center) and (at the far right) the composer Gordon Mumma (b. 1935). Members of the Merce Cunningham Dance Company perform behind them, with images projected against the backdrop. In this work, Cage called for the dancers to perform within a matrix of strategically placed microphones, making the sounds of the dancers' movements an integral part of the performance.

Source: Courtesy of Cunningham Dance Foundation, Inc.

"disciplined action": in one of his many performances of this work, the composer sliced vegetables, placed them in a blender, and drank the mix while standing very close to a microphone.

audiences heard stark, disembodied sounds created in a recording studio the Barrons had set up in their New York apartment, consisting of oscillators, mixers, filters, and tape recorders. By later standards, the equipment was primitive, but the sound, generated entirely by electrical sources, was distinctively new.

Computer music is music that has been generated, transformed, fully composed, or performed by a computer program. In its earliest form, computer music involved allowing a computer to determine how a work would unfold. Lejaren Hiller's *Illiac Suite* for string quartet (1957) is generally acknowledged to be the first work in which the computer actually emulated the process of composition itself. Hiller (1924–1994), working with the scientist Leonard Issacson, created the work on an Illiac computer at the University of Illinois, programming the machine to create a series of movements in specific styles, ranging from strict counterpoint to twelve tone to random. Hiller later collaborated with John Cage to produce *HPSCHD* (1967–69), a multimedia,

■ *Electronic works.* Cage was part of the first generation able to explore the possibilities of electronically generated sound. *Fontana Mix* (1959) combines aleatory principles with taped music, the mix being determined by the combination of various transparencies on which are graphically notated changes in amplitude, frequency, timbre, and so on.

■ *Writings.* Cage's book *Silence* (1961) was the first of several influential collections of essays, diary entries, and experimental writing. He invented a poetic form of acrostic called the mesostic (in which lines intersect other lines, rather than meeting at the ends), and created visual and plastic art, including the 1969 type-superimposed-on-plexiglass sculpture *Not Wanting to Say Anything About Marcel*, dedicated to Marcel Duchamp. Despite these artistic forays and his expertise in mycology, Cage never broke his promise to Arnold Schoenberg to devote his life to music.

Cage and his music consistently polarized listeners. Most of the audience at New York's Lincoln Center walked out of his *Atlas eclipticalis* (whose score superimposes transparent staff paper on star charts to determine pitches) when it was performed by the New York Philharmonic in 1964; even members of the orchestra hissed the composer. But Cage's provocative music and writings remained fresh over time, and toward the end of his life he was showered with honors. He delivered the prestigious Charles Eliot Norton lectures at Harvard University in 1988, continuing in the tradition of

Stravinsky, Hindemith, Copland, Boulez, Bernstein, and Berio. Some saw genius in his works, others charlatanism, but all were provoked by them to rethink the nature of music and its relationship to the world around us.

KEY DATES IN THE LIFE OF CAGE	
1912	Born September 5 in Los Angeles.
1930	After visiting Europe returns to the United States and studies piano and composition with Henry Cowell.
1934	Studies harmony and counterpoint with Arnold Schoenberg at UCLA.
1938	Begins a lifelong personal and artistic association with the dancer Merce Cunningham, collaborating on a series of "happenings," performances that combine music, dance, poetry, film, and other forms of expression.
1954	Concert tour of Europe with the pianist David Tudor.
1961	Publishes *Silence,* the first of his many books on music.
1972	Sixtieth birthday is marked by concerts at The New School for Social Research and at Lincoln Center.
1988–1989	Delivers the Norton Lectures at Harvard University.
1992	Dies August 12 in New York City.

five-hour collage of musical quotations from Mozart, Beethoven, Schoenberg, and others, the sounds of 52 tape recorders and 7 harpsichordists, all structured according to computerized models, all accompanied by 6,400 slides (5,000 from NASA, the rest abstract designs), and 40 films, producing a simultaneous or an asynchronous and exuberant anarchy of activity.[6] By the 1990s, digitized computer technology had largely replaced the tape recorder (thus bypassing the physical limitations of tape) and electronic synthesis (allowing for more sophisticated manipulation of sounds).

Seeking a remedy for the inherently variable and unpredictable nature of performance, composers of many different orientations welcomed electronic music as a way of achieving total control over the finished product. Viennese composer Ernst Krenek

---

6. Johanne Rivest, "In Advance of the Avant Garde: John Cage at the University, 1952–69, lecture given at the University of Illinois, April 22, 1999; online at http://emfinstitute.emf.org/articles/rivest99/rivestoncage991.html. Access April 18, 2008.

"I could specify something and hear it instantly." Milton Babbitt at the RCA Mark II Sound Synthesizer, Columbia-Princeton Studios, New York City, late 1950s. By today's standards, this synthesizer is limited. But in its time, it was one of the most advanced machines of its kind, and there were only a handful like it anywhere in the world. On several occasions, Babbitt praised the ability of machines like this one to realize rhythms to a degree not possible in most "live" performances. But the apparatus, containing 750 vacuum tubes, was cumbersome to control. "It had a paper drive," Babbitt recalled later, "and getting the paper through the machine and punching the holes was difficult. We were punching in binary. The machine was totally zero, nothing predetermined, and any number we punched could refer to any dimension of the machine. . . . It was basically just a complex switching device to an enormous and complicated analogue studio hooked to a tape machine. And yet for me it was so wonderful because I could specify something and hear it instantly." A sequencer (which generated a loop of pitches automatically and continuously) was of special appeal to integral serialist composers like Babbitt. The Mark II declined in use after the mid-1970s, its pride of place taken over by less cumbersome analog synthesizer types such as the voltage-controlled modular Buchla and the keyboard-controlled Moog.

Source: Photo courtesy Milton Babbitt

praised the "electronic medium, earlier denounced as a mechanistic degradation of music," for its ability to lend itself "to a kind of controlled compositional improvisation much more readily than the realm of live sound because the composer can mould the sound material while he is creating it."[7] Around the middle of the century, in fact, some people believed electronic music would sweep away the established instruments and performance venues of most, or even all, music in Western society. By century's end, however, it was clear that electronic music was not about to replace live performers. Instead, like serial composition, it would provide composers with another option for creating music, enriching the musical landscape with its possibilities without eliminating earlier practices.

---

7. Ernst Krenek, *Horizons Circled* (Berkeley and Los Angeles: University of California Press, 1974), p. 151.

Modernism in painting: Abstract expressionism. Abstract expressionism is nonrepresentational, making its effect through the interplay of shapes and colors. This painting— Number 1, 1950 (*Lavender Mist*)—is by Jackson Pollock, one of the leading abstract expressionist painters of his generation. Pollock began working in his "drip and splash" style in the late 1940s, applying paint with objects other than brushes and often simply by pouring it onto his canvases. The resulting style avoids any single point of emphasis and any hierarchy of shapes or forms. The immediacy and raw energy conveyed by this technique have often been compared to the literary and musical manifestations of expressionism.

Source: Jackson Pollock, "Number 1, 1950 (Lavender Mist)" oil, enamel and aluminum paint on canvas, 221 × 299.7 cm/National Gallery of Art, Washington, D.C., USA/© 2003 The Pollock-Krasner Foundation/Artists Rights Society (ARS), New York/The Bridgeman Art Library, New York

In retrospect, electronic music achieved its greatest impact when composers began to integrate it with live performance. Milton Babbitt's *Philomel* (1963) calls for a soprano soloist to perform live against a recorded tape running at the same time. By the 1980s, rock music and other types of concerts were routinely combining taped (or digitally recorded) and live music; a notated score of much popular music and jazz is in fact nothing more than an approximate transcription of an electronic original. The essential work exists not in the form of a notated score, but rather as a recording. The Pulitzer Prize Committee recognized this in 2004, no longer requiring a score to be submitted for consideration of a work (see Focus: The Pulitzer Prize in music; for more on this change, see the Epilogue.)

The recording studio also benefited from the technologies of electronic music. As early as the 1950s, technology had given artists the freedom to vary such elements as dynamics (by altering levels of amplification) and resonance (by altering reverberation). Overdubbing (originally known as "sound on sound") allowed musicians to superimpose an additional voice or voices over an existing one; each of these "voices" was called a "track." Popular music, particularly rock, embraced these techniques with extraordinary enthusiasm. Electronic technology was also applied to standard instruments of the rock band in live performances, most notably the piano and the guitar. By the late 1960s, the synthesizer had become a staple of rock bands and many jazz ensembles.

MINIMALISM

Minimalism, is a controversial term first applied to new music in the early 1960s. The problem with the term is its use as an "umbrella" for very different compositional approaches and styles, many of which have been categorized as "avant-garde" or "experimental." What they seem to have in common is their combination of reaction to and rebellion against the idea of a definitive work, whether in the form

FOCUS   The Pulitzer Prize in Music

The Pulitzer Prize in Music is awarded annually for a "distinguished musical composition of significant dimension by an American that has had its first performance in the United States during the year." Like any award, the acknowledgment is to some extent arbitrary, yet the roster of winners since the inception of the award in 1943 provides an index of the enormous diversity of American music since that time. Award winners have ranged from Aaron Copland's ballet *Appalachian Spring* (1945) to Elliott Carter's String Quartet no. 3 (1973) to Wynton Marsalis's *Blood on the Fields* (1994), an oratorio for vocalists and jazz ensemble. The list is also notable for the absence of prominent composers such as Leonard Bernstein, Morton Feldman, George Rochberg, Lou Harrison, Vincent Persichetti, Steve Reich, Philip Glass, and above all, John Cage. That there is considerable cynicism regarding this or similar prizes can be understood when, as occurred in 1965, the Pulitzer jury awarded the prize to Duke Ellington, but the Pulitzer Board refused to accept the ruling and awarded no prize that year.

1943	*Secular Cantata no. 2. A Free Song* by William Schuman
1944	*Symphony no. 4. op. 34* by Howard Hanson
1945	*Appalachian Spring* by Aaron Copland
1946	*The Canticle of the Sun* by Leo Sowerby
1947	*Symphony no. 3* by Charles Ives
1948	*Symphony no. 3* by Walter Piston

1949	Music for the film *Louisiana Story* by Virgil Thomson
1950	Music in *The Consul* by Gian Carlo Menotti
1951	Music in *Giants in the Earth* by Douglas S. Moore
1952	*Symphony Concertante* by Gail Kubik
1953	(No Award)
1954	*Concerto for Two Pianos and Orchestra* by Quincy Porter
1955	*The Saint of Bleecker Street* by Gian Carlo Menotti
1956	*Symphony no. 3* by Ernst Toch
1957	*Meditation on Ecclesiastes* by Norman Dello Joio
1958	*Vanessa* by Samuel Barber
1959	*Concerto for Piano and Orchestra* by John LaMontaine
1960	*Second String Quartet* by Elliott Carter
1961	*Symphony no. 7* by Walter Piston
1962	*The Crucible* by Robert Ward
1963	*Piano Concerto no. 1* by Samuel Barber
1964	(No Award)
1965	(No Award)
1966	*Variations for Orchestra* by Leslie Bassett
1967	*Quartet no. 3* by Leon Kirchner
1968	*Echoes of Time and the River* by George Crumb
1969	*String Quartet no. 3* by Karel Husa
1970	*Time's Encomium* by Charles Wuorinen

of a fully notated score or a "correct" interpretation. Musical logic as it had been understood since the Renaissance was turned on its aesthetic head.

These radical approaches have included the use of graphic score notation alone (Earle Brown, *Dec. 1952* from *Folio*), nontraditional or extended use of standard notation (Christian Wolff, *Duet I* for piano four hands, 1960), indeterminacy as group performance (George Brecht, *Card: Piece for Voice*, for 54 performers and a deck of cards, 1959), indeterminacy as solo performance (John Cage, *45′ for a Speaker*, 1954), multimedia (Nam June Paik and Charlotte Moorman, *TV Cello*, 1964), performance or action art (Toshi Ichiyanagi, *Music for Electric Metronome*, 1960), and politicized art (Yoko Ono, *Cut Piece*, 1964). Many contributors to these new genres were "outsiders": nonclassical musicians, poets, painters, video makers, and theatrical performers. Electronics were often part of the performances. Many of these works possess varying degrees of freedom for the performers or participants; many of the works have a element of play or gamesmanship, and some use the modular or mobile principle, in which a performer may choose what she or he performs next (as in Stockhausen's *Klavierstück XI*, 1956). The opposite extreme may be found in the fully notated compositions of Morton Feldman (1926–1987), whose music gradually became quieter, slower, longer,

1971	*Synchronisms no. 6 for Piano and Electronic Sound* (1970) by Mario Davidovsky	**1991**	*Symphony* by Shulamit Ran
1972	*Windows* by Jacob Druckman	**1992**	*The Face of the Night, The Heart of the Dark* by Wayne Peterson
1973	*String Quartet no. 3* by Elliott Carter	**1993**	*Trombone Concerto* by Christopher Rouse
1974	*Notturno* by Donald Martino	**1994**	*Of Reminiscences and Reflections* by Gunther Schuller
1975	*From the Diary of Virginia Woolf* by Dominick Argento	**1995**	*Stringmusic* by Morton Gould
1976	*Air Music* by Ned Rorem	**1996**	*Lilacs, for Voice and Orchestra* by George Walker
1977	*Visions of Terror and Wonder* by Richard Wernick		
1978	*Déja Vu for Percussion Quartet and Orchestra* by Michael Colgrass	**1997**	*Blood on the Fields* by Wynton Marsalis
		1998	*String Quartet #2 (musica instrumentalis)* by Aaron Jay Kernis
1979	*Aftertones of Infinity* by Joseph Schwantner		
1980	*In Memory of a Summer Day* by David Del Tredici	**1999**	*Concerto for Flute, Strings and Percussion* by Melinda Wagner
1981	(No Award)	**2000**	*Life Is a Dream, Opera in Three Acts: Act II, Concert Version* by Lewis Spratlan
1982	*Concerto for Orchestra* by Roger Sessions		
1983	*Symphony no. I (Three Movements for Orchestra)* by Ellen Taaffe Zwilich	**2001**	*Symphony no. 2 for String Orchestra* by John Corigliano
1984	*"Canti del Sole" for Tenor and Orchestra* by Bernard Rands	**2002**	*Ice Field* by Henry Brant
		2003	*On the Transmigration of Souls* by John Adams
1985	*Symphony, RiverRun* by Stephen Albert	**2004**	*Tempest Fantasy* by Paul Moravec
1986	*Wind Quintet IV* by George Perle	**2005**	*Second Concerto for Orchestra* by Steven Stucky
1987	*The Flight into Egypt* by John Harbison		
1988	*12 New Etudes for Piano* by William Bolcom	**2006**	*Piano Concerto: "Chiara in Mano"* by Yehudi Wyner
1989	*Whispers Out of Time* by Roger Reynolds	**2007**	*Sound Grammar* by Ornette Coleman
1990	*"Duplicates": A Concerto for Two Pianos and Orchestra* by Mel Powell	**2008**	*The Little Match Girl Passion* by David Lang

and more silent, culminating in the six-hour *String Quartet II* (1983). La Monte Young (b. 1935), whom many consider the first minimalist, edited *An Anthology* (1963, 1970)[8] of scores by many of the above creators, including his tersely described conceptual pieces; in later years he began exploring the possibilities of overtones (harmonic and nonharmonic) in works such as the monumental installation *The Well Tuned Piano 81 X 25* (1988), a collaboration with environmental light artist Marian Zazeela.

In the present discussion, minimal music is defined in relation to a simultaneous movement in painting, from which it got its name, around 1960. In many ways, the approaches were quite similar: both were reactions against opulence and complexity (in art, abstract expressionism; in music, integral serialism), and both applied the use of "simple forms" or multiple repetitions of small units (geometric or white painting; repetitive music). In music, such motivic repetition would change only gradually over long stretches of time. This kind of musical minimalism was by no means a new phenomenon: the centuries-old tradition of church bell change ringing uses a few

---

8. La Monte Young and Jackson Mac Low, *An Anthology* (New York: Heiner Friedrich, 1963; second ed., 1970). A collection of pages from a wider-ranging group of contemporary composers is found in John Cage, *Notations* (New York: Something Else Press, 1972).

CD15, Track 5
RILEY
In C
Score Anthology II/180

fixed pitches (one from each of three or more bells), repeated at different speeds in such a way that the resulting permutations create an apparently infinite number of combinations.

A similar strategy is at work in one of the earliest of all minimalist works, Terry Riley's *In C* (1964). The score consists of 53 brief thematic fragments to be played in any combination of any kind of instruments, although the composer recommends a group of about 35 if possible. Each player performs these ideas in the same sequence but is free to repeat each unit as often as he or she sees fit. "There is no fixed rule as to the number of repetitions a pattern may have,"[9] the composer notes in the score, although if a performance runs between 45 and 90 minutes, then each performer would ordinarily repeat each pattern for somewhere between 40 and 90 seconds.[10] "One of the joys of *In C*," the composer noted in his performing directions to the score, "is the interaction of the players in polyrhythmic combinations that spontaneously arise between patterns. Some quite fantastic shapes will arise and disintegrate as the group moves through the piece when it is properly played." The one constant element of the piece is an ostinato C octave played on the high range of a piano or mallet instrument. If a performance of *In C* runs to 90 minutes, this would mean repeating this particular figure as many as 15,000 times in succession. This might sound like a recipe for monotony, but the process of unfolding is such that the work remains constantly in motion and gradually transforms itself into whatever the performers decide it will become.

What kind of a work is *In C*? It resists classification. It bears many hallmarks of jazz (individual "riffs," enormous latitude for improvisation), yet it is essentially a canon at the unison. Riley notes that "all performers must play strictly in rhythm," and he even recommends that musicians "rehearse patterns in unison before attempting to play the piece to determine that everyone is playing correctly." In many respects, *In C* harks back to an earlier period of time—its open-ended instrumentation and the tremendous latitude given to performers seem in some respects more typical of the Renaissance or Baroque than the 20th century. "At the time I wrote *In C*, I was almost ready to drop out of music," the composer once explained. "Classical music was very mental; the mind governed the musical activity. I think the shift in what this music [*In C*] was doing was letting the heart back into the game. I wanted to make the score so minimal that it wasn't important anymore."[11]

Another manifestation of minimalism involves what has come to be known as **phase music** or **process music,** in which we can clearly hear the process by which the elements of a work gradually transform themselves into something new and different. In the 1960s and early 1970s, Steve Reich applied this principle to musique concrète (*It's Gonna Rain, Come Out*), music for live performers interacting with electronics (*Violin Phase, Pendulum Music*), and works for live performers (*Four Organs, Drumming, Music for Pieces of Wood*). Since 1973, Reich has made the phase process a compositional tool among many others, and his musical range and reach have expanded accordingly.

Piano Phase for two pianos or two marimbas (1967) is an early example of a non-electronic Reich phase piece. In his experience, Reich thought a performance would last around 20 minutes. (The Anthology presents the work's beginning.) Both pianists

9. Performance instructions in score of *In C* by Terry Riley. © 1964 Composed by Terry Riley. Published by Ancient Word Music, Administered by Celestial Harmonies.

10. A 1989 recording by the Shanghai Film Orchestra (on Chinese instruments) under Wang Yongji and supervised by Riley revealed an unexpected difficulty in performance. Apparently, the musicians "rushed" through the 53 fragments so that the piece was ready to end in just over 10 minutes; to compensate, the conductor brought back earlier fragments to extend the piece. In Riley's words, "I kept telling them to take as much time as they wanted, but they never went over 30 [minutes]. In fact, after 10 or 12 minutes, the conductor was down to the last patterns! So he did a lot of 'recapping.'" John Schaefer, liner notes to Terry Riley: *In C*, Celestial Harmonies 13026-2, 1989.

11. Terry Riley, quoted in Michael Walsh, "The Heart Is Back in the Game," *Time*, September 20, 1982, p. 60.

play in the same range throughout (E^1 up to D^2, ending on A^1 up to E^2). The piece is in three sections:

The parts begin by alternating two- (a fifth, on E^1) and three-note (a fifth and minor third, on $F\sharp^1$) to produce a 12-note ostinato figure; the tonal effect is of a Dorian mode on E. Opening alone, the first performer (Reich's term) holds a steady tempo through the first 25 of 32 "measures" (modules). Each module is repeated a predetermined number of times within a specified range. Once the first performer has established the steady state, the second performer takes the same interlocking ostinato figure, but "accelerates very slightly" between each module (each acceleration will itself take several repetitions by the first performer). By the end of each accelerating module, the second performer is to be one sixteenth "ahead" of the first performer. Twelve modular shifts are necessary before the unison returns. Once more the second performer drops out and the figure continues.

When the second performer reenters, its ostinato changes the ascending fifth to an ascending fourth (right hand), while the left hand changes the B^1 to A^1 and plays a 8-note ostinato. The shifting pattern begins again; although the process now takes only 8 modules, Reich starts asking for a larger number of repetitions per module, ranging from 16 to 32 times (versus 12 to 24 times in the first section).

In the third and final section, the second performer takes the lead initially before the first performer reenters. The ostinato is down to four notes, in what may be heard as a four-note scale on A^1. The phasing again returns to the second performer's part; only 4 modules are now required before unison is reachieved, although Reich again "compensates" for the shorter modular shift by increasing the number of repetitions to as many as 60. Once the 32nd and final module is satisfactorily achieved, the performers cue to end.

CD15, Track 6
REICH
Piano Phase
Score Anthology II/181

Like *In C*, *Piano Phase* is essentially a canon at the unison, but the element of tempo has become the primary compositional process, putting the canon through a subtle time warp. As Reich directs the performers, the point "is not to count repeats, but to listen to the two voice relationship and as you hear it clearly and have absorbed it, move on to the next bar."[12] The rate of change is so gradual and the pulsation so persistent that a listener experiences an unfolding, almost nonlinear sense of time, rather than the more familiar cause and effect of most Western music.

Are there any listening signposts along the way? Is the piece somehow "modulating" from E to A—or is the opening really E^7, going through a quartal E-A-D before "resolving" on A? Are the gradual changes in the length of the ostinato figures meant to suggest a push toward the end, or does the increasing number of repetitions (intentionally) defeat that feeling? The use of the same instrument and range complicates perception of the work's progress, but does the relative simplicity of the score lessen the complexity? As with many pieces built on the exchange of "fragments," the acoustics and interaction of a live performance are essential elements.

Minimalism, in spite of its name, often produces works of immense length. The quintessential minimalist film is Andy Warhol's *Empire* (1964), unedited and shot with a single stationary camera focused on the Empire State Building for eight hours. Changes of lighting, texture, and motion in this silent black-and-white film are subtle

---

PRIMARY EVIDENCE   Music as a Gradual Process

Steve Reich, a composer widely associated with the development of minimalism in the early 1960s, has written frequently about the relationship of composer, performer, and listener. The comments here, from an essay of 1968 entitled "Music as a Gradual Process," address the idea that processes in music should unfold slowly enough so as to be perceptible to listeners.

*   *   *

I am interested in perceptible processes. I want to be able to hear the process happening throughout the sounding music.

To facilitate closely detailed listening a musical process should happen extremely gradually.

Listening to an extremely gradual musical process opens my ears to *it*, but *it* always extends farther than I can hear, and that makes it interesting to listen to that

musical process again. That area of every gradual (completely controlled) musical process, where one hears the details of the sound moving out away from intentions, occurring for their own acoustic reasons, is *it*.

I begin to perceive these minute details when I can sustain close attention and a gradual process invites my sustained attention. By "gradual" I mean extremely gradual; a process happening so slowly and gradually that listening to it resembles watching a minute hand on a watch—you can perceive it moving after you stay with it a little while.

. . . While performing and listening to gradual musical processes one can participate in a particular liberating and impersonal kind of ritual. Focusing in on the musical process makes possible that shift of attention away from *he* and *she* and *you* and *me* outwards towards *it*.

Source: Steve Reich, "Music as a Gradual Process" (1968). From Steve Reich, *Writings About Music* (New York: New York University Press, 1973). © 1974 Steve Reich.

---

12. Steve Reich, Directions for performance, *Piano Phase* (London: Universal Edition, 1980).

FOCUS　　　Music Education in the 20th Century

Music education became an integral element of most elementary school curricula throughout the Western world during the course of the 20th century; rhythm bands, choral groups, and instrumental ensembles flourished at many schools. At the secondary level, most schools were able to establish one or more musical groups, such as a chorus, wind band, or orchestra. Although funding for these groups could become precarious at times, these ensembles have continued to provide an important component of musical education down to the present day. Research studies repeatedly confirmed the intellectual, social, and physical benefits of music-making in early childhood.

Three important figures stand out in the development of music education in the 20th century:

■ Zoltán Kodály (1882–1967), a Hungarian composer, was an inveterate collector of folksongs, and he believed that folksong should be the basis for the musical education of very young children. The "Kodály Method" moves children through a carefully graded sequence of skills, moving from simple to increasingly complex intervals and rhythms.

■ The German composer Carl Orff (1895–1982) gave the impetus to what came to be called the *Schulwerk* ("School Work"), an approach centered more on instruments than singing, with a special emphasis on dance. After learning a few basic patterns, beginning with rhythms and simple melodic cells, students are encouraged to improvise on their own.

■ The Japanese violinist Sin'ichi Suzuki (1898–1998) developed a method of musical education that emphasizes group participation (including parents as well as children), physical activity, and frequent repetition of a small number of basic units. The "Suzuki Method" originated with the violin but eventually extended to other instruments as well. It has exposed thousands of children across the world to music-making at a very young age.

By the end of the century, music education efforts were increasingly focused toward very young children. In 1998, Florida governor Lawton Chiles signed into law a bill requiring all state-funded child-care centers and preschools to play classical music and read to children for 30 minutes each day (the so-called Beethoven's Babies Law). A year later, Georgia governor Zell Miller negotiated a public-private partnership with the recording firm of Sony to send new mothers home from the hospital with a free copy of a classical music CD. The original *Build Your Baby's Brain Through the Power of Music!* included selections by Mozart, Handel, Beethoven, Schubert, and Bach. Sony has since issued a series of more specialized disks, focusing on the individual powers of Mozart, Beethoven, Bach, and, most recently, the Baroque. Other companies have focused attention on the mother-to-be or the daily activities of infancy. The efficacy of neonatal, even prenatal exposure to classical music has yet to be fully explored or examined.

yet constant. In similar fashion, the changes in works like Riley's *In C* and Reich's *Piano Phase* operate on a scale far different from that associated with the traditions of Bach, Beethoven, and Brahms—and, for that matter, Schoenberg, Stravinsky, and Bartók as well. Minimalism forces listeners to hear within a different set of standards, to value processes of change that are relatively slow, minimal, but no less powerful in their effect.

POSTMODERNISM

In 1979, the distinguished American composer Charles Wuorinen (b. 1938) published a treatise on composition that opened with these words:

> Most of the Western music we know from the past is representative of the tonal system. . . . But while the tonal system, in an atrophied or vestigial form, is still used today in popular and commercial music, and even occasionally in the works of backward-looking serious composers, it is no longer employed by serious composers in the mainstream.[13]

---

13. Charles Wuorinen, *Simple Composition* (New York: Longman, 1979), p. 3.

Postmodern architecture. In postmodern architecture, as in postmodernism in general, modernism coexists with ornamentation, humor, and overt references to past styles. The glass-and-stone body of Philip Johnson's AT&T Building (1978) in New York City is decidedly modern in its austere functionality, but the ornamental scrolled top provides a postmodern touch. It offers a whimsical and even ironic commentary on what lies beneath; to many observers, the building as a whole resembles a Chippendale-style chest of drawers.

Source: Richard Payne/Richard Payne, FAIA

Wuorinen's thoroughly modernist pronouncement is typical of the generation of composers who came of age in the 1950s and 1960s: it rests on the assumption that a chasm exists between "high" and "low" art, between "forward-looking" and "backward-looking" composers, and that no forward-looking serious composer would write in a tonal idiom, a stylistic remnant of the past. By the last quarter of the 20th century, however, **postmodernism** had made Wuorinen's claim seem remarkably dated.

Postmodernism, like modernism itself, is an aesthetic attitude rather than a particular style. It embraces the past (including modernism) but often in an eclectic manner, synthesizing a variety of approaches in a single work. In music, all approaches are equally valid within the postmodernist approach. Postmodernist composers felt obliged neither to avoid nor to use traditional forms and genres. On an even broader scale, postmodernism often abandons the pretension of art as an invariably serious enterprise.

Postmodernism emerged gradually over the last third of the 20th century, becoming particularly conspicuous in the field of architecture. For several decades in the mid-20th century, "serious" architects (to borrow Wuorinen's term) prided themselves on the elegant simplicity of steel-and-glass skyscrapers that conspicuously avoided anything that smacked of ornament. The mantra of such architects was the famous dictum of their Viennese colleague Adolf Loos: "Ornament is crime." When the Seagram Building, designed by Mies van der Rohe and Philip Johnson, opened in New York in 1958, critics hailed the purity and simplicity of its design as cool, impersonal, aloof. By the 1970s, however, at least some architects were beginning to rebel against the rigidity of such design. The "cool" of the late 1950s was increasingly perceived as cold. In the mid-1980s, the same Philip Johnson designed the quintessentially postmodern AT&T Building, also in Manhattan. It embraces the modern—most

Pop Art and postmodernism.
Pop Art was one of several movements that emerged in the 1950s and 1960s as a revolt against modernism, particularly abstract expressionism. This 1965 painting—*Reverie*—is by Roy Lichtenstein. Pop Art typically blurs the distinction between art and everyday life by repackaging common images—like those found in comic books—in a new manner, forcing us to look at "throw away" objects more carefully. Although widely reviled when it appeared (*Life* magazine once nominated Lichtenstein as "Worst Artist in the World"), Pop Art helped break down the perceived gulf between "high" and "low" art, and indeed between life and art in general. In this sense, it bears distinct parallels to the work of John Cage and other experimental composers who sought to bridge comparable gaps in music. The text within this particular work evokes a line from Hoagy Carmichael's celebrated love song *Stardust* (1927).

Source: Roy Lichtenstein (1923–1997), "Reverie," from the portfolio *11 Pop Artists,* Volume II, 1965, color serigraph on paper, 27 1/8 × 23 in./Smithsonian American Art Museum, Washington, D.C./Art Resource, NY/© Estate of Roy Lichtenstein

of the building conforms to the steel-and-glass formula—but its pediment evokes a Chippendale-style chest of drawers. The very top of this modernist skyscraper is ornamental, whimsical, and draws on the idioms of the past—all hallmarks of the postmodern aesthetic, which is intensely aware of the artificiality of art and language.

By the end of the 20th century, postmodernism had become the predominant aesthetic within the concert hall. For the first time in several decades, audiences were hearing substantial quantities of new music that could no longer be described as modernist or avant-garde. Some critics called this approach "the new lyricism" or "the new Romanticism." Shock was suddenly passé. *The People United Will Never Be Defeated* (1976) by the American composer Frederick Rzewski (b. 1938), for example, uses a decidedly tonal Chilean revolutionary song as the basis of a set of 36 variations, a decidedly old-fashioned form. Rzewski thus places his work conspicuously within the tradition of Bach's *Goldberg Variations* and Beethoven's *Diabelli Variations*. He uses a variety of stylistic and technical approaches in these variations; the set as a whole constitutes a veritable history of pianistic writing—some traditional, some not, some tonal, some not. This eclectic mixture of styles is typical of postmodernism, which in many respects represents the culmination of all pluralistic trends in 20th-century music. In the postmodern outlook, the very concept of a musical mainstream becomes irrelevant.

Like many composers of her generation, Thea Musgrave (b. 1928) cultivated but eventually moved beyond modernism, atonality, and serialism. Born in Scotland, she studied with Nadia Boulanger and eventually took a teaching position at the University of California, Santa Barbara. Her *Orfeo II* (1976), scored for solo flute and string ensemble, moves freely between tonal and atonal idioms. Long passages of its opening section ("Orfeo Laments") are centered on G and D. It would be misleading to say the

CD15, Track 7
MUSGRAVE
Orfeo II
Score Anthology II/182

Thea Musgrave. The composer rehearses her opera *Pontalba* (2003), with Robert Lyall, conductor of the New Orleans Opera Association. Musgrave was commissioned to write the work to celebrate the 200th anniversary of the Louisiana Purchase, and she chose to tell the story through the real-life character of Micaela Almonester, a New Orleans woman who became the Baroness de Pontalba. Musgrave has also written operas about Mary, Queen of Scots, Simon Bolivar, and Harriet Tubman—all of them, in the composer's own words, "feisty people."

Source: AP Wide World Photos

music is *in* either of these keys, but it has a strong sense of a tonal center. The tonality is reinforced rhythmically by the steady, repeated pattern of eighth notes in the opening in the lower voices, almost in the fashion of a Baroque ground bass.

At figure 4, the first violin intones the opening phrase of the most famous aria from Christoph Willibald Gluck's opera *Orfeo* of 1762, *Che farò senza Euridice?* ("What shall I do without Euridice?"), Orpheus's moving lament at the loss of his beloved wife (Example 23–2). This reminiscence from another musical world, the middle of the 18th century, has an eerie effect within the context of Musgrave's *Orfeo II*. When it

Example 23–2 Gluck, *Orfeo ed Euridice*, "Che farò senza Euridice?"

What shall I do without Euridice? Where shall I go without my beloved?

appears in the first violin at figure 4, it sounds like (and is) a fleeting memory. The flute soloist, representing Orpheus, listens to the fragments of this melody and tries to imitate them (just after figure 10 through figure 14) but cannot sustain the line. Orpheus's inability to recover the tonal melody parallels his inability to recover the dead Euridice.

References to past idioms, although frequently used in postmodern music, are not essential to its aesthetic. But what happens when modernism confronts popular music in the same work? Tania León's (b. 1943) *A la par* (1986), a three-movement work for percussion (including piano), offers one possible scenario. The second movement, "Guaguancó," mixes the rhythms of a Cuban popular dance with atonal harmonies. León calls this her attempt "to express the dichotomy between the folk-music traditions of my native Cuba and the Classical European training I received at the Havana Conservatory." In this particular movement, the repeated melodic-rhythmic figure in the bass line can be heard as representing the vernacular idioms of Cuban dance, while the other instrumental lines reflect the idiom of European modernism. Listen for the repeated melodic and rhythmic figure in the lower register of the piano. This kind of figure is typical of the Afro-Cuban dance known as the *guaguancó*.

The Spanish title *A la par* translates loosely as "at the same time as" or "on a par with," and it is a fitting description of the relationship between popular and modernist styles. Even though they are often quite distinct—each goes its own way—they nevertheless complement one another to create a whole larger than the sum of its parts. Every instrument seems to occupy its own space, yet in the end, everything is indeed *a la par*.

While León has turned to popular music for inspiration, others have turned to music of a much earlier era. Arvo Pärt (b. 1935), born in Estonia, wrote music using serialist and other modernist techniques during the early part of his career; the unpredictability of official Soviet reactions to his work led to a pattern of lengthy compositional silence interrupted by bursts of activity; his reputation began to go beyond Soviet borders with *Fratres* (chamber ensemble, 1976) and *Cantus in Memoriam for*

CD15, Track 8
LEÓN
A la par: Guaguancó
Score Anthology II/183

Tania León. In addition to composing, Tania León has conducted several of the world's leading orchestras, including the Leipzig Gewandhaus and the New York Philharmonic.

Source: Michael Provost/KMI Kaylor Management, Inc.

FOCUS   The Business of Composing in the 20th Century

Thanks to the introduction of meaningful international copyright laws, composers and recording artists of the early 20th century could make a decent living from their art if they pursued their careers over many years. By the late 20th century, the market potential of recorded sound was so great that composers could sometimes make a fortune from one recording of a single hit song.

Not surprisingly, a great deal of 20th-century musical talent gravitated toward the recording studio. And over the course of time, that studio became increasingly accessible. For most of the century, a recording was a major milestone for any composer, musician, or musical group. The barriers to be crossed were substantial: one had to secure a contract, rent a recording studio, and pay for pressings, packaging, and distribution. By the last decade of the century, the process had become so simple that musicians could record a CD in the privacy of their own homes and distribute the music almost instantly over the Internet. Even the music itself could be created by means of machines with few (if any) actual performers. Synthesizers that had taken up the space of half a basketball court in 1960 could now fit inside a laptop computer.

Composers of the 20th century also benefited from a new source of patronage: the university. Supported by a salary based on teaching, university composers were free to write the kind of music they wished to write, without commercial pressures. The arguments for and against such an arrangement have raged endlessly. Critics maintain that this "ivory tower" setting contributes to a sense of isolation between composer and society. Aaron Copland, for one, observed that it was not "healthy" for "the whole composing community to move within university walls," on the grounds that such individuals would find themselves cut off from stimuli that would otherwise enlarge their capacities as artists.[14] Others, like Milton Babbitt, argued that the university setting allowed at least a few composers to pursue more experimental kinds of composition, in the same way that many scientists pursue knowledge for its own sake rather than for its direct commercial applications (see Primary Evidence: "Who Cares If You Listen?"). Both sides would agree, however, that the phenomenon of the university composer has added even more diversity to the 20th-century musical scene, even as economic realities have curtailed the availability of such opportunities.

14. Howard Pollack, *Aaron Copland* (New York: Henry Holt, 1999), p. 286.

CD15, Track 9

PÄRT
O Weisheit
Score Anthology II/184

Benjamin Britten (string orchestra and bell, 1977). It was around this time that Pärt, who had delved into medieval and Renaissance vocal music as well as plainchant, discovered the concept of *tintinnabuli* (Latin, small bells). If plainchant could be heard as perfect unity (or, metaphorically, a stream of light), the simple triad was the most perfect realization of that unity when sent through a prism, revealing all colors: "The three notes of a triad are like bells. And that's why I call it tintinnabulation." For Pärt, this was a way to cope with "the complex and multifaceted," which "only confuses" him.[15]

Pärt emigrated in 1980, and has since received much attention in western Europe. (He now lives in Berlin.) Much of his music sets liturgical texts, although he usually writes for concert hall performances; his music has also been used in many film soundtracks. Although a score like "O Weisheit," from the *Seven Magnificat-Antiphons* (chamber choir, 1988, revised 1991) seems simple to a fault, the music has elements, both ancient and modern, that become audible: a relatively slow tempo, two durational values (half and whole note), harmony revolving around A major (although, when the lowest voices enter, the chord is in second inversion), and alternation between full 8-note chords (dividing each section in half) and 4-note chords (altos and tenors only). Phrasing of the text (the first of the Advent antiphons, sung before the Magnificat itself) is accomplished by one-measure rests.

The piece is indeed about unity, but the changing pitches (also in the middle voices) generate changes in overtones (much as a bell, continuing to vibrate after being struck, appears to be changing pitch). Although this is chantlike, there is no

15. Richard E. Rodda, liner notes for Arvo Pärt, *Fratres*, I Fiamminghi, The Orchestra of Flanders, Rudolf Werthen (Telarc CD-80387).

Arvo Pärt. Born in Estonia, the composer emigrated to the West in 1980 and has lived in Berlin since 1981.

Source: Universal Edition/Mats Ludqvist

melody per se; the voice leading is even less complex than early organum; and the dynamics are strictly *piano*, the only change occurring with the choral texture changes. "O Weisheit" is the first of seven short pieces; the complexities will expand gradually through the cycle, but the tintinnabular approach remains the essence of this and other Pärt works. He is not "rediscovering" the wheel of consonance; he is changing our perspective on it.

CONCLUSION

The decades immediately after World War II witnessed a second wave of modernism. Combinatoriality and integral serialism manifested a widespread desire to make a fresh start and explore new systems of composition that had not been widely used before the war. Aleatory music—music of chance—fulfilled these desires in an even more radical fashion, whereas electronic music opened up new possibilities of timbre and form in a way that gave the composer complete or nearly complete control over the musical work. By the late 1960s, however, at least some composers were beginning to turn away from the modernist aesthetic to embrace postmodernism, a more eclectic outlook that accepted the traditions of the past, including tonality, conventional forms, and established genres, as well as modernism itself. Minimalism, based on the extended manipulation of a limited number of musical ideas, offered yet another idiom running counter to the second wave of modernism. As will be seen in Chapter 24, other forms of music with origins outside the Western art music world came to dominate in the marketplace, developing in a variety of directions over the second half of the century and contributing to a musical scene that by the year 2000 was more diverse than at any previous time in the history of Western music.

Major Composers of the 20th Century

FRANCE

Erik Satie (1866–1925) was an iconoclast and an inspiration to many later composers, most notably **Claude Debussy** (see Composer Profile, Chapter 20). Satie cultivated mostly smaller forms, and many of his works are hauntingly beautiful. Others are openly challenging, even absurdist. His *Three Pieces in the Form of a Pear*, for piano, was a response to critics who said he had no sense of form; he indicated that another one of his piano pieces, *Vexations*, was to be played 840 times in succession (premiere, 1963). Satie collaborated with Sergei Diaghilev to produce the ballet *Parade* in 1917. His reminiscences, published in 1912, bear the title *Memoirs of an Amnesiac*.

Paul Dukas (1865–1935) is best remembered for his tone poem *The Sorcerer's Apprentice* (made famous by Mickey Mouse in Walt Disney's *Fantasia* and *Fantasia 2000*). An important figure for many decades as a composer, critic, and teacher, Dukas destroyed most of his compositions shortly before his death, leaving posterity relatively little to appreciate of his work. **Maurice Ravel** (1877–1937), along with Debussy, was the most outstanding exponent of impressionism. His piano music, particularly *Gaspard de la nuit* and *Miroirs*, is of outstandingly high quality. The celebrated *Boléro* manifests Ravel's talents as an orchestrator; his orchestral version of Mussorgsky's *Pictures at an Exhibition* is in fact better known than the piano original. Ravel also wrote two operas, several ballets (most notably *Daphnis et Chloé*), two piano concertos (one for the left hand alone, written for a pianist who had lost his right arm during World War I), a string quartet, and a number of songs for voice and orchestra.

The composers **Darius Milhaud** (1892–1975), **Francis Poulenc** (1899–1963), **Georges Auric** (1899–1983), **Arthur Honegger** (1892–1955), **Germaine Tailleferre** (1892–1983), and **Louis Durey** (1888–1979) were dubbed "Les Six" ("The Six") by the journalist Henri Collet in 1920. These six composers were only loosely connected in their individual styles, but all were united in their attempts to write in a distinctively French manner, to draw on subjects from everyday life, and to integrate styles from outside the so-called classical tradition into their music. Milhaud was a prolific and wide-ranging composer whose output encompassed chamber music (his 18 string quartets deserve to be better known), piano music (see Chapter 20), symphony, opera, and even electronic music. His *Création du monde* and *Le Boeuf sur le toit* use jazz elements to great effect. A brilliant pianist, Poulenc developed a highly idiomatic style for the instrument. His early works include a ballet for Diaghilev, *Les Biches* (1924). He later wrote a religious opera, *Dialogue of the Carmelites* (1957), that has held its own on the stage. Poulenc's *Gloria* is also frequently performed, as are many of his fine songs for voice and piano. Auric was a child prodigy: by the time he was 16 he had already written nearly three hundred songs. He wrote several ballets for Diaghilev, the best known of which is *Les Matelots* (1925). In 1946, he wrote the film score for Jean Cocteau's classic film *Beauty and the Beast*. Honegger is perhaps best known for *Pacific 231*, a musical portrayal of a steam locomotive, but he also wrote many works for the stage and for chorus. The cantatas *Le Roi David* (1921) and *Jeanne d'Arc au bûcher* (1938) are widely admired, as are his five symphonies and his many sonatas for various instruments. The only woman composer of Les Six, Tailleferre studied orchestration with Ravel and wrote in a number

of genres, both instrumental and vocal. Her *Concertino for Harp and Orchestra* was commissioned and premiered by the Boston Symphony Orchestra in 1927. Durey worked primarily in the area of chamber music and song but eventually turned to using music as a means toward political ends. He was active in the French Communist Party for many years, and his *The Long March* (1949), for tenor solo, chorus, and orchestra, uses a text by Mao Tse-tung.

Edgard Varèse (see Composer Profile, Chapter 20) and **Olivier Messiaen** (1908–1992) were important figures to an entire generation of composers coming of age after World War II. Most prominent among these was **Pierre Boulez** (b. 1925), who, along with the German Karlheinz Stockhausen and the American Milton Babbitt, was one of the first composers to embrace total serialism. From 1971 to 1977, Boulez served as music director of the New York Philharmonic and introduced an unprecedented quantity of new or recent music into that orchestra's repertory. From the early 1970s until 1992, he also directed France's Institute for Research and Coordination in Acoustics/Music (IRCAM), a major government-funded center for musical research and performance.

GREAT BRITAIN

Edward Elgar (1857–1934) is best known for his *Pomp and Circumstance March no. 2* (the theme song of graduations), but his style was on the whole far more chromatic. He was widely considered the leading English composer of his day. His concertos for violin and for cello, the oratorio *The Dream of Gerontius*, and the orchestral "Enigma" Variations remain in the repertory today. **Frederick Delius** (1862–1934), regarded as the finest English composer of the impressionist style, lived for a time in Florida but spent most of his life in France. His orchestrations are particularly noteworthy in such works as *Brigg Fair*, *Appalachia*, and *On Hearing the First Cuckoo in Spring*. His *Mass of Life* is an enormous work for soloists, chorus, and orchestra, set to texts by the German philosopher and poet Friedrich Nietzsche.

Ralph Vaughan Williams (1872–1958) was a leader in the 20th-century renaissance of English music. He was an active member of the English Folk Song Society, and many of his works incorporate folk tunes or folklike tunes. A number of his compositions evoke the modal counterpoint of another golden age of English music, the 16th century. His *Fantasia on a Theme by Tallis* for strings and his *5 Variants of "Dives and Lazarus"* are good examples of this kind of sound. Vaughan Williams's nine symphonies are significant contributions to the genre in the 20th century; he also wrote a substantial quantity of choral music that continues to be performed today, including several outstanding hymns. **Gustav Holst** (1874–1934) is best remembered for his suite *The Planets* (1916), brilliantly scored for an enormous orchestra, but his other works—for chorus and for orchestra alike—deserve wider exposure. **William Walton** (1902–1983) gained international attention with his witty music for *Façade*, a monologue with an equally witty libretto by the poet Edith Sitwell. But Walton went on to demonstrate mastery over a variety of styles and genres, from oratorio (*Belshazzar's Feast*) to concerto (one apiece for violin, viola, and cello) to film music.

Michael Tippett (1905–1998) composed several successful operas (including *Midsummer Marriage*, *King Priam*, and *The Knot*

Garden), but his most widely acclaimed work is *A Child of Our Time* (1941), written in the tradition of Bach's Passions but substituting African-American spirituals for Lutheran chorales. Tippett's four symphonies are also worthy of note. **Benjamin Britten** (1913–1976) is acknowledged as the greatest composer of opera in the English language since Henry Purcell. *Peter Grimes, Billy Budd*, and *The Turn of the Screw* have all become standards of the opera house. *The Young Person's Guide to the Orchestra* (1946) is a series of variations and a fugue on a theme by Purcell; each variation highlights a particular instrument or group of instruments in the orchestra. Britten's many vocal works retain a distinctly English sound, yet their appeal extends far beyond his native land; his masterpiece may well be the *War Requiem* (see Chapter 22). The music of **Peter Maxwell Davies** (b. 1934) synthesizes many different styles and idioms. His *Tenebrae pro Gesualdo* explores the chromaticism of the late Renaissance composer, and his opera *Taverner* centers on the 16th-century English composer. But Davies's most celebrated work by far is *Eight Songs for a Mad King* (1969), which calls for the instrumentalists to sit in birdcages, a reference to King George III's bullfinches and a metaphor for his mental imprisonment. **Harrison Birtwistle** (b. 1934) established his reputation with the opera *Punch and Judy* (1966–67), a re-creation of the classic puppet show using live performers. Birtwistle writes for most instrumental and vocal media, but his operas have gained the most attention, including *Down by the Greenwood Side* (1968–69), (1973–1984), *Gawain* (1990–92), and *The Last Supper* (1998–99).

Thea Musgrave (b. 1928), a native of Scotland, studied with both Nadia Boulanger and Aaron Copland. Her music has been enormously successful on both sides of the Atlantic. Well known for her many operas, including *The Voice of Ariadne* (1973), *Mary, Queen of Scots* (1977), and *Harriet, The Woman Called Moses* (1984), Musgrave has taught at Queens College in New York since 1987. **Andrew Lloyd Webber** (b. 1948), the most financially successful theatrical composer ever, has demonstrated time and again the appeal of modern musical theater, tackling an eclectic variety of subject matter and styles in hits such as *Jesus Christ Superstar, Evita, Cats, Phantom of the Opera*, and *Sunset Boulevard*.

ITALY

Giacomo Puccini (1858–1924) was widely hailed as the successor to Verdi in the tradition of Italian opera. He scored international successes with such works as *La Bohème* (1896, the point of departure for the 1996 Broadway musical *Rent*), *Madama Butterfly* (1904), *Tosca* (1901), and *Turandot* (unfinished at the composer's death, it was completed and premiered in 1926). Although his music is more chromatic and on the whole more polyphonic than Verdi's, Puccini was an equal master of lyricism. No subsequent Italian composer has captured the stage to the same degree.

Ottorino Respighi (1879–1936) and **Gian Francesco Malipiero** (1882–1973) are generally regarded as Neoclassicists, although this label does not do justice to the full variety of their music. Respighi's three sets of *Ancient Airs and Dances* (1916, 1923, 1931), based on chansons and dance music of the Italian Renaissance, exposed many listeners for the first time to the delights of this earlier music. Malipiero was the moving force behind the first modern edition of Monteverdi's complete works.

Luigi Dallapiccola (1904–1975) was one of the first Italian composers to embrace dodecaphonic composition. Many of his works are overtly political. The *Canti di Prigionia* (1941, "Songs of Prison"), for example, sets texts by three famous prisoners: Mary Stuart (Queen of Scots), Boethius, and Savonarola, a monk and Florentine leader who was martyred for his reformist beliefs. The opera *Il Prigioniero* (1948) addresses similar themes. Dallapiccola taught and traveled widely in the United States after World War II. **Luigi Nono** (1924–1990) was another composer who connected his music with politics. He embraced dodecaphonic composition and married Schoenberg's daughter Nuria. His later works incorporated aleatory and electronic techniques as well. His most significant composition, *Intolleranza* (1960, revised 1970), sets texts by Brecht, Sartre, and others in a condemnation of social inequity and imperialism. **Luciano Berio** (1925–2003) was the most prominent composer of the Italian avant-garde. His music is eclectic and consistently provocative. Berio's best known work is *Sinfonia* (1968) for voices and orchestra, which uses a number of collagelike techniques. Section II is a tribute to the memory of Martin Luther King, Jr., in which, as the composer explains, the eight voices "exchang[e] among themselves the sounds constituting the name of the black martyr until the point when his name is clearly enunciated." Section III uses the entire third movement of Mahler's Second Symphony as an underpinning above which Berio sets a dazzling array of thematic references to the works of other composers, from Bach to Boulez. He is also known for a series of challenging solo pieces, each called *Sequenza*.

SPAIN

Manuel de Falla (1876–1946) combined the musical idioms of his native Spain with an impressionistic style. He spent the years 1907 to 1914 in Paris and enjoyed the support of Debussy, Dukas, and Ravel, among others. He returned to Spain in 1914 but left for Argentina at the end of the Spanish Civil War in 1939. His most frequently performed works include *Nights in the Gardens of Spain* for piano and orchestra, the ballets *The Three-Cornered Hat* and *El Amor brujo*, and the *Siete canciones populares españolas*.

GREECE

Iannis Xenakis (1922–2001) began his academic work in Athens as an engineering student, but he then went to Paris to study composition with Messiaen. He combined these two fields when he helped the celebrated architect Le Corbusier create the Philips Pavilion for the 1958 Brussels World's Fair, for which both he and Edgard Varèse supplied electronic music (see Chapter 20). As a composer, Xenakis rejected both serialism and aleatory music, opting instead for an approach determined in large part by mathematical calculations.

GERMANY AND AUSTRIA

Composition in German-speaking countries was by no means dominated by atonalists and serialists in the first half of the 20th century. **Arnold Schoenberg, Alban Berg,** and **Anton Webern** (see Composer Profiles, Chapter 21) remain among the most celebrated composers of their era, but **Paul Hindemith** (1895–1963) achieved comparable renown as the leading German figure in the Neoclassical movement. A prolific composer in virtually every genre, he never abandoned tonality, although his works expand the concept of consonance well beyond that of earlier generations. Forced to resign his teaching position at the Berlin Academy of Music because of his refusal to divorce his Jewish wife, the couple emigrated first to Switzerland, then to the United States, becoming American citizens in 1946. Hindemith taught composition for many years at Yale University. His best known works include the symphonic suite derived from his opera *Mathis der Maler*, *Ludus tonalis* (a 20th-century counterpart to Bach's *Well-Tempered Clavier*), and the *Symphonic Metamorphosis on Themes by Weber*. He also wrote many sonatas and concertos for a variety of instruments. His song cycle *Das Marienleben* is a staple of the repertory.

Kurt Weill (1900–1950) wrote *The Threepenny Opera* (a thoroughly modernized version of the Gay and Pepusch classic from the 1720s) and *Rise and Fall of the City of Mahagonny* (Anthology) in collaboration with the poet and playwright Bertolt Brecht (1898–1956). Both works seek to realize Brecht's idea of "epic theater," in which emotional distance between the viewer and the events on stage is cultivated: the audience is repeatedly made aware of the artifice behind the illusion. With the rise of the Nazis to power in 1933, Weill emigrated to France and then to the United States, where he wrote several Broadway musicals.

Hans Werner Henze (b. 1926) is an eclectic, extremely prolific, and at times controversial composer. He intended his oratorio *The Raft of the Medusa* (1968), depicting the aftermath of on an infamous 1816 shipwreck of a French frigate, to be a memorial to Che Guevara, but some performers refused to perform with a portrait of Guevara hanging over them; the scandal helped make Henze an international figure (the work was finally premiered in 1971). Unlike his fellow Marxist Nono, Henze's political did not inspire an especially radical compositional style. **Karlheinz Stockhausen** (1928–2007) was a leading figure in the German avant-garde after World War II, leading the way for a new generation of composers seeking to distance themselves from the music of the war and prewar years. He embraced serialism, total serialism, electronic music, aleatory music, and spatially organized music with an unswerving confidence. He combined his compositional energies with an immense talent for organization and showmanship in the best sense of the word.

SCANDINAVIA

Carl Nielsen (1865–1931) cultivated the symphony (he wrote six of them) as well as the concerto (one apiece for violin, flute, clarinet). His harmonic idiom is more dissonant than Mahler's, but his music displays a comparable, sometimes Neoclassical sense of contrapuntal grandeur mixed with humor. The Finnish composer **Jean Sibelius** (1865–1957) also straddles the 19th and 20th centuries. Several of his best known works, such as *En Saga* and *Finlandia*, are overtly patriotic. After brief tours in Germany and the United States (where Yale University awarded him an honorary degree in 1914), he spent the remaining years of his life in semiseclusion and gave up composing altogether in 1929. His most important works are the seven symphonies, the last of which are written in an advanced chromatic idiom.

HUNGARY

Zoltán Kodály (1882–1967) collaborated with **Béla Bartók** (see Composer Profile, Chapter 20) in collecting folk music of eastern Europe, and his compositions reflect elements of this music as well. Kodály's best known work is the *Psalmus Hungaricus* (1923), written for the festivities celebrating the 50th anniversary of the union of the cities Buda and Pest. The orchestral suite from his opera *Háry János* is also frequently performed. But he is probably best remembered for developing the Kodály Method of teaching music to young children (see Focus: Music Education in the 20th Century).

György Ligeti (1923–2006) left Budapest in 1956 in the wake of the failed uprising against the Soviet Union and settled in Germany. His *Atmosphères* for orchestra (1961), used in Stanley Kubrick's film *2001: A Space Odyssey*, makes for a good introduction to the work of this remarkably versatile composer.

CZECHOSLOVAKIA/ CZECH REPUBLIC

Leoš Janáček (1854–1928), although born even before Mahler, did not begin to write his most important music until around 1900. It was then that he began to develop a theory of "speech melody" in which vocal lines more nearly resemble the natural contours of spoken language. His operas *Jenůfa*, *Kátya Kabanová*, *The Cunning Little Vixen*, and *The Makropoulos Affair* have all held the stage in Europe and to a lesser degree North America. His *Slavonic Mass* is also an important work. **Alois Hába** (1893–1973) began exploring the possibilities of microtonal music around 1920, dividing all half steps into two. He also developed what he called "nonthematic music," in which all voices are melodically unrelated. His String Quartet no. 3 (1922) uses both these techniques.

POLAND

Karol Szymanowski (1882–1937) absorbed a variety of styles: German late Romanticism (Richard Strauss), Russian mysticism (Scriabin), and impressionism (Debussy). His works, although tonal, flirt with atonality at times but always sustain lyrical interest and are almost invariably virtuosic. He wrote many works for solo piano (including a number of mazurkas), for piano and orchestra, and for orchestra, including three symphonies. He was an important influence for the remarkable generation of Polish composers who followed: **Witold Lutoslawski** (1913–1994), **Krzysztof Penderecki** (b. 1933), and **Henryk Gorecki** (b. 1933). Lutoslawski's earlier works are rather in the style of Bartók, drawing on Polish folk sources; he later explored ideas of aleatory and dodecaphonic composition. Penderecki (pronounced "Pen-de-ret-ski") has been particularly interested in exploring new possibilities of timbre, as is evident in his most celebrated work, *Threnody for the Victims of Hiroshima* (discussed in this chapter). He has written in many genres, for instruments and voices alike. After laboring in relative obscurity for many years, Gorecki ("Go-ret-ski") rocketed to fame in 1994 with his Symphony no. 3, a work he had written in 1976.

RUSSIA AND THE SOVIET UNION

Alexander Scriabin (1872–1915) is noted for his many piano miniatures, ten piano sonatas, and his large-scale orchestral works, especially *Le Poème de l'extase* ("Poem of Ecstasy") and *Prometheus, or the Poem of Fire*, the latter of which includes a part for a "color organ" designed to convert specific pitches or keys into colors (C major as red, F♯ major as blue, etc.). Productions of this work during the composer's life were unsuccessful for technological reasons. Scriabin's sense of advanced chromaticism eventually merged into a kind of free atonality around 1908. Despite his early death, Scriabin's "mystic chord" was a crucial influence on many atonalists seeking an organizing pitch principle, including Ruth Crawford.

Sergei Rachmaninoff (1873–1943), by contrast, continued in the 19th-century tradition of Tchaikovsky and Rimsky-Korsakov. He was hardly a modernist when compared with his countryman and younger colleague **Igor Stravinsky** (see Composer Profile, Chapter 20). Rachmaninoff's most popular works are the Piano Concertos nos. 2 and 3, the *Preludes* and *Études-Tableaux* for piano, and the *Rhapsody on a Theme of Paganini* for piano and orchestra. An internationally renowned pianist and conductor, he fled Russia after the Revolution in 1917 and eventually settled in Los Angeles. **Sergei Prokofiev** (1891–1953) spent much of his early career in France after the Revolution of 1917 but returned to the Soviet Union in 1932 and spent the rest of his life there working in an uneasy relationship with the regime. The communist authorities at first looked to Prokofiev as a kind of prodigal son who had voluntarily returned home from the "decadent" West, and the government bestowed many honors on him. That same government would later attack Prokofiev and his colleague **Dmitri Shostakovich** (see Composer Profile, Chapter 22) for their "decadence" and "formalism."

Aram Khachaturian (1903–1978), an Armenian, is noted for his use of exotic tone colors: the frenetic "Sabre Dance" from the ballet *Gayane* is a well-known example of his ability to incorporate timbres and modes that sound vaguely Asian yet still within the Western tradition. **Alfred Schnittke** (1934–1998) was an ethnic German born in Russia. His works cover a wide range of styles and media, from electronic music to more traditional genres such as concertos, suites, symphonies, and operas. His *Requiem* (1975) is particularly noteworthy. **Arvo Pärt** (b. 1935), born in Estonia, emigrated to Vienna in 1980, later moving to Berlin. Since the 1970s, he has applied the concept of *tintinnabuli* to produce triadically based, chantlike music full of changing overtones associated with the sound of bells. He is especially fond of setting Latin and Church Slavonic texts.

LATIN AMERICA

Like his near contemporaries Bartók and Vaughan Williams, the Brazilian **Heitor Villa-Lobos** (1887–1959) traveled throughout his native land to collect folk songs. He avoided direct quotation of these materials in his compositions, preferring instead to use them as a source of inspiration for his own ideas. In the celebrated *Bachianas Brasileiras*, a series of works for a variety of different instruments, he used such themes within a polyphonic texture reminiscent of Bach. **Carlos Chavez** (1899–1978) was the preeminent Mexican composer of his era. He, too, collected and drew on native musical sources for inspiration. His single best known work is the *Sinfonia India* of 1936. The Argentinian composer **Alberto Ginastera** (1916–1983) also drew on native idioms but cultivated a variety of other styles as well. His Second Piano Concerto (1972) is based on a 12-tone row derived from the dissonant chord in the finale of Beethoven's Ninth Symphony. His trilogy of operas about notorious Meditarranean figures (1964–1971) shocked audiences with their postexpressionistic sexual intensity. **Mauricio Kagel** (b. 1931), also from Argentina, has produced provocative works that are as much theater as music, even when performed in the concert hall.

UNITED STATES

Foremost among American modernists in the 20th century were **Charles Ives** (see Composer Profile, Chapter 20) and three Californians: **Henry Cowell** (1897–1965), **Harry Partch** (1901–1974), and **John Cage** (see Composer Profile, Chapter 23). Cowell, according to his student Cage, provided the "open sesame" for new music in America, experimenting with tone clusters and new timbres long before they became fashionable. Cowell was also an early champion of the music of Ives, at a time when few people knew the elder composer's work. Partch rejected almost every element of Western music and sought new models of sound in the music of ancient Greece and Asia; he also created an array of new musical instruments, including what he called a "gourd tree" and "cloud chamber bowls."

Often classified as "romantics" or "conservatives" (but perhaps Neoclassical in the essence of their styles), composers like **Virgil Thomson** (1896–1989), **Roy Harris** (1898–1979), and **Samuel Barber** (1910–1981) remained within the extended tonal idiom at a time when many of their contemporaries were embracing atonality and (later) serialism. Thomson is particularly known for his operas, which include *Four Saints in Three Acts* (to a libretto by Gertrude Stein) and *The Mother of Us All* (to a libretto, also by Stein, about Susan B. Anthony and the struggle for women's suffrage). He was also one of the finest music critics of his time. Harris is remembered primarily for his symphonies, most of which reflect some aspect of the American experience (no. 4 is the *Folksong Symphony*, with chorus; no. 6 the *Gettysburg Address*). Barber's lyricism, which won great praise in his time, is evident in his *Adagio for Strings* (taken from his second string quartet), his Violin Concerto, the opera *Vanessa*, and the song cycle *Knoxville: Summer of 1915* (for soprano and orchestra, to texts by James Agee).

Gian Carlo Menotti (b. 1911–2007) was born in Italy but spent most of his life in the United States. He is noted particularly for his operas *The Medium*, *The Telephone*, *The Consul*, and *Amahl and the Night Visitors*. His style is unpretentious but dramatically effective and generally within the technical reach of amateur opera companies. **Vincent Persichetti** (1915–1987) wrote in an idiom that was at once both modern and lyrical. His output includes nine symphonies and a number of concertos and sonatas.

Of the many American (and non-American) composers who took up jazz elements and mixed them into concert hall repertory, the most notable was **Leonard Bernstein** (1918–1990), who wrote his undergraduate thesis at Harvard on the use of jazz in classical music and went on to compose a number of works that did just that, including the musical *West Side Story* (1957). His other works include the operetta *Candide*, the *Chichester Psalms*, and three symphonies, notably no. 3 (*Kaddish*). In 1958, he became the first American-born permanent conductor of the New York Philharmonic Orchestra and used the position as a forum for a series of acclaimed broadcasts aimed at children. He was the first conductor to record all of Mahler's symphonies, and his recordings sold widely. His 1976 Norton Lectures were published in both book and video formats entitled *The Unanswered Question*.

Other composers developed an idiom not as immediately accessible to the wider public. **Roger Sessions** (1896–1985) wrote an opera at the age of 12 and entered Harvard University two years later; he was appointed to the faculty of Smith College at age 21. After eight years in Europe he returned to the United States to teach at UC Berkeley, Princeton, and Harvard. He established a reputation as a "composer's composer," one whose works were greatly admired by his colleagues yet never gained a wide following among audiences at large. His most important compositions are the eight symphonies, the Violin Concerto, the three piano sonatas, the opera *Montezuma*, and the suite from his incidental music to the play *The Black Maskers*. **Elliott Carter** (b. 1908) is another composer whose music is enormously admired by a devoted group of followers. He won the Pulitzer Prize twice, for his Second String Quartet in 1960 and again for his Third String Quartet in 1973. His early music tends toward the Neoclassical, but he later embraced serial composition. His music tends to be highly polyphonic and metrically complex.

Milton Babbitt (b. 1916) was at the forefront of two important developments around midcentury: total serialism and electronic music. His *Three Compositions for Piano* (Anthology) was the first work by any composer to serialize pitch and nonpitch elements alike, including rhythm, timbre, and dynamics. His *All Set* (1957) is a 12-tone work for jazz ensemble. Babbitt taught composition for many years at Princeton University and exercised a profound influence on subsequent generations of American composers. **George Crumb** (b. 1929), a native of West Virginia, taught at the University of Pennsylvania. His compositions explore a remarkable variety of timbres and constructive devices, and the graphic presentation of his scores is paramount in their interpretation. His most noted works include *Makrokosmos* for piano, *Echoes of Time and the River* (for which he won the Pulitzer Prize in 1968), *Black Angels* (for amplified string quartet), and *Ancient Voices of Children* (for soprano, boy soprano, and seven instrumentalists). In his vocal music, Crumb has frequently set texts of the poet Federico García Lorca.

Minimalists **Terry Riley** (b. 1935), **Steve Reich** (b. 1936), and **Philip Glass** (b. 1937) have all learned from John Cage and explored the musical implications of the dictum "less is more." All three of these younger composers have formed groups that perform their music in live concerts. Riley played in jazz ensembles in his early career, and his landmark work, *In C* (discussed in this

chapter), is based on the impulse toward improvisation. Reich studied composition at Mills College with Darius Milhaud and Luciano Berio before moving back to his native New York, where he has flourished as an independent composer. Glass won critical acclaim for his opera *Einstein on the Beach* in 1975, as well as the subsequent operas *Satyagraha* (1980) and *Akhnaten* (1983). His repetitive use of small units and his approach to form, rhythm, and texture have been shaped in part by his assimilation of certain Indian and African musical idioms. A younger generation has taken the minimalist approach in different direction; one of the best known is **John Adams** (b. 1947), who has demonstrated a flair for dramatic works (*Nixon in China*, *The Death of Klinghoffer*) as well as orchestral pieces (*The Wound-Dresser*, *Harmonium*). He won the Pulitzer Prize in Music in 2003 for *On the Transmigration of Souls*, composed in remembrance of the events of September 11, 2001.

A number of American women composers rose to great prominence in the second half of the century. **Pauline Oliveros** (b. 1932), born in Houston, has been a driving force behind the production and performance of new music in the San Francisco Bay Area for several decades. Some of her works involve group participation, blurring the distinction between performers and listeners. She has written for unconventional ensembles (for example, garden hoses and sprinklers) and for conventional ensembles in unconventional ways (for example, works in which the singers in a mixed chorus make all kinds of sounds with their mouths and hands); she has also composed for electronic media. **Joan Tower** (b. 1938), a native of New York, was a founding member of the Da Capo Chamber Players, one of the leading ensembles of its kind, specializing in contemporary music. She has received numerous grants and awards for her compositions, which have won a wide audience. **Ellen Taaffe Zwilich** (b. 1939) was the first woman ever to receive a D.M.A. (Doctor of Musical Arts) in composition from the Juilliard School (in 1975) and received the Pulitzer Prize in Music for her Symphony no. 1 in 1983.

Tania León (b. 1943) grew up in Havana and emigrated to the United States in 1967. She served as the first music director of the Dance Theater of Harlem and has conducted orchestras in the United States and abroad. Her opera *Scourge of Hyacinths* (1994) received performances in Europe and North America and has won widespread acclaim; her libretto is based on a radio play by the Nigerian Nobel-winning playwright Wole Soyinka. Her music reflects the diversity of her ancestry in a variety of cultures, including French, Spanish, Chinese, African, and Cuban. **Libby Larsen** (b. 1950) has established herself as one of the leading composers of concert and choral music. Academically trained (she holds a Ph.D. in composition from the University of Minnesota), she has remained largely independent of university positions, writing instead on commission from major orchestras and other ensembles. Women who have been active in the world of experimental and electronic music include **Laurie Spiegel** (b. 1945), **Laurie Anderson** (b. 1947), **Alice Shields** (b. 1943), **Wendy Carlos** (b. 1939), **Alison Knowles** (b. 1933), **Eve Beglarian** (b. 1958), and **Joan LaBarbara** (b. 1947).

The Popular Music of America and Its Influence

CHAPTER

24

istinctions between "popular" and "art" music are both problematic and useful. It is often difficult and sometimes impossible to separate the two into neat categories (see Appendix 4: "The Concepts of 'Popular' and 'Art' Music"), and yet these concepts highlight key differences between two broad categories of music in ways that can help us trace their historical development more readily. Popular music tends to have a wider appeal than "art" or "classical" music; in the 20th century and beyond, it is more likely to be transmitted in ways that bypass or supplement the medium of print. Popular music did not begin in the 20th century— any number of works considered earlier in this book might well be considered "popular"—but the advent of sound recording, radio transmission, and other electronic media over the last 125 years has created an economic market for this music that made popular music commercially lucrative (and thus attractive to composers and performers) to an extent that would have been unthinkable in earlier times. These same media have helped increrause public exposure to art music as well, although the number of similarly lucrative classical "hits" is small in comparison to the total variety of classical music recorded and broadcast.

Popular music has played a particularly important role in the musical culture of the United States. Repeated waves of immigration and westward expansion have created an unusually rich and diverse musical culture. And yet the resulting diversity of this country, so crucial to its cultural identity, makes any attempt to summarize its popular music a difficult task. Size is one immediate obstacle: how does one tackle regional differences when the regions themselves are larger than most other nations? The music of a resident population inevitably changes when a new group of people with their own language(s) and outlook(s) arrive on the scene. Internal relocations from one region of the country to another (for religious, social, or economic reasons) have caused American popular culture to shift and blend anew. Music is an area where such changes have become as current as the media that make them possible: what was once oral tradition and therefore regional in reach has become written down, listened to, and observed directly or electronically. Music is now so portable that any style can quickly become international in scope.

Virtually all music in the United States can be traced to its origins elsewhere, and often to multiple points of origin, because musical styles have constantly absorbed influences, often changing into something very different, even new. In the sketch of popular American music that follows, there will be two principal points of discussion: the development of a particular genre in the United States (including its foreign sources) and the way such a genre can experience the "ecstasy of influence" when a classical composer incorporates something from it.

BEFORE 1900

Europeans who came to North America from the 17th century onward did so in search of economic gain, freedom from religious persecution, or some combination of the two. The Pilgrims who landed at Plymouth Rock in 1620, in what is now Massachusetts, were English Separatist Puritans (Calvinists who "separated" from what they felt was the insufficiently reformed Anglican church). They had first fled to Holland and then, wishing to remain "English," traveled to New England. Other new colonies based on principles of religious freedom included Rhode Island (1636), and Pennsylvania; initially a refuge for persecuted Quakers, the colony also welcomed refugees of all faiths.

Except for the Quakers (who do not use music in their worship services), all of these groups continued the European traditions of sacred music. Indeed, it is no coincidence that the first book printed in British North America, the *Bay Psalm Book* (1640), was a collection of metrical Psalm texts intended to be sung. And it is no coincidence that in its earliest editions this book contained no notated music, because the congregations for whom it was intended already knew these tunes by heart; it is in this sense that this music might be considered "popular." (The *Bay Psalm Book* was first published with music in 1698.)

Other collections followed: the "Nonconformist" (later called Congregationalist) English pastor Isaac Watts's (1674–1748) psalms and hymns (the latter based on non-biblical texts), first published in *Hymns and Spiritual Songs* (1707) and later in America by Benjamin Franklin. Charles Wesley (1707–1788), a brother of Methodism's founder, John Wesley, wrote the lyrics for over 7,000 hymns, and the first group of American-born hymnodists (sometimes called the First New England school) included William Billings (see Chapter 13), Justin Morgan, Timothy Swan, Stephen Jenks, Jeremiah Ingalls, and Daniel Read.

Other factors encouraged the composition of hymnody. So-called singing schools began to crop up in New England in the 1720s, in which musicians would educate their students on the principles of score reading and singing (Billings operated such a school). A series of "Great Awakenings" brought open-air evangelism (advocated by American Congregationalist minister Jonathan Edwards and John Wesley and other English Methodists) to religious worship. These eras (ca. 1730–1760, ca. 1800–1830, ca. 1850–1900) produced new markets for hymnals and other religious songbooks. At the turn of the 19th century, singing-school teachers eased the learning process by inventing **shape-note singing,** replacing pitch staff reading with sol-fa syllables (recalling the Guidonian system), indicated by differing notehead shapes (Example 24–1):

Example 24–1 The sol-fa syllables used in shape-note singing (four-shape system)

fa   sol   la   fa   sol   la   mi   fa

Inspired by Billings's *The New England Psalm Singer* (1770) and similar collections, editors began compiling "sacred harp" collections, a reference to David the psalmist. The "sacred harp" style involves the use of "lining out" by a leader to cue a congregation for the next line of text, creating a **call and response** texture. The three most famous collections of this kind were the *Southern Harmony and Musical Companion* (1835, last revised 1854), its successor the *Christian Harmony*, using seven-shape notation (1866, now in two competing versions), and the *Sacred Harp* (1844), which was eventually published in four competing versions due to controversies over content. The most recently revised of these, the 1991 Denson volume, still contains 14 Billings tunes.

In 1867, three northern abolitionists published *Slave Songs of the United States*, an important vehicle for the preservation of African-American religious song from the antebellum era. Each of the 136 songs was presented as a melody with words; while the rhythms and pitches were probably homogenized to "European" standards, the power of text and music was not lost. In 1871, an ensemble of singers at Fisk University, a school for emancipated slaves in Nashville (founded 1866), was formed; dubbed the Fisk University Jubilee Singers, they began fundraising tours for their university in Europe and the United States, singing four-part harmonizations of these and other "slave songs."

The Fisk University Jubilee Singers, June, 1925. The world-famous choral group continued to make world tours after its initial visit to Europe in 1873. The members are waiting in a British rail station, from which they would travel to Windsor Castle to perform before King George V.

Source: © Hulton-Deutsch Collection/CORBIS. All Rights Reserved

Although many of these songs (and others borrowed from the oral traditions of African-American worship) would come to be known as **spirituals** or be categorized as **gospel music,** the terms were not originally limited to African-American music. Both Caucausian- and African-American religious worship were similarly ecstatic in nature during the height of the third Great Awakening. Churches, however, remained largely segregated, and practices varied widely. Some Caucasian-American congregations retained the sacred harp style, while others continued or resumed reliance on hymnals directed at specific Protestant denominations.

African-American services emphasized heterophonic singing and ecstatic exhortations and responses to express the fervor of belief. The process of codification has continued with the publication of the *African American Heritage Hymnal* (2001), a collection of "hymns, spirituals, and gospel songs" for the major historical African-American denominations (approximately 80 percent of black Christians). In addition to adding repertory previously ignored in Caucasian-American hymnals, the book hoped to reveal the style of performance of the "Euro-American authored hymns [that] in our use and singing [were] distinctly different from the musical notation in the hymnal."[1] This combination of goals reflects current attitudes toward performance practice as much as repertory. As the variety of gospel music categories in the Grammy Awards (see Chapter 19) suggests, African-American gospel music has continued to experience musical interchange with secular music since the beginning of the 20th century.

The references to hymns (and other genres) by Charles Ives has been discussed in Chapter 20. Ives did not merely use quotation because he "liked the tunes." He was attempting to re-create the experience of hearing different performances simultaneously, to portray in sound the thoughts of the 19th-century New England transcendental school of Emerson and Thoreau, and to express nostalgia and memory; but the sheer amount of quotation in "The Things Our Fathers Loved" suggests Ives's own mercurial personality.

African-American composers, on the other hand, wanted to make the religious music of their people a primary basis for concert hall music. Composers such as Harry T. Burleigh, William Grant Still, Margaret Bonds, J. Rosamond Johnson, Julia Perry, R. Nathaniel Dett, and Undine Smith Moore set spirituals as art songs; performers such as Roland Hayes, Marian Anderson, and Paul Robeson sang and recorded them. The same composers often wrote original songs with the flavor of the spiritual, or incorporated them into orchestral works.

RAGTIME AND BLUES

Music that developed largely through unwritten traditions found new audiences in the early 20th century through the media of sound recordings, radio, and printed music. Audiences that previously had little or no direct contact with such styles as ragtime, blues, jazz, and country music now had ample opportunity to hear this music.

Ragtime

Ragtime, which grew out of the largely unwritten tradition of African-American dance, flourished at the end of the 19th century and in the early decades of the 20th. The music is usually in duple meter and based on units of 8 or 16 measures. Syncopation is prevalent throughout, thrown into relief by the steadiness of the bass line

---

1. *African American Heritage Hymnal* (Chicago: GIA Publications, 2001), v.

typically heard in the banjo music of minstrel shows (see Chapter 16). A rag (that is, a piece in ragtime style) typically follows the form of a march: three or four different section with their own themes, each running to 16 measures, with connecting material between sections. In ragtime, the opening theme is often repeated after the second theme. The structure of Scott Joplin's *Maple Leaf Rag*, for example, follows the typical ragtime pattern of AA BB A CC DD.

Joplin himself was quite particular about how his music should be played. In 1908 he issued a primer on the subject, *The School of Ragtime*, in which he noted:

> It is evident that, by giving each note its proper time and by scrupulously observing the ties, you will get the effect. So many are careless in these respects. Play slowly until you catch the swing, and never play ragtime fast at any time. We wish to say here, that the Joplin ragtime is destroyed by careless or imperfect rendering, and very often good players lose the effect entirely, by playing too fast.[2]

Like its successors jazz and rock, ragtime met with considerable resistance, couched in complaints about its syncopated ("loose") rhythms and the purportedly loose morals of those who played and listened to it, but often grounded in unvarnished racism. One commentator, writing on the eve of World War I, called ragtime "a pernicious evil and enemy of true art," and urged readers to

> take a united stand against the Ragtime Evil as we would against bad literature, and horrors of war or intemperance and other socially destructive evils. In Christian homes, where purity of morals is stressed, ragtime should find no resting place. Avaunt with ragtime rot! Let us purge America and the Divine Art of Music from this polluting nuisance.[3]

Dances that originated in African-American folk culture remained little known elsewhere (although R. Nathaniel Dett wrote a "characteristic" piano suite of them, *In the Bottoms*, in 1913). However, middle- and upper-class white listeners saw ragtime as irresistibly primitive in the positive sense: spontaneous and genuine, in contrast to what many viewed as the overly refined and decadent idioms of the concert hall and opera house. Since at least the 1880s, there had been a growing sense that many of the most prominent composers—Wagner, Brahms, Debussy—had become too self-conscious and removed from the more elemental connections of music and time, music and the body. Music with a simpler, infectious beat, more direct harmonies, and more straightforward form was seen as a salvation from the hyperintellectualized, overly sophisticated styles of the late 19th century, and even more so from the musical modernism emerging in the early 20th century. Even Charles Ives, a stylistic maverick who railed against the excessively refined nature of the European tradition, wrote a set of ragtime dances.

This distinctly American idiom soon captured the imagination of European artists as well. Stravinsky became familiar with the style during World War I and wrote *Ragtime for Eleven Instruments* (1917). Debussy's "Golliwog's Cakewalk," from his *Children's Corner Suite* (1908), captures the rhythms of the style perfectly, even if the harmonies are at times distinctly chromatic. The cakewalk was a strutting dance

CD15, Track 10
JOPLIN
Maple Leaf Rag
Score Anthology II/185

CD15, Track 11
DEBUSSY
Golliwog's Cakewalk
Score Anthology II/186

---

2. Scott Joplin, *The School of Ragtime* (New York: Author, 1908).
3. Leo Oehmler, "Ragtime: A Pernicious Evil and Enemy of True Art," *Musical Observer* (September 1914), p. 15.

COMPOSER PROFILE   Scott Joplin *(1868–1917)*

Scott Joplin was not the first African-American composer, nor was he the first composer of ragtime music, but he was without question the most famous on both counts in his time. As a musician, he was largely self-taught and earned his early living by playing the piano in saloons, brothels, and music halls. His *Maple Leaf Rag* propelled him to instant fame: published in 1899, the piece sold 75,000 copies in its first six months and would eventually become the first million-seller hit in any musical genre or medium.

In spite of this and other successes, Joplin struggled to achieve his greatest dream: to integrate ragtime into the established forms of opera. The music to his first opera, *A Guest of Honor*, is lost, and if the work was performed publicly at all, it received little notice. Joplin published a piano-vocal score of a second opera, *Treemonisha*, at his own expense in 1911, but it was not well received in an underrehearsed backers' audition in Harlem in 1915. Its first staged performance did not take place until 1972, when it opened to rave reviews in Atlanta, GA.

Today we would call Joplin a **crossover** artist, taking one musical style into unfamiliar territory and creating a new subgenre. The black audiences of his own time seem not to have been prepared to hear a synthesis of popular African-American music with opera, although African-American musicals were filled with similar music. While Joplin's lack of success may have also been due to racial prejudices, many ragtime composers were white, as was his most sympathetic publisher. His style influenced many other composers, although Irving Berlin's huge hit, "Alexander's Ragtime Band" (1911) was less a rag than a relatively unsyncopated march. Ragtime had ceased to be popular by the time of Joplin's death.

Pianists began a revival of Joplin's music in the 1960s; this culminated in arrangements being successfully employed in the soundtrack to the movie *The Sting*. Today, his piano pieces are acknowledged, as one critic has observed, as the American counterparts to Chopin's mazurkas and Brahms's waltzes, both in musical quality and in the manner in which each captures the spirit of its time and place.

PRINCIPAL WORKS

Aside from two operas (see above), various songs, waltzes, and marches, Joplin's output consists of about 50 piano rags.

KEY DATES IN THE LIFE OF JOPLIN

1868	Born November 24 in Texarkana, Texas.
1882	Leaves home and earns a living in St. Louis and other towns by playing the piano in brothels, saloons, and variety halls.
1896	Settles in Sedalia, Missouri; enrolls in harmony and composition courses at George R. Smith College for Negroes.
1899	Publishes *Maple Leaf Rag* and achieves instant fame.
1907	Moves to New York City; begins work on his opera *Treemonisha* two years later.
1911	Publishes *Treemonisha* at his own expense; the work is performed in concert in 1915 but does not reach the stage until 1972.
1917	Dies April 1 in New York City.

Scott Joplin. A drawing of the composer and the title page from an early edition of his *Maple Leaf Rag*. Joplin rocketed to fame with the publication of this work in 1899. Legend has it that the publisher, John Stark, heard Joplin playing it in the Maple Leaf Club, a saloon in Sedalia, Missouri, and later offered him $50 plus royalties on the work. *Maple Leaf Rag* eventually sold more than a million copies.

Source: (left) © 2000 Bettmann/CORBIS; (right) Getty Images Inc.—Hulton Archive Photos that figured prominently in minstrel shows of the 19th and early 20th centuries and was itself a source of the ragtime style. Debussy adds a touch of irony to his work by incorporating into it (measures 61–63) an oblique reference to the celebrated "Tristan" chord of Wagner's *Tristan und Isolde* (see Chapter 17). He instructs the performer to play this passage haltingly, and "with great emotion," only to answer the quotation with a series of jaunty, disjointed eighth notes.

There are rhythmic elements in "Golliwog's Cakewalk" with wider stylistic implications as well. Using the jaunty 2/4 metric frame of ragtime as a foundation (four eighth-notes per measure), Debussy employs accent shifts throughout. An accent on the third eighth-note (measures 2 and 3) shifts to an even more dramatic *fortissimo* to the fourth eighth-note (measure 4). Amid the steady left hand in measures 5–8 there is another accent shift, from the third eighth-note (measure 6) to the second eighth-note (measure 8). These shifts amuse, but they also keep the listener from getting too comfortable within a "fixed" meter. In measure 41, the accompaniment becomes the entire texture, with no actual "melody" until the "Tristan" quotations (beginning measures 61 ff.). After the quotations, the opening three notes of the primary melody (measures 85 ff.) are isolated and shifted by one sixteenth into a downbeat figure before returning to their proper place in the return (measures 90ff.). The remainder of the piece recapitulates the opening section.

Even at this unpretentious level, Debussy is undermining rhythmic expectations within a straightforward pattern, in this case a popular music genre. When Stravinsky came to write his second ballet for Diaghilev, *Petrushka* (1911), he applied similarly shifting accents to otherwise "Russian" tunes (some original, some taken from published sources) and expanded the concept to shifting meters and ostinato layering. By the time he wrote *Le sacre du printemps* (see Chapter 20), Stravinsky was still using "Russian" tunes, but had added new contrapuntal and tonal complexities. The disorientation of rhythmic expectation is taken to greater extremes in *Le Sacre*: the displacement of melodic phrasing (the opening bassoon and English horn solos) and ostinato patterns (by themselves, rehearsal number 6; en masse, number 10). This resolves into the "Danse des Adolescentes" (number 13), written in a steady 2/4, full of unexpected accents, alternating with brief periods of rhythmic stability (number 14). The concluding Sacrificial Dance, the opening rhythm of which is presented as Example 20–5 ("Danse sacrale," page 529), expresses its violence (a dance to the death by the Chosen One) through the expectations raised by ostinato and ostinato-like fragments being dashed by relentlessly shifting meters and other disruptions.

What Joplin expresses within a stylistic principle (shifting syncopation against steady beat), Debussy turns into accentual displacement of melody and furthers by putting the accompanimental figure into the forefront. Stravinsky pushes these even further, to the point of creating a texture of ongoing metric disorientation, based on accompanimental (nonmelodic) ideas. Such a line of compositional influence, however conscious or unconscious, established an important 20th-century aesthetic: unpredictability tending toward nonpredictabiliy.

Blues

The broad repertory of music known as the **blues** were a particularly important force in American music, both as a genre in its own right and later for its enormous impact on the development of jazz. The text of a blues song is by definition a lament, bemoaning poverty, social injustice, fatigue, or, most famously of all, lost love. This type of song originated in the South among formerly enslaved African Americans and their descendants (although rural Caucasian-American musicians may have influenced the music also). Early recorded examples preserve the artistry of such individuals as "Blind Lemon" Jefferson (1894–1929), Blind Willie Johnson (1897–1945), and Robert Johnson (1911–1938). These musicians accompanied themselves with an acoustic guitar, with varying degrees of skill; the Johnsons (who were not related) were masters of the "slide guitar" style, playing with a piece of metal or a glass bottleneck instead of their left hands to create vibratos and glissandos. Blind Willie Johnson is a rare example of recorded "gospel blues," performing spirituals and hymns in a popular musical style, with up-to-date references to the 1918–19 Spanish influenza pandemic that killed at least 50 million people worldwide.

At the same time, a more urban style of blues was evolving, influenced on one hand by the vaudeville and tent tour circuits (providing more variety in the accompaniment) and on the other by songwriters who found in the blues a new and fruitful style to pursue. Ma Rainey (1886–1939) and Bessie Smith (1895–1937) were among the first to record this new "theatrical" blues style. The first to establish a reputation as a blues composer was William Christopher Handy (1873–1958).

The son of recently emancipated slaves, W. C. Handy was born in Florence, Alabama. He worked for a time as a schoolteacher but eventually became a professional musician, traveling throughout the South. It was not an easy life. In his autobiography, Handy (known as "The Father of the Blues") describes a period of homelessness in St. Louis when he took on a series of menial jobs. "I have always imagined that a good bit of that hardship went into the making of 'St. Louis Blues'," he noted. "I like to think that the song reflects a life filled with hard times as well as good times." "St. Louis Blues" (1914) is one of the earliest published blues numbers and among the most frequently recorded works of its kind.[4]

"St. Louis Blues" is constructed on a standard pattern known as the **12-bar blues form.** This consists of a series of variations on a repeated harmonic pattern of 12 measures in 4/4 time. Each of these 12-measure units is known generically as a **chorus** and is in turn divided into three groups of four measures each. The harmonic progression in "St. Louis Blues" follows a harmonic pattern typical for the blues:

Measure number	1	2	3	4	5	6	7	8	9	10	11	12
Harmony	I				IV		I		V		I	

CD15, Track 12

W. C. HANDY
St. Louis Blues
Score Anthology II/187

Like a great many blues number, "St. Louis Blues" opens with a **vamp,** a short progression of chords (and in this particular case, a melody as well) whose function is to introduce the basic harmonies, tempo, and mood of the whole. The vamp in "St. Louis Blues" is unusual in that it contrasts markedly with the chorus that follows. Handy explained this striking feature in his autobiography:

> When "St. Louis Blues" was written the tango was in vogue. I tricked the dancers by arranging a tango introduction, breaking abruptly then into a low-down blues. My eyes swept the floor anxiously, then suddenly I saw lightning strike. The dancers seemed electrified. Something within them came suddenly to life. An instinct that wanted so much to live, to fling its arms and to spread joy, took them by the heels. By this I was convinced that my new song was accepted.[5]

---

4. W. C. Handy, *Father of the Blues: An Autobiography*, ed. Arna Bontemps (New York: Macmillan, 1941), pp. 28–29.
5. W. C. Handy, *Father of the Blues: An Autobiography*, ed. Arna Bontemps (New York: Macmillan, 1941), p. 122.

PERFORMANCE PERSPECTIVE

A Blues Performance with Two Star Soloists
CD 15   Track 12

A classic collaboration on a recording of W. C. Handy's "St. Louis Blues" illustrates the extraordinary flexibility not only of the blues, but of jazz in general. The notated score gives only the barest of outlines for what the blues actually sound like in performance. Harmonies can be altered, enriched, or made to move at a faster speed, and melodies can easily be changed to accommodate the text. In performance, a blues song is fluid in spite of its underlying form. Vocalists are free to improvise, and the text, even if metered, can be declaimed irregularly, stretching the music to accommodate any number of syllables at any given point. The characteristic sound of the blues is shaped by the **blue note,** the slightly lowered third or seventh degree in the major scale. (For an especially clear example of this, listen to the first "ain't" in "It Don't Mean a Thing" as performed by Duke Ellington's band.)

When Bessie Smith (1895–1937) recorded "St. Louis Blues" in 1925 with the trumpeter Louis Armstrong, she omitted the vamp and altered many of the words in Handy's published score. The melodic line in this performance often bears only the faintest resemblance to the notated melody: Smith's plaintive sound and the slow tempo create something more nearly akin at times to speech. The simplicity of the arrangement—a reed organ (harmonium) provides the only accompaniment—focuses attention on the ongoing dialogue of the two soloists: Armstrong's mournful trumpet responds to each phrase of Smith's singing. This recording, which was marketed by Columbia as a "race record" (that is, music recorded by and intended for African Americans), helped further solidify Smith's reputation as "Empress of the Blues" and helped make her the highest-paid African-American entertainer in the United States at the time.

Bessie Smith. Her 1925 recording of "St. Louis Blues" with Louis Armstrong was so successful that the song's composer, W. C. Handy, later produced a short film (*St. Louis Blues*) in which Smith sings this number. The 1929 film features an entirely African-American cast and represents an early instance of a musician recording her art on film. "Talkies"—films with recorded soundtracks and thus music as well—had been introduced only two years before.

Source: Frank Driggs Collection

Elements of the blues, notably the emphasis on certain scale degrees and the bending of pitch, soon became basic to other musical genres. Jazz counted on blues as one of the crucial sources of its development (see discussion later in this chapter). Composers of dance and theater music also incorporated these elements. But the most versatile of these composers, who brought the crossover blend of blues, early jazz, and "concert hall" music to a peak of popularity, was George Gershwin (1898–1937), who began his career as a Tin Pan Alley song-plugger (an in-store or publisher's pianist who played through sheet music for potential customers) and writer. He began to write piano pieces ("Rialto Ripples," 1917), songs for other shows ("The Real American Folk Song is a Rag," 1918) hit songs ("Swanee," 1919), and musicals, mostly with his brother Ira (1896–1983), starting with *Lady Be Good* (1924) and including *Funny Face* (1927), *Girl Crazy* (1930), and *Of Thee I Sing* (1932; Pulitzer Prize for Best Play).

CD15, Track 13
GEORGE GERSHWIN
Prelude no. 2
Score Anthology II/188

Gershwin also wrote large-scale works with orchestra reflecting the crossover style, including *Rhapsody in Blue* (1924, with piano), *Concerto in F* (1925, with piano) *An American in Paris*, and the opera *Porgy and Bess* (1935).

Among Gershwin's small group of piano solos are the Three Preludes, composed and premiered in 1926 by the composer. Actually, five preludes were originally presented, but two were eliminated before publication. In fact, Gershwin had planned for a set of 24 preludes, after the examples of Bach and (more precisely) Chopin. The second, *Andante con moto e poco rubato* in E major, was described by Gershwin as a "blues lullaby"; a comparison with Chopin's prelude in A minor, op. 28, no. 1 (see Chapter 16) shows that this piece is clearly an homage to the Polish master.

POPULAR SONG

Even as many composers of the mid-20th century developed new harmonic idioms—both tonal and atonal—others continued to work within the boundaries of traditional triadic harmony. This trend is seen most remarkably in the genre of song, particularly in the United States. This country produced an unparalleled abundance of outstanding songwriters in the 20th century, most of who also worked in the musical theater and film. Most prominent among many are **Irving Berlin** (1888–1989), **Cole Porter** (1891–1964), **George Gershwin** (1898–1937), **Hoagy Carmichael** (1899–1991), and **Richard Rodgers** (1902–1979). All but Carmichael achieved success on Broadway and in the movies. Berlin and Porter are remarkable for having written their own lyrics as well. Berlin came to the United States as a child from his native Russia; Porter and Carmichael were both natives of Indiana; Gershwin, born in New York City, collaborated extensively with his brother Ira as lyricist; and Rodgers, also a New Yorker, teamed with lyricists Lorenz Hart and later Oscar Hammerstein II to write an astonishing string of Broadway hits. Although they are generally classified as popular rather than art music, the songs of these and other song composers in fact stand in a direct line of descent from those of Schubert, Schumann, Brahms, and Wolf.

CD15, Track 14
COLE PORTER
Night and Day
Score Anthology II/189

Porter's "Night and Day" and Ellington's "Sophisticated Lady," to take but two examples, reflect the traditions of the 19th-century song in remarkable ways. The harmonic vocabularies of these works, although essentially tonal, are richly chromatic and far from straightforward. The poetry is elegant and witty, the melodies unforgettable, and the union of the two represents the genre at its best. In Porter's "Night and Day," sung by Ella Fitzgerald, the juxtaposition of the wandering chromatic line in the bass against the repeated B♭ of the voice establishes the underlying tension between longing and insistency. Finally, after 35 iterations of B♭, the vocal line itself begins to rise and fall chromatically, gradually, languorously; the longing has become infectious. We do not feel a strong sense of tonic until the word "one" in the clinching phrase ". . . you are the one"[6] (measure 23). In measure 52, the music moves to a remote key (G♭ = ♭III), the repeated notes grow into a back-and-forth of a whole step (measure 57), and the tonic finally returns after a circuitous passage through a series of chromatic harmonies. Unlike Wagner in Act II of *Tristan und Isolde* (see Chapter 17) or Leonard Bernstein in the "Quintet" from *West Side Story* (see Chapter 22), Porter erases the differences between night and day: the lover here is indifferent to the setting and rising of the sun.

CD15, Track 15
DUKE ELLINGTON
Sophisticated Lady
Score Anthology II/190

Ellington's "Sophisticated Lady" uses advanced melodic and harmonic chromaticism to project the idea of a woman who has assumed a worldly attitude toward life

---

6. Quotation from lyrics, Cole Porter, "Night and Day." Published by Warner Bros.

Ella Fitzgerald in rehearsal.
"Lady Ella" (1917–1996) was among those who participated in the "Jazz at the Philharmonic" (JATP) concerts produced by Norman Granz. The superlative roster of musicians involved in JATP led to many invitations to perform abroad. Here, the group has just arrived in Stockholm (one of Europe's most jazz-enthusiastic cities) for a six-week concert gig. From left to right: Fitzgerald, Oscar Peterson (piano), Roy Eldridge (trumpet), and, standing in back, Max Roach (drums).

Source: © Bettmann/CORBIS. All Rights Reserved

and love. This chromaticism as well as the rhythmic freedom of Sarah Vaughan's interpretation emphasize the woman's exterior life of glamour and uncaring attitude ("Smoking, drinking, never thinking of tomorrow, nonchalant . . .").[7] Only with the final word of the text—"cry"—does the music arrive at its long-avoided resolution on the tonic. The chromaticism, in the end, is revealed as a mask covering the woman's true feelings.

Like many songs of this era, "Night and Day" and "Sophisticated Lady" have been subjected to countless arrangements, vocal and instrumental. Porter's "Night and Day" was first recorded by Fred Astaire for the movie *The Gay Divorcee* (1934), a comedy that revolves around mistaken identity and provides a platform for much singing and dancing. Within three months of the film's premiere, more than 30 artists had recorded the song. Within 25 years, the number had surpassed a hundred. And no two recordings are alike: the performance tradition of a song like "Night and Day" allows—and in fact encourages—performers to take considerable liberties with its rhythm, text, orchestration, harmonies, words, and even its melody. Astaire's version sounds very different from Frank Sinatra's, which in turn sounds very different from Ella Fitzgerald's. Nor can any of these renditions really be said to represent the composer's original intentions, because Cole Porter did not really conceive of the song as a fixed entity. The notion of an "authentic" version of this song is in fact vaguely ridiculous. Is it Cole Porter's original manuscript? The first edition? The first recording? As in jazz, improvisatory freedom plays such a basic role in this kind of music that the idea of an authentic text loses all relevance.

---

7. Quotation from lyrics, Duke Ellington, "Sophisticated Lady." Used by permission of Warner/Chappell Music, Inc.

FOCUS   Notable Song Composers of the 20th Century

■ **IRVING BERLIN** (1888–1989): "Alexander's Ragtime Band," "Always," "Blue Skies," "Puttin' on the Ritz," "How Deep Is the Ocean," "Marie," "God Bless America," "White Christmas," "There's No Business Like Show Business," "Easter Parade"

■ **COLE PORTER** (1891–1964): "Night and Day," "Anything Goes," "All through the Night," "Love for Sale," "Begin the Beguine," "Just One of Those Things," "I've Got You under My Skin," "Don't Fence Me In," "In the Still of the Night"

■ **GEORGE GERSHWIN** (1898–1937): "Swanee," "Strike Up the Band," "I Got Rhythm," "Someone to Watch over Me," "Embraceable You," "Fascinatin' Rhythm," "Love Is Here to Stay," "Let's Call the Whole Thing Off," "They Can't Take That Away from Me; and the opera *Porgy and Bess*, which includes "Summertime," "I Got Plenty o' Nuttin," "It Ain't Necessarily So," "Bess, You Is My Woman Now," and "A Woman Is a Sometime Thing"

■ **HOAGY CARMICHAEL** (1899–1991): "Stardust," "Georgia on My Mind"

■ **RICHARD RODGERS** (1902–1979): Songs from the musicals *Oklahoma!*, *South Pacific*, *Carousel*, *The King and I*, *The Sound of Music*, and *Flower Drum Song*

■ **HAROLD ARLEN** (1905–1986): "Stormy Weather," "It's Only a Paper Moon," and the songs for *The Wizard of Oz*, including "Over the Rainbow"

■ **HENRY MANCINI** (1924–1994): "Moon River," "Days of Wine and Roses," and the soundtracks for the *Pink Panther* movies

■ **BURT BACHARACH** (b. 1928): "Raindrops Keep Fallin' on My Head," "Walk on By," "What the World Needs Now," "Do You Know the Way to San Jose?"

■ **BOB DYLAN** (b. 1941): "Blowin' in the Wind," "The Times They Are A-Changing," "Mr. Tambourine Man," "Like a Rolling Stone," "Just Like a Woman," and the album *Blood on the Tracks*

■ **JOHN LENNON** (1940–1980) and **PAUL MCCARTNEY** (b. 1942): "I Want to Hold Your Hand," "Yesterday," "Ticket to Ride, "Revolution," "Let It Be," and the album *Sergeant Pepper's Lonely Hearts Club Band*

■ **CAROLE KING** (b. 1942): "Natural Woman," "Up on the Roof," "I Feel the Earth Move," "Will You Still Love Me Tomorrow?

■ **PAUL SIMON** (b. 1942): "Sounds of Silence," "Mrs. Robinson," "Bridge over Troubled Waters," and the album *Graceland*

■ **JONI MITCHELL** (b. 1943): "Woodstock," "Big Yellow Taxi," "Chelsea Morning," "From Both Sides Now," "Help Me," "You Turn Me On, I'm a Radio," "Free Man in Paris"

■ **ELTON JOHN** (b. 1947): "Your Song," "Rocket Man," "I Guess That's Why They Call It the Blues," "Candle in the Wind"

■ **JAMES TAYLOR** (b. 1948): "Carolina in My Mind," "Country Road," "Fire and Rain," "Lo and Behold," "Mexico," "Your Smiling Face"

■ **ALLAN MENKEN** (b. 1949): Songs from *Little Shop of Horrors*, *The Little Mermaid*, *Beauty and the Beast*, and *Aladdin*

Joni Mitchell performs in concert, September 7, 1979. Mitchell (b. 1943), a native of Saskatchewan, moved to the United States in 1965, and within two years had begun a career as a songwriter, singer, and performer in a modern folk style. Her early work was of the personal/confessional variety; albums from *Clouds* (1969) to the live *Miles of Aisles* (1974) exhibited increasing range in subject matter as well as popular success. Beginning with *The Hissing of Summer Lawns* (1975), Mitchell began to experiment with rock- and jazz-influenced arrangements and electronic instrumentation, and her lyrics were increasingly political. *Mingus* was a collaboration with the bassist/composer Charles Mingus, completed shortly after his death. Thereafter, Mitchell continued to release recordings that mixed her approaches, but after 1998's *Taming the Tiger*, she stopped recording new material, a hiatus recently broken with *Shine* (2007). In addition to Mitchell's songwriting, her unique and rich guitar style, based on open tunings, is a trademark of her musicianship.

Source: © Bettmann/CORBIS. All Rights Reserved

JAZZ: TO 1945

The rhythmic liveliness so characteristic of ragtime, combined with the use of expressive pitch distortion so typical of the blues, were particularly important forces in the development of **jazz.** The term (often spelled "jass" in the early decades of the 20th century) has been used to cover such an enormous range of musical styles that attempts at a concise definition seem futile. The trumpeter Louis Armstrong (1901–1971) once famously answered the question, "What is jazz?" by saying, "Man, man, if you gotta ask, you'll never know." Armstrong's response is at once evasive and revealing: he recognized that the term cannot be confined to a list of specific musical characteristics. Along these lines, more than one jazz musician has defined the art "not as a what, but a how." Jazz, in this view, is not so much a style of playing as an attitude, an approach toward music that embraces improvisation and rhythmic and intonational freedom, along with a general acceptance that the musical work exists in performance rather than in the form of a written score. Jazz musicians worked as hard as any other musicians to perfect their craft, of course, but the element of spontaneity (or at the very least, apparent spontaneity) has always played a key role in the world of jazz.

Like ragtime, jazz originated in the largely unwritten traditions of African-American dance and song, combined with other diverse influences such as marching band music, hymnody, and improvisatory storytelling. In the 1920s, it appealed as modernist art by virtue of its emphasis on rhythm, its freedom of improvisation, and what was perceived to be a kind of purity of spontaneous expression, seemingly devoid of calculated artifice.

Although blues is an important component of Armstrong's early body of work, the music itself embodies Dixieland jazz, a sound and style that had developed in Armstrong's native New Orleans in the early years of the 20th century. The typical Dixieland sound, said to have evolved out of the bands that accompanied funeral processions in New Orleans, is characterized by an ensemble in which the trumpet carries the melodic lead, the clarinet provides rapid counterpoint to the melodic line, the trombone helps carry the bass line, and the piano and drum set work together to emphasize the strong beats in duple meter, with the piano providing triadic harmonies on the off beats. An additional trumpet, a saxophone, banjo, and double bass often figure in Dixieland ensembles as well. Also typical of the Dixieland style (and for that matter, many other varieties of jazz) is the steady succession of soloists, each of whom improvises on at least one unit of the 12-bar blues chorus.

Louis Armstrong. After his enormously successful recording of "St. Louis Blues" with Bessie Smith in 1925, Armstrong would release at least six subsequent renditions of that song with various groups between 1929 and 1960. A recent (2004) film entitled *St. Louis Blues,* starring Sean Patrick Thomas, traces Armstrong's life from his impoverished childhood in New Orleans to worldwide fame.

Source: Getty Images, Inc./Hulton Archive Photos

CD15, Track 16
KING OLIVER
Snake Rag
Score Anthology II/191

After beginning his career in his home town, where he listened to recordings of Caruso and other opera singers on his Victrola (which "Little Nipper" also listened to; see "Prelude: The 20th Century"), Armstrong joined the exodus of jazz musicians to Chicago in 1923, working for the band of another cornettist, Joe "King" Oliver. Armstrong and Oliver developed an intricate duet style that sounded improvised but was in fact carefully worked out. This was an important new element of jazz: increasing emphasis on arrangement while continuing to delight in improvisational skill. This approach is amply evident in Oliver's "Snake Rag," recorded in 1923, with Lil Hardin (Armstrong's future wife) on piano and the Dodds brothers, Johnny and Warren ("Baby") on clarinet and drums.

Armstrong's career in the 1920s is in many ways typical of the way jazz musicians moved upward in their careers. He moved to New York in 1924, joining both the Fletcher Henderson Orchestra (primarily a dance orchestra) and Clarence Williams' Blues Five (which often served to back blues singers such as Bessie Smith). He returned to Chicago to begin leading his own groups, the Hot Five and Hot Seven; as the primary soloist, Armstrong recorded solos of considerable virtuosity and inventiveness, and his reputation as the greatest jazz soloist of his era was firmly established. From then on, he moved between Chicago and New York, joining the pit orchestra for Fats Waller's 1929 *Hot Chocolates* (and recording the show's "Ain't Misbehavin'"; see Chapter 22). By 1930, "Louis Armstrong and His Orchestra" had become the ensemble (usually 10 or so musicians) in which he would make his continuing contributions to jazz.

Duke Ellington's "It Don't Mean a Thing (If It Ain't Got That Swing)," written in 1932, represents jazz in the "Swing Era" of the 1930s and 1940s. Swing rhythm features a hard meter but a subtle avoidance of cadences and downbeats, with the soloist placing notes either just ahead or just behind the beat in a way that heightened the music's rhythmic suppleness. Swing was also dominated by the sound of what were called big bands, relatively large ensembles consisting of piano, drums, double bass, and a large complement of winds: saxophones (often five—two altos, two tenors, one baritone) and groups of three or four trumpets, trombones, and clarinets. Many of these bands also featured a vocal soloist: Ella Fitzgerald began her career with Chick Webb's band, and Frank Sinatra rose to prominence with the bands of Harry James and Tommy Dorsey. Each group sought to establish its own distinctive sound through its orchestration, often dictated by the leader's instrument and tastes—Duke Ellington's piano, Harry James's trumpet, Glenn Miller's trombone, Artie Shaw's clarinet, and, in the crossover Western swing style, Bob Wills's violin.

CD15, Track 17
DUKE ELLINGTON
It Don't Mean a Thing
Score Anthology II/192

Formally, the original song version of Ellington's "It Don't Mean a Thing" consists of an eight-measure instrumental introduction, followed by a two-measure vamp that can be repeated indefinitely before the entrance of the voice. The **verse** ("What good is melody . . .")[8] consists of 16 measures (2 × 8) that end on a half cadence leading to the song's chorus or principal melody. The chorus itself consists of four units of 8 measures each whose thematic content follows the pattern AABA. This pattern is so common in 20th-century song that it has come to be known as **song form**. The contrasting B section (here, from the words "It makes no diff'rence" through "ev'rything you got") is often known as the **bridge** because it connects statements of the A theme.

When Ellington recorded this number with his band in 1932, he substantially reworked the form of the piece. The recorded version omits the introduction and begins with 10 measures of the vamp, in which the singer (Ivie Anderson) uses her voice as

---

8. Quotation from lyrics, Edward Kennedy "Duke" Ellington, "It Don't Mean a Thing (If It Ain't Got That Swing)." Used with the permission of Warner/Chappell Music, Inc.

an instrument, singing syncopated nonsense syllables against the steady beat of the bass in a technique first popularized by Armstrong and Fitzgerald, **scat singing.** The 32-measure verse, expanded from the song's 16-measure version, is allotted to a solo muted trombone. The voice, in turn, presents the chorus in its full 32-measure form. At this point, the instruments take over with a series of quasi-improvised solos. In rehearsal, Ellington and his group would have planned who would play these solos and in what order. Beyond this, each instrumentalist was free to improvise at will, knowing in advance the basic chord progressions with which the band would support him. In this particular performance, we hear only one extended solo, given to the saxophonist (Johnny Hodges), who varies thematic elements of both verse and chorus. The full band then plays the opening of the chorus; the vocalist returns with the bridge passage, and the work concludes with the syncopated "doo-wah" fragmented on the muted brass.

Other performances of this same work by Ellington vary the number and sequence of the soloists, the order in which verse and chorus are first presented, the final cadence, and countless other features large and small. Jazz performances by their very nature represent a fusion of composed and improvised elements; only the limitations of a 78 rpm disk dictated the length of the 1932 performance found in the CD set.

As jazz ensembles became increasingly larger and their instrumental arrangements correspondingly complex, some listeners bewailed a loss of spontaneity. The noted critic Winthrop Sargeant took Ellington to task in 1943 for allegedly losing touch with the musical roots of jazz and having abandoned its "elemental" nature (see Primary Evidence: Jazz and the Question of Stylistic "Purity"). But Sargeant was guilty of assuming that jazz had always had and would always retain what he perceived to be a kind of stylistic purity, untouched by the same forces of musical change that had shaped every other form of Western music since the Middle Ages.

The writing down of jazz orchestrations in the 1930s and 1940s had a parallel, if not immediately obvious, with a new form of gospel music whose essence was more commercial than earlier styles. In the early 20th century, gospel music seemed to be reborn as a secular African-American entity: an a cappella vocal quartet whose counterpart in white culture was known as the barbershop quartet.[9] Although all-female groups sang (and still sing) in this style, the most successful groups of the 1930s and 1940s were gospel quartets of African-American men, who formed such groups as the Golden Gate Quartet, Fairfield Four, Dixie Hummingbirds, the Five Blind Boys of Alabama, and the Soul Stirrers (whose members included both Sam Cooke and Johnnie Taylor at different times).

JAZZ: AFTER 1945

In the decades just after World War II, a variety of jazz musicians began moving beyond established concepts of tonality, rhythm, and form. Foremost among these artists were the bassist Charles Mingus (1922–1979), the trumpeters Dizzy Gillespie (1917–1993) and Miles Davis (1926–1991), the saxophonists Charlie Parker (1920–1955) and John Coltrane (1926–1967), and the pianists Thelonious Monk (1917–1982) and Bud Powell (1924–1996).

---

9. For discussion of the possible African-American provenance of the barbershop quartet, see Jim Henry, "The Historical Roots of Barbershop Harmony," *The Harmonizer*, July/August 2003, pp. 13–17, online at http://www.barbershop.org/web/groups/public/documents/pages/pub_cb_00167.hcsp. Accessed April 27, 2008. Although white ensembles adopted the term "barbershop quartet" (and were so represented in a 1936 Norman Rockwell *Saturday Evening Post* cover), the term was associated with black performers from the beginning (ibid.).

COMPOSER PROFILE   Duke Ellington *(1899–1974)*

Ellington always struggled with musical labels. He resisted being categorized as a "jazz musician" and wrote in a variety of styles reflecting, at various times, the influences of the big band sound, swing, bop, cool jazz, rock, and many kinds of classical music. In his own way, Ellington synthesized as many styles as Stravinsky. But in the case of Ellington, critics were slow to accept this variety. When "The Duke" began to explore larger forms and more classically inspired idioms, disappointed listeners accused him of "abandoning jazz." Ellington himself insisted that "there are simply two kinds of music, the good kind and the other kind."[10]

In any event, Ellington was widely hailed in the 1930s as the leading jazz composer of his time. For almost fifty years, he was able to assemble and direct a remarkable group of musicians who toured the country and eventually the world. They could (and did) function as a dance band, but they went far beyond this. Their celebrated Carnegie Hall concert of 1943 included the premiere of *Black, Brown, and Beige*, a tone poem tracing the history of African Americans and suggesting, metaphorically, their eventual integration of American society. The concert concluded with the presentation of a plaque signed by Kurt Weill, Aaron Copland, Marian Anderson, Leopold Stokowski, and others. The entire event symbolized a bridging of both racial and musical barriers, although many of Ellington's

subsequent audiences, particularly in the South, would remain segregated until the 1960s.

Like his near contemporary, Aaron Copland, Ellington was hugely feted toward the end of his life, receiving the Presidential Medal of Freedom (1969) and some seventeen honorary degrees. The U.S. State Department sponsored a tour of the Soviet Union in 1970 at a period of intense tension between the two superpowers. In spite—or more likely because—of the Soviet government's tendency to discourage jazz, Ellington and his group were wildly received there: at some concerts, tickets sold for eight times their face value.[11]

PRINCIPAL WORKS

SONGS Ellington's most celebrated songs (many of which he wrote in collaboration with his colleague Billy Strayhorn) include "Mood Indigo," "Don't Get Around Much Anymore," "I Got it Bad (And That Ain't Good)," "Prelude to a Kiss," and "Satin Doll." Ellington made multiple arrangements of all his songs, both with and without lyrics.

INSTRUMENTAL MUSIC *Harlem* and *Black, Brown, and Beige* are tone poems that take as their subject the history of African Americans. Ellington also wrote extended works that highlighted his own instrumentalists, such as *Echoes of Harlem* and *Concerto for Cootie*, both created for his principal trumpeter, Cootie Williams. His film scores include *Anatomy of a Murder* (1959) and *Paris Blues* (1961).

Duke Ellington and His Orchestra, 1943. Ellington was able to keep his big band in operation from 1923 until his death, although there were many lean years. The first nadir occurred around the time this photograph was taken, during the American Federation of Musicians' strike against recording companies (1942–1943); the strike eliminated royalty payments, and forced many other bands to fold.

Source: © Michael Ochs Archives/CORBIS. All Rights Reserved

KEY DATES IN THE LIFE OF ELLINGTON

1899	Born Edward Kennedy Ellington on April 29 in Washington, D.C.; later nicknamed "Duke" because of his personal elegance and bearing.
1923	Moves to New York City and forms his first band.
1939	Begins collaborating with the songwriter and arranger Billy Strayhorn; together the two create some of the band's most memorable hits.
1943	First of several concerts at Carnegie Hall.
1965	First of a series of "Sacred Concerts," events for which Ellington wrote new music to sacred texts.
1970	Tours Soviet Union under the sponsorship of the U.S. Department of State as a "goodwill ambassador."
1974	Dies in New York on May 24.

10. *The Duke Ellington Reader*, ed. Mark Tucker (New York: Oxford University Press, 1993), p. 326.
11. John Edward Hasse, *Beyond Category: The Life and Genius of Duke Ellington* (New York: Simon & Schuster, 1993), p. 380.

PRIMARY EVIDENCE   Jazz and the Question of Stylistic "Purity" (1943)

W inthrop Sargeant, a highly influential music critic of the mid-20th century, was deeply sympathetic to jazz (he wrote a book on the subject in 1938), but his sympathy had a patronizing edge. The appeal of jazz, Sargeant argued, lay in its directness and simplicity. He was alarmed that jazz in its so-called pure form was beginning to mix too much with other styles of composition and thereby lose its essential, primitive, quality. What bothered Sargeant was what would trouble many others over subsequent decades, whether they admitted it or not: jazz was evolving in new directions, not remaining what it had once been. Ellington responded gracefully but with force.

SARGEANT'S CRITIQUE

The mistake of the fashionable jazz aesthetes has been to take jazz out of the simple sidewalk and dance hall milieu where it belongs and pretend that it is a complex, civilized art. In its own surroundings, jazz need make no apologies. It is the most vital folk music of our time; it is distinctly and indigenously American, and it speaks a new, infectious dialect that is fresher than anything of the sort Europe has evolved in centuries. It is, I think, something of a pity that, in a watered-down commercial form, jazz has virtually drowned out every other form of American popular music. . . . Curiously enough, the mass-produced, commercialized product is also tending to swamp what is left of real, improvised jazz. It is already obvious that the fresh, ingenuous type of jazz the Negroes of New Orleans and Chicago played a generation ago is unlikely ever to be heard again except in phonograph records. Thus, the original spring of jazz has run dry—and for very logical reasons. The musical dialect of jazz, like verbal dialects, owes its development to its remoteness from standardized education. One

of its most important ingredients has been the rather colorful awkwardness—the lack of technical polish—with which it is played. And that awkwardness, when genuine, is the fruit of ignorance.

Jazz appeared in the first place because the poor Southern Negro couldn't get a regular musical education, and decided to make his own homemade kind of music without it. His ingenuity has proved him to be one of the world's most gifted instinctive musicians. But as his lot improves, and with it his facilities for musical education, he is bound to be attracted by the bigger scope and intricacy of civilized concert music. Give him the chance to study, and the Negro will soon turn from boogie woogie to Beethoven.

ELLINGTON'S RESPONSE

Mr. Sargeant has evidently not been exposed to some of the more intelligent jazz, nor is he aware of the amazing musical background of some of our foremost composers and arrangers, in the popular field. . . .

He says that "harmony in jazz is restricted to four or five monotonous patterns," and names the blues, to substantiate this strange statement. I would be interested in knowing how he has managed to arrive at his classifications. Everyone knows that the blues is built upon a set pattern, as is, for example, the sonnet form in poetry. Yet this hasn't seemed to limit poetry to four or five monotonous patterns, nor do I think is jazz so limited. . . .

Most of all, I was struck by Mr. Sargeant's concluding statement, that given a chance to study, the Negro will soon turn from boogie woogie to Beethoven. Maybe so, but what a shame! There is so much that is good in a musical expression in the popular field.

Source: Winthrop Sargeant, "Is Jazz Music?" *American Mercury* 57 (1943): 403–9; Duke Ellington, "Defense of Jazz," *American Mercury* 57 (1944): 124. Reprinted with permission of the Enoch Pratt Free Library, in accordance with the terms of the bequest of H. L. Mencken.

A new style called **bebop** featured fast tempos, irregular chordal progressions, complex harmonies, and asymmetrical, often jagged melodies. Gillespie and Parker were the most celebrated of the bebop artists, renowned for their extraordinary improvisational abilities. At times both musicians also incorporated elements of what came to be known as Afro-Cuban jazz, which featured an expanded percussion section and emphasized ostinato figures and complex polyrhythms. Miles Davis's album *The Birth of the Cool* (1949) featured a style in which vibrato in the winds was held to a minimum, creating a distinctively "cool" sound that avoided the sentimentality and fullness so characteristic of the Big Band sound.

Davis was among those who, in the 1950s, contributed to a "modal" approach to jazz improvisation, in which scales or harmonic patterns became the underpinning for

Miles Davis performs in West Germany, ca. 1956–1957. By this time, Davis had a quintet that included John Coltrane and Paul Chambers, both of whom would appear in *Kind of Blue* (1959). In 1957 he recorded the soundtrack for Louis Malle's *Ascenseur pour l'Échafaud* (Elevator to the Gallows) in Paris.

Source: © Michael Ochs Archives/CORBIS. All Rights Reserved

CD15, Track 18
MILES DAVIS
Blue in Green
Score Anthology II/193

improvisation, rather than existing songs or standard progressions, without the pressure of bebop's harmonic complexities, and with the opportunity to "stretch" out in improvisational exploration, rather than having to "exchange choruses" on a regular basis. With tape recording and the long-playing record now commonplace technologies, jazz recording gained new freedom during this era as well. The most successful synthesis of these elements was Davis's 1959 recording *Kind of Blue*, which featured an all-star group of sidemen: Julian "Cannonball" Adderly, John Coltrane, Bill Evans (who was later credited as co-composer on one piece), Paul Chambers, Jimmy Cobb, and (on one track) Wynton Kelly. It is noteworthy that tempos in the five compositions are indicated either as "moderately" or "slowly."

The best-known tracks are "All Blues," a relaxed blues in 6/4, and "So What," a call-and-response between the bass (a nine-note solo) and the others (a two-chord reply mimicking "So what?"), with a 32-measure cycling of two scales; there is also a fairly traditional blues number ("Freddie Freeloader"). "Flamenco Sketches" is based on a repeated chord on C, while each soloist works through a series of five scales until satisfied. Finally, "Blue in Green" (recorded without Adderly), following a four-bar introduction by the pianist Evans, uses a 10-measure progression of chords (starting and ending on A) that the soloists improvise on (Davis twice, Coltrane twice, Davis twice); this pattern alternates with Evans performing the progression transposed a whole step down (to G), which occurs after the first Davis set and the Coltrane set (now "double time, rubato"); after the second Davis set, Evans's transposed double-time rubato version is played through twice before a cadence on D (an echo of the piano introduction).

The relative rigor of "Blue in Green" (improvisation based on a timed progression) is an antidote to the freedom of "Flamenco Sketches" (unlimited improvisation based on a series of scales); the mix of these with two tunes with catchy riffs and an otherwise straightforward blues resulted in a recording that has not only outsold all other jazz albums, but has had as much influence as any post–World War II jazz recording.

During the 1950s, Davis began exploring the possibilities of combining two mainstream idioms of music—jazz and classical—to create what came to be known as **third-stream music.** This approach attempted to find an independent path that bridged jazz improvisation and harmony with instruments and voice-leading techniques (particularly counterpoint) more commonly associated with classical music. The Modern Jazz Quartet, Dave Brubeck, Bill Evans, and Stan Getz were among the many other artists working in this vein throughout the 1950s and into subsequent decades. Gunther Schuller (b. 1925), composer and horn player who invented the term in 1957, collaborated with many of the leading practitioners. (He was also among those to orchestrate Joplin's *Treemonisha* after its rediscovery in 1970.) Wynton Marsalis's *Blood on the Fields* (1994), a three-hour jazz oratorio for an ensemble of three vocalists and 15 instrumentalists, represents a more recent manifestation of third-stream music. In this work, Marsalis (b. 1961) traces the experience of two African Americans in their struggle from slavery to freedom. *Blood on the Fields* won the Pulitzer Prize in Music in 1997.

Davis also played a central role in the emergence of a style known as **fusion.** With the growing popularity of hard rock in the 1960s, Davis, along with Cecil Taylor (b. 1933), Herbie Hancock (b. 1940), and Chick Corea (b. 1941), developed a type of jazz that used the textures, rhythms, and sonorities of rock and soul music, using such typical rock instruments as electric guitars and electric piano. Groups like the Mahavishnu Orchestra and Weather Report (both offshoots of the late 1960s Davis band) were among the most innovative ensembles of their kind in the 1970s.

By far the most radical and controversial of all jazz styles after World War II was the approach known as **free jazz.** Although improvisation had long been one of the characteristic features of jazz, free jazz extended the boundaries of the concept, eliminating such standard elements as improvisations on a given theme, fixed meters, chord progressions, and even tonality itself.

Dissatisfied with traditional forms of jazz and seeking a more distinctively Afro-centric voice, the saxophonist Ornette Coleman (b. 1930) assembled in 1960 a group of eight musicians—a double quartet, each consisting of a reed instrument (saxophone or bass clarinet), trumpet, bass, and drums—that included the saxophonist Eric Dolphy, trumpeters Don Cherry and Freddie Hubbard, and bassist Charlie Haden. The group began to improvise without a central theme, and the resulting "collective improvisation," as Coleman called it, runs 38 minutes without a pause. It was recorded in a single take, without splices or edits. The music blurs the line between solo and

Ornette Coleman in concert, 1982. Coleman's critical reception ranges from high praise to accusations of iconoclasticism. The "free nature" of his approach is hardly anarchic; his music is often composed in advance, his playing influenced by blues and bebop. His collaborators have included Charlie Haden, Don Cherry, Scott LaFaro, Freddie Hubbard, Eric Dolphy, Pat Metheny, Jackie McLean, Geri Allen, and James Blood Ulmer.

Source: Marc PoKempner/Lebrecht Music & Arts Photo Library accompaniment, another important distinction in more traditional jazz. It uses no established themes, chord patterns, or chorus lengths, and moves freely in and out of tonality. "The most important thing," Coleman wrote in the liner notes for the album, "was for us to play together, all at the same time, without getting in each other's way, and also to have enough room for each player to ad lib alone—and to follow this idea for the duration of the album. When the soloist played something that suggested a musical idea or direction to me, I played that behind him in my style. He continued his own way in his solo, of course."[12] As if to underline the interrelationship of modernist arts, the album cover of *Free Jazz* featured an abstract painting by the American artist Jackson Pollock (see Chapter 23).

Free Jazz created a firestorm of controversy among critics and listeners, many of whom accused Coleman of creating music that was not jazz at all. Others maintained that he had overintellectualized the art. The terms of the debate are eerily reminiscent of those in the exchange between Winthrop Sargeant and Duke Ellington in the 1940s (see Primary Evidence: Jazz and the Question of Stylistic "Purity"). It was a well-deserved tribute to Coleman and the integrity and quality of his creativity that his *Sound Grammar* (2005) received the 2007 Pulitzer Prize in Music.

COUNTRY MUSIC

Like jazz, country music embraces a variety of styles and represents the synthesis of many different musical traditions, most of them unwritten. The most important of these are Anglo-American folk song, hymnody, and traditional dance tunes. As early as the 17th century, country dancing in England was a lively type of social dance accompanied by one or two fiddles. Unlike courtly dance, these steps—reels, jigs, hornpipes, and the like—were often fast and physical. Transplanted to the American colonies, these musical traditions were cultivated with particular intensity in the rural South, especially in the Appalachian region. The singing and playing style of country music was decidedly uncultivated; its energetic and sometimes rough-edged quality gave it an emotionally authentic quality. There were also influences borrowed from and by African-American musicians, some of whom played in a similar style (in a segregated setting).

Country music was initially an unwritten tradition. When it began to be recorded for commercial purposes in the 1920s, it was marketed as "hillbilly music," but the term was viewed with the same wariness by its practitioners as "race record" was by its African-American counterparts. Eventually the term "old-time" or "old-timey" became the accepted nomenclature. Unlike piano rags and popular songs of the early 20th century, country music was played by "string bands," using the fiddle, banjo, guitar, mandolin, autoharp, and/or double bass—all of them readily mobile and capable of being played outdoors, in contrast to the piano, a parlor instrument associated more closely with the urban middle classes. The musicians themselves were quick to emphasize their rustic integrity and humble origins in the names of their bands: George Daniell's Hill Billies, The Skillet Lickers, and Uncle Dave Macon and His Fruit Jar Drinkers (so named because moonshine, whisky brewed illegally in the backwoods, was commonly drunk out of jars made for home canning of fruits).

As with traditional musicians throughout the world, country musicians were for the most part not professionally trained. One of the first big stars, Jimmie Rodgers (1897–1933), known as "America's Blue Yodeler," was a railroad worker from Mississippi

---

12. Liner notes to *Free Jazz* (Atlantic 1364), 1960.

Jimmie Rodgers and the Carter Family, Louisville, KY, ca. 1930. Mississippi's "Singing Brakeman" and the Virginia folk revivalists (left to right: Maybelle, Alvin P., and Sara Carter) made a number of country music recordings that had immense influence on later musicians. Maybelle Carter also developed a much-emulated guitar style (playing melodies in the lower strings). Her daughter, June Carter (1929–2003), married Johnny Cash (1932–2003), a highly successful songwriter and performer in his own right. Together, they continued the legacy of the first Carter generation.

Source: © Michael Ochs Archives/CORBIS. All Rights Reserved

who heard country blues singing and learned to play guitar while employed on a New Orleans–based line. When he caught tuberculosis and his railroad activities were curtailed, Rodgers decided to pursue an entertainment career; this became his sole focus after he left railroad work permanently in 1927. Rodgers soon found himself making records for the Victor Talking Machine Company, and when the first of his "Blue Yodel" recordings ("T for Texas") became a hit, his reputation was established. During his short career, he toured with Will Rogers and made a brief film, *The Singing Brakeman*, playing on his other nickname. Rodgers recorded approximately 100 "sides," most notably the series of 13 "Blue Yodels" that produced some of his biggest hits. One of the most intriguing, "Blue Yodel # 9 (Standing on the Corner)," was a collaboration with Louis Armstrong and Lillian Hardin Armstrong. Recorded in 1930, it marks a rare moment during the segregated era when superior musicians whose lives had taught them to value character over color came together to produce a crossover recording of such magnitude. Although Rodgers did not live to see the full impact of his contributions, his status as one of country's seminal musicians is undisputed.

With the rise of radio in the 1920s, the popularity of country music began to extend well beyond the South. On November 28, 1925, station WSM in Nashville, Tennessee, began broadcasting a local program called *The WSM Barn Dance*; its first performer, 77-year-old "Uncle" Jimmy Thompson, claimed he could "fiddle the bugs off a 'tater vine," was old enough to have fought in the Civil War.[13] The show changed its name to *The Grand Ole Opry* in 1928 to emphasize its distinction from the "high" art of grand opera. Yet as an institution, The Grand Ole Opry functioned very much like the great opera houses of Europe, for its impresarios launched many a career. By the late 1930s the weekly show, now performed before a large studio audience, was being broadcast nationwide. As the singer Loretta Lynn (b. 1935) put it, "If you've never played on *The Grand Ole Opry*, you haven't quite made it yet."[14]

---

13. http://www.southernmusic.net/grandoleopry.htm.
14. http://www.countryreview.com/GrandOleOpry.

Grand Ole Opry. Ryman Auditorium, a onetime church, served as the site for the Grand Ole Opry broadcasts on WSM in downtown Nashville, Tennessee, from 1943 to 1974. When the new Opry opened outside of the city, the Ryman fell into disrepair; a series of 1992 concerts by Emmylou Harris revived interest in the hall, and in 1994 it reopened as a performance space and small museum. The Opry now holds its winter season at Ryman.

Source: © Jason Moore/ZUMA/CORBIS. All Rights Reserved

CD15, Track 19
FLATT AND SCRUGGS
Foggy Mountain Breakdown
Score Anthology II/194

The Great Depression was as damaging to the old-time music industry as it was to the blues. Recording from the 1930s was more ethnomusicological in purpose, much of it funded by branches of the American government. Among those most active were John A. Lomax (1867–1948) and his son Alan Lomax (1915–2002). The elder Lomax, who told his story in *Adventures of a Ballad Hunter* (1947), began his career with a 1910 publication of material he had collected directly from the singers (*Cowboy Songs and Other Frontier Ballads*). Over the next 30 years, he became noted for his studies and field recordings, especially those made at southern "prison farms"; the inmates were primarily African Americans whose repertoire was vast and without racial barrier. He also helped Hudie Ledbetter (Lead Belly, ca. 1888–1949) launch a career as a singer-guitarist (and composer of "Goodnight, Irene," a huge hit for the Weavers, a folk group featuring Pete Seeger). Alan Lomax, who had begun working with his father in the 1930s, would pursue an international career, collecting traditional music in Great Britain, Italy, Spain, and the West Indies as well as the United States. Lomax made a 1937 field recording of fiddler W. H. Stepp's playing "Bonaparte's Retreat," which appeared in Lomax's 1941 book, *Our Singing Country*, and was the primary source for the "Hoe-down" finale of Aaron Copland's *Rodeo* (see Chapter 22).

"Foggy Mountain Breakdown," as recorded by Lester Flatt, Earl Scruggs, and the Foggy Mountain Boys in 1949, represents the country music subgenre of **bluegrass.** The style's name derives from the band in which Flatt and Scruggs first met, Bill Monroe and his Blue Grass Boys. The characteristic sound of bluegrass is an acoustic string ensemble of banjo, guitar, fiddle, and double bass. The banjo is picked (as opposed to strummed), and vocals tend to be pitched in the upper end of the singer's register, creating what has been described as a "high, lonesome sound." The characteristic syncopation of bluegrass anticipates the downbeat slightly, in contrast to jazz, in which performers often play just slightly behind the beat. The resulting rhythms are propulsive and infectious—"folk music with overdrive" as one commentator described it. In "Foggy Mountain Breakdown," Scruggs demonstrates his renowned technique of three-finger banjo picking. The virtuosity is dazzling, even within the relatively simple harmonic and metrical confines of this particular number. The piece also reveals formal similarities with the basic patterns of many blues and jazz numbers:

William H. ("Fiddler Bill") Stepp.
Stepp (1875–1947) was among a group of Kentucky fiddlers recorded by the Library of Congress's Archive of Folk Culture in the 1930s; other Stepp recordings include "The Drunken Hiccups," "Callahan," "Silver Strand," and "The Ways of the World."
Source: Courtesy Shanachie Records

soloists take turns improvising variations on a given theme or harmonic pattern. Like jazz, bluegrass and other forms of country music provided performers with a framework for improvisation.

The later fortunes of Flatt and Scruggs exemplify the development of country music over the decades that followed. The two toured and recorded successfully for many years, and their music attracted an even wider following through television and films. Their "Ballad of Jed Clampett" won fame as the theme song for the television series *The Beverly Hillbillies* (1962–1971), and "Foggy Mountain Breakdown" figured prominently in the blockbuster film *Bonnie & Clyde* (1968). But Flatt and Scruggs split up as a duo in 1969 over musical differences. Scruggs had pushed Flatt to explore new repertories, including such numbers as Bob Dylan's folk-rock song "Like a Rolling Stone." Flatt disliked performing such nontraditional repertory and established his own group, called Nashville Grass. Scruggs formed the Earl Scruggs Review with his sons, one of whom played electric guitar, and moved beyond the traditional bluegrass sound. He later won a Grammy® Award for Best Country Instrumental Performance with a rerecording of "Foggy Mountain Breakdown" for the 2000 film *O Brother, Where Art Thou?*

Like jazz, country music evolved in many directions. Bluegrass itself was a relatively late phenomenon that first emerged in the 1940s. Other new subgenres of country music included cowboy music (Gene Autry, Roy Rogers), western swing (Bob Wills), honky-tonk (Ernest Tubb, Hank Williams), rockabilly (Johnny Cash), country rock (Emmylou Harris), outlaw (Willie Nelson), and so-called new country (Garth Brooks); comparable genres emerged in other regions such as Texas (Tejano) and Louisiana (Cajun and zydeco). No musical style or genre has ever been immune from change, and country music has been no exception. Nashville, Tennessee, became the first major setting for the country music business, in its centrality as a songwriting and recording mecca not unlike New York's role in popular music during the Tin Pan Alley era and beyond.

Thomas Hart Benton, *The Sources of Country Music* (1975). Benton's mural, commissioned by the Country Music Hall of Fame in Nashville, Tennessee, captures the inherent contradictions between the sources and later development of the art. All of Benton's sources are true enough—the church choir, the dulcimer player, the dancers moving to the sound of the fiddle, the African-American banjo player, the cowboy strumming his guitar, the train racing across the landscape—but the image omits important technological components that have become just as powerful in the development of the art: radio, the phonograph, the recording studio, and television.

Source: Country Music Hall of Fame and Museum

Like jazz, country music has struggled with issues of stylistic "purity." For many of its followers, "true" country music is unadulterated by the pressures of commercialism and the technology of the recording studio. But the ideal of a wholly rural music untouched by the influences of electronic media and the marketplace ignores the reality of stars such as Hank Williams (1923–1953), a performer and songwriter in the honky-tonk mode, whose music was both a blend and a composite of country and noncountry styles and whose turbulent life was anything but pastoral. The "down-home" image of country music is not without foundation: many artists did grow up in households and communities in which one made one's own music, and there are performers outside the commercial country music business who have revived the old-time style. But none of them has remained unaffected by the power of radio, recordings, and the recording studio, not to mention the stylistic give and take between rock and country music that has continued for over a half century.

THE FOLK REVIVAL

Partly in reaction against the loud volume, insistent rhythms, and increasingly technological elements of rock and roll in the late 1950s and early 1960s, a number of musicians and their listening public gravitated toward a more natural sound, untouched (or only minimally so) by electronic manipulation. A broad category of music loosely known as "folk music" rode an enormous wave of popularity at this time. The repertory was derived from or created in the spirit of the traditional songs that had been cultivated by country musicians in previous decades. The folk sound rested on acoustic (not electric) guitars, limited use (or absence) of percussion instruments, and lyrical melody and texts that harkened back to an earlier era, extolling the virtues of simplicity and the enduring themes of love and loss. From the early 1950s into the 1970s, groups like the Weavers, the Kingston Trio, Peter, Paul and Mary, and Simon and Garfunkel, and individual artists like Bob Dylan, Joan Baez, Judy Collins, Joni Mitchell, John Denver, Gordon Lightfoot, and James Taylor more than held their own in the charts against Elvis, the Beatles, and the Rolling Stones.

The quintessential American folk musician is Pete Seeger (b. 1919), whose stepmother Ruth Crawford Seeger (see Chapter 23) was instrumental in preserving

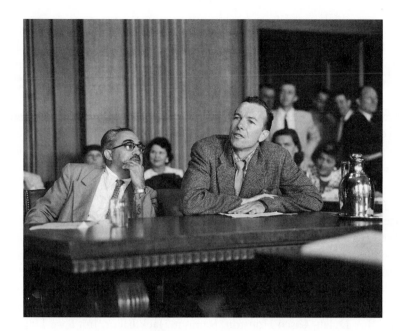

American folksong as an educational resource. He has been tireless as a folk song revivalist and supporter of social causes, taking over the mantle of Woody Guthrie (1912–1967, composer of "This Land Is Your Land") as a "singer to all the people" who brought songs of human dignity from all over the world to his audiences with just his voice and a banjo. As a member of the Weavers, he had several hit songs; but his career hit a roadblock when he was subpoenaed to testify in 1955 before the House Un-American Activities Committee. As he testified to the committee, "I resent very much and very deeply the implication . . . [that] . . . because my opinions may be different from yours [the committee members], that I am any less of an American than anybody else. I love my country very deeply."[15] He was subsequently blacklisted from all media outlets until the late 1960s, although his songs were covered successfully during this period by groups such as Peter, Paul and Mary and the Byrds (see above).

The relationship of the folk song to its sources remains much in dispute. Folk music, like traditional country music, operates under the (usually unspoken) premise that orally transmitted music is unadulterated by such commercial influences as radio and recordings and therefore has a greater value than music composed and performed by musicians who can read musical notation and are familiar with the immense capabilities of the recording studio. The untrained musician is somehow superior to those who have been trained (once again, shades of Sargeant and Ellington). In reality, few if any country musicians of the past 50 years have remained entirely free of the influences of the recording and broadcasting industries.

The ballad "Tom Dooley" illustrates the complexity of the relationship between the oral traditions of earlier times and the later realities of recording and broadcasting. "Tom Dooley" was originally a true folk ballad, a musical broadside that related the murder of one Laura Foster in 1865 in western North Carolina, allegedly at the hands of her lover, Tom Dooley. In 1938, the folklorist Frank Warner was traveling in that area and took down the song as performed in unaccompanied form by a local resident named Frank Proffitt, who had learned the song from his father, who in turn had learned it from his mother, who had witnessed the hanging of Tom Dooley. Warner passed his transcription on to his colleague Alan Lomax, who in 1947 published it in a

---

15. For the complete transcript of Seeger's testimony, go to http://www.peteseeger.net/HUAC.htm. Accessed May 14, 2008.

collection called *Folk Song U.S.A.*, crediting Warner as the collector. Eleven years later, the Kingston Trio made and recorded their own arrangement of "Tom Dooley," and scored their first big hit (selling over four million copies by 1962). Warner and Lomax contacted Proffitt, and the three filed suit against the Kingston Trio. The case was settled out of court, and those associated with *Folk Song U.S.A.* began to receive small royalties on the Kingston Trio's recording after 1962. The Kingston Trio "could have stayed out of trouble by learning the song from a **public domain** version,"[16] referring to work not under copyright and therefore available for all to use, but expert testimony confirmed the published version as the basis for the recorded version, and the group (and its record label) had little choice but to acquiesce.

The process of collecting and publishing folk music seems poised at times to turn the concept of oral tradition upside down: Should true (public domain) folksongs be allowed to be made private property, or should they be declared a permanent part of the public domain? A typical example of this situation involves "Buffalo Skinners," a ballad about the experience of hired hands working for a corrupt boss "on the plains of the buffalo." Versions of this song have been performed, arranged, recorded, and (in some cases) copyrighted by Woody Guthrie, Arlo Guthrie, Pete Seeger, Roger (Jim) McGuinn, Bob Dylan, Cisco Houston, Ramblin' Jack Elliot, Jim Kweskin, and John Renbourn. The song was not new neither when John Lomax published it in *Cowboy Songs and Other Frontier Ballads* (1910) nor when it was rearranged for publication in Silber and Robinson's *Songs of the Great American West* (1967).

Other artists wrote new works in the style of folk music. Bob Dylan (b. 1941), who at first considered himself a disciple of Woody Guthrie, initially wrote songs that drew on the traditional repertory through their uncomplicated, sometimes technically "incorrect" harmonies and less-than-perfect metrical blends of music and text. Dylan's singing style at first borrowed extensively from old-time and blues performers; it avoided any sense of traditional vocal beauty, instead sounding rough-hewn, half sung, half declaimed, and sometimes glaringly out of tune. No matter how many hours and studio recording takes were actually required to capture a song, Dylan still took as an ideal the AM radio impression of unvarnished immediacy.

As Dylan began to direct his attention to the political and social status quo, the absence of vocal beauty became its own act of protest against the Establishment. It was not merely the lyrics of Dylan's songs that decried; the voice itself was by extension the angry voice of the people, uncultivated and for that very reason all the more genuine and sincere. Dylan was also a traditionalist in using song as a vehicle of social protest. Ballads in 18th-century England had often protested against unpopular laws or court verdicts, and Dylan extended his work to protest against racial injustice, nuclear proliferation, and governmental repression.

Dylan's folk and protest music period gave way when he saw the success the California folk-rock band The Byrds had with his "Mr. Tambourine Man"; in a critic's words, he put down his acoustic and plugged in his electric guitar. His followers at first felt betrayed, but most of them (and many new fans) eventually supported the decision most symbolic of the end of the folk revival. As with other composer/performers who have survived the instability of musical fashion, Dylan's music has reflected a variety of styles—rock, country music, protest song, gospel, love song, blues—at different times and in different mixtures. His chameleon-like artistic path has scampered in many directions, only to return to a previous style; it is fair to say, however, that few were prepared to hear him actually croon on his 1969 country music album, *Nashville Skyline*.

---

16. Peter Irvine, "Folk, Copyright, and the Public Domain," 2003, online at http://www.peterirvinelaw.com/pdf/Folk_Music_Copyright_PD.pdf. Accessed on April 27, 2008.

The Byrds with Bob Dylan, Los Angeles, 1965. While Dylan had already recorded some songs with an electric backup, the success of the Byrds' cover of his "Mr. Tambourine Man" (released April 1965) convinced him to follow their path in his own way. Three months later, he became a "rock star" with his "Like a Rolling Stone." Members of the Byrds had made similar transitions: singer Gene Clark had been a member of the New Christy Minstrels (a hootenanny revival group), while Jim (later Roger) McGuinn, a sideman with the Chad Mitchell Trio, Judy Collins, and Simon and Garfunkel, brought the sound of the electric 12-string guitar (six courses, two strings apiece, like the Renaissance lute) to rock music.

Source: © Michael Ochs Archives/CORBIS. All Rights Reserved

RHYTHM, ROCK, AND RAP

When blues became an ensemble music by the 1940s, instruments imported from jazz (bass, drums) and the concept of "soloing," whether by the guitarist, a "mouth harp" (harmonica) player, or a reed or brass instrumentalist, increased its audience and made personality and presentation increasingly important. Performers like Howlin' Wolf (Chester Arthur Burnett, 1910–1976), Muddy Waters (McKinley Morganfield, 1915–1983), and B. B. King (b. 1925) used the louder sound (eventually amplified electrically) for new effects and greater vocal power.

At the same time, a piano-based fusion of ragtime, blues, and jazz became exceedingly popular. The style that became known as **boogie-woogie,** featured "walking" bass lines in left-hand octaves (usually broken up and syncopated) or other ostinato figures, while the right hand played chords, melody, or improvisational passages. The fusion of boogie-woogie's steady bass rhythms with the emotional intensity of the newly electrified blues led to a style known to African Americans as rhythm and blues and its slighter later hybrid, called rock and roll by Caucasian Americans.

The vocal sound of rock and roll (which persisted into rock music) typically rejected refinement in favor of immediacy, often involving an assertive, "unpretty" singing style and pointedly using words like "ain't" and "nohow." Backup singers often reinforced the rhythm with nonsense syllables like "shu-bop shu-bop" and "doo-lang doo-lang." But the formula for a memorable rock song remained essentially the same as that for any song from any period: a good tune and resonant lyrics.

Chuck Berry's "Roll Over, Beethoven" (1956) is typical of many early rock-and-roll songs of the 1950s and early 1960s. Its melodic range is limited, its formal structure and rhythms repetitive, its essential harmonies confined to the tonic, dominant, and subdominant—and for all these reasons, the work is mesmerizing. The lyrics themselves, urging the most revered of all classical composers to turn over in his grave, evoke a cultural war between so-called high and low art, contemplation and activity, old and young. (The lyrics are also amusing, their directive simple: "Dig these rhythm and blues!") The song spoke directly to a generation of teenagers, and it retains its elemental force today. Formally, "Roll Over, Beethoven" follows the 12-bar blues form. The published lead sheet provides only the barest outline of the melody,

CD15, Track 20
CHUCK BERRY
Roll Over, Beethoven
Score Anthology II/195

Chuck Berry. This image of Chuck Berry performing his signature duck walk captures two contradictory streams in the emergence of rock during the mid-1950s. What appealed to youth—and what parents found so threatening about this music—was its physical presence, its pounding rhythm, and the suggestive movements associated with it on the stage. The coat-and-tie outfit was a calculated effort to counter this. Berry was one of the first African-American rock-and-roll artists to be marketed directly to white youth, and the respectable clothing helped penetrate that market. In fact, this outfit remained standard for many rockers well into the 1960s. The Beatles, the Rolling Stones, and even the Doors made early appearances in such attire, and the male participants in Dick Clark's long-running *American Bandstand* television show were required to wear ties until the late 1960s.

Source: Michael Ochs Archives Ltd./Getty Images Inc—Los Angeles

harmonies, and words; a great many aspects of the music are left to the discretion of the performer or performers.

After the first few years of the 1960s, rock (as it would now come to be known) began moving in many different directions. The Beatles, building on the traditions of Elvis Presley, Little Richard, and others, emerged on the American scene in 1963 and paved the way for what would be called the "British Invasion" of similar groups, including the Dave Clark Five, the Rolling Stones, the Animals, and the Who. In 1970, the Who released the first significant rock opera, *Tommy*, which was transformed first into a film and later into a stage musical. Other subgenres of rock included folk-rock (discussed earlier in this chapter), surf rock, blues rock, and hard (or acid) rock. Surf rock was a curious mixture of styles; in some cases, it relied on close, sometimes intricate harmonies and counterpoint, as heard in Brian Wilson's music for the Beach Boys; on other occasions, a bold melody on lead guitar and an impression of surfing action (including wave sound effects) defined the style. Blues and blues rock were favored by British groups who studied the music of rediscovered African-American songwriters and placed them in more modern contexts, whether in a post-1940s-style band (Alexis Koerner, John Mayall) or within an electric guitar–dominated context (Cream, the Yardbirds). Hard rock or acid rock was characterized by a louder, more aggressive sound, often involving sonic distortion. Preeminent among these groups were Jefferson Airplane, the Grateful Dead, the Jimi Hendrix Experience, and Jim Morrison and the Doors.

Within a few years of their 1964 *Ed Sullivan Show* debut, the Beatles had expanded the boundaries of rock to include orchestral and non-Western instruments, more sophisticated and enigmatic texts, a broader range of harmonies and forms, and an increasingly sophisticated use of recording technology to create works that in effect could not be performed in a live setting in any recognizable fashion.

The manipulation of sound in the Beatles' "Strawberry Fields Forever" (1967), for example, is so basic to the work that it can be legitimately considered an example of electronic music. Beyond standard techniques of amplification, resonance, and overdubbing, "Strawberry Fields Forever" features electronic manipulation of the vocals that causes the pitch to drop, thereby contributing to the dreamy, other worldly quality of the sound. The technique is essentially the same as that used by Le Caine in his *Dripsody* (see Chapter 23). The cymbals and other percussion instruments were dubbed backward in places, creating a strange, unsettling effect. George Martin, the Beatles' producer at the time, deserves almost as much credit for these innovations as the Beatles themselves. "Strawberry Fields Forever" also features unusual harmonic, rhythmic, instrumental, and lyrical effects:

- *Harmony*. The opening harmonic progression, for example, moves from A to E minor to F♯ Major to D and only then back to A, and at the words "nothing is real," we hear a ♭V–VI progression.

- *Rhythm and tempo*. These are irregular at many points, set in a manner that speeds up and slows down quite unpredictably, with the instruments underneath playing cross rhythms against the voice, all of which captures the essence of the words perfectly. (This technique also helped to splice together adjoining parts of two takes that were not quite in tune with one another.)

- *Instrumentation*. In addition to the standard guitars and drums, the work uses orchestral instruments such as flutes and cellos, as well as a non-Western instrument (the svaramandal, an Indian harp).

- *Lyrics*. These are largely unrhymed and unmetrical in structure, the words are elliptical, elusive, partly nonsensical in content (or perhaps not), but in any case markedly different from the typical lyrics of rock songs at that time.

Representing the composer's intentions. Until relatively recently, a composer's intentions were preserved primarily in the written or published score, or through some combination of the two. The rise of recorded music in the 20th century created new ways for composers to realize their works. John Lennon and Paul McCartney's song "Strawberry Fields Forever" (1967) was created in the recording studio: there were few if any written sketches and no "autograph score," only studio takes and retakes. The published version of the song, shown here, thus represents little more than a transcription made by an anonymous professional arranger hired by the publisher. The song's recorded performance is the real "published" score, designated by the ℗ (phonogram) symbol; the studio outtakes are the aural "sketches," never intended for publication (although often made available surreptitiously).

Source: "Strawberry Fields Forever," words and music by John Lennon and Paul McCartney. Copyright 1967 Northern Songs Ltd. Copyright renewed. All rights controlled and administered by EMI Blackwood Music Inc. (BMI) under license from ATV Music (Maclen Music). All Rights Reserved

Such techniques are even more abundant in the Beatles' landmark album, *Sergeant Pepper's Lonely Hearts Club Band*, released in 1967. This concept album, revolving around the idea of a fictional band, was one of the first to be issued with a complete set of printed lyrics. The music moved well beyond standard harmonies and forms, borrowing from several non-rock genres; it spawned a subgenre of its own known as progressive rock. From the late 1960s through the early 1980s, groups like Frank Zappa and the Mothers of Invention, Pink Floyd, the Moody Blues, Jethro Tull, Yes, Genesis, Emerson, Lake and Palmer, and Tangerine Dream cultivated a type of rock that consistently emphasized unconventional harmonies, complex rhythms, polyphonic textures, and unusual sonorities. No resource was off limits: Gentle Giant's "On Reflection" (1975) begins as a four-part fugue, reminiscent of a 14th-century caccia; Pink Floyd, in true musique concrète fashion, occasionally integrated into their music recorded sounds made from household objects. Rock styles proliferated still further in the closing decades of the 20th century. Heavy metal bands from the late 1960s onward, like Led Zeppelin, Kiss, and Guns n' Roses emphasized an unprecedented volume of sound.

Disco, popular in the 1970s and 1980s, was developed to meet the needs of a new kind of popular dancing. It featured a relentless 4/4 beat (minus the backbeat of most postwar popular music) and sweeping melody, often played by violins. Disco evolved into several subgenres (among them "acid house," later simply house) that reflected different audience's lifestyles. Techno relied heavily on electronic and digital manipulation and made little or no effort to mimic traditional instruments in the process. By the 1990s disco-related music had become ubiquitous (although accented backbeats had been restored). Those unsympathetic to these styles went in disparate directions, producing melodic music recalling the popular music of the pre-rock era; adopting an unforgiving "back to basics" approach (grunge); or just turning off the electricity (unplugged acoustic concerts). And, much like rock music of the 1960s and 1970s, no issue was off-limits as lyrical content.

By the beginning of the new century, the ability of performers to get their music to the public through the Internet began to solve the problem of dealing with an ever-smaller number of mainstream companies with traditional profit motives and fewer resources for experimentation. Despite the difficulties, many companies previously unassociated with the record industry entered the Internet and traditional retail marketplaces. Popular music in general moved into its postmodern stage; appropriating earlier styles with or without irony became a common practice; continual redefinition of self became a mode of operation for some, while others pursued stylistic organicism and longevity.

In the 1950s, African-American musicians continued to suffer the indignity of watching their popular songs sell far more copies when performed by Caucasian-Americans with the backing of the largest record companies, while black labels were neither able to advertise their wares to the same degree nor break through racial barriers at most radio stations and performing venues. So in 1959, Berry Gordy, Jr. (b. 1929) founded a record label, Tamla; the following year he created Motown Records, named for his home city of Detroit (Motortown).

Motown flourished in Detroit, with African-American groups like the Temptations, Diana Ross and the Supremes, the Four Tops, and Smoky Robinson and the Miracles and individual artists like Stevie Wonder and Marvin Gaye. The Motown sound was characterized by close vocal harmony, soaring melody, call and response, and a steady beat; the house band that supported the singers was led by musicians of great skill and taste, the composers and producers were gifted and prolific. As in rock music of the era, the repeated riff (a short motif, whether in the bass part or as a melodic feature) became a signature element. This crossover style proved extremely successful with all audiences, and for the first time, popular African-American music was providing a

The Supremes, 1965. The Supremes (left to right: Florence Ballard, Diana Ross, Mary Wilson) symbolize the crossover success Motown Records owner Berry Gordy, Jr., had in bringing African-American music to an integrated audience. The three women were dressed in gowns, wore fashionable wigs, and moved with carefully choreographed grace. The vocal arrangements borrowed from 1950s doo-wop, even as a more modern rhythm and blues style was employed. Diane (later Diana) Ross became the lead singer with her more mainstream pop voice; she was increasingly featured in the staging of their shows, and in 1967 the group renamed itself Diana Ross and the Supremes.

Source: © (Photographer)/CORBIS. All Rights Reserved

financial windfall for African Americans, without the aid, well-intentioned or exploitative, of others.

The Motown style gave way to others, some more or less related to it than others. Soul music, with its roots in gospel and rhythm and blues, flourished from the early 1960s on, recorded primarily in Memphis, Tennessee, and in Muscle Shoals (Florence), Alabama. Among many others, Aretha Franklin, who came out of the church gospel tradition, brought that sound and a personal conviction to a more syncopated, energetic beat. Horns also began to reappear in the arrangements. Soul would develop a number of subgenres: psychedelic, which loosened up the song form and reflected greater social and political consciousness; funk, which relied increasingly on repetitive figures and more exaggerated syncopation; Philadelphia, which revived the 1950s group vocal sound in a more sophisticated context of lush orchestrations; and genres influenced by rock, jazz, disco, and, since the 1980s, hip-hop music.

Hip-hop evolved out of Jamaican roots and began with words being shouted over a disk on a turntable being manipulated by a disk jockey. But a steady rhythmic element, known as the "beat," came to the fore; patterns were devised from live, electronic, and sampled sources, the last borrowing from other popular music styles and using MIDI and other devices to create repetitive patterns. (This at times secretive practice initially raised issues of copyright, but such borrowing is now in the open and considered as much homage as a musical issue.) Over that wall of hip-hop sound, **rap** emerged, derived in part from the Jamaican practice of toasting and the American "talking blues"; both concentrated on creating and performing texts spontaneously while music was being played. Rappers soon synthesized the beats with rhymed poetry, using a vocal technique somewhat akin to *Sprechstimme*. Originally dominated by male African Americans and criticized for its politicized and sexual content as much as any perceived musical deficiency, rap has become a genre open to both sexes, all racial groups, and all nations. Increasingly, social concerns have become part of the discourse, as exemplified by Kanye West. Since speech is a common denominator, the musical content per se may seem less important in rap music; but the better the "beat" is constructed and the stronger the connection between words and music, the more successful the result will be.

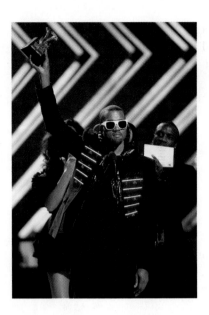

Kanye West. The rapper celebrates his 2008 Grammy® Award for Best Rap Album (for his third album, *Graduation*). Originally known as a rap producer, West uses a combination of eclectic, pitched-up samples (at the same speed but at a higher register than the original) and his voice, piano, and percussion to create his beats.

Source: © Mike Blake/Reuters/CORBIS. All Rights Reserved

CONCLUSION

The proliferation of approaches found in 20th-century art music was reflected in the rise of many new popular genres, notably jazz, which became the subject of serious discussion (not to mention disagreements) in short order. That a musical style born inside dance halls rather than concert halls could bring such enjoyment and be taken so seriously (and receive the label "America's classical music") testifies to significant influences on America's listening habits: international status, social change (notably integration), development of new media, and the sense that music could indeed be found anywhere. While some continued to criticize differences in taste (as had Hanslick and Wagner), others became more open to those differences; a sense of history much like that found in the study of classical music could be sensed in jazz, even after its vogue among certain classes passed on like any other "trend." Jazz has long been a fully legitimate subject for reference works, dissertations, critical essays, and recording reissues; significant improvisations (in some ways the most traditional aspect of jazz) are now transcribed for study.

Other music seemed to belong to both camps. Ragtime was a popular style that took itself seriously in Joplin's hands, was an influence on classical composers (more so than jazz, which had third-stream music as a short-lived fusion with classical music), and, by virtue of having been written down for commercial reasons, was revived successfully a half century after its heyday. Caucasian-American folk music survived in a similar fashion (although recordings, not sheet music, were the vehicle for this unwritten tradition); in emulation of several 19th-century European composers, 20th-century American composers borrowed melodies or imitated their style in "nationalist" compositions (Charles Ives and Henry Cowell was among the most prolific in this approach). Popular song continued in the art and domestic song traditions of the 19th century, and operetta had been replaced by the Broadway musical by the 1930s as another opportunity for the "hit song" to emerge (although "musicals" by Stephen Sondheim, William Finn, and others experimented by having little or no dialogue).

Another group of genres required no association with previous classical genres. Country music evolved from old-time music; while the oldest layers of country music have gone through a revival process (again, based on recordings), and offshoots such as bluegrass have endured, the (popular) country song has become its primary mode of expression. Since World War II, rhythm and blues, rock, and (most recently) hip-hop–based genres have blossomed into a potpourri or mosaic of styles, in many cases unique enough that the "revival" of a particular style may actually be considered a forward-looking trend, rather than retrospection. Country blues, so influential on those later genres, is, like old-time and early country music, a style that has continued to flourish, thanks to surviving recordings.

The emotional authenticity of jazz, country music, rhythm and blues, and others speaks directly to audiences weary of an art that to their minds had become overly refined. Unwritten traditions such as country blues and old-time music offer fresh alternatives to listeners. Both groups offer possibilities to composers interested in exploring new approaches to melody, harmony, and rhythm. And, with perhaps the least amount of fanfare, there is a genre as conscious of stylistic change as any other (see the variety of Grammy® Awards categories in Chapter 19) and whose emotional impact is unquestioned: gospel music, which in historical terms has the deepest roots of all American music: the hymns and psalms of the precolonial era and the call-and-response singing style of Africans enslaved in the New World.

DISCUSSION QUESTIONS

1. What factors outside music contributed to the growing diversity of musical styles in the 20th century?

2. Part of the appeal of jazz in the 1920s and 1930s lay in what was perceived to be its genuine and earthy nature, in contrast to the allegedly overrefined and decadent idioms of the concert hall and opera house. In what ways does this outlook resemble or differ from the move toward naturalness in the middle of the 18th century?

3. In what ways does Igor Stravinsky's description of his Octet (see Primary Evidence: Stravinsky on Musical "Objectivity," in Chapter 22) manifest the modernist aesthetic?

4. Tonality had long been a fundamental building block of musical form. In the absence of tonality, how did composers of the early 20th century working in the atonal idiom construct large-scale forms?

5. Does a composer adhering strictly to the principles of serial composition have more or less freedom than one not using the serial idiom?

6. How did the ideals of vocal beauty expand over the course of the 20th century?

7. Is John Cage's *4'33"* a work of music?

8. In what ways do Milton Babbitt's arguments in "Who Cares If You Listen?" (see Primary Evidence feature in Chapter 23) resemble those put forward by Boethius in the early medieval era (Prelude to the Medieval Era) that theory is superior to practice?

9. How did the transmission of musical works change over the course of the 20th century?

10. How did the relationship of the composer to his or her public change over the course of the 20th century?

Epilogue

Music at the Beginning of a New Century

The 21st century is too young to have defined itself musically, but for the moment at least, the pluralism and rapid changes of the 20th century continue. Musical genres and subgenres are still emerging and fading with remarkable speed. New styles explode into prominence, blend with other styles, fade, revive, and recombine with still newer styles.

Musical institutions continue to evolve accordingly. The recording industry, coping with declining sales for the first time after more than eight decades of uninterrupted growth, is seeking new ways to market music. Civic orchestras, which rose to prominence in the late 19th century, are adopting creative strategies to attract and retain new audiences. Concert venues accommodate increasingly diverse kinds of performances. In the 1930s and 1940s, when Benny Goodman's band and Duke Ellington's band performed at what had been a bastion of classical music—Carnegie Hall—critics hailed the events as landmarks in the history of jazz. In 2002, by contrast, when the hip-hop band Roots played in Avery Fisher Hall at Lincoln Center, the home of the New York Philharmonic Orchestra, the event created scarcely a stir.

Even the governing board of the Pulitzer Prize in Journalism and the Arts has begun to rethink the basis of its annual award for a "distinguished musical composition of significant dimension" (see p. 598). In June 2004, the board announced that nominees for the award in music would no longer be required to submit a score and a live recording of the work under consideration. Instead, only a recording—live or not—is needed. As Sig Gissler, administrator of the Pulitzer at Columbia University's Graduate School of Journalism, put it at the time, "We feel that we should broaden the prize a bit so that we can be more assured that we are getting the full range of the best of America's music, especially as the forms change, the categories erode, and composers move from one form to another."[1] The effect has been to open the prize to improvisational and electronic works as well as film music and music created in the recording studio; the jazz saxophonist Ornette Coleman won the 2007 award for his 2005 concert recording, released under the title *Sound Grammar* (see Chapter 24).

As styles continue to proliferate, some artists are combining them in ways that break down the borders between them. So-called crossover acts, intended to appeal to the audiences for more than one genre, are now so common that the term has begun to lose meaning. The African-American jazz violinist Regina Carter exemplifies the trend toward a deepening synthesis of musical traditions. In December 2001, she was invited by the city of Genoa, Italy, to play on the violin known as The Cannon, a 250-year-old instrument once owned and used by the 19th-century virtuoso Niccolò Paganini. Carter and her group played a mixture of jazz numbers, improvisations, and arrangements of popular songs. At one point, she wove allusions to works by Johann Sebastian Bach

and Arvo Pärt (b. 1935) into a cadenza within her arrangement of *Don't Explain*, a song written in the mid-1940s by Billie Holiday (1915–1959).

The erosion of meaningful distinctions between opera and musical offers yet another example of how genres can change and merge over time. Gian Carlo Menotti composed several operas for Broadway in the late 1940 and 1950, and received two Pulitzer Prizes in Music (*The Consul*, 1950; *The Saint of Bleecker Street*, 1955). Baz Luhrmann's 1990 production of Puccini's *La Bohème*, revived in 2002 for Broadway, presented the opera in its original Italian (with English translations running at the top and bottom of the stage) but with amplified sound. Elton John and Tim Rice's 1999 reworking of Verdi's *Aïda* was more radical, using the plot of Verdi's opera as the basis for an entirely new score. In 2003, the Italian rock musician Lucio Dalla premiered a reworking of Puccini's *Tosca* as *Tosca: Desperate Love*, in which singers perform against a recorded soundtrack. Some critics see the work as a "dumbing down" of traditional opera; others consider it part of a necessary transformation of a genre in danger of becoming ossified. This is not to say that transformations and reworkings of long-established operas will eventually supplant more traditional productions and venues. What seems more likely is that such works will add to the growing range of musical choices available to audiences. This in turn might well provide a necessary component for the survival of opera as a going enterprise, especially in the United States, which gives little or no public funding for it, as opera strives for a less elitist image.

Still, no one can predict music's future. History suggests only that it will change in ways we cannot today envision. Composers,

Regina Carter in Genoa. On December 30, 2001, Regina Carter played jazz on a violin built in the 1740s by Giuseppe Bartolomeo Guarneri of Cremona (see Chapter 10), owned and used in the 19th century by Niccolò Paganini (see Chapter 16) and now owned by the City of Genoa and played by invitation only. Note the microphone attached to the instrument's body near the tailpiece.

Source: Marco Scarpa/Marco Scarpa Photography

---

1. Justin Davidson, "Score One for Broad," *Newsday*, 1 June 2004, online.

FOCUS   The Beatles on a Cosmic Trip

According to the Associated Press:

Saturday, February 2nd 2008, 4:00 AM

WASHINGTON—The Beatles are about to become radio stars in a whole new way. NASA will broadcast the Beatles' song "Across the Universe" across the galaxy to Polaris, the North Star, on Monday. It's the first-ever beaming of a radio song by the space agency directly into deep space. NASA is celebrating the 40th anniversary of the song, the 45th anniversary of NASA's Deep Space Network—which communicates with its distant probes—and the 50th anniversary of NASA. The song, written by Paul McCartney and John Lennon, will be flying at the speed of light. But it will take 431 years to reach its final destination—Polaris is 2.5 quadrillion miles away.

performers, and audiences of the early 19th century could not have imagined the phonograph. Their grandchildren at the beginning of the 20th century, although familiar with recorded sound, could not have imagined the astonishing musical variety made possible by the electronic amplification and digital manipulation of sound. Even as recently as the 1960s, few would have predicted a medium with the potential and international scope of the Internet; the World Wide Web has provided new ways to promote and sell music, allowing individual artists to reach out to potential audiences directly, bypassing many traditional marketing approaches. And so, almost certainly, our children and grandchildren a hundred years from now will be listening to music unimaginable to us today—even as they enjoy the opportunity to explore the "golden oldies" of the early 21st century and thereby learn a little about us and our musical tastes.

Whatever form it takes, music will remain one of humanity's defining characteristics. Indeed the music of Bach, Beethoven, and Chuck Berry, among others, is now on its way out of our solar system, representing humanity to the universe. In August and September 1977, the United States launched two essentially identical spacecraft to explore the outer planets and beyond. On the chance that one or both of these craft might someday fall into the hands of an extraterrestrial civilization, the National Aeronautics and Space Administration (NASA) included in the payload a series of photographs of life on earth, texts, recordings of many sounds from earth (wind, water, animals), greetings in multiple languages, and a variety of musical selections from cultures around the world. These musical selections are as follows:

- J. S. Bach, Brandenburg Concerto no. 2, first movement.
- Java, court gamelan, *Kinds of Flowers*, recorded by Robert Brown.
- Senegal, percussion, recorded by Charles Duvelle.
- Zaire, Pygmy girls' initiation song, recorded by Colin Turnbull.
- Australia, Aborigine songs, *Morning Star* and *Devil Bird*, recorded by Sandra LeBrun Holmes.
- Mexico, *El Cascabel*, performed by Lorenzo Barcelata and the Mariachi México.
- Chuck Berry, *Johnny B. Goode*.
- New Guinea, men's house song, recorded by Robert MacLennan.

- Japan, shakuhachi, *Tsuru No Sugomori* ("Crane's Nest"), performed by Goro Yamaguchi.
- J. S. Bach, Gavotte en rondeaux from the Partita no. 3 in E major for Violin, performed by Arthur Grumiaux.
- W. A. Mozart, *The Magic Flute*, Queen of the Night's aria (no. 14).
- Georgian S.S.R., chorus, *Tchakrulo*, collected by Radio Moscow.
- Peru, panpipes and drum, collected by Casa de la Cultura, Lima.
- *Melancholy Blues*, performed by Louis Armstrong and his Hot Seven.
- Azerbaijan S.S.R., bagpipes, recorded by Radio Moscow.
- Igor Stravinsky, *Rite of Spring*, Sacrificial Dance.
- J. S. Bach, *The Well-Tempered Clavier*, Book 2, Prelude and Fugue in C, no. 1.
- Ludwig van Beethoven, Symphony no. 5, first movement.
- Bulgaria, *Izlel je Delyo Hagdutin*, sung by Valya Balkanska.
- Navajo Indians, *Night Chant*, recorded by Willard Rhodes.
- A. Holborne, instrumental selections from *The Fairie Round*.
- Solomon Islands, panpipes, collected by the Solomon Islands Broadcasting Service.
- Peru, wedding song, recorded by John Cohen.
- China, ch'in, *Flowing Streams*, performed by Kuan P'ing-hu.
- India, raga, *Jaat Kahan Ho*, sung by Surshri Kesar Bai Kerkar.
- *Dark Was the Night*, written and performed by Blind Willie Johnson.
- Ludwig van Beethoven, String Quartet in B, op. 130, Cavatina.

What any extraterrestrial creatures will make of this assortment is anyone's guess. But it will surely make clear to them music's central importance to the human race (see Focus: The Beatles on a Cosmic Trip).

Appendix 1

A Guide to Selected Research Materials in Music History

The literature on music can sometimes seem overwhelmingly vast, but with the help of a few key sources, you can navigate it confidently.

A good place to begin is with Vincent H. Duckles and Ida Reed, *Music Reference and Research Materials: An Annotated Bibliography*, 5th ed. (New York: Schirmer Books, 1997). This resource of resources lists and describes the domain of music reference materials by category, beginning with dictionaries and proceeding through music histories, guides to musicology, bibliographies of music and works about music, journal indexes, catalogs of music libraries, and more. The rest of this appendix provides only a brief overview of what can be found in abundance in *Music Reference and Research Materials*.

DICTIONARIES AND ENCYCLOPEDIAS

The basic English-language encyclopedia of music is *The New Grove Dictionary of Music and Musicians*, 2nd ed. (New York: Grove's Dictionaries, 2000). First published in three volumes in the late 19th century, *Grove* has grown to a substantial 29 volumes and is also available online (www.grovemusic.com). It has entries for musical terms, individual composer biographies, and biographies of other important figures in music history. Every composer biography includes a list of works with essential information—such as date of composition, date of first performance, and date of publication—on all the music a composer wrote.

The most important biographical dictionary is *Baker's Biographical Dictionary of Musicians* (New York: Schirmer Books, 2001). Thoroughly revised by the late Nicolas Slonimsky, the entries in this six-volume work are more concise than the biographical entries in *The New Grove*. Still more concise biographies can be found in a one-volume reference, *The Harvard Biographical Dictionary of Music* (Cambridge, MA: Harvard University Press, 1996).

The standard one-volume reference source for musical terms is *The Harvard Dictionary of Music* (Cambridge, MA: Harvard University Press, 2003).

JOURNALS

Journals (also known as periodicals) are collections of scholarly articles that appear on a regular schedule (such as monthly, three times a year, or yearly). A typical issue contains articles by several authors on a variety of subjects. Just how varied the subject matter is depends on the particular publication. The *Journal of the American Musicological Society*, for example, has a broad scope: a single issue might include an essay on the dissemination of Gregorian chant, another on the cantatas of Bach, and yet another on Wagner's early

operas. A journal like *19th-Century Music*, in contrast, publishes articles only on the music of a single century, and a journal like *Beethoven Forum* focuses even more narrowly on a single composer.

Many journals also include book reviews. The purpose of these reviews is not so much to persuade people to buy (or not to buy) a particular book, but rather to move forward scholarly debate on a particular subject. If the author of a new book makes a particularly startling claim about, say, the circumstances of Mozart's death, a book reviewer has the obligation not only to summarize the argument, but also to evaluate it. In this way, book reviews constitute an important part of an ongoing dialogue among scholars.

Some of the more important journals in the field of music history include the following:

Acta Musicologica	*Music Theory Spectrum*
American Music	*Music & Letters*
Early Music	*Musical Quarterly*
Journal of Music Theory	*19th-Century Music*
Journal of Musicology	*Notes: The Journal of the*
Journal of the American	*Music Library Association*
Musicological Society	*Popular Music*

JOURNAL INDEXES

Several excellent indexes, all of them regularly updated and available in both printed and online editions, provide a guide to the abundant information available in music journals:

- The *Music Index* lists the articles in a wide range of music periodicals published since 1949 categorized by subject and author (www.harmonicparkpress.com/musicindex.htm).

- The *RILM Abstracts of Music Literature* covers books as well as journals published since 1969. (*RILM* is the acronym for *Répertoire International de Littérature Musicale*, or "International Repertory of Musical Literature.") More scholarly and international in scope than *Music Index*, it also includes abstracts—brief summaries—of every book or article it indexes (www.rilm.org).

- The *Arts & Humanities Citation Index (A&HCI)*, which first appeared in 1980, indexes journal articles in a variety of fields, including music. In addition to the standard author and subject indexes, *A&HCI* also indexes every footnote appearing in each of these journal articles. This allows researchers to trace citations to a particularly central source or work. If, for example, you have identified a particular book or article as an important source for a topic you are researching, you can use *A&HCI* to find out what recent journal articles have cited that same source or work. This can often lead you to important new sources that you might not otherwise have found. For online access to *A&HCI*, consult your local library.

DISSERTATIONS

A dissertation is a book-length work written by a graduate student to earn a doctoral degree—in music either a Doctor of Philosophy (Ph.D.) or Doctor of Musical Arts (D.M.A.). Dissertations usually have a narrow focus. The standard guide to dissertations in music is Charles Adkins, *Doctoral Dissertations in Musicology*, available in printed form but more up to date in its online form (www.music.indiana.edu/ddm).

PRINTED LIBRARY CATALOGS

With the advent of computer catalogs, library card catalogs are easy to overlook, but they remain essential for the serious music scholar. A great deal of material in all disciplines issued before the 1970s has not yet found its way into any database. Some very large libraries, such as the New York Public Library and the British Library, have made the contents of their collections accessible through printed library catalogs. The New York Public Library's *Dictionary Catalog of the Music Collection* (Boston: G.K. Hall, 1964–1976) for example, consists of page after page of photographed catalog cards, most of which are still not represented in that institution's computer database. Other major collections have made their card catalogs available in a similar format; see Duckles and Reed's *Music Reference and Research Materials* for a list of the most important of these.

UNION CATALOGS

A union catalog shows the holdings of more than one library. The most important of these specifically for music-related materials is the *Répertoire international des Sources Musicales* ("International Repertoire of Musical Sources"), better known as *RISM*. This essential resource for anyone working with music written before 1800 lists the holdings of music manuscripts, prints, and books to be found in libraries throughout the world. The many volumes within this multifaceted series are indexed in Duckles and Reed's *Music Reference and Research Materials*.

Two catalogs that include music among many other disciplines are these:

■ *OCLC* (Online Computer Library Center), the world's largest online union catalog (www.oclc.org.).

■ *National Union Catalog of Pre-1956 Imprints* (London: Mansell, 1968–1981), a printed catalog of 754 volumes covering materials published prior to 1956. This catalog shows holdings from libraries throughout North America and is particularly useful for older materials that may not appear in any online databases.

THEMATIC CATALOGS

Thematic catalogs are an invaluable resource for research in music. A thematic catalog of the works of a particular composer lists the entire output of that individual and gives details on each work, including an *incipit* (the first few notes of the work or movement in musical notation, enough to identify it unambiguously), the location of the autograph score (if it still exists), first and early editions, and a bibliography of writings about a particular work. The best source for thematic catalogs is the works lists in the composer biographies in *The New Grove*.

STYLE MANUALS

Any standard style manual—such as Kate L. Turabian's *A Manual for Writers of Term Papers, Theses, and Dissertations*, 6th ed. (Chicago: University of Chicago Press, 1996), or the Modern Language Association's *MLA Handbook for Writers of Research Papers*, 6th ed. (New York: Modern Language Association of America, 2003)—can help you prepare a research paper. But music, like any discipline, has a specialized vocabulary and specialized stylistic conventions, and three useful guides address these:

■ Jonathan Bellman, *A Short Guide to Writing about Music* (New York: Longman, 2000).

■ D. Kern Holoman, *Writing about Music: A Style Sheet from the Editors of 19th-Century Music* (Berkeley and Los Angeles: University of California Press, 1988).

■ Richard J. Wingell, *Writing about Music: An Introductory Guide*, 4th ed. (Upper Saddle River, NJ: Prentice Hall, 2009).

Appendix 2

Evaluating Musical Editions

When you study or perform a work of music, which edition should you use? If only one is available, the question is easy to answer. But often, particularly in the case of major composers, we have many editions from which to choose. If you're using the library, you might be tempted to use the first edition you find, but then you'd be relying on luck, because the quality of musical editions varies greatly.

A good edition of music conveys as closely as possible the composer's intentions. Editors sift through a variety of musical sources and other evidence to determine those intentions. In the edition they identify their sources and make clear their reasons for choosing a particular reading in cases where the correct reading is in dispute. Ideally, they also include a **critical report** that establishes the relationship among those sources and the basis for their editorial choices. Critical reports are either appended to the back of a volume or issued as a separate volume.

The original manuscript score of a work in the composer's own hand—known as the **holograph, autograph score,** or simply **autograph**—is usually the most reliable guide to a composer's intentions. The autograph score of many works, however, has not survived. And even when it is available, it is by no means infallible. Composers, after all, make mistakes. Considering how complicated and intricate a four-movement symphony is, for example, it shouldn't be surprising that the composer of one might occasionally write, say, a natural sign where a sharp sign was clearly intended. Editors would not be doing their job simply to perpetuate such mistakes. Composers also take shortcuts, such as marking the phrasing of a frequently repeated figure only the first two or three times it occurs. Editors then must decide whether or not to apply that same phrasing to all subsequent occurrences. Composers also change their minds. The autograph score and the first edition of Mozart's six string quartets dedicated to Haydn are significantly different. Mozart was almost certainly involved with the production of this first edition, and in the process of seeing it into print, he appears to have had second thoughts about certain details of tempo, articulation, and other matters. Mozart's participation in the publication process makes the first edition an authoritative source, in this case one that is arguably more important than the autograph.

Yet even an authoritative first edition is not necessarily the last word. Hector Berlioz, for instance, tinkered with matters of orchestration repeatedly after hearing his works in performance, even after a work had been published, and he wrote about these changes in some of his letters. Anton Bruckner, in turn, undertook massive revisions of many of his symphonies. Which version represents a composer's final thoughts on any given passage? Conscientious editors have to identify and evaluate carefully all relevant sources of a particular work—autograph, early copies, first editions, later editions, comments in the composer's correspondence—to make a critical edition of that work. What is critical about these editions is the editor's attitude toward all the sources. Editors do not merely accept, uncritically, whatever sources happen to be the earliest or most widely disseminated, but rather subject each source to careful scrutiny.

For an example of what can result from uncritical editing, consider the case of the six string quartets by Joseph Haydn now known as Opus 33. The autograph score of these quartets no longer exists. Haydn probably gave it to his Viennese publisher, Artaria, who used it to engrave the first edition in 1782. This edition consisted of a set of parts; no full score of the work was issued until the early 19th century. The publisher then probably either threw the manuscript away or reused it for packaging. (Composer's autographs were not perceived as valuable until a decade or so later, and even then publishers continued to be astonishingly cavalier with them.) Artaria's first edition, then, is the most reliable source we have for Opus 33. We know through Haydn's correspondence that he worked with Artaria in producing this edition, and for this reason we can call it an authoritative source. Surviving copies of this edition, however, are exceedingly rare, probably because few were printed and because people would have used them mostly at home the way we use sheet music today.

Another edition, published a few years later by Hummel of Amsterdam, in contrast, seems to have been widely available. This edition was the first to designate the quartets as Opus 33. It is, however, thoroughly unreliable, beginning with the opus number, which is different from the one that appears on Artaria's authoritative edition. Haydn had nothing to do with the Hummel edition; he received no payment for it and would certainly have been outraged to have his work pirated. Although it was considered unethical in Haydn's time for a publisher to print a living composer's music without any payment, the practice was nonetheless common until the emergence of effective copyright laws in the late 19th century.

What, then, was the source for Hummel's edition? We cannot know for sure, but it was clearly corrupt, both ethically and textually. One possible scenario is that these corruptions originated with one of Haydn's copyists, who in an attempt to earn some extra money made an unauthorized additional copy, which he then sold to any unscrupulous publisher, like Hummel, who was willing to pay the right price. Haydn was aware of this practice and complained about it on more than one occasion, but he could do little to stop it. Because these unauthorized copies had to be made quickly and surreptitiously, they were likely to contain errors. Another possible scenario is that the corruption came from Hummel himself or someone working for him. Troubled by the strange opening in the first movement of op. 33, no. 1 (Example A2–1), Hummel may have "corrected" it by filling in what he thought were missing harmonies (Example A2–2). The result is musically disastrous.

Unfortunately, bad editions have a way of perpetuating themselves. The least expensive and most widely available edition of the Opus 33 quartets today is a reprint, an exact photographic reproduction, of an edition of these works published in the late 19th century, prepared by a German scholar named Wilhelm Altmann.

This is an uncritical edition: Altmann provides no indication of his sources. It is, however, clearly based on Hummel's unreliable early-19th-century edition. And because it is considerably less expensive, musicians are more likely to buy Altmann's edition than a critical edition of the quartets published as part of Haydn's complete works by the Haydn-Institut in Cologne, Germany. Thus Hummel's corrupt edition remains with us even today.

A note of caution: Many editions of music proclaim themselves as "Urtext" editions. *Urtext* is a German word that means "original text." Some of these self-proclaimed Urtext editions are in fact very carefully prepared critical editions, but others are not. The word itself has been used so indiscriminately that it is difficult to know when it really means something and when it is being used as a label to sell an item. Be critical in choosing an edition.

Example A2–1 The opening of the first movement of Haydn's String Quartet op. 33, no. 1, as it appears in Artaria's authoritative first edition

Example A2–2 The opening of the first movement of Haydn's String Quartet op. 33, no. 1, as it appears in Hummel's edition

Appendix 3

Writing about Music

"Don't write about the music," the jazz musician Miles Davis once advised. "The music speaks for itself."[1] Anyone who has ever tried to describe a piece of music in words knows exactly what Davis meant. Yet writing about music—the most abstract and elusive of all the arts—can help us better appreciate its subtlety and magic. Our words will never replace the music, but they can help us understand it.

Writing about the emotional power of music poses particular challenges. It is not easy to put into words the passion we feel when we hear a work of music that moves us, and no two listeners respond identically to the same performance. Gushing accounts are rarely helpful. To write that a specific passage is "powerful and awesome" does not, by itself, tell us anything; we need some justification for such a statement, some explanation of what it is that makes the passage remarkable.

To avoid such difficulties, some writers avoid the subjective and emotional aspects of music and restrict themselves to objective issues like harmony and form. But if writing that focuses on the emotional aspects of music can be overblown, writing that focuses solely on its technical aspects can be dry and tedious. The playwright George Bernard Shaw (1856–1950), who supported himself as a music critic early in his career, skewered this sort of analysis in the following passage, which begins with a hypothetical description of Mozart's Symphony in G minor, K. 550:

> Here is the sort of thing: "The principal subject, hitherto only heard in the treble, is transferred to the bass (Ex. 28), the violins playing a new counterpoint to it instead of the original mere accompaniment figure of the first part. Then the parts are reversed, the violins taking the subject and the basses the counterpoint figure, and so on till we come to a close on the dominant of D minor, a nearly related key (commencement of Ex. 29), and then comes the passage by which we return to the first subject in its original form and key."

How succulent this is; and how full of Mesopotamian words like "the dominant of D minor"! I will now, ladies and gentlemen, give you my celebrated "analysis" of Hamlet's soliloquy on suicide ["To be or not to be . . ."] in the same scientific style. "Shakespeare, dispensing with the customary exordium, announces his subject at once in the infinitive, in which mood it is presently repeated after a short connecting passage in which, brief as it is, we recognize the alternative and negative forms on which so much of the significance of repetition depends. Here we reach a colon; and a point pository phrase, in which the accent falls decisively on the relative pronoun, brings us to the first full stop."

I break off here, because, to confess the truth, my grammar is giving out. But I want to know whether it is just that a literary critic should be forbidden to make his living in this way on pain of being interviewed by two doctors and a magistrate, and hauled off to Bedlam [an infamous mental institution in London] forthwith; whilst the more a musical critic does it, the deeper the veneration he inspires.[2]

The technical and emotional elements of music go hand in hand: no work of music is completely devoid of emotion, and every work of music is built on technical foundations of some kind (even John Cage's *4'33"*). Composers fuse the technical and emotional in their work; a writer's job is to analyze and describe how these two elements function in tandem.

1. Gary Carner, ed., *The Miles Davis Companion: Four Decades of Commentary* (New York: Schirmer, 1996), p. 85.
2. George Bernard Shaw, *Music in London*, 3 vols. (London: Constable, 1932), II, 321. Originally published May 31, 1893.

Appendix 4

The Concepts of "Popular" and "Art" Music

Consciously or unconsciously, we often distinguish between music written for a serious purpose ("art" or "classical" music) and music whose function is primarily to entertain and that appeals to a broader public ("popular" music). Such distinctions have a long heritage in Western thought. Aristotle noted that certain rhythms "are noticeably vulgar in their emotional effects while others better suit freeborn persons" (see Prologue: Antiquity). And Johannes de Grocheo, writing around 1300, recommended that the motet "not be performed in the presence of common people, for they would not perceive its subtlety, nor take pleasure in its sound." He urged that motets be performed only "in the presence of learned persons and those who seek after subtleties in art" (see Chapter 2). The categories of art and popular music remain very much with us today and are fundamental to the way in which music is marketed.

Yet the distinction between popular and art music is conceptually fuzzy and impossible to define in any consistent way. To begin with, the two categories are not mutually exclusive. Just because a work of music is popular does not mean it cannot be a work of art, and just because it is a work of art does not mean it cannot be popular.

However art music is defined—as music that has survived the test of time, for example, or music with some serious purpose, or music written for an elite audience—we have no clear way to distinguish it stylistically from popular music. Works can easily shift from one category to the other over time. Take, for example, *The Beggar's Opera* (Anthology) by Pepusch and Gay in the 1730s. It was written, adapted, and readapted in many different guises over the course of the 18th century and composed in a style as different as possible from the prevailing serious opera of the upper classes. Yet it is now included in every discussion of opera from the period (as it is in Chapter 9 of this book). The same holds true for Mozart's *Magic Flute*, which premiered in 1791 in a theater that catered to a decidedly middle-brow if not low-brow public but is now performed routinely in every major opera house in the world. In the 20th century, Kurt Weill and Berthold Brecht adapted Gay's *The Beggar's Opera* into *Die Dreigroschenoper* ("Threepenny Opera"), a biting social satire. One number in particular from this work, *Mack the Knife*, became quite popular. Louis Armstrong and Frank Sinatra, for example, both recorded very different arrangements of it. Similarly the Doors, a rock group, included on one of their albums a rendition of the *Alabama Song* (Anthology) from another Weill/Brecht production, *The Rise and Fall of the City of Mahagonny*. And the Beatles, who were consistently marketed as popular musicians, produced music of enormous stylistic variety, ranging from the rock-and-roll *I Wanna Hold Your Hand* to *Revolution No. 9*, a montage of electronically manipulated sound clips that reflected trends in the world of avant-garde electronic music at the time.

Recognizing the inadequacy of the terms *art* and *popular*, some commentators have attempted to distinguish instead between "cultivated" and "vernacular" styles, but this distinction also breaks down on close inspection. Rock music, an ostensibly vernacular genre, is today produced and recorded with the most sophisticated audio equipment available; bands rehearse endlessly, and individual performers practice with as much intensity as any other kind of musician. Although vernacular music may convey an impression of spontaneity, it is often as carefully thought out—as cultivated—as any music in the ostensibly cultivated category.

But if no consistent difference exists stylistically between art and popular music, or cultivated and vernacular music, there is a difference in the attitudes composers, performers, and audiences bring to bear on music they assign (consciously or unconsciously) to one category or the other. Popular music is usually associated with a relatively relaxed approach toward the work at hand. Compare any two performances of almost any popular song and you will quickly realize they can differ enormously. Performers routinely change words, harmonies, instrumentation, even melody and form. Listeners, in turn, not only accept but welcome such changes. Ella Fitzgerald's rendition of Cole Porter's *Night and Day* differs markedly from Frank Sinatra's, and both take liberties with Porter's original. Sinatra, for example, begins one of his many recordings of the work with the chorus, ignoring the opening verse entirely. But even Porter, as a composer, expected performers to make such alterations.

Yet even here, differences in attitude cannot be assigned exclusively to one kind of music or another. Probably no one would think of 18th-century opera seria as popular music (see Chapter 9), yet composers, performers, and audiences all expected singers in this repertory to embellish da capo arias.

On the whole, however, such practices and attitudes are far less common within the repertory we tend to think of as art music or classical music, particularly in works written after the early 19th century. As we saw in Chapter 14, the respect and deference toward the composer's intentions that now characterize our attitude toward art music dates to roughly 1800, that is, to the generation of Beethoven. Mozart, a few decades earlier, had readily agreed to rewrite the music of several roles in *Don Giovanni*. He had originally composed the work for a specific cast of singers in Prague but willingly made significant changes to accommodate the strengths of the different cast that performed it in Vienna. Over the course of the 19th century, this kind of alteration became increasingly rare. Opera houses began to accommodate the composer, not the other way around.

From the 19th century onward, tradition has taught performers to approach certain repertories with a sense of veneration. Musicians go to great lengths to ascertain and execute the composer's intentions as accurately as possible, using the best edition available (see Appendix 2). Within this tradition, performers rarely change words, harmonies, form, or instrumentation. When Leonard Bernstein substituted a single word in the finale of

Beethoven's Ninth Symphony at the Berlin Wall in 1989—changing *Freude* (joy) to *Freiheit* (freedom)—critics debated the alteration at great length. Some considered it appropriate to the circumstances; others found it sacrilegious, a defilement of Beethoven's original score. What is significant is that this alteration of a single word aroused so much attention.

Works that have at various times been considered both classical and popular can also tell us something about the essence of this distinction. Performers have long felt at liberty to make fundamental changes to Gilbert and Sullivan's *Pirates of Penzance* (Anthology I/140), altering words, music, and orchestration to suit their immediate times, needs, and resources. One recent American production, for example, substituted "Coast Guard" for the original "Customs House" in order to make a particular passage more comprehensible to its audience. Joseph Papp's Broadway production of 1980 used electric guitars and synthesizers in addition to a standard orchestra. Unlike Bernstein's alteration of Beethoven's Ninth, however, these and other changes, because they are consistent with a long tradition of performance practice, elicited virtually no comment. In contrast, scholars are now preparing a critical edition of the work in an attempt to reconstruct the original version from autograph sources and the earliest editions.

Music of all kinds can be fruitfully studied and performed from both an art and popular point of view. Neither is superior to the other. Both are legitimate, and both represent valid ways of making—and listening to—music.

The Ordinary of the Mass

The ritual of the Mass,[1] as celebrated in the Catholic church since the medieval era, consists of certain unvarying elements—the Ordinary—and certain elements used in connection with specific seasons, weeks, or days—the Propers. The Ordinary, in other words, is that portion of the Mass that remains constant, whereas the Propers change throughout the year. Until the mid-1960s, all the elements of the Mass, both Ordinary and Propers, were always said (or sung) in Latin; most Catholic churches now use the vernacular, that is, the everyday language of the country in which the Mass is being celebrated. (Protestant sects, many of which retained the Mass in whole or in part, switched to the vernacular early on, during the Reformation in the 16th century.)

A Mass can be performed with no singing at all, but the five parts of the Ordinary that are typically set to music and have posed a challenge to generations of composers are these:

- The Kyrie, a supplication for mercy ("Lord have mercy upon us"). Its text is actually in ancient Greek, not Latin.

- The Gloria, a hymn of praise to the Holy Trinity (God the Father, God the Son, God the Holy Spirit).

- The Credo (creed), a statement of faith, detailing the essential elements of church doctrine.

- The Sanctus, a hymn of consecration at the moment when the Communion wine and bread are blessed.

- The Agnus Dei, a prayer for peace.

Kyrie

Kyrie eleison.	Lord, have mercy.
Christe eleison.	Christ, have mercy.
Kyrie eleison.	Lord, have mercy.

Gloria

Gloria in excelsis Deo.	Glory to God in the highest.
Et in terra pax hominibus bonae voluntatis	And on earth peace to people of good will.
Laudamus te.	We praise You.
Benedicimus te.	We bless You.
Adoramus te.	We worship You.
Glorificamus te.	We glorify You.
Gratiam agimus tibi propter magnam gloriam tuam	We give thanks to You for thy great glory,
Domine Deus, Rex coelestis.	Lord God, heavenly King.
Deus Pater omnipotens.	God the father almighty.

Domine Fili unigenite, Jesu Christe.	O Lord, the only begotten Son, Jesus Christ.
Domine Deus, Agnus Dei, Filius Patris	Lord God, Lamb of God, Son of the Father
Qui tollis peccata mundi,	Who takest away the sins of the world
miserere nobis	have mercy upon us.
Qui tollis peccata mundi,	Who takest away the sins of the world
suscipe deprecationem nostram.	Receive our prayer.
Qui sedes ad dexteram Patris	Who sittest at the right hand of the Father
miserere nobis.	have mercy upon us.
Quoniam tu solus sanctus.	For thou only art holy.
Tu solus Dominus.	Thou only art the Lord.
Tu solus altissimus, Jesu Christe.	Thou only art most high, O Jesus Christ.
Cum Sancto Spiritu, in gloria Dei Patris. Amen.	With the Holy Spirit, in the glory of God the Father. Amen.

Credo

Credo in unum Deum,	I believe in one God,
Patrem omnipotentem,	the Father almighty,
factorem caeli et terre,	maker of heaven and earth,
visibilium omnium, et invisibilium.	and of all things visible and invisible.
Et in unum Dominum Jesum Christum,	And in one Lord Jesus Christ,
Filium Dei unigenitum:	the only begotten Son of God,
et ex Patre natum ante omnia saecula;	born of the Father before all ages;
Deum de Deo, lumen de lumine,	God of God, light of light,
Deum verum de Deo vero;	true God of true God;
genitum, non factum,	begotten not made;
consubstantialem Patri;	being of one substance with the Father;
per quem omnia facta sunt.	by whom all things were made.
Qui propter nos homines,	Who for us men,
et propter nostram salutem,	and for our salvation,
descendit de caelis.	came down from heaven;
Et incarnatus est de Spiritu Sancto ex Maria Virgine;	and was incarnate by the Holy Spirit, of the Virgin Mary;
et homo factus est.	and was made man.
Crucifixus etiam pro nobis,	He was crucified also for us,
sub Pontio Pilato passus,	suffered under Pontius Pilate,
et sepultus est.	and was buried.
Et resurrexit tertia die,	And the third day he rose again
secundum Scripturas.	according to the Scriptures;

---

1. Ordinary of the Mass (Kyrie, Gloria, Credo, Sanctus, Agnus Dei) English translation, from *New Harvard Dictionary of Music*, ed. Don Michael Randel (Cambridge, MA: Belknap Press of Harvard University Press, 1986). Entry for "Mass."

Et ascendit in caelum,
sedet ad dexteram Patris.

Et iterum venturus est
cum gloria judicare
vivos et mortuos:
cujus regni non erit finis.

Et in Spiritum
Sanctum Dominum
et vivificantem,
qui ex Patre Filioque procedit.

Qui cum Patre et Filio

simul adoratur et
conglorificatur;
qui locutus est per Prophetas.
Et unam, sanctam,
catholicam et
apostolicam Ecclesiam.
Confiteor unum baptisma
in remissionem peccatorum.
Et exspecto
resurrectionem mortuorum,
et vitam venturi saeculi. Amen.

and ascended into heaven.
He sitteth at the right hand of
the Father;
and he shall come again
with glory to judge the
living and the dead;
and his kingdom shall have
no end.
And [I believe] in the
Holy Ghost,
the Lord and giver of life,
who proceeds from the Father
and the Son,
who together with the Father
and the Son
is adored and
glorified;
who spoke by the Prophets.
And [I believe in] one
holy catholic and
apostolic Church.
I confess one baptism
for the remission of sins.
And I await the
resurrection of the dead,
and the life of the world to
come. Amen.

Sanctus

Sanctus, sanctus, sanctus
Dominus Deus Sabaoth.
Pleni sunt caeli et
terra gloria tua:
Hosanna in excelsis.
Benedictus qui venit
in nomine Domini:
Hosanna in excelsis.

Holy, holy, holy,
Lord God of hosts.
Heaven and earth are
full of thy glory.
Hosanna in the highest.
Blessed is he that cometh
in the name of the Lord.
Hosanna in the highest.

Agnus Dei

Agnus Dei,
qui tollis peccata mundi,

miserere nobis.
Agnus Dei,
qui tollis peccata mundi,

miserere nobis.
Agnus Dei,
qui tollis peccata mundi,

dona nobis pacem.

Lamb of God,
who takest away the sins
of the world,
have mercy on us.
Lamb of God,
who takest away the sins
of the world,
have mercy on us.
Lamb of God,
who takest away the sins
of the world,
Grant us peace.

Glossary

Absolute music Instrumental music without a program or any other indication of a possible extramusical content.

Accompanied recitative Type of recitative accompanied by the orchestra.

Affect Predominant emotion of a text or musical work.

Air de cour Literally, "courtly air"; genre of secular song in late-16th-century and early-17th-century France that could be either polyphonic or homophonic (voice and lute).

Alberti bass Type of accompanimental figure used in much music of the Classical era and featuring frequent repetitions of a broken triad. The device is named after Domenico Alberti (1710–ca. 1740), an otherwise obscure Italian composer who favored its use.

Aleatory music From the Latin *alea* ("die," the singular of "dice"), music of chance, leaving one or more elements of performance to randomly determined or indeterminate circumstances such as a roll of the dice, sounds that happen to be present at given moment, or actions determined at the whim of the performer.

Ambient music Background music, the sonic equivalent of architecture, whose primary purpose is to shape actions and attitudes rather than to be the focus of the listener's attention.

Ambitus Range of a given melody or mode.

Antecedent and consequent Terms borrowed from grammar to describe the relationship of units within a phrase of music. The **antecedent** phrase comes first (*ante* = "before") and in its most basic form moves from tonic to dominant. The **consequent** phrase follows, and in its most basic form moves from dominant to tonic. See also **periodic phrase structure.**

Anthem Designation given to many motet-like works on English texts from the 16th century onward. The full anthem is for chorus throughout. The verse anthem alternates choral passages with passages for solo voice and instrumental accompaniment.

Antiphon Type of plainchant sung before (and sometimes after) the recitation of a psalm or other type of chant.

Antiphonal Type of performance featuring repeated alternation between two voices or groups of voices.

Antiphoner (*Antiphonale*) The liturgical book containing the texts (and, if notated, the chants) of the Mass Propers.

Arch form Symmetrical structure within which a unit of music progresses toward a midpoint and then more or less retraces its steps.

Arietta A song or aria of relatively small dimension.

Ars nova Literally, *The New Art*; the title of an early-14th-century theoretical treatise attributed to Philippe de Vitry and used, by extension, to describe French music of the period as well.

Atonality Melodic and harmonic idiom first cultivated in the early decades of the 20th century, characterized by the absence of a tonal center.

Augmentation Process by which the rhythmic value of a line is systematically increased.

Authentic mode Any of the melodic modes with an ambitus running an octave above the final note.

Autograph or **Autograph score** Score written in the composer's own hand; also known as a holograph.

Avant-garde From the French term for military vanguard, an elite group of artists considered far in advance of all others, leading the way to the future. The term, widely used in all the arts of the 20th century, is particularly associated with the phenomenon of modernism.

Ballade (1) One of the *formes fixes* in the music of the 14th and 15th centuries. The texts usually consist of three strophes of seven or eight lines, the last of which is a refrain. The rhyme scheme varies, but typical patterns include ababccdD, ababbcbC, ababcdE, and ababcdeF (the uppercase letter indicates the refrain, which remains constant from strophe to strophe). (2) Narrative poem, often set to music in the 19th century. (3) Instrumental work that reflects the narrative character of its poetic counterpart.

Ballad opera Type of opera popular in England during the 18th century, featuring contemporary songs (including, but not limited to ballads) mixed with dialogue.

Ballata (plural, **ballate**) Italian poetic and musical form of the 14th and early 15th centuries, formally similar to the French virelai of the same period. The form of the ballata is AbbaA, with a refrain (A) framing the internal lines of each strophe and returning unchanged in each strophe, both musically and textually.

Bar form Form associated with the repertory of the medieval minnesinger, consisting of two *Stollen* followed by an *Abgesang* (AAB).

Basse danse Type of dance popular in the 15th and early 16th centuries. The notated sources preserve only a series of long notes, around which other instruments were expected to improvise their own contrapuntal lines.

Basso continuo Literally, the "continuous bass"; the bass line of any work from the 17th or 18th century that incorporates not only the bass line itself but also the harmonies to be realized above that line. The term is also used to describe the performers playing this part: at a bare minimum, this would consist of a chordal instrument (such as organ or lute), ideally supported by one or more instruments capable of sustaining a bass line (such as viol or bassoon).

Basso ostinato Literally, "obstinate bass"; bass pattern repeated many times within the course of a movement or work.

Bebop In jazz, a style featuring fast tempos, irregular chordal progressions, complex harmonies, and asymmetrical, often jagged melodies.

Bel canto Italian for "beautiful singing," a term used to describe a style of Italian opera in the first half of the 19th century that emphasized lyrical melodic lines, legato phrasing, and a seemingly effortless vocal technique, even in passages of great technical difficulty. The emphasis throughout is on the voice: orchestral accompaniment in 19th-century bel canto opera is typically discreet, limited to harmonic underpinning with little or no counterpoint.

Binary form Any musical form that consists of two parts.

Bluegrass Style of country music that emerged in the 1940s, typically performed by an ensemble of banjo, acoustic guitar, fiddle, and double bass. The banjo is picked (as opposed to strummed), and vocals tend to be pitched in the upper end of the singer's register; the characteristic syncopation of the style anticipates the downbeat slightly, in contrast to jazz, in which performers often play just slightly behind the beat.

Blue note In blues and jazz, the slightly lowered third or seventh degree in the major scale; in natural minor, the slightly lowered third or seventh degree; in any scale, the slightly lowered diminished fifth (resolving to a fourth).

Blues Style of song that originated in the American South among African Americans who were slaves and the descendants of slaves. The standard **12-bar blues form** rests on a repeated harmonic pattern of 12 measures in 4/4 time, which in turn is divided into three groups of 4 measures each.

Boogie-woogie   Jazz piano style drawn from blues and ragtime, featuring syncopated "walking" or other ostinato bass lines in the left hand while the right hand plays melodic chords or improvisational passages.

Bourrée   Lively dance in duple meter with a prominent upbeat at the beginning of each section.

Branle   "Line dance," sometimes in duple meter (*branle simple*), sometimes in triple (*branle gay*).

Breve   In Franconian notation, the note value that subdivides the long.

Bridge   In popular song of the 20th century, the contrasting B section that connects statements of the A theme.

Cabaletta   Fast closing section of an aria.

Caccia (plural, **cacce**)   Poetic and musical form cultivated in 14th- and early-15th-century Italy, sometimes monophonic but more frequently for three voices, often with two canonic upper voices. The texts typically deal with hunting.

Cadence   Point of musical closure indicated by pitch, harmony, rhythm, or any combination of these elements.

Cadenza   Solo passage in a concerto movement or in an aria, usually toward the end, in which the soloist displays his or her virtuosic talents by embellishing themes heard earlier in the movement or aria; the orchestra remains silent throughout.

Caecilian movement   Tendency among certain 19th-century composers to restore Gregorian chant and the style of 16th-century a cappella polyphony as the ideals of church music.

Call and response   Musical texture in which a soloist (leader, minister) sings or cues ("lines out") a phrase to be answered by the choir (ensemble, congregation).

Canon   (1) Polyphonic work written in such a way that the imitating voice or voices follow the line of the original either exactly (a strict canon) or with small modifications (a free canon). (2) Rule or direction given at the beginning of such a composition to indicate the manner in which it is to be realized (e.g., the points at which the successive voices are to enter).

Cantata   In its broadest sense, a work to be sung (the Italian word *cantare* means "to sing"). More specifically, the term is used to denote a vocal work, usually sacred, for performance forces of varying size, from soloist and basso continuo to soloists, chorus, and orchestra.

Cantilena motet   Type of 15th-century motet that features a florid, lyrical top voice over slower moving lower voices.

Cantus firmus (plural, **cantus firmi**)   "Fixed melody" that serves as the basis of a composition. A cantus firmus can be newly composed for a work but is most often derived from an existing composition.

Canzona   Instrumental work of the late Renaissance or Baroque originally based on a vocal model, such as the chanson, but later often composed independently of any vocal model.

Castrato   Castrated male singer whose voice has never broken and who therefore sings in the soprano or alto range. Castrati were common in opere serie of the 17th and 18th centuries.

Cauda   The long melisma at the end of a conductus.

Cavatina   In Italian opera of the 19th century, the introductory aria sung by a main character. In German opera of the same period, a type of aria characterized by an introspective quality, free of virtuosic display.

Chaconne   Type of bass pattern used throughout the Baroque.

Character piece   Brief work for solo piano that seeks to portray the mood or "character" of a particular person, idea, situation, or emotion. These are sometimes specified, sometimes not. The character piece, which first appeared in the early 19th century, tends to be brief, sectional, and fairly simple in construction.

Chorale   A hymn, either in its harmonized form or as a melody alone. Chorales are associated particularly with the congregational music of the Protestant Reformation.

Chorus   In popular song of the 20th century, the principal tune or section.

Clausula (plural, **clausulae**)   Passages of measured organum that could be substituted at will into the appropriate textual section of a larger existing work of organum.

Coda   From the Italian word for "tail," a closing section of a work or movement.

Color   Melodic pattern of an isorhythmic tenor.

Combinatorial   Quality of certain 12-tone rows in which the hexachord of a row—its first six or last six notes—can be combined with one of the hexachords of an inverted, retrograde, or retrograde inverted form of the same row without producing any duplication of pitches.

Computer music   Music generated, transformed, composed, and/or performed by a computer.

Concertato madrigal   Type of madrigal that emerged in the early 17th century, using instruments (basso continuo with or without additional instruments) independently of the vocal part or parts.

Concertino   Small group of soloists within a concerto grosso, often consisting of two violins and basso continuo.

Concerto   Term used in the 17th century to indicate broadly any work consisting of multiple forces, such as voices and instruments. From the 18th century onward, the term was reserved primarily for works featuring a soloist or soloists contrasted against a larger ensemble.

Concerto grosso   Type of Baroque concerto typically featuring soloists (the concertino) and a larger ensemble (the ripieno). The term also encompasses the ripieno concerto, a work for large ensemble with no soloists.

Concert overture   Single-movement work for orchestra associated with a programmatic idea of some kind. The genre grew out of the 18th-century tradition of performing opera overtures in the concert hall; the concert overture is, in effect, an overture without an opera.

Concitato   See *genere concitato*.

Conductus (plural, **conductus or conducti**)   Genre of vocal monophony or polyphony cultivated in the 12th and 13th centuries. Conductus of one, two, three, or occasionally four voices were not based on borrowed musical material of any kind; their texts consist of freely composed poetry written in metered verse that lend themselves to syllabic and strongly metrical musical settings. In the polyphonic conductus, all voices move in roughly the same rhythm.

Conjunct motion   Melodic motion exclusively or predominantly by half or whole steps.

Consequent   See **Antecedent and consequent**.

Consort   Small ensemble of matched instruments with ranges from soprano to bass, in emulation of vocal groups.

Contenance angloise   Literally, "the English guise"; term used by the French poet Martin le Franc in 1442 to describe the music of Dunstable, Binchois, and Du Fay. This "new way of composing with lively consonances" probably refers to the triadic sonorities and panconsonance of their music.

Contratenor   Literally "against the tenor"; name first given in the 14th century to a voice line moving in the same range as the tenor.

Copyright   According to legal registration, the sole or shared ownership of any work of music or other art, often but not necessarily including the creator.

Countersubject   Contrapuntal theme played against the subject of a fugue.

Couplet In a rondo, a contrasting theme (B, C, D, etc.) within the pattern ABACADA. Also called an **episode.**

Critical edition Edition prepared by an editor who critically evaluates the relative merits of all sources for a work, such as the composer's autograph score, authorized copies, first and early editions, and later revisions by the composer. A critical edition is usually issued with a critical report.

Critical report Editor's report on all significant discrepancies between the critical edition and the various sources (autograph score, first edition, etc.) used to create that edition.

Crossover A term used from the mid-twentieth century onward to describe a musical style transferred to genre or medium in which it is not normally used; often used to indicate the use of an "art" style in "popular" music or vice versa.

Cross-relation Simultaneous or nearly simultaneous sounding of two pitches a half step apart.

Cyclical coherence Manner in which the various movements of a multi-movement cycle (sonata, quartet, symphony, etc.) are related to one another, through thematic ideas, distinctive textures, or other musical elements.

Cyclic Mass Cycle of all movements of the Mass Ordinary integrated by a common cantus firmus or other musical device.

Da capo aria Type of aria consisting of three sections: an opening A section, a contrasting B section, and a return of the A section. In performance, singers were expected to embellish and elaborate the notated music, particularly in the return of A.

Development In sonata form, the section following the exposition and preceding the recapitulation, so called because it develops the ideas originally presented in the exposition. The typical development manipulates themes, moves through a variety of keys, and avoids the tonic.

Diastematic neumes Neumes that indicate the relative relationship of notes (higher, lower, same) according to their vertical placement on the page. In early plainchant notation, diastematic neumes (also known as heightened neumes) were written without staff lines of any kind.

Discant organum See **measured organum.**

Dissonant counterpoint Species counterpoint emphasizing dissonant harmony and voice leading rather than consonance.

Divine Office (or **Office**) Series of eight services held daily in monastic communities from dawn through the middle of the night, consisting musically of the chanting of psalms and hymns.

Doctrine of ethos In ancient Greece, the belief that music had the power to elevate or debase the soul, to enlighten or degrade the mind, and to arouse in listeners certain kinds of emotions and behaviors.

Dodecaphony From the Greek *dodeca,* meaning "12." A method of serial composition based on a series or row of 12 pitches drawn from the chromatic octave (C, C♯, D, D♯, etc., up through B).

Double-exposition concerto form Type of sonata form found in many concertos of the late 18th and 19th centuries, in which the opening tutti exposition remains in the tonic and the subsequent solo exposition modulates from the tonic to a secondary key area.

Double leading-tone cadence Type of cadence favored in the 14th and early 15th centuries that featured two leading tones a fourth or a fifth apart resolving upward by half step.

Duplum From the Latin word for "second," the added second voice in organum and polyphony of the 12th and 13th centuries.

Empfindsamkeit The German word for "sensibility," used by some music historians to identify an aesthetic attitude prevalent in the mid-18th century and reflected in much music of that time as well. The style of *Empfindsamkeit* is associated with music that focuses on detail and avoids thick textures and grandiose gestures.

Episode (1) Nonimitative section within a fugue. (2) In a rondo, an extended passage that appears between entrances of the main theme (the refrain); also known as a **couplet.**

Equal temperament System of tuning that came into widespread use over the course of the 18th century, based on a division of the octave into 12 absolutely equal semitones.

Etude A work for solo instrument, originally designed to improve or expand technique in private; by the 19th century, a piece of great difficulty to be played for public approval.

Exit convention Convention of opera seria in which the singer who has just finished an aria leaves the stage.

Exposition (1) In a fugue, the opening section that introduces the subject in all voices. (2) In a sonata-form movement, the opening section that presents the principal themes of the movement over the course of a harmonic plan that typically moves from tonic to dominant or (in minor-mode works) from tonic to relative major.

Expressionism Broad artistic movement of the early 20th century that sought to give voice to the unconscious, to make manifest humanity's deepest and often darkest emotions. In Freudian terms, expressionist art bypasses the ego and aims straight for the id, the unconscious repository of primal urges.

Faburden Style of three-voice writing found in some English music of the 15th and 16th centuries, featuring one notated and two implied lines. The uppermost voice moves parallel to the notated voice at the interval of a fourth above; the lowermost voice moves in thirds and fifths below the notated line.

Fantasia Type of work that follows no structures of large-scale convention but follows instead (or at least gives the impression of following) the composer's free flight of fantasy.

Fauxbourdon Style of three-voice writing popular in the 15th century in which two voices are notated and a third, implied voice (the fauxbourdon) runs parallel to the uppermost notated line at the interval of a fourth below.

Figured bass Notational convention of the basso continuo in the 17th and 18th centuries using numbers ("figures") to indicate the desired intervals—and thus the harmonies—to be played above a given bass line.

Finalis Characteristic final note of a given mode.

Florentine Camerata Group of artists and noblemen who met in Florence between roughly 1573 and 1587 to discuss, among other things, the possible means of recreating the music of ancient Greece.

Folia Type of bass pattern used throughout the Baroque.

Formes fixes Literally, "fixed forms"; the poetic and musical structural patterns in French music of the 14th and 15th centuries. The most important of the *formes fixes* were the ballade, virelai, and rondeau.

Franconian notation Earliest system of mensural notation, used in the second half of the 13th century and ascribed to Franco of Cologne. Franconian notation assigned specific durational values for the first time to specific note forms.

Free jazz Subgenre of jazz that emerged in the early 1960s, characterized by extreme improvisation, often without a central theme, fixed meters, chord progressions, or even tonality itself.

Free organum See **unmeasured organum.**

French overture Type of overture that begins with a slow introduction featuring dotted rhythms and moves to a fast imitative section. Commonly used in French operas and opere serie of the 17th and 18th centuries.

Frottola (plural, **frottole**)   Secular Italian vocal genre of the late 15th and early 16th centuries. The texture tends to be chordal and the texts are often lighthearted, comic, or ironic.

Fugato   Passage within a work or movement that begins like a fugue but does not sustain itself after a series of initial entries.

Fugue   Type of composition that incorporates a series of imitative entries, usually on a single theme but capable of accommodating multiple themes as well.

Fusion   A type of jazz that borrows the textures, rhythms, and sonorities of rock and soul music, using instruments such as electric guitars and electric piano.

Galant   Term used by some historians to describe the musical style of the mid-18th century, emphasizing the music's lightness and grace.

Galliarde   Type of dance, similar to the saltarello but even more vigorous, with larger leaps by the dancers.

Gamut   In medieval theory, the entire range of available pitches, conceived of as a series of seven interlocking hexachords beginning on C, F, or G (see Example 1–4).

Genere concitato   Literally, the "agitated" or "warlike" manner; a style of writing, developed by Monteverdi, for evoking a mood of agitation or anger, often through the use of rapid repeated notes and fanfarelike figures.

Gesamtkunstwerk   German for "integrated art work"; Richard Wagner's ideal of the highest form of art, synthesizing music, drama, and gesture.

Gospel music   Hymns and other songs associated with American Christianity; more recently, a specific reference to African-African Christian music.

Gradual (**Graduale**)   (1) The liturgical book containing the texts (and, if notated, the chants) of the Mass Ordinary. (2) The second element of the Mass Propers.

Grand opéra   Type of French-language opera prevalent in the 19th century, usually in five acts, with elaborate staging, costumes, and ballet, often based on historic subjects.

Gregorian chant   Name often given to plainchant in honor of Pope Gregory I (later Saint Gregory), long believed to have been the originator of the repertory.

Ground bass   Short bass pattern that, repeated many times over the course of a movement or work, provides the structural basis for the voice or voices above it.

Guidonian hand   Mnemonic device attributed to the medieval theorist Guido d'Arezzo, used to teach solmization syllables.

Half cadence   Cadence on the dominant.

Harmonic rhythm   Rate of harmonic change within a given passage of music. A passage is said to have a slow harmonic rhythm if it maintains the same harmony over a relatively long span of time, such as a full measure or half a measure, depending on meter and tempo.

Harmonics   Effect created by a technique of string playing in which the performer touches the bowed string lightly at a designated point. The resulting sound is a harmonic overtone two octaves higher than the notated pitch, and the sound is light and ethereal.

Head motif   Thematic idea that occurs at the beginning of a movement or work and returns prominently throughout the course of the music that follows.

Heightened neume   See **diastematic neume.**

Hemiola   Brief passage of duple-meter rhythms within an otherwise triple-meter context.

Hexachord   Any grouping of six pitches. Through the Baroque era, a hexachord was conceived of as a series of six ascending notes, all separated by whole steps except the third and fourth notes, which are separated by a half step. In 20th-century dodecaphony (12-tone serial music), a hexachord is half of a 12-tone row.

Hip-hop   Originally a popular dance music based on "beats," combinations of musical samples and sounds produced in the recording studio; in combination with an adaptation of Jamaican "toasting" (speaking over the music), hip-hop is referred to as rap music.

Historicism   Approach to artistic creation that openly embraces the forms and styles of earlier generations even while presenting them in original ways.

Hocket   Passage featuring rapid-fire voice exchange, a favorite device of 14th- and early-15th-century composers.

Holograph   Score written in the composer's own hand; also known as an autograph score or simply as an autograph.

Homophony   Type of texture in which a principal melodic line is accompanied by a clearly subordinate voice or voices.

Humanism   A philosophical movement of the Renaissance committed to independent reasoning (without, however, rejecting faith), the study of ancient literature in its original language, and a reliance on original sources rather than secondhand commentary. Humanism was the successor to medieval scholasticism, which relied almost entirely on abstract thought and the accumulation of wisdom through disputation rather than empirical evidence or observation.

Hymn   Setting of a sacred but nonliturgical text, usually strophic and predominantly syllabic.

Idealism   System of thought based on the premise that objects in the physical world are a reflection of ideas in the mind. The rise of Idealism in the late 18th and early 19th centuries played a key role in the rising status of instrumental music.

Impressionism   Musical style that flourished in the period 1890 to 1920, associated chiefly with the French composer Claude Debussy and characterized by a blurring of distinct harmonies, rhythms, timbres, and forms.

Intabulation   Arrangement for keyboard or for a plucked stringed instrument—lute, guitar, vihuela, cittern, pandora—of a work originally written for voices.

Integral serialism   System of serial composition in which elements beyond pitch, such as rhythm and dynamics, are also subjected to serial treatment. Also known as **total serialism.**

Intermedio (plural, **intermedi**)   Dramatic work, often with music, performed between the acts of a larger theatrical presentation such as a play or opera.

Intermezzo   Sung dramatic work staged between the acts of a larger opera, usually an opera seria.

Inversion   Mirror image of a melodic line. The inversion of a line that moves up a major third and then down a minor second would be a line that moves down a major third and then up a minor second.

Isomelic   From the Greek iso ("the same") and melic ("melodic"), a term coined by 20th-century scholars to describe music of the Renaissance in which one or more voices in the various sections of a polyphonic work present a series of variations on the work's opening idea.

Isorhythm   Term coined in the 20th century to describe the rhythmic and melodic structure of certain tenor lines in polyphony of the 14th and 15th centuries. An isorhythmic tenor features a rhythmic pattern (the talea) and a melodic pattern (the color), each of which is repeated at least once. The talea and color may be of equal duration, but more often they are not.

Italian overture   Type of overture found in many operas and oratorios of the 18th century consisting of three movements in the sequence fast-slow-fast.

Jazz   Musical style that emerged in the early decades of the 20th century in the American South, covering a wide range of substyles connected by an approach toward music that embraces improvisation and rhythmic and intonational freedom, along with a general acceptance that the musical work exists in performance rather than in the form of a written score.

Jubilus   In plainchant settings of the Alleluia within the Propers of the Mass, the long melisma on the final syllable of the word *Alleluia*.

Klezmer   Type of instrumental music originally cultivated in the 19th century by the *klezmorim*, the professional Jewish musicians of eastern Europe, and characterized by a steady bass and rhythmically free winds above, often with chromatic passages in thirds, exaggerated accents, and repeated half steps back and forth.

Leitmotiv   German for "leading motif," a brief musical idea connected to some person, event, or idea in a music drama. The Leitmotiv distinguishes itself from the earlier device of the musical reminiscence by virtue of its malleability and its context within a network of related musical ideas. It was first pioneered in the music dramas of Richard Wagner.

Liber usualis   Literally, "Book of Use"; anthology of many different kinds of plainchant for both the Mass and the Office.

Lied   (pronounced "leet"; the plural, **Lieder,** is pronounced like the English word "leader") German term for the genre of song.

Ligatures   Notational signs used in plainchant and polyphony through the Renaissance to represent two or more pitches within a single unit. In mensural notation, ligatures were often used to indicate rhythmic values.

Liturgical drama   A liturgical passage in chant presented in a quasi-theatrical manner during the service, with individual portrayals of the protagonists.

Long   In Franconian notation, longest standard note value.

Lute song   Type of strophic secular song cultivated in England during the early 17th century for lute and voices (usually four). The lute could substitute for or double as many as three of the four voices.

Madrigal   Poetic and musical form first used in 14th-century Italy and then taken up later again in the 16th century. (1) The texts of 14th-century Italian madrigals usually consist of two or three strophes, each with three lines, plus a two-line ritornello (refrain) at the very end. (2) The 16th-century Italian madrigal is a poem of a single strophe using a free rhyme scheme and meter, such as an alternation of 7- and 11-syllable lines.

Madrigal comedy   Series of polyphonic madrigals loosely connected through plot and characters. The genre enjoyed its heyday in the closing decades of the 16th century.

Mannerism   Term used to describe an artistic style prevalent in the works of certain artists of the 16th and early 17th centuries—both in painting and in music—that emphasized unusual degrees of distortion, exaggeration, and unsettling juxtaposition for dramatic effect. In music, these devices could include extreme dissonance, unusual harmonic progressions, and exaggerated word-painting.

March   Genre of music originally intended to keep soldiers in formation during movement, characterized by duple meter and a steady tempo.

Masque   Theatrical genre of 17th-century England featuring a mixture of declaimed poetry, songs, scenery, dance, and instrumental music.

Mass   The central service of the traditional Christian liturgy, a ritualistic celebration of Christ's Last Supper with his disciples. The liturgy of the Mass consists of the Ordinary (fixed texts said or sung at every Mass) and the Propers (texts that vary according to the date within the liturgical year, such as a particular feast day or season).

Matrix   An interlocking numerical grid showing all four forms of a tone row at all transpositions.

Mean-tone tuning   System of tuning used widely in the Renaissance and Baroque eras in which perfect fifths were altered in such a way to make major and minor thirds more pleasing to the ear.

Measured organum   Type of organum in which all voices move at about the same speed. Also known as **discant organum.**

Melisma   Florid musical setting of several notes per syllable of text. The term is primarily used in connection with medieval plainchant.

Melismatic organum   Type of organum in which multiple notes in the added voice(s) run against the individual notes of an original chant.

Mélodie   French for "melody," also used for the genre of song in France from the 19th century onward.

Melodrama   A staged musical work or number in which a spoken voice is accompanied by the orchestra.

Mensural notation   System of musical notation that first emerged in the mid-13th century, in which rhythmic durations were indicated by distinct note shapes as opposed to ligatures. In its broadest sense, mensural notation is still in use today, but the term is generally understood to refer to the various forms of mensural notation used between approximately 1250 and 1600.

Mensuration signs   Notational devices used at the beginning of a work to indicate the mensural relationship of note values, such as the number of semibreves per breve or the number of minims to a semibreve.

Meta-art   The application of a mathematical, computer-generated, or other process to achieve artistic expression in any medium.

Microtones   Intervals smaller than a half step within the diatonic scale.

Middle entries   Those sections within a fugue that present a point of imitation, in contrast to **episodes,** which feature little or no imitation.

Minim   In Petronian notation, the note value that subdivides the semibreve.

Minimalism   Artistic movement that emerged in the early 1960s, relying on multiple repetitions of small units that differ only slightly or are varied only gradually over long stretches of time.

Minnesinger   Medieval German poet-composer-performer who sang songs of love.

Minstrel song   Type of song typically performed in the 19th and early 20th centuries by white performers in blackface. The songs themselves purportedly represent the perspectives of African-American slaves or their descendants.

Minuet   Dance form that became a common feature in instrumental cycles of the Baroque and Classical eras. The typical minuet consists of two binary forms, the first known as the *minuet proper,* the second as the *trio.* The minuet proper is repeated at the end of the trio.

Minuet proper   In a minuet, the opening and closing section (A) within a basic ABA form.

Mode   (1) Melodic mode—a scale type characterized by a specific pattern of whole steps and half steps. Melodies in any of the eight so-called church modes of the medieval era end on a characteristic pitch (the **finalis,** or final) and move up and down within a particular range (ambitus). (2) Rhythmic mode—in the medieval era, one of six consistent patterns of repeated units of long and short durations. (3) Since the early 18th century, one of the two principal forms—major and minor—of the diatonic scale.

Modernism   Artistic movement of the early 20th century that emphasized novelty at almost any cost, based on the conviction that the New must be as different as possible from the Old. Modernism in music frequently involved a rejection of tonality, conventional forms, and established genres.

Modified strophic form   Type of strophic form in which the music varies to some degree from strophe to strophe—through melodic embellishment, for example, or alteration of texture or harmony—but remains otherwise recognizably the same.

Monody   Any work of the 17th century consisting of a solo voice supported by basso continuo.

Monophony   Musical texture of a single voice or line, without accompaniment of any kind.

Moresca   "Moorish" dance, supposedly influenced by the Arabic cultures of northern Africa and Spain.

Motet   Polyphonic vocal work, usually sacred.

Motetus   In the 13th-century motet, the voice added above the tenor. Its counterpart in organum was known as the **duplum,** but with an underlaid text of its own in motets, this part became known as the motetus.

Motoric rhythm   Music in a rapid tempo and nonlegato, with notes struck on a constant rhythmic subdivision of the beat.

Musica ficta   Convention of the late medieval and Renaissance eras in which certain notes were sharped or flattened in performance according to various conventions, such as creating cadential leading tones or avoiding cross-relations between voices.

Musica reservata   Term used in the 16th and early 17th centuries to describe certain kinds of music "reserved" for connoisseurs and not intended for wide-scale distribution. These works were demanding for performers and listeners alike and often included unconventional elements of notation, chromaticism, or the use of ancient Greek genera.

Music drama (*Musikdrama*)   Term coined by Richard Wagner to distinguish traditional opera from what he felt to be his fundamentally new approach to sung drama. The music drama is characterized by the ideal of the *Gesamtkunstwerk*, in which music, words, and gesture are all inextricably linked yet at the same time self-sufficient.

Musique concrète   French term for "concrete music," used to denote music in which the sonic material to be manipulated is a recorded sound taken from everyday life. The sounds are thus real, or "concrete." Also known as electroacoustic music.

Musique d'ameublement (Fr., furnishing music)   Music designed by Erik Satie as background to other activities, the aural equivalent of wallpaper; a forerunner of Muzak and **ambient music.**

Mutation   In solmization, the process by which singers would shift from one hexachord to another.

Neoclassicism   Style that emerged in the 1910s and 1920s, characterized by a return to the tonal idiom, conventional genres and forms, the ideal of absolute music, conciseness of expression, and a general tendency toward transparent textures, lighter orchestration, and small ensembles.

Neumatic   Musical setting of two or more notes (i.e., a neume) per syllable of text. The term is used primarily in connection with plainchant.

Neume   Sign used in early chant notation to indicate pitch.

Nonretrogradable rhythm   Olivier Messiaen's term for a palindromic rhythmic unit—that is, one that is the same forward as backward and whose retrograde form is therefore identical to its original form.

Obbligato accompaniment   Style of homophony associated particularly with music of the later decades of the 18th century in which the accompanying voices contribute material essential to a work's musical fabric.

Octatonic scale   Scale that alternates between half and whole steps and contains within itself all possible intervals, from the minor second to the major seventh.

Office   See **Divine Office.**

Opera   In the narrowest sense, a drama sung entirely from beginning to end. In a looser sense, any drama consisting primarily of singing, as opposed to speaking.

Opera buffa   Literally "comic opera," a subgenre of opera that emerged in Italy out of the tradition of the intermezzo, based on humorous subjects and featuring everyday characters rather than the heroes, rulers, and gods typically found in opera seria.

Opéra comique   Type of opera in 19th-century France that incorporated spoken dialogue as well as music. In spite of its name, the subject matter of the genre was not always comic.

Opera seria   Literally, "serious opera." Type of opera cultivated in the period ca. 1680 to 1810, particularly in Italy. Its characteristic features were a strict division between recitative and aria, an emphasis on virtuoso singing, particularly in da capo arias, and the use of castrati. The librettos were typically drawn from ancient history or mythology.

Operetta   Lighter type of opera that emerged in the mid-19th century out of the traditions of the singspiel and the opéra comique. Operettas mix spoken dialogue with sung numbers and deal invariably with humorous and lighthearted subjects.

Oratorio   Genre of vocal music similar to opera in its musical elements (recitatives, arias, choruses, etc.) but performed without staging or costumes. Most oratorios revolve around religious subjects, but some are written on secular themes.

Organicism   A theoretical and analytical approach to music that attempts to demonstrate that elements audible on the surface manifest a deeper coherence, the work being treated as a "living form."

Organum (plural, **organa**)   Polyphonic work of the 9th to 12th centuries consisting of an original plainchant melody in one voice along with at least one additional voice above or below.

Ostinato   Figure presented repeatedly in succession.

Overture   Single-movement orchestral work, either independent or as the prelude to a sung drama.

Panconsonance   Style of writing associated with Dunstable and Du Fay in the early 15th century that makes ample use of triads and restricts the use of dissonance considerably, compared to the idioms of the 14th century.

Parallel organum   Type of organum in which the added voice or voices run parallel to an established plainchant melody at a constant interval.

Paraphrase   Free variation of an existing melodic line or polyphonic network.

Paratactic form   Any structure that consists of a series of more or less discrete units unrelated to one another musically. Paratactic form can be represented schematically as A, B, C, D, E, and so on.

Parisian chanson   Term coined by 20th-century scholars to describe a type of song that emerged in the French capital during the 1520s, featuring predominantly chordal textures.

Parlor song   So called because of its preferred place of performance in the 19th-century home, a type of song whose texts are invariably strophic and sentimental, and whose music is melodically and harmonically straightforward.

Passacaglia   Type of bass pattern used throughout the Baroque.

Passamezzo   (1) Type of bass pattern used throughout the Baroque. (2) Dance similar to the pavane, but with a lighter step.

Pasticcio   Work whose individual units are written by several different composers.

Pavane   Slow, courtly dance in duple meter.

Pentatonic scale   Any scale based on five notes.

Periodic phrase structure   Form consisting of many modular units of equal length, initially associated with dance music. See also **antecedent and consequent.**

Pervading imitation   Compositional technique in which a series of musical ideas are stated imitatively in all voices across the course of an entire work or section of a work. The technique first began to be cultivated in a widespread manner in the second half of the 15th century.

Petronian notation   System of mensural notation used in the late 13th and early 14th centuries, ascribed to Petrus de Cruce and based on the principles of Franconian notation, but including the shorter note values of the minim and semiminim and allowing for as many as nine semibreves within the duration of a single breve.

Phase music or process music   Subgenre of minimalism in which the listener can clearly hear the process by which the elements of a work gradually transform themselves into something new and different.

Picardy third   See *tierce de picardie*.

Pitch class   Any set of notes associated with a particular note regardless of register: any A, any B, any C, and so on.

Plagal mode   Any of the melodic modes with an ambitus running roughly a fifth above and a fourth below the final note.

Plainchant   Monophonic music of the medieval Christian church.

Point of imitation   Unit of music in which all the voices of a polyphonic composition take up more or less the same musical idea in succession. Points of imitation are a by-product of pervading imitation.

Polyphony   Musical texture of two or more voices essentially equal in importance.

Polytextual motet   Any motet with multiple texts performed simultaneously. The polytextual motet was cultivated most intensely in the 13th century.

Polytonality   Simultaneous juxtaposition of contrasting triads or keys.

Postmodernism   Aesthetic attitude that emerged in the last third of the 20th century, embracing the past (including modernism) but often in an eclectic manner, synthesizing a variety of approaches in a single work. Postmodernist composers felt obliged neither to avoid nor use tonality or atonality, conventional forms, and established genres.

Prepared piano   Instrument with sounds altered by inserting foreign objects (bolts, weather stripping, screws, wool, bamboo, coins) into selected strings. The prepared piano is played primarily on the keyboard, while the "string piano" and other extended techniques involve playing directly on the strings.

Prima prattica   Term coined in the early 17th century to describe an older attitude toward text setting in which the projection of a sung text was subordinated to the established conventions of good counterpoint. The *prima prattica* is closely associated (but not synonymous) with polyphony. Literally, the "first practice," so called because it existed before the emergence of the *seconda prattica*, the "second" (or newer) practice.

Primitivism   Aesthetic movement of all the arts in the early 20th century that consciously avoided the cultivated traditions of Western art. In music, primitivism gave special importance to rhythm, the most basic of all musical elements, and abandoned or substantially altered such arbitrary (so-called civilized) concepts as voice leading, triadic harmony, and the major and minor forms of the diatonic scale.

Process music   See **Phase music.**

Program music   Any instrumental work that in one way or another—through a title or accompanying poetry or prose—is connected with a story or idea that lies outside the music itself.

Prosula (plural, *prosulae*)   Type of trope in which words were added to an existing chant.

Psalm tone   Plainchant formula used to recite the psalms.

Public domain   Term applied to any creation (music, literature, artwork, invention, phrase, etc.) that never was or is no longer the property of an individual or organization; the main issue behind copyrighting "traditional" or "folk" music.

Quadruplum   From the Latin word for "fourth," the added fourth voice in organum and polyphony of the 12th and 13th centuries.

Quartal harmonies   Chords built on the interval of a fourth rather than a third.

Quattrocento   Italian term for the 15th century (literally, "the 1400s").

Ragtime   Style that grew out of traditions of African-American dance and flourished at the end of the 19th century and in the early decades of the 20th. Ragtime music is usually in duple meter and based on units of 8 or 16 measures. Syncopation is prevalent throughout, thrown into relief by the steadiness of the bass line.

Rap   See **Hip-hop.**

Recapitulation   In sonata form, the section following the development. In its simplest form, the recapitulation begins with a return of the opening idea of the movement in the tonic key; it continues by restating the entire exposition in the tonic, without modulation. In practice, recapitulations are not nearly so regular and often incorporate substantial changes in relation to the exposition.

Recitation tone   In plainchant, and particularly in psalm tones, a central pitch used repeatedly in immediate succession to declaim large quantities of text.

Recitative   Style of singing characterized by syllabic declamation, with greater emphasis on the projection of the text at hand than on melody, more nearly approximating the inflections of speech even while adhering to the basic musical elements of pitch and rhythm.

Refrain   (1) In the broadest sense, any theme and/or text that returns repeatedly over the course of a work after contrasting material. (2) In a rondo, the recurring theme (A) within the pattern ABACADA.

Reprise   Unit of music to be repeated in performance immediately after it has been first presented. A binary form often consists of two reprises.

Respond   Refrain portion of a responsorial chant, sung before the verse.

Responsorial chant   Any of the plainchants, such as the Gradual, Alleluia, and Tract, in which the chorus and soloist alternate.

Retrograde   Melodic line presented backward, that is, from its end to its beginning.

Revue   A theatrical presentation of a potpourri of acts following one another in quick succession, dominated by but not limited to song and dance; a successor to music hall and vaudeville performances.

Rhythm and blues   Popular music synthesis of electrified blues and boogie-woogie that in its up-tempo form is analogous to early rock and roll.

Rhythmic mode   See **mode.**

Ricercar   In the early 16th century, a freely composed work that is improvisatory and preludial in character, often for lute or keyboard. By the mid-16th century, the term had become identified with polyphonic works for keyboard or for instrumental ensembles. By the 18th century, the term was associated with fugues that used a large number or variety of contrapuntal devices.

Ripieno   Literally, "full"; designation used in the Baroque era for the large ensemble within a concerto grosso.

Ripieno concerto   Type of concerto for large ensemble, without soloists.

Ritornello   Literally, a "brief return"; musical idea that returns at several points over the course of a work, usually after contrasting material of some kind. The **ritornello principle** is the structural basis by which composers construct large-scale forms around successive returns of an opening idea. This principle is especially important in the genre of the concerto.

Rococo   Term borrowed from art history and used by some music historians to describe the musical style of the mid-18th century, emphasizing qualities of lightness and grace.

Romanticism   Mode of thought that emerged in the late 18th and early 19th centuries and placed unprecedented importance on imagination and subjectivity over reason and objectivity.

Rondeau (plural, **rondeaux**)   One of the *formes fixes* used in music of the 14th and 15th centuries. Each strophe consists of eight lines of text set to music following the rhyme scheme ABaAabAB (uppercase letters indicate refrains, which remain constant from strophe to strophe).

Rondellus   Type of polyphonic composition cultivated in the medieval era, in which the voices exchange extended phrases repeatedly (e.g., A over B, followed by B over A, followed by A over B, etc.).

Rondo   A type of movement associated largely with finales and found in many different instrumental genres of the late 18th and 19th centuries. It is composed in **rondo form,** a structure derived from dance music ("round dance") in which the basic pattern in its simplest form is ABACA, with the recurring theme (A) constituting the **refrain** and the contrasting themes (B, C, etc.) constituting the **episodes** or **couplets**.

Root position triad   Triad whose root or fundamental pitch appears in the lowest sounding voice.

Row   In serial composition, another name for the series of 12 different pitch classes.

Rubato   See **Tempo rubato.**

Saltarello   Lively dance that often follows a slower one.

Scat singing   Technique of singing in which the voice mimics an instrument, singing syncopated nonsense syllables against the steady beat of the bass.

Scherzo   From the Italian word for "joke," a movement type that emerged in the early 19th century and eventually supplanted the minuet within such multi-movement cycles as symphonies, quartets, and sonatas. Like the minuet, the scherzo is in ABA form; in contrast to the minuet, the scherzo is typically faster and at times humorous or even grotesque in its gestures.

Secco recitative   Literally, "dry recitative," accompanied by basso continuo alone; also known as *recitativo semplice* ("simple recitative").

Seconda prattica   Term coined in the early 17th century to describe a new attitude toward text setting in which all musical means were subordinated to the effective delivery of the text being sung. The *seconda prattica* is closely associated (but not synonymous) with the emerging practice of monody. Literally, the "second practice," so called because it appeared after the *prima prattica,* the "first" (or older) practice.

Semibreve   In Franconian notation, the note value that subdivides the breve.

Semiminim   In Petronian notation, half the note value of a minim.

Semi-opera   Type of theatrical entertainment that flourished in England during the second half of the 17th century. These were essentially plays with a large proportion of musical numbers, both vocal and instrumental.

Sequence   (1) Element of the Mass Propers, authorized for special feast days, appearing after the Alleluia. (2) Any musical idea repeated on successively different pitches.

Serial composition   Method of composition based on the repeated manipulation of an established row (series) of pitches and/or rhythms and/or dynamics. Transpositions and permutations of the series (inversion, retrograde, retrograde inversion) provide variety. Dodecaphony is the most common form of serial composition, based on a row of 12 different pitch classes.

Series   In serial composition, another name for the row of 12 different pitch classes.

Shape-note singing   Religious music read from a system combining standard notation with a set of differently shaped note heads related to solfège.

Singspiel (plural, **Singspiele**)   "Singing play"; German-language spoken drama with interpolated musical numbers (arias, duets, trios, etc.). The singspiel of the 18th century was an important forerunner of the later operetta and musical.

Socialist realism   Aesthetic doctrine espoused by Soviet bloc authorities in the 20th century to encourage artists to produce works in a readily accessible style. In music, works written under the influence of socialist realism typically incorporate folk or folklike elements and project an overwhelmingly optimistic tone.

Solmization syllables   Syllables associated with the pitches of a hexachord, in ascending order: *ut, re, mi, fa, sol, la.*

Solo concerto   Type of concerto featuring a soloist and a larger ensemble, as opposed to a ripieno concerto.

Sonata   Literally, "that which is sounded" (i.e., played on instruments). Term used in the Renaissance and Baroque in the broadest sense to indicate a work for an instrument or instruments of any combination. From the 18th century onward, the term was used to indicate a work for one or more solo instruments, usually in three or four movements.

Sonata da camera   Literally, "sonata of the chamber"; type of sonata featuring a series of dance-related movements, popular in the Baroque era.

Sonata da chiesa   Literally, "sonata of the church"; type of sonata featuring a slow first movement and at least one additional imitative movement, popular in the Baroque era.

Sonata form   Structural convention frequently found in first movements, slow movements, and finales of instrumental works, particularly from the second half of the 18th century and all of the 19th century. A movement in sonata form incorporates an **exposition**, a **development**, and a **recapitulation**. An introduction and coda are sometimes added but are not essential elements of the form.

Sonata form with varied reprise   Type of sonata form in which the exposition is not repeated note for note but instead written out and changed in subtle ways.

Sonata-rondo form   Type of rondo (ABACABA) in which B corresponds to the secondary key area of a sonata-form movement; that is, it is presented first in a contrasting key and then (toward the end) in the tonic, as in a sonata-form recapitulation.

Song cycle   Collection of songs ordered in such a way as to convey at least the outline of a story or idea.

Song form   A form frequently used in popular song of the 20th century, featuring four units of eight measures each, following the thematic pattern AABA.

Spiritual   African-American hymn developed from pre–Civil War songs; a primary influence on African-American popular as well as religious music.

Sprechstimme   Literally, "speech-voice," with "voice" understood here in the sense of "singing." A style of vocal declamation that lies midway between speech and song, cultivated particularly in the early 19th century by such composers as Arnold Schoenberg and Alban Berg.

Stop   On an organ, a lever that controls the flow of air through sets or combinations of sets of pipes, thereby altering the timbre of the instrument's sound.

Stretto   Overlapping entries in several voices of a fugue subject in shortened form, designed to increase the need for a final resolution of the fugue's tension.

Strophic   (1) In poetry, any text made up of stanzas (strophes), each of which has the same number of lines and follows the same rhyme scheme and meter. (2) In music, any setting of a strophic text in which each strophe is sung to the same music.

Sturm und Drang   Literally, "storm and stress"; designation, given by 20th-century scholars, to a style of writing that appears in certain works by Haydn, Mozart, Gluck, and others in the late 1760s and early 1770s. The characteristics of *Sturm und Drang* music include a predilection for the minor mode and such extreme gestures as large melodic leaps, jagged syncopations, and sudden dynamic contrasts.

Style brisé   Literally, "broken style"; style of writing for the keyboard that imitates the broken (arpeggiated) chords often played on a lute or guitar.

Subject   Theme of a fugue.

Suite   In the music of the Baroque and Classical eras, a series of dance or dance-like movements. Later, a collection of any kind of individual movements not falling into the standard pattern of the sonata, symphony, or other established genres.

Syllabic   Musical setting of one note per syllable of text.

Symphonic poem   Term coined by Franz Liszt in 1854 to replace the generic name of what had previously been called the **concert overture**, a one-movement work for orchestra with some kind of programmatic association.

Symphony   (1) In the 17th and early 18th centuries, a work or movement for large instrumental ensemble. (2) In the 18th century, an overture to an opera or stage play. (3) From about 1720 onward, a multimovement work for instrumental ensemble.

Syntactic form   Any formal structure that maintains one or more thematic ideas consistently across the course of an entire movement or work. Syntactic form involves an interrelationship of musical units in the same way that syntax relates to the functional relationship of a sentence's verbal units (nouns, verbs, etc.). Syntactic form is the opposite of paratactic form, in which the units of a movement are thematically unrelated.

Synthesized electronic music   Music consisting of sounds generated and manipulated entirely by electronic means, through an electronic oscillator or a modifying device like a synthesizer.

Tactus   From the Latin word for "touch," the basic unit of temporal measurement used in Renaissance music. One theorist of the late 15th century claimed the rate of the *tactus* was equivalent to the heartbeat of an adult man breathing at a normal speed—that is, roughly 60 to 70 times per minute.

Talea   Rhythmic pattern of an isorhythmic tenor.

Temperament   Manner of adjusting ("tempering") the intervals of a scale.

Tempo rubato   Literally, "robbed time"; practice of performing with subtle accelerations and decelerations of tempo not otherwise indicated in a score.

Tenor   (1) The high voice range of the adult male, running roughly from the G above middle C to the B slightly more than an octave below middle C. (2) In medieval and Renaissance music, the vocal part that "holds" (Latin, *tenere*) the chant melody.

Tenorlied   Type of secular song cultivated in Germany in the 16th century in which the principal melody appears in the tenor voice, with three contrapuntal voices surrounding it.

Tetrachord   Any grouping of four pitches, in particular, the interlocking descending successions of notes in the ancient Greek musical system.

Third-stream music   An style that bridges jazz improvisation and harmony with instruments and voice-leading techniques (particularly counterpoint) more commonly associated with classical music.

Through-composed   Term used to describe song settings that are not strophic—that is, settings that provide new music for each section of the text.

Tièrce de picardie   Literally, "Picardy third"; major third at the end of a work otherwise in minor mode. The raised third was not always notated but instead left to the discretion of the performer.

Toccata   Type of work for keyboard that is freely constructed, based on no preexistent material, and typically features rapid passagework.

Total serialism   See **integral serialism.**

Trecento   Italian term for the 14th century (literally, "the 1300s").

Triad   Chord of three notes whose adjacent pitches are separated by intervals of a major or minor third.

Trio   (1) Any work for three voices or instruments. (2) In a minuet or scherzo, the contrasting middle section (B) within a basic ABA form.

Trio sonata   Type of sonata for two instruments of a high range (violins, flutes, oboes, etc.) and basso continuo, popular throughout the 18th century.

Triplum   From the Latin word for "third," the added third voice in organum and polyphony of the 12th and 13th centuries.

Trope   Musical or textual addition to an existing plainchant. Tropes could be added to the beginning or end of a chant, or they could be interpolated into the chant itself.

Troping   Process of creating a trope.

Troubadours (fem., **trobairitz**), **trouvères**   The mostly wandering minstrels—often composer, poet, and performer in the same person—who entertained the courts of the nobility in southern (troubadour) and northern (trouvère) France in the 12th and 13th centuries.

Tutti   Literally, "all"; term used to indicate the large ensemble within a concerto grosso. Also used to designate the sections of the work played by this ensemble.

12-bar blues form   A series of variations on a repeated harmonic pattern of 12 measures in 4/4 time; the most common harmonic pattern is I-IV-I-V-I.

Unmeasured organum   A type of organum in which the added voice(s) move rapidly against the slower-moving notes of original chant. Also known as **free organum.**

Vamp   In popular song of the 20th century, a short progression of chords that can be repeated indefinitely before the entrance of the voice.

Variation suite   Set of contrasting dance-related movements based on one basic thematic idea.

Verse   In popular song of the 20th century, the opening section that leads into the song's chorus or principal melody.

Villancico   Principal genre of Spanish song in the Renaissance. The term was first used in the late 15th century to identify a poetic form equivalent to the French virelai (AbbaA).

Villanella   General term used to describe a variety of Italian song types of the 16th and early 17th centuries. These songs were often to bawdy texts and featured predominantly chordal textures.

Virelai   One of the *formes fixes* in the music of the 14th and 15th centuries. Each strophe consists of a variable number of lines but always begins and ends with the refrain, an unchanging unit of text and music. The general pattern of rhyme is AbbaA (the uppercase letter indicates the refrain).

Vocalize   To sing a melodic line to a vowel sound, without a text.

Voice leading   Manner in which two or more voices move in relationship to one another.

Volta   Vigorous "turning" dance (*voltare* means "to turn" in Italian), often in compound duple meter.

Whole-tone scale   Scale of six notes, each a whole tone apart.

Word painting   Use of musical elements to imitate the meaning of a specific passage of the text being sung at that moment, such as a falling melodic line to indicate descent, a leap to indicate jumping, and so on.

Index

Boldface page numbers refer to composer profiles.